Family Violence

Family Violence

Edited by
Lloyd Ohlin and Michael Tonry

Crime and Justice
A Review of Research
Edited by Michael Tonry and Norval Morris
with the Support of The National Institute of Justice

VOLUME 11

The University of Chicago Press, Chicago and London

This volume was prepared under Grant Number 85-IJ-CX-0016 awarded to the Castine Research Corporation by the National Institute of Justice, U.S. Department of Justice, under the Omnibus Crime Control and Safe Streets Act of 1968 as amended. Points of view or opinions expressed in this volume are those of the editors or authors and do not necessarily represent the official position or policies of the U.S. Department of Justice.

The University of Chicago Press, Chicago 60637
The University of Chicago Press, Ltd., London

ISSN: 0192-3234
ISBN: 0-226-80806-8

LCN: 80-642217

Library of Congress Cataloging-in-Publication Data

Family violence / edited by Lloyd Ohlin and Michael Tonry.
     p. cm.—(Crime and justice: a review of research; v. 11)
    Includes bibliographical references and indexes.
    ISBN 0-226-80806-8. ISBN 0-226-80807-6 (pbk.): $35.00 (est.)
    1. Family violence—United States. I. Ohlin, Lloyd E.
II. Tonry, Michael H. III. Series: Crime and justice (Chicago,
Ill.): v. 11.
HV6001.C672 vol. 11
[HQ809.3.U5]
364 $—dc19
[362.8'2]   88-17386
                                             CIP

The paper used in this publication meets the minimum requirements of American National Standard for Information Sciences—Permanence of Paper for Printed Library Materials, ANSI Z39.48-1984. ⊚

Contents

Preface

At different times and places particular types of criminal activity become the focus of public attention and of demands for prevention and control. Sometimes it is because the activity itself has become more pervasive or has assumed a more threatening form, as in the current concern about the transportation and sale of illicit drugs or in the shoot-outs between members of rival urban gangs. At other times it is because social and political movements raise to public saliency forms of criminal conduct that have remained hidden or whose harm and cost have gone unrecognized. It is this latter process that has brought various forms of family violence to public and official attention. Movements concerned with the rights of women and children have drawn support from both the right and the left of the political spectrum. These movements have exposed the prevalence of, and the harm resulting from, the physical and sexual abuse of women and children by other family members, and they have created widely shared demands for corrective actions.

These social and political developments also generated a surge of interest in family violence research and led the editorial board of *Crime and Justice* to consider developing a thematic volume on family violence. First, however, there was a problem to overcome. Though the board includes a diverse group of leading scholars on crime and justice problems, none of them claimed to know very much about the state of family violence research. Thus, notwithstanding an apparent commonality of interest, little interaction seems to have occurred between researchers in family violence and those concerned with crime and criminal justice in general. Accordingly, to determine whether family violence research was sufficiently advanced to support a *Crime and Justice* thematic volume, a meeting on family violence was convened in Washington, D.C., in October 1984, consisting of members of the *Crime and Justice* editorial board and leading family violence researchers and practitioners. Those attending were James Bannon, Leonard Berkowitz, Jeffrey Fagan, David Farrington, David Finkelhor, James Garbarino, Robert Hampton, Barbara Hart, Lois Herrington, Tom Lalley, Rolf Loeber, E. Michael McCann, John Monahan, Norval Morris, Eli Newberger, Lloyd Ohlin, Robert Pierce, Albert J. Reiss, Jr., Steven Schlesinger, Lawrence Sherman, James K. Stewart, Pamela Swain, Michael Tonry, Lenore Walker, Joseph Weis, and Franklin Zimring. Papers were commissioned from Jeffrey Fagan on the relation between family violence and violence outside of the family, from Lenore Walker on intervention by criminal justice agencies with respect to spouse abuse, from Joseph Weis on the incidence of various forms of family violence, and from James Garbarino on child maltreatment as a criminal justice problem.

Three conclusions emerged. First, previous interaction between criminological and family violence researchers was as limited as we had suspected. Second, the world of family violence research was itself highly specialized, with different communities of scholars studying different forms of family violence and with remarkably little interaction and exchange among them. Third, there was broad agreement that both criminological and family violence research would benefit from a careful effort to bring together within one volume a collection of major review essays on the central empirical, theoretical, and policy issues raised by family violence, with particular focus on the role of the criminal justice system and other formal legal controls.

This volume, many, many months later, is the result, thanks to generous support from the National Institute of Justice and steady encouragement from James K. Stewart, the institute's director. As is true of all *Crime and Justice* thematic volumes, each essay was commissioned, and all were discussed in detail by the authors and a dozen leading scholars and practitioners at a research conference. Not all of those commissioned survived for inclusion in the published volume, and all underwent substantial alterations in response to the comments and suggestions of critical readers.

Family violence is a research field that has only recently begun to overcome disciplinary insularity and to devote increased attention to problems of research methodology and design. Many talented scholars are actively at work, and an accumulating body of increasingly rigorous findings is emerging. We hope this volume contributes to these efforts.

Lloyd Ohlin and Michael Tonry

Family Violence in Perspective

No doubt acts of violence and willful neglect within families have been occurring for as long as there have been human families. During the four centuries since Europeans first colonized North America, there have been periods of heightened public and political awareness of family violence, especially involving wives and children; we are now in the midst of one such period.

Despite this history of acknowledgment of family violence as a subject of public concern, the recognition of family violence as a subject for social science research is much more recent. The systematic study of child abuse by social scientists is generally dated to the publication in 1962 of a now-classic article on the "battered child syndrome" by a group of physicians who documented evidence of repeated multiple bone fractures suffered by abused children (Kempe et al. 1962). Research on other forms of family violence is even more recent.

Since 1962, there has been steady, and steadily growing, attention on physical and sexual abuse of children as social problems. During the late sixties, most states enacted legislation requiring medical and social service workers to report cases of suspected abuse to state agencies. Various national organizations came into being to promote provision of services for abused and neglected children and to work for political and financial support for services. During the seventies and eighties, many more cases of child abuse were reported to law enforcement agencies than ever before, and many more criminal prosecutions were initiated.

Lloyd Ohlin is Touroff-Glueck Professor of Criminal Justice Emeritus, Law School, Harvard University. Michael Tonry is managing editor of *Crime and Justice: A Review of Research*.

To facilitate criminal prosecutions in child abuse cases, evidentiary and procedural rules have been changed in many places—for example, to permit use of videotaped questioning of child witnesses to make testifying less stressful, and to encourage use of "anatomically correct" dolls to make it easier for children to explain what happened to them.

Public and political attention on other forms of family violence has also increased in recent decades. Concern for spouse assault, especially when women are victims, has led to the growth of the shelter movement, to the formation of national and state political organizations, to law reform efforts aimed at both changing rape laws to encompass "marital rape" and at simplifying rape prosecutions—by eliminating corroboration requirements that some witness other than the alleged victim provide direct evidence and by forbidding testimony about the alleged victim's previous sexual conduct. The most radical doctrinal change in the substantive criminal law has been the recognition, primarily in case law, of the "abused spouse syndrome" defense in murder cases in which the husband-victim was not actively threatening the wife-assailant at the time he was killed.

Other forms of family violence have also received increased attention in recent years, but, lacking the visceral and emotional appeal of child victims and the political organization and ideological commitments of the women's movement, much less attention has been focused on them, many fewer specialized services and resources have been created, and there have been fewer associated statutory and case law developments. Violence between siblings, for example, may be the most common form of intrafamily violence, but it receives very little attention. As Mildred Pagelow (in this volume) shows, violent victimization of adolescents by parents is not uncommon but adolescents tend commonly not to be seen as sympathetic victims. Physical and financial abuse and neglect of the elderly by family members is apparently widespread, but again the social and public policy reactions have been much less vigorous than for child or spouse abuse.

Heightened public attention to various forms of family violence has raised public consciousness of these problems and in doing so has catalyzed development of a sizable number of distinct family violence research communities and a massive social science literature on the prevalence, incidence, and correlates of victimization (on marital violence, see Frieze and Browne [in this volume]; on child physical and sexual abuse, see Garbarino [in this volume]; on treatment programs for violence, see Pagelow [in this volume]); on treatment programs for abusers and victims (see Saunders and Azar, in this volume); on the causes of family violence (see Burgess and Draper, in this volume); and on the deterrent, incapacitative, and punitive deployment of criminal justice system resources (see Elliott, in this volume).

This literature suffers from a number of serious problems and it is in part these problems that led to the development of this volume. One problem is that the family violence literature has traditionally been fragmented. Different scholarly and research communities studied different forms of family violence, published in and read different journals, belonged to different professional and scholarly organizations, and attended different conferences and meetings. Child sexual abuse research, for example, was for long primarily within the province of medical researchers and social workers. Child physical abuse and neglect was studied preponderar.tly by medical, social work, and psychology-based researchers. Spouse assault was investigated by feminist activists and clinicians and by sociologists. Abuse of the elderly and of adolescents and violence between siblings were investigated by virtually no one until the last few years.

And all of these different groups of family violence researchers worked in near isolation from the sizable number of scholars of diverse disciplines who studied crime and the criminal justice system (see Hotaling, Straus, and Lincoln, in this volume). Conversely, criminologists made few systematic inquiries into violence inside the family and the major sources of data on crime, such as the National Crime Survey's victimization studies and the Uniform Crime Report data on reported offenses and arrests, shed little light on family violence (see Weis, in this volume).

This fragmentation of family violence research and the divide between family violence studies and criminological studies was regrettable because it balkanized knowledge and policy-relevant insights, but it was doubly regrettable because it impoverished theory and generated fundamentally incomplete accounts of different forms of serious antisocial behavior.

Various forms of stranger and nonstranger violence and other crimes against strangers often occur within the same family. The intellectual balkanization of the past quarter century of research has impeded efforts to understand the interaction among various forms of family violence and between crimes within families and crimes against strangers. For example, powerful evidence exists for the "intergenerational transmission of violence" hypotheses that people who are victims of child abuse are disproportionately likely themselves to become abusing parents (Herrenkohl, Herrenkohl, and Toedter 1983), and that children who witness violence within the house or grow up in houses where adults are criminally active are themselves disproportionately likely to be violent or criminally active (Mednick and Volavka 1980; Loeber and Stouthamer-Loeber 1986). There is evidence that some women who are victims of spousal abuse are themselves disproportionately likely to be perpetrators of child abuse. There is evidence that men who commit violence against their spouses can be divided into different types who match different profiles—some of whom are violent only within the house, others of whom are violent both inside the house and outside (Shields and Hanneke 1983).

Violence and crime are socially and psychologically complex phenomena and need to be investigated in all their complexity. Research on child abuse that fails to take account of the mother's own victimization, of violence between parents or between parents and siblings, of crimes committed by parents or by siblings, and of the interactions among all these behaviors inevitably presents an incomplete picture of the etiology, correlates, and natural history of child abuse. It is not impossible that members of the same family have, at different times, been subjects of child abuse research conducted by a medical research team, parenting skills research conducted by developmental psychologists, spouse assault research conducted by sociologists or clinical psychologists, and criminological research conducted by sociologists, economists, or operations researchers.

A second serious problem with family violence research is that it tends to be exceedingly weak methodologically. Choices of research designs and methodologies, of course, must be determined by reference to the topics being investigated. If the experiences of battered women in shelters are under investigation, a clinical sample of shelter residences is a sensible group to study. However, if the topics under investigation are the prevalence, incidence, and correlates of specific behaviors in the general population, clinical samples or "snowball" samples or samples recruited by media ads or notices posted in grocery stores are simply the wrong groups to study. Unfortunately, with the exception of the surveys conducted by the Family Research Laboratory at the University of New Hampshire (Straus and Gelles 1986; Hotaling, Straus, and Lincoln, in this volume), sampling problems are widespread in family violence research (see Weis, in this volume). Similarly, sample sizes are too often too small to support use of credible statistical analytic tools, and comparison groups are often poorly matched to experimental groups.

To be sure, family violence poses particular difficulty as a research subject. Ethical concerns and constraints are especially daunting, particularly for those researchers who have clinical backgrounds and have been reform activists. Considerations to prevent continuing or future harm to victims and to intervene decisively to reduce vulnerability to future harm often combine with ideological preferences to remove battered wives from the marital home and to initiate punitive actions against male assailants. Interestingly, in reference to child abuse, many researchers and activists hold the opposite view—that criminal justice intervention often does more harm than good—and give primacy to efforts to maintain or reestablish household stability (see Garbarino, in this volume). Together, these sorts of ethical considerations and ideological preferences make it very difficult for many researchers to take a detached interest in the integrity of research designs. Similarly, the belief that an intervention strategy may be effective makes many researchers reluctant to use random case assignment procedures for experimental purposes to assess the intervention's effects when doing so denies access to it by victims who might benefit.

Coupled with the relative newness of family violence research as an academic specialty, these two major problems—the traditional balkanization of family violence research and its lack of methodological rigor—have produced a literature that is extensive but not definitive.

The separation of family violence research from criminological research is, in retrospect, not surprising but ironic. It is not surprising because the roots of social science research on family violence can be found in the arenas of medical, social work, and clinical practice while American criminology found roots in the social problems focus of university departments of sociology. It is ironic because one overriding theme of family violence activists in recent years has been the assumption that acts of family violence are *crimes*, that criminal justice officials have been remiss in not treating them as crimes, and that—at least for marital violence directed at women—arrests and criminal prosecution are preferred intervention strategies.

The preceding overview no doubt contains overly broad generalizations and many of them, a careful reader may note, are phrased in the past tense. Communication has improved across the specialized research communities that made up the world of family violence research, and interaction between the worlds of family violence and criminology is increasing.

This volume is one among many efforts to break down these traditional artificial barriers and attempts to summarize in one place the best of current scholarship by family violence researchers from many subspecialties, by criminologists, and by scholars who are within neither group.

The balance of this essay introduces some of the recurring themes and policy dilemmas that characterize family violence as a social problem and as a research subject. Responding to recent cultural and political trends to "criminalize" family violence and to recognize that crime in the streets and home have much in common, the emphasis of this essay, and of this volume, is on family violence as crime.

It is difficult to know how much family violence there is, how it varies from one time period to another, or to what extent it is culturally sanctioned or tolerated. It seems reasonable to assume that the amount and types of family violence vary with socioeconomic conditions, with cultural norms, and with public concern. That there is too much family violence is clear. That family violence is much more common than formerly believed and is present in all social strata is also clear. Whether the prevalence of some or all forms of family violence is increasing, decreasing, or is stable is much less clear; there can be little doubt, especially concerning physical and sexual abuse, that compulsory reporting laws, improved official data systems, and greater public awareness have brought much more abuse to light than in earlier periods. This book explores what is known about such matters from research and from efforts at intervention and care.

From a policy perspective, the ultimate goal is to devise policies that have some likelihood of assisting families to function more effectively while providing better protection for past, present, and potential victims. A number of recurring tensions arise from efforts to achieve these goals of assistance and protection at the same time.

I. Goal Conflict in Responding to Family Violence

The basic tension in devising intervention strategies lies with the inherent contrasts between criminal justice and social service intervention strategies. To those activists and victims who insist that violence in the family is as criminal as if the same acts had occurred between strangers, the deterrent and protective properties of the criminal law are especially needed because of the constant exposure and vulnerability of victims of family violence. To those, however, who believe that the foremost public policy objective is to preserve the family, to build on its strengths, to heal its wounds, and to foster its nurturing and affectionate capabilities, bringing the police and the courts into family problems undermines family cohesion, exacerbates conflict, and impedes restoration of smooth functioning. Thus there are some whose primary concern is abuse of women or whose primary concern is abuse of children who favor a full criminalization approach to family violence, and there are others who see criminal justice intervention only as a last, desperate recourse after the best efforts of the social services have failed.

Another basic tension lies in the conflict between goals of protection of the privacy of family relationships and acknowledgment of the urgency of public intervention to protect victims of violence (see Zimring, in this volume). This tension varies in saliency between cultures and in different historical periods (see Pleck, in this volume). The emergence of demands for public intervention and a correlative reduced concern for family privacy appear to occur most strongly in periods of social change when movements focusing on the rights of women, children, or the elderly push to the forefront of public attention. We appear now to be in the midst of such social movements. The historic tensions in different approaches and perspectives on the family and its acts of violence are again stimulating public debate, controversy, and efforts at clarification.

II. State of Family Violence Research and Theory

It is perhaps characteristic of new fields of research or professional concern that the initial phase reflects the specialized capabilities and interests of those who become involved. One serious consequence, as noted above for family violence, is a fragmentation of effort and failure of communication of research, theory, and practical experience. There is a tendency to specialize in different types of family violence, to publish in different journals, and to report results to different professional audiences. Such tendencies make it difficult to obtain a comprehensive picture of the scope of family violence and its interactive nature in families where the initial cause of intervention or scrutiny is a specific concern with child abuse, spouse abuse, or the abuse of siblings or the elderly.

Recently there has appeared increasing recognition that different types of violence may occur in the same family and make effective treatment more difficult. Accordingly, many practitioners feel they need to understand and become more sensitive to the various forms of violence, to their interactions, and to their common roots. Similarly, research workers feel the need for more comprehensive surveys on the incidence and prevalence of violent acts within the same families and more comprehensive theoretical accounts. Since the early seventies, members of the Family Violence Research Program of the Family Research Laboratory of the University of New Hampshire, led by Murray

Straus, have recognized the need for more comprehensive approaches to treatment, research, and theory and have made major advances in promoting this perspective through their publications and the national conferences they convene.

Despite a growing sophistication about the need for more rigorous attention to research methodology and the requirements for procuring persuasive results, research on the incidence and prevalence of family violence, analysis of its demographic distribution, testing of competing theoretical accounts, and evaluation of the effects of interventions is still in a relatively primitive state with a few notable exceptions (see Weis, in this volume). There still remain serious problems in defining the various forms of family violence in terms of the seriousness of the assault, the amount of physical injury, sexual molestation, or neglect, and the extent of psychological trauma. The simple question of what constitutes a "family relationship" is complicated by the diversity of intimate nonmarital relationships in relatively stable arrangements. Consequently the lack of consensus on definitions of the object of study and measures of violence makes it difficult to compare or validate results from different studies.

The problems of sampling pose comparable difficulties. Many of the research studies draw on the case files of the courts or social service agencies. The samples tend to be small and are of limited generalizability because of the bias in the agency admission or selection process. National or local surveys of the general population overcome these limitations to a considerable extent but are themselves limited in other ways that have been catalogued by Joseph Weis (in this volume).

The problems of sampling and generalizability also apply to attempts to evaluate the effects of criminal justice system responses to family violence (see Elliott, in this volume) and to treatment programs for victims and offenders (see Saunders and Azar, in this volume). Following up agency samples where treatment interventions have occurred may show apparent success in reducing violence but the absence of control group follow-ups makes it difficult to determine the relative importance or effects of the treatment. The use of an experimental design to test a treatment hypothesis with careful definition of the target group and randomized controls is very rare in this field of research but efforts of this kind are increasingly recognized as critical for advancement of practice and knowledge of causal effects.

Despite these limitations, there is much to be learned about family violence from the existing body of literature on research and practice. It is understandable that the strongest initial response to the discovery of the extent and intensity of family violence was to do something about it. The early definitions of the problem thus came from clinical and social service practitioners, many of whom sought to advance conceptual understanding of the cases they were dealing with. This possibility helped to mobilize researchers with a strong interest in improving and augmenting available treatments. At the same time, it became apparent that better knowledge was needed about the extent of various forms of family violence, a need that has been addressed by two methods, the collection of data from agencies dealing with family violence problems, and the funding of national surveys on the incidence and prevalence of different types of family violence (concerning child physical and sexual abuse, see Garbarino [in this volume]; concerning marital violence, see Frieze and Browne [in this volume]; concerning other forms of family violence, see Pagelow [in this volume]; concerning the interaction between family violence and crime outside the family, see Hotaling, Straus, and Lincoln [in this volume]).

III. State of Criminal Justice Research

There are parallels between the development of research approaches in relation to crime and family violence. The early studies of crime in the United States grew out of case studies of offenders being subjected to various forms of criminal justice processing.

Particularly with the growth of the juvenile court movement, probation, social case work, the settlement house movement in depressed urban areas, and the advent of psychoanalytic theoretical and treatment perspectives, attention focused on the developmental histories of offenders and potential avenues for treatment (see Mennel 1973). Data on the amount of crime in the United States gradually became available with the collection by the FBI of arrest data from police departments in the 1920s. This generated a series known as the Uniform Crime Reports which have gradually been improved in coverage, reliability, and detail over subsequent years. The advantage of this type of data collection is that it provides benchmarks for assessing trends in police responses to crime despite difficulties introduced by including new agencies and sometimes new definitions over the years. The disadvantage of these data is that the extent of the crime problem is measured only by reports to the police or by arrests and thus fails to reflect the volume of crime that goes unreported or that does not result in arrests. Local (e.g., Farrington and West 1981) and occasionally national samples of youth (e.g., Chaiken and Chaiken 1982; Elliott and Huizinga 1983) and later of adult criminals (Greenwood and Abrahamse 1982), asked to report on their offenses, have provided substantially different pictures from those provided by arrest data, in terms both of the amount of criminal activity and of its demographic distribution. Police data thus underestimate the amount of crime and the distribution of offenders as measures of incidence or prevalence but do provide helpful benchmarks on police capabilities of response.

A further innovation for estimating the national or local incidence of crime was introduced by the President's Commission on Law Enforcement and Administration of Justice during its work from 1965 to 1967. The commission supported a national survey of crime (Ennis 1967) and several more intensive local surveys in which randomly selected household members were asked about their experience as victims of crime. Later institutionalized in the National Crime Surveys conducted by the Bureau of the Census on large, nationally representative samples of households at six month intervals, with funds provided by the Bureau of Justice Statistics, these surveys have now become established as a way of assessing dimensions of the crime problem independent of the response capabilities of the police (Sparks 1981; Gottfredson 1986). By taking periodic counts they are providing valuable data on trends that often differ substantially from those indicated by police data. Thus in assessing the type and nature of the crime problem, there now exist three independent windows (police, self-report, and victim data) for gauging the incidence of crime and to some extent its prevalence in particular samples.

Family violence research appears to be moving along a parallel track. The initial clinical and social service responses to family violence provided valuable insights into the dynamics of this process in violent homes but also raised new interest in the dimensions of the problem. This has led to efforts to collect data from agencies that typically encounter the problem through their intake processes, as, for example, the National Incidence Surveys of child maltreatment sponsored by the National Center on Child Abuse and Neglect (Burgdorf 1980). National surveys of representative samples of households, such as those undertaken by Murray Straus and his colleagues in 1975 and 1985 (e.g., Straus and Gelles 1986), have been conducted to obtain reports from potential victims. Though these provide essential pilot studies of the potential for sampling households, they have not yet been instituted as a regular survey series.

Family violence has not been generally acknowledged as a serious crime problem in this country until recently, and sources of national data on crime reflect that state of affairs. In the Uniform Crime Reports, for example, reports of family violence are merged with the statistics on simple or aggravated assaults. They can be identified separately in the National Crime Surveys, however, but their treatment is much less extensive than it could be and completely ignores crimes against children under age 12. In the past, police have exercised a great deal of discretion in reporting family violence calls. The pervasiveness of this pattern of discretionary decisions by the police was a major finding of the American Bar Foundation Survey of Criminal Justice in the United States (LaFave 1965). It revealed a tendency on the part of the police to take as little action as possible in family violence encounters. This tradition may be changing as the result of pressure from groups in the women's rights movement and from recent efforts to replicate or implement prescriptive arrest policies in spouse assault cases as a result of the findings of a spouse assault experimental study in Minneapolis that concluded that a policy of invariant arrest produced lower rates of repeated violence to original victims than did other police actions such as mediation efforts (Sherman and Berk 1984).

One of the important tasks for the future is to combine the interests of criminologists and family violence specialists in obtaining more careful delineation of the nature and extent of family violence and of the effects of different forms of prevention and intervention by social service or criminal justice agencies.

IV. The Special Nature of Family Violence
One barrier to closer collaboration between criminologists and family violence researchers in the past has been the tendency of both groups to view family violence as a special problem distinct from assaults outside the home. Accordingly, there have been few attempts to identify clearly what these forms of violence have in common or to what extent theories, concepts, and empirical descriptions are equally applicable. Many forms of abuse of spouses, children, siblings, parents, and the elderly in the home are of great importance to family specialists but do not reach the level of criminal violation. In the past, there has been a great reluctance to intervene in family affairs unless the ensuing violence mobilizes the attention of social service or law enforcement agencies and thereby commands official intervention.

This situation seems to be changing, however, with the increased sensitivity to the human and social costs of violence in the home. There is increasing recognition by criminologists and family violence specialists that new insights can be gained from collaborative studies of the nature, causes, extent, and patterns of violence in the home and its interactions with violence outside the home. There is increasing evidence that the violent experiences of both offenders and victims in the home predispose to crimes against others on the outside. Also, if—as appears to be the case—abused children are disproportionately likely to become involved in crime and violence in later life, there is a mutual interest in both prevention and effective forms of intervention on the part of the social services and law enforcement. Both groups need to collaborate to find out what kinds of intervention policies work best, while respecting strong cultural norms supportive of the integrity, privacy, intimacy, and mutual responsibility of family relationships.

Nowhere is the ambivalence about family violence as a special problem more evident than in considering the vulnerability of prior victims to future violence. Where maintaining the integrity of the family and building on its strengths is a primary objective, there is a risk that the battered wife or child may suffer further harm. Or where prosecution is successfully initiated, there is the possibility of reprisal or the internalization of deeply felt feelings of guilt. In the end, the goal is to bring about a cessation of family violence through either deterrence or dissuasion, but, so far, very little research has been conducted to demonstrate how to accomplish this so that the benefits outweigh the costs (see Fagan, in this volume).

V. Ethics and Research

In the past twenty years, much progress has been achieved in recognizing ethical issues and in establishing and observing ethical standards for the conduct of social research. It is now routine for research institutions conducting studies of human subjects to require clearance of the study design, research instruments, and procedures by a standing committee on research ethics. These committees require a showing that no harm will come to those who participate, that their informed consent will be obtained in advance of the inquiry, and that confidentiality of their responses will be protected. Research on family violence, like other research on human subjects, must comply with all such requirements, as must studies of criminal offenders and victims. However, some sensitive ethical problems have special prominence in family violence research.

One of these relates to the ethical obligation to report to the appropriate authorities knowledge of criminal violent abuse that has occurred or is continuing without official notice or intervention. This may involve reports from victims in interviews that severe physical assaults of spouses or sexual abuses of children are occurring. The victim may insist on confidentiality for fear of reprisals from the offender. To take no action to bring about intervention would be intolerable even though it might preclude further research or might result in more violent acts. This is not an uncommon situation in studies of criminal offenders and victims. Offenders in their self-reports will admit to many offenses for which they were never apprehended and victims will identify criminal acts and offenders that they refuse to report for a variety of reasons. Normally, researchers announce in advance of the interview that admissions should not include sufficient details to establish culpability. But obviously, the family violence context is especially sensitive since the situation of jeopardy is a continuing one.

The ethical obligations to report or to take actions to curb known abuses rests on the need to protect vulnerable victims from further abuse or to deter offenders from abusing current or future potential victims. The reporting obligation encounters tensions arising from the obligation to preserve confidentiality and to protect the integrity of the research process and its access to both offenders and victims. Usually in these situations, the researcher is not in possession of sufficient evidence to support arrest or prosecution and must rely on advice to and persuasion of the victim to take appropriate protective measures with the aid of social services or law enforcement. In some ways, the situation is not unlike that encountered in the study of organized crime. Researchers find that organized crime figures will often talk freely about their operations knowing that no hard evidence will emerge that law enforcement agencies do not already know or suspect. At the same time, victims often insist on confidentiality and, because of fear of reprisals, refuse to report to the authorities.

What tends to emerge in these situations is a differentiation of functions between various types of research and between research activities and remedial responses. Research designed to generate knowledge about the incidence, prevalence, and demographic distribution of family violence is unlikely often to obtain actionable evidence to trigger an obligation to report independent of the wishes of the victim. Evaluation research on the effectiveness of intervention and treatment programs takes place in a context in which reporting has already taken place.

Clinical studies of the dynamics of family violence also sometimes identify cases of abuse. There is still a need for sensitivity concerning confidentiality and the continuing vulnerability of prior victims in each of these research approaches to family violence, but the context in which it is conducted mitigates the ethical tensions noted above. Furthermore, recent experience has demonstrated the ability of medical, human services, and law enforcement agencies to activate discovery systems for identifying violence in the home through such channels as hotlines, shelters, emergency clinics, school guidance counselors, and family service workers.

VI. The Future of Family Violence Research

There has been some debate about whether family violence exhibits unique characteristics that distinguish it from other forms of violent assaults. However, our reliance on the family as a basic institution for the development of bonding capabilities, training in the management of emotions, relationships for the expression of intimacy, and the transmission of basic cultural norms, values, and beliefs would appear to justify special attention to major disruptions of these functions. We clearly need to know much more about family violence if we wish to be more effective in its prevention or cure. Though each essay in this volume details many issues on which more intensive research is needed, it may be appropriate here to underscore some of the major tasks to be accomplished.

A. State of Knowledge

We have noted above the somewhat fragmented organization of research activities involving different disciplines, theoretical perspectives, issues, goals, and reporting outlets. Though this is understandable and even desirable in the initial exploratory phases of knowledge accumulation and theory development, family violence studies have reached a point where a more comprehensive view of the various forms of family violence and their interrelationships would inform and quicken the development of knowledge and treatment effectiveness. This is now beginning to take place. This book was inspired by a desire to aid this process and, in particular, to explore the relation of family violence to crime and criminal justice generally. The essay by Hotaling, Straus, and Lincoln (in this volume) on intrafamily violence and crime and violence outside the family focuses specifically on this relationship.

B. Theoretical Development

Given the variety of disciplines involved in the study of family violence and the specialization of attention to its different manifestations, it is not surprising to find a rich and confusing array of explanations. All of the mainstream theories appear to have some relevance to some aspects of family violence. At times they appear to be competing explanations, and at others to complement or supplement one another. More attention now needs to be paid to explicit statements of underlying theoretical assumptions and the appropriate concepts and operational variables by which theoretical relevance can be tested. This may then facilitate the task of theoretical integration, an excellent example of which may be found in Burgess and Draper's essay (in this volume) on the role of biological, behavioral, and cultural selection in the explanation of family violence. This task would be greatly facilitated by more intensive efforts to reach some consensus on basic definitions of the dependent variable, violence or abuse, and the unit of analysis, the family.

C. Methodology

Family violence research is advancing steadily in its increasingly sophisticated attention to design and measurement problems. There is still much to be done to develop reliable studies of the incidence and prevalence of the various forms of family violence. Reviews of existing knowledge are forced to draw on small clinical studies and agency intake data in which for the most part the selection biases are unknown. This situation has been relieved somewhat in recent years by the introduction of survey research studies of the general population. A major goal, however, should be the initiation of long-term longitudinal cohort studies in which the family is the unit of analysis. This would permit advances beyond cross-sectional correlations of variables to examination of the sequential development of factors related to the emergence of the different forms of family violence and their relation to other forms of crime and serious antisocial conduct. The explanatory power of such designs would also be greatly enhanced by the coupling of longitudinal studies with experimental interventions (Farrington, Ohlin, and Wilson 1986). These, of course, are expensive undertakings involving long-term commitments from funding sources and research staff. At this stage of development, they should not preclude continuing resort to cross-sectional, agency and clinical studies from which many useful insights about the extent and dynamics of family violence can be obtained.

D. Experimental Intervention

Increased concern about family violence has generated a number of innovative efforts to deal with the problems of victims and, to a much lesser extent, of offenders. Evaluation of the relative effectiveness of these programs has been severely hampered by the difficulty or perceived limited usefulness of creating control groups. Understandably, the preoccupation has been to provide the most help possible to victims with the limited resources available and the need for services. However, in the long run, these resources could be expended much more effectively if we knew more about what works and what does not for different types of situations and victims. The difficulty of reaching evaluative judgments is amply demonstrated in the essays by Elliott (in this volume) and Saunders and Azar (in this volume) on criminal justice procedures and treatment programs. Experimental interventions involving random assignment to different groups are difficult to construct, and it is difficult to hold to the experimental design. But the payoff in knowing what works better than an alternative treatment would advance practitioners' knowledge and skill immeasurably. What is needed are opportunities to test comparatively those interventions for which we have the best theoretical and factual basis for hope of success.

E. Data Archives

As family violence research increases its data-gathering operations, the advancement of knowledge would be greatly facilitated by establishing a center for the archiving of data sets with appropriate confidentiality protections. This has proved a fruitful strategy in a number of fields including that of crime and criminal justice. It permits a parsimonious use of different types of research competence and facilitates more extensive analysis of expensively obtained data sets. Some persons are more adept at the design and fielding of research than at analysis of data. Archiving permits both sets of skills to function more effectively. In addition, it permits the costly data-gathering process to achieve maximum payoff by opening the data set to the exploration of different empirical enquiries and the testing of different theoretical interpretations which had not been foreseen by the field team.

Family violence offers an exciting field of research and practice innovation. There is deep public concern about the problem, its extent, causes, prevention, and treatment. Increasing amounts of public and private funds are becoming available to find out what is wrong and what can be done about it. The pioneers in research and treatment are in constant demand for conferences and workshops organized by persons eager to become informed about the current state of knowledge and to gain guidance on promising steps to be taken. It is our hope that this volume will facilitate this process by reflecting as objectively as possible what is known from research and practice about the problem. Gaps identified in our knowledge should be perceived as a spur to further work rather than as a commentary on this fledgling field of study and the inspiring efforts of its pioneers.

REFERENCES

Burgdorf, K. 1980. *Recognition and Reporting of Child Maltreatment: Findings from the National Study of the Incidence and Severity of Child Abuse and Neglect.* Washington, D.C.: National Center on Child Abuse and Neglect.

Burgess, R. L., and P. Draper. In this volume. "The Explanation of Family Violence: The Role of Biological, Behavioral, and Cultural Selection."

Chaiken, J., and M. Chaiken. 1982. *Varieties of Criminal Behavior.* Santa Monica, Calif.: Rand.

Elliott, D. S. In this volume. "Criminal Justice Procedures in Family Violence Crimes."

Elliott, D. S., and D. Huizinga. 1983. "Social Class and Delinquent Behavior in a National Youth Panel." *Criminology* 21:149–77.

Ennis, P. H. 1967. *Criminal Victimization in the United States: A Report of a National Survey.* President's Commission on Law Enforcement and Administration of Justice. Field Surveys no. 2. Washington, D.C.: U.S. Government Printing Office.

Fagan, J. In this volume. "Cessation of Family Violence: Deterrence and Dissuasion."

Farrington, D. P., L. E. Ohlin, and J. Q. Wilson. 1986. *Understanding and Controlling Crime: Toward a New Research Strategy.* New York: Springer-Verlag.

Farrington, D. P., and D. J. West. 1981. "The Cambridge Study in Delinquent Development." In *Prospective Longitudinal Research*, edited by S. A. Mednick and A. E. Baert. Oxford: Oxford University Press.

Frieze, I. H., and A. Browne. In this volume. "The Incidence and Prevalence of Violence in Marriage."

Garbarino, J. In this volume. "The Incidence and Prevalence of Child Maltreatment."

Gottfredson, M. R. 1986. "Substantive Contributions of Victimization Surveys." In *Crime and Justice: An Annual Review of Research*, vol. 7, edited by M. Tonry and N. Morris. Chicago: University of Chicago Press.

Greenwood, P. W., and A. Abrahamse. 1982. *Selective Incapacitation.* Santa Monica, Calif.: Rand.

Herrenkohl, E. C., R. C. Herrenkohl, and L. J. Toedter. 1983. "Perspectives on the Intergenerational Transmission of Abuse." In *The Dark Side of Families: Current Family Violence Research*, edited by D. Finkelhor and associates. Beverly Hills, Calif.: Sage.

Hotaling, G. T., M. A. Straus, and A. J. Lincoln. In this volume. "Intrafamily Violence, and Crime and Violence outside of the family."

Kempe, C. H., F. N. Silverman, B. B. Steele, W. Droegemueller, and H. K. Silver. 1962. "The Battered-Child Syndrome." *Journal of the American Medical Association* 181:17–24.

LaFave, W. 1965. *Arrest: The Decision to Take a Suspect into Custody*. New York: Little, Brown.

Loeber, R., and M. Stouthamer-Loeber. 1986. "Family Factors as Correlates and Predictors of Juvenile Conduct Problems and Delinquency." In *Crime and Justice: An Annual Review of Research*, vol. 7, edited by M. Tonry and N. Morris. Chicago: University of Chicago Press.

Mednick, S. A., and J. Volavka. 1980. "Biology and Crime." In *Crime and Justice: An Annual Review of Research*, vol. 2, edited by N. Morris and M. Tonry. Chicago: University of Chicago Press.

Mennel, R. 1973. *Thorns and Thistles: Juvenile Delinquents in the United States, 1825–1949*. Hanover, N. H.: University Press of New England.

Pagelow, M. D. In this volume. "The Incidence and Prevalence of Criminal Abuse of Other Family Members."

Pleck, E. In this volume. "Criminal Approaches to Family Violence, 1640–1980."

Saunders, D. G., and S. Azar. In this volume. "Treatment Programs for Family Violence."

Sherman, L. W., and R. A. Berk. 1984. "The Specific Deterrent Effects of Arrest for Domestic Assault." *American Sociological Review* 49:261–72.

Shields, N. M., and C. R. Hanneke. 1983. "Battered Wives' Reactions to Marital Rape." In *The Dark Side of Families: Current Family Violence Research*, edited by D. Finkelhor and associates. Beverly Hills, Calif.: Sage.

Sparks, R. F. 1981. "Surveys of Victimization—an Optimistic Assessment." In *Crime and Justice: An Annual Review of Research*, vol. 3, edited by M. Tonry and N. Morris. Chicago: University of Chicago Press.

Straus, M. A., and R. J. Gelles. 1986. "Societal Change and Change in Family Violence from 1975 to 1985 as Revealed by Two National Surveys." *Journal of Marriage and the Family* 48:465–79.

Weis, J. G. In this volume. "Family Violence Research Methodology and Design."

Zimring, F. E. In this volume. "Toward a Jurisprudence of Family Violence."

Elizabeth Pleck

Criminal Approaches to Family Violence, 1640–1980

ABSTRACT

American efforts to prevent or punish family violence began in New England in the 1640s with the passage of the first laws against family violence. Interest in criminalizing family violence since then has been episodic. There have been periods of American history that included reforms against family violence, including significant efforts to criminalize it; there have been other periods of decriminalization of family violence, and still others when there were significant judicial innovations in the handling of family violence cases without any comparable interest in the subject of domestic abuse. A social atmosphere favorable to the criminalization of family violence results from many factors, the most important of which is that family violence must be defined and perceived not just as a threat to individual victims but also as a danger to the social order. However, among the many reasons for the lack of interest in criminalizing family violence, the most significant is the view that family violence is primarily a domestic matter.

Many people think that family violence was discovered in the 1960s. It is true that the scale of effort on behalf of victims has been greater since that period than ever before. Yet there were earlier periods of reform against family violence in American history. From 1640 to 1680, the Puritans of colonial Massachusetts enacted the first laws anywhere in the world against wife beating and "unnatural severity" to children. A

Elizabeth Pleck is a research associate at the Center for Research on Women, Wellesley College. She wishes to acknowledge the anonymous reviewers' helpful comments on an earlier draft of this essay.

second reform epoch lasted from 1874 to about 1890, when societies for the prevention of cruelty to children (SPCCs) were founded, and smaller efforts on behalf of battered women and victims of incest were initiated. A modern era of interest came into its own in 1962, when five physicians published an article about "the battered child syndrome" in the *Journal of the American Medical Association* (Kempe et al. 1962). In the early 1970s, the women's liberation movement rediscovered wife beating and, somewhat later, marital rape. Since then many other types of family violence, from abuse of the elderly to sibling violence, have come to light.

The history of the criminalization of family violence is contemporaneous with, but not entirely parallel to, the rise (and fall) of these three periods of social interest. In each of them there were significant campaigns to increase the criminal penalties for domestic violence. The most recent period is somewhat mixed since it includes increasing efforts to criminalize incest, wife abuse, and marital rape but also retains persistent doubts about the wisdom of such efforts if they are applied to abused and neglected children. Even in periods when reform against family violence was quiescent, there have been important developments in the American judicial system affecting the handling of family violence criminal cases.

There has always been one necessary (although not sufficient) belief animating reform against domestic violence, namely, that the public interest in enforcement of the law against perpetrators of family violence outweighs the traditional rights of husbands or parents, or respect for domestic privacy. Whereas the state has long possessed the right to punish violators of the criminal law, it has often been claimed that family relationships require or deserve special immunity. Reformers have insisted that outside agencies have the right to intervene in the family and sometimes to take action to remove children from parental custody.

The greater the defense of the rights and privileges of the traditional family, the lower the interest in the criminalization of the family. When family violence is seen as a crime that threatens not only its victims but also the social order, support for criminalization of family violence increases. Thus, the conditions that most impede the criminalization of family violence are increased respect for family privacy, diminished enthusiasm for the state's responsibility to intervene in the family, and vigorous defense of the family ideal, a range of beliefs about the sanctity of the family that serves to shield the home from public view and state intervention. These beliefs include the view that parents have the right to discipline children physically; that a husband possesses the right to have sexual access to his wife; that nagging women or disobedient children often provoke the beatings they receive; that wives and children, as economic dependents, need a male provider; and that the law should not disrupt this traditional pattern of support, except in unusual circumstances.

Some forms of domestic violence have been more likely to be punished as crimes than others. Family murder and infanticide have always been regarded as serious crimes, although they have often been punished as manslaughter, rather than as homicide. Other types of domestic abuse, such as sibling violence and marital rape, have rarely been regarded as crimes. Criminal statutes have been passed to punish specific types of family violence. Many types of family violence have also been prosecuted as assault and battery, disorderly conduct, or breach of the peace. In general, wife abuse has been the type of family violence most likely to appear in court. This is because battered wives have been the victims of domestic violence most willing to complain to the police and to press charges. Sibling violence and marital rape have been the types of family violence least likely to be criminalized because sibling violence is often regarded as normal behavior, and rape laws have often exempted from criminal prosecution a husband's sexual assault on his wife.

This essay is organized as follows: Section I discusses seventeenth-century developments, with emphasis on both New England and the southern colonies of Maryland and Virginia. Sections II and III treat innovations in the nineteenth century. Section II focuses largely on the creation of new trial courts to which family violence cases could be brought and on appellate case law that contradicted or affirmed common-law rights of parents or husbands. Section III deals with the multiple social reform movements of the late nineteenth century that were concerned with family violence, including the most significant of these, societies for the prevention of cruelty to children. Section IV analyzes the development of the juvenile courts, beginning at the turn of the century. Section V briefly discusses the modern period of heightened interest in family violence, beginning around 1960 and subsiding somewhat by the 1980s, and compares the modern developments with their historical antecedents.

I. Seventeenth-Century American Laws and Courts

Unique features of the Puritan experiment in the New World encouraged the criminalization of family violence. The Puritans of New England believed that the family prepared children for a pious life and that it conveyed their religious values. An institution so necessary to the Puritan mission could not become a sanctuary for cruelty and violence. The Puritans classified verbal or physical assault, whether between strangers or family members, as "wicked carriage." Family violence was a sin; only if the Puritans maintained their watchfulness against sin would their godly experiment prosper.

The Puritans attacked family violence with the combined forces of community, church, and state. Conformity was expected, and meddling was considered a positive virtue. Neighbors watched each other informally for signs of aberration, which were often reported to the minister or local constable. The political freedom of the Massachusetts Bay Colony from direct English rule during the English Civil War also made it possible for the colony to embed its religious principles in the law.

The colony of New Haven enacted the first American law against family violence in 1639. The law punished incest with death by hanging. If the sexual union had been voluntary, then both parties were to be put to death. No one was ever prosecuted under this statute. Thus this and many other colonial laws, while extremely punitive, had a largely symbolic intent.

Two years later the first law against wife abuse anywhere in the Western world was written into a new criminal code of the Massachusetts Bay Colony. According to one of the provisions of the Massachusetts *Body of Laws and Liberties*, "Everie marryed woeman shall be free from bodilie correction or stripes by her husband, unlesse it be in his owne defence upon her assault" (Massachusetts Colony 1890, p. 51). A few years later, the law was amended to prohibit husband beating as well. Plymouth Colony was probably following Massachusetts Bay in enacting a law against spouse abuse in 1672 (Cushing 1977, p. 48). Wife beating was punished with a five-pound fine or a whipping, and husband beating with a sentence to be determined by the court. The Massachusetts *Body of Laws and Liberties* also protected the "liberties of children." A provision that prohibited parents from choosing their child's mate included a clause that forbade parents from exercising "any unnatural severities" toward children.

Since the Puritans are usually known for their scarlet A's and ducking stools, it may come as a surprise to find that their laws concerned wife beating and child abuse. The Puritans have not received the credit they deserve for their humanitarian ideas. These ranged from outlawing the torture of prisoners to prohibiting cruelty to animals. The *Body of Laws and Liberties* reflected a belief that women and children deserved certain rights; thus, the provision against wife beating was found in a section on the liberties of women; the clause against child abuse was contained in a section on the liberties of children.

New England Puritan attitudes toward wife beating reflected English Puritan ideas. As early as 1599 an English Puritan minister argued that a wife beater should be whipped because "he is worthy to be beaten for choosing no better" (Koehler 1980, p. 49). The English Puritan moral theologian William Gouge, who published a popular manual titled *Domesticall Duties* in 1622, argued that it was immoral for a husband to beat his wife (Stone 1977, p. 179). In his family advice book, the great Puritan preacher William Perkins opposed wife beating, as did another English Puritan writer, Richard Baxter (Stone 1977, p. 179). American Puritans followed English practice in condemning wife beating. In one of his sermons, the famous Boston minister Cotton Mather preached that for "a man to Beat his Wife was as bad as any Sacriledge. And such a Rascal were better buried alive, than show his Head among his Neighbours any more" (Koehler 1980, p. 49).

New England's Puritan laws were in advance of English law and attitudes. Yet English seventeenth-century ecclesiastical courts also punished wife beaters, and some Anglicans in England condemned wife beating. But when the English Puritans came to power under Cromwell, they did not pass legislation against wife beating. The freedom of the Massachusetts Bay Colony from English domination—along with Puritan humanitarian ideas—encouraged the enactment of the *Body of Laws and Liberties*.

The passage of the *Body of Laws and Liberties* occurred during a period of political freedom for the colony. Parliament had granted Massachusetts Bay permission to govern itself, in accordance with English law. When the English Civil War broke out in 1642, the colonies were left on their own. Taking advantage of their freedom from imperial domination, the Puritans set out to draft laws that reflected their religious principles. In the 1630s, freemen, resident stockholders in the investment company backing the colony, demanded a written constitution and a civil and criminal code to protect their liberties. They were concerned that royally appointed judges might misuse their discretionary powers and infringe on the civil liberties Englishmen had come to expect. Acting on their request, the colony's general court, the equivalent of a colonial legislature, appointed a committee to devise a written legal code that became the law of the colony, even though it was never sent to Parliament for approval. A draft by Puritan minister John Cotton was rejected because it contained too many provisions calling for capital punishment, including one specifying hanging for incest. The general court turned to Reverend Nathaniel Ward, a Puritan minister with English legal training. He pruned some of Cotton's capital provisions and added sections protecting the liberties of women, children, servants, and foreigners. As one of the founders of the New Haven Colony, Cotton was able to achieve enactment of a law against incest there (Haskins 1960, pp. 123–40).

In addition to the law against incest in New Haven, several other New England colonies punished incest as a crime. The Bible called for capital punishment of those who committed incest, but English law at the time did not. The colony of New Haven followed the Bible and made incest a crime punishable by death; the colony of Massachusetts Bay copied English law and omitted incest from its list of capital crimes. In all the New England colonies, the definition of incest was broader than our own; in addition to a father's sexual relations with his daughter, incest included consensual sex or even marriages between near relatives. Here again, the Puritans intended these laws merely to serve as a symbolic affirmation of biblical principles. One survey of seventeenth-century New England court records found only six cases of incest in the criminal courts, and no one was executed for having committed incest (Oberholzer 1956, p. 124).

Although there were humanitarian and religious dimensions to the Puritan legal code, the major purpose of their laws against family violence was to reinforce hierarchy within the family or in society. In the Puritan way of thinking, God ruled the state and the state governed the family. Within the family, the husband was sovereign over his wife, children, servants, and apprentices. As people who respected authority, the Puritans accepted and even justified the use of "legitimate" physical force by parents, masters, and husbands. A father was entitled to use "moderate correction" in the discipline of his children, servants, and apprentices. Occasionally, the state permitted a husband to punish an abusive wife or a disobedient child at home (presumably with a whipping). The courts never permitted a child to punish a parent, or a wife to punish a husband. The obvious reason for this difference is that the husband and father was the highest ranking figure in the household. Only he could act on the basis of authority delegated by the state.

Criminal laws against family violence were intended mainly to serve symbolic purposes—to define the boundary between saint and sinner, to demonstrate to God and community a vigilance against sin, and to shore up proper authority in the household and in society. While the Puritans passed laws against family violence, these were rarely enforced, and when they were, offenders usually received lenient sentences. In keeping with these motives, Puritan laws punished both abuses of authority and acts of disobedience or rebellion against legitimate authority.

The desire of the community to eradicate sin encouraged surveillance of families where violence was occurring. But the equally strong impulse to respect parental rights and authority and to preserve the family limited the number of persons arrested for domestic assault. If there were arrests or prosecutions, it encouraged the law to side with maintaining the nuclear family, rather than with permitting or encouraging single-parent households.

The few domestic assaults that were prosecuted were punished by a fine.[1] Court records indicate that some domestic assailants were fined and whipped, although a fine was usually offered as an alternative to a whipping (Koehler 1980, pp. 140–41). Magistrates believed that the disgrace of punishment and "holy watching" by neighbors would deter further violence. Repeat offenders were sometimes asked to post a bond of surety. If they failed to do so, they were sent to jail. If they did post a bond and committed another act of violence, the bond was forfeited.

How frequent was prosecution for family violence? In the court records of Plymouth Colony from 1633 to 1802, the only jurisdiction where the subject has been studied for a long period of time, there were only nineteen cases of wife beating, husband beating, incest, or assault by a child on parents. The single largest group of cases, twelve out of nineteen, concerned wife beating (Pleck 1987, p. 27). Another study of verbal as well as physical assault between spouses found that in six New England colonies between 1630 and 1699, fifty-seven wives and 128 husbands were tried in court on charges of assault (Koehler 1980, p. 160). The inclusion of verbal abuse explains the large number of

---

[1] Only the New England colonies of Massachusetts Bay and Plymouth enacted laws against spouse abuse. In the other New England colonies of Rhode Island, Connecticut, and New Hampshire, spousal assault was punished as assault and battery, although there was no specific statutory provision against it.

women—typically charged by their husbands with "nagging"—who were brought to court.

In cases of wife beating, judges tended to inquire whether a wife provoked her husband into beating her. On occasion, battered wives who complained to their neighbors that they were abused recanted their grievances in court. In the Essex County Quarterly Court in 1682, for example, Elizabeth Ela pleaded, "I have nothinge Agenst my husband to charge him with" (Dow 1911–21, pp. 272–73). In cases of abused servants, judges usually wanted proof that the servants had not been incorrigible (Ulrich 1982, p. 187).

No case of child abuse was ever prosecuted in the Plymouth courts. Indeed, despite the provision in the Massachusetts *Body of Laws and Liberties* permitting children to complain of their parents' unnatural severity, none ever did so. Moreover, no evidence of burning or scalding of children appears in New England colonial court records. Only one natural father was brought before any New England colonial court for having abused his child. Michael Emerson of Haverhill, Massachusetts, was charged with "cruel and excessive beating" of his eleven-year-old daughter with a flail swingle (a large wooden handle attached to a free-swinging stick that was used in the threshing of grain) and with kicking her. Six months later, the court abated Michael Emerson's fine and released him on a bond of good behavior (Dow 1911–21, pp. 139, 141).

Demos (1986, pp. 85–87) attributes the low incidence of reported child abuse to the nature of Puritan family and community life. In their relatively large households, Puritan children were cared for by siblings, as well as by other kin, thus reducing the stress on a single caretaker. As productive laborers from an early age, children were necessary to the work of the farm family. Parents regarded their child's destiny as a matter of fate or God's plan; they were not plagued with self-doubts and did not require their children to furnish them with proof of their personal esteem.

Contrary to this view, however, Pleck (1987, p. 28) and Ulrich (1982, p. 187) argue that acceptable punishment appears to have included those beatings and bruisings that fell short of maiming or *permanently* injuring the child. Puritans were expected to treat a servant as they would treat a child. Yet there were far more reports of servant abuse than of child abuse. Although a servant, the servant's relatives, and neighbors might complain against a cruel master, hardly anyone did more than issue threats and warnings to a brutal father or mother. The hesitancy to charge a natural father or mother with child assault or to remove an abused child from his or her natural parents can be attributed to the Puritans' reverence for the two-parent, father-dominated household and their belief in the parent-child bond. These explanations are more complementary than contradictory. That the Puritan domestic homicide rate was quite low suggests that family tensions rarely reached the boiling point (Pleck 1987, p. 219), and that there were more cases of servant abuse than of child abuse also suggests a reluctance to interfere with the parent's right to punish a disobedient child.

In the New England colonies, a second judicial system, the church court, existed alongside the magistrate's court. The most frequent cause of complaint in these courts was fornication. But church courts, on rare occasions, also tried cases of wife abuse, cruelty to children and servants, assaults, murder threats against parents, and child neglect.

Church courts relied much more on shaming and community censure than did the secular courts. The congregation of a church had to decide whether to accept a sinner's confession (Oberholzer 1956, pp. 120–21, 124). Sometimes they were asked to vote; at other times they were asked to raise their voices to indicate acceptance of a confession, or sometimes they were asked to keep silent to signal a rejection. If a congregation rejected an applicant, then the minister delivered a fearsome sermon on the evils of wrongdoing before pronouncing sentence. A church in Weston, Massachusetts, accepted the confession of a man who threatened to kill his father, while a minister in Cambridge, who threatened to take his mother's life, was suspended (Powers 1966, p. 162).

As Puritans became Yankees, the limited enforcement of domestic violence legislation disappeared altogether. In Plymouth, there were four complaints of wife assault between 1663 and 1682. Thereafter the number of accusations dwindled to only one complaint per decade from 1683 to 1702. In the first half of the eighteenth century, virtually no complaints of wife assault came before Plymouth magistrates, and in the second half of the century, there were at most two complaints per decade. By 1690, accusations of other types of family violence—husband beating, violence between servants and masters, a child beating a parent, or incest—disappeared from the Plymouth courts (Pleck 1987, p. 29).

At the top of the Puritans' prosecution list of moral crimes was fornication, that is, premarital or extramarital sex. Even here, however, Puritan interest began to recede. After 1650, presentments for fornication declined (Hartog 1976). Most of the defendants were mothers of illegitimate children; the courts no longer brought to trial couples who had committed the offense but who subsequently married.

The declining enforcement of the crime of fornication was accompanied by a waning belief in the community's responsibility to regulate activity that occurred in private (Hartog 1976). Legal thinkers in the eighteenth century distinguished between public and private behavior. In *Commentaries on the Laws of England*, first published between 1765 and 1769, William Blackstone stated his view that a crime was an act that produced mischief in civil society, while private vices were not the legitimate subject of law. Even the vice of drunkenness, if practiced in public, was an evil example deserving of prosecution, Blackstone argued. But disharmony in the home was no longer perceived as a threat to the social order. The family became a private institution, separated from public life. State interest in the enforcement of morality had been the reason for Puritan interest in family violence; the decline of that interest contributed to the lack of social attention, even among the Puritans, to family violence (Pleck 1987, p. 33).

All of the North American colonies shared a common English legal tradition. But the New England colonies differed from the rest because they were founded by religious dissenters—Puritans—who wanted to incorporate biblical doctrine and distinctive religious principles into their laws. Except for those in New England, American colonies showed no special concern about family violence. The victim of family violence had to turn to relatives, friends, or neighbors for aid; no help could be expected from the local constable. Anglican churches were established in the southern colonies, but apparently no church courts were established there.

While the colonies other than those in New England tended to replicate English patterns, Maryland and Virginia devised a unique institution, the orphan's court, that supervised the treatment of orphans. This court provided protection and supervision of the orphan's estate and placed the orphaned child with a guardian. It also had the power to remove a child from custody of abusive stepparents. Authority over estates and supervision of guardians gave the orphan's court powers greater than those common in English chancery courts at the same time (Carr 1977).

The orphan's court was a legal response to the high death rate in the southern colonies. Malaria and epidemics were prevalent in the Chesapeake region, a much less healthy region than New England. A child in colonial Maryland or Virginia had a 50 percent chance of spending his or her childhood in the household of a stepfather or guardian. Young children who had lost a father often did not have relatives living nearby to take care of them (Watson 1975; Carr 1977).

The orphan's court had the power to investigate complaints against guardians. In 1682, a grandfather protested to the Virginia orphan's court about the treatment accorded his three grandsons by their acting guardian. The children were dressed in rags and old clothes, given only salt, hominy, and a bit of meat to eat, and were put to work in the fields doing a man's labor, planting corn and suckering tobacco. One grandson, set to work from dawn to dusk at arduous physical labor, had few clothes, if any, and was "sadly beaten and abused by the overseer and tyed up by the hands and whipt" (Walsh 1979, p. 145). The chief judge of probate agreed that the orphans "have not the Common Care had of them as is usuall for planters to have of their meanest Servants or Slaves," and he recommended that the county court place them in their grandfather's custody. The judge made no specific reference to abuse of the child. Two years later, the children were finally placed in their grandfather's hands. It is not clear whether this long lapse of time in removing the child from a guardian was typical for the orphan's court.

In attempting to enforce a minimal standard of care for children, the orphan's court asserted governmental responsibility to protect children. The court only supervised stepfathers and guardians and left natural parents to govern their children as they saw fit. No case of child abuse ever appeared before a court in the southern colonies. Thus, in the colonial South as well as in New England, parental rights remained sovereign.

II. Criminal Justice, 1830–74

No laws against family violence were passed from the time of the Pilgrim statute against wife beating in 1672 until a law against wife beating was enacted in Tennessee in 1850 (State of Tennessee 1850). The whole of the eighteenth and half of the nineteenth century appears to have been a legislative vacuum. Indeed, there is little evidence, aside from an occasional divorce case on grounds of cruelty, to demonstrate even passing interest in this subject during the eighteenth century (Kerber 1980, pp. 170–72, 175–78). Although thinkers of the Enlightenment in the eighteenth century often decried "parental tyranny," they were referring to a parent's denial of a child's right to choose a mate or to a husband's excessive (but not necessarily violent) authoritarianism

(Fliegelman 1982). The general lack of interest in family violence can be attributed to the growing distrust of government interference in the family, the increasing respect for domestic privacy, and the waning zeal for state enforcement of private morality (Glenn 1984, pp. 63–83; Pleck 1987, pp. 31–33). The era from 1830 to 1874 was not a period of social concern about family violence. Nonetheless, the criminal approach to family violence progressed gradually during those years, as cities established police, alderman's, or hustings courts. In these general rather than specialized courts, cases of wife beating and child abuse were heard alongside prosecutions of pickpockets and public drunkards.

Because these courts had relatively simple procedures and were located in neighborhoods near the tenements where poor families lived, it was easy for victims and their relatives to bring a complaint to court. The police court was usually located in a small room in a corner of the neighborhood police station. The room reeked of stale cigar smoke and human sweat and was crowded with predatory male bondsmen, messengers, and lawyers soliciting clients. The judge was usually an elected official who had some legal training. A husband who beat his wife might be fined fifty dollars. But if a man could not pay his fine, he might be sent to city jail. Cases of aggravated assault, family murder, or incest were felonies tried in superior court (Steinberg 1981).

While it was relatively easy for women victims to bring a complaint to court, it was much harder to ensure that justice would be meted out. In the police court, on occasion, a brawling husband was fined but his wife was sent to jail! Abused wives who fled their homes, and thereby left their children behind, could be charged with desertion. A wife who decided to drop her complaint against an abusive husband could so enrage a police court judge that he would charge her with contempt of court (*Boston Morning Post* 1837, pp. 81–82, 84–86, 110–11, 121, 137–38, 180, 201–4).

The operation of police courts up to the 1870s has not been studied, largely because of the lack of available documents. Friedman and Percival (1981) examined the records of the Oakland, California, police courts from 1870 and 1920. There appear to have been no major changes in the procedures of police courts during that time. Thus this evidence appears applicable as well to the first seven decades of the nineteenth century. In Oakland, most cases of child and wife abuse were tried in the police court as violations of public order. About half of those arrested for such violations were convicted or pleaded guilty. Defendants usually had to choose between going to jail and paying a fine. Most chose jail because they did not have enough money to pay their fines. But a battered wife often dipped into her savings or borrowed money from friends to purchase her husband's release since she and her children were dependent on the husband for support (Friedman and Percival 1981, p. 131).

We do not know whether the conviction rate was lower in cases of family violence than it was in other crimes against the public order. It seems likely, however, that many district attorneys were unwilling to prosecute cases of family abuse. For their part, district attorneys frequently claimed that reluctance to prosecute belonged entirely to wives who withdrew the charges because "to imprison the defendant would only leave the families in want" (Adams 1886, p. 10). The lack of vigorous prosecution of crimes of domestic violence reinforced the police attitude against arresting domestic assailants. Police had the power to arrest if the victim filed a complaint, if they themselves saw the assault, or if there was a witness. One police captain in a New York City neighborhood explained his manner of handling the great number of "family quarrels" to which he was summoned in this way:

> I settled such quarrels in my own way, as other policemen were doing. Arresting a drunken wife beater wouldn't help the family. The wage-earner would be in jail, the children would be without food and the wife would come pleading to the court to discharge the husband so that the family wouldn't starve. No, there was a more effective method. Wherever a drunken man beat up his wife, I beat the man up myself and gave him a taste of his own medicine. Then I made him go to bed and stay there until he slept it off. [Feldberg 1985, pp. 123–24]

Some cities established alderman's courts, which were criminal courts roughly similar to police courts that handled complaints against public order. Allen Steinberg (1981) studied alderman's courts in mid-nineteenth-century Philadelphia. Such courts were found in cities that had an aldermanic system of municipal representation. The alderman presiding over the court was an elected official, usually lacking any legal training. He derived his income from the fees he assessed each complainant. Because complainants paid the costs of prosecution, the alderman had an interest in prosecuting cases, and fee-paying complainants had an incentive for pursuing their cases. Since fees were assessed on the basis of the number of charges that were brought, aldermen encouraged the filing of multiple complaints. Penalties varied with the frequency or the severity of the crime and ranged from commitment in lieu of bail, to a small bond to keep the peace, to a reprimand. Steinberg found that aldermen invariably accepted a woman's claim of physical abuse and took some action. But a husband might bring a countercharge of assault against his wife.

In hustings courts, local civil as well as criminal tribunals found only in Virginia, wife beaters were charged with breach of the peace. The local newspaper carried the names of men brought to court on these charges. A husband brought before the hustings court for wife beating was often fined or released on the promise of good behavior. A man was not released from jail until he posted a bond for a stipulated number of months; if the assault was repeated, the bond was forfeited. Matthew Scroggins appeared in the hustings court of Petersburg, Virginia, five separate times on the charge of breach of peace. His wife testified in court that her husband drank all day, gambled frequently, tried to stop her from earning a living to support their four children, and beat her. Each time Rosena Scroggins brought her husband to court for beating her, the court imposed a higher bond: the first time, $5, the second time, $150, the third, $200. Matthew Scroggins died at age forty-one of "dropsy," no doubt an alcohol-related death (Lebsock 1984, p. 35).

As these examples indicate, wife beating was punished as a crime in many American courts. Atypical judicial opinions are often cited to prove that wife beating was "not against the law" until the 1870s. Robert Calvert writes, "There is no specific time when the husband lost his authority to beat his wife" (1974, pp. 88–91). Many writers on family violence decry "the rule of the thumb" that permitted a husband to beat his wife with a stick no thicker than his thumb. In 1783, an English Judge Buller (characterized by a cartoonist as "Judge Thumb") first asserted the rule. But English legal authorities challenged him, and writers and cartoonists lampooned him (May 1978). No American judge ever endorsed the "rule of thumb," and before the Civil War, two American states passed statutes against wife beating: Tennessee in 1850, and Georgia in 1857 (Pleck 1979). There is no information about the sponsors of this legislation or the reasons why it was passed. It is not known whether the Tennessee law was enforced, although a few severe cases of wife beating were prosecuted under the Georgia law (Wyatt-Brown 1982, p. 281).

The idea that wife beating was not against the law in nineteenth-century America originates with three appellate court rulings issued between 1824 and 1868: one in Mississippi in 1824, and two others in North Carolina in 1864 and 1868 (Pleck 1979). According to these court rulings, a husband had the legitimate right to discipline his wife physically, as long as it was done in a moderate manner. In *Bradley v. State*, 1 Miss. 157 (1824), the Mississippi Supreme Court upheld the right of moderate chastisement, even though Calvin Bradley was found guilty of assault and battery on his wife, Lydia. In *State v. Black*, 60 N.C. 262 (1864), a lower court in North Carolina found Jesse Black guilty of assault and battery on his wife, Tamsey, but the state supreme court, in overturning the ruling and ordering a new trial, upheld the right of a husband "to use toward his wife such a degree of force as is necessary." Jesse Black's actions, they argued, did not constitute assault and battery. After his wife, Tamsey, had taunted him (accusing him of visiting Sal Daly, a prostitute, and calling him a hog thief), he had seized her by the hair and pulled her to the floor and held her there. Since he did not hit or choke her, the court decided he had not committed assault and battery. In *State v. Rhodes*, A. B. Rhodes gave his wife, Elizabeth, three licks with a stick the size of one of his fingers. The North Carolina Supreme Court upheld a lower court ruling that Rhodes was not guilty. Even so, the court rejected the claim "that the husband has the right to whip his wife much or little" but ruled instead that it would "not interfere with family government in trifling cases" (State v. Rhodes, 61 N.C. 453, 353 [1868]). A trifling case, the court seemed to suggest, was one where no permanent injury had been inflicted.

State v. Rhodes has been widely quoted, probably because the North Carolina justices issued a lengthy ruling. But the decision ran contrary to legal opinion of the time, as even they acknowledged. "Our opinion is not in unison with the decisions of some of the sister States," the judges wrote, "or with the philosophy of some very respectable law writers, and could not be in unison with all; because of their contrariety—a decent respect for the opinions of others has induced us to be very full in stating the reasons for our conclusion" (*State v. Rhodes*, pp. 353–54, 1868).

While police courts and state appellate court judges for the most part regarded wife beating as a crime, child abuse appeared to fall within the domain of legitimate parental right. A parent who committed assault and battery on a child could be brought into police court, and charged. But only two cases of child abuse were decided on appeal prior to the beginning of the Civil War. In *Johnson and Wife v. the State of Tennessee*, 21 Tenn. 183 (1840), Mrs. Johnson hit her daughter with a stick or a switch and her fists and slammed her daughter's head against the wall. The case was missing detail about why the Johnsons were beating their daughter or the extent of the injuries they caused. In sending the case back for retrial, the Tennessee court affirmed the Johnsons' right "to chastise their refractory and disobedient" daughter, but it also held that parents must not exceed the bounds of moderation by inflicting cruel and merciless punishment. In retrying the case, a jury decided that the Johnsons had exceeded the bounds of moderation. Their conviction was overturned, however, because the judge in the original trial had improperly instructed the jury.

At about the same time, the North Carolina State Supreme Court put forward an alternative and far more conservative judicial definition of child cruelty. *Pendergrass v. the State of North Carolina*, 19 N.C. 365, 367 (1837), concerned a schoolmistress who hit a misbehaving girl of six or seven on the arm and neck and also beat her with a large (but unidentified) instrument. The girl's marks and bruises disappeared after a few days. The jury found the schoolmistress, Rachel Pendergrass, not guilty. The court upheld the right of a teacher (or a parent) to correct a child moderately. The chastiser's intentions, they argued, had to be considered in deciding whether an act was cruel. In this ruling, cruelty was defined as those acts that endanger life, limbs, or health, or cause disfigurement or permanent injury. But causing the child only temporary pain was considered legitimate.

Only the most serious and life-endangering cases of child abuse were regarded as criminal in nature. Given these judicial attitudes, it is not surprising to find that very few cases of child abuse were ever brought to court. It is important to note that judges did not necessarily consider the home the best place to raise a child, and thus were not always opposed to removing a child from parental guardianship. In fact, mid-nineteenth-century writers and reformers extolled the virtues of the asylum and the house of refuge as homes for delinquent, orphaned, neglected, or abandoned children (Rothman 1971; Mennel 1973; Schlossman 1977).

Jacksonian era reformers, interested in institutions to house the mentally ill, the insane, and the criminal, established houses of refuge. These were private institutions for children, authorized by laws that permitted courts to commit abandoned, vagrant, destitute, and neglected children to the refuge along with child criminals. Rothman (1971) has traced the origins of the house of refuge to reformers' fears of social unrest and to their desire to impose middle-class morality on the poor, thereby recapturing the Puritans' sense of community watch-fulness. In the 1850s, Charles Loring Brace helped to establish the Children's Aid Society in New York City. It sought to rescue children from the city streets and place them with farm families or send them to the West. Most rescued children were presumed to be either runaways, homeless, abandoned, or orphans (Boyer 1978). The lack of inquiry into whether such children had families or relatives with whom they could live suggests a cavalier attitude toward the family life of the poor. But these children were placed, not *because* of parental malfeasance, but because they were believed to be growing up without any parental supervision.

Similarly, though antebellum judges were willing to remove children from homes where drunkenness or neglect occurred, they were unwilling to intervene in instances of physical abuse (Thomas 1972). The desire to respect family privacy and to safeguard the traditional rights of parents to discipline their children was far greater than the fear of social disorder or the desire to control the lives of the poor. There was nothing new in these views; in fact, they represented a continuation of the dominant attitude in most of the eighteenth century.

III. The High Point of Criminalization, 1875–90

A volcano of moral outrage at domestic abuse and of sympathy for its victims erupted around 1875 and continued for the next fifteen years. The first society to protect children from cruelty was founded in New York in December 1874 (McCrea 1910; Coleman 1924; Hawes 1971; Antler and Antler 1979). By the turn of the century there were more than 300 such societies in the United States. In the same quarter century judges and lawyers campaigned to punish wife beating with the whipping post (Pleck 1983*a*). Female advocates of temperance helped to pass laws giving tort protection to drunkards' wives and children. Since many drunken men also abused their families, these laws often benefited the victims of domestic violence. One final undertaking was a women's legal aid society in Chicago, which aided victimized women and girls (Pleck 1983*b*). All these efforts shared the view that family violence was a serious crime.

There were several reasons for the revival of interest in criminal sanctions against family violence that began in 1875. The late nineteenth century resembled the Puritan era in some ways: both were periods of heightened interest in the state's responsibility to enforce public morality. The native-born, middle-class public believed that a society that did not uphold the moral law—a single standard of appropriate behavior—would decay. To stave off calamity, the aroused citizenry looked to the police, courts, and to state legislatures to pass and enforce morals laws. Legislators and voluntary groups sought to prohibit the sale of alcohol, to close saloons on Sundays, to punish violators of the Sabbath, and to eliminate prostitution.

Family violence was also taken seriously because the public was fearful of crime (Boyer 1978, pp. 143–61). The New York millionaires who founded the world's first SPCC worried that neglected and abused boys would, as grown men, "swell the ranks of the dangerous classes," endangering "public peace and security," and that similarly abused girls would soon become young women lost in "body and soul" (New York Society for the Prevention of Cruelty to Children 1876, p. 6). These statements coupled the fear of crime and immorality with the implicit hope that the children of the poor could be molded into respectable citizens. But the fear of crime also reflected a statistical and social reality: after the Civil War, the violent crime rate soared (Pleck 1987, p. 242). Nor was the home spared the turmoil occurring outside it. In the one city for which figures are available, Philadelphia, the rate of husband-wife murders increased from one per million persons between 1839 and 1845 to 4.1 per million between 1874 and 1880 (Pleck 1983*b*, p. 454).

Middle-class fears of violent crime were joined with a desire to reimpose a rural, Protestant morality on an urban-industrial society. Northerners worried about immigrants, and Southerners about blacks, and the public in all regions looked with suspicion on vagabonds and tramps. Immigrants, blacks, and homeless men were seen as brutish by nature, and unable to control their aggressive and criminal impulses. The enemy of the social order was not the deviant individual, as it had been among the Puritans, but a frightening strata of society, the so-called dangerous classes. Anxieties about the dangerous classes could be marshaled to support the founding of anticruelty societies or the passage of whipping post legislation. At a time of national economic depression, the potential militance of a great army of the unemployed and the threat of a permanent criminal class fueled the demand for criminalizing family violence.

Some scholars attribute the origins of the SPCC to these multiple fears (Hawes 1971; Gordon 1988). As immigration from abroad revived after the Civil War, the American native-born wealthy and middle class worried about violence, depravity, disease, riots, and labor unrest among the urban poor. In the United States these fears were exacerbated by the fact that the poor were largely immigrant and Catholic. But the desire for a well-ordered society was rooted as much in the Civil War as in society's uneasy accommodation to the passing of the agrarian order. After a national bloodbath in which 600,000 men were killed, the public wanted a return to stability. Since strong centralized government had saved the Union, it could be trusted to take on the new responsibilities of enforcing middle-class morality and of punishing the criminal classes.

In addition to these motives, the founders of SPCCs were also genuinely concerned about the suffering of helpless children. The nineteenth century has been termed the "century of the child." Children came to be viewed as individuals, possessing their own rights, rather than as obedient servants to their parents. Children were also regarded as innocent, rather than as innately sinful, beings. The decline of Calvinism and the rise of Romantic thought contributed to this more benign view of the child and to greater concern about children's suffering at parental hands. If the child also had individual rights, then it was the responsibility of the state to help enforce those rights. The state also had a duty to protect the innocent and helpless child (Nelson 1983).

One additional explanation for the origins of the SPCCs (Gordon 1983–84) is that they represented a continuation of the campaigns against corporal punishment that began in the schools and in parental advice literature in the 1830s. Women writers of child-rearing advice and some male school reformers had urged parents to exercise restraint in discipline, using the rod only as a last resort. Less frequent resort to corporal punishment, Gordon has argued, spilled over into greater concern about protecting innocent children. At the same time, rhetoric about children's rights reflected the reality that adolescent children had acquired the right to choose a career or a mate on their own, rather than to await parental approval.

To be sure, while some SPCCs, such as the one in Boston, campaigned against corporal punishment in the home and schools, others, such as the one in New York, advocated corporal punishment of children and carefully distinguished between corporal punishment and cruelty. In city after city, founders of the SPCCs were often millionaires or conservative feminists who had little in common with those who favored milder punishment of children.

There is a similar problem in claiming that the SPCCs reflected a new, more enlightened view of the child. An embarrassingly long interval separates the "discovery of childhood" from the founding of the SPCCs. The idea of the innocence of the child can be traced back to Rousseau. The *Body of Laws and Liberties* had reflected the view that children had certain liberties. Therefore, there must have been some more immediate stimulus to the founding of the SPCCs than changing ideas about children. What was new was the view that the state had a responsibility to protect the innocent child and to guarantee the rights of the child against those of the parent (Nelson 1983, pp. 7–8, 53–56). In the post–Civil War era parents were seen as exercising authority delegated by the state. If they failed to fulfill their responsibilities to their children, then the state had the power and the duty to intervene in order to safeguard the interests of the child.

The SPCCs reflected both a growing respect for the power of the state and the desire to safeguard the rights of children. In 1882, Elbridge Gerry, the president of the New York SPCC, vehemently insisted that "at the present day in this country, children have *some* rights, which even parents are bound to respect" (Bremner 1970, p. 196). However, the SPCCs emphasized the state's responsibility to intervene in the home far more than they mentioned the protection of children's rights. In fact, the founders of SPCCs made no distinction between the child's rights and the state's responsibilities since they could not imagine a situation in which the child would need protection *from* the state.

The ground for SPCC intervention was prepared by appellate court rulings that expanded the definition of child cruelty. Between 1862 and 1874, there were nine state appellate decisions concerning child cruelty. In these cases, only one reverted to the narrow *Pendergrass* definition of child cruelty as acts that endanger life or cause permanent injury, and it was decided by the same North Carolina State Supreme Court that had ruled in *Pendergrass*. However, all other state appellate courts held that child cruelty was whatever exceeded moderate standards of correction, irrespective of whether the parent had caused bruises, marks, or burns or had threatened the child's life (Pleck 1987, p. 77).

The SPCCs did not leave the matter there, however. They introduced in many states child cruelty statutes that considerably broadened the definition of child cruelty. In these statutes, child cruelty consisted of exploitation of the child, neglect, and abuse. In Pennsylvania's statute, child cruelty included physically mistreating a child, employing a child to beg, or permitting a child to sing in a dance hall or a concert hall, or in a theater in which liquor was sold. Typical additional grounds in other states were neglecting to provide reasonable food, clothing, shelter, and protection, exposing children during inclement weather, and forcing a child to beg. Child cruelty statutes specified criminal penalties for abuse and removal of the child from parental guardianship. Thus the SPCCs helped to criminalize child cruelty, taking it from the realm of case law. They also created private agencies with statutory powers to enforce these new laws—both to prosecute abusive and neglectful parents and to bring cases to court that required termination of parental guardianship and placement of the child out of home. Other statutes granted SPCCs the power to arrest abusive parents, temporarily to remove children from parental custody, and to place children in the society's temporary home or in an orphanage.[2]

These extraordinary police powers made the SPCCs unpopular. When children ran away from home or were lost in an immigrant neighborhood, their parents sometimes worried that their children had been snatched away by "the Cruelty," as the SPCC was often called. Actually, the majority of complaints to the SPCC resulted not from the independent inquiries of its agents but from complaints made by neighbors and relatives of victims. Because they have failed to examine the actual case records of these agencies, historians have presented an exaggeratedly fearsome image of the operation of the agencies during their Victorian heyday (Antler and Antler 1979). Examination of the case records of late nineteenth-century SPCCs in Boston, Philadelphia, New York City, and Chicago has shown that in comparison with early twentieth-century SPCCs, those of the late nineteenth century actually made less frequent use of the courts. The societies often removed neglected children from home but rarely removed abused children (Pleck 1987; Gordon 1988). Probation and casework services with families had not yet been "invented." Usually a case that did not result in the removal of a child was simply dismissed.

In the nineteenth century, there were hundreds of societies to protect children from cruelty but only one society to protect wives from cruelty. Children were innocent and helpless; women were not. Although Victorians recognized that women often suffered unjustly at the hands of brutish, drunken men, they also believed that women should sacrifice themselves for the sake of the family. Nonetheless, although

---

[2] In New York, agents of the SPCC could arrest abusive parents (Pleck 1987, p. 82). In Boston, the Massachusetts SPCC's agent was accompanied by a police officer, who made the arrest (Gordon 1988).

the level of effort on behalf of victimized women was far less than that on behalf of children, there were similar reasons for the interest in the abuse of wives and in children. Humanitarianism, the fear of crime, and the desire to create a single standard of morality motivated all the efforts against family violence of the late nineteenth century. The campaigns against the abuse of adult women had two separate ideological sources, however, one in law enforcement, the other in feminism, temperance, or women's community activism.

The law enforcement ideology is revealed most clearly in the campaign to punish wife beating with the whipping post. To modern observers an effort of this kind appears highly bizarre. Yet it expressed a desire to punish family violence as a serious crime and to hold domestic abusers accountable for their actions. The leaders of this campaign emphasized criminal punishment for wife beating rather than civil remedies for women victims. Arguing that the criminal penalties of fines and imprisonment had been insufficient, they advocated corporal punishment of wife beaters (Pleck 1983a). Between 1876 and 1906, bills to punish wife beaters with the whipping post were introduced in twelve states and the District of Columbia. Most of the supporters of the whipping post were eminently respectable, mostly Republican male lawyers, district attorneys, and grand juries. The heads of anticruelty societies and several important suffragist leaders favored the idea.

The whipping of wife beaters was an English idea, first proposed in Parliament in 1854 and unsuccessfully reintroduced there three more times by 1875. The punishment of flogging appealed to the fear of the "dangerous classes" on both sides of the Atlantic. Industrialization had created a large number of vagabonds, tramps, and thieves who preyed on the public and threatened to disrupt the social order. Nonetheless, the public was not fearful enough to demand the reintroduction of corporal punishment. The U.S. Congress (in 1906) and most state legislatures that considered the matter defeated whipping post legislation because they regarded it as uncivilized and barbaric.

Three states passed laws to punish wife beating with the whipping post: Maryland (1882), Delaware (1901), and Oregon (1906). Unique circumstances explain the passage of whipping post legislation in Maryland and Delaware.[3] Most states had abolished the whipping post as a general punishment around the time of the American Revolution or

---

[3] No information is available about the proponents of the whipping post in Oregon, or the reason for the bill's passage there.

during the early nineteenth century. Delaware had resisted the national trend, retaining both the pillory and the whipping post. Maryland legislators were familiar with Delaware's use of the whipping post, and appear to have decided that the flogging of criminals in their neighboring state had effectively deterred crime. It might have made sense for them to follow Delaware in punishing a number of crimes with flogging, but the sponsor of the bill in Maryland was concerned only with punishing wife beating. Though Delaware had punished many crimes from horse stealing to barn burning with the whipping post, wife beating was not among them. Delaware legislation to punish wife beating provided the opportunity to extend the penalty of flogging to yet another crime.

In both Maryland and Delaware, only a few wife beaters were ever flogged. The Maryland law punished wife beating with up to forty lashes or a year in prison. In the first year after the Maryland law was enacted, no one was prosecuted under the statute, although 156 husbands were charged with the lesser offense of "assault upon wives." The following year a black man was convicted under the act and sentenced to seven lashings. After a one-year lapse, a white man convicted under the statute was sentenced to twenty lashes and a year in jail. By the turn of the century, however, Maryland's whipping post had fallen into disuse, although it was not officially abolished until 1948. In Delaware, the law punished wife beating with five to thirty lashes at the whipping post. Between 1901 and 1942, twenty-one men were flogged for wife beating, with the largest number of floggings occurring in the early twentieth century (Caldwell 1947, p. 131). In a state where blacks constituted only 13 percent of the population in 1940, two-thirds of the men flogged for wife beating were black.

Although several feminists and female advocates of temperance supported the effort to punish wife beating with the whipping post, they gave greater priority to protection and assistance to women victims than to the punishment of male abusers. Their efforts included expanding tort protection for battered wives and, in Chicago, the establishment of a legal aid society for battered women and victims of incest and rape. The ideas behind these efforts combined feminism with belief in family stability and Victorian morality.

Feminists of the late nineteenth century argued that wife beating, wife murder, rape, and incest constituted "crimes against women." Lucy Stone was the leading American feminist of her day. Three times she tried unsuccessfully to introduce legislation in Massachusetts to increase access to separation and protective orders for battered women (Pleck 1983*b*). Exasperated with the failure to pass this legislation, Stone joined the coalition in favor of punishing wife beating with the whipping post. In her view, wife beating was rooted in drunkenness, male licentiousness, and a husband's ownership of his wife as his personal property. Crimes committed by women, such as infanticide or murders that were crimes of passion, she attributed to male lust.

By contrast, women's temperance organizations, which did not espouse feminist ideas, sought to protect vulnerable women, to stabilize the family, and to enforce their vision of morality. They believed women were not men's equals but their moral superiors. They tended to blame drink, rather than patriarchy, for wife beating. Women had to shore up the traditional family, they argued, by forcing men to assume their rightful responsibilities (Giele 1961, pp. 120–25, 142–49). The criminal and civil law could aid these efforts by compelling men to give up alcohol and increasing the penalties for drunkenness.

Late nineteenth-century judges in several states refused to permit wives or children to sue husbands or fathers for damages arising from an assault on the grounds that such torts would sow the seeds of discord and clog the courts with what they regarded as trivial cases. Yet leaders of the Women's Christian Temperance Union, the largest women's organization in the nineteenth century, helped to pass legislation to expand tort protection for victims of domestic violence. This legislation permitted an injured party to sue the saloonkeeper or the owner of the saloon for damages caused from injury inflicted by an intoxicated person. In 1873, New York and Arkansas passed the first of these laws. In all, twenty states from Maine to New Mexico enacted such legislation, and the last of these laws was passed in 1891. In some states, only the wife could sue for damages, although in others, several injured parties could do so, including a husband, child, parent, or employer. In order to be awarded damages, the law generally required the wife to notify the saloonkeeper in advance not to serve her husband alcohol (Black 1892, pp. 277–377).

Only a few drunkards' wives could afford to hire a lawyer to sue, but in the few cases that reached the courts, wives generally won their suits and were awarded damages. Ann J. Wilson of Genessee, Michigan, had informed the town saloonkeeper not to serve her husband. When her husband finally came home from the saloon, he attacked her in front of their children and struck her on the head with a chair. She was awarded damages, although the amount of the award was not stated. Courts also upheld other legal transactions that favored the assaulted wife. One Illinois husband who pleaded with his wife not to separate from him signed a note promising to pay her $600 if he became drunk or abused her. He did, and she sued him for divorce. The Illinois Supreme Court upheld the validity of his promissory note (Blackwell 1877).

Female temperance reformers helped battered women achieve greater legal protection, but they did not carry their work to the next logical step of providing women victims with legal assistance. This oversight was due mainly to their interest in many issues, of which providing legal remedies for drunkards' wives was a minor one. Instead, the origins of legal aid to women victims of domestic violence arose out of the women's club movement. These organizations, established throughout the United States, sought to develop community institutions to meet the needs of women.

Beginning after the Civil War, local women's clubs had organized "protective agencies" to provide working girls and women consumers in poor neighborhoods with legal aid. In Chicago in 1885, the local women's club, along with the Women's Christian Temperance Union, helped to establish a society that devoted special attention to the protection of victimized women and girls. The Protective Agency for Women and Children in Chicago, as the society was called, helped battered wives to secure property held in their husbands' names. It assisted victims of rape or incest, encouraged them to bring their cases to court, and attended court with them. The Protective Agency took credit for oversight of the courts, with the result that rape charges were no longer dismissed or reduced to a lesser charge of disorderly conduct.

The initial policy of the Protective Agency was never to encourage divorce, but the case of a stepfather who raped his two stepdaughters forced them to give legal assistance to the girls' mother in securing a divorce. Eleven years after its founding, the Protective Agency merged with a larger, better funded, predominantly male organization, the Bureau of Justice, which furnished legal aid to indigent male and female clients. In the agreement of consolidation with the Bureau of Justice, the women asked for, and received, sole jurisdiction over the cases affecting women and children since they believed it "a self-evident truth that women can do better work for the wronged of their own sex than men can do" (Protective Agency for Women and Children 1897, p. 14). As a result of the merger, the caseload of the agency grew rapidly. The agency began to provide assaulted wives who had children with legal assistance in securing a divorce, rather than with just legal separations.

In 1905, the agency merged a second time to form the Legal Aid Society of Chicago. It wanted to join an even larger, better-funded organization that would nonetheless provide it with a necessary guarantee of autonomy. The Protective Agency still maintained its separate identity and was represented as officers and on the board of directors of Chicago Legal Aid. According to the terms of the merger, the president of the Protective Agency became the vice president of Legal Aid, and half the directors of the society were women. By 1912, however, reports of its work disappeared from the annual report of Chicago Legal Aid. Rape cases were being handled by other agencies. By the 1920s, the official policy of Chicago Legal Aid was to discourage divorce and urge reconciliation whenever possible.

IV. Decline of Interest in Criminal Approaches to Family Violence during the Progressive Era, 1900–1920

By the 1890s, the perception of family violence as a serious crime began to fade. The last legislative attempt to punish wife beating with the whipping post occurred in 1906. In the period between 1875 and 1890, the view that family violence was a serious crime had coincided with zeal for "law and order." Support for criminalization of family violence had capitalized on fears of violent crime and of the dangerous classes. Those fears could be channeled to support strong punishments, such as the whipping post, to threaten abusive parents with the removal of their children, and, when combined with feminism or temperance, to provide legal assistance to victimized mothers or their daughters. When ideas of rehabilitation and prevention of crime replaced a belief in punitive sanctions, there was less interest in criminal punishment of family violence.

There was no comparable retreat to domestic privacy, as there had been in the 1700s. But instead, the state's responsibility, while much expanded, was defined in terms of recreating family privacy, rather than in terms of enforcing the criminal law (Rothman 1980). By the early twentieth century, judges of family courts and heads of SPCCs came to view criminal prosecution and police-like methods as unprofessional and outmoded. They believed that social casework methods were more efficient, humane, and better suited to handling the complicated dynamics of abusing families. Ironically, the greater the scrutiny in the family character of domestic violence, the lower the interest in its criminal side.

The juvenile court represented one additional step toward decriminalizing child abuse and strengthening social casework intervention in abusive and neglectful families. A voluminous body of literature has been concerned with either the origins or actual operation of these courts in the early twentieth century (Platt 1969; Schlossman 1977; Ryerson 1978; Rothman 1980; Tiffin 1982). Was it fear of the city, the desire to exert expert control over social problems, or the old middle-class interest in transforming the poor into bourgeoisie that prompted the Progressives to found juvenile courts? Even Schlossman (1977), who finds the juvenile courts similar in many ways to their Jacksonian era predecessors, has identified some unique features, such as the court's emphasis on probation and family-centered treatment for youthful offenders. If the juvenile delinquent could be rehabilitated at home, he or she would not have to be sentenced to reform school. In reality, however, Schlossman found that despite the rhetoric of reformers about cooperating with parents, the day-to-day actions of the juvenile court were often extremely punitive.

While juvenile courts were mainly interested in juvenile delinquency, child neglect was a much lower, but still important, priority. Child neglect was more important to the SPCCs, which, during the Progressive Era, worked closely with the juvenile courts. In terms of the sheer number of cases, child neglect had always been a much larger phenomenon than physical abuse, even in the Victorian era. But SPCCs and the juvenile courts virtually swept aside the problem of physical abuse in favor of child neglect. The category of child neglect fitted with their thinking about social problems and with the remedies they favored.

Progressive Era thought had dual strands: an environmentalism that located social problems in poverty and poor housing, and a eugenicism that rooted the same problems in genetic inferiority. The SPCCs favored social reforms, such as children's playgrounds and mothers' pensions, to remove the social conditions that bred neglect, casework to uplift the family environment through expert (yet friendly) counsel, but also sterilization of the mentally retarded and laws preventing their marriage. They portrayed all of these efforts as preventive remedies, superior to the law enforcement methods of the Victorian SPCCs (Gordon 1988).

The rhetorical emphasis of the Progressives on preserving the child's home has given the impression that most neglected children were left at home under parental supervision. The juvenile court established separate procedures for handling cases of abuse and neglect. While probation was common for juvenile delinquents, removal to foster homes or industrial schools was frequent for abused and neglected children. In fact, the rate of removal of such children was actually higher in the Progressive Era than in the supposedly punitive and legalistic era of the Victorian SPCCs (Pleck 1987, pp. 131–32). However, Progressive Era efforts to reform the character of perpetrators, rather than simply to condemn them as monstrous brutes, also had implications for the manner of handling abused and neglected children who were not removed from home (Garland 1985). Fewer cases of abuse and neglect were simply dismissed, and more families were placed under supervision, receiving occasional visits from caseworkers.

Social work practice and the way juvenile courts, psychological clinics, and social agencies operated have all been criticized for their punitive treatment and cultural arrogance toward their clients, most of whom were working class or poor and immigrant (Platt 1969; Donzelot 1977; Schlossman 1977; Tiffin 1982). These studies have not dealt with abused and neglected children but rather with the ideas and origins behind the juvenile court. But since the courts handled such cases, the general criticism of their work would presumably apply to their handling of abuse and neglect cases. The implication is that family violence was a social label imposed by experts and outsiders, rather than a problem perceived by the poor or the working class themselves.

Gordon (1988) and Pleck (1987) have insisted that it was both. Outside intervention could offer legal threats to shore up one's bargaining position in the courts in child custody or divorce cases, or it could offer compassion and concrete economic assistance. These gains far outweighed the potential losses. Moreover, since outside intervention more often came to the aid of weaker, more dependent members of the family, it represented an agent of change in family power relations more often than it did a reinforcement of the status quo. The bad side of the courts could not always be separated from their good side. The same type of agency action might be intended to provide, and might result in, *both* humanitarian assistance and increased manipulation of the lives of the poor.

V. The Rediscovery of Family Violence, 1955–80

Family violence persisted from the Progressive Era until the 1960s, but interest in it did not. Social agencies still came across such cases but often classified them as problems of economic hardship, family maladjustment, or mental illness. In the Progressive Era, the etiology of domestic violence was often attributed to moronic tendencies and genetic inferiority, during the Great Depression, to economic hardship, and in the 1940s and 1950s, to family problems or psychiatric illness (Gordon 1988).

The rediscovery of "child cruelty" is usually dated to 1962, when C. Henry Kempe, a Denver pediatrician, and four of his medical colleagues published an article in the *Journal of the American Medical Association* entitled "The Battered Child Syndrome" (Kempe et al. 1962). This landmark publication can be seen more as a result than as a cause of the discovery of child abuse. In the mid-1950s, the specter of violent teenagers menacing the public compelled social workers to abandon their professional offices and reach out to troubled youth. Aiding the neglected child was justified as a means of combating juvenile delinquency. The American Humane Association (AHA), under the leadership of Vincent DeFrancis, pioneered in the development of "aggressive casework," intervention in neglectful families when the caseworker had not been invited. They also surveyed the problem of child neglect. In turn, the AHA alerted the U.S. Children's Bureau to the prevalence of the problem, and the bureau funded the research of Kempe and others. Kempe's survey of the prevalence of severe battering of infants and young children was then used to demonstrate that a new and serious social problem existed (Nelson 1983).

Certainly, the modern era is the first time physicians became major participants in reform against child abuse or neglect. Battered babies were patients of pediatricians and radiologists; the reason for their injuries was uncovered through X-ray evidence. The problem of child abuse and neglect was not confined to hospitalized children, yet their suffering, dependency, and helplessness made a powerful claim on the medical conscience. Stephen Pfohl (1977) has given much of the credit for the rediscovery of child abuse to radiologists. Beginning in the early 1950s, radiologists used X-ray evidence of multiple fractures in young children at various stages of healing in order to cast doubt on parents' explanations that a child had been injured as a result of a single mishap. Pfohl notes that radiology was considered a low-status medical specialty. He attributes the interests of radiologists in child battering to a desire to increase their professional status and to an eagerness to demonstrate that they, too, saved lives.

The social atmosphere of the late 1950s and early 1960s also contributed to the rediscovery of child abuse. Child abuse emerged as a social issue during the height of the civil rights movement, as the nation was prodded by black protest to protect the constitutional rights of minorities. A small but vocal group of advocates of children's rights took up a similar call on behalf of children (Feshbach and Feshbach 1978).

Reform against child abuse led to increased funding for research about its causes, to expanded services to abusive and neglectful families, and to the hiring of additional personnel. The growth of public and professional concern about battered children occurred in the early 1960s, at a time of renewed support for social welfare legislation. National economic prosperity and optimism about government's capacity to solve social problems moved Congress to appropriate large sums for social welfare programs, including those aimed at helping children (Nelson 1983).

The dominance of physicians and social workers in the reform effort against child abuse dampened interest in criminalization of child abuse. Most social workers, doctors, and even many lawyers and judges agreed that imprisoning abusive parents—other than those who had murdered their children—was counterproductive. Police and judges were not qualified to handle family problems, it was claimed. Monrad G. Paulsen, the dean of the University of Virginia Law School, reasoned that "all in all, criminal sanctions can do little to help a child. The major problems concern his care and custody" (Paulsen 1962, p. 43). A legal definition of abuse, Paulsen argued, demanded punishment, rendering the parent's rehabilitation difficult, if not impossible. Prosecution would snuff out any hope of preserving the child's home and would make parents so resentful that casework with them would be imperiled. If charges were brought, it would be difficult to find any witnesses. Fines, it was argued, robbed the family of valuable financial resources. Furthermore, imprisonment would separate the parent from the child (Thomas 1972, p. 341). The law, it was believed, imposed adversarial methods on troubled parents and children in need of counseling.

As a result of media attention and the lobbying efforts of pediatric associations, every state in the nation between 1963 and 1967 passed laws requiring physicians (and sometimes other professionals) to report instances of child abuse to police or social agencies, such as children's protective services (DeFrancis 1966; Costa and Nelson 1978). Reporting laws increased public awareness of child abuse and neglect and led to increased reporting of such cases. Reporting laws were actually criminal statutes since a physician's failure to report child abuse was generally punishable as a misdemeanor under the criminal law (Thomas 1972, p. 331). The Children's Bureau, proposing a model statute, favored mandatory reporting to the police because they were on call twenty-four hours a day. Initially, most reporting statutes designated the police as the agency to receive mandatory reports; subsequent legislation more often designated a child protective service as the reporting agency (Paulsen 1966).

Once cases were reported, the tendency was to rely on civil, rather than on criminal, procedures and on social casework, supplemented by resort to the courts, if necessary. These were the approaches developed during the Progressive Era. The dislike of arrest, prosecution, and punishment of abusive and neglectful parents arose from the objections stated above and from the emphasis of all the parties involved, including the courts and police, on rehabilitating the abusive or neglectful family.

Sociologists and psychiatrists put the spotlight on sibling violence, and social workers, nursing professionals, and psychologists brought elder abuse to light. These were types of family violence that had previously escaped any efforts at reform and had rarely been reported to SPCCs. Of all the types of family violence to receive attention in the period since the mid-1950s, child abuse received the most, followed by wife abuse. Although many women campaigned against child abuse, the problem of child abuse was defined as a public health matter, not a feminist issue. In the early 1970s, the only common ground shared by feminists and advocates of children was concern about victims of incest and sexual molestation.

While reformers against child abuse opposed criminal sanctions against perpetrators, reformers against wife abuse and marital rape favored them and tried to pressure the police and courts to respond adequately to the complaints of women victims. The medical and social work professionals who dominated child abuse reform defined child battering as a psychological illness of the parents requiring social services and psychological treatment. The feminist activists and lawyers who led the campaign against wife beating and marital rape rooted the problem in the inequality of women and in the lack of proper law enforcement.

Wife beating and marital rape were considered crimes, rather than manifestations of mental illness (although many experts emphasized both etiologies). The battered women's movement sponsored legislation to increase the criminal penalties for wife beating, to strengthen civil remedies, and to make it easier for women victims to file criminal charges against their assailants (Schecter 1982). There were no mandatory reporting laws for wife abuse or marital rape similar to those on behalf of child abuse and neglect. But the greater publicity given the problem, the establishment of social service and feminist advocacy groups, and the founding of shelters for battered women encouraged victims to complain to the police and to persist in the arrest, prosecution, and punishment of their assailants.

There were several similarities between the contemporary period of concern about family violence and the two earlier reform epochs. From the sponsors of the *Body of Laws and Liberties* to the founders of the SPCCs, reformers had sought to protect the rights of women and children. Feminists of the Victorian era advocated greater legal rights for married women, along with increased protection in civil and criminal law. The liberation movements for children and women, beginning in the 1960s, also led the way in expanding the legal rights of women and children.

A small, concerned group rather than the public at large has always been the major force behind reform against family violence. The Puritan effort against family violence was not a voluntary social movement as much as a state (and minister-initiated) reform. But in the late nineteenth century and from the mid-1950s through the 1980s, small, private organizations of professionals (mainly lawyers in the late nineteenth century and physicians and social workers in the 1960s and 1970s) championed the children's cause. Similarly, in both of these periods, individual feminists and women's organizations drew attention to "crimes against women" and often found themselves allied with male law enforcement officials, who were desirous of stamping out violent crime.

In all three eras, the fear of violence and of dangerous criminals animated reform. Puritans worried that pirates, heretics, and malcontents would destroy their divinely sanctioned undertaking. Since they did not distinguish between public and private crime, they were as disturbed about violent assaults in the home as they were about theft, corruption, or usury. The late nineteenth-century fear of "the danger-ous classes" expressed unease about the new industrial order—the un-welcome presence of Catholic immigrants in cities, tramps in the coun-tryside, and worry about union militants stirring up strikes. The SPCCs hoped to protect young children, so that the future generation could be saved from a life of crime or prostitution. The first reawaken-ing of interest in child abuse and neglect in the mid-1950s came not from pediatricians but from social workers, responding to public fears about an upsurge in juvenile delinquency. In hearings about national legislation against child abuse in 1973, experts pointed out that many violent criminals and assassins had been abused as children (Pleck 1987, p. 177).

In the 1970s as in the 1870s, wife beating began as a women's rights issue and picked up support as a law and order issue. In both centuries, women activists sought to pressure the police and district attorneys to arrest male perpetrators and to prosecute them, and they decried the lenient sentences judges handed down. Feminist organizations accom-panied women victims to court and sought to provide them with legal aid. Victorian and some contemporary male law enforcement officials, seeking to strengthen the state's control over violent criminals, recog-nized that previous criminal efforts to deal with wife beating had not worked. They called for new sanctions (the whipping post in the nineteenth century or court-ordered therapy in the 1970s and 1980s).

If there were many similarities, there were also some important dif-ferences. In the modern period, reform was broader, more successful, and national in scope. Puritan reform against domestic violence was confined to the New England colonies. Even at the turn of the century, most cities did not have an SPCC, and the efforts on behalf of abused women were limited to a few places. Moreover, the range of social services to abusive families—from therapy to child care—was far greater in the present than in the past. The numerous self-help groups for victims, former victims, or perpetrators were without precedent.

Nonetheless, as in previous eras of reform, disillusionment began to set in and interest started to wane. In the mid-1970s, influential lawyers and psychiatrists attacked child abuse programs for denying parental rights of due process and for excessive and deleterious removal of chil-dren (especially children of the poor and minorities) from their parents (Wald 1975, 1976; Goldstein, Freud, and Solnit 1979). The general argument asserted that abused and neglected children were worse off in foster care or in group homes than they would have been if they had been left with their biological parent(s).

This counterfactual statement was almost impossible to prove or disprove. It must surely have been true in some cases and untrue or mixed in others. But the appearance of this rhetoric can best be read as a sign of disillusionment with the results of state intervention in the family (Ross 1980, pp. 77–81). Once it became clear that child abuse reform also led to greater state intervention in the family (which could mean increasing the number of children removed from parental home), medical language and good intentions could no longer conceal the controversial nature of the issue.

In the mid-1970s, the controversy was limited to the experts, who disagreed about the merits of child abuse programs. Five years later, it had spread to segments of the general public. In 1980, New Right groups across the country, disturbed about the prevalence of abortion and the "breakdown of the American family," targeted for defeat federal domestic violence legislation. It would have provided federal funds for battered women's shelters, social service and advocacy programs on behalf of battered women, and research (Gelb 1983). New Right groups believed battered women's shelters encouraged women to get divorces and thereby undermined the traditional family. Domestic violence legislation also had to justify itself in light of the desire to reduce the number and size of federal social welfare programs. In 1984, national legislation, funded at drastically reduced levels, was nonetheless enacted.

The resurgence of conservatism targeted not only domestic violence legislation but also child abuse laws. In 1979, one conservative Republican senator, Paul Laxalt of Nevada, introduced a Family Protection Act that had been written by the executive director of a New Right lobbying group, the Moral Majority. Among other provisions, it eliminated federal expenditures specially designated for child abuse prevention and reallocated funding to the states, where such programs would compete with other social service programs. It further proposed to amend the definition of child abuse to exclude corporal punishment of a child by a parent or parental designate. It also stipulated that no federal law, grant, program, or directive would broaden or supersede existing state laws relating to spousal abuse. The Family Protection Act, which never had much chance of being passed, was intended mainly to remind liberal legislators and their sympathizers of the strength of feelings of many conservative groups concerning these issues.

Domestic violence was no longer a "safe" issue. Diminished funding for these programs, including cutbacks in needed personnel, encouraged a lack of public concern. The morning papers and the evening news still carried stories about marital rape, child molestation, sexual abuse at day-care centers, or elder abuse. But attention was more likely to be fleeting.

Yet the ideas that underlay reform implicitly attacked the importance of preserving the family at all costs, of safeguarding domestic privacy, and of allocating special rights to husbands and parents. Legitimate concerns about failures and mistakes in current social policy were mixed with ideological defenses of the traditional family and of domestic privacy. Further, it would cost money to establish battered women's shelters, victim advocacy programs, child protective services, hotlines, and the rest. The national mood favored lower levels of public funding for all social welfare programs and a defense of "the family," namely, parental rights, family autonomy, and domestic privacy. These abstract ideals, however worthy, have always been in conflict with the state's responsibility to protect its weakest and most vulnerable members. The lesson of the past is that the greater the emphasis on the "family" character of domestic violence, the lower the interest and support for criminalization of family violence. This generalization appears to apply equally as well in the 1980s.

REFERENCES

Adams, Robert. 1886. *Wife Beating as a Crime, and Its Relation to Taxation.* Philadelphia: Social Science Association.

Antler, Joyce, and Stephen Antler. 1979. "From Child Rescue to Family Protection: The Evolution of the Child Protective Movement in the United States." *Children and Youth Services Review* 1:177–204.

Black, Henry C. 1892. *A Treatise on the Laws Regulating the Manufacture and Sale of Intoxicating Liquors.* St. Paul, Minn.: West.

Blackstone, William. 1765–69. *Commentaries on the Laws of England.* Oxford: Oxford University Press.

Blackwell, H. B. 1877. "Drunkard's Wives, Take Notice!" *Woman's Journal* (April 19).

Boston Morning Post. 1837. *Selections from the Court Reports originally published in the "Boston Morning Post" from 1834 to 1837.* Boston: Otis, Broaders.

Boyer, Paul. 1978. *Urban Masses and Moral Order in America, 1820–1920.* Cambridge, Mass.: Harvard University Press.

Bremner, Robert H., ed. 1970. *Children and Youth in America: A Documentary History*, vol. 2. Cambridge, Mass.: Harvard University Press.

Caldwell, Robert G. 1947. *Red Hannah: Delaware's Whipping Post*. Philadelphia: University of Pennsylvania Press.

Calvert, Robert. 1974. "Criminal and Civil Liability in Husband and Wife Assaults." In *Violence in the Family*, edited by Suzanne K. Steinmetz and Murray A. Straus. New York: Dodd, Mead.

Carr, Lois G. 1977. "The Development of the Maryland Orphans Court, 1654–1715." In *Law, Society, and Politics in Early Maryland*, edited by Aubrey C. Land, Lois G. Carr, and Edward C. Papenfuse. Baltimore: Johns Hopkins University Press.

Coleman, Sydney H. 1924. *Humane Society Leaders in America*. Albany, N.Y.: American Humane Association.

Costa, Joseph J., and Gordon K. Nelson. 1978. *Child Abuse and Neglect: Legislation, Reporting, and Prevention*. Lexington, Mass.: Heath.

Cushing, John D. 1977. *The Laws of the Pilgrims: A Facsimile Edition of the Book of the General Laws of the Inhabitants of the Jurisdiction of New Plymouth, 1672 and 1685*. Wilmington, Del.: Glazier.

DeFrancis, Vincent. 1966. *Child Abuse Legislation: Analysis and Study of Mandatory Reporting Laws in the United States*. Denver: American Humane Association.

Demos, John. 1986. *Past, Present, and Personal*. New York: Oxford University Press.

Donzelot, Jacques. 1977. *The Policing of Families*. New York: Random House.

Dow, George F., ed. 1911–21. *Records and Files of the Quarterly Courts of Essex County, Massachusetts*. Vol. 8. Salem, Mass.: Essex County Historical Society.

Feldberg, Michael. 1985. "Police Discretion and Family Disturbances: Some Historical and Contemporary Reflections." In *Unhappy Families: Clinical and Research Perspectives on Family Violence*, edited by Eli H. Newberger and Richard Bourne. Littleton, Mass.: P.S.G.

Feshbach, Norma D., and Seymour D. Feshbach. 1978. "Toward an Historical, Social and Developmental Perspective on Children's Rights." *Journal of Social Issues* 25:1–7.

Fliegelman, Jay. 1982. *Prodigals and Pilgrims: The American Revolution against Patriarchal Authority, 1750–1800*. Cambridge: Cambridge University Press.

Friedman, Lawrence M., and Robert V. Percival. 1981. *The Roots of Justice: Crime and Punishment in Alameda County, California, 1870–1910*. Chapel Hill: University of North Carolina Press.

Garland, David. 1985. *Punishment and Welfare: A History of Penal Strategies*. Brookfield, Vt.: Gower.

Gelb, Joyce. 1983. "The Politics of Wife Abuse." In *Families, Politics, and Public Policy: A Feminist Dialogue on Women and the State*, edited by Irene Diamond. New York: Longman.

Giele, Janet. 1961. "Social Change in the Feminine Role: A Comparison of Woman's Suffrage and Woman's Temperance, 1870–1920." Ph.D. dissertation, Radcliffe College, Department of Sociology.

Glenn, Myra C. 1984. *Campaigns against Corporal Punishment: Prisoners, Sailors, Women, and Children in Antebellum America*. Albany: State University of New York Press.

Goldstein, Joseph, Anna Freud, and Albert J. Solnit. 1979. *Before the Best Interests of the Child*. New York: Free Press.

Gordon, Linda. 1983–84. "Child Abuse, Gender, and the Myth of Family Independence: Thoughts on the History of Family Violence and Its Social Control, 1880–1920." *Review of Law and Social Change* 12:523–37.

———. 1988. *Family Violence and Social Control*. New York: Viking Press.

Hartog, Hendrik. 1976. "The Public Law of a County Court: Judicial Government in Eighteenth Century Massachusetts." *American Journal of Legal History* 20:282–329.

Haskins, George L. 1960. *Law and Authority in Early Massachusetts: A Study in Tradition and Design*. New York: Macmillan.

Hawes, Joseph M. 1971. *Children in Urban Society: Juvenile Delinquency in Nineteenth Century America*. New York: Oxford University Press.

Kempe, C. Henry, Frederic N. Silverman, Brandt F. Steele, William Droegemuller, and Henry K. Silver. 1962. "The Battered Child Syndrome." *Journal of the American Medical Association* 181:17–24.

Kerber, Linda K. 1980. *Women of the Republic: Intellect and Ideology in Revolutionary America*. Chapel Hill: University of North Carolina Press.

Koehler, Lyle. 1980. *A Search for Power: The "Weaker Sex" in Seventeenth-Century New England*. Urbana: University of Illinois Press.

Lebsock, Suzanne. 1984. *The Free Women of Petersburg: Status and Culture in a Southern Town, 1784–1860*. New York: Norton.

McCrea, Roswell C. 1910. *The Humane Movement*. New York: Columbia University Press.

Massachusetts Colony. 1890. *The Body of Liberties of 1641*. Boston: Rockwell & Churchill.

May, Margaret. 1978. "Violence in the Family: An Historical Perspective." In *Violence and the Family*, edited by J. P. Martin. Chichester: Wiley.

Mennel, Robert M. 1973. *Thorns and Thistles: Juvenile Delinquents in the United States, 1825–1940*. Hanover, N.H.: University Press of New England.

Nelson, Barbara J. 1983. *Making an Issue of Child Abuse: Political Agenda Setting for Social Problems*. Chicago: University of Chicago Press.

New York Society for the Prevention of Cruelty to Children. 1876. *First Annual Report*. New York: Styles & Cash.

Oberholzer, Emil, Jr. 1956. *Delinquent Saints: Disciplinary Action in the Early Congregational Churches in Massachusetts*. New York: Columbia University Press.

Paulsen, Monrad G. 1962. "The Delinquency, Neglect, and Dependency Jurisdiction of the Juvenile Court." In *Justice for the Child*, edited by Margaret K. Rosenheim. New York: Free Press.

———. 1966. "The Legal Framework for Child Protection." *Columbia Law Review* 66:679–717.

Pfohl, Stephen. 1977. "The Discovery of Child Abuse." *Social Problems* 24:310–21.

Platt, Anthony M. 1969. *The Child Savers: The Invention of Delinquency*. Chicago: University of Chicago Press.

Pleck, Elizabeth H. 1979. "Wife Beating in Nineteenth-Century America." *Victimology* 4:60–74.

———. 1983*a*. "The Whipping Post for Wife Beaters, 1876–1906." In *Essays on the Family and Historical Change*, edited by Leslie P. Moch and Gary D. Stark. College Station: Texas A & M University Press.

———. 1983*b*. "Feminist Responses to 'Crimes against Women, 1868–1896.'" *Signs* 8:451–70.

———. 1987. *Domestic Tyranny: The Making of Social Policy against Family Violence from Colonial Times to the Present*. New York: Oxford University Press.

Powers, Edwin. 1966. *Crime and Punishment in Early Massachusetts, 1620–1692: A Documentary History*. Boston: Beacon.

Protective Agency for Women and Children. 1897. *Eleventh Annual Report of the Protective Agency for Women and Children*. Chicago: Privately published.

Ross, Catherine J. 1980. "The Lessons of the Past: Defining and Controlling Child Abuse in the United States." In *Child Abuse: An Agenda for Action*, edited by George Gerbner, Catherine J. Ross, and Edward Zigler. New York: Oxford University Press.

Rothman, David J. 1971. *The Discovery of the Asylum: Social Order and Disorder in the New Republic*. Boston: Little, Brown.

———. 1980. *Conscience and Convenience: The Asylum and Its Alternatives in Progressive America*. Boston: Little, Brown.

Ryerson, Ellen. 1978. *The Best-laid Plans: America's Juvenile Court Experiment*. New York: Hill & Wang.

Schechter, Susan. 1982. *Women and Male Violence: The Visions and Struggles of the Battered Women's Movement*. Boston: South End Press.

Schlossman, Steven L. 1977. *Love and the American Delinquent: The Theory and Practice of "Progressive" Juvenile Justice, 1825–1920*. Chicago: University of Chicago Press.

State of Tennessee. 1850. *Acts of the State of Tennessee, Laws, Statutes, etc., for the Years 1849–1850*. Nashville, Tenn.: Kennie & Watterson.

Steinberg, Allen. 1981. "'The Spirit of Litigation:' Private Prosecution and Criminal Justice in Nineteenth Century Philadelphia." Paper read at the annual meeting of the Social Science History Association, Nashville, Tenn., October.

Stone, Lawrence. 1977. *The Family, Sex and Marriage in England, 1500–1800*. New York: Harper & Row.

Thomas, Mason P. 1972. "Child Abuse and Neglect: Historical Overview, Legal Matrix and Social Perspectives." *North Carolina Law Review* 50:327–49.

Tiffin, Susan. 1982. *In Whose Best Interest? Child Welfare Reform in the Progressive Era*. Westport, Conn.: Greenwood.

Ulrich, Laurel. 1982. *Good Wives: Image and Reality in the Lives of Women in Northern New England, 1650–1750*. New York: Knopf.

Wald, Michael S. 1975. "State Intervention on Behalf of 'Neglected' Children: A Search for Realistic Standards." *Stanford Law Review* 27:985–1040.

———. 1976. "State Intervention on Behalf of 'Neglected' Children: Standards for Removal of Children from Their Homes, Monitoring the Status of Children in Foster Care and Termination of Parental Rights." *Stanford Law Review* 28:673–706.

Walsh, Lorena S. 1979. "'Till Death Us Do Part': Marriage and Family in Seventeenth-Century Maryland." In *The Chesapeake in the Seventeenth Century: Essays on Anglo-American Society*, edited by Thad W. Tate and David L. Ammerman. Chapel Hill: University of North Carolina Press.

Watson, Alan D. 1975. "Orphanage in Colonial North Carolina; Edgecombe County as a Case Study." *North Carolina Historical Review* 52:105–19.

Wyatt-Brown, Bertram. 1982. *Southern Honor*. New York: Oxford University Press.

Robert L. Burgess and Patricia Draper

The Explanation of Family Violence: The Role of Biological, Behavioral, and Cultural Selection

ABSTRACT

The nonrandom pattern of both marital violence and child maltreatment across cultures suggests that such behaviors may have been adaptive in certain past environments. Biological and psychosocial concepts and principles form the basis for a biosocial theory of family violence. In evolutionary theory, the twin concepts of parental investment and paternity certainty suggest the existence of endemic conflicts of interest within marital pairs and between parents and offspring. A biosocial perspective suggests that the probability of marital violence increases when ecological instability leads to the erosion of structural buffers (such as kin support or sex segregation), to changes—or perceived changes—in the marital balance of power, and to the development of coercive patterns of marital communication. Common social indicators of marital violence, underemployment, financial pressures, anxiety, and alcohol abuse can be conceptualized as markers of ecological instability or its consequences. Child maltreatment may have functioned in circumstances of ecological instability to optimize the reproductive fitness of parents. Even when maltreatment of children is nonadaptive or maladaptive, it occurs more frequently under conditions marked by ecological disturbances associated with rising levels of stress and reliance on coercion in family relationships. Mating and parenting behavior should be especially sensitive to circumstances indicative of ecological instability.

Robert L. Burgess and Patricia Draper are, respectively, professor and associate professor of human development, Pennsylvania State University. The authors appreciate critical comments and suggestions from Lloyd Ohlin, Michael Tonry, Richard Will, Richard Gelles, James Q. Wilson, Don Ford, Henry Harpending, Jeff Kurland, Robert Plomin, Emil Pensky, and Lise Youngblade.

For many of us, the family is thought to function as a "haven in a heartless world" (Lasch 1977). Research over the past quarter century, however, suggests that Doris Lessing (1973) may be a particularly sensitive observer when she observes that "behind every door there is a disaster." The issue of violence in families became part of our general social and scientific consciousness over twenty-five years ago in a now-classic paper by Kempe et al. (1962), a group of physicians who coined the term "the Battered Child Syndrome." This work was a result of awareness by these physicians of evidence of repeated, multiple bone fractures that were appearing in the x-rays of a substantial number of children. Their purpose in writing the article was to alert other physicians to the problem in order to facilitate the detection of abuse. A virtual explosion of publications on child abuse followed. Most of this was initially by psychiatrists (e.g., Merrill 1962; Steele and Pollock 1968; Fischoff, Whitton, and Pettit 1971). Out of this grew a medical model of child maltreatment that emphasized the psychopathology of abusers. Abusive parents were described as being psychopathic and emotionally immature (Kempe et al. 1962), irrational, rigid, and compulsive (Merrill 1962), emotionally disordered, and subject to unresolved dependency needs (Steele and Pollock 1968). These efforts to explain child abuse show the influence of Freud's 1919 essay, "A Child Is Being Beaten," in which he used his theoretical formulations to describe the dynamics of a child abuser.

Several problems existed with this early work. There was an almost exclusive emphasis on extreme, bizarre cases, often involving torture. Reports were almost always based on inadequate or biased clinical samples with no control groups. For example, Steele and Pollock (1968, p. 95) say of their sample, "It is our impression that with few exceptions our patients had emotional problems of sufficient severity to be accepted for treatment had they presented themselves at a clinic or psychiatrist's office." The proposed causal model was unidirectional. The idea that certain children may have traits that make them more susceptible to abuse was not considered until the 1970s (e.g., Gelles 1973).

The second major step in the history of research on violence toward children in the United States occurred when scholars from other areas and disciplines began to work on the problem, in part as a response to the defects seen in the first wave of studies. Researchers began to design their studies with more care, with better samples, and with appropriate control groups. From this work, we learned that most of the earlier psychiatric profiles of abusive parents were inaccurate. Of the many psychiatric traits of parents who abuse children, the only ones that have stood the test of time are depression and anxiety (Wolfe 1984). It is worth noting that these traits are common reactions to sudden or chronic stress (Burgess and Youngblade 1988), a point to which we return later. This focus on stress was a frequent feature of research by social workers and sociologists who emphasized correlates of abuse such as poverty and unemployment (e.g., Gil 1970; Gelles 1973). The idea was that any of us could abuse our children if we were subjected to the stress associated with loss of job, poverty, having too many children, or being a single parent. Survey research indicated that, while child abuse is found in all social strata, it is more prevalent in blue-collar, less well educated families. Straus, Gelles, and Steinmetz (1980), for example, found rates of abuse 40 percent higher in blue-collar than in white-collar families and 62 percent higher in families earning less than $6,000 annually.

When scholars from other disciplines turned to the problem of child abuse, a major outcome was a growing awareness of correlates of abuse operating on levels of analysis quite different from the personalities of abusive parents. Thus, at one level, it has been argued that societal values and norms may lead to the acceptance, if not the condoning, of child abuse (Gil 1970). Within our society, there is ample evidence that we readily accept violence in certain contexts, perhaps especially in the family (e.g., Stark and McEvoy 1970; Geis and Monahan 1975).

At a different analytical level, it has been reported that parents isolated from important social support systems in their neighborhoods and elsewhere are especially likely to be violent toward their children (Garbarino and Crouter 1978). Other research has documented the importance of the social structure of the family itself. For example, families with four or more children are found disproportionately in abuse statistics. Similarly, rates of abuse are higher in single-parent households and in households with step-relations (Daly and Wilson 1980; Burgess et al. 1981).

To complicate matters further, other documented correlates of child abuse include characteristics of parents such as depression and anxiety (Wolfe 1984) and autonomic hyperreactivity (Vasta 1982), as well as characteristics of abused children themselves, such as difficult temperaments (Johnson and Morse 1968; Frodi 1981), mental retardation (Sandgrund, Gaines, and Green 1974), and hyperactive and other difficult-to-handle behaviors (Reid, Patterson, and Loeber 1982).

Given multiple correlates operating on different levels of analysis, some investigators have attempted to organize all of the presumed determinants in a conceptually or theoretically significant way (e.g., Parke and Collmer 1975; Garbarino 1977; Burgess 1979; Belsky 1980). Garbarino (1977) and Belsky (1978, 1980) have each drawn on Bronfenbrenner's (1977) ecological model of human development. With some differences, these writers conceptualize child maltreatment as being multiply determined by forces at work in the individual, the family (the microsystem), the community (the exosystem), and the culture (the macrosystem) and assert that these multiple determinants are ecologically nested within one another. This perspective is important because it explicitly recognizes that the various correlates of maltreatment operate on different analytical levels. Belsky (1980) has done a particularly thorough job of grouping the principal predictors of maltreatment within various ecological levels.

As it stands now, however, the ecological model of child maltreatment suffers from several deficiencies. First, it is not clear what it means to say that the various multiple correlates of abuse are "ecologically nested" within each other. Does this mean more than the assertion that there are important interactions between these variables? But, second, and perhaps more important, there seem to be no theoretical reasons for postulating that factors operating on one level of analysis may be more important than those operating on another. Admittedly, this is a difficult issue but it is one that any theory worth its salt must attempt to answer. Third, as currently used, the model is simply a descriptive or taxonomic system. It alerts us to various social indicators that we should examine but proposes no causal mechanisms or processes responsible for the nesting of these correlates. In all fairness, however, the model may not have been designed as an explanatory device.

In this essay, however, we take a modest step in the direction of identifying explanatory principles of violence in families. For several reasons, taking this step is not easy. First, the task is difficult because there are ambiguities in the use of key concepts such as abuse, battering, and violence. Following Gelles and Straus (1979, p. 554), the concept of violence as we use it is equivalent to physical aggression: "an act carried out with the intention of, or perceived as having the intention of, physically hurting another person." The harm can range from the minor pain produced by a slap to systematic torture or murder.

A second problem is that some theoretical approaches have focused largely on what medical researchers refer to as "marker variables," whereas others emphasize causal mechanisms or processes (Burgess 1986). Marker variables simply tell us where to look for probable causal processes. Examples of such marker variables include depression, low self-esteem, alcoholism, family size, social isolation, and various manifestations of poverty. While these factors, and others like them, have been found to be reliably associated with violence in families—especially the maltreatment of children—they do not, in and of themselves, explain why or how it is that some, and only some, people with such characteristics express violent behavior.

Third, where attention has been given to causal mechanisms or processes, the theories used have differed markedly in terms of the units of analysis employed and of underlying premises or assumptions. Gelles and Straus (1979) have discussed these efforts under the headings of "intraindividual," "social psychological," and "sociocultural" theories. Given the cogency of their analysis, we describe only the major highlights of each of the theories mentioned in their review. The reader is directed to their original paper for a more comprehensive treatment.

In their analysis of *intraindividual theories*, that is, theories that attempt to explain family violence as a function of an individual's characteristics, Gelles and Straus (1979) focus on two widely used explanations of family violence: psychopathology and alcohol and drugs. Notably, Gelles and Straus chose to omit biologically based characteristics from their discussion of theories at this level of analysis. In any case, the psychopathology explanation postulates that violence is the result of a psychological abnormality (e.g., inadequate self-control, sadism, psychopathic personality, or mental illness) that occurs in some individuals. The major application of this theory to the family has been with respect to child abuse (e.g., Kempe et al. 1962; Steele and Pollock 1968). There are several important drawbacks to using this theoretical approach. There is inadequate scientific evidence to support this theory; the theory does not adequately explain which abnormal personality traits are associated with violence (in fact, only a very small proportion of mentally ill persons are violent); and, by using acts of violence as indicators of mental illness, such theories are often used tautologically.

Alcohol and drug use explanations have similarly focused on characteristics of individuals. The alcohol and drug use theory postulates that these substances act as disinhibitors that release the violent tendencies existing in humans. Again, there are several problems associated with this approach to explaining family violence. Most important, there is little rigorous scientific support for it. While some analyses of family violence (e.g., Snell, Rosenwald, and Robey 1964) observe that participants in domestic violence are often drinking or drunk prior to attacking, the theory does not explain where the violent tendencies that exist in humans originate or why alcohol and drugs do not act as violence disinhibitors for everyone. Others (e.g., Gelles 1974) have proposed that the association between alcohol and violence is probably not a function of the disinhibiting properties of alcohol but, rather, that being drunk may provide an excuse for violent behavior.

Dissatisfaction with intraindividual theories led some investigators to explore the utility of social psychological and sociocultural theories. The function of *social psychological theories* is to explain the interaction of individuals with their social environments, that is, with other individuals, groups, and organizations. Gelles and Straus (1979) describe seven theories that fall under this rubric: frustration-aggression theory, social learning theory, self-attitude theory, "a Clockwork Orange" theory, symbolic interaction theory, exchange theory, and attribution theory.

Frustration-aggression theory (Dollard et al. 1939; Miller 1941) posits that the tendency to respond aggressively is innate in humans and that aggressive behavior results when some purposeful activity is blocked. That is, humans tend to be aggressive toward objects that interfere with important goals, or to displace the aggression to a "safer" object. This theory does not explain under what conditions frustration leads to aggression, does not account for societal differences (e.g., in some societies frustration is followed by passive withdrawal [Mead and MacGregor 1951]), and does not differentiate physical aggression from verbal abuse and aggression. Nonetheless, when viewed as a special case of social learning theory (i.e., the link between frustration and aggression occurs only if the individual has been reinforced for an "aggressive" response to frustration), it does explain why the tendency to respond to frustration by aggression is so common. It also helps explain family violence, according to Gelles and Straus (1979), because the family is the focus of high personal involvement and of high frustration.

Social learning theory (e.g., Burgess and Bushell 1969; Bandura 1973; Patterson 1982b) postulates that violence is a learned phenomenon. That is, the individual learns about the response (violence) and which stimuli typically follow the response (when violence is appropriate). This learning process is accomplished via three mechanisms: modeling/imitation, direct tuition, and reinforcement/punishment. Applied to the family, this theory would posit that the family serves as a training ground for violence by providing both exemplars for imitation and role modeling and contingencies of reinforcement and punishment that (often unintentionally) encourage violence (Patterson 1982a). We describe below research documenting the importance of these theoretical ideas.

Self-attitude theory (Kaplan 1972), a modification of social learning theory, postulates that violence occurs when an individual struggles to cope with negative self-attitudes that arise out of adverse psychosocial experiences. In a society, culture, or group that values violence, persons of low self-esteem may seek to bolster their images in the eyes of themselves and others by carrying out acts of violence. While this theory explains the propensity to violence of those for whom society makes it difficult to achieve an adequate level of self-esteem, Gelles and Straus (1979) point out that its propositions are not sufficient to explain the high level of violence in the family and why family members are likely victims of individuals who have experienced self-devaluing experiences.

A "Clockwork Orange" theory (Gelles and Straus 1979) includes the variety of explanations that locate the cause of violence in boredom and the urge to seek thrills. Basically, it proposes that there is an optimal level of stress or tension and that, if life circumstances do not provide this level, aggression and violence will occur as a means of moving toward the optimal level. In application to the family, this theory tries to explain "senseless" aggression and violence that can occur in highly integrated, smoothly functioning groups, such as an apparently model family. Farrington (1980) also used the notion of an optimal stress level in developing a theory specifically related to intrafamily violence. Farrington defined stress as an imbalance between the demands with which an individual or family is faced and the response capabilities available for use in dealing with those demands. He posits that all individuals and families come to develop personal and unique optimal stress levels at which they function most comfortably. In situations in which the balance of demands to response capabilities either exceeds or falls short of the usual stress level, the probability of intrafamily violence is increased.

Gelles and Straus (1979) include under the rubric of social psychological theories three conceptual frameworks that, while they have not been used specifically in reference to intrafamily violence, do offer potential for such a use. The first is symbolic interactionism. A symbolic interactionist approach disregards notions of biological drives and focuses instead on the symbolic, subjective meaning of social life. With respect to family violence, its focus would be on the nature of meanings of violence, how these meanings are built up, how they persist, how they are modified, and the consequences of these meanings in situations. Applied to family relations, Gelles and Straus (1979) speculate, this approach might concern itself with the evolving social meanings and role expectations among family members.

The second of these frameworks is exchange theory, which assumes that interaction is guided by the pursuit of rewards and the avoidance of costs (punishments) and that an individual who supplies reward services to another obliges that other to fulfill an obligation to furnish benefits to the first individual (Blau 1964). Interaction will continue, then, to the extent that the reciprocal exchange of rewards occurs. When reciprocity is not achieved the interaction will end. Further, exchange theorists argue that individuals expect rewards to be proportional to investments ("distributive justice"; e.g., Homans 1967), and they contend that costs and rewards are evaluated in the light of alternatives (Thibaut and Kelley 1959). Exchange theory can be seen as a special application or elaboration of social learning theory (Burgess and Nielsen 1974). Applied to family violence, it helps explain the growth of resentment, anger, and hostility. Such reactions are made more probable when the rule of distributive justice is violated.

The third and final framework described under the heading of social psychological theories is attribution theory (e.g., Kelley and Thibaut 1969; Kelley 1971). As a perspective on family violence, attribution theory seeks to describe the processes used by individuals to impute motivations to others. With respect to intrafamilial violence, it would posit that the structure of family relations is such that there is a high probability of malevolent intent attributed to the actions of other family members, which sets in motion an escalating cycle of resentment and aggression (Gelles and Straus 1979).

At a macrolevel of analysis, Gelles and Straus (1979) review six sociocultural theories that purport to examine individual violence as a function of such social structures or arrangements as norms, values, institutional organization, and systems operations. These theories, while focusing on macrolevel variables, also include concepts and processes that exist at the intraindividual and psychosocial levels as well. The theories reviewed are functional, culture-of-violence, structural, general systems theory, conflict theory, and resource theory.

The basic proposition of functional theory is that violence fulfills certain functions, such as a sense of achievement, a danger signal, and, for observers, a catalyst for action (Coser 1967). With respect to the family, this theory asserts that violence can be important for maintaining the adaptability of the family to changing circumstances and is thus important to its survival. One particularly interesting application of functionalist theory to intrafamilial violence is Bakan's (1971) assertion that the widespread use of violence toward children may be seen as a case of population control through filicide. We have more to say about such an evolutionary application later.

Culture-of-violence theory assumes that violence is unevenly distributed in the social structure, most notably in the higher rates of violence in the lower socioeconomic status sectors of society (Coser 1967). Further, this theory proposes that the differential distribution of violence is a function of different cultural norms and values concerning violence and that violence is a learned response and reflects effective socialization into that subculture's value systems and norms. With respect to family violence, the family can be viewed as a training ground for violence because it is a major unit in transmitting subcultural values (Steinmetz and Straus 1974). An important limitation of culture-of-violence theory, however, is that it does not explain how the subcultural values originate, nor does it explain how these values can be modified or changed over time. Even so, this theory is useful in pointing to the different cultural or subcultural rules that legitimize or require violence.

A structural theory approach to violence also assumes that violence/deviance is unevenly distributed in the social structure (Durkheim 1951), with violence more common among those of low socioeconomic status. This theory proposes that violence is a result of unequal distribution of some of the major causes of violence (stress and frustration) and of the differential learning experiences that provide models, norms, and values that legitimize the use of violence. An obvious advantage of this theory is that it integrates many of the ideas emphasized in other theories (e.g., stress, frustration reduction, and learning experiences).

General systems theory applied to family violence (Straus 1973) seeks to account for violence between family members by viewing the family as a goal-seeking, purposive, adaptive system. Violence is thus treated as a system product or output rather than as a product of individual pathology. "Positive feedback" processes produce an upward spiral of violence, and "negative feedback" processes serve to maintain or dampen the level of violence. This theory also examines the morphogenic processes that alter the role structure of the family in pursuit of various goals. General systems theory has been used principally in explanations of the maintenance of family violence, but it has not been used systematically to analyze the beginning or termination of family violence.

Conflict theory (Dahrendorf 1968) views individual actors, groups, and organizations as seeking to further their own "interests" rather than as consensus-equilibrium-seeking systems. The focus is on conflict management rather than on system maintenance. Violence occurs as a mode of conflict resolution when other modes of pursuing individual or group interests break down. The family can be viewed as an arena of confrontation and conflicting interests (Sprey 1969). Again, using a conflict perspective, violence is likely to occur because it is a powerful mode of advancing one's interests when other modes fail (Steinmetz and Straus 1974).

Finally, Gelles and Straus (1979) review intrafamilial resource theory (Goode 1971), which asserts that violence is an important resource by means of which individuals (or groups) can maintain or advance their interests. Goode (1971) argues that the greater the resources a person can command, the more force the person can muster. However, the more resources a person can command, the less likely it is that force will be deployed in an overt manner. Violence is thus used as a resource when other resources are lacking.

As brief as our account of each of these theories has been, it should, nevertheless, be evident that they are not simple competitors in a theoretical contest. They, instead, may be viewed as potential collaborators that have directed our attention to different correlates, aspects, and manifestations of family violence. Moreover, from our perspective, these theories differ among themselves with respect to the level of generality they assume. Only some theories have identified causal mechanisms (e.g., social learning theory) while others have focused on social indicators or marker variables (e.g., structural theory).

At this stage of theoretical development, the most important problems facing us involve efforts to explain why conflicts of interest appear to be inevitable, especially in families; to identify the linkage that connects proximate causal mechanisms to the distal and macro factors associated with violence in families; and to explain why violence toward women and children has been so common in human family history. If undertaken properly, attempts to answer these questions should provide the added benefit of revealing the interconnections between the various theories described above.

To accomplish these tasks, our essay departs from the usual social science approach. The long history of violence across species and cultures has led us to conclude that we need to try to develop theoretical propositions and concepts that derive from a broadly historical perspective, that transcend interspecific differences, that are sufficiently general to permit parsimonious interpretations of the diverse data currently available, yet that are precise enough to generate specific predictions. In Section I we maintain that modern evolutionary theory meets these criteria. Our position is that knowledge of the evolutionary and ecological factors associated with the relationship between parents and offspring can reveal much about parent-child conflict (Trivers 1974) as well as about marital conflict.

A position similar to our own is found in Bolton's (1983) family resource theory. Although his is primarily a clinical theory, it shares certain assumptions with the biosocial theory we describe in this essay. For example, family resource theory assumes that there is the potential for violence in us all and that parental effort can ultimately be explained in terms of its contribution to parents' reproductive success. The theory postulates that the attachment bond between parents and offspring has evolved as a primary mechanism to insure parental care for children. The theory identifies a variety of factors that can short-circuit the bonding process, including an inability to bond either by the parent or the child, environmental pressures that exacerbate parent-child competition for resources, and dysfunctional patterns of family communication.

This essay differs from most treatments of family violence (including family resource theory) in still another way: we consider carefully the cross-cultural record. In Sections II and III, we describe data drawn from cross-cultural studies that illustrate that relations between spouses and between parents and offspring show a great deal more variability than is apparent to social scientists whose field of analysis is limited to complex, stratified Western societies. For example, when seen from our current moral values, behaviors such as child abuse appear to be profoundly pathological. However, our values are entrenched in a stable, centralized political system and an economy that distributes huge surpluses with a surprising degree of equity among individuals who are no longer connected to each other by long-standing ties of shared residence and kinship. Humans have not experienced for long the geographical mobility, affluence, and political stability of our current society. Indeed, the industrial revolution and the biomedical advances that reduce mortality are only recent embellishments on earlier inventions that have had even more profound consequences for the human social condition. Because of the rapidity of technological advance and the geometric increase in the world population in the last few hundred years, it is easy to forget that social relationships, including family relationships, were structured in significantly different ways from those to which we have become accustomed.

Throughout most of history, the individual's "rights" to life and to some measure of satisfaction were a function of being born into an established group based on ties of kinship. This preexisting group provided economic and political security for new members; it was also a buffer against other similarly structured groups that, depending on circumstances, could constitute a serious competitive threat. For our ancestors, families or kindreds were a necessity for survival and reproduction (van den Berghe 1979). In order to maintain a competitive advantage or to expand against the interests of other groups, families (particularly their senior members) had to be able to allocate resources efficiently among kin and other individuals related by marriage. Families both nurtured members and culled from them. Ample examples come from European traditions in the form of primogeniture, of sending surplus children into monasteries and convents, of "selling" children into indentured servitude, and of apprenticing children for periods of years to nonfamily members (Dickemann 1979). In other, more final, ways, parents discriminated among children, keeping some and "letting go" of others by recourse to distant wet nurses in the notorious rural baby farms of seventeenth- and eighteenth-century Europe (Aries 1970; Langer 1972; DeMause 1974).

We mention these recent practices (which seem abhorrent by modern standards) because in the following pages we frequently reiterate that human family relationships cannot be assumed to be inevitably benign. Competition for access to scarce resources is a fact between families and within families (Trivers 1974). It is in this context that the cross-cultural record is most valuable. Good ethnographic descriptions are available of societies ranging from technologically simple hunter-gatherers, through tribal economies based on horticulture and animal husbandry, to peasant intensive-land-use systems. All human societies provide a normative system within which mating, parenting, and ties of kinship develop. By looking at diverse societies, one can see the interplay between individual behavior, family goals, environment, and social institutions. Broadening one's understanding of family interaction by looking at different cultural settings has many advantages. In particular, one can analyze how human universals such as sex, age, competition/hierarchy, and biological kinship constitute a core around which human families operate. At the same time, one can determine how extrafamilial and nonbiological factors such as environment, climate, population density, and the economy affect the expression of these underlying universals.

Finally, our discussion of family violence differs from many others in that we try to describe the causal chain that links evolutionary principles to actual violence in specific families. The biosocial theory we propose emphasizes the importance of two ecological conditions: cultural norms and the stability or instability of the environment in which family members find themselves. In addition, we present data to illustrate how certain interpersonal contingencies of reinforcement and punishment may function as proximate mechanisms that translate conditions of ecological instability into intrafamily violence. In this way, we hope to balance evolutionary theory's emphasis on group differences against developmental analyses that are concerned with the identification of individual differences.

I. Evolutionary Theory

To set our argument into the proper evolutionary context, we should like to point out the major concepts of evolutionary theory. These concepts are used later to construct the most general theoretical propositions for our analysis of violence in families.

A. *Basic Concepts and Learning Rules*

Evolutionary theory assumes that all of life from the beginning of time has been subjected to a continual process of *natural selection*, that is, *differential reproductive success*. An individual's evolutionary fitness is defined in terms of reproductive success relative to others. On average, individuals better adapted to their physical and social environment have higher fitness. Individuals continually affect one another's fitness in that they both compete for and create resources that, necessarily, are finite (Williams 1966a). *Inclusive fitness* can sometimes be facilitated by behaving altruistically toward genetically related others. There is evidence that most animals have evolved to be altruistic especially toward their genetic relatives, that is, members of their kin group (Alexander 1979a, 1979b). We believe that many of the behaviors associated with family life, including the tendencies to produce and care for offspring, to establish relatively enduring social-emotional bonds, to mourn the loss of loved ones, and even to exhibit violent behavior toward family members, can ultimately be explained in terms of the contributions those behaviors make to inclusive fitness. We should perhaps emphasize our use of the adverb "ultimately" in the preceding sentence. A complete explanation of a behavior also requires attention to potential causal mechanisms; throughout this essay we refer to important proximate processes that have originated in other theoretical perspectives.

It is a common part of the parlance in evolutionary ecology to describe patterns of behavior as "strategies"—for example, reproductive, life-historical, or foraging strategies. This is a convenient metaphor meant to emphasize the nonrandom and goal-directed aspects of alternative behavioral processes. It is not therefore assumed that the individual displaying such a "strategy" is either conscious of its goals or is cognitively deciding the best course of action. Some behavioral strategies, however, may necessitate more cognition than had been initially assumed (e.g., Cheney, Seyfarth, and Smuts 1986). Although the ultimate goal of behavioral strategies is assumed to be increased inclusive fitness, each strategic analysis seeks to explicate more immediate, proximate goals such as time minimization, energy maximization, increased access to members of the opposite sex, and so forth (see the review in Krebs and Davies [1987]). *Parental investment*, a concept drawn from evolutionary theory, is central to our understanding of family violence (Trivers 1972). Parental investment refers technically to behavior displayed by a parent that increases the reproductive potential of the child toward whom the behavior is directed, at the cost of similar investment by the parent toward other or future offspring. Implicit is the notion that a parent has limited resources and a finite life span to expend those resources in the rearing of children. Another key concept we use is *parental certainty* (Kurland and Gaulin 1984). Because females have virtually complete certainty of parenthood, whereas males do not, we are especially concerned with the concept of *paternity certainty*. This concept from evolutionary theory is central to an understanding of family organization and process, including parental investment.

Our intention in this essay, then, is to use evolutionary reasoning and arguments about evolutionary fitness to try to make sense of the often puzzling phenomena of marital violence and child maltreatment. This is not an easy task, in part because many of the central concepts are difficult to operationalize. Fitness, for example, is the touchstone of evolutionary biology, and yet it is difficult to measure or operationalize

(Wallace 1958). Here we use success in reproduction—that is, completed fertility—as an index of evolutionary fitness.

Some of the controversy surrounding our approach stems from the old and, in our opinion, sterile debate about "nature and nurture" or "heredity and environment" in the human sciences. Yet, when the domain of discussion passes from the general to that of specific problems, issues, or phenomena in the behavioral sciences, there is not substantial disagreement to be found among working scientists. Variation in human behavioral development results from nurture, but the way that an organism transforms environmental signals into behavioral phenotypes is the result of its evolutionary history (see, e.g., reviews in Bateson [1982]; Dawkins [1982]; and Alcock [1984]).

One of our goals, thus, is to elucidate learning rules, evolutionary algorithms that mediate between the environment, broadly defined, and an organism's response to it. For example, rats learn easily to avoid foodstuffs that lead to nausea, but they find it difficult to learn to avoid foods that result in electric shock (Garcia and Koelling 1976). Rats learn food avoidance, yet the learning rule used is a sensible consequence of their evolutionary past: avoiding food with peculiar taste and odor because these are indicative of tainted food. Individuals in the past who avoided such tainted or rotten foods were likely to avoid poisonous or sickening substances that would either kill or debilitate them and therefore they were better able to survive to reproduce. Learning is not an arbitrary concatenation of cue and reward but is itself shaped by the evolution of adaptive sensory, motor, and cognitive physiology.

Another factor that contributes to the controversy of applying evolutionary theory to human behavior is the assumption that the theory seems to imply that all behavior must be adaptive. However, the theory suggests something quite different. It suggests, first of all, that many, but not necessarily all, attributes (behavioral as well as morphological) evolved because they contributed to reproductive success in previous species-typical historical circumstances. Thus evolutionary biologists often act as historians attempting to determine why a particular trait might have been adaptive (Alexander 1979b). Second, the theory allows for the possibility that some attributes may simply be by-products or incidental consequences, that is, nonadaptations of other attributes that were the product of selection pressures. Third, the theory does not rule out the possibility that some attributes are actually maladaptive. The theory would, of course, lead to the prediction that truly maladaptive traits would eventually be selected against precisely because they inter-fere with reproductive success.

Our attempt to use evolutionary theory to explain family violence does not assume that such violence is necessarily adaptive for anyone. Rather, we argue that the apparently nonrandom pattern of both marital violence and child maltreatment suggests that such behavior may have been adaptive in certain past environments. The major point here is that nonadaptive and maladaptive behavior may be grounded in an underlying evolutionary logic. Thus even pathological behavior may allow tests of evolutionary hypotheses in that they, in effect, may make more apparent the constitutional, circumstantial, psychological, and developmental factors associated with the behavior under analysis (Symons 1979, 1986). Therefore we are prepared to argue that violence in some family contexts has been a part of the repertoire of behaviors of our ancestors. But we also suggest that violence is elicited easily by certain environmental conditions and that the way humans perceive their environment is an evolved charac-teristic worthy of investigation in those terms. Our evolutionary model assumes that (1) humans have learning rules and perceptual rules, (2) these rules are best understood at this stage in the development of behavioral science as products of our evolution, (3) these rules are neither always nor even usually adaptive in contemporary environ-ments, and (4) these rules are not necessarily "conscious" or accessible to introspection by the actors.

B. Evolution, Reproduction, and Ecology

Any evolutionarily successful organism must balance its allocation of time, energy, risk, and other resources between growth and mainte-nance (somatic effort) and mating and parenting (reproductive effort) (Pianka 1970; Daly and Wilson 1983; Kurland and Gaulin 1984). Or-ganisms adapted to transient resources or unstable environments, where selection favors prolific breeders who can momentarily take ad-vantage of an open niche, will make the greatest genetic contribution to the next generation. Such organisms are referred to as "r-strategists," in that they manifest traits associated with a high "r," the intrinsic rate of increase of a population conforming to the logistic growth equation. In contrast, some organisms are "K-strategists," evolving traits associated with alterations in the maximum population size that can be accom-modated by the organisms interacting with the environment, that is, the "carrying capacity" of logistic population growth, symbolized by "K." Although r-strategists are expected to have a large number of cheaply produced progeny who will opportunistically settle new habitats, the K-strategists are expected to invest heavily in each off-spring making them "durable" and competitive in stable and saturated environments. From our perspective, the key distinction between r- and K-strategists is the low parental effort of the former and the rela-tively higher parental effort of the latter. The terms are relative, so that, for example, the weeds in your yard are r-strategists when com-pared to your apple tree but are K-strategists when compared to the prodigious masting output of a chestnut oak. Among mammals, pri-mates are relative K-strategists, but, among the primates, humans are extreme K-strategists, although given the current human population explosion, our closest living animal relative, the chimpanzee, is even more of a K-strategist than we are. In any case, the r/K-strategy con-tinuum of life-historical and reproductive traits underscores the con-stellation of mating and parenting tactics. Some consequences of this adaptation in our species are that (1) Immaturity is very prolonged. Humans require fifteen to twenty-five years to reach reproductive ma-turity. (2) Parental care in humans is prolonged. It lasts from approxi-mately two to thirty or so years in various human societies. This is almost an order of magnitude longer than for other mammals. (3) Ex-tensive learning is necessary for successful survival and reproduction. (4) Males provision and otherwise provide resources for females and dependent offspring. There is a great deal of variation in the amount of parental effort by fathers across human societies, but there is almost always some.

These consequences are obviously interrelated. We list them to em-phasize the unprecedented place that parental provisioning, nurture, and, especially, the teaching of immature young have in our species. Humans are evolved specialists in child raising and child care. But as one would predict, there is a dark side to this specialization. Individuals who spent their resources on either offspring of low viability or, worse, immatures who were not their own left few descendants. We expect, then, that highly evolved and specific learning rules and perceptual algorithms are designed into our species. For example, male sexual jealousy is apparently a cultural universal, but it varies widely in prom-inence and expression. Our understanding is that male sexual jealousy is learned, yet it is very easily learned. There is, we propose, an evolved learning propensity that makes human males sensitive to the sexual behavior of their mates. There are, perhaps, perceptual rules that govern this learning rule. It is interesting that the consequences are probably not adaptive (i.e., optimal) in human societies today. Kurland (1979) shows that an optimally adapted male would divert resources to his sisters' offspring rather than to his wife's at a level of paternity uncertainty far higher than the level of uncertainty currently found in any human society.

It has become increasingly apparent in evolutionary ecology that mating systems are related to species characteristics, habitat, resource distribution, and the ease with which resources can be stored or defended (Kleiman 1977; Wittenberger 1980; Kleiman and Malcolm 1981; Vehrencamp and Bradbury 1984). The key issue in unraveling the associations among these factors is offspring survival. Under some circumstances, females can rear young without direct provisioning from males, for example, where resources can be independently harvested by her. Another such circumstance is one in which pressure from predators can be handled by her alone or by associating with other females in protective herds or burrows. In these situations, males may facilitate offspring survival in an indirect manner, as in the case of territorial defense, which insures the female and her brood the ability to gather food and to give birth to young without intense competition from conspecifics. Most mammals have mating systems of this type.

In other cases, where the sexes form durable pair bonds, it is commonly thought that the paternal role in protecting offspring evolved because it promoted male fitness. According to current evolutionary thinking, high male parental investment cannot evolve (or be "facultatively" expressed) except where benefits to males outweigh costs in terms of forgone mating opportunities (Zeveloff and Boyce 1980; reviewed in Kurland and Gaulin [1984]). In mammals, the extreme inequality of reproductive investment by the sexes rewards competition by males for access to multiple mates; for this reason monogamy is rare in mammals. The (infrequent) occurrence of monogamy among mammals is explained in terms of species morphology, characteristics of young, and distribution of resources such that the fitness interests of both the male and female are best served by combining efforts in the form of establishing an exclusive mating relationship, cooperating in nest-building or home-territory defense, and in rearing of young.

Because of the anatomy and physiology of reproduction in mammals, there are asymmetries between the sexes in the amount of time, energy, and risk devoted to reproduction (Trivers 1972; Maynard-Smith 1974; Dawkins 1979; Kurland and Gaulin 1984). Mammalian physiology requires at minimum almost no parental investment from males, while females must commit much. This asymmetry of parental investment leads to mammalian sex differences in patterns, or "strategies," of reproductive behavior. Unlike the male, whose reproductive success (from the perspective of evolutionary biology) may be furthered by impregnating as many females as possible, the female's reproductive success is limited by the time, energy, and risk costs of ovulation, conception, successful parturition, and, in the case of relatively helpless (altricial) young, the constraints of nurturing her offspring until they can survive on their own. Given a lower ceiling on ultimate reproductive potential for females than for males, females of most mammalian species are expected to show greater discrimination regarding mate choice and timing of reproduction than is shown by males, and greater commitment to parental effort.

Similarly, the sexes differ in their modes of interacting with the opposite sex. The male in most species, in some ways, takes the initiative in sexual contact; for example, in establishing a base from which to attract females by courtship displays and in discouraging other males. The female approach seems in many species to consist of choice and discrimination, whenever this is possible or useful. Where this choice is impossible or pointless, the female may engage instead in passive but powerful signaling, for example, with the pheromones released during estrus.

Males can vary their commitment of resources between the extremes of maximizing copulation with a large number of females, the "cad strategy," and maximizing provision of parental care to their offspring, the "dad strategy." Among mammals, the empirical correlates of the cad strategy are male dominance hierarchies, male-male aggression and violence, and high morphological dimorphism between the sexes because, in this situation, the fitness of a male seems to be determined primarily by competition with other males. Well-known examples of species with cad mating organization are elephant seals (LeBouef 1974), anubis baboons on the savannah (DeVore 1963), and most herd ungulates. In contrast, when male parental effort is high, the empirical correlates for numerous species are relatively stable, male-female monogamous associations, reduced male-male competition for access to females, and reduced dimorphism (Draper and Harpending 1982). Familiar examples include gibbons, beavers, mongoose, and wolves in some areas (Kurland and Gaulin 1984).

There is a corresponding strategy spectrum for females. In the face of males who will not provide parental effort, females may maximize reproductive success by minimizing time loss. They then reproduce early, with little or no concern for their mate or mates. Hrdy (1981) suggests that, in many social species, selection has favored outright promiscuity in females, thus defusing tendencies in males to harm or kill infants in the future. At any rate, with her large reproductive commitment and her limited reproductive potential, female investment in each offspring ought to be great relative to that of the male, and this is in fact what is observed.

By contrast, in populations in which males invest heavily in offspring, females may delay sexual bonding and refuse any male save one who will be a reliable partner and provisioner for her and the offspring of the mating. This strategy will favor the ability of females to predict the behavior of males, and it will favor sexual reticence and coyness in females. These abilities allow the female to avoid pregnancy without a stable mate and to assure the mate that he is in fact the father of offspring born (Trivers 1972). In species where such a cautious reproductive style is practiced, there is considerable courtship prior to mating. The female tests the qualities of the male as a potential mate, and the male assures himself during the same period that the female is not already pregnant by some other male.

The perspective of evolutionary ecology on mating, parenting, species morphology, and habitat characteristics can be usefully applied to social processes in humans. In the case of humans, of course, simple knowledge of habitat characteristics does not produce much predictive power because humans remain morphologically quite generalized and "specialize" behaviorally in a variety of adaptive ways (Washburn 1978). For humans, technology is one of the critical variables that must be understood in calculating the relationship between human groups and their local environment. Humans, insofar as cultural practices go, do not uniformly adhere to monogamous mating practices. Indeed, polygyny is more common among the ethnographically described human societies than is monogamy (van den Berghe 1979). Moreover, if pre-, extra-, and postmarital sex are added, as well as divorce and remarriage, concubinage, and prostitution, it becomes apparent that humans are, and have long been, effectively polygamous or serially monogamous.

Just as we find variation in mating and marriage across societies and cultures, so, too, are there variations in parenting practices. For example, although male parental investment is normatively expressed in all known human societies, it varies among individual males from those who show virtually no parental involvement after insemination to those who provide direct nurturance well into adulthood. It is our view that ecological conditions affect human reproductive (mating and parenting) effort in important ways. We explore two ecological conditions in this essay: cultural norms and the stability or instability of the environment in which families find themselves.

II. Marital Violence

Cultural norms influence the occurrence and kinds of violence between spouses. Ecological stress is another important influence on marital violence. Differences between individuals in rates of offending are related to interpersonal contingencies for coping with instability in the environment.

A. Cultural Norms and Marital Violence

Species with male parental investment share certain characteristics as a subclass. The mated pair isolates itself, particularly during the mating season, and is generally intolerant of opposite-sex individuals. Human social organization is unusual among higher mammalian species in that it combines living in heterosexual, mixed-age groups with a mating system based on more or less permanent ties between individuals. This seems commonplace enough to us, but other mammals who form pairs do so in isolation from others of their species.

For example, gibbons and beavers form devoted pairs, and each partner is active in driving away other beavers. (Often the female ousts other females, the male, other males.) Wolves and wild dogs appear to be an exception: they pair-bond and consort in packs; closer inspection reveals that typically only one female is reproductively active and a single pack male is her designated mate. The sexual capabilities of other adult pack members are suppressed (Altmann and Altmann 1979; Packer and Pusey 1982). In comparison with other pair-bonding mammals, humans seem to be "borrowing trouble" by combining sexually exclusive partnerships with all the temptations of group life.

There is a propensity among human groups to stress patriarchal values and the sexual double standard that holds females disproportionately responsible for sexual fidelity (Symons 1979; Daly and Wilson 1983). Without passing judgment on the ethics or worth of this value, there is an underlying "sexual contract" inherent in mating practices that incorporate high degrees of male parental investment in offspring: females give evidence of paternity certainty in return for male parental investment. Males in species where male parental investment has been favored may have been selected to be intolerant of cuckoldry. This factor may help account for marital violence and explain why males are overwhelmingly the perpetrators of severe violence on females, not the other way around. This observation in no way endorses the brutalization of women by their mates. However, it is relevant in the context of the theoretical perspective adopted in this essay to point out that it is in the fitness interests of men to keep their women away from other men. Marital violence researchers persistently find that perpetrators are largely men who command few resources relative to their wives and who can give little evidence of the ability to provision a wife and offspring (Allen and Straus 1980). If we can assume that human sexual behaviors have been influenced by natural selection, we would predict that economic or psychological insecurities in men would translate readily into sexual insecurity. The same perspective leads one to assume that, given reasonable alternatives, women should not remain permanently attached to a mate who cannot contribute to her support and that of her offspring. Along these lines, Wilson (1987, pp. 96–98) has developed a "male marriageable pool index" that shows a strong association over time between the decrease in the number of employed black males per 100 black women, controlling for age, and the steady increase among blacks in the United States of female-headed households. For two related applications of this proposition, see Dickemann (1983) and Draper and Harpending (1982).

The concepts of certainty of paternity, male parental investment, and sexual jealousy are pertinent to the many studies of marital violence that mention the Western cultural ideology of male dominance as a factor in the victimization of women (see, e.g., Fagan, in this volume; Frieze and Browne, in this volume). Researchers also report that men with a history of wife battering hold more conservative sex-role attitudes in comparison with their wives and in comparison with nonbattering men (cited in Davidson [1978]).

Established notions that husbands and fathers have authority over women and children are found throughout regions of the Judeo-Christian faith and among other world religions such as Islam, Buddhism, and Confucianism. These values are not just the inventions of the politically centralized Western and Asiatic societies but are found in many societies of the world. The assumption of patriarchal rule by males is common though not universal in its application (Quinn 1977; Leacock 1978). A high proportion of societies imbue the adult male role with authority to coerce the behavior of dependent women and children. These powers are generally limited, however, by familial and community standards regarding the nature of sanctions the husband can bring to bear for particular offenses. Young men are similarly under the authority of senior male kinsmen. Women and children, because of their physical limitations, have always been in a weak position to take an individual stand against domination by one male or several allied males.

The social structure can insure the subordination of women in other ways, although this is variable (Rosaldo and Lamphere 1974; Reiter 1975). Women in a majority of world societies find their formal authority undermined by the common practice of organizing domestic groups around related males. For example, households and village segments are often composed of an older man and his wife, their adult sons with their wives, and the grandchildren. The pattern is one in which daughters marry out of their natal group as they reach maturity, joining their husbands in the village or territory in which the husband has grown up. This postmarital residence pattern is known as "patrilocality." The kinship system that emphasizes links through males and ignores female kin is called "patrilineality" (Keesing 1975).

These social forms are justified (both by the people who live in the systems and by social scientists who analyze the occurrence of this pattern) on various economic and political grounds. For example, where critical economic resources, such as land and rights to land, water rights, or domestic stock, are owned and managed by males, it is economical to keep the cooperating males together. Wives are brought in from other nearby groups, and daughters and sisters are sent off to live with men in other groups also based on descent in the male line. Similarly, keeping related males together has been thought to promote group defense. Some have argued that conditions of endemic warfare engender patrilocal residence on the grounds that a fighting force composed of male kin and men with long friendships is more effective against political and military adversaries (Otterbein and Otterbein 1965; Bigelow 1969; van den Berghe 1979). Ethnographic examples of societies organized in this way come from many parts of the world: East Africa (Gulliver 1963); Japan (Smith and Wiswell 1982); Taiwan (Wolf 1972); Circum Mediterranean (Campbell 1964); and India (Minturn and Hitchcock 1966).

A consequence of these residence and marriage patterns is that women typically begin their adult lives as newcomers into groups in which primary economic and social control is in the hands of males. It is true that other women are also living in such groups. However, their own structural position is such that they do not ally themselves with a young wife. Older women, for example, will be the mothers of the adult men and so will have interests in common with their sons and grandchildren. Other women, already married in, and senior to, the new wife (her sisters-in-law, for example), will be mothers of young children and dependent on their husbands and the husbands' kindred for economic and social support. Each new wife who joins such a patrilocal group of male kindred is in a position of marked subordination not only to her husband and other men but also to senior women. Upper-class groups throughout India show these patterns; a particularly rich description of Rajput domestic life illustrates the structural constraints under which women live (Minturn and Hitchcock 1966).

The sexes in such societies occupy markedly sex-segregated spheres of activity and interest (Whiting and Whiting 1975). The lives of adult women and children are separated so that work, leisure, rest, eating, and ritual participation often occur in same-sex groups. Women carry out their domestic and economic roles with relatively limited access to their husbands and males-in-law. The work of women is organized by senior women and delegated across villages and within households. One effect of this segregation is to reduce social contact between women and their husbands (or between women and their males-in-law). Although women are formally under the control of men, in daily life the reality of male dominance is often not highly salient. Women inhabit a women's sphere that buffers them from male coercion (Fernea 1965; Mernissi 1975; Abu-Lughod 1985).

Many of the societies found practicing slash and burn agriculture in the tropical forests have institutionalized sex segregation. The Mundurucci of lowland Venezuela (Murphy and Murphy 1985) and highland New Guinea groups (Meggitt 1964; Strathern 1972) carry the formal separation of the sexes to an extreme where adult males sleep, eat, work, and conduct leisure activities in separate men's houses in separate areas of the village.

The probability that male sexual jealousy will be aroused is minimized by the spatial segregation of the sexes. From the point of view of men who fear cuckoldry by their wives, the female hierarchy serves male interests in patrilocal societies. In many sex-segregated societies, wives are under the more or less continuous surveillance (if not outright control) of a mother-in-law who can be expected to discourage their contact with other men. Such customs, known as female claustration, are common in large parts of North Africa, the Middle East, and among Hindu and Muslim groups in Asia (Vreede-de Stuers 1968). They find extreme expression in purdah, the residential seclusion of women of reproductive age. In groups practicing purdah, women remain in the women's quarters of extended family dwellings. Only men related as husbands, sons, or nephews to the women may socialize with the women (Abu-Lughod 1985). Women leave their seclusion only for unusual circumstances, such as weddings or funerals. They go about in public heavily veiled and accompanied by their husbands or other men of their husband's group (Fernea 1965; Minturn and Hitchcock 1966; Mernissi 1975; Schilkroudt 1978).

In modern industrialized society, norms governing public and private contact between men and women are ostensibly diametrically opposed to those just described. In theory, the sexes mix in an egalitarian and sex-blind manner, though under the surface we see evidence of age-old insecurities and doubts. For example, single women often go to some effort in public to sustain the appearance of respectability by such artifices as not going out alone at night, not entertaining men alone in their private quarters, and dressing in a manner that will not unduly attract masculine attention. It is easy to see, however, that modern society has relaxed many of the customs that historically have operated simultaneously to make sexual philandering difficult (for women) and to reassure men about the fidelity of their mates. It can be predicted that contemporary men of low status or who have low self-esteem, or both, will be most likely to react with anxiety, defensiveness, and violence to the relative absence of restrictions that modern women enjoy (see, e.g., O'Brien 1971).

Whereas restrictions such as sex-segregation clearly affect female autonomy most directly, in kin-based societies there are other factors that ameliorate the low status of wives and children. Wives, for example, maintain strong affective ties with their own kin, visiting them and receiving visits in turn. Husbands find many reasons for maintaining good relations with their in-laws. Typically, in-laws live not too far away and are a second source of support (after husband's kin) for economic or political assistance. In societies in which polygyny is permitted, a husband can hope that if he treats his first wife well he may gain a second wife from among his senior wife's kinswomen. The wife's kindred and their potential value to the husband create restraints to the ideal of legitimate authority over wives vested in husbands. In this way a woman, although jurally subordinate to her husband, is protected from extreme and persistent maltreatment because of the nearness of her kin, the frequency of their visits, and the flow of information and gossip.

This may be one of the ways in which postindustrial societies have created problems for the marital relationship. Some of the traditional "safeguards" that simpler social systems have built into their institutions and that have the effect of buffering women from extreme male violence are no longer common. Similarly, in less technologically developed societies, there is not the degree of privacy and social isolation of spouses from other kin and neighbors that exists in modern Western societies such as the United States. Violent confrontations between spouses are heard by others and attract bystanders who may intervene to stop a beating that is deemed excessive by community standards.

Women in technologically simple societies are valued above all for their fertility. Not only are cultural values overwhelmingly pronatalist, but people say explicitly that they want children because of the economic value their work will contribute to the family and because they represent a form of social security to parents in their elder years (Mamdani 1972). A wife, aside from characteristics of her health or personality, is valued for her ability to bear and rear children. Women in highly patriarchal societies achieve social esteem because of their role as mothers of the children claimed by their husband's descent group. Women know that through their fertility and their ability to nurture children they can claim tolerance and support from their in-laws (Caldwell 1976, 1978, 1980). In our own society, the economic value of children has disappeared along with the agrarian lifestyle of the nineteenth and early twentieth centuries. Rising levels of state-supported education and high geographical mobility may have eroded, in some families, the economically meaningful reciprocal ties of mutual dependency between parents and offspring. Women in modern times do not find their childbearing capabilities as highly valued as formerly.

There are other societies in which the social structure does not confer the same degree of unequal political and economic advantages on men that we have been discussing. For example, in societies in which descent and coresidence are calculated in the female line (matrilineal and matrilocal societies), women remain together on land they have inherited through their mothers (Schneider and Gough 1961). It is husbands who change residence at marriage and who move in as strangers among an established group of cooperating women (Richards 1950; Schneider and Gough 1961; Douglass 1969). Such societies are much less common than the patrilineal and patrilocal variant. Matriliny generally occurs in the context of low technology, low population density, and low levels of warfare. Women are usually the major food producers. The economic contribution of men is typically less important and time-consuming than that of the women. The men engage in long-distance trade and are away from home for long periods. When they are at home, men supplement family foods with fishing and hunting (Schneider 1961).

The matrilineal kinship organization does not mean, however, that women are politically superior to men. Positions of political leadership in matrilineal societies are still monopolized by men who are the heads of kinship groups composed of the descendants of women (Basehart 1961). Nonetheless, women form solidary groups with their sisters and mothers, while their brothers and uncles act as political and ritual leaders on their behalf. Thus the de facto autonomy of women in matrilineal systems is greatly increased (Schlegel 1972). Women look to their own kindred (men and women) for economic and social support; the authority of men as husbands is reduced and they find it difficult to coerce women. Similarly, men cannot coerce children since children belong to the mother's kinship group. In these situations, men, as husbands, are in a structurally weak or impotent position somewhat analogous to women's position in patrilineal and patrilocal societies. Marriages in matrilineal systems are fragile and the sanctions against extramarital female philandering are less severe than in patrilineal societies. The combination of female autonomy, fragile marriages, and reduced male parental investment is found in matrilineal societies in culturally unrelated parts of the world. Ethnographic reports from the Zuni (southwestern United States) and the Tonga (central Africa) show the ease with which women can sometimes rid themselves of husbands and move in and out of divorced, widowed, and married statuses with few economic or psychological disruptions to themselves or their children (Colson 1958; Schlegel 1977).

Notice, however, the relationship between male parental investment and the presence of the sexual double standard. We mentioned earlier that in species in which males invest in females and young, both partners to the pair bond, but especially the male, are intolerant of other sexual competitors. In all known human societies, customs regulate sexual activity, and in all cases the primary intent is restraint on female sexuality. In both monogamous and polygamous societies, sanctions are stronger against female than against male infidelity.

That this applies to our own society is evident from a number of studies of marital violence. For example, Greenblat (1985) attempted to ascertain under what circumstances the use of force against a spouse was considered appropriate. Respondents displayed generally low levels of acceptance of the general proposition that it is appropriate to hit one's spouse. Nonetheless, self-defense, retaliation, and the spouse's known or suspected sexual infidelity were circumstances mentioned as those that would make the use of violence appropriate. This analysis may help explain a finding by Berk et al. (1983) that white males as batterers are responsible for particularly brutal attacks regardless of the ethnic background of the females with whom they have a relationship. The values of the dominant group in American society expect white men to perform as heads of households. White men in financial straits presumably find their role failure especially demeaning and may be especially intolerant of and sensitive to potential signs of defection in their mates.

Just as the tendency for women's autonomy to be eclipsed by effective male dominance in everyday life is limited in societies practicing matriliny, a similar pattern holds for most hunting and gathering groups (who recognize bilateral kinship), in which the requirements of foraging and the scattered nature of plants and game require regular residential moves and shifting combinations of families. Both husbands and wives, over much of the year, live in groups where some of the primary kin of each also live (Draper 1975). In these more "democratically arranged" societies, residence, work, leisure, and social and religious life are not organized in a stable fashion over time to keep lines of related males together. Living in contexts more genealogically diversified, women and children receive the backing of their own kin and lifelong allies and cannot be coerced as readily by their mates as in patrilineal cultures. These same factors influence the susceptibility of women to marital violence in complex societies. For example, Straus (1980) has argued that abused women are found disproportionately among women who have less power by virtue of not being in the labor market, who are excluded from decision making in the family, and who have less education.

To summarize, the occurrence of marital violence seems to be related significantly to the existence of patriarchal norms and values where men control the wealth and have, thereby, a power advantage over women. What is most important to recognize, however, is that societies are often organized in this way because such structural arrangements have functioned to reduce threats to the certainty of paternity while minimizing the use of physical force. The next issue to be addressed, then, is the circumstances that lead to an increasing likelihood of physical violence.

B. Ecological Instability and Marital Violence

Our central thesis is that transitional states marked by instability in the environment in which families live increase the probability of marital violence and child maltreatment. Human groups have historically been exposed to ecological changes that signal improvement or degradation of their life situation. Examples of such signals include food abundance or famine, adequate rainfall or drought, safety from large animals or the threat of predation, and peace or war. Because of this history, natural selection should favor sensitivity to such environmental cues, especially those directly related to reproductive success. Thus, among the behavioral systems most affected would be mating (and parenting) because they are so closely related to inclusive fitness.

Using the concept of ecological instability, a family can be conceptualized as an ecosystem, that is, a group interacting with its habitat. Under normal conditions, we may assume that an ecosystem will be in a state of dynamic equilibrium so that there is a fairly equal balance, or even an excess, of resources to stress. To the extent that the resources a family can marshall decrease or are perceived to decrease in proportion to the demands with which it must cope, stress will occur, and conflict and violence become more likely (Burgess and Youngblade 1988). Actual or perceived decreases in individual and family resources are often observed during transitional periods, marked by rapid social change, when there is typically increased uncertainty and associated disintegration of normal social control mechanisms (e.g., Erlich 1966).

We maintain that many of the social indicators of marital violence should be regarded as markers of ecological instability; they represent circumstances in which the level of stress often exceeds the couple's resources. For example, researchers in the United States have frequently examined the relevance of socioeconomic status for rates of marital violence. Included in this research has been a focus on factors such as level of education and occupational prestige (e.g., Gelles 1974) and status inconsistency or underachievement in the workplace (Hornung, McCullough, and Sugimoti 1981). This body of research indicates that marital violence is found across all social classes, but rates are higher in lower socioeconomic status, blue-collar families, especially those marked by underemployment and unemployment (Straus, Gelles, and Steinmetz 1980). Circumstances associated with low socioeconomic status, such as poor living conditions and financial pressures, can clearly lead to stress within the family.

Such stress can also originate within the family itself. As first noted by Gelles and Straus (1979), certain characteristics intrinsic to family life can set the occasion for violence and other forms of aggressive behavior. The importance of these family characteristics is probably exacerbated in modern Western societies in which many traditional buffers such as sex segregation and close and frequent contact with kin are missing. Among the characteristics identified by Gelles and Straus (1979) is the great amount of time the nuclear family spends in face-to-face contact. One consequence of spending a lot of time in close interaction with someone is that small annoyances can easily be exaggerated in importance, perhaps because of their sheer predictability. Another is that the more time individuals spend together, the greater the overlap of their interests and activities. These, in turn, may become events around which conflicts of interest arise, leading to disputes and disagreements. Conflicts of interest may be magnified in situations such as the loss of employment in which resources become increasingly scarce. As Burgess put it, "These conflicts of interest are infinite in number and are the grist for escalating disengagement, disaffection, and domestic guerrilla warfare" (1979, p. 144).

Another important characteristic is the belief that family members hold that they have the right to influence and control each other's behavior. Especially in today's society, household structure insulates the family from the social constraints of other individuals and groups; dissatisfaction with the conduct of another family member, including one's mate, may be compounded by inept or aggressive attempts to change that person's behavior. This hypothesis, that characteristics unique to family life increase the likelihood of aggressive exchanges, is supported by studies that show that we tend to be more polite, gentle, and approving with strangers of the opposite sex than with our spouses (Birchler, Weiss, and Vincent 1975).

Our thesis, then, is that the family functions like an ecosystem in which changes originating outside the family (such as loss of employment), when combined with changes occurring within the family (e.g., shifts in the balance of power), can lead to ecological instability in which the levels of stress exceed personal and family resources. Of course, not everyone responds to excessive stress by being violent. For this reason, researchers have also attempted to isolate interindividual differences in rates of violent behavior.

C. Coercive Interpersonal Contingencies and Marital Violence

The earliest research of this kind was carried out by psychologists who tended to look at marital violence as a symptom of individual psychopathology. These studies were usually of a clinical nature and focused on a variety of personality traits of violent husbands, such as conservatism and rigidity (Davidson 1978), alcohol use or alcoholism (Gayford 1975), and violence in the family of origin (Gayford 1975). One of the few psychological traits of violent husbands that has withstood the use of proper control groups is low self-esteem (see, e.g., Boyd and Klingbeil 1979).

The other predictor at the individual level that has received some empirical support is having witnessed violence in one's family of origin. For example, Straus, Gelles, and Steinmetz (1980) found that 39 percent of violent husbands had observed violence in their families of origin whereas only 26 percent of nonviolent husbands had. The pattern was the same for women: 30 percent of violent wives had witnessed violence in their childhood homes while only 17 percent of the nonviolent wives had. Violence in the family of origin included observing the father hitting the mother as well as having been beaten as a child. In a more recent study, however, O'Leary and Arias (1987) found that only 13 percent of the violent men and 12 percent of the violent women reported interparental violence in their families of origin. Moreover, the correlation between this history and violence toward one's partner was significant for the men in their sample but not for the women.

One important feature of the research on marital violence is that it has tended to focus on what we earlier called "marker variables." This is the case whether the investigator has been chiefly concerned with social-structural correlates of marital violence or with personality traits. By conducting largely marker-variable research, there has been a tendency sometimes to forget that these predictors do not invariably lead to violence. We all know, of course, that, even without the structural buffers found in some societies, not all men who have lost their jobs, who have low self-esteem, or who suspect their wives of infidelity go so far as to beat them. Better research is clearly needed to help identify the circumstances under which these conditions of ecological instability do and do not lead to marital violence. In particular, more information is needed about the specific proximate processes that lead to escalating conflict and violence.

A promising beginning is seen in marital research conducted by researchers working within a behavior-theory tradition (e.g., Gottman 1979; Rosenbaum and O'Leary 1981; O'Leary 1987). Controlled studies suggest that patterns of marital communication discriminate between distressed and nondistressed couples (Gottman 1979; Margolin and Wapfold 1981). This research suggests that verbal and nonverbal actions marked by negative affect are the best predictors of marital distress (cf. Schaap 1984).

As part of a longitudinal study of marital violence, Vivian and O'Leary (1987) report that aggressive couples tend to be more negative both in affect and content when they communicate. For example, they disagree more frequently in the course of problem-solving interaction and they tend to criticize their partner more often. Negative affect was found to be the dimension of communication that best distinguished aggressive from nonaggressive couples.

Social-learning theorists conceptualize communication patterns in terms of interpersonal contingencies of reinforcement and punishment. The importance of this conceptualization can be seen in the finding that aggressive couples are more likely to reciprocate one another's negative affect behavior than are other couples and to do so for extended interchanges (Vivian and O'Leary 1987). As Gottman (1979) has pointed out, effective problem solving has three phases: (1) agenda building, when the couple defines the problem, expresses their feelings about it, and tries to determine each other's feelings; (2) arguing, when the couple disagrees and defends their respective positions, and (3) negotiation, when alternative solutions are proposed, discussed, evaluated, and tried. Nondistressed couples tend to move through each of these successive stages. Distressed couples prolong the agenda-building phase by "cross-complaining," that is, by responding to statements of problems with countercomplaints rather than by attempting to understand each other's position. Similarly, nondistressed couples move quickly through the arguing phases, whereas distressed couples keep repeating themselves rather than moving ahead.

Finally, research from a behavioral or social learning tradition also indicates that there is an important relation between verbal and physical aggression. In short, the frequency of verbal aggression is positively correlated with the frequency of physical aggression (Margolin 1988), and verbal aggression in the early stages of a relationship precedes the development of physical aggression later on in a marriage (Murphy and O'Leary 1987).

The style of communication that a couple develops probably also plays a critical role in determining whether conditions of ecological instability and associated conflicts of interest escalate into marital violence. Thus these interpersonal contingencies of reinforcement and punishment may serve as the missing theoretical links that allow us to determine when low income, joblessness, suspected infidelity, and so on, are likely to explode into violence. A growing amount of evidence supports our position. For example, Walker (1979) reports that wife batterers are found to have an "intrusive style" of interaction, they are easily angered, and they display extreme jealousy, fears of abandonment, and violent outbursts in response to the perceived loss of their authority.

We explore further the relations among fitness concerns, social norms, ecological instability, and coercive interpersonal contingencies in the next section of this essay.

III. Child Maltreatment

Child maltreatment has existed in some form and with varying frequency in virtually all known cultures. Evidence suggests that such behavior may, in some circumstances, have adaptive significance. Ecological instability, especially in the social environment, can affect parenting behavior and result in higher levels of child maltreatment. Not all responses to environmental stress, however, produce maltreatment. We refer to those factors that may explain differences in behavioral responses to stress as coercive interpersonal contingencies.

A. *Cultural Norms and Child Maltreatment*

When discussing cultural norms that differentially influence parental effort, including the maltreatment of children, we must recognize that customs that seem clearly harmful to children are often benign from the parents' perspectives; they are simply following practices that form a part of the traditional ways in which a child becomes a member of the social group. Cassidy (1980), for example, has used the concept of "benign neglect" to emphasize that many weaning customs of nonindustrialized people potentiate malnutrition. Ethnographic studies indicate that there are many customs that contribute to the malnutrition and associated secondary infections of children. Some parenting customs do this indirectly by permitting or encouraging caretakers and toddlers to engage in interpersonal relationships that exacerbate the psychological stress associated with weaning or directly by permitting or encouraging the imposition of dietary restrictions and food competition between age and sex groups (Cassidy 1980).

In many societies the child is abruptly weaned from the mother's breast. Events surrounding this change in the mother-child relationship include forcible separation of toddler and mother and punishment for the expression of dependency behaviors. The mother may put bitter substances on her nipples, slap her child, burn its arms with caustic plant juice, and ignore its cries (Levine and Levine 1963). Many societies have customs that exacerbate the psychological stress of weaning, including the promotion of the maternal deprivation syndrome. Symptoms following such deprivation include insomnia, anorexia, weight loss, increased susceptibility to infection, and even death (Bowlby 1951; Rohner 1975). Food competition takes many different forms. In some societies, a newly weaned toddler is expected to compete on an equal basis with older siblings and even adults. In Malaya, for example, parents have attributed independence and responsibility to young children and explained their extreme thinness by simply saying the child "refuses to eat" (Wolff 1965). Wolff attributes high toddler malnutrition and mortality to these practices. In many societies, it is common for toddlers to receive a disproportionately small share of total family food because the traditional food-flow patterns favor adults, especially economically productive males (e.g., Cuthbertson 1967). These dietary practices usually assume certain predictable patterns. For example, in most societies, the weaning customs favor males (Cassidy 1980). It is important that the child who is weaned later is less at risk of malnourishment.

A number of different theoretical approaches have been offered to explain these fairly common practices. It has been suggested, for example, that the experience of malnutrition in early childhood may be biologically adaptive because it biases developmental plasticity toward hunger resistance in societies where food is often scarce. It has been found that individuals from societies where malnutrition is common grow more slowly, are shorter, and generally require less food (Newman 1961). Thus, in this case, long-term advantage may accrue despite the short-term damage of malnutrition. Another explanation of these practices is that toddler malnutrition and associated higher mortality rates function as population control mechanisms because they remove individuals from the population directly by causing their deaths (Scrimshaw, Taylor, and Gordon 1968). This is perhaps best seen in cases where preferential treatment (better or more nutritious foods and delayed weaning) is given to males. Given the "normally" higher mortality rate of male children, such special favors may serve the function of creating adaptive sex ratios (Fisher 1958; Trivers 1985) without implying unlikely group-selection mechanisms (Williams 1966b).

Were we to witness similar behavior in our own society, we would probably explain it as being due either to "ignorance" of appropriate child-rearing techniques or to an underlying lack of affection. To be sure, prescientific conceptions are often at odds with the recent discoveries of Western scientific medicine. Moreover, there is some evidence that, as parents become more educated, the use of traditional methods declines as does the frequency of malnutrition (Sanjur et al. 1970).

Concerning the "lack of affection" explanation, most of the ethnographic literature reports that parents in nonindustrialized societies are generally nurturant and affectionate toward their children (Cassidy 1980). Moreover, apparent parental rejection may, in some societies, be common yet not culturally preferred. For example, given a history of malnourishment for both mother and child, a cycle of unresponsiveness may develop in which mother and child display progressively deteriorating behavior patterns. Children of malnourished mothers are found to be of lower birth weight, they demonstrate lower resistance to infection and are less responsive to maternal stimulation. By being less responsive, these children may fail to signal their needs to their mothers (Pollitt 1973).

In a study of 101 societies reported in the Human Relations Area Files, Rohner (1975) finds that both affection and rejection occur in all societies. He suggests a cultural continuum. At one extreme are societies with child care customs that primarily emphasize affection (e.g., Papago) and at the other are those that emphasize rejection (e.g., Ik). But perhaps most important, Rohner distinguishes rejection that is relatively constant, generalized, and expected to have major maladaptive effects on child development from sporadic, short-term rejection that is associated with specific events of child rearing. He calls the latter form of occasional rejection "molecular": molecular rejection occurs in settings that otherwise emphasize affection. This concept is important because it illustrates that neglect can simply be a technique for socialization rather than a global parental attitude and tactic indicating disinterest or hostility toward a child.

One interesting feature of harmful dietary and weaning customs is that they illustrate that cultural practices can interpose time and space between actions that are harmful to a child's welfare and the child's actual death. Because of this, the relation between cause and effect can be circuitous and not apparent. For example, systematically denying children access to protein-rich food may produce subclinical malnutrition that may weaken them so that they fall victim to severe diarrhea. Gastrointestinal disease and dehydration will be recorded as the cause of death, not the predisposing malnutrition and food practices due to parental neglect. Similarly, severe infection of ritually inflicted wounds associated with puberty rites may appear several days later, resulting in death, especially when ashes or other substances are rubbed into the wounds for desired cosmetic effects (Linton 1936). Scrimshaw (1984) notes that seeking psychological distance through temporal and spatial distance occurs even among infanticidal parents who often abandon rather than directly murder their children.

There is a considerable amount of evidence that progenicide—action that selectively reduces the probability of survival of children of all ages (McKee 1984)—has been widely practiced throughout history in many societies. For example, in much of western Europe throughout the fifteenth to the nineteenth centuries, it was customary to send newborn infants to live with rural wet nurses for nine months to a year or more. Some of these wet nurses were reported to nurse two or three infants at once (Sussman 1975). Mortality rates for these infants were appallingly high. In Britain in the 1870s, the overall infant mortality rate was approximately 15 percent, but the mortality rates of infants living with "baby farmers" reached 90 percent (Sauer 1978).

While deliberate progenicide may not be a statistically common event, it has been observed for all the major groups of higher primates, including humans (Dickemann 1979; Hrdy 1979; Daly and Wilson 1983). For humans, especially, it has commonly been associated with control of the sex ratio. Drawing on the concepts and principles of evolutionary biology, Dickemann (1979) describes an abundance of historical data that bear on her argument that male preference and the pattern of hypergamy, where females prefer and tend to mate with males of higher status, are ultimately linked to greater variance in male than in female reproductive success. Using ideas from Trivers and Willard (1973), she argues that skewed sex ratios represent the outcome of reproductive strategies that increase the inclusive fitness of the individual parent. For example, differential investment in a high-quality male gains a mother, whose socioeconomic status is high, more grandchildren because that male will be able to compete successfully with other males for access to females. Conversely, investment in daughters is a useful strategy for lower-socioeconomic-status mothers because, while their sons will not fare as well in competition with other males, their daughters may be attractive to higher-status males. Because sex-differential mortality ensures an excess of females at all social levels, it would be predicted that high-status families would be more likely to commit infanticide toward their daughters and find brides for their sons among lower-status families who will pay a dowry for a daughter's alliance with a high-status male. The data fit this model rather well (e.g., Miller 1981).

The phenomenon of progenicide makes it clear that actions harmful to children are found throughout the historical and cultural record; that such practices do not necessarily imply individual or cultural pathology; and that these practices may be adaptive from an evolutionary perspective—that is, they may contribute to the parents' inclusive fitness under the ecological conditions in which they find themselves. It should not be assumed, however, that we make conscious calculated assessments of actions that may affect our reproductive success. This is probably seldom, if ever, the case. Instead, a multitude of proximate mechanisms undoubtedly bridge the gap between changing ecological conditions and patterns of child rearing. Social norms, values, and beliefs may well rank among these mechanisms. An example would be cultural norms prescribing that male infants should be breastfed longer than female infants. Beliefs may develop around such rules. For instance, in rural Taiwan, mothers apparently believe that earlier weaning assures their daughters of an earlier menopause and a welcome end to the round of childbearing (Wolf 1972). In the Ecuadorian highlands, there is a widespread belief that, if a girl is nursed past one year, she will, at sexual maturity, become boy crazy and rebellious (McKee 1977). These can be seen as examples where biological and cultural evolution are complementary. As Durham (1976) has argued, both biological and cultural attributes of human beings result, to a large degree, from the selective retention of traits that enhance the inclusive fitness of individuals in their environments, despite differences between the mechanisms of selection and regardless of the relative importance of those mechanisms in the evolution of a trait.

To return to our central point, the role of such cultural norms and beliefs may be especially important in explaining normative child maltreatment. They may be of less importance, however, when looking at harm to children that is culturally proscribed. It is not yet known whether there are significant differences between child maltreatment that is prescribed normatively and that which is proscribed. It is even possible that one precludes the other. In other words, the kinds of actions that we consider abusive in our society may exist, in part, because infanticide and, to some extent, abortion are prohibited.

B. Ecological Instability and Child Maltreatment

As with marital violence, cultural norms can set the occasion for child maltreatment. Once again, however, instability in the environment can contribute to increases in the probability of maltreatment. Our premise is that turbulence in the environment can affect parenting just as it does mating behavior. Given the length of time and amount of effort required for child care, human parents, especially, should be sensitive to improvements in, or degradation of, resources necessary for successful reproductive effort.

Because no organism inhabits a completely predictable environment, natural selection has produced capabilities for facultative adjustment of behavior in organisms, allowing them to alter their responses to changing environments adaptively. In the case of K-strategists, in which the individual requires a long time to reach reproductive maturity and in which small numbers of young are produced, the importance to the individual of being able to "track" or adjust to changes in environmental quality is critical. This is especially true in humans, for example, where mistaken judgments by parents can lead to death of one or all offspring. Unstable diversity in environments is precisely where facultative behaviors enjoy the greatest advantage over obligate, environmentally insensitive ("instinctive"), behavioral strategies (Alcock 1984). Because those traits with larger effects on inclusive fitness are expected to be under the most intense selection pressures, humans ought to be sensitive to cues indicating changes in the availability of critical resources. Therefore, both parenting and mating are among the key behavioral systems affected by such changing perceptions because they are so closely related to inclusive fitness.

The critical role of ecological instability for parenting is seen in studies of nonhuman primates. For example, an increased frequency of infanticide has been associated with factors as diverse as increasing population density, changes in dominance hierarchy, decreased parental control of vital natural resources, uncertain parenthood, and disturbances of the ecology of primate groups by humans (Hrdy 1979).

These very general issues are related directly to human parenting. Dickemann (1979), in her analysis of infanticide, has also recognized the importance of drastic changes in ecology. She has argued that periodic catastrophes and resource scarcities typically raise mortality rates for males because of their increased susceptibility to life-threatening birth defects and infectious diseases, particularly those of the digestive and respiratory tracts (Preston 1976). Because infant mortality rates of males are especially sensitive to economic conditions, females tend to become the more numerous sex whenever environmental conditions for child rearing are less than optimal (Preston 1976). Under these conditions, preferential treatment for males arises. Thus male preference may have been the preferred parental strategy for humans given the general unpredictability of the environment (Dickemann 1979). As McKee (1984, p. 95) comments, "It is ironic that female biological strength may be one factor promoting the development of social systems oppressive to women." In any case, conditions of ecological instability may produce a postcatastrophe sex ratio highly favoring males due to more intense female infanticide. This, in turn, may lead to the subsequent need for males to colonize less populated areas, which, in turn, can lead to ecological instability in the new areas (see Bigelow 1969).

Many of the common correlates or marker variables associated with child maltreatment can be conceptualized as indicators of ecological instability. For example, it has been reported that parents isolated from important social support systems in their neighborhoods are more likely to be violent toward their children (Garbarino and Crouter 1978). Low income and joblessness have also been associated with higher levels of child maltreatment (e.g., Straus 1980). Other research has documented the importance of the social structure of the family itself. Large families, for example, are found disproportionately in abuse statistics. Similarly, rates of abuse are higher in single-parent households and in households with step-relations (Daly and Wilson 1980; Burgess et al. 1981).

Many macro, social-structural correlates of child abuse should be regarded as markers of ecological instability in that they represent situations in which the level of stress often exceeds the family's resources. Among examples of such situations are many of the circumstances surrounding low socioeconomic status, including below-average family income, chronic joblessness, and all the problems these conditions produce—such as suboptimal housing in neighborhoods marked by high crime rates and high migration, less than adequate diets, and frequent disputes with creditors. Similarly, at the community level, parents who do not have ready access to the resources associated with effective support systems are going to find themselves experiencing considerable stress. Certain features of family structure and organization are associated with chronic or periodic stress, such as large family size, single parenthood, and step-relations in a family (see e.g., Belsky 1980; Straus, Gelles, and Steinmetz 1980; Burgess et al. 1981). All of these factors have been found to be predictive of higher rates of child maltreatment (Burgess 1979).

Wahler (1980) has shown how the conditions outlined above increase the likelihood that a person will frequently have aversive exchanges with others outside as well as within the family (analogous conditions can also contribute to marital violence; see Fagan [in this volume]). Indeed, Wahler and Hahn (1984) have found that, rather than interacting with people who form a warm, supportive network and who provide assistance, empathy, and problem-solving help, these parents more often interact with others who are experiencing similar levels of stress. The outcome is that instead of helping each other, they often simply match "war stories," thus exacerbating rather than ameliorating the aversive nature of the interactions they have outside the family. To the extent that these interactions are aversive for the abusive parent, the parents will tend to avoid them, perhaps interacting only under duress. In this way, the abusive parent becomes more and more isolated from useful social supports, and violence becomes even more likely.

C. Coercive Interpersonal Contingencies and Child Maltreatment

Of course, these indicators of ecological instability do not always lead to abuse. It is essential to consider factors that can allow us to account for individual differences in responses to accumulating stress. The first factors to be considered are the individual traits of both the abuser and the abused child. Parental characteristics that have been associated with child abuse include, for example, depression and anxiety (Wolfe 1984) and autonomic hyperreactivity (Vasta 1982). Characteristics that have been linked to the abused children themselves include difficult temperaments (Johnson and Morse 1968; Frodi 1981), mental retardation (Sandgrund, Gaines, and Green 1974), and hyperactive or otherwise "difficult-to-handle" behavior (Reid, Patterson, and Loeber 1982).

As important as these individual traits may be, we still need to identify the conditions under which they, in turn, are actually converted into violent behavior. Our suggestion is that key principles of social learning theory (or behavior theory), operating through interpersonal communication, serve as important causal mechanisms linking social indicators of ecological instability and individual traits to the occurrence of aggression and violence within the family.

As Skinner (1981) has pointed out, in both evolutionary and behavior theory, selection is the primary causal mechanism. In evolution, traits are selected because they contribute to differential reproduction, that is, fitness. In behavior theory, behaviors are selected because they increase the probability of positive reinforcement or the avoidance of punishment. Similarly, cultural practices may be selected because of the beneficial consequences they produce for the group as a whole or for a dominant subgroup.

We can see interpersonal contingencies of reinforcement and punishment in operation when we look at research that has examined interaction or communication patterns in abusive families. In these studies, investigators have tried to determine whether there are certain styles of interaction that seem to culminate in violence and other forms of child maltreatment. Abusive parents are often very poor observers of their children's behavior (Burgess et al. 1981). This lack of effective and accurate monitoring may be due either to the parents' lack of skills (Patterson 1980, 1985), lack of resources (Wolfe 1984), or both. In either case, one outcome of poor observing skills is that such parents tend to respond to their children in ways that are functionally noncontingent (Patterson 1979; Dumas and Wahler 1985; Wahler and Dumas 1986). Apart from making life unpredictable for children, this circumstance has serious consequences for the parent-child relationship. Rewards that are consistently provided on a noncontingent basis may eventually lose whatever ability they had to function as positive reinforcers (Bijou and Baer 1961). Imagine, for example, a family in which the parents, perhaps due to their failure to track their child's behavior accurately, are as likely to give their approval when their child misbehaves as when the child behaves properly. Later on, attempts to use their approval in a deliberate effort to regulate the child's behavior will be likely to fail. Under the circumstances, their approval is not functioning as a positive reinforcer for their child. Because of this, parents who respond noncontingently to their children are thereby depriving themselves of one major source of influence over their children, that is, the use of positive incentives (Burgess and Richardson 1984). This may account for the fact that abusive parents exhibit lower frequencies of positive behavior toward their children than do nonabusive parents (Burgess and Conger 1978). In other words, their efforts to use positive behaviors to control their child's behavior may have been weakened as a result of lack of success. This history of ineffective child management may also account for the finding that abusive parents view children and child-related activities less positively than do nonabusive parents (Disbrow, Doerr, and Caulfield 1977). These parental views are not without meaning. Patterson (1982*a*), for example, found a close relationship between a mother's labeling of her child as deviant and her rejection of the child. Such rejection makes the child a more likely target for abuse (Burgess, Garbarino, and Gilstrap 1983).

Given the normal conflicts of interest that characterize family life, coupled with a low rate of positive reinforcement, parents must inevitably turn to other measures. This may explain the higher frequency of punitive behavior directed by abusive parents to their children. Reid (1984) reports, for example, that abusive mothers display approximately twice the rate of punitive behavior as nonabusive parents with child management problems and nearly four times the rate found in nondistressed families. Other investigators have found a similar pattern (e.g., Bousha and Twentyman 1984).

Interestingly, there is evidence that an abusive parent's use of punishment is often a function of events other than the child's behavior. For instance, Dumas and Wahler (1984) have shown that higher rates of punitive behavior are especially common when the parent has had a "bad day." On those days when an abusive mother has negative interactions with social agencies, neighbors, her husband, or boyfriend and is especially irritable, she is most likely to exhibit high rates of punitive behavior, perhaps even abusive behavior, toward her child, regardless of what the child is doing. Punishment that is provided noncontingently becomes increasingly ineffective, at least at levels acceptable to society (Parke, Deur, and Saivin 1970). Thus at those times when the parent is very irritable, matters can quickly get out of hand. This would be particularly likely if the child reciprocated the parent's abusive behavior or if there were a flare-up in fighting among siblings. Both possibilities are more common in abusive families (Burgess and Conger 1978; Burgess et al. 1981; Reid, Patterson, and Loeber 1982).

As exchanges within the family become increasingly negative, emotions flare (Vasta 1982), and it becomes more and more difficult to terminate the aversive interchanges. The evidence shows that abusive mothers are much less successful in their child-management efforts than nonabusive mothers. In one study, it was reported that nondistressed mothers were successful in 86 percent of their discipline attempts; nonabusive mothers with child-management problems were successful 65 percent of the time; abusive mothers were effective in only 46 percent of their discipline attempts (Reid, Taplin, and Loeber 1981). These abusive parents were also less likely to use positive acts such as teasing or humor and more likely to use physical coercion in their attempts at discipline.

Over time, then, interactions within the family become less and less positive, and more negative. Indeed, there is growing evidence of a significant relation between the frequency of mildly aversive interchanges and the rate of intensely aversive interchanges between parents and children (e.g., Reid 1984). The more often a parent exhibits mild forms of aversive behavior, the more likely it is that significantly abusive behavior will occur. Consequently, violent attacks may result not only from strong situational or personal stress but also from the outcome of progressively more aversive exchanges between a child and a parent who is frequently and easily irritated and who is unskilled at quickly resolving conflicts of interest and discipline confrontations. It is possible, of course, that the probability of an abusive assault is greatest on those days when levels of stress are high and the parent's effectiveness at child management is especially low.

In any case, this tendency to be negative and hostile will, of course, contribute to the reduction of exchanges marked by positive emotions. Because these exchanges become unpleasant, the impetus for family interaction becomes extinguished, except during occasions when contact is necessary. The overall effect, then, will be lowered frequencies of family interaction, which is a pattern found in abusive families (Burgess and Conger 1978).

IV. General Conclusions

This essay began by noting that both marital violence and child maltreatment have been found to be reliably associated with a multitude of correlates operating on very different levels of analysis. Family violence researchers have used virtually every extant theory of human behavior in their efforts to explain violence in families. In this essay, we have tried to show that the multiple correlates of marital violence and child abuse constitute an integrated whole when examined through the prism of evolutionary ecology.

Our analysis began by our assuming that human reproductive behavior—including courtship, mating, marital interaction, fertilization, and parental care—has been responsive to a continual process of natural selection. Given anatomical and physiological differences between the sexes, we have seen that there are different optimal reproductive strategies for males and females. These different strategies help us to understand why conflicts of interest are so common in families and why they affect both mating and parenting tactics.

With regard to mating, the different strategies are reflected in the fact that females tend to prefer to mate with males of a social status higher than theirs and that there is greater variance in reproductive success for males than for females. These two tendencies, when combined with others, such as the special sensitivity of male infant mortality rates to adverse environmental conditions, may contribute to the tendency for human societies to be male dominated and for women to be the chief victims of marital violence.

Given a balance of power that favors males, as a class, over females, and given, further, that males are often expected to provide resources and protection for females and dependent offspring, men should be expected to take steps to increase their certainty of paternity. In many societies, kinship systems have evolved culturally to maintain the power imbalance, to reduce threats to paternity certainty, yet also to minimize the use of physical and psychological coercion. According to the biosocial theory of family violence that we have described, marital violence becomes more likely if the following conditions are met: (1) structural (e.g., kinship) buffers are eliminated, (2) changes or perceived changes in the balance of power occur (e.g., during times of rapid individual and social change), and (3) coercive patterns of marital interaction develop. Each of these conditions is a predictable outcome of the circumstances associated with what we have called ecological instability.

Differences between males and females with regard to strategies that optimize reproductive access also affect parental behavior. For example, given heavy, "obligate" maternal investment in women (gestation, parturition, lactation, and rearing) and the low reproductive potential of women in comparison to men, the prediction from comparative evolutionary ecology is that women will have a more conservative and tenacious attitude toward offspring than will men. It is also predicted that women will try harder to keep children alive but that they, too, will reach a point at which costs exceed benefits. In the language of fitness, a woman would have a high likelihood of curtailing investment in any offspring who impairs her ability to support other living children, unborn children, or both. As described by our biosocial theory, women (as well as men) should be sensitive to indicators of changes in environmental resources. Given the enormous metabolic and energetic investment necessary to rear any offspring to maturity, a parent who produces an excessive number of offspring under unfavorable conditions may, in fact, successfully rear fewer reproductive offspring than another parent with fewer offspring. Under conditions present throughout most of human history, natural selection should have favored the ability of parents to adjust fertility to current or expected resources. The "adjustment" could be prenatal (infertility, miscarriage, etc.) or postnatal in the form of infanticide or varying degrees of neglect or abandonment (Lack 1954, 1968). In either case, the stage is set for the victimization of children.

Drawing on these evolutionary concepts and cross-cultural studies, we have suggested that the maltreatment of children, in some circumstances, may have contributed, paradoxically, to the inclusive fitness of the abusing parents. Examples discussed include infanticide and dietary practices that favor male children over female children. Such practices may function in certain conditions to create adaptive sex ratios. This especially might be the case in times of ecological instability such as droughts, famines, natural catastrophes, epidemics, and warfare, when the naturally higher mortality rates of male infants may lead to skewed sex ratios. We should remember, however, that cultural practices like these do not require conscious attention to matters of inclusive fitness. This is unnecessary because cultural norms can serve as proximate mechanisms leading to biologically adaptive behavior. As we have seen, belief systems often grow around cultural norms to guarantee compliance.

Even today, in our society, differential rates of child abuse suggest the past adaptiveness of child maltreatment. Examples include the disproportionately higher rates of maltreatment found for stepchildren. We may, in short, be biologically "prepared" to act in hostile ways under certain circumstances to children who share none of our genes. This might especially be the case when resource competition develops between half brothers and half sisters. Similarly, the higher rates of maltreatment found in large, low-socioeconomic-status families as well as in single-parent families would be predicted by our biosocial theory. In those situations, competition for resources is exacerbated, and the costs associated with parental investment may be higher than normal. Finally, the higher rates of abuse found among children who were born prematurely, who are difficult to manage, or who are physically, intellectually, or emotionally handicapped are, likewise, consistent with our theoretical principles in that such youngsters are poor prospects for investment that will lead to their successful reproduction as adults. As Bolton (1983) has observed, all of these conditions may highlight the child's role as a competitor with parents and encourage the parents to concentrate on the costs rather than the benefits of parenthood.

We need to emphasize, however, that we are not arguing that child maltreatment (or marital violence) is necessarily adaptive biologically in all or even in most cases. It is possible that some of our behavior today is biologically maladaptive. An example of this might be the lowered fertility associated with the demographic transition. Demographers use that term to refer to three distinct stages that modern industrial societies seem to have gone through. The first is marked by high mortality and high fertility. The second stage, associated with technological improvements in food production and sanitation, is identified by low mortality and high fertility. The third stage evidences both low mortality and low fertility. A perplexing problem for evolutionary theory is how to explain the especially low fertility of middle- and upper-middle-socioeconomic-status couples.

We cannot, in this essay, examine this matter in detail, but we can at least suggest the possibility that many of the historically proximate means to reproductive success have become ends in themselves. For example, given the discovery of easy and effective contraceptive techniques, we can now control our fertility more directly yet still derive the benefits of our propensity to enjoy sex. This decoupling of proximate means and ultimate reproductive ends could easily lead to the trends we see in modern industrial societies, such as delayed age at marriage, cohabitation, postponed childbirth, and higher rates of childlessness (Davis 1985). It may also lead to increased preoccupation with such ancillary aspects of reproductive effort as resource accumulation. In short, bearing children may be judged to be less attractive than other valued ends such as avoiding the pain of childbirth, the inconvenience of parenthood, the pursuit of an advanced education, a career, or the maximization of economic comfort (Barkow and Burley 1980). If there is any merit to this argument, it should also apply to the parental effort one directs toward children. In other words, disproportionate attention to immediate proximate mechanisms of reproduction itself, at the expense of parental investment, may lead to an increased likelihood of child abuse and neglect because the progeny themselves may jeopardize success in the dating or mating "games."

Two points should be emphasized here. First, we cannot assume, a priori, that violence toward a mate or the maltreatment of children are universally adaptive or maladaptive. They clearly can be either (or nonadaptive), depending on prevailing ecological circumstances. Second, the theory of evolution is as relevant for the explanation of nonadaptive and maladaptive reproductive effort as it is of adaptive effort. All these cases are grounded in the underlying logic of the theory (Symons 1979, 1986).

Whether specific incidents of family violence contribute to the aggressor's inclusive fitness or not, we have argued that the probability of violence increases with increasing ecological instability. Many of the common correlates of family violence clearly involve circumstances where a family's resources are stretched or are perceived to be stretched, to the limit and where stress becomes increasingly difficult to manage. Examples discussed include poverty, joblessness, living in high crime neighborhoods, and the absence of social support systems. A similar analysis, of course, could be applied to the pressures associated with relative deprivation and conspicuous consumption in the higher social classes. An important part of our biosocial theory is the idea that it is biologically adaptive to be sensitive to changes in the ecology that signal improvement in, or degradation of, available environmental resources. Because mating and parenting behavior are so closely tied to inclusive fitness, they should be especially sensitive to circumstances indicative of ecological instability.

Critics of the application of evolutionary theory to human behavior sometimes claim that evolutionists ignore individual differences. We have tried to address the issue of individual differences by identifying proximate processes that seem to govern whether conditions of ecological instability are actually translated into family violence.

The proximate processes that we have selected to emphasize in this essay are interpersonal contingencies of reinforcement and punishment. We have suggested that coercive interpersonal contingencies are proximate mechanisms connecting social indicators of ecological instability to actual occurrences of family violence. This connection is not simple, however. Because these interpersonal contingencies have developed within the family, it follows that violence may occur even in the absence of most or all of the marker variables so long as the interpersonal contingencies operating in the family have become progressively coercive (Burgess and Richardson 1984). There is also the possibility that the common indicators of ecological instability denote circumstances that place family members at risk for violence because they increase the likelihood of conditions that can lead to coercive interpersonal contingencies. Our guess is that both possibilities occur. In any case, the effects of ecological instability on families are transmitted through these patterns of family interaction (Burgess 1986).

The theoretical perspective we have taken represents an attempt to apply evolutionary concepts to a problem, family violence, that intuitively appears inconsistent with notions of inclusive fitness. An important feature of our biosocial theory is that we have also attempted to identify intermediate-level circumstances that link ultimate issues of inclusive fitness to proximate causes of child maltreatment. We have conceptualized these circumstances as manifestations of ecological instability in which the level of stress exceeds available resources.

Our evolutionary-ecological perspective addresses the issue of individual differences by attempting to specify mechanisms by which macroindicators of ecological disturbance such as socioeconomic status can lead to microlevel processes that culminate in violence and other forms of maltreatment. Coercive patterns of family interaction represent the principal causal pathway that connects ecological instability to violence within families. This raises the possibility that some of the common correlates of such violence are themselves reactions to sudden or chronic ecological instability. For example, alcoholism, depression, and anxiety may be responses to ecological stresses in the family, such as loss of employment, excessive financial debt, or divorce. Consequently, violence toward one's mate or children may be a direct result of ecological instability, or it may be mediated through the personal traits described above. Thus there is the intriguing possibility that these individual traits (e.g., problem drinking), which have previously been assumed to precipitate violent behavior, may actually be the result of the same factors that lead to family violence itself: ecological instability and the uncertainty of successful reproductive effort.

REFERENCES

Abu-Lughod, L. 1985. "A Community of Secrets: The Separate World of Bedouin Women." *Signs* 10:637–57.
Alcock, J. 1984. *Animal Behavior: An Evolutionary Approach.* Sunderland, Mass.: Sinauer.
Alexander, R. D. 1979a. *Darwinism and Human Affairs.* Seattle: University of Washington Press.

———. 1979*b*. "Natural Selection and Social Exchange." In *Social Exchange in Developing Relationships*, edited by R. L. Burgess and T. L. Huston. New York: Academic Press.

Allen, C. M., and M. A. Straus. 1980. "Resources, Power, and Husband-Wife Violence." In *The Social Causes of Husband-Wife Violence*, edited by M. A. Straus and G. T. Hotaling. Minneapolis: University of Minnesota Press.

Altmann, S. A., and J. Altmann. 1979. "Demographic Constraints on Behavior and Social Organization." In *Ecological Influences on Social Organization*, edited by E. Smith and I. Bernstein. New York: Garland.

Aries, P. 1970. *Centuries of Childhood: A Social History of Family Life*. New York: Knopf.

Bakan, D. 1971. *Slaughter of the Innocent: A Study of the Battered Child Phenomenon*. San Francisco: Jossey-Bass.

Bandura, A. 1973. *Aggression: A Social Learning Analysis*. Englewood Cliffs, N.J.: Prentice-Hall.

Barkow, J. H., and N. Burley. 1980. "Human Fertility, Evolutionary Biology, and the Demographic Transition." *Ethology and Sociobiology* 1:163–80.

Basehart, H. 1961. "Ashactic." In *Matrilineal Kinship*, edited by D. Schneider and K. Gough. Berkeley: University of California Press.

Bateson, P. G. 1982. "Preferences for Cousins in Japanese Quail." *Nature* 295:236–37.

Belsky, J. 1978. "Three Theoretical Models of Child Abuse: A Critical Review." *Child Abuse and Neglect* 2:37–49.

———. 1980. "Child Maltreatment: An Ecological Integration." *American Psychologist* 35:320–35.

Berk, R. A., S. F. Berk, D. R. Loeseke, and D. Rauma. 1983. "Mutual Combat and Other Family Violence Myths." In *The Dark Side of Families: Current Family Violence Research*, edited by D. Finkelhor and associates. Beverly Hills, Calif.: Sage.

Bigelow, R. 1969. *The Dawn Warriors: Man's Evolution toward Peace*. Boston: Little, Brown.

Bijou, S. W., and D. M. Baer. 1961. *Child Development*. Vol. 1, *A Systematic and Empirical Theory*. New York: Appleton-Century-Crofts.

Birchler, G. R., R. L. Weiss, and J. P. Vincent. 1975. "Multi-method Analysis of Social Reinforcement Exchange between Maritally Distressed and Nondistressed Spouse and Stranger Dyads." *Journal of Personality and Social Psychology* 31:349–60.

Blau, P. M. 1964. *Exchange and Power in Social Life*. New York: Wiley.

Bolton, F. G., Jr., 1983. *When Bonding Fails: Clinical Assessment of High-Risk Families*. Beverly Hills, Calif.: Sage.

Bousha, D. M., and C. T. Twentyman. 1984. "Mother-Child Interactional Style in Abuse, Neglect, and Control Groups: Naturalistic Observations in the Home." *Journal of Abnormal Psychology* 93:106–14.

Bowlby, J. 1951. "Maternal Care and Mental Health." *World Health Organization Bulletin* 3:355–534.

Boyd, V., and K. Klingbeil. 1979. *Behavioral Characteristics of Domestic Violence*. Seattle: University of Washington.

Bronfenbrenner, U. 1977. "Toward an Experimental Ecology of Human Development." *American Psychologist* 32:513–31.

Burgess, R. L. 1979. "Child Abuse: A Social Interactional Analysis." In *Advances in Clinical Child Psychology*, edited by B. B. Lahey and A. E. Kazdin. New York: Plenum.

———. 1986. "Social Incompetence as a Precipitant to and Consequence of Child Maltreatment." *Victimology: An International Journal* 10:72–86.

Burgess, R. L., E. A. Anderson, C. J. Schellenbach, and R. Conger. 1981. "A Social Interactional Approach to the Study of Abusive Families." In *Advances in Family Intervention, Assessment, and Theory: An Annual Compilation of Research*, edited by J. P. Vincent. New York: Columbia University Press.

Burgess, R. L., and D. Bushell, Jr. 1969. *Behavioral Sociology: The Experimental Analysis of Social Process*. New York: Columbia University Press.

Burgess, R. L., and R. D. Conger. 1978. "Family Interaction in Abusive, Neglectful, and Normal Families." *Child Development* 49:1163–73.

Burgess, R. L., J. Garbarino, and B. Gilstrap. 1983. "Violence to the Family." In *Life Span Developmental Psychology: Non-normative Life Events*, edited by E. J. Callahan and K. McCluskey. New York: Academic Press.

Burgess, R. L., and J. M. Nielsen. 1974. "An Experimental Analysis of some Structural Determinants of Equitable and Inequitable Exchange Relations." *American Sociological Review* 39:427–43.

Burgess, R. L., and R. A. Richardson. 1984. "Coercive Interpersonal Contingencies of Reinforcement as a Determinant of Child Abuse: Implications for Treatment and Prevention." In *Behavioral Parent Training: Issues in Research and Practice*, edited by R. F. Dangel and R. A. Polster. New York: Guilford.

Burgess, R. L., and L. M. Youngblade. 1988. "Social Incompetence and the Intergenerational Transmission of Abusive Parental Practices." In *Family Abuse and Its Consequences: New Directions in Family Violence Research*, edited by R. Gelles, G. Hotaling, D. Finkelhor, and M. Straus. Beverly Hills, Calif.: Sage.

Caldwell, J. C. 1976. "Toward a Restatement of Demographic Transition Theory." *Population Development Review* 2:321–66.

———. 1978. "A Theory of Fertility: From High Plateau to Destabilization." *Population and Development Review* 4(4):553–77.

———. 1980. "The Wealth Flows Theory of Fertility Decline." In *Determinants of Fertility: Theories Re-examined*, edited by C. Hohn and R. Mackensen. Liège: Ordina.

Campbell, J. K. 1964. *Honor, Family, and Patronage: A Study of Institutions and Moral Values in a Greek Mountain Community*. Oxford: Clarendon.

Cassidy, C. M. 1980. *Benign Neglect and Toddler Malnutrition: Social and Biological Predictors of Nutritional Status, Physical Growth, and Neurological Development*. New York: Academic Press.

Cheney, D., R. Seyfarth, and B. Smuts. 1986. "Social Relationships and Social Cognition of Nonhuman Primates." *Science* 234:1361–66.

Colson, E. 1958. *Marriage and the Family among the Plateau Tonga*. Manchester: Manchester University Press.

Coser, L. A. 1967. *Continuities in the Study of Social Conflict*. New York: Free Press.

Cuthbertson, D. P. 1967. "Feeding Patterns and Nutrient Utilization: Chairman's Remarks." *Proceedings of the Nutrition Society* 26:143–44.

Dahrendorf, R. 1968. *Essays in the Theory of Society.* Stanford, Calif.: Stanford University Press.

Daly, M., and M. I. Wilson. 1980. "Abuse and Neglect of Children in Evolutionary Perspective." In *Natural Selection and Social Behavior*, edited by R. D. Alexander and D. W. Tinkle. New York: Chiron.

———. 1983. *Sex, Education, and Behavior.* North Scituate, Mass.: Duxbury.

Davidson, T. 1978. *Conjugal Crime.* New York: Hawthorne.

Davis, K. 1985. *Contemporary Marriage: Comparative Perspectives on a Changing Institution.* New York: Russell Sage.

Dawkins, R. 1979. *The Selfish Gene.* London: Oxford University Press.

———. 1982. *The Extended Phenotype: The Gene as the Unit of Selection.* Oxford: Oxford University Press.

DeMause, L. 1974. "The Evolution of Childhood." In *The History of Childhood*, edited by L. DeMause. New York: Psychohistory Press.

DeVore, I. 1963. "Mother-Infant Relations in Free-ranging Baboons." In *Maternal Behavior in Mammals*, edited by H. L. Rheingold. New York: Wiley.

Dickemann, M. 1979. "Female Infanticide, Reproductive Strategies, and Social Stratification: A Preliminary Model." In *Evolutionary Biology and Human Social Behavior*, edited by N. Chagnon and W. Irons. North Scituate, Mass.: Duxbury.

———. 1983. "Female Choice, Male Life Histories, and Male Celibacy in U.S. Black Ghettos." Paper presented at a workshop on the Application of Life History Strategies Models to the Study of Human Development, University of California, Los Angeles, May.

Disbrow, M. A., H. O. Doerr, and C. Caulfield. 1977. "Measures to Predict Child Abuse." Project report. Seattle: University of Washington.

Dollard, J., L. W. Doob, N. E. Miller, O. H. Mowrer, and R. R. Sears. 1939. *Frustration and Aggression.* New haven, Conn.: Yale University Press.

Douglass, M. 1969. "Is Matriliny Doomed in Africa?" In *Man in Africa*, edited by M. Douglass and P. Kayberry. London: Tavistock.

Draper, P. 1975. "Cultural Contrasts in Sex Role Egalitarianism in Foraging and Sedentary Contexts." In *Toward an Anthropology of Women*, edited by R. Reiter. New York: Monthly Review Press.

Draper, P., and H. Harpending. 1982. "Father Absence and Reproductive Strategy: An Evolutionary Perspective." *Journal of Anthropological Research* 38(3):255–73.

Dumas, J. E., and R. G. Wahler. 1985. "Indiscriminate Mothering as a Contextual Factor in Aggressive-oppositional Child Behavior." *Journal of Abnormal Child Psychology* 13(1):1–17.

Durham, W. H. 1976. "The Adaptive Significance of Cultural Behavior." *Human Ecology* 4(2):89–121.

Durkheim, E. 1951. *Suicide: A Study in Sociology.* Translated by J. A. Spaulding and G. Simpson. New York: Free Press.

Erlich, R. S. 1966. *Family in Transition: A Study of 300 Yugoslav Villages.* Princeton, N.J.: Princeton University Press.

Fagan, J. In this volume. "Cessation of Family Violence: Deterrence and Dissuasion."

Farrington, K. 1980. "Stress and Family Violence." In *The Social Causes of Husband-Wife Violence*, edited by M. A. Straus and G. T. Hotaling. Minneapolis: University of Minneapolis Press.

Fernea, E. W. 1965. *Guests of the Sheik*. Garden City, N.Y.: Doubleday.

Fischoff, T., C. F. Whitton, and M. G. Pettit. 1971. "Psychiatric Study of Mothers of Infants with Growth Failure Secondary to Maternal Deprivation." *Journal of Pediatrics* 79:209–15.

Fisher, R. A. 1958. *The Genetical Theory of Natural Selection*. New York: Dover.

Freud, S. 1919. "A Child Is Being Beaten: A Contribution to the Study of the Origin of Sexual Perversions." *Collected Papers*, Vol. II. New York: Basic.

Frieze, I., and A. Browne. In this volume. "The Incidence and Prevalence of Violence in Marriage."

Frodi, A. M. 1981. "Contributions of Infant Characteristics to Child Abuse." *American Journal of Mental Deficiency* 85:341–49.

Garbarino, J. 1977. "The Human Ecology of Maltreatment: A Conceptual Model for Research." *Journal of Marriage and the Family* 39(4):721–35.

Garbarino, J., and A. Crouter. 1978. "Defining the Community Context of Parent-Child Relations: The Correlates of Child Maltreatment." *Child Development* 49:604–16.

Garcia, J., and R. A. Koelling. 1976. "Relation of Cure to Consequence in Avoidance Learning." *Psychonomic Science* 4:123–24.

Gayford, J. J. 1975. "Wife Battering: A Preliminary Summary of 100 Cases." *British Medical Journal* 1 (January): 195–97.

Geis, G., and J. Monahan. 1975. "The Social Ecology of Violence." In *Man and Mortality*, edited by T. Likona. New York: Holt, Rinehart, & Winston.

Gelles, R. J. 1973. "Child Abuse as Psychopathology: A Sociological Critique and Reformulation." *American Journal of Orthopsychiatry* 43:611–21.

———. 1974. *The Violent Home*. Beverly Hills, Calif.: Sage.

Gelles, R. J., and M. A. Straus. 1979. "Determinants of Violence in the Family: Toward a Theoretical Integration." In *Contemporary Theories about the Family*, edited by W. R. Burr, R. Hill, I. K. Nye, and I. L. Reiss. New York: Free Press.

Gil, D. G. 1970. *Violence against Children: Physical Abuse in the United States*. Cambridge, Mass.: Harvard University Press.

Goode, W. J. 1971. "Force and Violence in the Family." *Journal of Marriage and the Family* 33:624–36.

Gottman, J. M. 1979. *Marital Interaction: Experimental Investigations*. New York: Academic Press.

Greenblat, C. S. 1985. "Don't Hit Your Wife . . . Unless: Preliminary Findings on Normative Support for the Use of Physical Force by Husbands." *Victimology* 10:221–41.

Gulliver, P. H. 1963. *Social Control in an African Society: A Study of the Arusha: Agricultural Masais of Northern Tanganyika*. Boston: Boston University Press.

Homans, G. C. 1967. "Fundamental Social Processes." In *Sociology*, edited by N. Smelser. New York: Wiley.

Hornung, C. A., B. C. McCullough, and I. Sugimoti. 1981. "Status Relationships in Marriage: Risk Factors in Spouse Abuse." *Journal of Marriage and the Family* 43:675–92.

Hrdy, S. B. 1979. "Infanticide among Animals: A Review, Classification, and Examination of the Implications for the Reproductive Strategies of Females." *Ethology and Sociobiology* 1:13–40.

———. 1981. *The Woman That Never Evolved*. Cambridge, Mass.: Harvard University Press.

Johnson, B., and H. A. Morse. 1968. "Injured Children and Their Parents." *Children* 15:147–52.

Kaplan, H. B. 1972. "Toward a General Theory of Psychosocial Deviance: The Case of Aggressive Behavior." *Social Science and Medicine* 6:593–617.

Keesing, R. 1975. *Kin Groups and Social Structure*. New York: Holt, Rinehart, & Winston.

Kelley, H. H. 1971. *Attribution in Social Interaction*. Morristown, N.J.: General Learning Press.

Kelley, H. H., and J. W. Thibaut. 1969. "Group Problem Solving." In *The Handbook of Social Psychology*, 2d ed., edited by G. Lindzey and E. Aronson. Reading, Mass.: Addison-Wesley.

Kempe, C. H., F. N. Silverman, B. F. Steele, W. Droegemueller, and H. K. Silver. 1962. "The Battered-Child Syndrome." *Journal of the American Medical Association* 181:17–24.

Kleiman, D. G. 1977. "Monogamy in Mammals." *Quarterly Review of Biology* 52:39–69.

Kleiman, D. G., and J. R. Malcolm. 1981. "Evolution of Male Parental Investment in Mammals." In *Parental Care in Mammals*, edited by D. J. Gubernick and P. H. Klopfer. New York: Plenum.

Krebs, J. R., and N. B. Davies. 1987. *An Introduction to Behavioral Ecology*. Sunderland, Mass.: Sinauer.

Kurland, J. A. 1979. "Paternity, Mother's Brother, and Human Sociality." In *Evolutionary Biology and Human Social Behavior*, edited by N. A. Chagnon and and W. Irons. North Scituate, Mass.: Duxbury.

Kurland, J. A., and S. J. C. Gaulin. 1984. "The Evolution of Male Parental Investment: Effects of Genetic Relatedness and Feeding Ecology on the Allocation of Reproductive Effort." In *Primate Paternalism*, edited by D. M. Taub. New York: Van Nostrand.

Lack, D. 1954. *The Natural Regulation of Animal Numbers*. Oxford: Oxford University Press.

———. 1968. *Ecological Adaptation for Breeding in Birds*. London: Methuen.

Langer, W. L. 1972. "Checks on Population Growth: 1750–1850." *Scientific American* 226(2):92–99.

Lasch, C. 1977. *Haven in a Heartless World*. New York: Basic.

Leacock, E. 1978. "Women's Status in Egalitarian Society: Implications for Social Evolution." *Current Anthropology* 19:247–74.

LeBouef, B. J. 1974. "Male-Male Competition and Reproductive Success in Elephant Seals." *American Zoologist* 14:163–76.

Lessing, D. 1973. *The Golden Notebook*. New York: Bantam.

Levine, R. A., and B. B. Levine. 1963. "Nyansongo: A Gusii Community in Kenya." In *Six Cultures, Studies of Child Rearing*, edited by B. B. Whiting. New York: Wiley.

Linton, R. 1936. *The Study of Man*. New York: Appleton-Century.

McKee, L. 1977. "Differential Weaning and the Ideology of Gender: Implications for Andean Sex Ratios." Paper read at the seventy-sixth annual meeting of the American Anthropological Association, Houston, April.

———. 1984. "Sex Differentials in Survivorship and the Customary Treatment of Infants and Children." *Medical Anthropology* 8(2):91–108.

Mamdani, M. 1972. *The Myth of Population Control: Family, Caste, and Class in an Indian Village*. New York: Monthly Review Press.

Margolin, G. 1988. "Interpersonal and Intrapersonal Factors Associated with Marital Violence." In *Family Abuse and Its Consequences: New Directions in Research*, edited by R. Gelles, G. Hotaling, D. Finkelhor, and M. Straus. Beverly Hills, Calif.: Sage.

Margolin, G., and B. E. Wampold. 1981. "Sequential Analysis of Conflict and Accord in Distressed and Nondistressed Marital Partners." *Journal of Consulting and Clinical Psychology* 49(4):554–67.

Maynard-Smith, S. J. 1974. "The Theory of Games and the Evolution of Animal Conflicts." *Journal of Theoretical Biology* 47:209–21.

Mead, M., and F. C. MacGregor. 1951. *Growth and Culture: A Photographic Study of Balinese Children*. New York: Putnam.

Meggitt, M. J. 1964. "Male-Female Relationships in the Highlands of New Guinea." *American Anthropologist* 66:204–24.

Mernissi, F. 1975. *Beyond the Veil: Male-Female Dynamics in a Modern Muslim Society*. New York: Wiley.

Merrill, E. J. 1962. "Physical Abuse of Children: An Agency Study." In *Protecting the Battered Child*, edited by V. De Francis. Denver: American Humane Association.

Miller, B. 1981. *The Endangered Sex: Neglect of Female Children in Rural North India*. Ithaca, N.Y.: Cornell University Press.

Miller, N. 1941. "The Frustration-Aggression Hypothesis." *Psychological Review* 48:337–42.

Minturn, L., and J. T. Hitchcock. 1966. *The Rajputs of Khalapur*. New York: Wiley.

Murphy, C. M., and K. D. O'Leary. 1987. "Verbal Aggression as a Predictor of Physical Aggression in Early Marriage." Paper presented at the Third Family Violence National Conference, University of New Hampshire, Durham, July.

Murphy, Y., and R. Murphy. 1985. *Women of the Forest*. 2d ed. New York: Columbia University Press.

Newman, M. T. 1961. "Biological Adaptation of Man to His Environment: Heat, Cold, Altitude, and Nutrition." *Annals of the New York Academy of Sciences* 91:617–33.

O'Brien, J. E. 1971. "Violence in Divorce-prone Families." *Journal of Marriage and the Family* 33:692–98.

O'Leary, K. D. 1987. "Physical Aggression between Spouses: A Social Learn-

ing Perspective." In *Handbook of Family Violence*, edited by V. B. Van Has-
seet, R. L. Morrison, A. S. Bellack, and M. Hersen. New York: Plenum.

O'Leary, K. D., and I. Arias. 1987. "Marital Assessment in Clinical Practice."
In *Assessment of Marital Discord: An Integration of Research and Clinical Practice*,
edited by K. D. O'Leary. Hillsdale, N.J.: Erlbaum.

Otterbein, K. F., and C. S. Otterbein. 1965. "An Eye for an Eye, a Tooth for a
Tooth: A Cross-cultural Study of Feuding." *American Anthropologist*
67:1470–82.

Packer, C., and A. Pusey. 1982. "Cooperation and Competition within Coalitions of Male Lions: Kin Selection or Game Theory?" *Nature* 296:740–42.

Parke, R. D., and C. Collmer. 1975. "Child Abuse: An Interdisciplinary Analysis." In *Review of Child Development Research*, vol. 5, edited by M. Hethering-
ton. Chicago: University of Chicago Press.

Parke, R. D., J. L. Deur, and M. Saivin. 1970. "The Intermittent Punishment
Effect in Humans: Conditioning or Adaptation?" *Psychonomic Science* 18:193–
94.

Patterson, G. R. 1979. "A Performance Theory for Coercive Family Interaction." In *The Analysis of Social Interactions: Methods, Issues, and Illustrations*,
edited by R. B. Cairns. Hillsdale, N.J.: Erlbaum.

———. 1980. "Mothers: The Unacknowledged Victims." *Monographs of the
Society for Research in Child Development*, vol. 45, no. 5, serial no. 186. Chicago:
University of Chicago Press.

———. 1982*a*. "The Unattached Mother: A Process Analysis." In *Social Relationships: Their Role in Children's Development*, edited by W. Hartup and Z.
Rubin. Harwichport, Mass.: Harwichport Conference.

———. 1982*b*. *Coercive Family Process.* Eugene, Oreg.: Castalia.

———. 1985. "Beyond Technology: The Next Stage in the Development of
Parent Training." In *Handbook of Family Psychology and Psychotherapy*, edited
by L. Abate. New York: Dow-Jones-Irwin.

Pianka, E. R. 1970. "On r- and K-Selection." *American Naturalist* 104:592–97.

Pollitt, E. 1973. "Behavior of Infant in Causation of Nutritional Marasmus."
American Journal of Clinical Nutrition 26:264–70.

Preston, S. 1976. *Mortality Patterns in National Populations with Special Reference
to Recorded Causes of Death.* New York: Academic Press.

Quinn, N. 1977. "Anthropological Studies of Women's Status." *Annual Review
of Anthropology* 6:181–225.

Reid, J. B. 1984. "Social-interactional Patterns in Families of Abused and Nonabused Children." In *Social and Biological Origins of Altruism and Aggression*,
edited by C. Zahn-Waxler, M. Cummings, and M. Radke-Yarrow. Cambridge: Cambridge University Press.

Reid, J. B., G. R. Patterson, and R. Loeber. 1982. "The Abused Child:
Victim, Instigator, or Innocent Bystander?" In *Response Structure and Organization*, edited by D. J. Bernstein. Lincoln: University of Nebraska Press.

Reid, J. B., P. S. Taplin, and R. Loeber. 1981. "A Social Interactional
Approach to the Treatment of Abusive Families." In *Violent Behavior: Social
Learning Approaches to Prediction, Management, and Treatment*, edited by R.
Stuart. New York: Bruner/Mazel.

Reiter, R. 1975. *Toward an Anthropology of Women*. New York: Monthly Review Press.

Richards, A. I. 1950. "Some Types of Family Structure amongst the Central Bantu." In *African Systems of Kinship and Marriage*, edited by A. R. Radcliffe-Brown and C. D. Forde. Oxford: Oxford University Press.

Rohner, R. P. 1975. *They Love Me, They Love Me Not*. New Haven, Conn.: Human Relations Area Files Press.

Rosaldo, M. Z., and L. Lamphere. 1974. *Woman, Culture, and Society*. Stanford, Calif.: Stanford University Press.

Rosenbaum, A., and K. D. O'Leary. 1981. "Marital Violence: Characteristics of Abusive Couples." *Journal of Consulting and Clinical Psychology* 49:63–71.

Sandgrund, A. K., R. Gaines, and A. Green. 1974. "Child Abuse and Mental Retardation: A Problem of Cause and Effect." *American Journal of Mental Deficiency* 79:327–30.

Sanjur, D. M., J. Cranoito, L. Rosales, and A. vonVeen. 1970. "Infant Feeding and Weaning Practices in a Rural Preindustrial Setting: A Sociocultural Approach." *Acta Paediatrica Scandinavia*, suppl. 200.

Sauer, R. 1978. "Infanticide and Abortion in Nineteenth Century Britain." *Population Studies* 32(1):81–93.

Schaap, C. 1984. "A Comparison of the Interaction of Distressed and Nondistressed Married Couples in a Laboratory Situation: Literature Survey, Methodological Issues, and an Empirical Investigation." In *Marital Interaction: Analysis and Modification*, edited by K. Hahlweg and N. S. Jacobson. New York: Guilford.

Schilkroudt, E. 1978. "Age and Gender in Hausa Society: Socio-economic Roles of Children in Urban Kamo." In *Sex and Age as Principles of Social Differentiation*, edited by J. S. LaFontaine. London: Academic Press.

Schlegel, A. 1972. *Male Dominance and Female Autonomy*. New Haven, Conn.: Human Relations Area Files Press.

———. 1977. "Male and Female in Hopi Thought and Action." In *Sexual Stratification: A Cross-cultural View*, edited by A. Schlegel. New York: Columbia University Press.

Schneider, D. M. 1961. "The Distinctive Features of Matrilineal Descent Groups." In *Matrilineal Kinships*, edited by D. Schneider and K. Gough. Berkeley: University of California Press.

Schneider, D. M., and K. Gough. 1961. *Matrilineal Systems*. Berkeley: University of California Press.

Scrimshaw, N. S. 1984. "Infanticide in Human Populations: Societal and Individual Concerns." In *Infanticide: Comparative and Evolutionary Perspectives*, edited by G. Hausfater and S. Hrdy. New York: Aldine.

Scrimshaw, N. S., C. E. Taylor, and J. E. Gordon. 1968. *Interactions of Nutrition and Infection*, Geneva: World Health Organization Monograph Series 57.

Skinner, B. F. 1981. "Selection by Consequences." *Science* 213(4507):501–4.

Smith, R. J., and E. L. Wiswell. 1982. *The Women of Saye Mura*. Chicago: University of Chicago Press.

Snell, J. E., R. J. Rosenwald, and A. Robey. 1964. "The Wifebeater's Wife: A Study of Family Interaction." *Archives of General Psychiatry* 11:107–13.

Sprey, J. 1969. "The Family as a System in Conflict." *Journal of Marriage and the Family* 31:699–706.

Stark, R., and J. McEvoy III. 1970. "Middle Class Violence." *Psychology Today* 4:52–65.

Steele, B. F., and C. B. Pollock. 1968. "A Psychiatric Study of Parents Who Abuse Infants and Small Children." In *The Battered Child*, edited by R. E. Helfer and C. H. Kempe. Chicago: University of Chicago Press.

Steinmetz, S. K., and M. A. Straus. 1974. *Violence in the Family*. New York: Dodd, Mead.

Strathern, M. 1972. *Women in Between: Female Roles in a Male World: Mount Hagen, New Guinea*. London: Seminar Press.

Straus, M. A. 1973. "A General Systems Theory Approach to a Theory of Violence between Family Members." *Social Science Information* 12:105–25.

———. 1980. "Wife-Beating: How Common and Why." In *The Social Causes of Husband-Wife Violence*, edited by M. A. Straus and G. T. Hotaling. Minneapolis: University of Minnesota Press.

Straus, M. A., R. J. Gelles, and S. K. Steinmetz. 1980. *Behind Closed Doors: Violence in the American Family*. Garden City, N.Y.: Doubleday.

Sussman, G. 1975. "The Wet-nursing Business in Nineteenth Century France." *French Historical Studies* 9(2):304–28.

Symons, D. 1979. *The Evolution of Human Sexuality*. New York: Oxford University Press.

———. 1986. "Sociobiology and Darwinism: Commentary." *Behavior and Brain Sciences* 9:208–9.

Thibaut, J. W., and H. H. Kelley. 1959. *The Social Psychology of Groups*. New York: Wiley.

Trivers, R. L. 1972. "Parental Investment and Sexual Selection." In *Sexual Selection and the Descent of Man*, edited by B. Campbell. Chicago: Aldine.

———. 1974. "Parent-Offspring Conflict." *American Zoologist* 14:244–64.

———. 1985. *Social Evolution*. Menlo Park, Calif.: Benjamin/Cummings.

Trivers, R. L., and D. Willard. 1973. "Natural Selection of Parental Ability to Vary the Sex Ratio of Offspring." *Science* 179:90–92.

van den Berghe, P. 1979. *Human Family Systems: An Evolutionary Perspective*. New York: Elsevier.

Vasta, R. 1982. "Physical Child Abuse: A Dual-Component Analysis." *Developmental Review* 2:125–49.

Vehrencamp, S., and J. W. Bradbury. 1984. "Mating Systems and Ecology." In *Behavioral Ecology: An Evolutionary Approach*. 2d ed., edited by J. R. Krebs and N. B. Davies. Oxford: Blackwell Scientific.

Vivian, D., and K. D. O'Leary. 1987. "Communication Patterns in Physically Aggressive Engaged Couples." Paper presented at the Third National Violence Research Conference, University of New Hampshire, Durham, July.

Vreede-de Stuers, C. 1968. *Purda: A Study of Muslim Women's Life in Northern India*. Assen, India: Van Gorcum.

Wahler, R. G. 1980. "The Insular Mother: Her Problems in Parent-Child Treatment." *Journal of Applied Behavior Analysis* 13:207–19.

Wahler, R. G., and J. E. Dumas. 1986. "Maintenance Factors in Coercive

Mother-Child Interactions: The Compliance and Predictability Hypotheses." *Journal of Applied Behavior Analysis* 19:13–22.

Wahler, R. G., and D. M. Hahn. 1984. "The Communication Patterns of Troubled Mothers: In Search of a Keystone in the Generalization of Parenting Skills." *Journal of Education and Treatment of Children* 7:335–50.

Walker, L. E. 1979. *The Battered Woman.* New York: Harper & Row.

Wallace, B. 1958. "The Comparison of Observed and Calculated Zygotic Distributions." *Evolution* 12:113–15.

Washburn, S. 1978. "Human Behavior and the Behavior of Other Animals." *American Psychologist* 33:405–18.

Whiting, J. W. M., and B. Whiting. 1975. "Aloofness and Intimacy: A Cross-cultural Study of the Relations between Husbands and Wives." *Ethos* 3:183–207.

Williams, G. C. 1966a. *Adaptation and Natural Selection.* Princeton, N.J.: Princeton University Press.

———. 1966b. "Natural Selection, the Costs of Reproduction, and a Refinement of Lack's Principle." *American Naturalist* 100:687–90.

Wilson, W. J. 1987. *The Truly Disadvantaged: The Inner City, the Underclass, and Public Policy.* Chicago: University of Chicago Press.

Wittenberger, J. F. 1980. *Animal Social Behavior.* Boston: Duxbury.

Wolf, M. 1972. *Women and the Family in Rural Taiwan.* Stanford, Calif.: Stanford University Press.

Wolfe, D. A. 1984. "Behavioral Distinctions between Abusive and Nonabusive Parents: A Review and Critique." Paper presented at the Second Family Violence Research Conference, University of New Hampshire, Durham, July.

Wolff, R. J. 1965. "Meanings of Food." *Tropical and Geographical Medicine* 17:45–51.

Zeveloff, S. I., and M. S. Boyce. 1980. "Parental Investment and Mating Systems in Mammals." *Evolution* 34(5):973–82.

Joseph G. Weis

Family Violence Research Methodology and Design

ABSTRACT

Research on family violence is in its early days. The quality of research
is uneven, and findings are often inconsistent. Better studies and more
accurate data are needed to improve our understanding of family violence
and to develop more effective prevention and control strategies.
Unfortunately, insufficient attention has been given to methodological
issues that need to be investigated and resolved before more valid and
reliable estimates of the prevalence and correlates of family violence can
be expected. Definitional problems include wide variations in the
boundaries of the domain of family violence and in the elements of
definitions. Crucial methodological problems that affect research findings
on family violence include issues related to the research context, data
sources, sample characteristics, research designs, and measures and their
validity.

Family violence is not a new social phenomenon, but it did not become
a proper topic of inquiry by the research and policy communities until
the 1960s, for child abuse, and the 1970s, for spousal violence. In one
leading scholarly research journal on the family, not one article was
published before 1970 with the word "violence" in the title (O'Brien
1971). After 1970, research publications appeared at a rapid rate: 1,170
journal articles and books appeared between 1972 and 1980 (Wolfgang
and Weiner 1981). Unfortunately, the evidence accumuiated from this
literature has been described as "clouded," "limited," "rudimentary,"
"primitive," and not meeting "traditional standards of scientific inquiry" (Gelles 1973; Gerbner, Ross, and Zigler 1980; Gelles 1983).

Joseph G. Weis is professor of sociology and director of the Center for Law and
Justice at the University of Washington.

The proliferation of research on family violence has produced a dif-
fuse literature characterized by uneven quality. Little empirical research has been published on what Gelles and Straus (1979) call the
most critical issues in family violence research: prevalence and incidence (how much is there?); correlation (how is it distributed?); and
cause (how is it explained?).[1] Bolton et al. (1981, pp. 535–36) have
estimated that through 1978 only 20 percent of the literature on child
abuse could be considered "research," with more than three-fourths of
those research studies relying on official case records or aggregate statistics and only 3 percent focusing on prevalence and incidence and 11
percent on psychosocial correlates.

Placed within the broader context of empirical research on violence
in general, the state of family violence research appears even more
bleak—only a small percentage of all research works on violence addresses some variation of family violence. For example, a quantitative
meta-analysis[2] of empirical studies of violence carried out between 1945
and 1983 shows that only 18 percent address general family violence,
only 4 percent focus on spousal violence, and only 11 percent treat
violence against children (Bridges and Weis 1984). Most research attention has been on criminal violence in general, without differentiating
the various forms of violence that are defined by a critical feature that
sets family violence apart from other forms of violence—the intimate
social and personal relationship between victim and offender. The
scant empirical research has generated findings that are sometimes contradictory, often discrepant, and generally unreliable.

Substantial discrepancies among estimates of the prevalence, inci-

[1] There are, of course, other critical issues in the study of family violence, e.g., the
consequences and impacts of family violence on victims, offenders, family, and society,
and the effectiveness of prevention and control policies and programs. This essay focuses
on the three issues identified by Gelles and Straus (1979) because the evaluation literature
is reviewed in other essays in this volume and most of the methodological and design
problems identified here also apply to policy-directed and evaluation research.
[2] A quantitative meta-analysis is a quantitative method of reviewing and assessing
empirical research literature (Hunter, Schmidt, and Jackson 1982). Here, empirical
findings on violence reported in the literature between 1945 and 1983 were aggregated,
coded, and analyzed. The basic unit of analysis, the dependent variable, is the reported
empirical *relation* between violence and other variables, such as social class, race, and
gender. The analysis attempts to account for variations in the relations by using study
design characteristics (e.g., differences in data sources, research designs, and measures)
as independent variables (cf. Tittle, Villemez, and Smith 1978). A comprehensive literature search of more than 23,000 articles, monographs, and theses on violence was performed, and extensive information on study design characteristics and findings was coded
and analyzed statistically on a subset of eligible studies (see Bridges and Weis [1988] for a
more complete description of this quantitative meta-analysis of violence).

dence, and correlates of family violence compromise the usefulness of the research results. Prevalence and incidence estimates of the extent of child abuse differ dramatically. One of the earliest surveys of officially recorded child abuse conducted before most states had enacted reporting laws for child abuse and neglect reported only 6,000 cases nationwide (Gil 1970), while a self-report survey of a national representative sample of families estimates that 1.5–2 million children may be the victims of physical harm every year (Straus, Gelles, and Steinmetz 1980). Even more pronounced differences in prevalence estimates are evident in studies of spousal violence. Extrapolations from official records have produced estimates ranging from thousands to millions of battered wives per year, while more direct survey methods report that 28 percent of couples (approximately fifteen million) experience violence at some point during their marriage (Straus 1978). Discrepant estimates of prevalence and incidence also make it difficult to determine with any degree of confidence that the rate of family violence is increasing or decreasing. At the national level, although official criminal, health, and social service statistics suggest increases in violence against spouses and children, victimization surveys show more stability in rates, while self-report surveys report decreases (Straus and Gelles 1986).

Even more important to our understanding of family violence are the apparent discrepancies in the reported correlates of family violence. There are differences in the estimates of the correlates of family violence and of general criminal violence, as well as among studies of family violence. The correlates of gender, race, and socioeconomic status illustrate the nature of these discrepancies.

Most research on the relation between gender and general violence suggests greater male involvement, both as perpetrators and victims, except as victims of sexual violence (Simon 1975; Hindelang 1976; Smith and Visher 1980; Johnson 1986). However, there are studies of family violence that report findings to the contrary. Coleman and Straus (1980) report that more mothers than fathers relate that they have engaged in violence against their children. For spousal violence, Steinmetz (1977) reports a slightly higher rate of wife perpetrators and husband victims. Regarding child victims, Rosenblatt (1980) and Rhoades and Parker (1981) have found that more girls than boys report more serious injury as victims of parental violence, particularly at the hands of their mothers. By contrast, Maden and Wrench (1977) report that boys are slightly more likely to be victims of parental violence.

The relation between race and general violence suggests greater involvement among blacks than whites, both as perpetrators and victims, particularly of the more serious types of violent behavior, like homicide and aggravated assault (Wolfgang and Ferracuti 1967; Hindelang 1978; Hindelang, Gottfredson, and Garofalo 1978; Sampson 1985), although the nature of the effect of racial inequality on violent crime is not clear (Golden and Messner 1987). However, some research shows that (1) parental violence has no relation with race (Rhoades and Parker 1981; Daley and Piliavin 1982), (2) a slightly higher level of violence exists against children among blacks (Holter and Friedman 1968), or (3) a weak relation exists between being a white parent and violent child abuse (Rosenblatt 1980).

The research literature on general violence suggests that there is more violence among members of the lowest socioeconomic strata (Wolfgang, Figlio, and Sellin 1972; Elliott and Ageton 1980), although there is also considerable ambiguity about the strength and meaning of the correlation (Brownfield 1986; Weis 1986b). Again, the research on family violence shows somewhat different relations that vary with the severity of injury and the characteristics of the offender. For example, Pelton (1978) and Straus, Gelles, and Steinmetz (1980) report that the higher the social status, the less prevalent the parental violence. But Coleman and Straus (1980) discovered differences in the relation for mothers and fathers; less serious and physically harmful violence was not related to the father's socioeconomic status but was related to the mother's. Daley and Piliavin (1982) report no relation between parental education and income and the severity of injury in cases of child abuse. For spousal violence, Schulman (1979) discovered a slight drop in the incidence of violence among the wealthy and those in professional and managerial occupations.

A quantitative meta-analysis of research findings on violence (Bridges and Weis 1985) helps to clarify the discrepancies in correlations across studies. It indicates that study findings, including the strength of correlates, do indeed vary by the "form" of violence under consideration. For example, the overall mean correlation between gender and violence across all study findings in the analysis is only .073, suggesting that males, surprisingly, are not much more violent than females. However, when findings on family violence are analyzed separately, the correlation drops to .030, while for other kinds of violence it increases to .136. This indicates that gender differences in violent behavior are negligible when the offenders and victims are intimates but are more substantial when violence occurs among nonintimates.

Similar differences in correlations by form of violence are apparent for race and socioeconomic status. The overall mean correlation for race is .109, indicating slightly more involvement in violent behavior among blacks. However, it seems that the race difference is greater for general criminal violence (.155) than it is for family violence (.041). That is, whites and blacks are almost equally likely to engage in spousal or parental violence, but blacks appear to be more involved in other types of violence. The mean correlation for socioeconomic status is −.109, suggesting slightly more violence in the lower socioeconomic strata. But, as with race, it seems that lower class involvement is greater for general criminal violence (−.142) than it is for family violence (−.070) (Bridges and Weis 1985; Sederstrom 1986). Thus these three major sociodemographic variables—gender, race, and socioeconomic status—appear to be more weakly related to family violence than to other forms of violence.

Of course, the question is to what extent the differences in correlates reflect "actual" differences in violent behavior and etiological factors or, instead, differences in the characteristics of the studies that produced them. It is likely that different types of studies are generating different correlates of violent behavior. Variations in study design characteristics—including data sources, samples, research designs, measures, and levels of analysis—may account for many of the discrepancies in findings on important correlates of violence and in estimates of its prevalence and incidence (Bridges and Weis 1988). These discrepancies seriously complicate and jeopardize the development and testing of theory since different measurement methods should be in agreement on the "actual" characteristics of the phenomenon to be explained. Without consistency across studies in the correlates of violence, the precise "causes" of violent behavior will remain uncertain. Gelles (1983) has concluded from a review of theories of family violence that empirical research on correlates and causes is not yet adequate for rigorous theory development and that methodological problems, especially with operational definitions of violence and sample composition, have delayed the development of adequate multidimensional causal models.

Research on family violence is plagued by inaccurate and inconsistent information on the basic facts of violent behavior among family members. Greater consensus on the facts of family violence should improve our understanding of the phenomenon and our capacity to develop more effective prevention and control strategies. However, it is not clear that there is widespread recognition of the need, and support, for research on the factors that are responsible for discrepant estimates of prevalence, incidence, and correlates. Among policymakers, until quite recently, this type of research has not been a high priority. For example, among the twenty-two areas where national research efforts were recommended by the U.S. Attorney General's Task Force on Family Violence (1984), not one addresses the measurement or estimation of the prevalence, incidence, or correlates of family violence. There is widespread agreement that more complex and accurate data are needed. Unfortunately, there is less recognition of the many methodological issues that need to be investigated and resolved—especially those that may be responsible for many of the inconsistencies—before valid and reliable data on family violence can be expected.[3]

Given the dearth of empirical research on family violence, the discrepancies in estimates of prevalence, incidence, and correlates, and the inattention to the methodological sources of these inconsistencies, this essay selectively and briefly addresses some of the important conceptual and methodological problems and limitations in the measurement of family violence. Section I discusses conceptual and definitional issues, focusing on the boundaries of the domain of family violence and the elements of rigorous definitions. Section II addresses a variety of methodological problems that affect research findings on family violence, including issues related to the research context, data sources, sample characteristics, research designs, and measures and their validity. Finally, Section III discusses a number of research needs and priorities that may lead to improvements in family violence research.

I. Conceptual and Definitional Issues
Two related conceptual problems have jeopardized the comparability, generalizability, and reliability of research findings on family violence—underdeveloped theory and imprecise nominal and operational definitions.

Since family violence is a relatively new subject of scientific inquiry, it is not surprising that theory construction and testing are at an early stage of development. A major review of available theories identified fifteen perspectives, most of them borrowed from the sociology of deviance and crime, the social psychology of aggression, and abnormal psychology (Gelles and Straus 1979). Unfortunately, this theoretical diversity brings with it a variety of definitions of independent and dependent variables and very few empirical tests of theory to reduce

---

[3] This is not to suggest that family violence research is "necessarily" inadequate or deficient but, rather, that much of the research is not as rigorous or refined as in other fields of inquiry.

the conceptual confusion to a simpler empirical reality. As Gelles (1980) and others have pointed out, the field is, with a few exceptions (Garbarino 1977; Burgess 1979), characterized by descriptive work, with little hypothesis testing, causal modeling, or attempts to construct and test integrated theories of the different types of family violence.

Imprecise nominal and operational definitions of variables specified by theories have been conceptual obstacles to sound theorizing and empirical research. When attention has been paid to definitions, it is usually on the characteristics of the violence that is to be explained. These definitions can vary dramatically by theory, types of family violence, legal jurisdiction, and culture over time, across studies, and even within some studies. Consequently, the diversity and ambiguity of definitions confuse and compromise the research findings on the amount and distribution of family violence. It is very difficult to compare the results of different studies, accumulate knowledge, and generalize beyond any one study.

Examples of the impact that variations in definition have on research findings are illuminating. When the National Study of the Incidence and Severity of Child Abuse and Neglect used an operational definition of "child maltreatment" that did not specify the amount of harm required to qualify as a case, 30 percent of children were classified as victims of maltreatment. Later, when the definition was narrowed to cases where a minimum degree of harm was specified and apparent, the estimate dropped to *1* percent (Burgdorf and Eldred 1978). The effect on correlates of changes in definition is similar, particularly when the seriousness of violent behavior or degree of harm is included and varied in a definition. For example, studies that define violence solely in terms of serious assaultive acts causing physical injury or harm to victims find a much stronger correlation between race and violent behavior than studies using definitions that include less harmful behaviors (Hindelang 1978; Bridges and Weis 1985).

More precise and, perhaps, even standardized definitions are needed, but less clear are the proper domain and elements of the definitions and how they should be employed in research and practice. To establish the boundaries of the domain, one needs to specify *who* should be included as offenders and victims and *what* kinds of behavior should be considered violent. Unfortunately, even at the most general level the domain of "family violence" is ambiguous—the rubric includes family violence, domestic violence, intrafamilial violence, intimate violence, and non-stranger violence. The offenders and victims represented in studies range from parents, children, siblings, husbands, wives, relatives, intimates, lovers, friends, neighbors, and work associates to nonstrangers. The behaviors range from shouting, slapping, emotional trauma, verbal threats, spanking, aggressive gestures, intimidation, shoving, forced sex, stabbing, punching, and shooting to burning. To include all of these disparate actors and acts within the domain of family violence (or whatever one chooses to call it) does a disservice to the pursuit of rigorous inquiry.

Clarifying the units of analysis is an essential first step—who is family and what is violence? In general, family violence is considered that violence that is perpetrated by family members against one another. But beginning with the *family*, it is not always clear what criteria differentiate the family from other social units. The nature of the "relationship" between the victim and offender is probably the most important characteristic. First, when violence occurs in the traditional family unit,[4] properly called *family violence*, the offenders and victims share a *kin* relationship by being related through birth or marriage; second, practically all of them share an *intimate* relationship in that they know each other in a close, personal way; and third, many of them share a *domiciliary* relationship by virtue of living together in the same household. This conceptualization would include spousal violence, sibling violence, parental violence, and violence against parents and other relatives.

However, there are other types of relationships between victim and offender where all three of those elements may not be present. These relationships have not been, but perhaps should be, included in the domain of family violence research.[5] Depending on theoretical, re-

[4] The traditional family is typically defined by sociologists in broad terms as a group "linked by blood or marriage who live together, cooperate economically, and share responsibility for bringing up their collective offspring" (Federico 1979, pp. 355–56).

[5] There are eight "logical" types of relationships between victim and offender that define concomitant types of violence.

Relationship between Victim and Offender

Type of Violence	Intimate	Kin	Domiciliary
Family violence	Yes	Yes	Yes
Extended family violence	Yes	Yes	No
Intimate domiciliary violence	Yes	No	Yes
Intimate violence	Yes	No	No
Kin violence	No	Yes	No
Domiciliary violence	No	No	Yes
Domiciliary kin violence	No	Yes	Yes
General violence	No	No	No

search, or practical purposes, the most likely candidates for inclusion are the violent acts that happen between emotionally close kin who do not live together—for example, between brothers who have their own families, ex-spouses, cousins, and absentee fathers and resident mothers, or what might be called *extended family violence*. Another is the violent behavior between unmarried couples who live together or among friends who are housemates, or *intimate domiciliary violence*. Last, *intimate violence* takes place between people who have a close, personal relationship but do not regularly share the same domicile, such as lovers and good friends.[6]

These types of family violence are to be distinguished from the kind of violence that occurs among offenders and victims who are not related to each other, do not know each other well, and who do not share living arrangements. It is the "other" *general violence* that occurs among strangers, mere acquaintances, and the recognizable. This kind of violence is certainly not family violence.

More attention has been devoted to defining the *violence* in family violence, but, paradoxically, it is more apparent "who" should be included in the domain of family violence research than "what." If the objective is to study bona fide "violence," the broad range of behaviors must be narrowed. There also is considerable confusion over the similar but not synonymous terms that are commonly used to identify categories of unacceptable behaviors. Otherwise put, it is not clear how violence differs from abuse, maltreatment, battering, beating, and so on. Comparing violence and abuse, some acts considered abuse are, indeed, violent, but in many instances they are not. For example, Gil (1970) defines child abuse as violence against children or a physical attack or injury ranging from minimal to fatal injury inflicted on a child by a person having caretaking responsibilities for him. For Baldwin and Oliver (1975) there are very specific clinical, medical criteria of injury that define child abuse: death, skull or facial bone fractures, bleeding

---

[6] The other logical possibilities do not share the critical dimension of an intimate relationship between victim and offender or its powerful combination with a domiciliary relationship. *Kin violence* occurs between kin who are distant socially, personally, and, perhaps, geographically, e.g., a violent act between distant cousins who are virtual strangers. *Domiciliary violence* happens among those who merely live in the same domicile, e.g., boarders or residents of a dormitory, apartment building, or house, who share little in way of personal relationships. The most unusual kind of violence, and probably *only* a logical possibility, would be *domiciliary kin violence* because it occurs among kin who are not socially and personally close but who share living arrangements. This might occur in living situations where an obscure, distant relative moves in with a family and violence ensues.

into or around the brain, two or more instances of mutilation requiring medical attention, three or more instances of fractures or severe bruising, or multiple fractures or severe internal injuries. Among some survey researchers (Straus, Gelles, and Steinmetz 1980), abuse refers to violent acts with a high probability of causing physical harm to a victim.

More common are definitions that confound abuse and violence by including behavior that is not clearly violent, such as failure to thrive (Egeland and Brunnquell 1979), malnourishment (Giovannoni and Becerra 1979), and emotional deprivation (Tuteur and Glotzer 1966), among a variety of other nonviolent phenomena. Combinations of violent and nonviolent behavior, or physical and nonphysical harm, are mixed in categories of violence, abuse, and maltreatment. The conceptual confusion is complicated because terms like "abuse" are evaluative attributions that can be applied to practically any violent or nonviolent action or consequence.

Conceptual clarity in family violence research would be improved substantially if the focus of inquiry were restricted to violent behavior and physical injury. For example, violence has been defined by Gelles and Straus (1979) as an act carried out with the actual or perceived intention of physically hurting another person. A slightly more general definition is offered by Megargee (1976) as acts characterized by the use or threat of force that is likely to result in injury. Finally, it is behavior occurring in a natural setting directed against another person, which is intended to cause physical pain or injury, or an overt threat intended to create fear of injury in forcing another's behavior compliance (Weis and Bridges 1983). These definitions are typical of those used by many researchers and point to a number of the critical elements that should be included in definitions of violence.

Behavior, intent to harm, and injury seem to be basic elements, but the specification of each element may vary depending on how narrowly or broadly one wants to focus inquiry. For example, the three representative definitions given above propose that actual, attempted, or threatened behavior that is intended to cause physical injury or create the fear of injury (particularly, to force someone to do something), and that actually does or is likely to cause injury or pain, should be included in definitions of violence. Which variations of each of the major elements are included in a definition depends on one's research purposes and preferences, but the precise delineation of each, though difficult, is

necessary for rigorous and comparable research findings on family violence.[7]

Even more important than the specific content of any definition of
violence is the congruity between nominal and operational definitions
of the phenomenon. For example, as the nominal definition is used in
research, there should be adequate measurement of each of the basic
elements as they vary in the definition. The nominal definition helps
establish conceptual boundaries and clarify distinctions that may be
useful in forging the operational definitions that are the grist of empirical research. What the phenomenon is named is less critical than how it
is operationalized and measured. The conceptual and measurement
problems created by sloppy definitions are sufficiently bothersome that
Besharov (1981) has proposed that definitional issues should become an
explicit methodological concern among many others in family violence
research.

II. Methodological Issues

Research on family violence is saturated with methodological problems
and limitations, many generic to social science research but some
unique to family violence research. Progress in resolving many of these
problems has been achieved in research on "sensitive" topics in other
areas, especially the measurement of criminal behavior and victimization (Hindelang, Hirschi, and Weis 1981; Weis 1986a). There follows a
discussion of methodological issues related to the research context, data
sources, sample designs and compositions, research designs, and validity and reliability of measures.

A. Research Context

Research on family violence is research on a sensitive topic in a
sensitive setting. The family is a difficult social institution to study, and
made more difficult when the topic of inquiry is violent behavior between offenders and victims who typically have close, personal relationships.

1. *The Family.*   There are a number of characteristics of the family
that are usually considered hindrances to good research on family vio-

---

[7] This is not a call for one "standard" definition but for the specification and elaboration of the elements included in definitions of "family" and "violence" that are used in
family violence research. Otherwise, meaningful comparisons across studies are extremely difficult, if not impossible, with any precision.

lence (Gelles 1978; Gelles and Straus 1979). First, the family is a *complex* social organization consisting of multiple roles and statuses that create a complicated social system and different perceptions of intrafamilial experiences that make it difficult to penetrate and objectify.

Second, the family is also a very *private* social group with most interaction and behavior invisible to outsiders, particularly the variety of "private" acts, ranging from sexual intimacy to violence against one's children, that take place behind closed doors. These acts typically become known only when victims or other interested parties report them to authorities or to researchers. One of the most frequent reasons that victims of family violence give for not reporting it to the police is that it is a "private matter" (Hindelang 1976; Gottfredson and Gottfredson 1980; Timrots and Rand 1987).

Third, social interaction among family members is *intimate* and, therefore more intense, emotional, and consequential than other interaction. This intimacy of relationships reinforces privacy norms because there are personal and private experiences that occur only among intimates, including violence. Consequently, there is a tendency to insulate the family from prying outsiders, including researchers.

These characteristics of the traditional family unit that make research difficult also apply to the other kinds of violence and relationships that fall within the domain of family violence. For example, violence between lovers who live together is hardly traditional family violence, but the unit of analysis can be conceptualized as the violence that occurs between an offender and victim who share an intimate relationship and live in the same household.

2. *Violence as a Sensitive Topic.* The difficulties in doing research within the context of the family and other intimate relationships are exacerbated when a *sensitive topic* like violence is the object of investigation. In general, people want to keep violent behavior private because public exposure could lead to legal sanctions, stigmatization, shame and guilt, loss of respect and self-esteem, and other consequences that reflect negatively on the offender (and sometimes on the victim). Consequently, it is the kind of behavior that one does not want open to public scrutiny and judgment and is less likely to reveal about oneself than more positive acts.

The fear that research subjects may experience in sharing private and socially unacceptable aspects of their lives with outsiders is even more salient in research on family violence because of the intimate relationship of the offender and victim. For example, the victim of a brutal sexual assault may feel anxious about disclosing information about it, including the identity of the offender, because she may also fear reprisal from the offender with whom she has a personal relationship. The two reasons given most often for not reporting these victimizations to the police are that it is a private matter and that there is fear of reprisal from the offender (Hindelang 1976; McDermott 1979; Timrots and Rand 1987). Both self-report and victimization surveys vastly underestimate assault and rape between offenders and victims who know each other (Skogan 1981), perhaps for the same reasons.

Unfortunately, these types of response effects, as well as others to be discussed, may have the most substantial detrimental effects on precisely those types of violent behavior that constitute the core of family violence. The survey measurement of assault and rape, particularly among offenders and victims who know each other, is so inadequate that Gove, Hughes, and Geerken (1985, p. 415) have concluded that official crime data provide more valid rate estimates for assault and rape than do victimization surveys and that it is "quite clear that for rape and assault, the measures of 'crime' in the victimization surveys and in the Uniform Crime Reports are completely different." Given the reliance on survey research on family violence, this evidence is particularly troublesome. It suggests that the predominant acts of violence—assaults and rape—are measured less accurately than other illegal acts by survey measures and also less accurately than official measures. In short, differences in data sources seem to affect study findings.

B. Data Sources

> Current knowledge about the incidence of family violence is based mostly on estimates. Effective responses to the problem require more accurate data. There is no shortage of figures, yet estimates . . . vary greatly. In addition, experts regard family violence to be among the most underreported of any crime. The task of understanding family violence requires the collection of accurate and complete data. [U.S. ATTORNEY GENERAL'S TASK FORCE ON FAMILY VIOLENCE 1984, p. 82]

Probably the primary source of conflicts among findings on the prevalence, incidence, and correlates of family violence is the variety of data sources and their concomitant research methods and procedures. Studies using different measurement approaches often produce discrepant conclusions about intrafamilial violence. These discrepancies reverberate to the detriment of theory construction and testing, policy-making, program design and implementation, and even evaluation.

There are three basic uses for data on family violence: the social indicator purpose is to produce accurate estimates of the amount of violence; the etiological purpose is to measure the distribution of family violence by a variety of social, demographic, psychological, and other characteristics; and the evaluation purpose is to monitor and assess policy and program developments. Knowing the volume of family violence in the community can be useful policy-relevant information, but beyond confirming that there is a substantial problem it is not as useful as data on the characteristics of offenses, offenders, and victims or on prevention and control efforts. A broader consideration of the measurement of family violence, including the social indicator, etiological, and evaluation purposes of data collected from a variety of official and unofficial sources, is necessary.

There are five major alternative sources of data on family violence: *official records* (criminal justice, social service, and health); *self-reports* of violent behavior; reports of personal *victimization; informant* reports; and direct *observation.*

1. *Official Records.* Most research on family violence, particularly before 1970, has relied on official record data gathered from criminal justice, mental health, social work, and clinical records, both public and private. Not surprisingly, given the different orientations to the problem and different reporting and recording requirements and practices, there is very little coordination across these data sources.

Of the public agency records, criminal justice data are probably used most frequently, especially police arrest figures at both the local and national levels, for documenting family violence between adults. These data are much less useful for measuring violence against children. Case studies using clinical record data, both medical and psychological, have been more typical of research on child abuse. Criminal justice records may be the most critical official data sources for a number of reasons: they are collected regularly and systematically, with legal constraints on reporting and recording procedures and practices; they are widely available, from community to community and nationally in the annual Uniform Crime Reports (UCR); and they may become more necessary in research because of recent efforts to "criminalize" family violence.

Criminal justice data produce biased samples of offenders and offenses that underrepresent all crimes, varying by type of offense and offender characteristics (Weis 1983). Unfortunately, the underrepresentation is apparently worse for assaults and rapes, particularly when offenders and victims know each other (Hindelang 1976; McDermott 1979; Skogan 1981). Of course, these characteristics of the offense and the relationship between offender and victim describe family violence, meaning that underestimations of prevalence and incidence are even greater for family violence than for other types of violence or crime. Incomplete and inaccurate records may also contribute to the underestimation problem. For example, approximately 20 percent of local arrests are "missing" from state and federal record systems, while 20 percent of the available records are "inaccurate" (Doernberg and Zeigler 1980; Sherman and Glick 1984; Belair 1985). If there is a "dark figure" of unknown crime, there may be a veritable "black hole" of unknown family violence.

Criminal justice data are incomplete in other ways, particularly regarding the sociodemographic characteristics of the offender and victim, the relationship between them, and situational characteristics of the incident. For example, the most widely used national source of official data on criminal violence, the UCR, includes information on only six violent offenses (homicide, rape, aggravated assault, simple assault, sex offenses, and offenses against the family and child) that can be considered family violence. It does not include, except for homicide, information on the age of the individual offender and victim or on the specific nature of the relationship between the two. This kind of information could differentiate family violence from other forms of violence, enhancing the utility of this important data source in research on family violence. These limitations of the UCR are even more severe regarding child offenders and victims since no distinction is made between a young child and an older juvenile.

This would not be a simple task, nor would a rigorous codification of the relationship between offender and victim necessarily lead to accurate recording. Zahn and Riedel (1983) report only a 50–60 percent "agreement" in specifications of victim-offender relationships for homicide between local police records and medical examiner records for the same jurisdictions and sizable discrepancies between local police records and FBI Supplemental Homicide Reports for the same cities and time periods. So, even for homicide, a crime with a very high clearance rate and more information than usual collected about the circumstances of the crime, there is substantial disagreement regarding the "relationship" between the victim and offender. And the distinctions coded are much less precise (family, friends, strangers, unknown) than are required for empirical specification (e.g., father and son) of the relationship.

Better police record data may be one of the unanticipated consequences of recent legislation in a number of states that have "criminalized" family violence by attempting to limit the discretion of police officers in handling "domestic disturbance" cases. For example, the Washington State Domestic Violence Protection Act of 1984 requires police to make an arrest whenever there is probable cause to believe a domestic assault has occurred. The sample of arrestees should constitute a more representative group of persons whose violent behavior against another family member has been reported to the police. In other states that still handle domestic cases in the traditional fashion, police would more likely attempt to reconcile the offender and victim and not report an offense (Berk and Loseke 1981). When police are required to treat violence in the family like other cases, more cases are reported and there is an apparent specific deterrent effect on future violence (Sherman and Berk 1984), although some research raises doubts about the magnitude of the effect (see Elliott, in this volume). This suggests that there may be positive consequences of the criminalization of family violence, one hoped for—a deterrent effect—and one unanticipated—better data.

There are discrepancies between official data sources on the basic characteristics of family violence because they are compiled for different reasons and focus on different aspects of the phenomenon. Criminal justice records register violent *offenders* and their offenses primarily for the purpose of crime control, whereas social service, mental health, and medical records register *victims* of violence and their injuries, whether social, psychological, or physical, primarily for the purpose of serving and protecting the victim. In recent years, social service and health records have probably been used less often in research than criminal justice records because they are either unavailable or so incomplete as to render them unreliable. For example, there are no systematically collected national health data on nonfatal physical injury resulting from family violence. At the local level, medical and clinical records are more available, including those compiled by medical examiners (Zahn 1975), emergency rooms (Martin 1976; Lion 1985), clinics (Walker 1979), and medical offices (Sgroi 1977). However, these data typically are narrow in focus, contain little systematic information on the violent event and the offender, suffer from selective sampling biases, and cannot be generalized beyond the particular study population. However, many acts of family violence that are not reported to the police often end up in medical facilities, particularly county and city hospital emergency rooms (Stark, Flitcraft, and Frazier 1979). For example, in a Swedish study of 192 patients treated in a hospital for serious knife wounds, 42 percent were not reported to the police (Wikstrom 1985), and it is likely that a substantial proportion of those occurred between intimate offenders and victims. This suggests that health records, though limited as a primary source of data on family violence, may be useful in exploring the extent and nature of unreported serious violent acts, providing data for exploratory research on etiological factors, and constituting samples of subjects about whom more comprehensive information would be collected by other methods.

Public social service records have been used more often than health records, particularly in research on violence against children. Historically, the efforts to protect children and prevent abuse have produced separate social welfare, juvenile court, and child protective service records on neglect, dependency, and abuse among children. These records have been used in a variety of studies, but the small and selective samples drawn from clients of these agencies produce unreliable findings that, again, cannot be generalized to those who have not received assistance (Plotkin et al. 1981).

The only national social service records on family violence are on "child abuse." Since 1968, and reinforced in 1974 by the Federal Child Abuse Prevention and Treatment Act, child protection statutes have required the reporting of suspected abuse and neglect, as well as central "registers" of those reports that may include information on the victim, suspected perpetrators, family circumstances, and characteristics of the event (Besharov 1978). These data could provide useful information on violence against children, particularly that which is not brought to the attention of the criminal justice system initially or after it is reported to child protective services.

However, as with other large-scale state or national reporting systems, there are a variety of problems with central registers. The definitions of abuse and neglect vary by state, thus reducing the comparability of statistics. Perhaps most troublesome is that they probably underrepresent the population of abused and neglected children even more than criminal justice records underrepresent criminals because there is more unbridled discretion among caseworkers than among criminal justice agents and there are low levels of "substantiated" reports. Some states, like Washington, may have only one-in-twenty reported cases substantiated—that is, the suspected abuser admits the act or is convicted in court. This is much lower than police clearance rates for most crimes, especially crimes of violence.

Besharov (1977) has concluded that central registers have not fulfilled their intended monitoring, diagnostic, and data collection tasks because of incomplete and inaccurate records, cumbersome reporting procedures, and confidentiality restrictions that inhibit research and other access to the records. The assessment of the extent, location, and severity of injury, critical information in deciding whether a violent and physically harmful act has occurred, is typically inadequate (Thiesen 1978). In short, the central registers that currently exist in practically all states have an unfulfilled potential to be a very useful data source on violence against children. There are indications that it may be possible through interagency coordination to establish cross-indexed registers of criminal justice, social service, health, and education information on apparent cases of abuse and neglect (Zill, Peterson, and Moore 1984).

In addition to public sources of records on family violence, there are also a few private agency sources. For example, private social work agencies (Gelles 1980), shelters and crisis centers for victims of spousal violence including rape (Dobash and Dobash 1979; Walker 1979), private mental health clinics, psychiatrists, and counselors have all been used to identify prospective subjects or to collect data from their records. The typical case studies based on these private clinical records can be useful in gaining insights on the dynamics and causes of family violence. However, the samples are usually so small and selective, and the data so variable and questionable, that private records are probably best suited to preliminary, exploratory data collection. There are better data sources if one is interested in investigating the types of victims of family violence who avail themselves of the services provided by private agencies or professionals.

2. *Self-reports of Violent Behavior.*   Much contemporary research on family violence is likely to use one of two survey methods of collecting data, both based on self-disclosure of information, either about one's own behavior—commonly referred to as "self-report surveys"—or about one's personal victimization—commonly referred to as "victimi-

zation surveys." The self-report survey is more popular, with a variety of methods of administration, including the self-administered questionnaire (Weis and Bridges 1985) or an interview (Straus 1979), phone interview (Straus and Gelles 1986), randomized response (Tracy and Fox 1981), and diary (Steinmetz 1977). Respondents are simply asked if they have engaged in a variety of violent acts, as well as in other behaviors of interest. Self-report studies show that violence is much more common than is represented in official records (Straus 1979; Elliott and Ageton 1980; Hindelang, Hirschi, and Weis 1981). While national surveys of personal victimization show that violence among adult family members, using a broad definition of intrafamilial violence, is relatively infrequent (Hindelang, Gottfredson, and Garofalo 1978), a national self-report survey of a representative sample of family members, using a broad definition of intrafamilial violence, reports that it is so commonplace that approximately one-half of the households in America is the scene of family violence at least once a year (Straus, Gelles, and Steinmetz 1980).

Since its inception in research on juvenile delinquency in the mid-1950s (Short and Nye 1958), the self-report method of measurement has been open to criticism. The central issue is why anyone, even if they could remember accurately, would tell the truth about their criminal behavior. Consequently, self-reports may be susceptible to distortion from inaccurate recall, differential interpretation of questions, and motivated or unconscious response error. When the questions are about one's involvement in family violence, these problems may be especially severe—the norms regarding family privacy, along with respondents' fear of the consequences, may produce socially desirable responses. The direction of error may not always be predictable; respondents may underreport their violence in most cases (e.g., a father reporting his violence toward his daughter) but overreport in other cases (e.g., a younger brother reporting his violence toward his older brother). In short, the self-report method is currently a preferred source of data on family violence, but it is not immune to many of the problems of survey research.

3. *Reports of Personal Victimization.*   Surveys of personal victimization within the family are rare. More typical, though not frequently carried out, is a general survey that includes both self-reports of violent behavior and of personal victimization, and that may ask about the relationship between the offender and victim (Straus 1979; Weis and Bridges 1985). The annual National Crime Survey (NCS) of the

Bureau of the Census and the Department of Justice is a national source of victimization data on crime, including violence between intimates.

The NCS shows that interpersonal violence is a relatively infrequent crime, although more prevalent than official records indicate. A comparison of the violent offenses recorded in the UCR and violent victimizations reported in the NCS suggests that between two to three times the number of violent crimes occur than are reported to the police (Hindelang 1976; Langan and Innes 1986). However, it has been shown repeatedly that these victimization surveys have trouble measuring interpersonal violence (Gove, Hughes, and Geerken 1985). Because the interviews have been carried out within the household, perhaps within earshot of the perpetrator, respondents may be less likely to report the transgression of a loved one or a potentially vindictive offender, although analyses of the British Crime Survey (Gottfredson 1984) suggest that the presence of others may increase reported victimization due to prompted recall. There is also evidence (Skogan 1981) that the NCS does not measure adequately "series victimization," where a victim experiences a number of similar crimes over a relatively short period of time.[8] An example of a series victimization is a woman who repeatedly is the victim of violence by her spouse, to the extent that she cannot discriminate one incident from another (Bureau of Justice Statistics 1984, p. 1). This type of chronic, frequent victimization is typical of violence against many spouses and children (Steinmetz 1977; Gelles and Straus 1979). The intimacy and privacy in the relationship of offender and victim, as well as the long-term, high frequency, shameful, illegal conduct, all combine to threaten the validity of responses to victimization survey items (Weis 1986a).

The most critical limitation of the NCS in research on violence against the child may be the twelve-year-old minimum age for subjects. Younger children, who are even more likely to be victims of their parents or siblings, are excluded from the sample.[9] It is assumed that it is difficult to collect data on sensitive topics from younger children, but recent experience suggests the contrary with drug use (Keyes and Block 1984) and with respondents between five and eight years old who an-

[8] Specifically, a respondent has experienced three or more victimizations of a similar type within a six-month recall period and cannot remember the details of discrete victimizations. Series victimizations are likely to be concentrated in two crimes—less serious assault and household larceny (Dodge 1984, p. 2).

[9] The minimum age for respondents is fourteen; twelve- and thirteen-year-olds have proxy interviews completed for them by a parent, while children eleven years old and younger are excluded from the sample.

swered questions about their involvement in deviant conduct (Weis and Worsley 1982). If the hurdle of parental consent can be overcome, children may provide useful data on intrafamilial victimization.

A combination of both the self-report and victimization survey techniques deserves special attention because of its centrality to survey research on family violence. The "conflict tactics" measures developed by Straus (1979) are self-reports of the behaviors—rational, verbal, and violent—that are used to resolve conflict within the family. The procedure asks the respondent to report both one's behavior and victimization, so there is a primary measure of the respondent's own violent behavior and a secondary measure of victimization. Gelles (1978) reports that both spouses are more likely to report their own victimization than their own use of violent behavior. Unfortunately, only aggregate spouse comparisons can be made because the national sample included only one spouse per sampled family, so comparisons are between *unrelated* "husbands" and "wives" rather than between members of a couple. Szinovacz (1983) has used the conflict tactics measures in research on couples, primarily to test validity, but has discovered quite variable estimates of the incidence of spousal violence; husbands tend to underreport *both* their victimization by their wives and their violence against their wives, particularly for acts like biting and kicking. Browning and Dutton (1986) report similar differential reporting with the conflict tactics scale by husbands and wives, with the former perceiving the relationship as mutually violent and the latter as more husband violent. They conclude that within couples there is "considerable disparity in recall for violence." A strong social desirability response effect may, in part, be responsible for those underreports because no "real man" gets beaten up by his wife or resorts to kicking and biting her (a "wimp effect?"). Overall, these secondary measures of victimization produce higher estimates of involvement in family violence than do self-reports, suggesting their viability as an additional source of useful data on family violence and as a means to validate self-reports of family members.

4. *Informant Reports.*   Research on family violence has relied on informants to report on the violent behavior of neighbors, parents, children, students, and friends. Gil (1970) used the "neighbor informant technique" in a National Opinion Research Center survey of child abuse. When the 1,520 respondents were asked if they had physically injured their own children, only six admitted they had; but when asked if they knew neighbors who had harmed their children, eight times as many responded affirmatively. Of course, whether the respondent had

direct knowledge of the neighbors' violence is uncertain. However, a potentially better source of informant data is a family member; spouses observe or know a great deal of the behavior that is intentionally concealed from public view, including violence (Rosenbaum and O'Leary 1981; Fagan, Hansen, and Stewart 1983).

Children are often witnesses to the violent behavior that occurs between their parents. One Scottish study reports that approximately 50 percent of the witnesses in cases of wife beating that are reported to the police are children (Dobash 1977), and it is likely that the proportion of child witnesses in cases not reported is much higher. Straus (1974) asked college students about the violent behavior of their mothers and fathers and discovered higher estimates of the incidence of parental violence than the self-reports of the parents and more violence on the part of the fathers than mothers.

Standardized informant checklists have been used in research on aggression and violence among children (Achenbach and Edelbrock 1979), asking parents to report on their children's behavior or teachers to report on their students' behavior. Techniques have also been developed to use peer informants in collecting data on crime among juveniles (Schwendinger and Schwendinger 1985), and there is no reason, at least technically, why these techniques could not be adapted to the measurement of family violence. It is also possible to combine self-report, victimization, and informant methods in one survey instrument. Respondents are simply asked about their own violent behavior and personal victimization, as well as that of designated others, for example, parents and siblings.

5. *Direct Observation.*   Whereas informants report their observations of violence to a researcher, direct observation depends on the researcher's own observations of the phenomenon under study. The observation may range from rigorous coding of discrete behaviors in experimental settings to participant observation in natural settings. Observation studies are rare, probably less than 5 percent of current empirical research on the family (Gelles 1978) and even less on family violence. Most of the direct observation studies of family violence are typically performed within the home and report an even greater incidence of violence than self-report or victimization surveys or official measures (Burgess and Conger 1978; Patterson, Stouthamer-Loeber, and Loeber 1979). However, these types of studies usually use amenable subjects and broad, sometimes vague, definitions of violence and aggression. They focus on less serious aggression, hostility, and con-

flict, particularly among children. Serious, harmful, violent behavior is not a focus of observation, simply because it is a low base-rate phenomenon and not committed in front of outsiders. It is also more difficult to do observations of families who live in high crime rate neighborhoods and who may be less cooperative subjects (Weis and Sumi 1985). Therefore, the kind of violent crime, particularly committed by adults, that could lead to criminal justice sanctions is not to be seen.

It is not evident that direct observation studies add much to what we learn about harmful acts of serious violence among children and adults from other data sources that take less time and money and offer at least equal scientific rigor. Observation studies may be more useful for specific research purposes—for example, to enrich evaluation research on the dynamics of family relationships or to augment more general etiological research. As a source of complementary data on predisposing factors to more serious violence in later years, an observation study may be most appropriate, particularly if the families are selected on the dependent criterion to begin with—for example, observation of "stress" in violent families sampled from criminal justice records. Otherwise, there is typically very little data collected on the dependent variable of interest here, but much more on a variety of independent variables. Indeed, a strength of observation research is in the study of "normal" families from whom much can be learned about the prevention and control of violence. In short, if one wants to study less serious, aggressive behavior, especially among children, direct observation is adequate. But if the focus is serious, potentially criminal, violent behavior among family members, including adults, direct observation is less adequate. In general, other methods will produce more, and often better, data in less time for less money.

These data sources—official records, self-reports, victimization reports, informants, and observation—produce discrepant estimates of prevalence, incidence, and correlates of violence. For example, research using official record samples of violent families supports the view that violence occurs disproportionately among families that are poor (Pelton 1978; Monahan 1981; Fagan, Hansen, and Stewart 1983), but studies using self-reports of violence typically find weaker relationships between violence and social class (Johnson 1980; Straus, Gelles, and Steinmetz 1980; Hindelang, Hirschi, and Weis 1981; Brownfield 1986). These differences are, in good part, a consequence of the differences in basic methods of measurement that are typical of each of the data sources (Bridges and Weis 1988). These inconsistencies confuse the basic "facts" on family violence, hampering empirical research, theorizing, and control efforts. However, many of these discrepancies can be reconciled as they have been in the more general criminological research on measurement (Hindelang, Hirschi, and Weis 1979)—if more attention is devoted to other methodological limitations that are more specific to research on family violence.

C. Samples

Most of the samples in empirical research on family violence have been small, nonrepresentative, purposive, or convenience samples of "official" offenders, clients, or patients from the records of criminal justice, social service, or health agencies (Spinetta and Rigler 1972; Bridges and Weis 1985). Control groups are usually not included in the sample design, and the selection and matching criteria and procedures are usually rudimentary when attempts are made to generate a purposive sample based on matching "official" subjects with others (Plotkin et al. 1981).

These kinds of samples, produced by "sampling on the dependent variable" (Hirschi and Selvin 1967), limit the ability to generalize to those involved in family violence who do *not* become patients, clients, or offenders—and the research evidence shows that the majority do not. It was not until the early 1970s that general population samples were used in family violence research (e.g., Straus 1979), although samples in family violence research are seldom randomly selected. Given the relatively low base rate of serious violence, nonprobability samples, based on known-group, snowball, stratified, or cluster sampling procedures of identified or at-risk families or individuals, will be necessary in most research, with the exception of large, well-funded projects. Consequently, researchers must be careful to specify the relation between the sample and the population from which it is drawn, otherwise the ability to generalize may be no better than that from samples of official offenders or victims.

Other ways of constituting study samples—monitoring police radio calls for family disturbances, following up on newspaper reports of police activities, pursuing legal notices of divorce actions, placing ads in newspapers or magazines for subjects (Gelles 1978)—have been suggested or tried, but with the same kinds of problems of nonrepresentativeness, diminished generalizability, and limited utility of findings.

Even the best national probability sample of over 2,000 married couples in 1975 (Straus, Gelles, and Steinmetz 1980) has problems regarding sample characteristics. The sample includes respondents from "intact" families only, the children are between thirteen and seventeen years old, and interviews were done with husbands in half of them and wives in the other half. Consequently, intrafamilial violence in single-head-of-household families, transitional or unstable families, or nontraditional family organizations is not represented. Likewise, a disproportionate amount of child abuse, including murder, happens to children under three years old (American Humane Association 1978). These sample characteristics also limit the self-reports to parents only, and to only one of them, which means that the violent behavior of only one parent, who may or may not be the primary offender, is reported.

The 1985 "ten years after" version of this national survey has corrected most of these sample deficiencies, except for the last—sampling only one partner in a couple (Straus and Gelles 1986). This eliminates individual-level offender and victim comparisons and analyses since data have to be aggregated across "unrelated" husbands and wives. It also introduces an uncontrolled source of measurement error—the different perceptions of violence experienced by a "couple" that are reported by only one of its members. Female respondents will tend to overreport, while male respondents will tend to underreport, both perpetration and victimization. Since the over- and underreporting will vary by couple, aggregating across individual representatives of a couple may produce invalid statistics. If one had couple data—for example, a "couple score" representing the mean value of violence—there might be different results (cf. Szinovacz 1983; Browning and Dutton 1986).

A meta-analysis of the effects of study design characteristics on correlates of violence shows that the type of sample is second to the data source in its effects on empirical research findings. For example, the average correlation across studies between social class and family violence is weaker in studies that use probability samples. Even studies that use probability samples in combination with official data produce weaker correlations between social class and family violence than studies that use purposive samples (Bridges and Weis 1985, p. 16). Drawing subjects from groups of officially identified offenders or victims of family violence is more likely to generate an inverse relation between social class and violence than probability sampling, *even if* official data are used in both to measure violence (Sederstrom 1986). Overall, inadequate samples typify research on family violence, but even studies with more rigorous sampling procedures produce research findings that may be affected by the characteristics of the sample design, as well as by the research design.

D. Research Designs

The cross-sectional nonexperimental design has been predominant in empirical studies of family violence. This is probably due to the overwhelming reliance on official data sources to constitute small convenience samples of subjects known to be involved in the type of family violence under investigation—for example, child victims of violence. Unfortunately, cross-sectional designs are more limited than experimental designs in their capacity to study etiological factors, particularly the temporal ordering of causal effects on behavior. A good cross-sectional design (e.g., Straus and Gelles 1986) can produce a variety of invaluable findings but is generally limited to producing static relations between variables or dynamic relations that are dependent on the haphazard and faulty recall of respondents. For example, even studies of the intergenerational transmission of violence—a concept that is theoretically and empirically dependent on the emergence of etiological factors and violent behavior over long periods of time—typically use cross-sectional designs and the memories of respondents to recall details of their abuse as children or the violence of their parents or spouses (Straus 1979; Pagelow 1981; Rosenbaum and O'Leary 1981; Herrenkohl, Herrenkohl, and Toedter 1983). Of course, long-term retrospective recall, especially over many years and about the violent behavior of intimates, can be quite inaccurate and compromise the validity of research findings (Weis 1986a).

The research designs that compensate for the weaknesses of cross-sectional designs—longitudinal and experimental—are extremely rare in research on family violence, particularly on serious violence that is committed by adults. For example, it has been estimated that less than five percent of the empirical research studies on family violence use some form of control or comparison group (Bolton et al. 1981). And most of the experimental research, though using control groups, is on the relation between child abuse and aggressive behavior in children (Reidy 1977; Kinard 1980; Bousha and Twentyman 1984) and usually collects data at one time or at two times separated by a short interval, in some cases only a couple of hours.

Longitudinal designs—whether panel, time series, or cohort designs—are more useful in examining temporal changes and developmental processes that may be related to family violence, perhaps over many years and across generations. Three sources of national, annual time series data have been discussed—the Uniform Crime Reports, National Crime Survey, and Central Registers of child abuse and neglect. Another source—if data collected at two times ten years apart on two samples qualify as a time series—is the National Survey of Family Violence, 1975 and 1985 (Straus and Gelles 1986). Because of very similar study designs and almost identical measures, comparisons of findings between the two surveys are possible—a critical feature of time series data. There are also more local time series data—for example, the records of police, social welfare, and health agencies—but they are limited in scope and reliability.

Most time series are based on official record data and are useful for assessing changes in aggregate prevalence rates. They are quite limited, however, in the kind of information on offenders, victims, and incidents that is necessary to investigate developmental processes and etiology. Survey time series data are better in this regard, but the NCS is still inadequate in the measurement of independent variables, and other surveys, like the National Family Violence Survey, are not done often enough to investigate possible changes in etiological factors over time.

Beyond these incomplete and flawed time series of data on violence—most of it is not on family violence per se—there are even fewer empirical studies that have used longitudinal designs in research on family violence, particularly panel or cohort designs. Prospective designs are scarce, and those that incorporate experimental components—considered one of the most powerful research designs available for etiological research on crime (Farrington, Ohlin, and Wilson 1986)—are virtually nonexistent. Most of the longitudinal research on family violence focuses on the cycle of violence or the relation between early and later violence. Specifically, studies have investigated the relation between one's victimization as a child and later aggressive or troublesome behavior (Kinard 1980) or later juvenile delinquency (Gutierres and Reich 1981; McCord 1983).

Retrospective design studies (Lewis and Shanok 1977; Alfaro 1978) are typical, usually employing reverse record checks to investigate abuse in the history of a sample of official delinquents. Prospective design studies of the emergence of juvenile or adult violence out of childhood abuse are very rare (Bolton, Reich and Gutierres 1977). Most of the retrospective and prospective design studies are purposive samples of officially designated offenders or victims, making control groups even more desirable. However, with few exceptions (Lewis and Shanok

1977; McCord 1983) control groups are not used, which compromises the external validity of findings. The inadequacies of official record data may also compromise the validity of longitudinal studies. For example, youngsters who have records of crime and of abuse may have acquired both for the same etiological reasons—that is, abuse in early childhood may not cause juvenile delinquency, but, rather, poor parenting could be responsible for both (Newberger, Newberger, and Hampton 1983).

Prospective longitudinal designs are more evident in contemporary research on crime (e.g., Elliott and Ageton 1980), in part because of the difference in base rates of crime and family violence. Because perhaps 25 percent of juveniles acquire police records in many communities, including many who have committed a serious crime, a probability sample of fewer than 1,500 subjects will produce sufficient juvenile crime over a number of years to make the study worthwhile (Hindelang, Hirschi, and Weis 1981). Violence is the least frequent of crimes, particularly serious violence between intimates. Consequently, a much larger sample would need to be drawn even for a cross-sectional study; for example, the 1985 National Family Violence probability sample consisted of 6,002 households (Straus and Gelles 1986). For a prospective longitudinal study, perhaps over many years, the sample size might have to be so big as to be unwieldy and prohibitively expensive.

With purposive sampling of the panel in a prospective design, some of the problems created by probability sampling may be overcome, but other more generic problems remain. For example, one does not see prospective studies of adult violence emerging out of childhood histories of abuse because of the time required to follow a panel from childhood to mature adulthood. This entails a substantial professional and personal commitment from the researcher and costly extramural support in the provision of money and resources. These types of studies are extremely expensive in many important ways.

They are also difficult to implement and maintain over long periods of time. Research support is not usually granted for more than a few years at a time, making a study of intended longer duration vulnerable to the loss of grant support with changes in agency policy, personnel, priorities, and budget. Subject attrition can be difficult to manage if the sample is relatively large, dispersed geographically, mobile, and must be followed over a number of years. Monitoring, tracking, and recapturing the sample for wave after wave of data collection is a daunting management task. The erosion of design integrity over time is also troublesome, particularly if the design includes an experimental component requiring random allocation of subjects to study and control groups. Changes in the sources of extramural support may lead to changes in design or even in the substantive focus of the study, while trying to maintain some semblance of the original study design and sample. Additionally, there may be pressures in the implementation environment that compromise the research design, for example, subjects who categorically refuse to accept a feature of the design—the parents of aggressive boys who absolutely refuse to be randomly assigned to anything. Finally, the confounding of age, period, and cohort effects over many years can diminish the validity of research findings unless there is an experimental component to the research design, multiple cohorts are utilized, or statistical corrections are made in analyses to control for their possible independent and interactive effects on findings (Klepinger and Weis 1985).

Longitudinal, prospective designs including experimental components and multiple cohorts are considered the designs of the future by some criminologists (Farrington, Ohlin, and Wilson 1986). Whether they can be applied to studies of even rarer phenomena, even more sensitive topics, and even more fragile research contexts is not clear. They certainly are not without problems and limitations, particularly if multiple cohorts and experimentation are included; these additional features make implementation, monitoring, and data collection even more difficult (Kerr 1984). Some critics of longitudinal designs suggest that the benefits in additional knowledge derived from them do not justify the large investments of money that they require. Gottfredson and Hirschi (1986) argue that cross-sectional designs are preferable because they can produce the same kinds of results in much shorter periods of time for much less money. In summary, the flawed research designs of most studies on family violence are obstacles to good research.

E. Measurement: Measures and Validity

One other major study design characteristic can affect the validity and reliability of findings—the measurement of study variables. There are many measurement issues and problems in the current empirical research on family violence, but the characteristics of the measures and their validity will be the focus of discussion here.

The most fundamental question is, What to include in the *measures,* or operational definitions, of family violence? Official records provide their own answer—what you see is what you get—and they are extremely difficult to modify so as to include information that is not routinely collected for agency record-keeping purposes. However, survey measures are under the direct and immediate control of the researcher, and, consequently, there are practically as many different measures as there are researchers. Some measures reflect a conceptualization of family violence as a unidimensional phenomenon (e.g., Straus 1979), while others represent it as more multidimensional (e.g., Weis and Bridges 1985; Fagan and Wexler 1985). The former focuses on violent "acts rather than on outcomes," while the latter includes behavior, outcomes, and situational characteristics in a more comprehensive characterization. This is not simply a matter of arbitrary preference but, rather, reflects the complexity of the context within which family violence occurs. If one wants accurate descriptions of a complex phenomenon, a number of factors need to be measured. The critical multidimensionality of criminal incidents has been recognized for many years by criminologists, leading to the development of measures that take into account the legal seriousness of the offense, the number of offenders and victims, the presence of weapons, the nature and degree of injury, and so on (e.g., Sellin and Wolfgang 1964). Multidimensional measures of family violence should include many of these kinds of factors, as well as others.

To define the domain of family violence adequately, the meaning of family violence must be specified, both nominally and operationally. The measurements of "family" in family violence are often inadequate or entirely missing in a variety of data sources (e.g., the UCR and NCS) and studies. The nature of the *relationship* between the offender and victim needs to be determined. The measurement of "violence" needs to be sensitive to social context.

Measures of the behavior, its consequences, and situational characteristics are necessary to sort out sources of systematic error. Beginning with *behavior*, many studies do not distinguish between completed, attempted, or threatened acts. This is an important distinction because many attempted or threatened acts of violence are not carried out; instead of asking how many times in the past year a respondent has "stabbed someone," "attempted to stab" might be added in order to tap more of this often unmeasured violence.

Consequences are also critical to the description of family violence, particularly the characteristics of physical injury and degree of harm, and formal and informal social reactions to the violence. Without measures of the type and seriousness of injury, there is no way to know whether a self-reported "hitting or punching" is a trivial or serious violent act or, in legal terms, whether it is a simple or aggravated assault. Measures of formal and informal social reactions aid in assessments of the "perceived" seriousness of the violence by victims, witnesses, interested parties, and, perhaps, even offenders. For example, violent behavior reported to the police is perceived by the complainant as sufficiently serious and harmful to be reported, and it may also be more serious in its consequences for the offender and the victim. Less formal reactions might include medical attention for the physical injury or the escape of a victim of spousal violence to a shelter. Measurement of both types of consequences—physical injury and social reaction—provides information on both the actual and perceived seriousness of the violence.

There are also a number of *situational characteristics* that, if not measured, threaten the validity of findings on family violence. Unlike official crime data, survey measures often do *not* distinguish between offender and victim, aggressor and defender, or perpetrator and defendant. For example, a respondent may report that she punched her husband, but the resulting data will not indicate whether she intentionally initiated the violence or was simply defending herself. The social and legal distinctions between aggression and self-defense are crucial, as are their implications for measurement.

Use of a weapon in a violent situation is often an aggravating circumstance in the law and is also an indicator of the seriousness of the act. Ascertaining the type of weapon, how it was used, and with what effect is essential. Otherwise, a respondent may report the "use" of a knife in a violent confrontation, which could range from falsely telling a victim he had a knife in his pocket to stabbing the victim in the stomach.

More generic situational characteristics are not as necessary to rigorous measurement but are useful in describing other important features of the social context—for example, where the violent behavior occurred, the number and characteristics of people present, when the incident happened, and its duration. Poor measurement of those types of factors can also distort study findings.

Perhaps the most important measurement issue is the *validity* of the data collected. How accurate are the measures of offenders, victims, and incidents, of their critical characteristics, and of other variables of interest? Validation research has taken a backseat to the quest for prevalence estimates of family violence, and factors associated with it. In the long run, the validation of measures is the critical foundation on which are built better research, explanations, policy decisions, and program outcomes. Unfortunately, validation research on the measurement of family violence is rare and not particularly rigorous, and it is apparent that there are a number of threats to the validity of measures, and obstacles to doing validation research.

Each of the five major data sources has its own validity problems. Official records suffer from variations in definitions, different reporting and recording practices, and biased samples of violent behaviors and persons. Observations are intrusive, restricted to front room behavior, focus on less serious violence, and may be affected by observer and sample biases. Informants can only report on behavior and individuals they know, which places severe restrictions on the usefulness of the data. Victimization surveys are victim based rather than offender based, and their validity is threatened by the interview context and the intimate relationship between victim and offender. Finally, even though self-report surveys have become a favored measurement approach, critics do not believe that valid and reliable research can be based on self-reports of intrafamilial violent behavior (Pelton 1978).

Since self-reports play a central role in current empirical research on family violence and have a greater potential for modification and improvement than, say, official records, they are the primary focus of discussion here. Special attention is devoted to the self-report technique used in the National Family Violence Surveys, the conflict tactics scale (Straus 1979). It represents a model of survey measurement on family violence; there is some research available on its validity and reliability, and if it represents the best the field has to offer, the magnitude of validity problems for other survey measures should be apparent.

Research on measures of sensitive topics, including crime, shows the self-report technique to be quite reliable (Straus 1979; Hindelang, Hirschi, and Weis 1981). However, when using survey measures of intrafamilial violence, the validity of answers must be a predominant concern. Gelles (1978) suggests that the most persistent question in the study of sensitive topics is whether the subjects told the truth. Unfortunately, no study has examined thoroughly the validity of the reported prevelance and incidence estimates and correlates of family violence. And studies of family violence typically use weak validation criteria. For example, Bulcroft and Straus (1975) used parents' reports to assess the validity of college student children's reports of violence in the home, a procedure that leaves it unclear who is perceiving, remembering, and telling the most truth. It is clear that parents who engage in violence are unreliable informants—they tend to overestimate the degree of violence in their families (Marsh, Johnston, and Kovitz 1983). Violent youngsters also see their families as violent, even though independent evidence suggests they are not (Fagan and Wexler 1984). Overall, Straus (1979, p. 83) has concluded that there is "no definitive evidence supporting the validity of the conflict tactics scales. Neither, however, is there complete lack of evidence." Surely, however, the burden of proof is to provide sufficient empirical evidence of the data's validity, not of its invalidity.

There is little use in family violence research of external validation criteria, whether based on "known group differences" as defined by official records or on direct comparisons in individual cases of self-reports with official records. This reciprocal validation of self-reports and official records is common procedure in validation research on crime generally (e.g., Hindelang, Hirschi, and Weis 1981) but is extremely rare in research on family violence crimes.

Direct comparisons of the incidence estimates and correlates produced by different methods of measurement are rare in family violence research, even though this could often be done. For example, it is known that the apparent relation between social class and child abuse is different for official and self-report measures (Gelles and Straus 1979), but comparative analyses of both measures within the same study on the same sample of respondents are unknown in family violence research. This type of correlational validity is crucial for any rigorous overall assessment of validity because it both uses an external validation criterion and represents a comparison of two different methods. When comparisons using the same method are made—for example, the comparisons of parent and children survey reports (e.g., Bulcroft and Straus 1975)—the validity of coefficients may be inflated because of a same-method effect. At minimum they will represent a much weaker test of concurrent, correlational validity than would comparisons of different methods.

The common reliance on a single family member, typically the mother, as a respondent, contributes to inaccurate reports because there is differential validity by respondent characteristic; husbands, wives, and children perceive and report different rates of spouse and child abuse (Szinovacz 1983). Unfortunately, it is difficult to know which family members provide the most accurate accounts of various kinds of incidents. There is evidence that the accuracy of reporting varies with the respondent's education and income and with the ratio of husband-to-wife power. However, these types of apparent response effects have been noted but not investigated in any detail (Bradburn and Sudman 1979).

The dearth of "response effects" research on survey measures of family violence is alarming, particularly because the characteristics of family violence have the potential to distort survey responses and, therefore, compromise the validity of research findings (Loftus 1980; Torangeau 1984; Weis 1986a). Family violence is an especially "sensitive" topic; violent behavior among intimates is emotionally charged and traumatic; violence is a high salience behavior because it is relatively low in frequency but can produce serious, harmful consequences; intrafamilial violence is often "serial" or chronic, which means that similar behaviors are committed over long periods; victimizing one's loved ones is highly undesirable behavior that can bring shame and guilt on the perpetrator, as well as on the victim, and perhaps even formal sanctions; and alcohol seems to be involved in a large percentage of cases of family violence.

Schulman (1979) reports that the administration of Straus's Conflict Tactics Scale by telephone interview yielded a weaker relation with social class than did administration by face-to-face interview. This suggests that there may be task-related response effects; how surveys are administered may produce different correlates. Respondent effects on validity are unfortunately only paid lip service in much family violence research. Many researchers mention that the topic of intrafamilial violence may cause respondents to give less than accurate answers because they fear the consequences or because they want to provide socially desirable responses (Gelles 1978). However, these and other response effects, including method of administration, anonymity of respondent, question wording and content, specificity of questions, recall periods, response categories, salience of the question topics, and respondent characteristics that may affect responses, are not investigated systematically (cf. Torangeau 1984).

Given the relatively regular occurrence of violent acts within some families, substantial detrimental response effects should be expected (cf. Weis 1986a). Violence against children, for example, is often a chronic series of events, with single incidents accounting for only 6 percent of all cases and the average number of assaults of victims being about eleven per year (Gelles and Straus 1979). And 20 percent of women victims of spousal violence are regular, chronic victims (Steinmetz 1977). Perpetrators and victims are less likely to provide accurate answers to queries about this kind of situation than about other violent incidents. No one wants to remember much less disclose much family violence, regardless of the circumstances.

One final major obstacle to validation research is the lack of isomorphism or similarity between behaviors in different data sources and studies in terms of measured content, seriousness, and degree of harm (Hindelang, Hirschi, and Weis 1979). That is, the domains of intrafamilial violent behavior as represented in the various data sources are not the same; there may not be sufficient overlap even to consider assessment of validity by comparing their correlates. For example, the conflict tactics "violence" scale items range from throwing an object or grabbing someone to using a knife or gun on someone (Straus 1979). Many of these types of acts, particularly the less serious and less harmful ones, will not appear in police records because they are not actionable. The effect on study findings is obvious—they will differ because the violent behaviors represented in each data source also differ. Methodological adjustments, particularly standardizing on content and seriousness of behaviors, that have been made in validation research on crime (Hindelang, Hirschi, and Weis 1981) are lacking in family violence research. However, if such adjustments are made in the future, many of the discrepancies in the correlates produced by different measures of family violence may be resolved, leading to complementary and confirming findings on the basic facts of family violence and, therefore, more consistent and useful information for research, policy decisions, and program planning.

III. Strategies to Improve Research

Much has been learned over the past two decades about family violence, but the field remains underdeveloped. There is confusion regarding the basic facts of family violence, due in good part to methodological problems. A useful first step toward improving research on family violence is the development of long-term research strategies. A strategy is not a prescription but a plan to accomplish a goal. It defines the boundaries within which more concrete means to the end will be applied. The goal here is to build a stronger scientific data base for family violence theory, policy, and practice. Specifically, what needs to be done *methodologically* to build knowledge and enhance our understanding of family violence?

Obviously, many things that would improve family violence research are essential to good research in general. Good methodology is requisite to good science. So the most general strategy, to put it simply, is to do good research. However, as discussed earlier, there are also unique methodological issues, questions, and problems in family violence research, and they require special consideration and, perhaps, empirical investigation. There is a pervasive need for more methodological research on family violence; without it, many methodological issues cannot be resolved. Some of them seem particularly important to improving research on family violence.[10]

One fundamental methodological issue is whether family violence is empirically and theoretically distinct from other kinds of violence. What are the relations between, and causes of, family violence and general violence? If they are correlated, and if their correlates are the same, then, on methodological grounds, separate studies of family violence and general violence may be unnecessary if the only important difference between samples is the difference in the relationship between victim and offender. Of course, there are other good grounds for research on family violence—for example, policy formulation, prevention, and control—and there is evidence that the correlates of family violence and general violence are indeed different (Bridges and Weis 1985). However, much more theoretical research attention needs to be focused on both the conceptual *and* empirical distinctions between family violence and general violence. Theories of family violence and related empirical research should produce more compelling scientific evidence of the need for a separate research enterprise on family violence. Otherwise, research in the field will probably not be taken as seriously as it should be, while continuing to suffer from the methodological limitations that have hampered it in the past.

Precise theoretical constructs and definitions of the various types of family violence should be a primary concern to researchers, policymakers, and practitioners alike. Efforts to standardize or at least agree on the critical elements of definitions of "family" and "violence" would go far to improve theory and research, facilitate comparisons of findings

---

[10] This does not mean that they are necessarily the most critical methodological issues in the field or that their attendant research strategies are the only, or correct, way to attempt to resolve them.

and studies, and provide the basis for building cumulative knowledge on family violence. Since theories are the beginning of the research process, systematic efforts to test existing theories of family violence and to construct new theories are needed. Research, when possible, should be designed to test theories since one of the limitations of current knowledge in the field is reliance on untested theories borrowed, in whole or part, from a variety of disciplines and other substantive areas.

Given the critical importance of national and state data sources on family violence to a variety of research purposes, concerted and continuous efforts should be made to consider family violence data requirements in the design of general data collecting and reporting efforts. For example, the Uniform Crime Reports should be modified to facilitate the systematic collection of data on the age of the offender and victim and the specific relationship between the two for all six crimes of interpersonal violence that are family related. The UCRs should also be modified to facilitate the recording of "incidents" of family violence, whether they lead to arrest or not. The National Crime Survey data collection procedures should be modified, for at least some subsample surveys, so that interviews are carried out in complete privacy and it is made clear that victimizations do not necessarily have to be perceived as crimes before they can be reported. Special efforts should also be made to survey respondents under twelve years old, perhaps in special pilot studies in order to develop the research methodologies necessary to collect valid and reliable reports from this type of respondent.

There is a need for coordinated statistics on all aspects of each of the types of family violence, such as the individual states' registers of child abuse and neglect. There have been recent efforts to coordinate federal-level information on children and families (Zill, Peterson, and Moore 1984); the *Sourcebook of Criminal Justice Statistics* (e.g., U.S. Department of Justice 1987) is a good model for a compilation of the statistics on family violence that may come out of these coordinated efforts.

Because research on family violence is carried out for different reasons by different types of researchers, a long-term research agenda should include a variety of study designs rather than only the apparently most rigorous (or popular) design. A great deal of descriptive and exploratory research needs to be done, perhaps with study design characteristics that would be inadequate for theory testing purposes. Research should proceed on a number of fronts but with awareness of both the strengths and weaknesses inherent in any particular study design and, therefore, the validity and utility of the research results.

For example, clinical studies may be well suited to exploring causes of spousal violence and, thereby, developing better survey measures. Or a cross-sectional design using police record data can be used to describe and understand law enforcement handling of child abuse cases. If researchers who study family violence educate themselves about the differential methodological adequacy of various study designs, the field will be well served.

The measures used in family violence research are a particularly perplexing design problem. Progress in the field depends on more precise measurement. Fundamental substantive issues—for example, the dimensionality of family violence or the temporal properties of chronic spousal violence—simply cannot be addressed, much less resolved, unless more attention is paid to the psychometric properties of measures and their validity and reliability.

A variety of measurement approaches should be used, tested, and refined. Given the often contrary findings and the validity problems that typify this subject, multimethod and multiple-indicator research should be encouraged and used more often. This is particularly true for those data collection techniques that are not favored because they are difficult to use and have more apparent validity problems. For example, both observation and informant methods of measurement hold great promise as techniques to validate self-report data and to tap the more personal and intimate aspects of family violence that a questionnaire or agency-generated record simply cannot provide.

Experimental research on different methods of measuring family violence is needed to assess the accuracy and consistency of the various data collection techniques that produce what we consider "facts" about family violence. There is not one validation study of family violence with the kind of experimental design and comparison of measures on the same sample that would allow a rigorous assessment of relative validity. This type of research has been done on measures of crime and general violence but not on family violence. A focus of this type of validation research should be the conflict tactics measures because they have been used often, subjected to some validity and reliability testing, and provide the potential for standardized survey measurement.

Research on the validity and reliability of data and findings needs to be treated as integral to good research on family violence. This is sufficiently important that a separate research and development project on measurement strategies and methods would be useful. One might also consider a requirement that all federally funded research on family violence devote a fixed percentage of budget to assessing and demonstrating the validity and reliability of data and findings.

For both self-report and victimization survey methods, research should address the variety of potential "response effects" that seriously threaten the validity of answers to questions. Research in the context of the family on the kinds of violent criminal behavior that are typically frequent, emotionally traumatic, and perpetrated among offenders and victims who are intimates seems to be unusually vulnerable to the whole range of response effects in survey research.

Finally, rather than focus attention and resources on the improvement of estimates of prevalence and incidence, more research needs to be done on the correlates and causes of family violence. It does little good to know that there is a certain volume of family violence in our society if we do not know who is doing it, where and when it is happening, how and why it is being done, and whether our interventions are effective. The answers to these kinds of questions are, ultimately, crucial to preventing and controlling family violence and, thereby, reducing its prevalence and incidence.

REFERENCES

Achenbach, T. M., and C. Edelbrock. 1979. "The Child Behavior Profile: II." *Journal of Consulting and Clinical Psychology* 47:223–33.

Alfaro, J. 1978. *Child Abuse and Subsequent Delinquent Behavior.* New York: Select Committee on Child Abuse.

American Humane Association. 1978. *National Analysis of Official Child Neglect and Abuse Reporting.* Englewood, Colo.: American Humane Association.

Baldwin, J. A., and J. E. Oliver. 1975. "Epidemiology and Family Characteristics of Severely Abused Children." *British Journal of Preventive Social Medicine* 29:205–21.

Belair, R. R. 1985. *Data Quality of Criminal History Records.* Washington, D.C.: U.S. Government Printing Office.

Berk, S., and D. Loseke. 1981. "Handling Family Violence: The Situational Determinants of Police Arrests in Domestic Disturbances." *Law and Society Review* 15:317–46.

Besharov, D. J. 1977. "Delinquency Patterns in Maltreated Children and Siblings." *Victimology* 2:349–57.

———. 1978. "Legal Aspects of Reporting Known and Suspected Child Abuse and Neglect." In *Abused and Neglected Child: Multidisciplinary Court Practice,* edited by Douglas J. Besharov. New York: Practicing Law Institute.

————. 1981. "Toward Better Research on Child Abuse and Neglect: Making Definitional Issues an Explicit Methodological Concern." *Child Abuse and Neglect* 5:383–90.

Bolton, F. G., Roy H. Laner, Dorothy S. Gai, and Sandra P. Kane. 1981. "The Study of Child Maltreatment: When Is Research . . . Research?" *Journal of Family Issues* 2:535–39.

Bolton, F. G., J. W. Reich, and J. E. Gutierres. 1977. "Delinquency Patterns in Maltreated Children and Siblings." *Victimology* 2:349–57.

Bousha, D. M., and C. T. Twentyman. 1984. "Mother-Child Interactional Style in Abuse, Neglect, and Control Groups: Naturalistic Observations in the Home." *Journal of Abnormal Psychology* 93:106–14.

Bradburn, N. M., and S. Sudman. 1979. *Improving Interview Methods and Questionnaire Design.* San Francisco: Jossey-Bass.

Bridges, G. S., and J. G. Weis. 1984. "A Meta-analysis of Correlates of Violence." Paper presented at the annual meeting of the American Society of Criminology, Cincinnati, November.

————. 1985. *Study Design and Its Effects on Correlates of Violent Behavior.* Seattle: University of Washington, Center for Law and Justice.

————. 1988. "Measuring Violent Behavior: Effects of Study Design on Reported Correlates of Violence." In *Violent Crime, Violent Criminals*, edited by Marvin E. Wolfgang and Neil A. Weiner. Beverly Hills, Calif.: Sage.

Brownfield, D. 1986. "Social Class and Violent Behavior." *Criminology* 24:421–38.

Browning, J., and D. Dutton. 1986. "Assessment of Wife Assault with the Conflict Tactics Scale: Using Couple Data to Quantify the Differential Reporting Effect." *Journal of Marriage and the Family* 48:375–79.

Bulcroft, R., and M. A. Straus. 1975. "Validity of Husband, Wife, and Child Reports of Intrafamily Violence and Power." Durham: University of New Hampshire, Family Violence Research Program.

Bureau of Justice Statistics. 1984. *The National Crime Survey: Working Papers, Volume II: Methodological Studies.* Washington, D.C.: U.S. Government Printing Office.

Burgdorf, K., and C. Eldred. 1978. *System of Operational Definitions.* Rockville, Md.: Westat.

Burgess, R. L. 1979. "Family Violence: Some Implications from Evolutionary Biology." Paper presented at the annual meeting of the American Society of Criminology, Philadelphia, November.

Burgess, R. L., and R. D. Conger. 1978. "Family Interaction in Abusive, Neglectful, and Normal Families." *Child Development* 49:1163–73.

Coleman, D. H., and M. A. Straus. 1980. "Alcohol Abuse and Family Violence." In *Alcohol, Drug Abuse, and Aggression*, edited by E. Gottheil, K. A. Druley, T. E. Skoloda, and H. M. Waxman. Springfield, Ill.: Thomas.

Daley, M. R., and I. Piliavin. 1982. " 'Violence against Children' Revisited: Some Necessary Clarification of Findings from a Major National Study." *Journal of Social Science Research* 5:61–81.

Dobash, R. E. 1977. "Relationship between Violence Directed at Women and

Violence Directed against Children within the Family Setting." Scotland: Select Committee on Violence in the Family.

Dobash, R. E., and R. Dobash. 1979. *Violence against Wives*. New York: Free Press.

Dodge, R. W. 1984. "Series Victimization—What Is to Be Done?" In *The National Crime Survey: Working Papers, Volume II: Methodological Studies*, edited by the Bureau of Justice Statistics. Washington, D.C.: U.S. Government Printing Office.

Doernberg, D. L., and D. H. Zeigler. 1980. "Due Process vs. Data Processing: An Analysis of the Computerized Criminal History Information Systems." *New York University Law Review* 50:1110–1230.

Egeland, B., and D. Brunnquell. 1979. "An At-Risk Approach to the Study of Child Abuse: Some Preliminary Findings." *Journal of American Academy of Child Psychiatry* 18:219–35.

Elliott, D. S. In this volume. "Criminal Justice Procedures in Family Violence Crimes."

Elliott, D. S., and S. S. Ageton. 1980. "Reconciling Race and Class Differences in Self-reported and Official Estimates of Delinquency." *American Sociological Review* 45:95–110.

Fagan, J. A., K. V. Hansen, and D. K. Stewart. 1983. "Violent Men or Violent Husbands? Background Factors and Situational Correlates of Domestic and Extra-domestic Violence." In *The Dark Side of Families*, edited by David Finkelhor and associates. Beverly Hills, Calif.: Sage.

Fagan, J. A., and S. Wexler. 1984. "Family Origins of Violent Delinquents." Paper presented at the Second National Conference for Family Violence Researchers, University of New Hampshire, Durham, July.

———. 1985. "Complex Behaviors and Simple Measures: Understanding Violence in Families." Paper presented at the annual meeting of the American Society of Criminology, San Diego, November.

Farrington, D. P., L. E. Ohlin, and J. Q. Wilson. 1986. *Understanding and Controlling Crime: Toward a New Research Strategy*. New York: Springer-Verlag.

Federico, R. C. 1979. *Sociology*. Reading, Mass.: Addison-Wesley.

Garbarino, J. 1977. "The Human Ecology of Child Maltreatment." *Journal of Marriage and the Family* 39:721–35.

Gelles, R. J. 1973. "Child Abuse as Psychopathology: A Sociological Critique and Reformulation." *American Journal of Orthopsychiatry* 43:611–21.

———. 1978. "Methods for Studying Sensitive Family Topics." *American Journal of Orthopsychiatry* 48:408–24.

———. 1980. "Violence in the Family: A Review of Research in the Seventies." *Journal of Marriage and the Family* 42:873–85.

———. 1983. "An Exchange/Control Theory." In *The Dark Side of Families*, edited by David Finkelhor. Beverly Hills, Calif.: Sage.

Gelles, R. J., and M. A. Straus. 1979. "Determinants of Violence in the Family: Toward a Theoretical Integration." In *Contemporary Theories about the Family*, edited by Wesley R. Burr, Reuben Hill, F. Ivan Nye, and Ira L. Reiss. New York: Free Press.

158   Joseph G. Weis

Gerbner, G., C. S. Ross, and E. Zigler, eds. 1980. *Child Abuse and Agenda for Action*. Oxford: Oxford University Press.

Gil, David G. 1970. *Violence against Children: Physical Child Abuse in the United States*. Cambridge, Mass.: Harvard University Press.

Giovannoni, J. M., and R. M. Becerra. 1979. *Defining Child Abuse*. New York: Free Press.

Golden, R. M., and S. F. Messner. 1987. "Dimensions of Racial Inequality and Rates of Violent Crime." *Criminology* 25:525–41.

Gottfredson, M. 1984. *Victims of Crime: The Dimensions of Risk*. London: H.M. Stationery Office.

Gottfredson, M., and D. Gottfredson. 1980. *Decision-making in Criminal Justice: Toward the Rational Exercise of Discretion*. Cambridge, Mass.: Ballinger.

Gottfredson, M., and T. Hirschi. 1986. "The True Value of Lambda Would Appear to Be Zero: An Essay on Career Criminals, Criminal Careers, Selective Incapacitation, and Related Topics." *Criminology* 24:213–34.

Gove, W. R., M. Hughes, and M. Geerken. 1985. "Are Uniform Crime Reports a Valid Indicator of the Index Crimes? An Affirmative Answer with Minor Qualifications." *Criminology* 23:451–505.

Gutierres, S. E., and J. A. Reich. 1981. "A Developmental Perspective on Runaway Behavior: Its Relationship to Child Abuse." *Child Welfare* 60:89–94.

Herrenkohl, E. C., R. C. Herrenkohl, and L. J. Toedter. 1983. "Perspectives on the Intergenerational Transmission of Abuse." In *The Dark Side of Families*, edited by David Finkelhor and associates. Beverly Hills, Calif.: Sage.

Hindelang, M. J. 1976. *Criminal Victimization in Eight American Cities*. Cambridge, Mass.: Ballinger.

———. 1978. "Race and Involvement in Common-Law Personal Crimes." *American Sociological Review* 43:93–109.

Hindelang, M. J., M. R. Gottfredson, and J. Garofalo. 1978. *Victims of Personal Crime: An Empirical Foundation for a Theory of Personal Victimization*. Cambridge, Mass.: Ballinger.

Hindelang, M. J., T. Hirschi, and J. G. Weis. 1979. "Correlates of Delinquency: The Illusion of Discrepancy between Self-Report and Official Measures." *American Sociological Review* 44:995–1014.

———. 1981. *Measuring Delinquency*. Beverly Hills, Calif.: Sage.

Hirschi, T., and H. C. Selvin. 1967. *Delinquency Research: An Appraisal of Analytic Methods*. New York: Free Press.

Holter, J. C., and S. B. Friedman. 1968. "Child Abuse: Early Case Findings in the Emergency Department." *Pediatrics* 42:128–38.

Hunter, J. E., F. C. Schmidt, and G. B. Jackson. 1982. *Meta-analysis: Cumulating Research Findings across Studies*. Beverly Hills, Calif.: Sage.

Johnson, R. E. 1980. *Juvenile Delinquency and Its Origins*. Cambridge: Cambridge University Press.

———. 1986. "Family Structure and Delinquency: General Patterns and Gender Differences." *Criminology* 24:65–84.

Kerr, D. 1984. "Changing Schools to Prevent Delinquency." Paper presented at the annual meeting of the American Psychological Association, Toronto, August.

Keyes, S., and J. Block. 1984. "Prevalence and Patterns of Substance Use among Early Adolescents." *Journal of Youth and Adolescence* 13:1–14.

Kinard, E. M. 1980. "Emotional Development in Physically Abused Children." *American Journal of Orthopsychiatry* 50:606–96.

Klepinger, D. H., and J. G. Weis. 1985. "Projecting Crime Rates: An Age, Period, and Cohort Model Using ARIMA Techniques." *Journal of Quantitative Criminology* 1:387–416.

Langan, P. A., and C. A. Innes. 1986. "Preventing Domestic Violence against Women." Washington, D.C.: U.S. Department of Justice, Bureau of Justice Statistics.

Lewis, D. O., and S. S. Shanok. 1977. "Medical Histories of Delinquent and Nondelinquent Children." *American Journal of Psychiatry* 134:1020–25.

Lion, J. R. 1985. "Clinical Assessment of Violent Patients." In *Clinical Treatment of the Violent Person*, edited by Loren H. Roth. Washington, D.C.: U.S. Department of Health and Human Services.

Loftus, E. F. 1980. *Memory*. Reading, Mass.: Addison-Wesley.

McCord, J. 1983. "A Forty Year Perspective on Effects of Child Abuse and Neglect." *Child Abuse and Neglect* 7:265–70.

McDermott, M. J. 1979. *Rape Victimization in 26 American Cities*. Washington, D.C.: U.S. Department of Justice.

Maden, M. F., and D. F. Wrench. 1977. "Significant Findings in Child Abuse Research." *Victimology* 2:196–224.

Marsh, E. J., C. Johnston, and K. Kovitz. 1983. "A Comparison of the Mother-Child Interactions of Physically Abused and Nonabused Children during Play and Task Situations." *Journal of Clinical Child Psychology* 12:332–46.

Martin, D. 1976. *Battered Wives*. San Francisco: Glide.

Megargee, E. 1976. "The Prediction of Dangerous Behavior." *Criminal Justice and Behavior* 3:3–21.

Monahan, J. 1981. *Predicting Violent Behavior: An Assessment of Clinical Techniques*. Beverly Hills, Calif.: Sage.

Newberger, E. H., C. M. Newberger, and R. L. Hampton. 1983. "Child Abuse: The Current Theory Base and Future Research Needs." *Journal of the American Academy of Child Psychiatry* 22:262–68.

O'Brien, J. E. 1971. "Violence in Divorce Prone Families." *Journal of Marriage and the Family* 33:692–98.

Pagelow, M. D. 1981. "Factors Affecting Women's Decisions to Leave Violent Relationships." *Journal of Family Issues* 2:391–404.

Patterson, G. R., M. Stouthamer-Loeber, and R. Loeber. 1979. "Parental Monitoring and Anti-Social Behavior." Eugene: Oregon Social Learning Center.

Pelton, L. H. 1978. "Child Abuse and Neglect: The Myth of Classlessness." *American Journal of Orthopsychiatry* 48:608–17.

Plotkin, R. C., S. Azar, C. T. Twentyman, and M. G. Perri. 1981. "A Critical Evaluation of the Research Methodology Employed in the Investigation of Causative Factors of Child Abuse and Neglect." *Child Abuse and Neglect* 5:449–55.

Reidy, T. J. 1977. "The Aggressive Characteristics of Abused and Neglected Children." *Journal of Child Psychology* 33:1140–45.

Rhoades, P. W., and S. L. Parker. 1981. "The Connections between Youth Problems and Violence in the Home: Preliminary Report of New Research." Salem: Oregon Coalition against Domestic and Sexual Violence.

Rosenbaum, A., and K. D. O'Leary. 1981. "Marital Violence: Characteristics of Abusive Couples." *Journal of Consulting and Clinical Psychology* 49:63–71.

Rosenblatt, G. C. 1980. "Parental Expectations and Attitudes about Childrearing in High-Risk vs. Low-Risk Child Abusing Families." New York: Century Twenty-One.

Sampson, R. J. 1985. "Structural Sources of Variation in Race-Age-Specific Rates of Offending across Major U.S. Cities." *Criminology* 23:647–73.

Schulman, M. A. 1979. *A Survey of Spousal Abuse against Women in Kentucky.* New York: Harris & Associates.

Schwendinger, H., and J. S. Schwendinger. 1985. *Adolescent Subcultures and Delinquency.* New York: Praeger.

Sederstrom, J. D. 1986. "Social Class and Violent Behavior: A Meta-analysis of Empirical Findings." Doctoral dissertation, University of Washington, Department of Sociology.

Sellin, T., and M. E. Wolfgang. 1964. *The Measurement of Delinquency.* New York: Wiley.

Sgroi, S. M. 1977. "Kids with Clap: Gonorrhea as an Indicator of Child Sexual Assault." *Victimology* 2:251–67.

Sherman, L. W.,and R. A. Berk. 1984. "The Specific Deterrent Effects of Arrest for Domestic Assault." *American Sociological Review* 49:261–72.

Sherman, L. W., and B. D. Glick. 1984. *The Quality of Police Arrest Statistics.* Washington, D.C.: Police Foundation.

Short, J. F., Jr., and I. Nye. 1958. "Events of Unrecorded Juvenile Delinquency: Tentative Conclusions." *Journal of Criminal Law and Criminology* 49:296–302.

Simon, R. J. 1975. *Women and Crime.* Lexington, Mass.: Heath.

Skogan, W. 1981. *Issues in the Measurement of Victimization.* Washington, D.C.: U.S. Government Printing Office.

Smith, D. A., and C. A. Visher. 1980. "Sex and Involvement in Deviance/ Crime: A Quantitative Review of the Empirical Literature." *American Sociological Review* 45:691–701.

Spinetta, J. J., and D. Rigler. 1972. "The Child-abusing Parent: A Psychological Review." *Psychological Bulletin* 77:296–304.

Stark, E., A. Flitcraft, and W. Frazier. 1979. "Medicine and Patriarchal Violence: The Social Construction of a 'Private Event.' " *International Journal of Health Services* 9:461–93.

Steinmetz, S. K. 1977. *The Cycle of Violence: Assertive, Aggressive, and Abusive Family Interaction.* New York: Praeger.

Straus, M. A. 1974. "Leveling, Civility, and Violence in the Family." *Journal of Marriage and the Family* 36:13–29.

———. 1978. "Wife Beating: How Common and Why?" *Victimology* 2:443–58.

———. 1979. "Measuring Intrafamily Conflict and Violence: The Conflict Tactics (CT) Scales." *Journal of Marriage and the Family* 41:75–88.

Straus, M. A., and R. Gelles. 1986. "Societal Change and Change in Family Violence from 1975 to 1985 as Revealed by Two National Surveys." *Journal of Marriage and the Family* 48:465–79.

Straus, M. A., S. K. Steinmetz, and R. Gelles. 1980. *Behind Closed Doors: Violence in the American Family*. Garden City, N.Y.: Doubleday.

Szinovacz, M. E. 1983. "Using Couple Data as a Methodological Tool: The Case of Marital Violence. *Journal of Marriage and the Family* 45:633–44.

Thiesen, W. M. 1978. "What Next in Child Abuse Policy? Improving the Knowledge Base." *Child Welfare* 57(7):415–21.

Timrots, A. D., and M. R. Rand. 1987. *Violent Crime by Strangers and Non-strangers*. Special Report no. NCJ-103702. Washington, D.C.: U.S. Department of Justice, Bureau of Justice Statistics.

Tittle, C. R., W. Villemez, and D. A. Smith. 1978. "The Myth of Social Class and Criminology: An Empirical Assessment of the Empirical Evidence." *American Sociological Review* 43:643–56.

Torangeau, R. 1984. "Cognitive Sciences and Survey Methods." In *Cognitive Aspects of Survey Methodology*, edited by Thomas B. Jabine, Miron L. Straf, Judith Tanur, and Roger Torangeau. Washington, D.C.: National Academy Press.

Tracy, P. E., and J. A. Fox. 1981. "Validation of Randomized Response." *American Sociological Review* 2:187–200.

Tuteur, W., and J. Glotzer. 1966. "Further Observations on Murdering Mothers." *Journal of Forensic Sciences* 11:375.

U.S. Attorney General's Task Force on Family Violence. 1984. *Final Report*. Washington, D.C.: U.S. Attorney General.

U.S. Department of Justice. 1987. *Sourcebook of Criminal Justice Statistics*, edited by Timothy J. Flanagan, David J. van Alstyne, and Michael R. Gottfredson. Washington, D.C.: U.S. Government Printing Office.

Walker, L. E. 1979. *The Battered Woman*. New York: Harper & Row.

Weis, J. G. 1983. "Crime Statistics; Reporting Systems and Methods," In *Encyclopedia of Crime and Justice*, edited by Sanford J. Kadish. New York: Free Press.

———. 1986a. "Issues in the Measurement of Criminal Careers." In *Criminal Careers and "Career Criminals": Volume II*, edited by Alfred Blumstein, Jacqueline Cohen, Jeffrey A. Roth, and Christy A. Visher. Washington, D.C.: National Academy Press.

———. 1986b. "Social Class and Crime." In *Positive Criminology*, edited by Michael R. Gottfredson and Travis Hirschi. Beverly Hills, Calif.: Sage.

Weis, J. G., and G. S. Bridges. 1983. "Improving the Measurement of Violent Behavior." Proposal to Center for Studies in Antisocial and Violent Behavior, National Institute of Mental Health.

———. 1985. *Improving the Measurement of Violent Behavior: Draft Instruments*.

Adult Personal Interview, Juvenile Self-Administered Questionnaire. Seattle: University of Washington, Center for Law and Justice.

Weis, J. G., and D. Sumi. 1985. "Sampling and Collecting Data from High-Risk Families in High Crime-Rate Neighborhoods: Interviews, Observations, and Official Records." Seattle: University of Washington, Center for Law and Justice.

Weis, J. G., and K. Worsley. 1982. "The Measurement of Deviant Behavior among Children." Seattle: University of Washington, Center for Law and Justice.

Wikstrom, P. O. 1985. *Everyday Violence in Contemporary Sweden: Situational and Ecological Aspects.* Stockholm: National Swedish Council for Crime Prevention.

Wolfgang, M. E., and F. Ferracuti. 1967. *The Subculture of Violence: Toward an Integrated Theory in Criminology.* London: Tavistock.

Wolfgang, M. E., R. M. Figlio, and T. Sellin. 1972. *Delinquency in a Birth Cohort.* Chicago: University of Chicago Press.

Wolfgang, M. E., and N. Weiner. 1981. *Domestic Criminal Violence: A Selected Bibliography.* Washington, D.C.: U.S. Department of Justice.

Zahn, M. A. 1975. "The Female Homicide Victim: A Test of Two Hypotheses." *Criminology* 13:400–415.

Zahn, M. A., and M. Riedel. 1983. "National versus Local Data Sources in the Study of Homicide: Do They Agree?" In *Measurement Issues in Criminal Justice,* edited by Gordon P. Waldo. Beverly Hills, Calif.: Sage.

Zill, N., J. L. Peterson, and K. A. Moore. 1984. *Improving National Statistics on Children, Youth, and Families.* Washington, D.C.: Child Trends, Inc.

Irene Hanson Frieze and Angela Browne

Violence in Marriage

ABSTRACT

Societal attitudes about marital violence have changed in the last twenty
years. Battered wives have much more legal protection available than even
a few years ago. There is now a substantial body of research on battered
women and their marriages; less is known about violent men and the
reasons for their violent behavior toward wives. Although studies of
marital violence have inevitable methodological problems, survey data on
the prevalence of violence in marriage suggest that as many wives hit
husbands as husbands hit wives but that the degree of physical injury
tends to be far greater for women than for men. Numerous studies have
attempted to find a relation between various characteristics of the battered
wife and the violence she experiences, but most of this work has not been
replicated. Studies of men have similarly failed to find many consistent
predictors of their violence. Marital rape and a lack of affection between
spouses, once violence becomes established, characterize violent
marriages. The use of violence is correlated with other forms of
interpersonal power in the violent spouse. The relation of alcohol to
marital violence is more complex. Alcohol abuse may be a symptom of
men with the tendency to use violence rather than a direct causal factor in
their battering. The literature on reactions of victims of all types has not
focused on understanding battered women and their reactions.

Assault between family members is not a new phenomenon, although it
has become a part of the public awareness in this country only during
the last decade. During the history of our country, laws about spousal
violence have undergone major changes (Pleck, in this volume). Today,
no American jurisdiction legally permits one spouse to strike another.
Physical attacks against marital partners fall under various assault stat-

Irene Hanson Frieze is professor of psychology at the University of Pittsburgh.
Angela Browne is professor in the College of Criminal Justice, Northeastern University.
The authors are grateful to Joel Garner and Edward Gondolf for their many helpful
comments on an earlier version of this essay.

utes, depending on the jurisdiction: assault and battery, assault and infliction of serious injury, felonious assault, assault with intent to do great bodily harm, assault with intent to commit murder, and assault with intent to maim. State legislatures have adopted laws to aid women who are physically abused by their husbands, and many have mandated new procedures for the handling of family violence cases. Some of these changes result from lawsuits brought against police departments or prosecutors for inaction or discrimination in spouse abuse cases. Others result from the impact of social science research on specific procedures and policies (e.g., Sherman and Berk 1984). Some new laws authorize police to make arrests in family assault but not in nonfamily assault (Goolkasian 1986).

Although these changes are now being put into effect, both the policies and their implementation vary widely between jurisdictions. Laws established for the protection of "all people" are still not applied evenly to the victims of family violence (Lerman 1981; U.S. Commission on Civil Rights 1982). Although our legal system has become less accepting of the physical assault of wives, especially of severe cases, a husband's assault of his wife continues to carry fewer legal sanctions than a similar assault from a stranger in many jurisdictions. Police officers and prosecutors may still classify assaults between partners as misdemeanors, rather than as major offenses (Tong 1984; Goolkasian 1986), thus typing the case from the beginning as less "serious," and more acceptable, than other types of assaults. Similarly, police officers responding to the scene of a "domestic disturbance" in most jurisdictions rarely arrest the assailant unless severe injury has occurred or the assailant is drunk or assaultive or rude to the officers themselves (Berk and Loseke 1981; Ford 1983; Berk, Berk, and Newton 1984; Worden and Pollitz 1984).[1]

Such policies discriminate against those assaulted by their partners, no matter how legitimate their complaints, and extend a sort of legal protection to individuals who abuse their intimates, rather than extending this protection to the victims. Policies and practices that treat assaults against wives as less serious than other assaults may stem in part from ancient codes and customs that permitted the use of violence by husbands against wives (Dobash and Dobash 1978). There is also a continuing widespread belief that family matters are private and that

---

[1] See Elliott (in this volume) for a review of research on the handling of family violence cases by police, prosecutors, and courts.

outsiders, such as the police, should not interfere (Goolkasian 1986). Effective responses by the criminal justice system to spouse abuse have been made more difficult by a lack of knowledge about the prevalence, seriousness, and patterns of marital violence. Section I of this essay surveys attitudes about victims and victim blame. Empirical research on marital violence is evaluated in Section II. Section III presents incidence and prevalence data on violent marriages along with information on the seriousness of violence between partners and the characteristics of violent partners. Risk factors associated with violence in marriage, including sexual relations, differences in power and decision making, and alcohol and drug abuse, are examined in Section IV. Victim responses to physical assault and threat are described in Section V. Section VI offers conclusions about what we still need to know about violence in marriage and how such information can be obtained.

I. Attitudes about the Victim

Gradual legal changes concerning family violence reflect public attitudes. In 1970, Stark and McEvoy reported on data from a *Psychology Today* magazine reader survey on attitudes about violence; about 25 percent of their male sample and 17 percent of their female sample would approve of a husband slapping his wife under certain circumstances. In a later study done in the mid-1970s with a battered woman sample and a comparison sample in the Pittsburgh area, a large majority of the women (86 percent) reported that it is "never" okay for a husband to hit his wife (Frieze 1980). In a study, using the same methodology, of forty-four men from the Pittsburgh area who responded to a newspaper ad requesting volunteers for a study of "men's attitudes about violence," 84 percent felt that it was never okay for a husband to hit his wife (Frieze, McCreanor, and Shomo 1980).

Greenblat (1983) more recently found low levels of acceptance of marital violence among her sample of 80 recently married adults contacted through random digit telephone dialing in the New Brunswick, New Jersey, area. Eighty-six percent of men and 91 percent of women disagreed with the statement that "there are some conditions under which it is okay for a husband to slap his wife." There was slightly more tolerance of wives slapping husbands. However, people in this study did cite self-defense, retaliation, and sexual infidelity as acceptable reasons for violence toward one's spouse. These findings were replicated in a later study with 124 college students using scales rather than open-ended questions (Greenblat 1985). Seventy-eight percent approved of a husband slapping his wife in self-defense, while 24 percent approved in the case of her having an outside sexual affair. Those students with more traditional attitudes about sex roles were more approving of husband-to-wife violence than were those with less traditional attitudes.

Saunders et al. (1987) attempted to make research on attitudes about marital violence more standardized by developing a scale to assess such beliefs. The Inventory of Beliefs about Wife-Beating contains five subscales that were devised and validated on student samples:

1. *Wife-Beating is Justified.*   Items refer to whether a husband has the right to beat his wife and when he is justified in doing so.

2. *Wife Gains from Abuse.*   Items suggest that wives may like to be beaten or that they are responsible for being beaten.

3. *Help Should Be Given.*   Items ask whether the person should help battered women and if social agencies should do so.

4. *Offender Should Be Punished.*   Items refer to the appropriateness of arrest for husbands who assault wives and the husband's responsibility.

5. *Offender Is Responsible.*   Items include some of those from the previous subscales and others assessing husband responsibility for violence.

In general, female students and those working in shelters or other agencies providing services to battered women were more supportive of battered women and less supportive of the violent husbands on these scales than were male students and abusers. The scales were also found to correlate with scales measuring traditional sex-role attitudes showing that those who are more traditional are more tolerant of wife battering.

This work on attitudes about marital violence suggests that public attitudes have changed. There is no longer casual acceptance of violence against women. Many people, however, are still not completely sympathetic to battered wives and may believe that they "allow themselves" to be battered (Greenblat 1985; Saunders et al. 1987). These beliefs are consistent with research on all types of victims that has shown a tendency to blame the victim for his or her fate (Taylor 1983; Frieze, Hymer, and Greenberg 1987). This blaming tendency may be especially strong for female victims of assault or sexual aggression from an intimate (Schur 1984; Frieze 1987).

There are many explanations for this phenomenon of blaming the victim. One way to conceptualize the issue is to assess the feelings of the person observing the victim. When we learn that someone has been victimized, our assumptions about the world are threatened (Janoff-

Bulman and Frieze 1983). For example, many people believe that the world is basically just and fair and that good people are rewarded and bad people are punished (Lerner 1980; Smith and Green 1984). When we learn that someone has been victimized, we may interpret the events leading to the victimization in such a way as to maintain our belief in a just world (Wyer, Bodenhausen, and Gorman 1985). This may involve blaming the victim in some way so that this person is seen as somehow deserving of what has happened. One form of victim blaming is to see the wife as provoking violence against herself (Greenblat 1985). Shakespeare's play, *The Taming of the Shrew*, provides a good example. Or battered women can be seen as somehow liking the violence (and possibly therefore provoking it) (Shainess 1984; Greenblat 1985; Saunders et al. 1987).

Victim blame can also be a method of coping with discomfort arising from learning about a victim who is similar to oneself (e.g., Shaver 1970). Very few people believe that they are potential victims before a victimizing event occurs (Perloff 1983). Instead, people generally see themselves as less likely than others to have bad things happen. When someone who is similar to us is victimized, our sense of personal safety is threatened. By distancing ourselves from the victim, we can maintain a feeling of personal safety (Frieze, Hymer, and Greenberg 1987). It is also threatening for much the same reasons to think that someone had been victimized randomly. If negative events are random, no one can feel safe.

There are other ways to respond to our discomfort in learning about someone who has been victimized (Frieze and McHugh 1986). We can deny that such things happen with any frequency. This is relatively easy to do for domestic violence because such victimization is often hidden, "behind closed doors" (Pagelow 1984). Another response is to deny the gravity of such events. Trivialization or laughter is not an uncommon response to mention of marital violence; it is still joked about in the media and elsewhere (Frieze and McHugh 1986).

II. Empirical Research on Marital Violence
Social scientists began to study family violence in the 1960s, with an emphasis on child abuse (e.g., Kempe et al. 1962; Steele and Pollock 1968; Gil 1970). Pagelow (1984) claims that violence between family members was earlier either ignored or seen as too controversial for serious research (cf. Parnas 1967). In the early seventies, a number of social scientists began to do research on assaults between marital part-

ners (e.g., O'Brien 1971; Straus 1971, 1973; Gelles 1974). There have now been many studies of battered women, of marital violence, and of violent families (see Pagelow [1984] for a comprehensive review).

A. Defining Marital Violence[2]

Much of the research on marital violence focuses on the "battered woman." However, "battering," "abuse," and "violence" are used in quite varying ways across studies. This creates confusion and may be one reason for inconsistencies across various research projects. Browne (1987) suggests that "violence" connotes physical force, whereas "abuse" can include both nonviolent and violent interactions; she urges that the terms "battering" and "beating" be restricted to repeated, physically forceful actions.

Another issue is whether there must be evidence of an intent to harm before an action is considered to constitute marital violence (Steinmetz 1977; Walker 1979; and Pagelow 1981). But, since intent is difficult to measure, many look only at the *level* of violent behavior. Perhaps the major advocate of this position is Murray Straus. Straus's Conflict Tactics Scale (formerly called the Conflict Resolution Technique Scales; Straus 1979) has been the instrument most used for assessing the occurrence of violence between family members. This scale is ordered along a continuum from nonviolent tactics, such as discussing an issue calmly, to overtly violent acts, such as using a knife or a gun (Straus 1980). Assaultive actions on this scale are divided into categories of relatively "minor" violence (throwing something at another person; pushing, grabbing, or shoving; slapping) and "severe" violence (kicking, biting, hitting with fist, hitting with an object, beating up, threatening with a knife or gun, using a knife or a gun). The Conflict Tactics Scale does not assess what *kind* of an object was thrown at another person, the repetition of specific actions during a particular assault, the forcefulness with which these actions are carried out, or the relative strength of the perpetrator and victim.[3]

The idea of "battering" or "abuse" contains several important components. First, both the types of violent actions and the harm done should be considered. The *force* with which an act is carried out, the number of

---

[2] See Weis (in this volume) for a general discussion of definitional and methodological issues in the study of family violence.

[3] The strengths and weaknesses of the Conflict Tactics Scale are complex and beyond the scope of this essay. For criticisms, see Dobash and Dobash (1979) and Pagelow (1981). For responses, see Straus (1979, 1981).

repetitions, and the *clustering* of different acts together play a major role in determining the amount of damage done (Browne 1987). Both the repetition of violent acts and a clustering of types of acts within a single incident increase the potential for injury, as victims are overwhelmed by the rapidity of events and are unable to recover in time to protect themselves from the next blow (cf. Reid, Taplin, and Loeber 1981; Patterson 1982). The clustering of acts during an assault also frequently produces a distinctive *pattern* of injuries in battered women, characterized by multiple injury sites; a concentration of injuries to the central part of the body (head, face, neck, throat, chest, and abdomen), rather than the extremities, and multiple types of injuries from one event, particularly abrasions and contusions not seen in male victims of abuse by wives (Stark et al. 1981).

Sonkin, Martin, and Walker (1985) provide perhaps the most comprehensive definition of battering. Four types of violence are outlined: physical, sexual, property, and psychological. Forced sexual acts and marital rape are associated with other forms of marital violence, as is the destruction of property belonging to the abused. Marital violence also includes psychological abuse such as threats of violence, pathological jealousy, mental degradation, and controlling the freedom of movement of the spouse so that she is not free to go where she wants or do what she wants.

All of these definitions seem to be based on the idea of extreme forms of violence and seem wrongly to exclude mild violence. Any use of violence in a marriage can have psychological effects on the marital partners. Though women who are assaulted "only once" are rarely labeled as battered and still less often are studied, any use of violence can dramatically alter the balance of power in a relationship; a sense of openness and trust on the part of the woman may be destroyed and result in a permanent sense of inequality, threat, and loss (Walker 1979; Dobash and Dobash 1984; Pagelow 1984; Straus and Gelles 1986). Repeated assaults by a partner seem to have a cumulative effect on women victims that builds on the shock of the first assault and takes them through a progression of emotions and attributions as they attempt to reinterpret their lives and their relationships in light of a pattern of continued attacks.

B. *Studying Battered Women*

Most research on marital violence has focused on battered female victims rather than on their male assailants or on men abused by their wives. Recently, there have been some studies of violent husbands (e.g., Sonkin, Martin, and Walker 1985; Sonkin 1987), but these are limited in scope and tend to be based on small samples of men in treatment or men who have been identified as assailants by the criminal justice system. There is also some evidence that there is a small proportion of male victims of marital violence (e.g., Klaus and Rand 1984). However, such men rarely use social service agencies for help and are, thus, unavailable for most research projects (Fagan et al. 1980).

There is an extensive body of research on battered women. Some of the major studies are briefly outlined in table 1. These studies represent a variety of research techniques. In all of this research, though, a primary issue is the identification of the sample. Nearly all studies rely on the self-report of the women. In most cases, they have defined themselves as battered before being included in the research. In other studies of the general population, battered groups are identified through their responses to interview questions. Such studies raise a number of methodological issues.

1. *Defining the Research Sample.*   In any research project, the selection of the study participants depends on the questions one wishes to ask. If the goal is to understand violent husbands, it is probably best to interview these men directly. However, few studies have done this (Sonkin, Martin, and Walker 1985). Instead, it is typically the battered women who are studied. This is fine for certain types of research questions. For instance, if the subject being investigated is the feelings of physically abused women or how they view their marriages, then it may be quite appropriate to only interview women. However, this sample group is probably not appropriate for other types of questions, such as why the men are violent.

Even with battered women as the target group, it may be difficult to identify an appropriate sample. It may be necessary to question women who can be reached through shelters or safe houses or through referrals from therapists or social service agencies (e.g., Gelles 1974; Gayford 1975; Carlson 1977; Hilberman and Munson 1978; Walker 1979). Another technique is to seek a sample through advertising. Such a technique was utilized by Doran (1980) to identify battered women from middle and upper-middle class areas who, it was felt, might not want to go to shelters. This technique does introduce other forms of bias. It eliminates women who do not read newspapers or who do not want to volunteer as a research subject. Responding to a newspaper survey demands more of the subject than agreeing to a verbal request to be a study participant.

TABLE 1

Studies of Self-Identified Battered Women

Researchers	Battered Women Sample	Comparison Group	Data-Collection Technique
Berk et al. (1983)	262 police calls in California	None	Analysis of police records
Bowker (1983a)	146 Wisconsin women, newspaper ad	None	In-depth interviews
Browne (1987)	42 women who tried to kill husbands	205 battered women, no lethal action	In-depth interviews
Dobash and Dobash (1978)	109 "violently" beaten women	None	In-depth interviews
Doran (1980)	294 New Jersey newspaper readers	318 New Jersey newspaper readers	Survey (and 172 interviews)
Dvoskin (1981)	31 Tucson women, married	144 Tucson women, married	Interviews in a waiting room
Eberle (1982)	390 Denver area women, ads and referrals	None	In-depth interviews
Frieze (1980, 1983, etc.)	137 southwestern Pennsylvania women; shelters, ads, legal action	137 southwestern Pennsylvania women, neighborhood match	In-depth interviews
Gelles (1974)	40 couples, agency referrals	40 couples, neighborhood match	Interviews
Hilberman and Munson (1978)	60 rural North Carolina women, psychiatric referrals	None	Data collected informally during counseling
LaBell (1979)	512 Florida women, shelterees	None	Admission and departure interviews
Pagelow (1981)	350 California and other areas, shelters and volunteers	None	Surveys and in-depth interviews
Roy (1977)	150 New York city women, hotline callers	None	In-depth interviews
Shaud (1983)	33 Minneapolis women, treatment referrals	61 area women, domestic relations court and 55 area women, child care court referrals	Mailed questionnaires
Shields and Hanneke (1983)	92 Midwest women, agency referrals	None	In-depth interviews
Walker (1979)	120 women, 300 partial interviews	None	In-depth interviews
Walker (1983)	403 Rocky Mountain women, newspaper ad	Same women in other relationship	In-depth interview

Another frequent means of identifying a battered-women group is to use referrals of women in psychotherapy (e.g., Hilberman and Munson 1978; Walker 1979) or social service agency clients (e.g., Gelles 1974; Shields and Hanneke 1983). This type of group consists of those who have felt that they need psychological help and may overrepresent those with coping problems or psychopathology. Women who are functioning well without such help will not be represented in such a sample. There is also some evidence that battered women who blame themselves for their marital problems are particularly likely to seek psychological help (Frieze 1980).

Police records are another source of data about battered women. Berk et al. (1983) studied 262 domestic incidents between couples in Santa Barbara, California, drawn from police records of "domestic disturbance" calls. Another less often used technique for identifying battered women for study is to use medical records of emergency room patients seeking treatment for marital violence (Stark et al. 1981). Stark et al., in reviewing medical records, estimated that 21 percent of the women using emergency surgical services were victims of assaultive acts by a male partner. Such estimates are based on the observations of medical staff members and reports of the injured women themselves. Since it is quite likely that other beaten women may not have wanted to identify the cause of their injuries, the actual percentages of such women in emergency rooms are probably higher.

Police records and medical reports are not subject to the same biases as interviews of shelter residents or women seeking psychological help, but they have other built-in forms of bias. Such sources of information are still based on women who have sought some type of help from institutionalized sources. Low socioeconomic status groups are likely to be overrepresented here as with other samples since women with more financial resources may have more private sources of help.

In a formal attempt to compare the types of women who might be found using different solicitation techniques, Washburn and Frieze (1980) compared three samples of self-identified battered women in the southwestern Pennsylvania area. One group consisted of women who had filed a legal action to remove their husbands from their homes because of the husband's physical abuse. Names of all women who had filed under the Pennsylvania Protection from Abuse Act 218 were listed in public court records. These women were telephoned and asked to participate in the study. A second group included women who had sought help at one of the area shelters for battered women. Finally,

TABLE 2

A Comparison of Battered Women from Three Subject Sources

	Legal Action (N = 36)	Shelterees (N = 50)	Posted Ads (N = 49)
Marital Status (percent):			
Married	39	28	49
Separated	44	58	8
Divorced	14	4	33
Race (percent):			
White	81	74	92
Black	19	26	8
Employment Status (percent):			
Full-time work	42	22	49
Part-time work	22	10	27
Unemployed	36	68	24
Average Income:*			
Husband	4.55	3.24	3.66
Wife	2.14	1.77	2.12
Education (percent):			
Grade school	19	37	4
High school	33	49	39
Some college	44	14	47
Postgraduate education	3	4	10
Level of Injury (percent):			
First injury serious	31	38	18
Worst injury serious	75	66	51

SOURCE.—Washburn and Frieze 1980.

* Average income is scored 1–5 with 5 being high.

some of the battered women were recruited through notices posted in laundromats, stores, and restrooms. Each of these groups of battered women had distinct characteristics (see table 2).

Women from the women's shelters were more often separated from their partners, black, and unemployed. They were younger, had lower incomes and less education than the other groups, and had more small children. These women appeared to have the fewest resources and to be the most in need of the public assistance provided by the shelter. Some of the wealthier battered women in the study sample in fact commented that they would be quite reluctant to go to a shelter and would instead seek temporary housing at a motel or with a friend if they needed shelter.

Women who had filed legal action tended to be the intermediate group. They, too, had a high rate of separation, and their racial breakdown was similar to that in the general area (19 percent black).

Many of them worked full-time, and they had higher levels of education than the shelter group. Their husbands had the highest incomes of any of the groups of battered women. These women also had more school-age children than the other groups and more often lived outside the city. Although the worst physical harm experienced by the women from the shelters and those who filed legal restraining orders was comparable, the frequency of the violence delivered by the second group of women toward their husbands was greater than that of the other groups. Other differences also emerged. The women from the legal action group repeatedly expressed a belief that they were helping themselves to change their situations. They also expressed fewer feelings of powerlessness.

The women who had responded to posted advertisements were most often still married to their abusers. They were more likely to work full-time, were better educated, and earned somewhat larger incomes than the shelter group. They were also more often white. The majority of women recruited from the public advertisements had not been battered recently. Either the violence had not occurred for a long time, or the relationship had ended prior to the interview. The women responding to posted notices had experienced the least violence, although, even with this group, over 50 percent sustained severe or permanent injuries.

These data suggest that there are indeed differences in the battered women identified from various sources. Although the particular differences found by Washburn and Frieze (1980) may not generalize to other locations, this study does point out the need for researchers of domestic violence to be acutely aware of the potential biases that may be built into their work by decisions made about how to choose the sample population. Other studies have indicated that battered women do not form a homogeneous group (e.g., Snyder and Fruchtman 1981).

Because samples of battered women may differ from one another systematically as a function of how they are identified or the types of interview questions they are asked, it is especially important that a comparison groups be used if general conclusions are drawn about the characteristics of battered women. Unfortunately, this requirement is seldom met. As shown in table 1, most studies include no comparison group. Even when a comparison sample is included, it must be carefully selected. In research employing a comparison group, the nature of the comparison group and the variables that need to be matched or controlled must be clearly identified (Parlee 1981; Sanders and Pinhey 1983).

Frieze (1980) developed a control sample by matching each battered woman to another married or formerly married woman from the same neighborhood. Gelles (1974) used a similar procedure of developing a neighborhood match for each of his violent agency referral couples. Walker (1983) interviewed only battered women but was able to generate a comparison group by asking the women to describe their abusive relationship *and* a relationship with another man that was not abusive. Stark et al. (1981) used injured women seeking medical attention who did not cite domestic assault as the cause of their injuries as a control group for battered women seeking emergency medical attention. More sophistication is seen in the work of Rosenbaum and O'Leary (1981), who studied abused wives and abusive husbands in a treatment group for domestic violence. To test for effects due to treatment seeking, the violence couples were compared to other couples in marital therapy but with no reported violence. In addition, neighborhood controls were used for the violence group. A similar matching strategy was used by Shaud (1983).

Although all of these are interesting comparison groups, the characteristics of each of the comparison groups is likely to be quite different. Neighborhood matches may control to some degree for demographic characteristics such as socioeconomic status or ethnicity. But, they do not control for the effects of seeking treatment or other help. Treatment-based controls may differ on demographic factors. Other variables, too, that are not being measured will also vary between the groups.

2. *General Population Studies.*   Problems of self selection are avoided when a representative random sample is used. In a large survey of the general population, battered women can be identified in the course of a brief interview (e.g., Schulman 1979; Straus, Gelles, and Steinmetz 1980; Straus and Gelles 1986). Data on domestic violence have also been collected by the National Crime Survey (Langan and Innes 1986). However, such large random samples are difficult to obtain and may incorporate other biases (e.g., O'Brien 1985). Because of the time constraints in most survey interviews, the number of questions that can be asked must be severely limited. Screening questions such as those used in the National Crime Survey may eliminate those who do not think of family assaults as crimes (Klaus and Rand 1984). Other research has

also shown that how one asks questions greatly affects the answers given (e.g., Frieze 1983). Through in-depth interviews, questions can be asked in different ways and definitional issues may not be as great an issue. But, in rapid screening interviews, a "no" response may mean that the questions are not asked again in another form.

Survey studies relying on brief interviews may affect responses in other ways too. With such procedures, there is little time to build rapport between interviewer and interviewee. Women may be reluctant to discuss as personal an issue as physical abuse by their husbands in a short survey format (Klaus and Rand 1984). This may be especially true in a telephone interview, although Kilpatrick et al. (1985) report great success with this technique for interviewing rape victims.

In the study of violence between adult partners, research based on random samples has given us the most valid estimates of the incidence of violent actions. These data also suggest relations between the perpetration and victimization by violence and various other variables (e.g., Schulman 1979; Straus, Gelles, and Steinmetz 1980; Straus and Gelles 1986). These studies have not, however, been able to provide detailed information about the context within which particular acts occurred, about the outcomes of specific acts and incidents in terms of injuries or other consequences, or about the development of patterns of violence over time (e.g., Dobash and Dobash 1979). The findings in random sample surveys must thus be interpreted and reported only for what they are. They can tell us little about the dynamics of a particular phenomenon. These must be investigated in smaller, more focused studies.

3. *When and Where to Interview.*   Marital violence is a complex, repeated crime. Reactions of the victims and the perpetrators may change over time. This raises a number of questions for the researcher. When should the victim of such violence be interviewed? How does the timing of the data collection influence the resulting data?

Most marital violence research studies battered wives who have identified themselves in some way by seeking help. But, if we find that a battered woman interviewed at a shelter where she has sought temporary refuge is quite depressed and anxious (e.g., Hughes and Barad 1983), does this tell us that such emotions are typical of battered women or only of those who have felt the need to go to a shelter? An alternative interpretation is that being at a shelter causes women to be depressed and anxious. When interviews of battered women are done at shelters, we have no way of knowing the sources of their feelings. In general, people's memories of previous events are affected by their current mood state (Bower 1981). Women interviewed after successfully "beating wife beating" (Bowker 1983*a*) might be more positive in their feelings since they have defined themselves as escaping their victim status. This focus on a positive outcome may cause the battered woman to remember other positive aspects of her life. She will appear much less upset than a woman who feels fearful and remembers other negative aspects of her early childhood or other parts of her life.

Thus, interviews of women who have left their husbands may yield quite different patterns of data than studies of women leaving shelters to return to their husbands, women in emergency rooms, or those who have recently called the police. The circumstances of the interviews need to be more carefully scrutinized. By looking for generalities across circumstances, we can better understand the underlying dynamics of violent marriages.

Another question is where interviews should be done. If the assailant is present, the responses of a battered woman are likely to be quite different than they would be if he were not present. Failure to control for the presence of other family members has been identified as one of the reasons for underreporting of family violence in the National Crime Survey (Klaus and Rand 1984). Telephone interviewers need to be especially sensitive to this issue, since the physical presence of the husband or other family members may not be known to the interviewer.

III. Dynamics of Violent Marriages

Early studies on criminal victimization focused primarily on violent incidents occurring outside of the home. Newspapers and other media emphasized the more sensational crimes and criminals, and a common impression was formed that the risk of personal injury was greatest from individuals outside one's circle of intimates. Crimes that occurred within the family were rarely reported, and those that became known were viewed as oddities. The "average" family, it was assumed, afforded nurturance and protection of its members (Walker 1986).

A. *How Common Is Marital Violence?*

Numerous studies show that physical assaults between married and cohabiting partners are a serious problem (see table 3). In one early study, Gelles (1974) interviewed families located from social service agencies' records and neighborhood controls and found that 56 percent

TABLE 3
Reported Incidence of Marital Violence

Type of Sample	Sample Size	Rate of Violence (per 100 people)		
		Husband or Male Partner	Wife or Female Partner	Couple
National random samples:				
Straus, Gelles, and Steinmetz (1980):	2,143 couples			
For entire length of study		27	24	28
For last 12 months only		12.1	11.6	16
Straus and Gelles (1986) (last 12 months only)	3,520 couples	11	12	16
Klaus and Rand (1984) (yearly average)	60,000 households, National Crime Survey	.27	.02	...
Regional random samples:				
Hornung, McCullough, and Sugimoto (1981)	1,553 women in Kentucky (from Schulman 1979)	...	...	16
Nisonoff and Bitman (1979):	297 Long Island residents			
All reports		16	11	...
Victim reports only		13	19	...
Russell (1982)	644 women in San Francisco, ever married	26	...	...
Schulman (1979):	1793 women in Kentucky			
For entire length of study		21	...	...
For last year only		10	...	...
Other samples:				
Frieze et al. (1980)	137 southeastern Pennsylvania women, ever married comparison group	34	27	...
Levinger (1966)	600 divorce applicants	37	...	...
Mason and Blankenship (1987)	107 women and 48 men, Michigan under-graduates	1.8	2.2	...

of the husbands and wives were physically aggressive with one another during marital arguments. Gelles found that husbands were more violent in every category of violence he looked at except "hitting with something" (which was one of the milder forms of violence). In earlier studies, physical assault of wives by their husbands showed up as a cause of divorce (O'Brien 1971). Levinger (1966) in a study of 600 divorce applicants found that 37 percent of the wives listed physical abuse as the reason for divorce.

In a national survey of over 2,000 homes conducted in 1975, Straus, Gelles, and Steinmetz (1980) asked married couples about violence directed toward one another and found that more than one-quarter (28 percent) of those interviewed reported at least one instance of physical assault in their relationships; 16 percent reported violent incidents in the year just prior to the study. Of these incidents, over a third were serious assaults involving such acts as punching, kicking, hitting with an object, beating up, and assaults with a knife or gun. A follow-up survey conducted in 1985 found the same percentage reporting violent incidents in the twelve months prior to the study (Straus and Gelles 1986). These estimates are supported by the results of a Harris poll using similar questions, which found that 21 percent of 1,793 women respondents in the state of Kentucky had been physically attacked by a male partner at least once. This figure was much higher for those who had been recently separated or divorced; of these women, two-thirds reported violence in their former relationships (Schulman 1979).

Estimates in the Straus, Gelles, and Steinmetz (1980) study suggest that over 1.5 million women are physically assaulted by their male partners each year. In a report on data from the National Crime Survey (NCS) for the years 1978–82, Bureau of Justice statisticians Langan and Innes (1986) estimated that 2.1 million women were victims of domestic violence at least once during an average 12-month period. Langan and Innes noted that compared with victims of stranger violence, these women victims of a male partner's violence also faced an unusually high risk of reoccurrence of the violence. Of those assaulted by a partner, 32 percent were victimized again within six months of the "initial" (first reported) victimization, compared with only 13 percent of the victims in stranger-to-stranger crime who were revictimized by a stranger within a six-month period.

Other studies of violence between adult partners conducted in particular locations confirm these percentages. In a random sample of women in San Francisco, 21 percent of the women who had been or were currently married reported at least one occasion of physical abuse by their mates (Russell 1982). A telephone survey of Long Island, New York, residents yielded lower figures of 16 percent of men and 11 percent of women having "hit" their spouses (Nisonoff and Bitman 1979). Although there were few divorced or separated individuals in the sample, the reported rates of violence for those previously married was higher than the rates for those who were currently married. In another study, researchers found that 34 percent of a general comparison group of ever-married women (chosen as battered women's matches) reported being attacked at least once by a male partner (Frieze et al. 1980).

As table 3 shows, rates found in other studies vary greatly. The age of the population and the types of questions asked appear to be factors affecting rates. Studies of college students (Mason and Blankenship 1987) give especially low rates, as do those from the National Crime Survey (Klaus and Rand 1984). Many suspect that even the higher percentages are too low because of reluctance on the part of some interviewees to report incidents of violence between themselves and an intimate (Lentzner and DeBerry 1980; Straus, Gelles, and Steinmetz 1980; Langan and Innes 1986). But, even if actual figures are no higher than the findings, it is clear that, counter to the pervasive image of assaultive violence as primarily occurring in the streets, for many people, their time of greatest risk is in the home.

B. How Serious Is Violence between Partners?

Assaults by adult partners are often quite serious. In 1980, a study based on data from the National Crime Survey (Lentzner and DeBerry 1980) compared violent crimes involving intimates with crimes involving strangers and found that, when the attacker was a stranger, 54 percent of the victims were injured. However, when the attacker was related, three-fourths of the victims sustained injury. Three-fifths of the attacks by relatives occurred at night, so most of these victims were "home safe" at the time the assault occurred. Again using NCS data, Langan and Innes (1986) note that, although the majority of domestic violence incidents would technically fall into the "misdemeanor" category in police statistics, and thus appear less serious, the extent of physical injury was not a factor in the classification of these crimes.

How mutual is the violence between romantic or married partners? When violent assaults occur in relationships, are men or women more likely to be the perpetrators? Are there differences between men and women when one looks at relatively minor physical assaults, compared with more serious actions and injuries?

Probably the best type of data to answer these questions comes from national samples using male and female respondents. In their study of American families, Straus, Gelles, and Steinmetz (1980) found that half (49 percent) of those who reported violence said that both partners had used some kind of force; in 27 percent of the cases, only the husband had been assaultive, and in 24 percent, only the wife had been assaultive. However, Straus and his colleagues noted that men's greater average size and physical strength and their tendency toward greater aggressivity can give the same acts quite different effects when done by a woman and a man in terms of pain, injury, and threat (Straus and Gelles 1986). The same finding has been reported by others (Russell 1982; Greenblat 1983). Men are also more able to avoid physical victimization than are women. As Pagelow (1984, p. 274) asserts, "Men are, on the average, larger and muscularly stronger than women, so if they choose to strike back they can do greater physical harm than is done to them, they can nonviolently protect themselves from physical harm, or they can leave the premises without being forcibly restrained."

Despite the seemingly equal appearance of assaultive behavior by men and women when looked at in isolation, Straus, Gelles, and Steinmetz (1980) and Straus and Gelles (1986) found that men had a *higher* rate of using the most dangerous and injurious forms of violence, such as physically beating up a partner or using a knife or gun, and that when violent acts were committed by a husband, the acts were repeated more often than they were by wives. Another analysis of the same data indicated that the average number of severely violent assaults by a husband against a nonviolent wife was three times greater than the average number of wives' assaults on nonviolent husbands (Straus 1980). In addition, a large number of violent attacks against wives occurred when the women were pregnant, thus increasing the risk of injury and of miscarriage or stillbirth (Straus, Gelles, and Steinmetz 1980, p. 43).

Although the Straus, Gelles, and Steinmetz (1980) study has often been cited as evidence for the *mutuality* of domestic violence, this interpretation is questionable for several reasons. First, their sample was restricted to couples who were currently living together, thereby excluding recently separated or divorced couples. Separated couples report much higher rates of violence in other research (e.g., Klaus and Rand

1984). Second, information on violent acts was gathered from only one member of each couple, without corroboration from the other partner or from other sources and without a means for ascertaining possible differences in the reports of the victims and the perpetrators of violence (Szinovacz [1983] critiques this methodology). The study did not ask about injuries sustained from the violence or about what proportion of the acts were in response to violence initiated by the other or in self-defense. Finally, questions about violence were set in a context of settling disputes in a conflict situation and, therefore, may not have elicited information about attacks that seemed to come "out of the blue." These are crucial questions for assessing the mutuality of combat, and some of them have been investigated in more depth by other researchers.

Separated and divorced couples appear to have extremely high rates of violence, especially violence that is perpetrated by husbands. Thus a greater impression of "mutuality" may result when studies examine only intact couples than when divorced or separated couples are included. In the Bureau of Justice Statistics report on family violence (Klaus and Rand 1984), for instance, 91 percent of all reported violent crimes between spouses were victimizations of women by husbands or ex-husbands, while only 5 percent were victimizations of husbands by wives or ex-wives.

The identity of the person doing the reporting also seems to be important in assessing what weight to give responses. Studies of crime victims show that they have a surprising tendency to forget or not to report even fairly serious attacks (e.g., Schneider 1980; Block and Block 1984). Experience with women victims of a partner's violence confirms this. Battered women, especially those who have been victimized over a long period, tend to underestimate both the frequency and the severity of the violence they experience when their reports are compared to the reports of witnesses or to hospital and other records. Similarly, experts working with abusive men note that they greatly *underreport* their violent actions, minimizing or denying assaultive behavior against their wives and claiming more involvement by the victim in justification of their violence than is suggested by witness or police reports (Ganley and Harris 1978; Sonkin and Durphy 1982, 1985; Szinovacz 1983; Deschner 1984; Ewing, Lindsey, and Pomerantz 1984). A study combining estimations of violence by male perpetrators and women victims may make male perpetrators appear less violent and more victimized, and their female victims appear less seriously assaulted and more likely to victimize their partners, than an observer would corroborate.

Empirical studies using a variety of methodologies suggest that men are more likely to assault their female partners, especially seriously, than are women to assault male partners (Dobash and Dobash 1978; Frieze et al. 1980; Pagelow 1981; Sonkin and Durphy 1985). For instance, in analyzing official records on almost 900 cases of family violence, Dobash and Dobash (1978) found that, when the sex of the victim was known, females were the victims in 94 percent, and males in 6 percent, of the cases. Almost the exact same proportions were found in records of the Minnesota Department of Corrections for 966 assaults; 95 percent were women victimized by men with whom they were or had been living, and 5 percent were men victimized by women partners.

No doubt there are couples who engage in "mutual combat" with roughly equal levels of aggression. Studies of severely battered women suggest, however, that they are not typically violent toward their mates, especially not in initiation and usually not in response. Their perception of danger is too great. It appears to be the "mildly battered" women who fight back. Interview studies of battered women have found that, for those women who do fight back, the husbands' level of violence is typically higher than that of their wives (Frieze et al. 1980; Saunders 1986).

Another factor in assessing the mutuality of violence is whether injuries result. Partners may "trade punches," but they rarely "exchange" injuries (Berk et al. 1983). Even when both partners are injured in an altercation, the woman's injuries are usually more serious (Berk and Loseke 1981; Stark et al. 1981).

We recognize that there may be differences in the patterns and rates of violence occurring in heterosexual relationships of various types. For example, long-term cohabiting relationships may exhibit different forms and frequencies of violent conduct than do more short-term or episodic relationships. As we have already indicated, most of the serious violence is directed by males against females, and the literature on male offenders is very sparse. For this reason, the remainder of this essay focuses on battered *women* and their marriages or relationships. For ease of writing, we refer to these relationships as marriages and to the partners as husbands and wives.

C. Characteristics of Violent Marriage Partners

Interview studies of battered women have provided most information about the characteristics of their marriages and violent husbands and battered wives. Certain common patterns have been identified in severely battered women's marriages (Frieze et al. 1980; Pagelow 1984; Browne 1987). Male initiation of violence is typical, but, over time, some wives will fight back (Saunders 1986). Once violence has occurred, it tends to be repeated. Over time, the violence becomes more severe and more frequent. Other correlates of violence include high levels of alcohol use by the husband (but not by the wife); a controlling style in the husband, in which he closely monitors the wife's whereabouts and makes all major decisions; disrupted sexual relations; and, possibly, marital rape. The battered woman feels socially isolated and has control of few resources. Within these violent marriages, there is often also physical or sexual abuse of children. Although either the wife or the husband may be physically abusive toward the children, husbands are more often the highly abusive parent.

Other patterns of marital violence have been identified. Bowker's (1983*a*) newspaper-generated sample of women who had "beaten wife-beating" divided into four groups as a function of the level of overall violence and the number of years that the violence had been happening. Thirty percent of his sample had continued in a relationship of low violence over many years. Nearly half of the sample was characterized by high levels of violence, but only 18 percent of the total sample had been in relationships with high levels of violence over many years. His sampling technique was probably responsible for the high proportion of couples with low levels of reported violence (51 percent). Less than 1 percent of this group had gone to a shelter after the worst violent incident. Thus, Bowker's population is probably quite different than samples drawn from shelters.

Frieze et al. (1980) also drew battered samples from other sources than shelters and found couples with low levels of violence. Many of these were found in her neighborhood matches, but 34 percent of the shelter women, 25 percent of the legal action women, and 41 percent of the women responding to posted notices were classified as belonging to relationships with levels of "mild violence." To be considered "severe violence," there had to be at least one incident in which the wife received severe injuries (severe bruises, cuts or burns that required medical attention, or more serious violence). Many differences were found between the mild violence and severe violence groups. Major effects centered around the characteristics of the violent men. Less violent men drank less and were less likely to have grown up in a family in which parents fought violently than were the more violent men. The wives of the less violent men had more decision-making power in their marriages than the severely battered women but less than did women in marriages without violence.

Although there is general agreement about the general outlines of the very violent marriage, other patterns do exist. There is less agreement about the personality and background characteristics of the men and women in violent relationships. In a review of a fifty-two case comparison study involving statistical analyses of husband-to-wife violence, Hotaling and Sugarman (1986) found that, of the forty-two characteristics or "risk markers" studied in female victims, only one—having witnessed violence between parents or care givers in childhood—was consistently correlated with being the victim of a male partner's violence. Variables *not* found to be consistently related to spouse-abuse victimization for women included being a full-time housewife, alcohol use, income or education level, personality integration, hostility, self-esteem, or the use of violence toward her children. Conversely, for husbands who were violent toward their female partners, three risk markers—witnessing of parental violence while growing up, sexual aggression toward the wife, and use of violence toward the children—were consistently found. Alcohol use, income level, occupational status, education level, and assertiveness were also consistent risk markers, although less strong. Hotaling and Sugarman (1986) note that the characteristics of the men were much better violence predictors than were the women's characteristics. In examining couples' characteristics, frequency of verbal altercations and marital dissatisfaction were consistently associated with marriages in which there was wife abuse. Low family income or social class, marital status (divorced, separated, cohabiting, and reconstituted couples), and religious incompatibility were also consistent risk markers of relationships having husband-to-wife violence.

IV. Violent Marriage Risk Factors

In this section, we look in more detail at some of the "risk factors" associated with marital violence against women. First is an analysis of affectionate and sexual relationships as a measure of marital dissatisfaction; then we turn to differences in resources between the husbands and wives and decision making; finally, we analyze the complex data on alcohol and marital violence.

A. *Sexual Relations and Affectionate Behavior*

Interview studies of battered women indicate that there is generally less affectionate behavior (physical affection, giving presents, having a good sexual relationship, etc.) in their marriages than in those of women in nonviolent comparison groups (e.g., Frieze et al. 1980). At the same time, clinicians working with battered women have observed that they often appear to love their abusive husbands and very much value signs of love and affection (Walker 1983).

1. *Origins of Love in Battering Relationships.*   Many battered women's positive feelings toward their husbands may result from feelings generated before the relationships became violent. In most of the studies of battered relationships, the majority of battered women—73 to 85 percent—do not experience physical assault until after they have made a major commitment to their abuser or married him (Dobash and Dobash 1978; Pagelow 1981; Rosenbaum and O'Leary 1981; Bowker 1983a; Mason and Blankenship 1987). Assaults before marriage tend to be isolated incidents, often related to the man's jealousy or to the woman's attempt to end the relationship, and are seen as atypical of the overall interaction. On the basis of clinical observations, Browne (1987) and Walker (1984) report that before the onset of violence the women felt that their partners were extremely attentive and affectionate. They showed constant concerns with the woman's whereabouts and activities, a desire to be with them all the time, intense expressions of affection, and wanted an early commitment to a long-term relationship. Such behaviors may be difficult to distinguish from idealized romantic interactions. Over time, though, such behavior is increasingly seen by the woman as intrusive, possessive, and controlling. She begins to feel isolated as she becomes separated from former friends and family networks. By the onset of the first violence, strong emotional bonds have typically been formed between the couple. The woman's social isolation makes her especially vulnerable and unable to get help (Walker 1979, 1984; Pagelow 1984; Browne 1987).

Over time, behaviors that battered women initially viewed as evidence of affection can become the triggers that lead to their assaults. The women report that the men's constant desire to know where they are may escalate into a requirement that they account for every hour of their time. Violent reprisals may occur if their explanations do not satisfy their partners. Battered women also frequently report extreme and delusional jealousy on the part of their partners, leading to increasing levels of isolation and risk in contacts with others (e.g., Frieze et al. 1980; Hotaling and Sugarman 1986).

2. *Marital Rape.*   Marital rape is a form of marital violence not measured by Straus, Gelles, and Steinmetz (1980) and many other re-

searchers. Marital rape is sometimes reported in relationships in which no other type of physical abuse occurs (Russell 1982; Finkelhor and Yllo 1983). However, it seems to be most frequently reported as a form of physical domination in otherwise violent relationships (Russell 1982; Frieze 1983). Incidence and prevalence estimates vary greatly, depending on the nature of the sample, the wording of key questions, and what definition is used. Studies use varying definitions of marital rape, and any reporting of empirical findings must be accompanied by an explanation of how sexually abusive behavior was defined for that sample.

Until the mid-1970s in the United States, rape of one's wife was not a crime. One typical statute (Pennsylvania's) defined rape as follows: "A person commits a felony of the first degree when he engages in sexual intercourse *with another person not his spouse:* (1) by forcible compulsion; (2) by threat of forcible compulsion that would prevent resistance by a person of reasonable resolution; (3) who is unconscious; or (4) who is so mentally deranged or deficient that such person is incapable of consent" (emphasis is added).

By 1980, only three states had completely eliminated the marital rape exemption from their laws, and five states had modified it. However, by 1982, thirteen other states had *extended* their exemptions to include cohabiting couples as well as those legally married (Mettger 1982). The reasons for the marital rape exemption can be seen in the history of rape laws and historical conceptions of the meaning of marriage (New York University Law Review 1977). Marriage has traditionally been seen as implying consent by the wife to grant sexual relations to her husband whenever he desires them. This means that the husband is seen as having a right to force his wife, through extreme force if necessary, to have sexual relations with him. In many states, this implied consent exists even when a couple is separated, so long as they are still legally married.

Researchers have not been so reluctant to define forced sex in marriage as rape. For instance, Pagelow (1984, p. 419) defines rape as "unwanted sexual contact accomplished by force, intimidation, or coercion that results in vaginal, anal, or oral sexual intercourse or penetration of a woman's body." Russell (1982, p. 43), in her survey on rape, followed a fairly strict legal definition that included forced anal and oral sex (if the subjects volunteered this information) but excluded sexual fondling. Other definitions are much broader. Bowker (1983*b*, p. 348) defined marital rape as "any sexual act forced on a woman against her will by violence or threat of violence." Doran (1980) asked respondents,

"Has your spouse or lover ever used violence or the threat of violence to force you to have sexual intercourse?" but did not specify other sexual acts.

Women have great difficulty in responding to questions about violent or forced sex in marriage. Even when asked specific questions, many victims experience an extreme sense of shame and humiliation that makes it difficult for them to disclose the existence of rape by a partner, even when assured anonymity (Gelles 1979; Russell 1982; Finkelhor and Yllo 1983; Pagelow 1984; Walker 1984). Russell (1982, p. 39) concluded that obtaining "honest disclosure of unwanted sexual experiences in marriage was more difficult . . . than disclosure of sexual abuse by all other categories of people, including the victims of incestuous abuse."

3. *Incidence and Prevalence.*   How common is marital rape? Data on marital rape tends to come from two sources: incidence studies on sexual assault conducted in the general population and research on physically abused wives in which some of the respondents report sexual assault by their partners.

In a random sample survey of 930 women in San Francisco, Russell (1982) asked questions to determine how many had been sexually abused by strangers, husbands, and other family members and found that 14 percent of the women who had ever been married (87 out of 644) reported rape by a husband or ex-husband. Respondents were asked to describe any kind of "unwanted sexual experiences" they had had, and then researchers excluded from the analyses those that did not meet the legal definition of rape. Thus the word "rape" was not used. When the results were tabulated for completed (as opposed to attempted) rapes, women reported more rapes by husbands and ex-husbands than by acquaintances or strangers. In fact, more than twice as many women reported sexual assaults by husbands as by strangers. Similarly, Finkelhor and Yllo (1983), in a representative sample of 326 women in Boston, found that 10 percent of women who had been married or lived with a partner reported at least one sexual assault by that partner. In this study, sexual assault was defined as sex in response to force or threat. Again, more than twice as many women reported sexual assault by husbands (10 percent) as reported assaults by a stranger.

Other studies, using less representative samples, found lower percentages. Doran (1981), in a sample of 612 respondents to a newspaper survey in northern New Jersey, found that 8 percent of women reported sexual activity with husbands or lovers in which violence or the threat of violence was used.

Research on severely violent relationships indicates that often the most violent assaults include sexual as well as physical attack (Browne 1987) and that battered women who are sexually assaulted by their husbands have typically experienced more severe nonsexual assaults than have other battered women (Doran 1980; Bowker 1983*b*; Frieze 1983; Shields and Hanneke 1983; Browne 1987). Bowker (1983*b*) conducted a study of marital rape in 146 battering relationships using a volunteer sample (most respondents were white and middle class) and found that in 23 percent of the relationships there had been sexual as well as nonsexual assault. Prescott and Letko (1977) noted that about a third of their sample of battered women reported sexual abuse in addition to battering. Pagelow (1980*b*) found that 37 percent of her sample of 325 battered women reported that their abusers had sexually assaulted them. (Respondents were asked, "Were you ever sexually assaulted by [your husband]?" and were advised, "Forcible rape *is* an assault.") Pagelow (1984) further observed that many of the women in her 1980 study who reported that they had *not* been raped said that they had submitted to sexual demands in order to prevent beatings or out of fear of the partner. Some women reported physical assaults during sexual activity as extreme as being choked until they lost consciousness, yet they did not define the behavior as *sexually* assaultive.

Higher percentages were found by two other studies of battered women. Walker (1984), using two separate measures of sexual assault in her study of 435 self-identified battered women, reported that 51 percent of the women responded affirmatively when asked if they had ever been "forced to have sex" by their abusers. In addition, 49 percent said that they had been asked or forced to participate in unusual sex acts. Similarly, in Shields and Hanneke's (1983) study of the wives of violent men, 46 percent of women whose husbands were violent within the family reported that they had experienced marital rape.

At least two studies have attempted to study marital rape apart from other marital violence. But, in both, marital rape was typically found in otherwise violent relationships. In Russell's random sample survey, 10 percent (63 of 644) of the women who had ever been married reported both rape and other types of assault by a partner, 4 percent (24 of 644) reported only wife rape, and 12 percent (75 of 644) reported physical assaults but not marital rape (1982, p. 89). (Thus the prevalence for nonsexual assaults of wives in the sample was 21 percent, compared to 14 percent for sexual assaults.) In a study of physically abused women conducted in Pittsburgh, Frieze (1983) compared a group of self-identified battered women ($N = 137$) with battered ($N = 48$) as well as nonbattered ($N = 89$) matched controls. Over one-third of the battered group reported being raped by their husbands, and over two-thirds felt they had been pressured into having sex with their husbands. Over 40 percent also reported that sex was unpleasant for them because of being forced. In those relationships in which the husband had not been violent in other ways, marital rape was rare. Frieze concluded that marital rape is most frequently associated with battering and may be "one of the most serious forms of battering" (1983, p. 552).

These marital rapes have serious consequences. Russell's (1982) data suggest that women who have been raped by their husbands perceive these sexual assaults as having more damaging long-term effects on their lives than do sexual assaults by strangers. Frieze (1983) found that marital rape was more predictive of a woman wanting to leave the marriage than severe violence alone. Marital rape victims suffer many of the reactions of other rape victims and need treatment for these symptoms that include sexual dysfunction as well as other stress responses (Hanneke and Shields 1985).

B. Power and Decision Making

Power differences among family members are often mentioned by family violence researchers as another factor in the violence, although the research findings are not entirely consistent (Hotaling and Sugarman 1986). One reason for the difficulty of generalizing studies is that each study uses its own conceptualization of power. Power has been defined in terms of dominance, decision making, and relative levels of resources (Frieze and McHugh 1981). The concept of power is central to Finkelhor (1983), who defines abuse as the stronger taking advantage of the weaker. Power was also central for Lystad (1986), who points out that the most powerless groups in society, the women and children, are most vulnerable to domestic abuse. One might also add the elderly to this list of vulnerable groups.

Violence or the threat of violence is an effective mechanism for controlling other people. Violence is used in this way among family members (Straus, Gelles, and Steinmetz 1980). Straus (1978) argues that one episode of violence toward a wife can cause a permanent change in the balance of marital power toward a strongly husband-dominant pattern. Other researchers have noted the instrumental nature of violence by husbands. Hilberman and Munson (1978) found in their study of battered women that the husbands were likely to become violent whenever they did not get their way.

The possession of resources such as money, education, social status, and friends is one measure of power. Violent men appear often to lack resources outside the home (Straus, Gelles, and Steinmetz 1980; Dvoskin 1981; Frieze and McHugh 1981; Finkelhor 1983). They may use violence against weaker family members to compensate for feelings of weakness outside the home (Finkelhor 1983). Walker (1983) and Hotaling and Sugarman (1986) also cite differences in resources as a causal factor in violence. Presumably, the husband feels a need to use violence to assert his power in the family to make up for his lack of status-related resources.

Power differentials were hypothesized as a correlate of domestic violence by Berk et al. (1983), who assessed power as a function of demographic characteristics. White men married to Hispanic women, who were assumed to be lower status than their husbands, were found to be more violent when other variables were controlled for in their study of domestic violence calls to the police. However, a similarly hypothesized relationship based on power as a function of the age difference in the couple was not found to be significant. In another study of relative resources, Hornung, McCullough, and Sugimoto (1981), in an analysis of a random sample of Kentucky women (from Schulman 1979), found that the risk of physical abuse was 1.3 times greater for women married to men who were underachievers in relation to their education level. Risk rates of 1.5 and 1.2 were associated, respectively, with women whose occupational attainments were low relative to their husbands or whose relative attainments were high. Similar patterns of risk were found for psychological abuse.

Decision making is another measure of family power. Frieze and McHugh (1981) found that decision making was highly related to the husbands' levels of violence. The most violent husbands tended to make most of the decisions about where the couple went together, whose friends they would see, and what major household purchases they should make. The most equalitarian marriages found by Frieze and McHugh were in the control group, in which there was no marital violence. Coleman and Straus (1986), in an analysis of the national household study data, found that equalitarian and divided-power marriages were the least violent. Such relationships may be similar to the low-violence marriages reported by Frieze et al. (1980), in which there was relatively equal low-level violence between husbands and wives. In these marriages, there appeared to be more equality between spouses than in the severely violent marriages that were much more husband dominant.

Another way in which battering men exert power is by controlling their wives' freedom of movement. Frieze and McHugh (1981) found that battered wives had less freedom to go where they wanted and tended to remain at home much more than women married to nonviolent men. The severe batterers also controlled family finances the most closely. Walker (1983) found that abusing men closely monitored where their wives were. Her explanation for such behavior is that violent men are basically insecure and feel a need for this type of control over their wives. Of course, it is their violence or the threat of such violence that allows them to exert this type of dominance. Other men who felt similarly insecure would not have the same means of enforcing these restrictions on their wives.

The issues surrounding power and violence are quite complex. It is never clear how much the use of physical force changes the power dynamics of the marriage and the characteristics of the man and woman involved. Do battered women have less influence over marital decision making because they are fearful of repeated violence, or are less assertive women more likely to be beaten? Such questions cannot be answered with confidence without longitudinal data. There is also the intriguing question of how moderately and highly violent relationships differ on various power dimensions. Although we do not yet understand as much about power as we would like, it appears that this is a fruitful variable for further investigation.

C. Alcohol and Drug Abuse

The drunken husband coming home and beating his wife is a common image in fiction. Such behavior on the part of the man is at least partially excused because he was drinking. Many feel that his drinking causes his violence. The wife's alcohol consumption is also seen as important in understanding the dynamics of family violence. A woman who is beaten when she has been drinking is more likely to be blamed for the violence. Her drunken behavior is seen as provoking the violence whereas a woman who is sober is less likely to be blamed for her husband's violence (Richardson and Campbell 1980).

Abusive men with severe alcohol or drug problems are apt to abuse their partners both when drunk and when sober, are violent more frequently, and inflict more serious injuries on their partners than do abusive men who do not have a history of alcohol or drug problems. They are also more apt to attack their partners sexually and are more likely to be violent outside of the home (Roy 1977; Frieze and Knoble 1980; Walker 1984; Browne 1987).

Seven of nine studies that investigated this question using some sort of a comparison group found that abusive men were more likely to abuse alcohol than were nonviolent men (Hotaling and Sugarman 1986). These studies ranged from nationally representative samples to small, matched samples using multiple comparison groups. In contrast to the clear pattern of results of alcohol abuse in male batterers, however, only 1 of 6 studies of abused wives that used control or comparison groups found greater alcohol use by battered women than by nonabused women (Hotaling and Sugarman 1986). Coleman and Straus (1983) analyzed national survey data to determine the relation of marital violence and alcohol abuse. A general correlation of "drunkenness" and spousal violence was found. However, those who showed evidence of extreme alcohol abuse were not the most violent. This finding was interpreted as indicating that those who were most often drunk were "anesthetized" to an intolerable world. Frieze and Knoble (1980) also found that the men who most often drank alcohol were not the most violent husbands, perhaps because alcoholics have less physical control over their bodies.

Other studies of special populations indicate a relation between the use of alcohol and marital violence, although these studies usually focus on help-seeking populations or couples involved with the police or the courts—both groups that would be expected to use alcohol at higher rates than in the population at large. For example, in a sample of 150 women who had called a hotline for help and advice about problems relating to the violence they had been subjected to by their husbands, Roy (1977) found that 85 percent of the men had alcohol or drug problems. These men were violent, but they were not always drunk when they were violent. Of the occasional drinkers, 80 percent beat their wives only when drinking. Thus, alcohol appeared as a direct cause of violence only for the men who were *not* heavy drinkers.

Rosenbaum and O'Leary (1981) found that alcohol abuse was a greater problem in abusive men who refused to enter a program for treatment of marital violence than for those abusive men who did enter treatment. This latter group did not differ from other nonviolent control groups in drinking behavior. Another study of 512 women in a Florida shelter for battered women found a high correlation between alcohol and the husbands' use of violence. Seventy-two percent of the men were reported as having drinking problems (compared to 8 percent of the women), and 28 percent of the men (and 5 percent of the women) reportedly had problems with drug abuse (LaBell 1979).

Using an entirely different type of sample, Orford et al. (1975) found that the wives of men referred to a clinic for suspected drinking problems frequently reported that violence was a problem in their marriages. Forty-five percent of these women reported being physically beaten and 27 percent reported that their husbands had attempted to inflict serious injuries on them. Additionally, 72 percent of these wives of suspected alcoholics reported being threatened with violence by their husbands.

An association of alcohol and marital violence also shows up in police data. In one such study of 1,388 police calls in inner-city New York, Bard and Zacker (1974) found that the batterer (who was typically male) was drinking in 30 percent of the calls for family disputes, while the person being assaulted was drinking in 26 percent of the cases. But, in cases where there was *clear physical evidence* that an assault had taken place (through visual inspection of the injuries received), only 21 percent of the cases showed evidence that one or both of the parties had been drinking. Alcohol was more common in cases where there was less injury. Bard and Zacker speculated that when the husband was drinking and seemed about to become violent, the wife then called the police to prevent an attack. These findings were replicated in a Norwalk, Connecticut, study of 344 police calls for domestic disturbances (Zacker and Bard 1977).

In another study of 1,790 police calls in Ontario, Canada, Gerson (1978) found more marital violence in families in which one or both spouses had been drinking. Of 411 marital assaults in which alcohol use was reported, both partners had been drinking in 44 percent of the cases, while in another 44 percent only the violent spouse had been drinking. In 13 percent of the cases, only the victim had been drinking.

Another study of a special population (Byles 1978) found a relationship between alcohol and violence through an analysis of records of 139 families who had appeared in family court in Ontario, Canada, often for problems relating to divorce. For these couples, the most frequently cited problem area was violence, usually by the husband against the wife. Alcohol-related problems were the third most common type of problem. However, there was also more violence in the alcohol problem families. Nearly three-fourths of the ninety-five alcohol problem families also had problems with violence, while less than a third of the families without alcohol problems had violence problems.

It is not surprising that alcohol should be linked to marital violence in our culture since there is a good deal of evidence that alcohol use is related to physically aggressive behavior in men. Alcohol use is reported to be common in cases of assault (e.g., Nicol et al. 1973; Mayfield 1976) and homicide (Wolfgang and Strohm 1957; Virkkunen 1974), as well as in crimes in general (Fitzpatrick 1974; Sobell and Sobell 1975). Laboratory research supports this relation. Subjects given alcohol in the laboratory who are then given an opportunity to administer shocks to another subject show higher levels of aggressive responding than do nondrinking subjects (Taylor and Gammon 1975; Zeichner and Pihl 1979). However, at least some of these effects may be related to feelings that socially unacceptable behavior is more permissible when drinking (Goldstein 1975).

Alcohol may also have physiological effects that would lead to increased aggression. Alcohol causes a decline in conceptual abilities that can cause a misinterpretation of actions of other people (Hull and Bond 1986). Also, individuals who already have aggressive or sociopathic tendencies are especially likely to become violent when under the influence of alcohol (Powers and Kutash 1978).

Although a strong association has consistently been found between substance abuse and violence, some have argued that alcohol should be viewed as a disinhibiting, but not a causal, factor (e.g., Pagelow 1981; Walker 1984; Sonkin, Martin, and Walker 1985). The use of alcohol and other drugs may serve a multitude of purposes for individuals involved in abusive interactions. Walker (1979), in an in-depth interview study of battered women, found that, although the battering men were reported to have drinking problems, and the most severe violence was done by alcoholic men, specific violent incidents did not always involve alcohol. Inconsistencies in the relation between alcohol use and violence have also been noted by Dvoskin (1981) and Eberle (1982). To differentiate batterers who abuse alcohol more systematically from those who do not, Eberle did a series of discriminant analyses using various characteristics of violent men as reported by her self-identified battered woman sample. Results indicated that nonalcohol users were younger and that their wives drank less. These nondrinkers were also less violent overall.

Gelles (1974) has speculated that perpetrators of violence may drink to excuse their own conduct. This may be particularly effective when the excuse of intoxication is also accepted by others. A number of researchers have discussed the tendency of abused women to blame the drinking, rather than their violent assailant, for the abusive incidents (Roy 1977; Frieze and Knoble 1980; Pagelow 1981; Russell 1982; Bowker 1983*a*). By saying that the violence is caused by alcohol use, family members do not have to admit that they are engaging in socially unacceptable or deviant behavior. Many people believe that intoxicated persons have a period of "time-out" during which they are not expected to follow normal social rules (Richardson and Campbell 1980). Besides providing battered wives with an explanation for their husband's violence, the alcohol attribution also gives them hope that, if their mates could stop drinking, the violence would also cease (Frieze and Knoble 1980; Walker 1984; Browne 1987).

Sonkin and Durphy (1985), in their work with violent men, also suggest that aggressive men may use substances such as alcohol or recreational drugs in part to dull the guilt and sadness they feel for their abuse of loved ones, although this connection is hard to establish since other evidence of contrition appears to decrease over time.

V. Reactions to Physical Assault and Threat by the Victim

Studies of victims of crimes, accidents, environmental disasters, and harassment have all found common emotional stress reactions (Janoff-Bulman and Frieze 1983). Psychiatrists have identified these reactions in the *DSM-III* as "Post-traumatic Stress Disorder." Common manifestations of this stress include feelings of anger, shock, disbelief, confusion, fear, and anxiety. Victims often feel helpless and insecure (e.g., Figley 1985). Such reactions are also seen in battered women.

A. *Emotional Reactions to Victimization*

Like other victims, battered women respond emotionally to violence. There are common emotional reactions a battered woman may have after a violent incident. She may be upset about the experience but hopeful that things will be better in the future. She may be fearful of future violence being even more severe—perhaps severe enough to threaten her life or that of her children. She may feel helpless to change her situation (Frieze 1980).

Emotional reactions by a battered woman to an assault may be greater than those of some other victims of stranger crime or natural disaster. For the battered woman, the victimization is often repeated, and the victim is intimately involved with the victimizer (Miller and Porter 1983). Her situation may be more analogous to that of the prisoner of war (Romero 1985) or a torture victim (Chandler 1986) than to victims of other crimes. Chandler's phenomenological analysis of battered women's experiences suggests that overriding fear and a loss of a sense of self characterize the severely battered woman. Other empirically based data show elevated anxiety scores and high levels of depression in a sample of forty-seven Arkansas shelter women (Hughes and Barad 1983). Many of the general models of reactions and coping of victims appear to apply to battered women (Hilberman 1980).

B. Cognitive Coping Strategies

In addition to emotional responses to victimization, victims employ a variety of coping strategies.

1. *Redefinition of the Event.*   Whether an individual feels victimized after experiencing a potentially victimizing event depends, in part, on an assessment of what happened (Folkman 1984). For any situation, many interpretations are possible. One of the first responses to any type of stress is to analyze the event to decide how serious it is. Cancer patients, for example, may compare their own situation to others who are less fortunate (Wood, Taylor, and Lichtman 1985); those cancer patients who see themselves as not having a very serious case feel better, independent of their realistic situation. Similarly, rape victims who redefine the rape as "not really a rape" appear to have fewer negative symptoms afterward (Scheppele and Bart 1983). These data suggest that denial can be an effective coping strategy. However, such denial can cause even more serious problems if the "victim" does not receive needed help (Roth and Cohen 1986).

This strategy has often been reported by those who work with battered women. Battered women often deny that anything serious has happened to them, at least at first. For example, as Chandler (1986) points out, denial may be a factor in why women marry men who have already been violent early in their relationship. Counselors also note that battered women often deny their own experiences.

Another form of denial is to discount or minimize what has happened. Battered women may discount what has happened as caused by unusual circumstances that will not happen again (Frieze 1980). Since battering is likely to recur, such discounting is probably particularly ineffective as a coping strategy for battered women. Battered women's denial of the violence may also account for the underreporting of family violence that many researchers have hypothesized.

Another way of redefining the event is to look at the experience as having a greater meaning—a test of personal strength and character or a message from God. This search for meaning is a common response in incest victims (Silver, Boon, and Stones 1983). One form of the search for meaning in the battered woman is for her to see herself as being called on to help her obviously needy husband (Chandler 1986).

2. *Self-Blame.*   Research dealing with the reactions of *all* types of victims shows a general tendency for victims to blame themselves. It is not uncommon, for example, for victims of unprovoked sexual assaults to take personal responsibility for the crime. Thus, a rape victim may focus on the clothing she was wearing or on not being vigilant enough in observing others around her (Janoff-Bulman 1979; Scheppele and Bart 1983). Following the same pattern, a battered woman may say to herself, "If only I had gotten dinner ready on time."

Common sense might suggest that holding oneself responsible for one's victimization would be self-defeating and maladaptive. However, there is some research indicating that such self-blame can be quite functional (Janoff-Bulman 1979). This is especially true if the self-blame is behavioral rather than characterological. Characterological self-blame attributes one's victimization to relatively permanent aspects of one's personality. Such characterological attributions give a woman little confidence that she can avoid future victimization and can produce feelings of depression and helplessness. Rape victims who made characterological attributions also tended to feel they *deserved* the rapes. Not only did they see themselves as the types of women who get raped, but also as the types of people who should be raped (Janoff-Bulman 1979).

Rape victims who attributed their rapes to behavioral factors were more confident about avoiding future attacks. By seeing particular actions or behaviors they had done as responsible (such as saying they should have been more careful about going out alone at night or dating someone they did not know well), they were able to take psychological control over the event; to avoid future victimization it is necessary for them only to act in a different way (Frieze 1987).

Other research has suggested that self-blaming may not always be adaptive (Meyer and Taylor 1986). Rape victims who blamed themselves were more likely to experience sexual dissatisfaction and depression after the rape. This was true whether the self-blaming was behavioral or characterological. Schultz and Decker (1985) also failed to find that self-blaming was adaptive for victims of spinal-cord injuries. Gilbert and Mangelsdorff (1979) provide a possible explanation for these discrepancies. They found that people who feel that they have more control over their daily lives tend to feel more stress. Perhaps self-blaming is adaptive only if it truly gives victims a sense that they can control their lives in the future and can prevent further victimization.

Battered women have often been reported to blame themselves for the violence they receive (Frieze 1979; Miller and Porter 1983). Such attributions may give the battered woman a feeling of control and hopefulness for the future. However, a battered woman might make such an attribution and still fear that the violence might get worse, especially if she felt that concrete measures, such as changing her own behaviors or getting help for her husband, were needed before the violence would stop and that the violence might get worse before these measures could take effect. Also, it should be kept in mind that even though battered women may see themselves as doing something that contributes to their husbands' violence, they see their husbands as ultimately responsible (Frieze 1980; Porter 1983). But, at the same time, many battered women feel shame about the violence (Chandler 1986).

Rather than asking "Why me?"—the question posed by other victims—they may instead ask, "What did I do tonight that set him off?" (Miller and Porter 1983). Once this question is answered, battered women may go to great ends to attempt to change their behaviors so that they will not precipitate the violence again. Although this may make them feel that they have some control over the violence, often they do not. The more likely scenario is that the violence will escalate (Hilberman and Munson 1978; Walker 1978, 1984; Frieze 1980). Thus, behavioral self-blame as a coping response for battered women does not appear to be a successful long-term strategy.

That self-blaming can have at least short-term benefits shows up in clinical studies. Battered women who saw some relation between their own behavior or personality and their partner's violence were rated as more effectively coping by shelter counselors in a study of fifty shelter residents in San Jose, California (Porter 1983). These "self-blamers" also rated themselves as happier than other battered women at the same shelter.

Miller and Porter (1983) have identified another form of self-blame that appears to be effective for battered women who have left their husbands. Such women feel a need to understand why they were in such a relationship so that they can avoid another one. In such cases, Miller and Porter found battered women making attributions to a "former self." They saw some aspect of themselves as permitting the violence to occur, but this aspect was seen as no longer part of them.

3. *Feelings of Helplessness.*   Another reaction identified as one of the general responses to victimization is to feel helpless (Brickman et al. 1982). Attributions to factors that are unchangeable and continuing

have been theorized as leading to feelings of helplessness (Abramson, Seligman, and Teasdale 1978). If one further sees oneself as the cause of an unchangeable, negative situation, the helplessness is further confounded with low self-esteem (Abramson, Seligman, and Teasdale 1978). An example of the type of attribution that would be expected to lead to feelings of helplessness in a battered woman would be a belief that she was the type of woman who deserved to be beaten (Frieze 1979). Such feelings would give her little hope for the future. This image of the passive, self-depreciating, depressed battered woman is one of the common images in the media today and one that is being labeled as the stereotypic battered woman profile by researchers in the field (Walker 1979). Another type of belief that would be associated with feelings of helplessness would be the belief that all men are violent toward their wives, no matter what their wives do. This, too, would give the battered woman little reason to hope for a nonviolent future relationship, no matter what she did.

Clinical studies have identified such feelings in battered women. With repeated unsuccessful attempts to control the battering, some battered women begin to demonstrate many of the signs of generalized feelings of helplessness and a perception of being unable to control their lives (Walker 1979, 1984). As this occurs, they become less and less able to change their situations for the better.

However, just as there has been found to be more than one type of battered woman, there are clearly battered women who do not show evidence of a generalized feeling of helplessness. Shaud's (1983) study of Minneapolis battered women indicated that when asked to respond to a scale measuring generalized feelings of helplessness, there was very low inter-item consistency. Thus, although the battered women may have felt helpless to control some aspects of their lives, this was not a pervasive reaction to all aspects of their lives. Further study is needed to isolate the variables that determine when battered women will show helplessness. One hypothesis is that this is most likely for severely battered women who have also been victims of child abuse or sexual assault and who have few economic resources. As will be discussed below, most battered women try to seek help and make continued efforts to change their situations.

C. Behavioral Reactions

Behavioral responses in all types of victims tend to take one of three major forms: withdrawal from others, lashing out and aggression, or seeking help from others (Janoff-Bulman and Frieze 1987). Such reactions show strong sex differences. As a response to their fear or shock, female victims are especially likely to retreat into their homes, not going out and not seeing others. Such forms of withdrawal do not appear to be adaptive although they are not uncommon (Burgess and Holmstrom 1979; Meyer and Taylor 1986). A more productive strategy also used more by women is to seek help. Men are more likely to demonstrate aggressive responses.

    1. *Seeking Help from Others.* Many crime and accident victims turn to others for help—for medical assistance, emotional support, information, or assistance with physical tasks resulting from the victimization (Frieze, Hymer, and Greenberg 1987). Others tell no one. Those who reach out to other people may not receive the assistance they want. Friends and acquaintances as well as bystanders may ignore victims, whom they see as "losers" or because they fear guilt by association (Bard and Sangrey 1979). Or, they may not know how to help (Wortman and Lehman 1985). Others avoid victims because victims are so often depressed, and most people prefer not being around unhappy people (Coates, Wortman, and Abbey 1979).

    Social support, if effective, can be a major determinant of successful coping for the victim (e.g., Schultz and Decker 1985), especially for female victims (Holahan and Moss 1985). Janoff-Bulman and her associates (Janoff-Bulman, Madden, and Timko 1983; Janoff-Bulman 1985) argue that positive social support is of special importance to women because being victimized by another human being decreases their belief that the world is benevolent and caring. This part of their worldview has to be rebuilt over time with the help of caring others.

    Most battered women do seek help for the violence or, more generally, for marital problems (Frieze 1979; Pagelow 1981). For example, in Schulman's (1979) Kentucky sample, 43 percent of the respondents who had been abused had told no one. Forty-three percent of the 146 battered women in a Milwaukee study received help from family members and 52 percent from friends (Bowker 1984). Similar findings were reported by Frieze et al. (1980), who found that 55 percent of the self-identified battered women in their sample had sought help from relatives, 52 percent from friends, and 39 percent from ministers or priests; 42 percent had sought psychological help. None of these resources was rated by the women as especially helpful overall (average helpfulness was between 3, "no effect," and 4, "helped"). Although sometimes adding to her frustrations, social support can be quite important for the battered woman in trying to cope with her victimization and in avoiding future battering (Mitchell and Hodson 1982). According to Bowker (1983*a*), material assistance was given to battered women by family members in 50 percent of the cases he examined. Friends were also likely to give such concrete forms of help. Both of these groups also allowed the battered woman to talk about her situation and solutions to the problem.

Shelters are probably one of the most important sources of institutionalized help for battered women. Women's shelters are now available in many areas of the country for battered women (Center for Women Policy Studies 1980). Ten percent of the women in Bowker's sample went to a shelter after the first incidence of abuse but, with repeated abuse, 29 percent sought their help (Bowker 1983*a*). Shelters provide physical protection as well as other services. A study of twenty residents of a New Haven, Connecticut, shelter showed clear evidence of less depression and more hopefulness in the women after living two weeks in the shelter (Sedlak 1983).

One commonly utilized service of shelters is self-help groups in which women talk with other battered women. Others who have dealt with the same problems provide models (Bowker 1983*a*) and a basis of social comparison (Coates and Winston 1983).

2. The Police and the Criminal Justice System.   Victims of all types of crimes also seek help from the criminal justice system. Overall, about one-third of all crimes are reported to the police (Zawitz 1983). Notifying the police reduces the crime victim's stress in several ways. The victim's sense of injustice, outrage, or offense can be reduced by reporting and a sense of control restored if the police catch the offender, especially if the offender is convicted, punished, or forced to make restitution (Ruback, Greenberg, and Westcott 1984). This is especially true for battered women. One factor that may be effective in keeping violent husbands from further beating their wives is arresting them (Langan and Innes 1986; Sherman and Berk 1984). When the police do agree to intervene, there is some evidence that this may prevent further recurrences of the assaults, at least for some abusers. However, the effectiveness of police interventions is still under investigation (see Elliott, in this volume).

That the majority of crime victims do not report their victimization to the police suggests that the police are not seen as a source of help by many victims. Indeed, two of the most frequently cited reasons that crime victims give for not calling the police are that "nothing can be done" and that "the police would not want to be bothered" (Zawitz 1983). Similar patterns are seen with battered women. In Bowker's (1983a) sample of women who had "beaten wife beating," 9 percent had called the police after the first violent incident. This percentage rose to 38 percent after the worst violence occurred. Frieze et al. (1980) asked their study participants if they had ever called the police. Only 38 percent of the self-identified battered women had ever called the police; 10 percent had called them "often." However, the battered women identified in the comparison sample had been more reluctant to seek help from the police. Only 13 percent of this group had ever called the police for help with their violent mates. Few of the women in either group filed formal charges against their mates even after calling the police. When asked why they did not press charges, common responses were fears of retaliation from their mates and not thinking that formal charges would help their situations.

Wife-abuse victims often have difficulties with the police. In two studies, abused wives rated the police as the *least* helpful of available sources of help (Frieze et al. 1980; Bowker 1983a). There are a number of reasons for this. Police officers may not think of women as victims of violent crime, and they may refuse to arrest the abusive husband even when the wife requests them to do so (Bowker 1983a). Women reporting assaults or threats by partners are familiar with being referred for personal mental health counseling or asked why they do not leave their homes, rather than being offered effective alternatives.

3. *Violent Responses by Battered Wives.*   Aggressive responses, such as trying to find and punish one's assailant or becoming violent toward family members are not uncommon responses of victims, especially male victims (Carmen, Ricker, and Mills 1984; Singer 1986). Other aggressive responses that might be more typical in women victims would include anger at men, buying a gun and learning to use it, or enrolling in a self-defense class. The most aggressive response to being victimized is to kill the victimizer. Such a response does sometimes occur in battered women.

National data indicate that a substantial proportion of U.S. homicides occur within the family (see Wolfgang [1958], Wilbanks [1982, 1983], and Zimring, Mukherjee, and Van Winkle [1983] for more localized reports). Browne and Flewelling (1986) found that, from 1980 to 1984, approximately 25 percent of all one-on-one cases of murder and nonnegligent manslaughter—or 18,712 homicides—were between family members over the age of eighteen. About 62 percent of these intrafamily homicides, or the deaths of 8,196 people, occurred between heterosexual partners (spouse, common-law, or ex-spouse). Of these homicides, the majority of the victims were female; 58 percent were women killed by male partners, and 42 percent were men killed by their women partners. Women were more at risk of homicide victimization from a male partner than from other family members, or from all other categories of persons outside of the partnership combined. Over half (52 percent) of murdered women are killed by their male partners, compared to only 12 percent of murdered men who are killed by their female partners. Men are more likely to be killed by acquaintances or strangers than are women (78 percent of male victims vs. 40 percent of female victims). Similarly, for male-perpetrated homicides, 55 percent are of acquaintances, 18 percent of strangers, and 16 percent of female partners. For female-perpetrated homicides, only 4 percent involve strangers, 28 percent are of acquaintances, and 55 percent involve partners.

These national data do not give us information about the contexts within which these murders occur. Other literature on spousal homicide provides some basis for speculation about the gender-based differences in homicide involvement for men and women. One thesis is that women kill primarily their male partners because it is these men from whom they are most at risk. In his early study of homicide in Philadelphia, Wolfgang (1967) notes that 60 percent of the husbands killed by wives had "precipitated" their own deaths—that is, were the first to use physical force, strike blows, or threaten with a weapon, compared with only 5 percent of the wife victims. Wilbanks (1983), in his study of all men and women arrested for homicide in Dade County, Florida, during 1980, also reported that the victims of female perpetrators were much more likely to have been the first to use force or threat than were the victims of male offenders.

Research on more specialized samples adds further information about the context of these crimes. Chimbos (1978), in a study of spousal homicides in Canada, observed that interspousal homicides were usually the endpoint of an ongoing series of assault and threats. Chimbos further notes that nearly all of the women charged with the deaths of their mates had previously been beaten by them. In such cases, it is the abusive mate who becomes the final victim. A 1977 study at the Women's Correctional Center in Chicago revealed that 40 percent of the women serving time there for murder or manslaughter had killed husbands or lovers who they reported had *repeatedly* attacked them (Lindsey 1978). In a study of women incarcerated in California for killing their mates, Totman (1978) reported that 93 percent of the women reported being physically abused by their partners, and 67 percent said that the homicide was in defense of themselves or a child.

City data indicate that there were many "cries for help" prior to the lethal incident in the majority of homicide cases between partners. A review of homicide records in Detroit and Kansas City revealed that, in 85 percent to 90 percent of the cases, police had been called to the home at least once during the two years before the incident, and in half (54 percent) they had been called five or more times (Police Foundation 1976). In the 1977 study at the Chicago Women's Correctional Center, all the women who had killed abusive mates reported that they called for police help at least five times before taking the man's life, and many said the violence they endured became more, rather than less, severe after their attempts at gaining assistance (Lindsey 1978).

Browne (1986, 1987) compared forty-two cases in which battered women were charged with the death or serious injury of their mates with 205 abusive relationships in which no lethal incident had oc-curred; several factors were found that distinguished the homicide rela-tionships from the nonhomicide relationships. Significantly more men in the homicide group became intoxicated every day or almost every day by the end of the relationship (80 percent vs. 40 percent), used street drugs (29 percent vs. 8 percent), and had made threats to kill (89 percent vs. 59 percent). Physical attacks occurred with greater fre-quency in the homicide group, and the women sustained more, and more severe, injuries as a result of these attacks than did women in the nonhomicide group. In addition, over 75 percent of women in the homicide group reported that they had been raped by their mates on at least one occasion (compared to 59 percent in the nonhomicide group), and 62 percent (vs. 37 percent) said that their mates had forced or urged them to perform other sexual acts against their will.

Browne (1987) conducted a discriminant function analysis that identified seven variables that in linear combination best differentiated the relationships of battered women who had killed or seriously injured their abusers from those who had not. These variables include fre-quency of intoxication by the man, drug use by the man, the frequency with which abusive incidents occurred, severity of the woman's in-juries, forced or threatened sexual assault by the man, the man's threats to kill, and the woman's threats to commit suicide. Although 92 percent of the men in the homicide group tended to have a history of misdemeanor and criminal arrests, most women in the homicide group had no history of violent, or even illegal, behavior. Yet, in these cases, the women's attempts to survive with an increasingly violent and unpredictable mate eventually resulted in an act of violence on their parts as well. Homicides that result from abusive relationships remind us of the seriousness of marital violence and highlight how a lack of intervention strategies and responsiveness by all facets of society can exacerbate the dangers already present in these situations (Browne 1987).

4. *Leaving the Relationship.*   Many ask why battered women remain in such relationships. The reasons are complex and vary with the individual (Gelles 1976). Some of the common beliefs of battered women and the lack of physical resources that keep them in these marriages are outlined below.

Leaving by battered women tends to take one of two forms. First, the woman may leave for a brief period and then return to her violent mate. Or, she may leave permanently and establish a new life-style. Looking first at temporary leave-taking, the battered woman who feels in immediate danger may be most likely to do this. This would be especially likely in those women who blame the husband for the violence (rather than themselves) and feel that they have no way of controlling an immediate outburst of violence. One other consideration here, though, is whether she had somewhere to go. Having money, a car, nearby friends, or family who could shelter her, or having a "safe house" or woman's shelter would be essential so that she would have the option of leaving. Isolated rural women may have the most difficulty in finding somewhere to go. Leaving on a temporary basis would also be a more likely response if the woman fears that the next violent incident will consist of extreme violence (Frieze 1980).

A number of factors may inhibit women from leaving permanantly. Some women cannot leave because of economic dependence on their husbands; others have nowhere to go because they lack resources of their own simply to pack up and drive to a motel, and they have no other source of shelter that would not require money (Frieze et al. 1980; Pagelow 1981). This situation is further complicated if the woman has children she would want to take with her. Other factors that might make it difficult to leave would be loss of her job and social status and fear of disapproval from family or friends (Pagelow 1977). By leaving, a woman gives up her identity as a wife, risks social disapproval, loses economic support, and loses any love she feels from her husband (Waites 1978).

Another fear that keeps women in abusive relationships is a fear of retaliation (Ridington 1978). The battered wife may fear that her husband will retaliate against her, their children, or her other family members if she tries to leave. Abused women's fear that their abuser will find them and retaliate against their leaving is justified. Some women who have left an abusive partner have been followed and harassed for months or even years, and some have been killed (Lindsey 1978; Jones 1980; Pagelow 1980a; Browne 1987). Evidence suggests that, in many cases, the man's violence continues to escalate after a separation (Fields 1978; Fiora-Gormally 1978; Lewin 1979; Pagelow 1980a, 1981). One of the best empirical predictors of women's leaving is the severity of the violence. Women, themselves, also cite this as one of the major factors in wanting to leave (Frieze et al. 1980). The severely battered woman may leave her husband, often because she is in fear of her life or that of her children if she stays (Walker 1978; Frieze 1979). Women who are battered *and* raped by their husbands suffer some of the strongest negative reactions; it is not surprising, therefore, that this group is most likely to leave their abusive mates (Frieze 1983).

VI. Conclusions

There is now much research on battered women. A good deal is known about the prevalence of marital violence and about some of the dynamics of violent marriages. Although both men and women engage in violent behavior toward one another, men tend to inflict more damage than women. Such violence can be quite severe, although it does not have to be. But any level of violence appears to affect the power relationships within the couple. Sexual violence accompanies other forms of violence in some relationships.

Our knowledge of marital violence does have some major limitations. Many studies gather data only from the battered woman. We need to learn more about violence from the battering male's orientation, although there are enormous practical and ethical difficulties in finding and interviewing the violent spouse. Another subject about which very little is known is whether there are battered men—men who are seriously injured by female mates over a long period of time who do not inflict similar injury on their mates. If such men exist, it is perhaps not surprising that they would be reluctant to report given the general reticence of male victims (Janoff-Bulman and Frieze 1987) and the social stigma of being assaulted by a woman.

There are a number of methodological problems in the existing body of empirical data as well. Most data are gathered at one time. The particular time chosen may affect the responses of the interviewee. We are handicapped in being able to describe the sequential processes, the background, and the situational variables that would support stronger theoretical positions about causes and correlates of various forms of spouse abuse. Consequently, more longitudinal work is desperately needed (see Weis [in this volume] for a review of methodological issues in family violence research).

Another weakness is that much of the existing research is characterized by a descriptive format. Reports of battered women are tabulated and reported. Occasionally, an attempt is made to correlate various components of their marriages. What is lacking is theory that would enable us to better understand how violent relationships develop and why victims make the responses they do. In this essay, we have made some preliminary attempts to outline theoretical frameworks that might be useful for researchers in this area: attribution theory and theories about the causes of reactions to any form of victimization. Some of the research on power also draws from important sociological theories of marital power and decision making. We look forward to the development of these theoretical models and the formulation of others to assist all of us in better understanding marital violence.

Such models will better enable us to identify the differing types of battered women. Empirical analyses of descriptive data clearly show that not all battered women are alike (e.g., Snyder and Fruchtman 1981), but without better theory, it is difficult to identify the crucial differentiating variables.

A thorough knowledge of the dynamics of marital violence is a critical prerequisite for the design and implementation of new policies and more effective interventions. Enhanced theoretical understanding would also assist service providers. We hope that this essay can be one step in this direction.

REFERENCES

Abramson, L. Y., M. E. P. Seligman, and J. D. Teasdale. 1978. "Learned Helplessness in Humans: Critique and Reformulation." *Journal of Abnormal Psychology* 87:49–74.

Bard, M., and D. Sangrey. 1979. *The Crime Victim's Book.* New York: Basic.

Bard, M., and J. Zacker. 1974. "Assaultiveness and Alcohol Use in Family Disputes." *Criminology* 12:281–92.

Berk, R. A., S. F. Berk, D. R. Loseke, and D. Rauma. 1983. "Mutual Combat and Other Family Violence Myths." In *The Dark Side of Families: Current Family Violence Research,* edited by D. Finkelhor and associates. Beverly Hills, Calif.: Sage.

Berk, R. A., S. F. Berk, and P. J. Newton. 1984. "An Empirical Analysis of Police Responses to Incidents of Wife Battery." Paper presented at the second national conference of Family Violence Researchers, University of New Hampshire, Durham, July.

Berk, S., and D. Loseke. 1981. "Handling Family Violence: Situational Determinants of Police Arrest in Domestic Disturbances." *Law and Society Review* 15:317–44.

Block, C. R., and R. L. Block. 1984. "Crime Definition, Crime Measurement, and Victim Surveys." *Journal of Social Issues* 40:137–60.

Bower, G. H. 1981. "Mood and Memory." *American Psychologist* 36:129–48.

Bowker, L. H. 1983a. *Beating Wife-Beating.* Lexington, Mass.: Lexington.

———. 1983b. "Marital Rape: A Distinct Syndrome?" *Social Casework* (June), pp. 347–52.

———. 1984. "Coping with Wife Abuse: Personal and Social Networks." In *Battered Women and Their Families,* edited by A. R. Roberts. New York: Springer.

Brickman, P., V. C. Rabinowitz, J. Karuza, D. Coates, E. C., and L. Kidder. 1982. "Models of Helping and Coping." *American Psychologist* 37:368–84.

Browne, A. 1986. "Assault and Homicide at Home: When Battered Women Kill." In *Advances in Applied Social Psychology,* vol. 3, edited by M. J. Saks and L. Saxe. Hillsdale, N.J.: Erlbaum.

———. 1987. *When Battered Women Kill.* New York: Free Press.

Browne, A., and R. Flewelling. 1986. "Women as Victims or Perpetrators of Homicide." Paper presented at the annual meeting of the American Society of Criminology, Atlanta, November.

Burgess, A. W., and L. Holmstrom. 1979. "Adaptive Strategies and Recovery from Rape." *American Journal of Psychiatry* 136:1278–82.

Byles, J. A. 1978. "Violence, Alcohol Problems and Other Problems in Disintegrating Families." *Journal of Studies on Alcohol* 39:551–53.

Carlson, B. 1977. "Battered Women and Their Assailants." *Social Work* 22:455–60.

Carmen, E. H., P. P. Ricker, and T. Mills. 1984. "Victims of Violence and Psychiatric Illness." *American Journal of Psychiatry* 141:378–83.

Center for Women Policy Studies. 1980. *Programs Providing Services to Battered Women.* 3d ed. Washington, D.C.: Center for Women Policy Studies.

Chandler, S. 1986. "The Psychology of Battered Women." Doctoral dissertation, University of California, Berkeley, Department of Education.

Chimbos, P. D. 1978. *Marital Violence: A Study of Interspousal Homicide.* San Francisco: R & E Research Associates.

Coates, D., and T. Winston. 1983. "Counteracting the Deviance of Depression: Peer Support Groups for Victims." *Journal of Social Issues* 39(2):169–94.

Coates, D., C. B. Wortman, and A. Abbey. 1979. "Reactions to Victims." In *New Approaches to Social Problems: Applications of Attribution Theory*, edited by I. H. Frieze, D. Bar-Tal, and J. S. Carroll. San Francisco: Jossey-Bass.

Coleman, D. H., and M. A. Straus. 1983. "Alcohol Abuse and Family Violence." In *Alcohol, Drug Abuse, and Aggression*, edited by E. Gottheil, A. Durley, I. E. Skolada, and H. M. Waxman. Springfield, Mass.: Thomas.

———. 1986. "Marital Power, Conflict, and Violence in a Nationally Representative Sample of American Couples." *Violence and Victims* 1:141–57.

Deschner, J. P. 1984. *The Hitting Habit*. New York: Free Press.

Dobash, R. E., and R. P. Dobash. 1978. "Wives: The 'Appropriate' Victims of Marital Violence." *Victimology* 2:426–42.

———. 1979. *Violence against Wives*. New York: Free Press.

———. 1984. "The Nature and Antecedents of Violent Events." *British Journal of Criminology* 24:269–88.

Doran, J. B. 1980. "Quantitative and Qualitative Perspectives on Violent and Non-violent Intimate Relationships." Paper presented at the annual meeting of the American Psychological Association, Montreal, August.

———. 1981. "Multiple Victimizations: Those Who Suffer More than Once." Paper presented at the first national conference for Family Violence Researchers, University of New Hampshire, Durham, July.

Dvoskin, J. A. 1981. "Battered Women—an Epidemiological Study of Spousal Violence." Doctoral dissertation, University of Arizona.

Eberle, P. 1982. "Alcohol Abusers and Non-abusers: A Discriminant Function Analysis." *Journal of Health and Social Behavior* 23:260–71.

Elliott, D. S. In this volume. "Criminal Justice Procedures in Family Violence Crimes."

Ewing, W., M. Lindsey, and J. Pomerantz. 1984. *Battering: An AMEND Manual for Helpers*. Denver, Colo.: Littleton Heights College.

Fagan, J., I. Frieze, V. Lewis, and D. Stewart. 1980. *National Evaluation of the LEAA Family Violence Demonstration Program: Process Evaluation*. San Francisco: URSA.

Fields, M. D. 1978. "Does This Vow Include Wife-Beating?" *Human Rights* 7(20):40–45.

Figley, C. R., ed. 1985. *Trauma and Its Wake: The Study and Treatment of Post-traumatic Stress Disorder*. New York: Brunner/Mazel.

Finkelhor, D. 1983. "Common Features of Family Abuse." In *The Dark Side of Families: Current Family Violence Research*, edited by D. Finkelhor and associates. Beverly Hills, Calif.: Sage.

Finkelhor, D., and K. Yllo. 1983. "Rape in Marriage: A Sociological View." In *The Dark Side of Families: Current Family Violence Research*, edited by D. Finkelhor and associates. Beverly Hills, Calif.: Sage.

Fiora-Gormally, N. 1978. "Battered Wives Who Kill: Double Standard Out of Court, Single Standard In?" *Law and Human Behavior* 2:133–65.

Fitzpatrick, J. P. 1974. "Drugs, Alcohol, and Violent Crime." *Addictive Disorders* 1:353–67.

Folkman, S. 1984. "Personal Control and Stress and Coping Processes: A Theoretical Analysis." *Journal of Personality and Social Psychology* 46:839–52.

Ford, D. A. 1983. "Wife Battery and Criminal Justice: A Study of Victim Decision-Making." *Family Relations* 32:463–75.

Frieze, I. H. 1979. "Perceptions of Battered Wives." In *New Approaches to Social Problems: Applications of Attribution Theory*, edited by I. H. Frieze, D. Bar-Tal, and J. S. Carroll. San Francisco: Jossey-Bass.

———. 1980. "Causal Attributions as Mediators of Battered Women's Responses to Battering." Part of the final report to the National Institutes of Health for Grant no. 1 R01 MH30193, University of Pittsburgh.

———. 1983. "Investigating the Causes and Consequences of Marital Rape." *Signs* 8:532–53.

———. 1987. "The Female Victim: Rape, Wife Beating, and Incest." In *Cataclysms, Crises, and Catastrophes: Psychology in Action*, edited by G. R. Vanden-Bos and B. K. Bryant. Washington, D.C.: American Psychological Association.

Frieze, I. H., S. Hymer, and M. S. Greenberg. 1987. "Describing the Crime Victim: Psychological Reactions to Victimization." *Professional Psychology* 18:299–315.

Frieze, I. H., and J. Knoble. 1980. "The Effects of Alcohol on Marital Violence." Paper presented at the annual meeting of the American Psychological Association, Montreal, August.

Frieze, I. H., J. Knoble, C. Washburn, and G. Zomnir. 1980. "Types of Battered Women." Paper presented at the annual research conference of the Association for Women in Psychology, Santa Monica, Calif., March.

Frieze, I. H., M. McCreanor, and K. Shomo. 1980. "Male Views of the Violent Marriage." Paper presented at the annual research conference of the Association for Women in Psychology, Santa Monica, Calif., March.

Frieze, I. H., and M. C. McHugh. 1981. "Violence in Relation to Power in Marriage." Paper presented at the annual meeting of the American Psychological Association, Los Angeles, August.

———. 1986. "When Disaster Strikes." In *Everywoman's Emotional Well-Being*, edited by C. Tavris. New York: Doubleday.

Ganley, A. L., and L. Harris. 1978. "Domestic Violence: Issues in Designing and Implementing Programs for Male Batterers." Paper presented at the annual meeting of the American Psychological Association, Toronto, August.

Gayford, J. 1975. "Wife Battering: A Preliminary Survey of 100 Cases." *British Medical Journal* 1:194–97.

Gelles, R. J. 1974. *The Violent Home: A Study of Physical Aggression between Husbands and Wives*. Beverly Hills, Calif.: Sage.

———. 1976. "Abused Wives: Why Do They Stay?" *Journal of Marriage and the Family* 38:659–68.

———. 1979. *Family Violence*. Beverly Hills, Calif.: Sage.

Gerson, L. W. 1978. "Alcohol-related Acts of Violence: Who Was Drinking and Where the Acts Occurred." *Journal of Studies on Alcohol* 39:1294–96.

Gil, D. G. 1970. *Violence against Children*. Cambridge, Mass.: Harvard University Press.

Gilbert, L. A., and D. Mangelsdorff. 1979. "Influence of Perceptions of Personal Control on Reactions to Stressful Events." *Journal of Counseling Psychology* 26:473–80.

Goldstein, J. H. 1975. *Aggression and Crimes of Violence*. New York: Oxford University Press.

Goolkasian, G. A. 1986. *Confronting Domestic Violence: A Guide for Criminal Justice Agencies*. Washington, D.C.: U.S. Department of Justice, National Institute of Justice.

Greenblat, C. S. 1983. "A Hit Is a Hit Is a Hit . . . or Is It? Approval and Tolerance of the Use of Physical Force by Spouses." In *The Dark Side of Families*, edited by D. Finkelhor and associates. Beverly Hills, Calif.: Sage.

———. 1985. "'Don't Hit Your Wife . . . Unless'; Preliminary Findings on Normative Support for the Use of Physical Force by Husbands." *Victimology* 10:221–41.

Hanneke, C. R., and N. A. Shields. 1985. "Marital Rape: Implications for the Helping Professions." *Social Casework* (October), pp. 451–58.

Hilberman, E. 1980. "Overview: The 'Wife-Beater's Wife' Reconsidered." *American Journal of Psychiatry* 137:1336–47.

Hilberman, E., and K. Munson. 1978. "Sixty Battered Women." *Victimology* 2:460–71.

Holahan, C. J., and R. H. Moss. 1985. "Life Stress and Health: Personality, Coping, and Family Support in Stress Resistance." *Journal of Personality and Social Psychology* 49:739–47.

Hornung, C. A., B. C. McCullough, and T. Sugimoto. 1981. "Status Relationships in Marriage: Risk Factors in Spouse Abuse." *Journal of Marriage and the Family* 43:675–92.

Hotaling, G. T., and D. B. Sugarman. 1986. "An Analysis of Risk Markers in Husband to Wife Violence: The Current State of Knowledge." *Violence and Victims* 1:101–24.

Hughes, H. M., and S. J. Barad. 1983. "Psychological Functioning of Battered Women and Their Children: A Preliminary Investigation." Paper presented at the ninety-first annual meeting of the American Psychological Association, Anaheim, Calif., August.

Hull, J. G., and C. F. Bond, Jr. 1986. "Social and Behavioral Consequences of Alcohol Consumption and Expectancy: A Meta-analysis." *Psychological Bulletin* 99:347–60.

Janoff-Bulman, R. 1979. "Characterological versus Behavioral Self-Blame: Inquiries into Depression and Rape." *Journal of Personality and Social Psychology* 37:1798–1809.

———. 1985. "Criminal vs. Non-criminal Victimization: Victims' Reactions." *Victimology* 10:498–511.

Janoff-Bulman, R., and I. H. Frieze. 1983. "A Theoretical Perspective for

Understanding Reactions to Victimization." *Journal of Social Issues* 39(2):1–17.

————. 1987. "The Role of Gender in Reactions to Criminal Victimization." In *Women and Stress*, edited by R. Barnett, L. Biener, and G. Baruch. New York: Free Press.

Janoff-Bulman, R., M. E. Madden, and C. Timko. 1983. "Victims' Reactions to Aid: The Role of Perceived Vulnerability." *New Directions in Helping* 3:21–42.

Jones, A. 1980. *Women Who Kill*. New York: Fawcett Columbine.

Kempe, C. H., F. N. Silverman, B. F. Steele, W. Droegemueller, and H. Silver. 1962. "The Battered Child Syndrome." *Journal of the American Medical Association* 181:107–12.

Kilpatrick, D. G., C. L. Best, C. J. Veronen, A. E. Amick, L. A. Villeponteaux, and G. A. Ruff. 1985. "Mental Health Victimization: A Random Community Survey." *Journal of Consulting and Clinical Psychology* 53:866–73.

Klaus, P. A., and M. R. Rand. 1984. *Family Violence*. Washington, D.C.: U.S. Department of Justice, Bureau of Justice Statistics.

LaBell, L. S. 1979. "Wife Abuse: A Sociological Study of Battered Women and Their Mates." *Victimology* 4:258–67.

Langan, P. A., and C. A. Innes. 1986. "Preventing Domestic Violence against Women." Washington, D.C.: U.S. Department of Justice, Bureau of Justice Statistics.

Lentzner, H. R., and M. M. DeBerry. 1980. "Intimate Victims: A Study of Violence among Friends and Relatives." Washington, D.C.: U.S. Department of Justice, Bureau of Justice Statistics.

Lerman, L. G. 1981. "Criminal Prosecution of Wife Beaters." *Response* 3:1–19.

Lerner, M. J. 1980. *The Belief in a Just World: A Fundamental Delusion*. New York: Plenum.

Levinger, G. 1966. "Sources of Marital Dissatisfaction among Applicants for Divorce." *American Journal of Orthopsychiatry* 26:803–7.

Lewin, T. 1979. "When Victims Kill." *National Law Journal* 2:2–4, 11.

Lindsey, K. 1978. "When Battered Women Strike Back." *Viva* 58/59:66–74.

Lystad, M. 1986. "Interdisciplinary Perspectives on Family Violence: An Overview." In *Violence in the Home: Interdisciplinary Perspectives*, edited by M. Lystad. New York: Brunner/Mazel.

Mason, A., and V. Blankenship. 1987. "Power and Affiliation, Motivation, Stress, and Abuse in Intimate Relationships." *Journal of Personality and Social Psychology* 52:203–10.

Mayfield, D. 1976. "Alcoholism, Alcohol, Intoxication, and Assaultive Behavior." *Diseases of the Nervous System* 37:288–91.

Mettger, Z. 1982. "A Case of Rape: Forced Sex in Marriage." *Response* 5(2):1–2, 13–16.

Meyer, C. B., and S. E. Taylor. 1986. "Adjustment to Rape." *Journal of Personality and Social Psychology* 50:1226–34.

Miller, D. T., and C. A. Porter. 1983. "Self-Blame in Victims of Violence." *Journal of Social Issues* 39(2):139–52.

Mitchell, R. E., and C. A. Hodson. 1982. "Battered Women: The Relationship of Stress, Support, and Coping to Adjustment." Paper presented at the annual meeting of the American Psychological Association, Washington, D.C., August.

New York University Law Review. 1977. "The Marital Rape Exemption." *The New York University Law Review* 52:306–23.

Nicol, A. R., J. C. Gunn, J. Gristwood, R. H. Foggitt, and J. P. Watson. 1973. "The Relationship of Alcoholism to Violent Behavior Resulting in Long-Term Imprisonment." *British Journal of Psychiatry* 123:47–51.

Nisonoff, L., and I. Bitman. 1979. "Spouse Abuse: Incidence and Relationship to Selected Demographic Variables." *Victimology* 4:131–39.

O'Brien, J. 1971. "Violence in Divorce Prone Families." *Journal of Marriage and the Family* 33:692–98.

O'Brien, R. M. 1985. *Crime and Victimization Data.* Beverly Hills, Calif.: Sage.

Orford, J., S. Guthrie, P. Nicholls, E. Oppenheimer, S. Egert, and C. Hensman. 1975. "Self-reported Coping Behavior of Wives of Alcoholics and Its Association with Drinking Outcome." *Journal of Studies on Alcohol* 36:1254–67.

Pagelow, M. D. 1977. "Secondary Battering: Breaking the Cycle of Domestic Violence." Paper presented at the annual meeting for the Sociologists for Women in Society Section of the American Sociological Association, California.

———. 1980a. "Does the Law Protect the Rights of Battered Women? Some Research Notes." Paper presented at the annual meeting of the Law and Society Association of the ISA Research Committee on the Sociology of Law, Madison, Wis., June.

———. 1980b. "Double Victimization of Battered Women: Victimized by Spouses and the Legal System." Paper presented at the annual meeting of the American Society of Criminology, San Francisco, November.

———. 1981. *Woman-Battering: Victims and Their Experiences.* Beverly Hills, Calif.: Sage.

———. 1984. *Family Violence.* New York: Praeger.

Parlee, M. B. 1981. "Appropriate Control Groups in Feminist Research." *Psychology of Women Quarterly* 5:637–44.

Parnas, R. J. 1967. "Police Response to Domestic Violence." *Wisconsin Law Review* 31:914–60.

Patterson, G. 1982. *Coercive Family Processes.* Eugene, Oreg.: Cataglia Press.

Perloff, L. S. 1983. "Perceptions of Vulnerability to Victimization." *Journal of Social Issues* 39(2):41–62.

Pleck, E. In this volume. "Criminal Approaches to Family Violence, 1640–1980."

Police Foundation. 1976. *Domestic Violence and the Police: Studies in Detroit and Kansas City.* Washington, D.C.: Police Foundation.

Porter, C. A. 1983. "Coping and Perceived Control in Battered Women." Doctoral dissertation, University of British Columbia, Department of Psychology.

Powers, R. J., and I. L. Kutash. 1978. "Substance-induced Aggression." In *Violence: Perspectives on Murder and Aggression,* edited by I. Kutash, S. B. Kutash, L. B. Schlesinger, and associates. San Francisco: Jossey-Bass.

Prescott, S., and C. Letko. 1977. "Battered Women: A Social Psychological Perspective." In *Battered Women: A Psychosociological Study of Domestic Violence*, edited by M. Roy. New York: Van Nostrand Reinhold.

Reid, J. B., P. S. Taplin, and R. Loeber. 1981. "A Social Inter-actional Approach to Treatment of Abusive Families." In *Violent Behavior: Social Learning Approaches to Prediction, Management and Treatment*, edited by R. B. Stuart. New York: Brunner/Mazel.

Richardson, D. C., and J. L. Campbell. 1980. "Alcohol and Wife Abuse: The Effects of Alcohol on Attributions of Blame for Wife Abuse." *Personality and Social Psychology Bulletin* 6:51–56.

Ridington, J. 1978. "The Transition Process: A Feminist Environment as Reconstructive Milieu." *Victimology* 3:563–75.

Romero, M. 1985. "A Comparison between Strategies Used on Prisoners of War and Battered Wives." *Sex Roles* 13:537–47.

Rosenbaum, A., and K. D. O'Leary. 1981. "Marital Violence: Characteristics of Abusive Couples." *Journal of Consulting and Clinical Psychology* 49:63–71.

Roth, S., and L. J. Cohen. 1986. "Approach, Avoidance, and Coping with Stress." *American Psychologist* 41:813–19.

Roy, M. 1977. "Research Project Probing a Cross-Section of Battered Women." In *Battered Women: A Psychosociological Study of Domestic Violence*, edited by M. Roy. New York: Van Nostrand.

Ruback, R. B., M. S. Greenberg, and D. R. Westcott. 1984. "Social Influence and Crime-Victim Decision Making." *Journal of Social Issues* 40(1):51–76.

Russell, D. E. H. 1982. *Rape in Marriage*. New York: MacMillan.

Sanders, W. B., and T. K. Pinhey. 1983. *The Conduct of Social Research*. New York: Holt, Rinehart & Winston.

Saunders, D. G. 1986. "When Battered Women Use Violence: Husband-Abuse or Self-Defense?" *Victims and Violence* 1:47–60.

Saunders, D. G., A. B. Lynch, M. Grayson, and D. Linz. 1987. "The Inventory of Beliefs about Wife Beating: The Construction and Initial Validation of a Measure of Beliefs and Attitudes." *Violence and Victims* 2:39–58.

Scheppele, K. L., and P. B. Bart. 1983. "Through Women's Eyes: Defining Danger in the Wake of Sexual Assault." *Journal of Social Issues* 39(2):63–80.

Schneider, A. 1980. "Methodological Problems in Victim Surveys and Their Implications." In *Victimology Research Agenda Development*, vol. 1, edited by J. Dahman and J. Sasfy. McLean, Va.: Mitre Corporation.

Schulman, M. 1979. *A Survey of Spousal Violence against Women in Kentucky*. Study no. 792701 for the Kentucky Commission on Women. Washington, D.C.: U.S. Department of Justice, Law Enforcement Assistance Administration.

Schultz, R., and S. Decker. 1985. "Long-Term Adjustment to Physical Disability: The Role of Social Support, Perceived Control and Self-Blame." *Journal of Personality and Social Psychology* 48:1162–72.

Schur, E. M. 1984. *Labeling Women Deviant: Gender, Stigma, and Social Control*. New York: Random House.

Sedlak, A. J. 1983. "The Use and Psychosocial Impact of a Battered Women's Shelter." Paper presented at the annual meeting of the American Psychological Association, Anaheim, Calif., August.

Shainess, N. 1984. *Sweet Suffering: Woman as Victim.* New York: Bobbs-Merrill.

Shaud, K. A. 1983. "The Bind of the Battering Relationship: A Study of Learned Helplessness and No-Win Binds in Battered Women." Paper presented at the annual meeting of the American Society of Criminology, Denver.

Shaver, K. 1970. "Defensive Attribution: Effects of Severity and Relevance on the Responsibility Assigned for an Accident." *Journal of Personality and Social Psychology* 14:101–13.

Sherman, L. W., and R. A. Berk. 1984. "The Specific Deterrent Effects of Arrest for Domestic Assault." *American Sociological Review* 49:261–72.

Shields, N., and C. R. Hanneke. 1983. "Battered Wives' Reactions to Marital Rape." In *The Dark Side of Families*, edited by D. Finkelhor and associates. Beverly Hills: Calif.: Sage.

Silver, R. L., C. Boon, and M. H. Stones. 1983. "Searching for Meaning in Misfortune: Making Sense of Incest." *Journal of Social Issues* 39(2):81–102.

Singer, S. I. 1986. "Victims of Serious Violence and Their Criminal Behavior: Subcultural Theory and Beyond." *Violence and Victims* 1:61–70.

Smith, K. B., and D. N. Green. 1984. "Individual Correlates of the Belief in a Just World." *Psychological Reports* 54:435–38.

Snyder, D. K., and L. A. Fruchtman. 1981. "Differential Patterns of Wife Abuse: A Data-based Typology." *Journal of Consulting and Clinical Psychology* 49:878–85.

Sobell, L. C., and M. B. Sobell. 1975. "Drunkenness, a 'Special Circumstance' in Crime and Violence, Sometimes." *International Journal of the Addictions* 10:869–82.

Sonkin, D. J., ed. 1987. *Domestic Violence on Trial: Psychological and Legal Dimensions of Family Violence.* New York: Springer.

Sonkin, D. J., and M. Durphy. 1982. *Learning to Live without Violence: A Handbook for Men.* San Francisco: Volcano.

———. 1985. *Learning to Live without Violence: A Handbook for Men.* Rev. 2d ed. San Francisco: Volcano.

Sonkin, D. J., D. Martin, and L. E. Walker, eds. 1985. *The Male Batterer: A Treatment Approach.* New York: Springer.

Stark, E., A. Flintcraft, D. Zuckerman, A. Grey, J. Robinson, and W. Frazier. 1981. *Wife Abuse in the Medical Setting: An Introduction to Health Personnel,* Monograph Series no. 7. Washington, D.C.: National Clearinghouse on Domestic Violence.

Stark, R., and J. McEvoy. 1970. "Middle Class Violence." *Psychology Today* 4:52–65.

Steele, B., and C. Pollock. 1968. "A Psychiatric Study of Parents Who Abuse Infants and Small Children." In *The Battered Child*, edited by R. Helfer and C. H. Kempe. Chicago: University of Chicago Press.

Steinmetz, S. 1977. *The Cycle of Violence: Assertive, Aggressive, and Abusive Family Interaction.* New York: Praeger.

Straus, M. A. 1971. "Some Social Antecedents of Physical Punishment: A Linkage Theory Interpretation." *Journal of Marriage and the Family* 33:658–63.

————. 1973. "A General Systems Theory Approach to a Theory of Violence between Family Members." *Social Science Information* 12(3):105–25.

————. 1978. "Wife Beating: How Common and Why?" *Victimology* 2:443–58.

————. 1979. "Measuring Intrafamily Conflict and Violence: The Conflict Tactics (CT) Scales." *Journal of Marriage and the Family* 41:75–88.

————. 1980. "Victims and Aggressors in Marital Violence." *American Behavioral Scientist* 23:681–704.

————. 1981. "Re-evaluation of the Conflict Tactics Scale." Paper presented at the first national conference for Family Violence Researchers, University of New Hampshire, Durham, July.

Straus, M. A., and R. J. Gelles. 1986. "Societal Change and Change in Family Violence from 1975 to 1985 as Revealed by Two National Surveys." *Journal of Marriage and the Family* 48:465–79.

Straus, M. A., R. J. Gelles, and S. K. Steinmetz. 1980. *Behind Closed Doors: Violence in the American Family.* Garden City, N.Y.: Doubleday.

Szinovacz, M. E. 1983. "Using Couple Data as a Methodological Tool: The Case of Marital Violence." *Journal of Marriage and the Family* 45:633–44.

Taylor, S. E. 1983. "Adjustment to Threatening Events: A Theory of Cognitive Adaptation." *American Psychologist* 38:1161–73.

Taylor, S. P., and C. B. Gammon. 1975. "Effects of Type and Dose of Alcohol on Human Physical Aggression." *Journal of Personality and Social Psychology* 32:169–75.

Tong, R. 1984. *Women, Sex and the Law.* Totowa, N.J.: Rowman & Allenheld.

Totman, J. 1978. *The Murderess: A Psychological Study of Criminal Homicide.* San Francisco: R & E Research Associates.

U.S. Commission on Civil Rights. 1982. *Under the Rule of Thumb: Battered Women and the Administration of Justice.* Washington, D.C.: U.S. Government Printing Office.

Virkkunen, M. 1974. "Alcohol as a Factor Precipitating Aggression and Conflict Behavior Leading to Homicide." British Journal of Addictions 69: 149–54.

Waites, R. E. 1978. "Female Masochism and the Enforced Restriction of Choice." *Victimology* 3:535–44.

Walker, L. E. 1978. "Battered Women and Learned Helplessness." *Victimology* 3:525–34.

————. 1979. *The Battered Woman.* New York: Harper & Row.

————. 1983. "The Battered Woman Syndrome Study." In *The Dark Side of Families,* edited by D. Finkelhor and associates. Beverly Hills, Calif: Sage.

————. 1984. *The Battered Woman Syndrome.* New York: Springer.

————. 1986. "Psychological Causes of Family Violence." In *Violence in the Home: Interdisciplinary Perspectives,* edited by M. Lystad. New York: Brunner/Mazel.

Washburn, C., and I. H. Frieze. 1980. "Methodological Issues in Studying Battered Women." Paper presented at the annual research conference of the Association for Women in Psychology, Santa Monica, Calif., March.

Weis, J. G. In this volume. "Family Violence Research Methodology and Design."

Wilbanks, W. 1982. "Murdered Women and Women Who Murder." In *Judge, Lawyer, Victim, Thief: Women, Gender Roles and Criminal Justice*, edited by N. H. Rafter and E. A. Stanko. Boston: Northeastern University Press.

———. 1983. "The Female Homicide Offender in Dade County, Florida." *Criminal Justice Review* 8(2):9–14.

Wolfgang, M. E. 1958. *Patterns in Criminal Homicide*. New York: Wiley.

———. 1967. "A Sociological Analysis of Criminal Homicide." In *Studies in Homicide*, edited by M. E. Wolfgang. New York: Harper & Row.

Wolfgang, M. E., and R. B. Strohm. 1957. "The Relationship between Alcohol and Criminal Homicide." *Quarterly Journal of Studies on Alcohol* 17:411–25.

Wood, J. V., S. E. Taylor, and R. R. Lichtman. 1985. "Social Comparison in Adjustment to Breast Cancer." *Journal of Personality and Social Psychology* 49(5):1169–83.

Worden, R. E., and A. A. Pollitz. 1984. "Police Arrests in Domestic Disturbances: A Further Look." *Law and Society Review* 18:105–19.

Wortman, C. B., and D. R. Lehman. 1985. "Reactions to Victims of Life Crises: Support Attempts That Fail." In *Social Support: Theory, Research and Applications*, edited by I. G. Sarason and B. R. Sarason. Dordrecht: Martinus Nijhoff.

Wyer, R. S., Jr., G. V. Bodenhausen, and T. F. Gorman. 1985. "Cognitive Mediators of Reactions to Rape." *Journal of Personality and Social Psychology* 48:324–38.

Zacker, J., and M. Bard. 1977. "Further Findings on Assaultiveness and Alcohol Use in Interpersonal Disputes." *American Journal of Community Psychology* 5:373–83.

Zawitz, M. W., ed. 1983. *Report to the Nation on Crime and Justice: The Data.* Washington, D.C.: U.S. Department of Justice.

Zeichner, A., and R. O. Pihl. 1979. "Effects of Alcohol and Behavior Contingencies on Human Aggression." *Journal of Abnormal Psychology* 88:153–60.

Zimring, F. E., S. K. Mukherjee, and B. J. Van Winkle. 1983. "Intimate Violence: A Study of Intersexual Homicide in Chicago." *University of Chicago Law Review* 50:910–30.

James Garbarino

The Incidence and Prevalence of Child Maltreatment

ABSTRACT

Data sources for the development of credible estimates of the prevalence
and incidence of various forms of child maltreatment, including physical,
sexual, and emotional abuse and physical and emotional neglect, are as
yet underdeveloped. The National Incidence Study and American
Humane Association reports provide incidence estimates, and upper and
lower bounds for prevalence estimates can be obtained by extrapolation
from these incidence estimates. Victimization by various forms of child
maltreatment is distressingly common and is especially likely to occur in
low-income households. Most individual incidents are not in themselves
highly serious but may be indicators of underlying family stresses. Many
practitioners are skeptical about the wisdom of "criminalizing" child
maltreatment, and, perhaps as a result, most studies on patterns
of reporting show that many suspected maltreatment incidents go
unreported. There is considerable evidence that active delinquents
are disproportionately likely to have suffered maltreatment.

Before any phenomenon can be studied it must be defined. Thus far,
no single definition of child abuse has been widely adopted. A variety
of definitions of child abuse have been offered, and none is free of
ambiguities. Social meanings of events flow from analyses of the intentions of actors, the consequences of acts, the value judgments of observers, and the source of the standard for that judgment. These four
elements—intentionality, effect, evaluation, and standards—present
the fundamental issues in defining abuse.

James Garbarino is president of the Erikson Institute, Chicago, Illinois.

Researchers have approached the interlinked issues of intention and harmful consequences as elements of abuse in a number of ways. Helfer and Kempe (1974) define abuse as nonaccidental physical injury resulting from acts or omissions of parents or guardians. From this viewpoint, the adult need only intend to do the thing that causes the injury and need not intend to harm the child. David Gil (1975) suggests that abuse is any intentional, nonaccidental use of force aimed at hurting, injuring, or destroying the child. For Gil, an adult need not intend to injure a child in order to abuse him or her. This definition would label "spanking" as abuse, and thus the term "abusive" might apply to most parents. Many researchers reject this approach on the grounds that it is too broad. Other scholars believe that cultural support for the use of force against children is at the heart of the child-abuse problem (Straus, Gelles, and Steinmetz 1980).

The judgments of observers and the standards that guide these judgments make up the third and fourth elements of social definitions of child abuse. Some investigators look to community standards for the criteria with which to define child abuse. For example, included in the Giovannoni and Becerra (1979) definition of abuse is parental or guardian behavior that violates community standards of how to treat children. Although such standards vary between communities, there is a marked degree of consensus among ethnic groups in America (Giovannoni and Becerra 1979).

In defining child abuse, it is sometimes necessary to look beyond culturally approved child-rearing norms to our best scientifically informed understandings of parent-child relations. The evaluation must be based on *both* science and culture. Informed scientists agree, for example, that rejection can be injurious to the psyche of a developing child. Some researchers, but not all, are convinced that the evidence demonstrates a connection between the use of physical punishment and impaired psychological development and social competence; the empirical evidence is debatable. "Abuse" is a socially mediated conclusion drawn about family life, and it must be based on a mixture of community standards and professional knowledge.

Child maltreatment can be defined as acts of omission or commission by a parent or guardian that are judged by a mixture of community values and professional expertise to be inappropriate and damaging (Garbarino and Gilliam 1980). This definition covers the four issues mentioned earlier. "Inappropriate" describes parental action; "damaging" covers consequences for the victim. Both are defined by social judgments based on community standards and professional expertise.

Inappropriate parental behavior may produce physical, emotional, or sexual damage. Although we cannot always accurately predict what effects maltreatment will produce, victims most often suffer multiple damage, and individual susceptibilities to harm differ. Also, while each type of maltreatment is distinct in principle, in practice there is so much overlapping that few cases are observed in which only one type of abuse is present, at least when a troubled family is observed over a long period. This overlap is one reason why abuse and neglect are often linked under the broader term "maltreatment."

In practice, neglect and abuse often are found in the same family; some estimates indicate they occur together 50 percent of the time over the life of a child. They may occur in sequence when neglect by one parent exposes the victim to abuse by the other (e.g., in cases of sexual abuse). Whether the terms "abuse and neglect" or "maltreatment" are used, the central policy issue is to devise ways to protect the child or teenager from damage and exploitation by setting and enforcing high standards of care for children and youth. The notion of inappropriateness is particularly important in respect to adolescent abuse. Things that might be appropriate in rearing young children lose their meaning and appropriateness for teenagers. Parents commonly face difficulty in changing habits formed while rearing young children when those children become adolescents. Teenagers are far more capable of abstract thought than are children and can independently evaluate their own motives as well as those of others. This capability demands that parents reason and consult with their adolescent children when making family decisions and setting rules. This may be hard to do at a time when adolescents are first asserting their independence, and it produces disturbance even among otherwise smoothly functioning families. Most parents eventually recognize the need for some adjustment to the new situation of having adolescent children. Some do not and are special risks for abusing their teenagers (Garbarino et al. 1986).

Special attention must be directed to patterns of behavior that would cause most normal children and teenagers to suffer some biological, social, or psychological harm. The consequences of abuse and neglect are not well documented, and the resilience of human beings rules out any simple cause and effect relationship between maltreatment and impaired development (Martin 1984).

Child-abuse activists and researchers often use a fever analogy to explain the meaning of child abuse and neglect. Abuse and neglect are seen as indicators of underlying problems within the family, just as a fever indicates infection in the body. Most fevers are not, in themselves, intrinsically dangerous and pose no direct threat to the organism. Very high fevers, however, particularly among very young children, are dangerous, like serious child abuse and neglect. Most of the physical damage done by abusive and neglectful parents, while socially distressing, morally unconscionable, and requiring attention, is not in itself a threat to the long-term health of the child. Only the most extreme instances of abuse and neglect are life-threatening or produce substantial physical impairment. Most injuries are less serious than the impaired relationships they reflect.

No one with any moral sensibility can ignore a battered child or even a bruised one. What is more important, however, is "developmental damage." Garmezy (1983) argues that the effects of child abuse (defined primarily as physical assault) are neither so simple nor so absolute as many public pronouncements would have us believe. Many victims of child abuse, probably most, survive it and avoid repeating the pattern in their own child rearing (Kaufman and Zigler 1988). The crucial issue is the overall pattern of parent-child relations and the probable impact of that pattern on the development of social, intellectual, and moral competence.

Physical force raises different issues for young children than it does for teenagers, and emotional abuse may take one form in childhood and another in adolescence. Focusing on inappropriateness and developmental damage draws the study of abuse and neglect back into the mainstream of issues in human development.

"Maltreatment" is thus intrinsically a social label. It is not enough that patterns of behavior are damaging in some objective sense. They must also violate norms of appropriateness. In North America we damage children in many ways that do not constitute maltreatment. We circumcise baby boys. We pierce the ears of little girls. We expose young athletes to elevated risks of physical harm. We feed children high-cholesterol diets. We make children anxious and guilty about masturbation. These forms of damage are not now defined as inappropriate, but definitions of the "appropriateness" of parental actions can change. For example, infant car seats are standard, whereas once they were optional and, still earlier, unavailable. It is today commonly considered inappropriate for an adult to travel in an automobile with an infant on his or her lap, whereas once it was entirely appropriate. Thus, an infant death in an automobile accident while riding on a parental lap is now "neglect related." Once it was a "preventable accident." Still earlier, it was merely a "random accident." Similarly, paddling a child and shaking an infant were once considered "benign discipline" but now are sometimes considered to be high-risk assaults. In both cases "perpetrators" are still generally absolved from "intent to damage" the child.

Must behavior be both "inappropriate" and developmentally damaging to be considered "maltreatment?" Practical definitions of maltreatment must be limited to behaviors that seriously violate one criterion and at least moderately violate the other to constitute maltreatment. Neither criterion is sufficient by itself. Both are necessary, but the more serious the violation of one criterion, the less serious the other violation need be.

This essay examines current knowledge about the prevalence and incidence of various forms of child maltreatment and comments on issues raised by recent calls for the "criminalization" of child maltreatment. Section I reviews empirical evidence on the trends in, and the incidence and prevalence of, child maltreatment in the United States. Section II describes recent calls for greater involvement of the criminal justice system in the handling of child maltreatment cases, reviews research on compliance with laws requiring the reporting of suspected incidents of child maltreatment, and summarizes research on the relations among child maltreatment, victimization, and delinquency. Sections III and IV discuss research and policy issues presented by recent increases in criminal justice system involvement in public responses to child maltreatment.

I. Incidence and Prevalence

Data on the incidence and prevalence of child maltreatment come from two principal sources: large-scale surveys and small-scale intensive studies of particular communities or agencies. In this essay, I use the term "incidence" to refer to estimates of the number or rate of new cases occurring in a given period, usually a year. I use the term "prevalence" to refer to estimates of the proportion of a population that has been victimized during childhood. Unfortunately, neither the National Crime Survey's victimization data nor the FBI's Uniform Crime Reports provide useful estimates of the incidence or prevalence of various forms of child maltreatment. Most of the data on the incidence of child maltreatment come from the National Incidence Study (NIS) sponsored by the National Center on Child Abuse and Neglect and from annual collections of child maltreatment official reports compiled by the American Humane Association (AHA). Estimates of prevalence come from a small number of national surveys and a larger number of local surveys and studies.

A. *Incidence Studies*

The NIS collected data on abuse and neglect occurring in a randomly selected sample of twenty-six U.S. counties located in ten states (Burgdorf 1980). Funded by the National Center on Child Abuse and Neglect, the NIS was conducted by Westat, a private consulting firm. Child protective service agencies, schools, hospitals, police, and courts were surveyed. This resulted in the identification of what would be projected nationally to be approximately 652,000 distinct cases—212,400 known to protective services, 71,400 known to other investigatory agencies (but not protective services), and 368,200 known to other professionals. The NIS provided a basis for estimating the annual incidence of various forms of maltreatment of children under eighteen in the United States. Table 1 sets out a summary of the estimates developed by the NIS.

The NIS estimates of maltreatment, though startlingly high—one child per 100 is estimated to be the victim of maltreatment—are likely to be underestimates (Peters, Wyatt, and Finkelhor 1986, p. 18). Many cases of child maltreatment, perhaps most, are never reported to official agencies and thus are not reflected in studies like the NIS. Other problems suggest that NIS data should be interpreted with caution. First, definitions of abuse vary from state to state, agency to agency, and professional to professional. Second, the extent of cooperation with the NIS by state agencies varied considerably (Gelles and Cornell 1985, p. 48).

The NIS study is being replicated, but results are not available at this writing. The 1979–80 NIS data are examined in depth below. First, however, the AHA's compilations of official cases dealt with by mandated child protective service agencies should be examined.

The AHA's National Study of Child Abuse and Neglect Reporting tabulates and analyzes cases reported to (and "accepted" by) official child protective service agencies, as compiled on a state-by-state basis (approximately 80 percent of the states participate). Data are available for the period 1976–84. In 1985, the study was reduced in scope—only five states were included. The study has subsequently been restored to its earlier form for 1986 data (not yet analyzed). The overall volume of reporting since the AHA reports began with the 1976 data has reflected growing public and professional awareness of child maltreatment.

TABLE 1

Estimated Number of Recognized In-Scope Children
(per 1,000 per year)*

Form of Maltreatment and Severity of Injury/Impairment	Number of In-Scope Children	Incidence Rate (per 1,000)†
Form of Maltreatment:‡		
Total, all maltreated children	652,000	10.5
Total, all abused children:	351,100	5.7
Physical assault	207,600	3.4
Sexual exploitation	44,700	.7
Emotional abuse	138,400	2.2
Total, all neglected children:	329,000	5.3
Physical neglect	108,000	1.7
Educational neglect	181,500	2.9
Emotional neglect	59,400	1.0
Severity of Child's Injury/Impairment:		
Fatal	1,000	.02
Serious	136,900	2.2
Moderate	410,300	6.6
Probable	101,700	1.6

SOURCE.—Burgdorf (1980, p. 37).

*National incidence estimates by major form of maltreatment and by severity of maltreatment-related injury or impairments.

†Numerator = estimated number of recognized in-scope children; denominator = 61,900, the estimated total number (in thousands) of children under 18 in the United States in December 1979.

‡Totals may be lower than sum of categories since a child may have experienced more than one in-scope category of maltreatment.

However, like the NIS data and for similar reasons, the AHA reports are likely to be substantial underestimates of the occurrence of child maltreatment. The percentage increase in reported cases has ranged from 25 percent, from 1976 to 1977, to 3 percent in the 1981–82 comparison. Overall, when changes are computed on the basis of rate of reported cases per 1,000 children, the pattern is as shown in table 2. It reveals ebbs and flows in the rate of increase that appear to reflect both actual changes in reported cases *and* artifacts of state record keeping and participation in the project. As Peters, Wyatt, and Finkelhor (1986, p. 18) note, "Most people consider the rise in incidence figures . . . to be primarily a product of new education, awareness, and professional attention to the problem." Informal tallies suggest a big increase for 1986.

TABLE 2

Estimated and Reported Rates of Child Abuse

Year	Estimated Number of Abused Children (in Thousands)	Annual Increase (in Percent)	Reported Number of Abused U.S. Children (per 1,000 Children)
1976	669	. . .	10.1
1977	838	25.3	12.8
1978	836	− .2	12.9
1979	988	18.2	15.4
1980	1,154	16.8	18.1
1981	1,225	6.2	19.4
1982	1,262	3.0	20.1
1983	1,477	17.0	23.6
1984	1,727	16.9	27.3
1985	1,928	11.6	30.6

SOURCE.—American Humane Association (1987, pp. 3–4).

Recent changes in the rate of increase may mean a stabilizing of the various community reporting systems with respect to physical abuse and neglect, ups and downs caused by economic changes, alterations in record keeping and classification schemes, a saturation of some state systems that has resulted in less willingness to "accept" cases for investigation, and the process of reporting systems absorbing the flood of sexual abuse reports touched off by public awareness initiatives in the early 1980s. It is impossible to know precisely the role of each factor in affecting the data. As of 1976 there were thirty-one "fully participating" states involved in the AHA study. "Fully participating" meant that the state was using AHA's reporting form or that it used compatible forms that provided the same categories and background data on families and intervention. By 1983, participation was essentially complete across the United States. And yet, we still do not know a great deal about trends. We can say some things about the sources and character of the reports.

The American Humane Association's report identifies the sources of the reports of child maltreatment. Law enforcement provides about 11 percent of the reports. Half the reports come from private citizens, principally friends, neighbors, and relatives (American Humane Association 1984). This distribution has been quite stable over the last decade, and it highlights that public awareness and public participation

TABLE 3

Types and Distribution of Child Maltreatment

Type of Maltreatment	Percent of Child Population Maltreated		
	1983 (N = 397,785)*	1984 (N = 304,993)†	1985 (N = 225,360)‡
Major physical injury	3.2	3.3	2.2
Minor physical injury	18.5	17.7	15.4
Unspecified physical injury	5.2	3.6	4.1
Sexual maltreatment	8.5	13.3	11.7
Deprivation of necessities (neglect)	58.4	54.6	55.7
Emotional maltreatment	10.1	11.2	8.9
Other maltreatment	8.3	9.6	10.2

SOURCES.—American Humane Association (1985, 1987).

*The distribution for 1983 is based on twenty-three states constituting 46 percent of the U.S. child population.

†The distribution for 1984 is based on sixteen states constituting 41 percent of the U.S. child population.

‡The distribution for 1985 is based on four states constituting 24 percent of the U.S. child population.

in child protective services play major roles in the day-to-day operation of the system.

The AHA patterns of types of maltreatment differ significantly from the NIS finding. Both data sources, unfortunately, can offer only crude indicators of the behaviors they attempt to measure. Nonetheless, especially with regard to palpably disturbing adult behaviors like sexual exploitation and serious physical abuse of children, both studies, whatever their other weaknesses, suggest that these behaviors are distressingly common. As table 1 shows, the NIS identified physical assault as the most common form of maltreatment (3.4 cases per year per 1,000 children under eighteen), followed by educational neglect (2.9), emotional abuse (2.2), physical neglect (1.7), emotional neglect (1.0), and sexual exploitation (0.7) (Burgdorf 1980, p. 37). Table 3 shows a breakdown of the American Humane Association's data by types of maltreatment. Neglect is the largest category, followed by minor physical injury. Tables 4 and 5 show somewhat different patterns for "major physical injuries" and "sexually maltreated children" in 1984. Compared with physically abused children, sexually abused children are (at the time of report, at least) older, more likely to be female, more likely

TABLE 4

Reported Characteristics for Children with Major Physical Injuries,
1984

Average age	5.3	Relationship to perpe-trator:		Employment: Caretakers	
Sex:					
Males	54.2	Own child	82.9	unemployed	37.4
Females	45.8	Other relative	5.1	Single female-	
Race:		Other	12.1	headed families	27.8
White	57.5	Children in household:			
Black	21.9	Reported children	2.0		
Hispanic	11.2	All U.S. households	1.9		
Other	9.5				

SOURCE.—American Humane Association (1985).
NOTE.—All numbers indicate percentages except for "Average Age" and those under "Children in Household."

to be white, less likely to be the perpetrator's child, and less likely to be living with unemployed care givers. Sexual abuse is less likely to include other forms of abuse when it is the principal allegation.

As public attention to problems of family violence generally and child maltreatment specifically has increased, there appears to have been a trend toward greater overall involvement of the courts. Table 6 provides data over the last decade on court involvement with reported protective service cases. But the AHA analyses suggest that this is not evidence for neglect. Rather, the overall rise in court involvement appears to stem from the rising number of sexual abuse reports (which are

TABLE 5

Reported Characteristics for Sexually Maltreated Children, 1984

Average age	9.3	Relationship to perpe-trator:		Employment: Caretakers	
Sex:					
Males	21.7	Own child	55.6	unemployed	27.7
Females	78.3	Other relative	18.7	Single female-	
Race:		Other	25.7	headed families	24.5
White	74.7	Children in household:			
Black	13.0	Reported children	2.0		
Hispanic	8.8	All U.S. households	1.9		
Other	3.5				

SOURCE.—American Humane Association (1985).
NOTE.—All numbers indicate percentages except for "Average Age" and those under "Children in Household."
"Children in Household."

TABLE 6

Comparison of Cases Receiving Court Action over Time (Percent)

Year	All Reported Maltreatments Receiving Court Action	Deprivation of Necessities Receiving Court Action
1976	22	20
1977	21	21
1978	20	20
1979	15	18
1980	14	26
1981	18	25
1982	20	34
1983	24	33
1984	30	26

SOURCE.—American Humane Association (1985).

more likely to receive court action) and the aggressive efforts of criminal justice systems (with leadership from the federal government) to criminalize child maltreatment (as compared with a pre-1980 focus on the problem in social service/child welfare/mental health terms).

This review tells us where things stand within the formal public agencies mandated to provide child protective services. To find out more about the larger community system for dealing with child maltreatment, the National Incidence Study warrants further consideration.

The NIS is notable for employing clear operational definitions of child abuse and neglect. It proceeded from the following overall description. "A child maltreatment situation is one where, through purposive acts or marked inattention to the child's basic needs, behavior of a parent/substitute or other adult caregivers caused foreseeable and avoidable injury or impairment to a child or materially contributed to unreasonable prolongation or worsening of an existing injury or impairment" (Burgdorf 1980, p. 4). The NIS notes particularly that its definition was designed to highlight an emphasis on consequences for the child, and further specified that "injury or impairment must be of 'moderate' or 'serious' severity at minimum" (Burgdorf 1980, p. 4). It also observes that the resulting operational definitions do not include some (perhaps many) situations in which "protective or other services might be appropriate" (e.g., institutional maltreatment, in-home assault by someone other than a parent or caretaker, dangerous behavior that did not cause injury or impairment, hazards the parent was not financially capable of eliminating, and lack of care resulting from the parents' unavoidable absence from the home). Table 1 presented the overall distribution of physical assault, sexual exploitation, emotional abuse, physical neglect, educational neglect, and emotional neglect. Note that, of some 470,500 maltreated children substantiated by child protective service agencies in the target communities, only 212,400 of these children meet all NIS criteria for inclusion in the study (Burgdorf 1980, table 3-5). This discrepancy has led to criticism of the NIS, as has the inclusion of so many cases of "educational neglect"—some 20 percent of the total.

Where do the reports come from that ended up as child protective services agencies cases *and* met NIS criteria for inclusion? Table 7 presents these data. Law enforcement accounted for 12 percent of all the reports to child protective services agencies and had a high substantiation rate, as did schools. However, if cases of "educational neglect" are excluded from the schools reports, then law enforcement agencies reports had the highest substantiation rates.

The reporting pattern shown in the NIS data closely parallels AHA findings. The 12 percent of reports from police in the NIS corresponds to 11 percent in AHA data. Medical sources represent 10 percent of NIS reports and 11 percent of AHA reports. Parents, friends, and neighbors are the sources of about half of the reports in both data sets.

Why did child protective services agencies substantiate some cases and not others? Table 8 data show that law enforcement's allegations were termed "invalid" by child protective services agencies less often than other sources (except the schools). Table 9 presents national estimates based on the counties sampled and the sampling of agencies within those counties. The NIS has been criticized on this point because the small number of large, urban counties in the sample and the small number of agencies sampled within each county created the possibility of serious distortion. Indeed, some critics charge that this did happen because several large hospitals did not participate, although they were appropriately included in the design. Note again the large role played by investigatory agencies.

The NIS provides some information about incidence of child maltreatment as a function of socioeconomic and demographic factors. Table 10 presents some of these data. The most striking difference is in the incidence figures for poor versus affluent families—27.3 percent versus 2.7 percent. This reflects a more general research finding linking poverty to child maltreatment (Pelton 1978; Garbarino et al. 1986).

TABLE 7

Number and Percent of Family Reports to Child Protection Services (CPS) and Percent Substantiated by Source of Report: National Estimates of Reports to CPS Agencies, May 1, 1979–April 30, 1980

Source of Reports to CPS	National Estimate		
	Number of Reports to CPS, Including Duplicates	Percent of All Reports to CPS	For This Source, Percent of Reports Substantiated by CPS
Department of Social Services/Welfare Department	43,000	6	45
Law enforcement (police, sheriff, courts/corrections, coroners, etc.)	88,200	12	56
Medical (hospitals, clinics, physicians, public health departments, etc.)	74,500	10	53
Schools (public and private)	100,300	14	57
All other agencies (preschool, day care, mental health, social services, etc.)	57,800	8	49
Other (nonagency) sources (child, parents, neighbors, anonymous, etc.)	354,500	49	35
Total	718,300	100	44

SOURCE.—Burgdorf (1980, p. 13).

TABLE 8

Primary Reason Report Is Not Substantiated by Child Protection Services (CPS) by Source of Report: National Estimate of Number and Percent of Family-Level Reports Not Substantiated by CPS Agencies

Source of Report to CPS	Number of Nonsubstantiated Reports	Reason Report Not Substantiated by CPS (Percent)			
		Allegation Invalid	Not Serious Enough	Insufficient Evidence	Unable to Investigate
Department of Social Services/ Welfare Department	23,600	48	20	14	18
Law enforcement agencies	38,600	38	39	13	10
Medical sources	34,800	52	29	9	11
Schools	43,400	34	39	16	11
All other agencies	29,500	49	28	13	10
Other (nonagency) sources	228,800	60	16	13	11
Total	398,700	53	23	13	11

SOURCE.—Burgdorf (1980, p. 14).
NOTE.—All reports not substantiated by CPS add to 100 percent for each source, with minor variations due to rounding.

TABLE 9

National Estimates of Annual Number of Suspected Maltreatment Victims Identifiable from Non-CPS Agencies, by Type of Agency

Type of Non-CPS Agency	Suspected Victims Identifiable to Study	
	Total Number, Including Duplicates*	Unduplicated Number†
Investigatory Agencies:		
Juvenile probation department	76,800	55,100
Police/sheriff's department	83,900	50,200
Coroners/medical examiners	300	0
Public health department‡	19,900	11,900
Total	180,900	117,200
Other Study Agencies:		
Hospitals	48,000	25,900
Public schools, elementary	375,800	282,400
Public schools, secondary	258,300	200,700
Mental health agencies‡	37,100	26,900
Other social service agencies‡	28,800	21,800
Total	748,000	557,700
Total, all non-CPS agencies encompassed by study	928,900	674,900

SOURCE.—Burgdorf (1980, p. 15).

*Total number of child-level data forms received from participating agencies over four-month study period in sampled counties, weighted: (a) to adjust for sampling and/or nonparticipation of agencies in study counties; (b) to convert from four-month to twelve-month period; and (c) to represent all U.S. counties.

†For each row, children also known to CPS or to agencies in previous rows are subtracted from the total number of suspected victims identified to the study by agencies in the row. Thus, each entry represents *additional* children over and above those known to CPS or to previously listed agencies.

‡Because of nonrandom selection procedures used with these agencies, estimates for public health, mental health, and other social service agencies are based only on participating agencies, with no adjustment for agency sampling or nonparticipation.

TABLE 10

National Incidence Estimates by Selected Household Geographic Characteristics: Estimated Number of Recognized In-Scope Children per 1,000 per Year

Characteristic	Number of Children in the United States	National Estimate		Incidence Rate (per 1,000)
		Study Estimate of Number of Maltreated Children*		
Total	61,900,000	652,000		10.5
Estimated annual family income† (percent known = 81):				
Under $7,000 per year	10,200,000	278,200		27.3
$7,000–$14,999	17,500,000	255,700		14.6
$15,000–$24,999	20,900,000	81,500		3.9
$25,000 or more	13,300,000	35,800		2.7
Number of children in family (percent known = 89):				
1	11,600,000	158,400		13.7
2–3	36,800,000	340,000		9.2
4 or more	13,500,000	153,500		11.4
Type of county (percent known = 100):‡				
Urban	27,300,000	297,600		10.9
Suburban	15,300,000	134,800		8.8
Rural	19,300,000	219,600		11.4

SOURCE.—Burgdorf (1980, p. 21).

*Whenever more than 1.0 percent of study cases have missing data, estimates are adjusted to 100 percent assuming missing-data cases have same percentage distribution as "known" cases.

†Census estimate based on 1977 data, the most recent available information about number of children by annual family income category. Study estimate is based on respondent's estimate of family's annual income and is of unknown validity.

‡Estimates for all U.S. children are based on estimated child populations for individual study counties, weighted by the inverse of the county's selection probability.

Table 11 shows the full range of "in-scope" maltreatment and corresponding severity of effect data. Those data reveal significant, even dramatic, differences. For example, neglect cases in the study seem to be particularly serious (32 percent of the neglect cases versus 12 percent of the abuse cases are judged "serious").

Table 12 presents this same "severity" issue in a somewhat different form. Here we see that emotional and physical neglect are most serious (not counting the 1,000 fatalities). We also see that fatalities cluster among children aged birth to five and fifteen to seventeen.

In conclusion, the NIS is valuable in shedding light on the different levels of social reality that exist in child abuse as a public phenomenon. In particular, NIS reveals the important role played by law enforcement agencies in identifying cases of child maltreatment. It sheds some light on the world of child maltreatment beyond the official reports received and investigated by state child protective services (and compiled by the AHA). Nonetheless, a separate study by AHA revealed that its compilation of reports and NIS results reveal much congruity in the demographics and socioeconomics of child maltreatment (American Humane Association 1983).

Straus, Gelles, and Steinmetz (1980) conducted a national probability survey of families with two adults in parental roles ("two-parent families") and at least one child three years of age or older and replicated this survey in 1985 (see Straus and Gelles 1986). Their results are generally cited as primary data on the prevalence and incidence of family violence. Their "violence index" includes all forms of assault, while the "severe index" excludes "throwing something at another person, pushing, shoving, or grabbing, and slapping or spanking" and includes only "kicking, biting, punching, hitting with an object, beating up, threatening with a knife or a gun, and the use of a knife or gun" (Straus, Gelles, and Steinmetz 1980, p. 259). Data are only partially analyzed for the 1985 study (however, sibling-to-sibling and child-to-parent violence analyses are available in Hotaling, Straus, and Lincoln, in this volume). When the socioeconomic and demographic correlates of violence are examined in the Straus, Gelles, and Steinmetz (1980) data, they generally reveal the same patterns evident in the reported abuse cases, that is, poverty is a risk factor, as are "life stress" and "stressful history." Sibling-to-sibling violence is especially high (see Pagelow [in this volume] for a review of research on sibling violence). By all accounts, this is rarely dealt with as a criminal justice system issue.

TABLE 11

Estimated Number of Recognized In-Scope Children and Severity Percentage Distribution by Major Form and Subcategory of Maltreatment

Form and Subcategory of Maltreatment	Number of In-Scope Children	Percentage of Severity of Child's Injury/Impairment*			
		Fatal†	Serious	Moderate	Probable
All forms, total	652,000	.16	20	63	16
Abuse, total:	351,100	.20	12	69	19
Physical assault:	207,600	.34	9	78	12
Assault with implement/foreign substance	79,400	.30	8	76	16
Other and unspecified	131,500	.33	6	78	15
Sexual exploitation:	44,700	.02	15	30	54
Intrusion	21,400	0	16	17	67
Molestation with genital contact	16,000	0	6	16	78
Other and unspecified	8,400	0	7	43	50
Emotional abuse:	138,400	0	16	66	17
Verbal/emotional assault	120,200	0	15	63	22
Close confinement	3,300	0	4	23	73
Other (e.g., threatened or attempted physical or sexual assault)	19,100	0	2	90	8

Neglect, total:	329,000	.08	32	55	13
Physical neglect:	108,000	.25	46	35	19
Abandonment	6,700	0	1	7	91
Other refusal of custody	18,900	0	4	31	65
Refusal to allow/provide care for diagnosed health condition	40,600	0	25	75	0
Failure to seek medical care for serious health condition	16,300	1.06	86	0	12
Inadequate physical supervision	6,800	1.22	86	0	13
Disregard of avoidable hazards in home	2,800	.43	99	0	0
Inadequate nutrition, clothing, hygiene	17,800	0	85	0	15
Other	3,400	0	85	0	16
Educational neglect:	181,500	0	14	77	9
"Permitted" chronic truancy	120,300	0	8	88	4
Other (e.g., kept child home, refused to enroll)	61,400	0	10	72	18
Emotional neglect:	59,400	0	74	12	10
Inadequate nurturance (e.g., failure to thrive)	26,000	0	85	0	12
"Permitted" chronic maladaptive behavior	14,000	0	93	0	5
Other	20,000	0	47	30	17

SOURCE.—Burgdorf (1980, p. 23).

NOTE.—More than one subcategory may apply to an individual child.

* The severity measure for maltreatment subcategories is the severity of the injury/impairment resulting from acts/omissions in the particular subcategory. Severity measure for major categories is the most serious injury/impairment resulting from all in-scope maltreatment events during the study period. Percentages for severity measures all add to approximately 100 percent with minor variations due to rounding.

† Percentages are expressed to two decimals.

237

TABLE 12

Severity of Maltreatment-Related Injury or Impairment by Form of
Maltreatment and Age of Child: Estimated Percentage Distributions
by Severity Category

Form of Maltreatment and Age of Child	Severity of Injury or Impairment				
	Fatal	Serious	Moderate	Probable*	Total
Estimated number of children	1,000	137,400	411,600	102,000	652,000
Form of maltreatment:					
Physical assault	72	14	40	24	32
Sexual exploitation	1	5	3	24	7
Emotional abuse	0	16	22	24	21
Physical neglect	28	36	9	20	17
Educational neglect	0	19	34	15	28
Emotional neglect	0	34	1	6	9
Total†	101	124	109	113	114
Age of child:					
0–2	49	16	5	10	8
3–5	25	7	9	13	9
6–8	2	17	18	15	17
9–11	0	19	18	20	19
12–14	1	14	23	20	21
15–17	23	27	27	22	26
Total	100	100	100	100	100

SOURCE.—Burgdorf (1980, p. 25).

*"Probable" should not be interpreted as less serious than "Moderate." Incest, aban-
donment, extreme close confinement and other "probable" injury situations are considered to be at least as serious as many situations where there are known injuries of
moderate or even serious dimension (e.g., a black eye or laceration resulting from a slap).

†Percentages sum to more than total since a child with a given severity of injury may
have experienced more than one form of maltreatment.

B. Prevalence Estimates

The National Incidence Study on child abuse and neglect estimated
that 3.4 children per thousand (or roughly 0.34 percent of all children)
are known to suffer demonstrable physical harm at the hands of a
parent or other in-home caretaker in this country each year (Burgdorf
1980, pp. 1, 4). The report also estimated that 5.7 children per thousand are victims of some type of abuse—physical, sexual, and/or emotional—and 5.3 children per thousand endure physical, educational,
and/or emotional neglect (Burgdorf 1980, p. 4). Among the low-income
populations, the rate of maltreatment (abuse and neglect combined) was
estimated at twenty-seven children per thousand (Burgdorf 1980, p.
10). Of course these rates are incidence figures per year. At issue in this

discussion is the total *prevalence* rate—how many children experience maltreatment over the course of their childhood (until age eighteen under law).

The overall prevalence rates are, of course, higher than the yearly incidence rates. How much higher? If each case identified by the National Incidence Study was a "once-in-a-childhood" situation, and if maltreatment typically begins to occur with equal frequency across the age span from birth to age eighteen, then we might simply add up the incidence rates for each of the eighteen years involved to get a total prevalence rate. Using the NIS data this would result in figure of a 61.0 per 1,000 children (6.1 percent) overall. This figure is very unlikely, however. For example, most estimates of the proportion of adolescent victims who are the recipients of maltreatment for the first time in adolescence average around 50 percent. This alone would lower the figure to 48.2 per 1,000 (4.8 percent). Also, most cases of child maltreatment are long-term. Thus, the *same* children who were identified as two-year-old victims might (if undetected or if detected but not treated successfully) be picked up as four-year-old or six-year-old or eight-year-old victims in succeeding years. We can thus expect that the 6.1 percent prevalence rate is an upper limit, and that a significantly lower figure is more likely.

Several surveys of the prevalence of sexual abuse have reported a lifetime rate of approximately 25 percent for females and 10 percent for males (Peters, Wyatt, and Finkelhor 1986). Of course, this includes all forms of sexual molestation and includes sexual assaults perpetrated by strangers and other adults not typically included in the definition of child abuse (i.e., acts by a parent or guardian). Nonetheless, the inclusion of sexual abuse may push up the possible upper prevalence limit.

If the child maltreatment incidence rate of 2.7 percent for low-income children is extrapolated to an upper limit prevalence rate of 55 percent, problems of estimation also arise. The link between low income and maltreatment seems to operate mostly during childhood (particularly infancy and early childhood) and to diminish dramatically in adolescence (Garbarino et al. 1986). This would mean that most low-income-related cases would occur early in childhood and tend to be chronic. A plausible estimate is an overall prevalence of 30 percent for very poor children and youth (based on an initial 2.7 percent incidence rate then declines gradually to a 1 percent incidence rate by age seventeen). All the figures reflect guesses about the relation between incidence and prevalence, of course.

In addition to the estimates provided by the NIS and the AHA reports on the incidence of child maltreatment on which the preceding extrapolations have been based, there have been many studies of the prevalence of various forms of maltreatment. The prevalence estimates are generally substantially higher than the incidence estimates. Peters, Wyatt, and Finkelhor (1986) provide a comprehensive review of the prevalence research on child sexual abuse, and Gelles and Cornell (1985) provide an overview of research on child abuse generally. Although the earliest prevalence studies involved research subjects who were either volunteers or college students (see also Pagelow, in this volume), more recent studies have involved random or stratified probability samples (e.g., national surveys in Canada [Badgley et al. 1984] and the United States [Timnick 1985a, 1985b]). These studies report prevalence estimates for child sexual abuse ranging from 6 percent to 62 percent for females and from 3 percent to 31 percent for males. The lowest rates suggest that child sexual abuse is not an uncommon experience. The highest rates suggest a social problem of staggering dimensions. There are a variety of explanations for variations in estimated prevalence rates. Studies vary in the restrictiveness of their definitions of child sexual abuse, they vary in their sample selection strategies, and they vary substantially in methodology.

II. Governmental Responses to Child Maltreatment

Small-scale studies of child abuse appear in an increasingly wide variety of journals. Reports are published frequently in *Child Abuse and Neglect: The International Journal*, *Social Work*, *Child Welfare*, the *Journal of Marriage and the Family*, and the *American Journal of Orthopsychiatry*, to name but a few sources. Numerous edited volumes, a growing number of monographs, and large numbers of unpublished project reports complete the picture. Some efforts are being made to provide comprehensive, "handbook" reviews of this work (e.g., Finkelhor et al. 1986; Cicchetti and Carlson 1988). These small-scale studies introduce a series of questions concerning child abuse as a criminal justice problem.

A. Criminal Justice System

A criminal justice model for child abuse was proposed in the 1984 report of the U.S. Attorney General's Task Force Report on Family Violence. Two premises for that report were (1) that family violence (to include child abuse) was to be considered a crime, and (2) that the legal response to family violence must be guided primarily by the nature of the abusive act and not the relationship between the victim and the abuser. A Justice Department official has noted, "The rationale provided for taking what may be considered a much stronger position on child maltreatment was simple justice" (Modzeleski 1987, p. 201).

The criminal justice system currently deals with child maltreatment in three ways: it is part of the front-line system for reporting and investigating child maltreatment cases, it is called on to prosecute cases of child maltreatment, and it contends with the consequences and sequelae of child maltreatment in the form of juvenile delinquents and adult criminals (as well as runaways and other status offenders).

By the mid-1980s virtually all police forces had developed some capacity for responding to child maltreatment cases. But most police departments in the United States have twenty or fewer sworn officers; only sixteen states have "full service" state police forces. This means that the typical "law enforcement" response is likely to be in the hands of nonspecialists in many settings, but in the hands of specialist teams in others (Shepherd 1988). Of course, law enforcement and the criminal justice system are involved in all the multiple-perpetrator/multiple-victim cases of sexual abuse (Finkelhor 1986, personal communication).

A comparison by the American Humane Association of its National Study on Child Neglect and Abuse Reporting and the NIS reveals that law enforcement personnel constitute the source of reports to child protective services in 11.6 percent of the AHA's annual compilation of reports and 12.5 percent of the NIS cases known to protective services (American Humane Association 1983). In the NIS data, law enforcement personnel constitute 18.4 percent of the cases known but not reported to child protective services.

In a study of Arizona, Montana, North Carolina, and Rhode Island, Greeneveld and Giovannoni (1977) reported that police investigated about 6.6 percent of the child maltreatment cases. Criminal action was recommended or initiated in 17.1 percent of these cases (and more rarely still in cases investigated by child protective services). Brown, Miller, and Burke (1977) conducted an in-depth exploration of how protective services and police operate in response to reports of child maltreatment in one major metropolitan area. In Cook County, Illinois, police investigated about 20 percent of the reported child maltreatment cases (although almost all reports *eventually* reached the protective services agency). Most (75 percent) of the cases reported to the police (77 percent of which came from the general public, as opposed to professionals) involved neglect rather than abuse. Nationwide, neglect cases outnumber abuse cases by approximately this same two-to-one ratio.

The role of police in neglect cases may result from their twenty-four-hour-a-day accessibility as much as anything else, since most neglect reports are for "lack of supervision." Interestingly, the reason why police were selected for identification as the recipients of reports in the earliest model reporting laws was not "ideological" but simply "practical"—the police maintained twenty-four-hour-a-day phone coverage (Besharov 1981).

If we are to understand the role of law enforcement in reporting child abuse, however, we must understand the general role of professionals in reporting. We must understand what motivates and impedes reporting if we are to be able to predict the impact of any change in the degree of "criminalization" in the process of child protective services.

B. Issues in Reporting

Advocates for battered wives seem united in their belief that the best interests of a battered woman lie in formal actions, particularly law enforcement intervention (see Elliott, in this volume). In contrast, many child advocates are skeptical about reliance on criminal justice approaches for dealing with child maltreatment in general, and some advocates even oppose these techniques altogether. These advocates emphasize the critical importance of parent-child attachment and psychological continuity for the child's development to proceed. They fear that the punishment orientation of the criminal justice system puts it at odds with children's needs for family stability, even in cases of child maltreatment. Punishing parents separates children from their families, as does any protective removal of the child. In this view, only the most extreme risk justifies an intervention that forces parent-child separation. Even in such an eventuality, however, the child-oriented concern is for permanency in a new or reconstituted, stable family rather than punishment of the perpetrator of abuse. This must be understood in examining the behavior of child abuse reporters, for even in the non-criminalized contexts in which most reporters operate there are many concerns expressed that reporting will initiate a process that leaves children worse off than they were before intervention.

Depending on one's point of view, reporting a suspected case of child maltreatment may be interpreted as an ethically necessary act, as a violation of confidentiality, as the simple meeting of a legal responsibility, as an act of physical courage, as a threat to one's livelihood, as an act of naive faith, or even as an act of folly. Researchers must sort out how these various interpretations reflect the actions of professionals faced with instances of child maltreatment, and how they may bear on child abuse as a criminal justice issue.

Every study conducted to date of reporting by professionals validates the widespread observation that professionals do not report all—and in some cases, even most—of the cases of child maltreatment with which they come in contact. The NIS, for example, attempted to discover the degree to which professionals were aware of cases of child maltreatment but did not report them to their local child protective services agency. Overall, only about one-third of the cases known to professionals were reported to child protective services. The NIS projected that of the 652,000 cases identified by professionals across the United States, only about 212,400 were in child protective service agency records (Burgdorf 1980).

In the NIS, the likelihood that a case known to a community's professionals would be reported to protective services varied as a function of characteristics such as the age of the child (cases involving young children were reported more often than cases involving adolescents), type of agency (hospitals were more likely to report than were schools), and type of maltreatment (at 56 percent, sexual abuse was more likely to be reported than were other forms of abuse and neglect).

Hampton and Newberger (1985) conducted further analysis of the NIS data to explore the roles of hospitals as reporters of child maltreatment—primarily abuse. They found underreporting of white, higher income, older parents involved in emotional abuse and neglect, particularly with adolescents. In a small-scale study of the reporting practices of 307 Virginia physicians, Saulsbury and Campbell (1985) reported congruent results with respect to type of maltreatment (i.e., emotional maltreatment was underreported). They also found that 38 percent of the physicians justified nonreporting on the grounds that a report should not be filed until diagnosis was certain, and 30 percent did so on the basis that the physician believed that he could solve the problem by working with the family rather than seeking outside intervention. This reluctance may be magnified when it is based on anticipation of law enforcement intervention.

A number of small-scale surveys of professionals and their child-abuse reporting patterns bolster the probable validity of the NIS findings with respect to the existence of a reporting gap (as it applies to professionals). These studies often involve projected responses to hypothetical cases presented by the investigator. The magnitude of the reporting gap varies from study to study, however, with most being smaller than that indicated in the NIS.

Twenty years ago, Silver, Barton, and Dublin (1967) reported that more than 20 percent of the physicians they surveyed said they would *not* report cases of suspected physical child abuse that came to their attention. More recently, James, Womack, and Strauss (1978) found that 62 percent of a sample of pediatricians and family physicians said they would decline to report a case of sexual abuse brought to their attention unless the family agreed that such a report should be made. In this and other studies to be reviewed it is unclear what, if any, effect there would be of substituting law enforcement for protective services as "investigators." Such a study is needed.

In a study of eighteen psychiatrists and eighty-three psychologists, pediatricians, and family counselors, Attias and Goodwin (1984) found that more than half of the psychiatrists but less than a third of the other clinicians said they would *not* report a family to child protective services in the case of an 11-year-old girl who graphically describes to her school counselor fellatio and cunnilingus with her natural father, ongoing for more than two years, if the child later retracted the allegation. The authors link this in part to widespread misunderstanding of the likelihood that such retractions, rather than the original allegations, are false.

Muehleman and Kimmons (1981) found that 81 percent of the psychologists they studied said they would report the hypothetical physical child-abuse case presented by the investigators. This represented an increase from an earlier study by Swaboda et al. (1979) in which 87 percent said they would not report the same hypothetical case. In a more highly developed form of the same procedure, Williams, Osborne, and Rappaport (1985) used a four point scale (4 = certainly would report; 1 = certainly would not report) and randomly offered four different hypothetical cases to a range of professionals (varying combinations of type of abuse—psychological or physical—and "privileged vs. nonprivileged communication").

Overall, most of the professionals indicated likelihood of reporting (an average score of 2.95 on the four-point scale), with the case of physical abuse in the nonprivileged communication condition being most likely to be reported (average score 3.68). Among the professional groups studied, school nurses and ministers were most likely to report (average scores of 3.35 and 3.32, respectively), and psychologists were least likely to report (with an average score of 2.42). Teachers (2.90), psychiatrists (2.87), and physicians (2.85) stood in between these extremes. Law enforcement personnel were not included in this study.

Interestingly, on a separate test of knowledge about reporting statutes, ministers scored highest and nurses lowest, suggesting that knowledge of reporting obligations under the law was not the decisive factor in differentiating among the professional groups. Whether the case involved privileged communication (i.e., information given in the context of therapy) made a significant difference in likelihood of reporting. As the investigators point out, this is particularly interesting because the child abuse reporting statute in the state in which the study was conducted specifically excludes privilege (excepting attorney-client relationship; Williams, Osborne, and Rappaport 1985).

As in all social problems containing a "moral" dimension, the distance between the hypothetical and socially desirable "should" and the actual day-to-day "do" can be quite large. Chang et al. (1976) reported the results of a survey of 1,367 physicians in which more than 90 percent said they agreed with the statement "physicians in your community should report cases." Slightly more than half (61 percent) said physicians in their community usually report cases. About 30 percent said they had actually seen cases of abuse in the preceding year (1973), but only one-third of these cases were "referred to a community agency." This suggests that an even smaller number were actually reported to child protective services.

Using the National Incidence Study as a basis for comparison, it seems safe to say that reporting has improved since the 1960s and 1970s. Nonetheless, a recent study of professionals' reporting of sexual abuse cases suggests that the issue is still quite alive. Using a self-selected sample of professionals with special interest, responsibility, or both, for sexual abuse cases in New England, Finkelhor (1984) found that 64 percent said they reported such cases to protective services when faced with them. The range across professional groups was from 48 percent (for mental health professionals) to 76 percent (for school personnel). Who you are (at least institutionally) seems to affect what you do about reporting.

What else do we know about influences on reporting? A recent report by Morris, Johnson, and Clasen (1985) involved a study of how physicians' attitudes toward discipline affected reporting. The fifty-eight Ohio physicians in the study indicated a significant differentiation between parental action they classified as "inappropriate" and action they would report. For example, while 98 percent identified "bruising with a belt" as inappropriate discipline, only 48 percent said they would report it to protective services as child abuse. In general, the higher the physician's tolerance for physical punishment, the less likely they were to report abuse (using a common set of ten hypothetical cases as the standard for comparison). "Personal experience with the family through previous visits" was an important factor in deciding whether to report abuse for 57 percent of the physicians participating in the study, only 30 percent of whom had in fact reported more than one case of suspected abuse in the preceding year.

These results come from physicians who agreed to participate in the survey, of course. Given that they represented a little less than half (43 percent) of the physicians originally contacted, we can expect that their responses reflect a "better" than average awareness of and commitment to the issue of intervention in child maltreatment. This is true of most (virtually all) of the surveys of professionals, which usually have a participation rate of approximately 50 percent.

What can we learn from this review? Three conclusions emerge. First, the reporting gap for child maltreatment is an empirical fact of life. Every expectation is that the results of the replication of the National Incidence Study will mirror the findings from 1979–80 that a major proportion of the professionally identified child maltreatment "caseload" is being dealt with outside of the legally mandated child protective service system. Has the reporting gap changed? Results of the NIS replication should shed some light on this issue. Due principally to the dramatic increase in identified cases of sexual abuse, the total number of child maltreatment cases reported to child protective service units has increased significantly in the period since the first NIS. The most recent data from the American Humane Association's National Study of Child Abuse Reporting suggest a reduction in the rate of increase, however (American Humane Association 1987).

Is reporting catching up with case identification? This is an empirical question capable of being answered in the NIS replication. However, Alfaro's 1985 survey of 243 professionals mandated by New York State law to report suggests that the problem remains significant (and may even be growing as frustration with the ability of overburdened child protective service agencies grows). In his survey of 131 school employees, sixty-two hospital employees, and fifty law enforcement employees, Alfaro (1985) found that the most important impediments to reporting abuse was a fear of reprisal against the child and doubts about the efficacy of child protective services. Forty percent of the school personnel, 18 percent of the hospital personnel, and *8 percent of the police* acknowledged instances of nonreporting. Alfaro found that "professional judgment," not the state reporting law, is the most decisive factor in reporting. Only 19 percent indicated "the law was the most important factor in the decision to make a report." We can speculate that law enforcement personnel are most directly affected by the law, however, given their low rate of nonreporting.

Second, moving beyond the "narrow" issue of professional reporting, there is a "broader" issue of professional case identification. Child maltreatment is intrinsically a social problem. It exists, not as some objective entity, but as the result of an on-going social process of negotiation between community standards including values, beliefs, ethical principles, conceptions of the rights of children, concepts of human nature and folk wisdom, and professional expertise including research findings, theoretical deduction, and clinical insight (Garbarino and Gilliam 1980; Garbarino, Guttmann, and Seeley 1986). Thus, the very existence of child maltreatment as a category of human experience is not fixed.

The definition of child maltreatment changes and develops as professional knowledge increases and community standards change. Acts that were once considered "accidental injuries" (such as deaths of infants in automobile accidents while riding on the laps of their parents) may become definitionally transformed as knowledge increases (and these deaths come to be defined as "preventable accidents"). As the knowledge-values negotiation proceeds, these same events may eventually be seen as culpable acts of maltreatment. And, the probability of criminal justice system intervention increases correspondingly.

A similar history is evident with respect to the use of violence against children—which once was generally accepted as "positive discipline" but came to be seen first as "corporal punishment," and more recently as "physical assault," en route to being defined as "physical abuse."

Gaps in reporting may exist because of gaps between case conceptualization and identification and legally mandated responses. The lower limit for criminal justice intervention should be set higher than the limit for mental health or social service intervention. A more fully resolved "negotiation" between community values and scientific evidence and expertise is needed to justify the police function than is required to authorize the public health function. This is particularly evident in the matter of psychological maltreatment, where such a two-tiered approach is generally recommended (Garbarino, Guttman, and Seeley 1986; Brassard, Germain, and Hart 1987).

The last twenty years have seen a dramatic improvement in case identification. As Alfaro's (1985) evidence suggests, however, the practical implications of this change are not clear-cut. We must differentiate between professional responses that obstruct further therapeutic and protective action (e.g., by suppressing case identification with its implied moral imperative to intervene) and responses that facilitate such intervention. This, of course, is a "higher" rendering of the commonly asserted differentiation between a criminal justice system response and a social service, or mental health system, response. This differentiation must at least be made conceptually. In legal matter of fact, of course, there is usually no such distinction.

Legal realities do not always correspond to social and psychological realities. Even a cursory look at the processes and outcomes of litigation and criminal prosecution demonstrates this. There is an important empirical question of whether child protective service involvement results in more and better intervention for children. In its extreme form, this concern underlies Goldstein, Freud, and Solnit's (1980) objection to protective intervention in all except the most dire circumstances. This provides the context for exploring the impact of further "criminalization" of child maltreatment (and correspondingly greater reliance on law enforcement for investigation).

For sexual abuse, particularly, many service providers hypothesize that involving the child protective service machinery (particularly if it invokes a law enforcement response) produces unnecessary negative consequences for the child that outweigh any benefits. Certainly, many respondents to Alfaro's (1985) survey believe this to be the case. Most respondents cited "quality of CPS intervention" as a concern that dissuaded them from meeting their legal mandate to report child maltreatment. Newberger (1985) has been outspoken in articulating the view that, when official intervention is iatrogenic in the sense that the treatment itself is harmful (as it tends to be, in his opinion, when criminal prosecution is involved), professional intervention will be pushed outside the law. Of course, it is an empirically unresolved issue as yet, whether criminal justice's reputation for *powerful* intervention is more significant in affecting reporting than the stereotype commonly held by professionals from social services and mental health that criminal justice intervention is iatrogenic.

Different solutions are required to deal with reporting that stems more from negative motivations (i.e., from a self-interested refusal to "get involved" or a tolerance for maltreatment) than from positive beliefs that the best interests of the child are served by intervention outside the context of reports to child protective service agencies or criminal justice systems. Nonreporting of the first type can and should be dealt with by education, training, and legal sanction. But such nonreporting appears to be only part, and probably the smaller part, of the current problem.

Narrowing the reporting gap does not appear to depend principally on further training of professionals with respect to their legal obligations or further criminalization of child maltreatment. Neither does it depend on simple exhortation. And, even allowing for the motivational impact of showcase prosecutions of nonreporting professionals, it does *not* depend on more active implementation of current legal mandates to report.

Rather, the answer seems to lie with raising the standard of response by child protective services and their allied investigatory and enforcement agencies. Existing evidence suggests that this should work. What we need, of course, is an experimental study demonstrating that actual and perceived improvement in the quality of protective services results in a corresponding decrease in well-intentioned resistance to reporting. This study should also test the hypothesis that the increased involvement of the criminal justice system results in better child protection and in community perception of better child protection.

Even a retrospective study demonstrating a correlational link between quality of protective services and willingness to report would be a valuable contribution (and one the NIS replication currently being conducted could provide). Some case studies are consistent with the hypothesis that better child protective service performance reduces resistance to reporting (Goodwin and Geil 1982; Alfaro 1985).

The key to better reporting lies in a quality of official response that meets three criteria. First, it must reinforce reporting by being responsive to the reporter's need for feedback, follow-up, and participation in the process that reporting initiates (Alfaro 1985). Will criminal justice intervention do this? Some fear that the more stringent rules of evidence and due process protections invoked by criminal justice system involvement will undermine such changes. Second, better reporting methods must significantly reduce iatrogenesis, go to great lengths to explain and understand such effects when they do occur, and include good faith efforts to prevent such effects where they do occur (Newberger 1985). Here too, there are grounds for concern that the greater power of the criminal justice system will lead to greater abuses of power. Third, it must assemble a convincing data set to demonstrate the comparative benefits of reporting and of intervention not accompanied by reporting (Goodwin and Geil 1982), including a demonstration of any adverse consequences of intervention undertaken in the absence of reporting to child protective services.

Burnett et al. (1976) reported on a pilot program to team police and social workers to intervene in domestic disturbance calls. Data from the program's first year of operation showed that "parent/child" problems constituted 26 percent of the 577 calls answered (as opposed to 20 percent for "runaway," 17 percent for "suicide/depression," 9 percent for "marital," 8 percent for "neighborhood problems," and 20 percent for "other"). Other programs involve training police in methods of dealing with "domestic disturbances" (Bard and Zacker 1971).

A study by Andrews and Cohn (1978) reported that when police investigate reports of neglect they are likely (or at least were when the study was done in the 1970s) to begin a process that results in the youth being labeled a status offender. Of 121 cases of neglect studied, 75 percent eventually were declared persons in need of supervision (PINS). Some 53 percent of the nonneglected youth studied eventually were declared PINS.

Labeling is a recurring issue associated with criminal justice system interventions. Particularly where adolescents are concerned, the "same" youth can be defined differently depending on who does the initial intake. For example, Farber and Kinast (1984) report that a comparison between a group of adolescents classified as "runaways" and a group classified as "abuse victims" revealed no significant difference in the experience of violence in the home—both groups came from violent homes as assessed using the Conflict Tactics Scale employed by Straus, Gelles, and Steinmetz (1980) in their national survey. In a similar vein, Brown, Miller, and Burke (1977) report that the action taken by police when responding to protective service cases depends to a great extent on the options open to them. For example, if they can call on emergency homemakers they are less likely to remove children who are unsupervised. This cautions against overgeneralization to speak of the law enforcement response or the criminal justice approach.

C. Child Maltreatment and Juvenile Delinquency
One way to establish the role of the criminal justice system in the child maltreatment problem is to assess the association between

maltreatment and delinquency. This can be accomplished by demonstrating that juvenile delinquents have experienced maltreatment at a rate higher than that of the general population.

Studies of juveniles involved in delinquent acts have consistently found that these juveniles have endured child abuse and neglect at far greater rates than estimates for the population as a whole and for the low-income groups in particular. Five studies serve to illustrate the range of these findings.

1. Case files of 863 delinquent male adolescents incarcerated in Ohio showed that 26 percent had been physically abused, and 85 percent of this group had been abused more than once (Kratcoski 1982).

2. Child abuse had been noted in the medical records of 15 percent of eighty-one delinquents of both sexes incarcerated in a Connecticut correctional school (Shanok and Lewis 1981).

3. At a private residential treatment program in New Hampshire for court-referred delinquents, 66 percent of 150 youths referred over an eight-year period were found to have been abused or severely neglected (Sandberg 1983).

4. Two hundred juvenile offenders being held in a Denver detention center after being picked up by the police for the first time were interviewed about their backgrounds. Eighty-four percent of 100, whose statements later were confirmed, and 72 percent of 100, whose statements could not be confirmed, reported being abused or neglected before the age of six. Of the confirmed-report group, 92 percent had been bruised, lacerated, or had had at least one bone fractured by their parents within eighteen months prior to being picked up (Steele 1975, 1976).

5. When medical records for 109 delinquents referred to a Connecticut juvenile court were matched with those of 109 nondelinquents, it was found that 9 percent of the delinquents, compared with 1 percent of the nondelinquents, had received services from a nearby hospital for child abuse injuries (Lewis and Shanok 1977).

Frequently a link between maltreatment and delinquency is forged when victims of maltreatment attempt to remedy their situation by retaliating or running away—either choice being considered a delinquent act and raising the prospect of bringing the adolescent into the criminal justice system as a perpetrator. While no studies report on the proportion of abused children who leave home while still under age, several studies indicate that a large proportion of adolescent runaways have been abused, and that many left home because of the abuse.

1. In a study of 308 adolescents served by a runaway program in

Connecticut, 11 percent of the boys and 12 percent of the girls left home directly because of abuse; incest had been the precipitating factor for 4 percent of the girls (Gullotta 1977).

2. Reports from youths at an Ohio runaway shelter indicated that 75 percent had been victims of significant physical maltreatment (McCord 1983).

3. Five percent of a national sample of runaway youths indicated that physical abuse by an adult had been a major reason for running away (National Statistical Survey on Runaway Youth, cited in Youth Development Bureau 1978).

4. Nearly two-thirds of 200 homeless teens served by a Boston youth project reported having been abused by their parents (Cunningham 1983).

It should be noted that while many adolescents leave home voluntarily to escape abuse, there is evidence that some "runaway" delinquents are actually "castaways" or "throwaways": children put out of their homes by their parents. These victims of extreme child neglect constitute a special class of cases in which maltreatment "causes" delinquency. (1) In the Connecticut runaway housing program, 24 percent of the 308 adolescents studied were found to be castaways (Gullotta 1977). (2) Of 33,000 youths served by the Department of Health, Education, and Welfare runaway projects in 1976–77, 10 percent had been pushed out of their homes by their parents or legal guardian (Youth Development Bureau 1978).

The frequency with which physical abuse leads to physical retaliation rather than running away is not well studied, but some evidence is available. (1) Twenty-six percent of 223 abused delinquents incarcerated in Ohio had directed violence toward immediate family members or caretakers, while 12 percent of 640 nonabused incarcerated delinquents had attacked a family member. Of those youths who had committed a violent offense against any person, 45 percent of the abused and 18 percent of the nonabused had acted against a family member (Kratcoski 1982). (2) Case studies of four juveniles who fatally shot their adult caregivers showed that all four were victims of on-going physical abuse, and two of the killings occurred during an abusive episode (Post 1982). (3) In another study of five youths who had killed or threatened to kill a parent, researchers concluded that parental brutality had led to at least two killings (Duncan and Duncan 1971).

Thus, from a variety of perspectives, it seems clear that delinquent children are disproportionately likely to have been victims of child maltreatment. Whether one experience causes the other or both are consequences of deeper etiological processes is not yet well established.

III. Research Issues

There are four major researchable issues involved in defining child maltreatment as a criminal justice problem. (1) Does the threat and/or use of criminal penalties increase the likelihood that perpetrators will participate in rehabilitative programs? (2) Does court-ordered participation in rehabilitative programs result in greater or lesser success in such programs? (3) Does early involvement of the criminal justice system (particularly police) increase or decrease the likelihood of accurate diagnosis and appropriate initial governmental response to suspected cases of child maltreatment? (4) To what extent does the victim's (and perpetrator's) developmental and life-course stage influence the appropriateness and likely effectiveness of intervention by the criminal justice system?

The first three of these issues are conceptually clear and relatively straightforward. This is not to say that they have been adequately researched. Indeed, there are assertions and anecdotal reports in support of *both* sides of each issue. None is definitely resolved. Some say criminalization increases participation but decreases effectiveness of rehabilitative programs. Others contend the opposite. Similarly, the debate continues over whether police involvement early in the process of investigation and diagnosis improves system performance, protects children, and preserves families. We need new research in these areas (see Saunders and Azar [in this volume] for a review of evaluation research on many of these issues).

The fourth researchable issue—"developmental and life-course stage" considerations—requires additional conceptualization before it can be subjected to empirical research. Researchers, practitioners, and policymakers are beginning to identify the elements of a life-course perspective on maltreatment. This first involved efforts to differentiate spouse abuse from child maltreatment. More recently, there have been efforts to differentiate still further the concept of domestic violence so as to identify distinct aspects of abuse and neglect directed towards four different groups—adolescents, the frail elderly, children, and spouses (Garbarino et al. 1986). But many differences exist among these four groups; one of the most salient is power—the ability to determine one's own behavior and influence the action of others. Children and the frail elderly are nearly powerless (though their behavior can have a significant effect on what happens to them). Teenagers gain power because of the increases in the ability to think, argue, and act that adolescence brings. Just as wives in a patriarchal and sexist society are powerful enough to threaten the authority of husbands but weak enough to be victimized, teenagers challenge parental authority yet are liable to victimization.

Because children and the elderly are powerless they are perfect victims for two reasons: they are especially vulnerable, and they elicit sympathy once they are abused. Teenagers are closer to wives in being imperfect victims, in both respects. One evidence of the greater power of abused teens and wives is the fact they sometimes are involved in reciprocal assault. Obviously, children and elderly cannot match the strength of the parent generation, but abuse has been identified as a contributing factor in many assaults by adolescents, from relatively minor incidents to parricide (Garbarino and Gilliam 1980). Likewise, wives who murder their husbands do so often in retaliation for abuse, usually as the culmination of a long period of mutual assault in which they are the chronic losers (Straus, Gelles, and Steinmetz 1980). Straus, Gelles, and Steinmetz (1980) reported serious assault by youth against their parents in 9 percent of a national sample of American families. The likeness between adolescent and wife abuse extends beyond these power dynamics, of course. The two groups are likely to face similar psychodynamic issues, including ambivalence about dependency and separation in their relationships with family authority figures. For the frail elderly there is the additional issue of whether abuse represents a "paying back" for earlier perpetration of abuse by the elders when they were in the parental role (see Pagelow [in this volume] for a review of research on abuse of the elderly).

For the present purpose, one additional concern is the degree to which the appropriateness and effectiveness of involving criminal justice agencies differs as a function of life course and development stage. Certainly one commonality linking wife and adolescent abuse, and differentiating them from the mistreatment of elders and young children, is that any issues of placement involving wives and adolescents *must* be decided in a negotiated fashion. Unilateral decisions made by professionals are easily sabotaged by nonconsenting wife and adolescent victims. Placement of dependent children and frail elderly raises issues of custodial care that require a high level of institutional resources.

IV. Policy Issues
Most of the policy issues involved in changing or maintaining current patterns of intervention by the criminal justice system in child maltreatment cases depend to a great extent on the research issues dis-

cussed earlier. Policy recommendations concerning more or less police investigation and more or less prosecution depend on observation of how such intervention affects families. However, there remain some issues that are not so much a matter of empirical research as they are of values, ideology, and priorities.

There are two major policy issues involved in decisions to change current patterns of intervention by the criminal justice system in the problem of child maltreatment.

One issue is the extent to which it is possible to protect children from traumatic experiences as witnesses and still evaluate the validity of their testimony so as to meet constitutional requirements for due process and protect the rights of the accused.

The other issue is the extent to which the community is willing to adapt to the requirements for an active prevention approach in which parents receive nurturance and feedback, as embodied in the concept of "community as parent to the family." This approach is in contrast to a purely reactive approach that maximizes family privacy and parental discretion and relies on intervention by the criminal justice system to apprehend, prosecute, and seek to rehabilitate or terminate parental rights in families that fail to meet community standards of child care.

Fersh offers a clear statement of the rationale for a broad-based criminalization of all forms of sexual abuse: "I would prefer, on legal and psychological grounds, to subsume all such cases simply under assault. Whether the child is assaulted with a broken bottle, a penis, or a finger, and whether the assault takes place in the ear, in the vagina, or in the mouth, and whether by father, or by stranger, or by some other person, where there is force or coercion they are all serious matters and ought to be treated as such" (1980, p. 305). Conte and Berliner (1981) report that such criminalization (and thus "treatment" by the law enforcement system) *can* lead to service-oriented intervention. In their study of eighty-four offenders charged with sexual assault against a child, a majority remained in the community (75 percent) and received counseling (52 percent) as a consequence of criminal charges. A majority (74 percent) also pleaded guilty and avoided a trial (with its attendant stress on children and parents involved).

This latter finding is a significant one. One of the major concerns of those who oppose law enforcement involvement in child maltreatment cases is that children will be traumatized in the process. Anecdotal reports abound of the intervention being itself harmful to the child. These iatrogenic problems include being removed from the home,

256   James Garbarino

being defined by other family members as the cause of the family's
ensuing social, psychological, and economic problems, and being
humiliated in the court-related interrogations and cross-examinations.
Although measures have been proposed and implemented to minimize
or prevent these problems, "horror stories" abound.

There are many issues of policy and research involved here (see
Goodman 1984). How can children participate in criminal prosecution
in a way that respects *both* their limited ability to conform to conventional rules of evidence *and* the need to meet constitutional guarantees
for the accused? Do children fabricate accusations of abuse with
sufficient frequency to warrant an adversarial approach in the legal
system? Can criminal justice agencies intervene in ways that use
methods that do not further victimize child victims? Other essays in
this volume address these issues. The point here is that they require
effective attention before mental health and social service professionals
will be reassured concerning the psychological effects of involving children in criminal prosecutions of child-abuse cases (leaving aside the
issue of its effect on parent-child relationships in abusive families).

If we are to shift away from a reactive, law enforcement approach to
a more "proactive" prevention-oriented approach that involves the
criminal justice system, we must contend with some fundamental cultural issues. The prevention of child maltreatment is bound up in
mechanisms for social control (Garbarino 1984). More than that, however, it is bound up in the joining together of social nurturance and
social control. This is the essential element of intervention in child
maltreatment, and it flows directly from the concept of support systems
as articulated by Caplan (1974). The key is nurturance and feedback,
social resources and social control. This becomes transparently important in dealing with child maltreatment, where families are likely to
face a deficit of both nurturance and feedback (Garbarino and Gilliam
1980). Families involved in maltreatment are likely to be cut off from
positive support systems—in part because of their own "distancing"
behaviors and lack of social skills, in part because they are cut off by
people around them. If the community is parent to the family, then
positive societal support provides an appropriate model. It offers just
what most high-risk families need—at least initially, when the issue is
whether the family *can* be stabilized in a pattern of relating that does
not involve maltreatment.

However, many voices are raised to dispute the concept of community "parenthood" of the family. The preferred orientation is commu-

nity as parent-of-last-resort. This authority figure requires a "clear and present" danger to the child before "violating" the privacy of the family and the "rights" of the parents.

Some ask, Who owns the children? That question must be rejected if the idea of children as *property* is rejected in favor of the idea of children as citizens, as junior partners in the life of the community. The better question is, Who has custody of the children? One model replies, Parents do. Another asserts, Parents have custody but the community has visiting rights. Yet another states, Parents and the community have joint custody. How this issue is resolved has enormous implications for the role of the criminal justice system in dealing with the problems of child maltreatment. Many express concern that the criminal justice system has difficulty operating as a "support system" for families, as opposed to as a "guard" in a "prison-like" state. This distinction sets the agenda for intervention and evaluation.

There is no clear and simple answer to the question of whether criminalization of child maltreatment is a wise course of action likely to improve the quality of life for children. Our society is experiencing deteriorating social conditions for children (e.g., increasing prevalence of poverty, reduced parental involvement and support, greater demands for performance brought on by factors such as early withdrawal of adult supervision). In such social environments it seems unlikely that a criminal justice approach to child maltreatment is likely to be any more effective than it is in halting other areas subject to criminalization such as prostitution and substance abuse. It may in fact be irrelevant. We certainly need research to address this issue.

REFERENCES

Alfaro, J. 1985. "Impediments to Mandated Reporting of Suspected Child Abuse and Neglect in New York City." Paper presented at the Seventh National Conference on Child Abuse and Neglect, Chicago, November.
American Humane Association. 1983. *Comparison of the National Study of Child Abuse and Neglect Reporting and the National Incidence Study*. Denver: American Humane Association.
————. 1984. *National Analysis of Official Child Abuse and Neglect Reports*. Denver: American Humane Association.
————. 1985. *National Analysis of Official Child Abuse and Neglect Reports*. Denver: American Humane Association.

————. 1987. *Highlights of Official Child Neglect and Abuse Reporting, 1985.* Denver: American Humane Association.

Andrews, R., and A. Cohn. 1978. "Report for the New York State Assembly, 1974." *New Yorker* 54:55.

Attias, B., and J. Goodwin. 1984. "Knowledge and Management Strategies in Incest Cases: A Survey of Physicians, Psychologists and Family Counselors." Paper presented at the Fifth International Congress on Child Abuse and Neglect, Montreal, September.

Badgley, R., H. Allard, N. McCormick, P. Proudfoot, D. Fortin, D. Ogilvie, Q. Rae-Grant, P. Gelinas, L. Pepin, and S. Sutherland. 1984. *Sexual Offenses against Children*, vol. 1. Ottawa: Canadian Government Publishing Centre.

Bard, M., and J. Zacker. 1971. "The Prevention of Family Violence: Dilemmas of Community Intervention." *Journal of Marriage and the Family* 33:677–82.

Besharov, D. 1981. "What Physicians Should Know about Child Abuse Reporting Laws." In *Child Abuse and Neglect*, edited by N. Ellerstein. New York: Wiley.

Brassard, M., R. Germain, and S. Hart. 1987. *Psychological Maltreatment of Children and Youth.* New York: Pergamon.

Brown, F., B. Miller, and P. Burke. 1977. *A Study of Policies and Practices of the Cook County Juvenile System in Child Abuse and Neglect.* Chicago: University of Illinois at Chicago Circle, Jane Addams College of Social Work.

Burgdorf, K. 1980. *Recognition and Reporting of Child Maltreatment: Findings from the National Study of the Incidence and Severity of Child Abuse and Neglect.* Washington, D.C.: National Center on Child Abuse and Neglect.

Burnett, B., J. Carr, J. Sinapi, and R. Taylor. 1976. "Police and Social Workers in a Community Outreach Program." *Social Casework* 57:41–49.

Caplan, G. 1974. *Support Systems and Community Mental Health.* New York: Behavioral Publications.

Chang, A., A. Oglesby, H. Wallace, H. Goldstein, and A. Hexter. 1976. "Child Abuse and Neglect: Physicians' Knowledge, Attitudes, and Experiences." *American Journal of Public Health* 66:1199–1201.

Cicchetti, D., and V. Carlson, eds. 1988. *Child Maltreatment: Research and Theory on the Causes and Consequences of Child Abuse and Neglect.* New York: Cambridge University Press (forthcoming).

Conte, J., and L. Berliner. 1981. "Prosecution of the Offender in Cases of Sexual Assault against Children." *Victimology* 6:102–9.

Cunningham, S. 1983. "Abused Children More Likely to Become Teenaged Criminals." *American Psychological Association Monitor* 38(1):26–27.

Duncan, J. W., and G. M. Duncan. 1971. "Murder in the Family: A Study of Some Homicidal Adolescents." *American Journal of Psychiatry* 127:1498–1502.

Elliott, D. S. In this volume. "Criminal Justice Procedures in Family Violence Crimes."

Farber, E., and C. Kinast. 1984. "Violence in Families of Adolescent Runaways." *Child Abuse and Neglect* 8:295–99.

Fersch, F. 1980. *Psychology and Psychiatry in Courts and Corrections.* New York: Wiley.

Finkelhor, D. 1984. *Child Sexual Abuse*. New York: Free Press.

———. 1986. Personal communication.

Finkelhor, D., S. Araji, L. Baron, A. Browne, S. D. Peters, and G. E. Wyatt. 1986. *A Sourcebook on Child Sexual Abuse*. Beverly Hills, Calif.: Sage.

Garbarino, J. 1984. "Is the Community Parent to the Child?" Unpublished manuscript. Department of Individual and Family Studies, Pennsylvania State University at University Park.

Garbarino, J., and G. Gilliam. 1980. *Understanding Abusive Families*. Lexington, Mass.: Heath.

Garbarino, J., E. Guttmann, and J. Seeley. 1986. *The Psychologically Battered Child*. San Francisco: Jossey-Bass.

Garbarino, J., C. Schellenbach, and J. Sebes, and Associates. 1986. *Troubled Youth, Troubled Families*. New York: Aldine.

Garmezy, N., ed., 1983. *Stress Coping and Development in Children*. New York: McGraw.

Gelles, R. J., and C. P. Cornell. 1985. *Intimate Violence in Families*. Family Studies Text, ser. 2. Beverly Hills, Calif.: Sage.

Gil, D. 1975. "Unraveling Child Abuse." *American Journal of Orthopsychiatry* 43:611–21.

Giovannoni, J. M., and R. M. Becerra. 1979. *Defining Child Abuse*. New York: Free Press.

Goldstein, J., A. Freud, and A. Solnit. 1980. *Before the Best Interests of the Child* New York: Free Press.

Goodman, G., ed. 1984. "The Child Witness," special issue. *Journal of Social Issues*, vol. 40 (no. 2).

Goodwin, J., and C. Geil. 1982. "Why Physicians Should Report Child Abuse: The Example of Sexual Abuse." In *Sexual Abuse: Incest Victims and Their Families*, edited by J. Goodwin. Boston: Wright.

Greeneveld, L., and J. Giovannoni. 1977. "Disposition of Child Abuse and Neglect Cases." *Social Work Research and Abstracts*, p. 17.

Gullotta, T. P. 1977. "Runaway: Reality or Myth?" Paper presented at the annual meeting of the American Association of Psychiatric Services for Children, Washington, D.C., November.

Hampton, R., and E. Newberger. 1985. "Child Abuse Incidents and Reporting by Hospitals: Significance of Severity, Class and Race." *American Journal of Public Health* 75:56–60.

Helfer, R., and H. Kempe. 1974. *The Battered Child*, 1st ed. Chicago: University of Chicago Press.

Hotaling, G. T., M. A. Straus, and A. J. Lincoln. In this volume. "Intrafamily Violence, and Crime and Violence outside the Family."

James, J., W. Womack, and F. Strauss. 1978. "Physician Reporting of Sexual Abuse of Children." *Journal of the American Medical Association* 240:1145–46.

Kaufman, J., and E. Zigler. 1988. "The Intergenerational Transmission of Child Abuse and the Prospect of Predicting Future Abusers." In *Child Maltreatment: Research and Theory on the Causes and Consequences of Child Abuse and Neglect*, edited by D. Cicchetti and V. Carlson. New York: Cambridge University Press (forthcoming).

Kratcoski, P. C. 1982. "Child Abuse and Violence against the Family." *Child Welfare* 61:435–44.

Lewis, D. O., and S. S. Shanok. 1977. "Medical Histories of Delinquent and Non-delinquent Children: An Epidemiological Study." *American Journal of Psychiatry* 134:1020–25.

McCord, W. D. 1983. "Ohio Project Uncovers Abuse/Runaway Links." *Midwest Parent-Child Review*, pp. 8–9.

Martin, H. 1984. "The Consequences of Being Abused and Neglected: How the Child Fares." In *The Battered Child*, 3d ed., edited by C. H. Kempe and R. Helfer. Chicago: University of Chicago Press.

Modzeleski, W. 1987. "Abused Handicapped Children in the Criminal Justice System." In *Special Children and Special Risks: The Maltreatment of Children with Disabilities*, edited by J. Garbarino, P. Brookhouser, and K. Authier. Hawthorne, N.Y.: Aldine de Gruyter.

Morris, J., C. Johnson, and M. Clasen. 1985. "Physicians' Attitudes toward Discipline and Child Abuse." *American Journal of Diseases of Children* 139:194–97.

Muehleman, R., and C. Kimmons. 1981. "Psychologists' Views on Child Abuse Reporting, Confidentiality, Life, and the Law: An Exploratory Study." *Professional Psychology* 12:631–38.

Newberger, E. 1985. "Prosecution Is Not the Best Response to Ending Child Abuse." Paper presented at the Seventh National Conference on Child Abuse and Neglect, Chicago, November.

Pagelow, M. D. In this volume. "The Incidence and Prevalence of Criminal Abuse of Other Family Members."

Pelton, L. E. 1978. "Child Abuse and Neglect: The Myth of Classlessness." *American Journal of Orthopsychiatry* 48:608–17.

Peters, S. D., G. E. Wyatt, and D. Finkelhor. 1986. "Prevalence." In *A Sourcebook on Child Sexual Abuse*, edited by D. Finkelhor, S. Araji, L. Baron, A. Browne, S. D. Peters, and G. E. Wyatt. Beverly Hills, Calif.: Sage.

Post, S. 1982. "Adolescent Parricide in Abusive Families." *Children Welfare* 61:445–55.

Sandberg, D. N. 1983. "The Relationship between Child Abuse and Juvenile Delinquency." Testimony submitted to the Senate Subcommittee on Juvenile Justice, Washington, D.C., October 19.

Saulsbury, F., and R. Campbell. 1985. "Evaluation of Child Abuse Reporting by Physicians." *American Journal of Diseases of Children* 139:393–95.

Saunders, D. G., and S. T. Azar. In this volume. "Treatment Programs for Family Violence."

Shanok, S. S., and D. O. Lewis. 1981. "Medical Histories of Abused Delinquents." *Child Psychiatry and Human Development* 11:222–31.

Shepherd, J. 1988. "Law Enforcement's Role in Family Violence." In *The Battered Child*, 4th ed., edited by C. H. Kempe and R. Helfer. Chicago: University of Chicago Press (forthcoming).

Silver, L., W. Barton, and C. Dublin. 1967. "Child Abuse Laws: Are They Enough?" *Journal of the American Medical Association* 199:65–68.

Steele, B. 1975. "Child Abuse: Its Impact on Society." *Journal of Indiana State Medical Association* 68:191–94.

———. 1976. "Violence within the Family." In *Child Abuse and Neglect: The Family and the Community*, edited by R. E. Helfer and C. H. Kempe. Cambridge, Mass.: Ballinger.

Straus, M. A., and R. J. Gelles. 1986. "Societal Change and Change in Family Violence from 1975 to 1985 as Revealed by Two National Surveys." *Journal of Marriage and the Family* 48:465–79.

Straus, M. A., R. J. Gelles, and S. Steinmetz. 1980. *Behind Closed Doors.* New York: Doubleday.

Swaboda, J., A. Elwork, B. Sales, and D. Levine. 1979. "Knowledge of and Compliance with Privileged Communication and Child Abuse Reporting Laws." *Professional Psychology* 10:448–57.

Timnick, L. 1985a. "22% in Survey Were Child Abuse Victims." *Los Angeles Times* (August 25), p. 1.

———. 1985b. "Children's Abuse Reports Reliable, Most Believe." *Los Angeles Times* (August 26), p. 1.

U.S. Attorney General's Task Force on Family Violence. 1984. *Final Report.* Washington, D.C.: U.S. Attorney General.

Williams, H., Y. Osborne, and N. Rappaport. 1985. "Child Abuse Reporting Laws: Professionals' Knowledge and Compliance." Unpublished manuscript. Department of Psychology, Louisiana State University, Shreveport.

Youth Development Bureau. 1978. *Runaway Youth.* DHEW Publication no. OHDS 78-26054. Washington, D.C.: U.S. Government Printing Office.

Mildred Daley Pagelow

The Incidence and Prevalence of Criminal Abuse of Other Family Members

ABSTRACT

The bulk of family violence research and policy discussion focuses on marital violence and child abuse. Violence against elders, abuse of adolescents by parents, and violence by children in the family receive much less attention. Violence against elders is likely to increase because the proportion of elderly people in our population is growing, and there has been a cutback in the social services needed for prevention. Elder abuse is especially prevalent in the middle and lower middle classes and involves psychological maltreatment, financial exploitation, and physical neglect more often than actual battery. Although adolescents constitute about half the population of abused children, they are unlikely to tell anyone of their abuse; when they do, they are often disbelieved or blamed. Sibling violence, including sexual exploitation, occurs more frequently than any other type of family violence yet is the least likely to be reported to authorities.

Spouse abuse and child abuse are the most notorious and studied forms of family violence. Other forms of family violence are as common and as worthy of public concern but receive much less attention from policymakers and researchers. This essay discusses the elderly who are abused by their in-home caretakers, adolescents who are abused by parents, and adolescents who are violent toward parents and siblings.

Public interest in crimes against the elderly concentrates largely on

Mildred D. Pagelow is adjunct research professor of sociology, California State University, Fullerton.

crimes by strangers or on maltreatment in board and care homes and in nursing homes, even though only about 6 percent of the elderly are institutionalized. The vast majority of the elderly are not in danger of that kind of maltreatment; they either live alone (30 percent) or they live in families (63 percent) and thus constitute the population at risk of abuse by family members (U.S. Bureau of the Census 1979). Elderly parents are maltreated in the same ways that children are maltreated, but they are also victimized by financial exploitation, a crime children are unlikely to suffer (Shell 1982).

The literature on child maltreatment most commonly addresses victimization of infants and young children, invoking the publicized image of the "battered child syndrome" (Allen et al. 1969; Bennie and Sclare 1969; Kempe et al. 1962). Yet almost half the reported victims of abuse by parents or parent-figures are children between the ages of twelve and eighteen (Libbey and Bybee 1979). Very few studies have examined sibling violence, although the national survey by Straus, Gelles, and Steinmetz (1980) found that the highest rates of intrafamily violence occurred between siblings. Violence by adolescents in the family is all but invisible in the literature (Pagelow 1984).

Thus, the categories largely overlooked in scientific research are comprised of people whose older ages make them of less interest: abused adolescents are older among child victims, and abused parents are older among adult victims. They generally are ignored as long as they remain in the confines of the home, but once elders are abused on the streets or in institutions, or when the adolescents' violence spills out to the street or school yard (David and David 1980), then the public and the scientific community become interested and sometimes enraged. Abused teenagers usually remain invisible victims until they grow old enough for emancipation. But some join the bands of homeless youths, become prostitutes, or counterattack their abusers. When these actions are taken, they gain the attention of social scientists, the criminal justice system, and the general public.

This essay attempts to summarize empirical research on the prevalence, incidence, and characteristics of elder abuse, abuse by and against adolescents, and sibling violence. Section I examines the research on victimization of the elderly in the home. Section II addresses what has been learned about adolescent victims of violence perpetrated by parents. Section III focuses on violent adolescents and their relationships with other family members. Section IV, the conclusion, draws together themes developed in the first three sections.

I. Violence against Elders in the Family

Abuse of elderly people within the family is much more common than either media attention to the subject or research on family violence would suggest. Some middle-aged parents are also victims of violence by their children but the issue has been ignored by researchers, with a few exceptions (Warren 1979). A small proportion (3.5 percent) of the parents interviewed in the Straus, Gelles, and Steinmetz (1980) national survey reported being attacked by their teenaged children. Usually the public and the law are unconcerned except when a nonelderly person is physically or mentally disabled. Some states, for example, such as California, have passed laws encouraging or mandating reporting suspicions of abuse of the dependent adult population, aged eighteen through sixty-four. Children's attacks on parents who are not elderly and not handicapped usually receive attention only when the violence is extreme or lethal.

Most of the conclusions presented in this section are tentative. Most of the research discussed involved small, unrepresentative, clinical samples of cases. There is substantial congruence in findings in the existing research, however, and while the unrepresentativeness of samples makes it difficult to generalize from the research to the general populations, there is little reason to question the basic patterns of victimizing and victimization that the research reveals.

A. Defining Elder Abuse

There is confusion and disagreement on definitions of *abuse*, but the concept *elderly* is generally defined chronologically and refers to persons aged sixty-five or older (Pagelow 1984). In this essay, the terms elderly and aged are used interchangeably to refer to persons sixty-five or older, although some writing on elder abuse has included persons under sixty-five (Block and Sinnott 1979; Lau and Kosberg 1979). Social scientists generally classify persons between fifty-five to seventy-five years as the "young old" and those beyond seventy-five as the "old old."

Defining *abuse* presents more serious difficulty (Pedrick-Cornell and Gelles 1982; Pagelow 1984). In 1980, congressional hearings identified the following forms of elder abuse: physical abuse, negligence, financial exploitation, psychological abuse, violation of rights, and self-neglect (U.S. Congress Select Committee on Aging 1980). A California Department of Social Services report defined the following forms of adult abuse.

Physical abuse—willful infliction of corporal punishment or injury. It includes, but is not limited to direct beatings, sexual assault, unreasonable physical constraints, or prolonged deprivation of food or water.

Fiduciary abuse—a person in a position of trust who willfully steals money or property, or secretes or appropriates money or property not in keeping with that trust.

Neglect—failure to exercise the degree of care a reasonable person would exercise. Neglect includes but is not limited to the failure to assist in personal hygiene, provide food and clothing, provide medical care for physical and mental health needs, protect from health and safety hazards, prevent malnutrition.

Abandonment—unreasonable desertion or willfully forsaking an elder.

Mental suffering—deliberately causing fear, agitation, confusion, severe depression, or severe emotional depression through threats, harassment, or intimidation. [CALIFORNIA DEPARTMENT OF SOCIAL SERVICES 1985, pp. 4–5][1]

Most researchers agree that acts must be intentional to be considered abusive (Block and Sinnott 1979; O'Malley et al. 1979). Douglass categorized abuse into verbal/emotional or physical, and neglect into "passive" or "active" (deliberate). For Douglass, "passive neglect" includes both physical neglect (not providing food, clothing, and medication), and psychological neglect (ignoring and isolating the victim). Neglect is passive when it is caused by the "ineptness or inability of the caregiver" (Douglass 1983, p. 398). Douglass reported more cases of passive neglect in his study than any other type of maltreatment.

Other definitional problems become evident when comparing findings from the few published research reports. One study's definition of abuse included nonaccidental physical abuse or neglect, but excluded psychological abuse or neglect and financial exploitation (Rathbone-McCuan 1980). Acts defined as physical abuse and physical neglect in some studies are partitioned by other researchers into direct and indirect physical abuse, with no neglect category (Block and Sinnott 1979; Lau and Kosberg 1979). It is not productive to "search for a common

---

[1] Although they may appear to coincide, the U.S. Congress Select Committee on Aging included self-neglect in its definition, which is not listed by California, but accounted for over 40 percent of the reported elder abuse cases during the month of July 1984 (California Department of Social Services 1985).

etiology, prevention, and cure" (Pagelow 1984, p. 58) when abuse and neglect are not conceptually distinguished. This frustrates efforts to determine promising intervention methods because the causes of physical violence are often different from the causes of neglect (Pedrick-Cornell and Gelles 1982).

The lack of a common definition of abuse is a serious difficulty in studying and generating statistics on the extent and prevalence of the different types of crimes against the elderly. For example, financial exploitation and denial of medicine and medical care may or may not be considered abuse (Fulmer and Cahill 1984; Giordano and Giordano 1984), depending on the definition used. The following acts have been treated differently or have not been included at all in various studies of elder abuse: withholding food and water from the nonambulatory; infantilization; overmedicating elders to sedate them; threatening to abandon elders; being slow to change clothing or bedding for the incontinent; locking elders in their rooms or tying them to their beds (Gentry and Nelson 1980; Beck and Ferguson 1981; Oliveira 1981). Definitional inconsistency results in extreme variation in incidence statistics: the broader the definition, the larger the incidence rate, and vice versa.

B. Incidence and Prevalence

Witnesses at congressional hearings in 1980 on domestic abuse of the elderly estimated that each year between 500,000 and 2.5 million persons over the age of sixty-five are abused by their caretakers, even though there had only been a few, largely exploratory, studies on which to base these ideas (Pagelow 1984). Estimates of the proportion of elderly persons who are abused ranged from 4 to 10 percent. The 10 percent estimate came from the Lau and Kosberg (1979) investigation of 404 clients at the Chronic Illness Center in Cleveland. The 4 percent estimate was from the Block and Sinnott (1979) study of twenty-six elders; on the basis of this small study, the researchers suggested there may be a million abused elders in this country. Block and Sinnott (1979, p. 80) hypothesize that the incidence rates for victims at both ends of the life span—the young and the old—may be similar. If that is correct, aged victims of family violence, because of the rapidly increasing numbers of elderly people, will soon outnumber child victims.

Official statistics are another source of data on elder abuse. In 1980, only twelve states had enacted mandatory reporting laws, but by 1983, five more states had passed such laws (King 1983). Connecticut requires reporting of suspected abuses of anyone over the age of sixty; in the first three years, 3,300 cases were reported (King 1983). In the first year after passing of California's law in 1983, 8,627 cases of abused noninstitutionalized persons aged sixty-five and over were reported (California Department of Social Services 1985). This represents only a tiny fraction of the state's 2.4 million residents sixty-five or older, but officials believe for a number of reasons, including the newness of the reporting system, that it grossly underreports abuse.

This may be correct because 373 cases of elder abuse were reported in 1984 in Orange County, California, which is an average of thirty-one per month. However, for the following year and the first five months of 1986, forty-nine cases per month were reported, an increase of 58 percent. While this shows that the problem is not uncommon, these figures include only a miniscule proportion of the almost 225,000 elders living in Orange County.

There is no way to know how many elderly persons are abused annually in this country because of the lack of reliable incidence statistics. The few studies that have been conducted were small, nonrandom, and largely exploratory, and show the need for more and larger studies using more rigorous research techniques. However, there is sufficient evidence to show that crimes of violence against the aged by their in-home caretakers are a serious problem that will continue to grow as the numbers of persons at risk increases.

C. Characteristics of Abused Elders and Their Abusers

At a family violence conference in 1981, Odacir Oliveira, a psychologist who has spent many years working with the elderly, presented this profile of the likeliest abuse victims among the aged: white women between the ages of seventy-five and eighty-five, who are middle to lower middle class, Protestant, and suffering some form of physical or mental impairment. This characterization is generally supported by the available research.

1. *Age and Sex of Victims.* Victims are mostly in the "old old" category and the vast majority (from 69 to 81 percent) are female (Sengstock and Liang 1983; California Department of Social Services 1985). Their ages range from seventy-five years and beyond; their median ages are about seventy-five to seventy-eight years (Block and Sinnott 1979; Shell 1982; Sengstock and Liang 1983; California Department of Social Services 1985). The dependent elderly are at higher risk of abuse, and dependency increases with age; after age seventy-five impairments increase and people begin to become the "frail elderly" (Cazenave 1981).

The greater longevity and dependency of women are two major reasons why approximately three out of four abused elders are female. More than 28 million Americans are over the age of sixty-five (an increase of 4 million in five years). By the end of this century, "the greatest increase, 53 percent, will occur among those 75 and older, which has important implications since this group is most vulnerable to physical, mental, and financial crises requiring the care of their family and society" (Steinmetz 1981a, p. 6). Of the population over age sixty-five in 1984, the ratio of women to men was ten to seven, and this ratio is growing (U.S. Bureau of the Census 1985). On the average, women outlive men by seven years; the proportion of women increases with age.

Women are more likely than men to become dependent as they age due to widowhood and economics. Women tend to marry men older than themselves (Rawlings 1978), and widowers are seven times more likely than widows to remarry. Most elderly men (77 percent) live with their spouses, whereas only 36 percent of elderly women live with husbands. Thus, two out of three older women have a choice of either living with others, usually relatives, or living alone, which is more expensive (Sommers 1982).

2. *Impairments, Socioeconomic Status, and Abuse.* While only 26 percent of elderly persons are limited in their activities because of health reasons and even fewer (16 percent) are unable to carry on major activities of daily living, a formidable 81 percent of persons over sixty-five have one or more chronic diseases or conditions (Schaie 1982). Dependency increases after age seventy-five as persons lose the ability to function independently; the more physical or mental losses they suffer, the greater the burden they become to their caretakers. The greater the burden, the more the stress on the caretaker (Steinmetz 1981a), and the more the stress, the greater the likelihood of abuse (Sengstock, Barrett, and Graham 1984). The more affluent stay healthier longer and obtain better medical care when they are ill than the poor. The highest medical expenses occur in the last few years of life, and chronic or acute illnesses (theirs or their mates) drain lifetime savings rapidly.

Even if the elderly are in relatively good health, financial problems cause many to share housing with their children. Elderly women are much more likely to be poor than are elderly men (U.S. Bureau of the Census 1983), and many must give up their independence to stretch limited budgets. Older minority women are even more likely to be poor, but reports show that the majority of abuse victims are white

(Block and Sinnott 1979; California Department of Social Services 1985) and Protestant (Sengstock and Liang 1983). Of course, the majority of the population is also white, and the research has not been done to establish whether abuse of the elderly is disproportionately prevalent among members of different racial groups. Nonetheless, the available research supports Oliveira's clinically based portrait of victims of elder abuse.

Poverty alone does not lead to elder abuse; one of the few studies of the relation between social class and elder abuse reports that a majority of the cases were from the middle class (Block and Sinnott 1979). Oliveira (1981) is likely to be correct when he suggests that abuse of elders occurs more often among middle-class families than in either the upper or lower classes. The upper class can provide in-home nursing and services, spacious homes with greater privacy for other family members, and access to quality nursing home care. Lower-class homes often lack privacy even before an old person moves in, so the effect can be less traumatic. The lower class usually has greater contact with social services and may know where to turn for help when needed. Further, when poor old persons require full nursing care, they are more likely to be eligible for admission to public institutions.

The middle class, however, may not be able to afford in-home maintenance and respite care, and may lack the option to institutionalize the elderly because they cannot afford quality nursing care homes but are not eligible for public nursing homes. They also may be unaware of social services in the community or unable to qualify for them. Even if their homes are sufficient for the nuclear family, the strain of cramped quarters causes stress and friction, which in turn can be directed against the elders as the source of their unhappiness. The process is described in a speech by one expert:

> Families grudgingly accept the burden of keeping elderly relatives in their homes because of lack of alternatives, but they resent the intrusion into their lives . . . the stage is set for overt or covert hostility . . . teenagers may refuse to vacate the bathroom for anxious grandparents. Because of physiological changes, old people must use the bathroom more frequently, often causing several trips at night, and they also require less sleep. Frequently, since they are excluded from family activities, they retire early and awaken at three or four in the morning, only to disturb the rest of the family by rattling utensils in the kitchen, getting their own

breakfasts. This is the "Pots and Pans Syndrome." It is
interpreted by the others as a sure sign of disorientation and the
onset of senility, and soon they are presented to physicians or
mental health workers who quickly diagnose them as "confused"
or "disturbed," whereupon they are prescribed unneeded
medication. We hook the elderly into abusing drugs! When they
fight back, they are seen as "difficult" and medication is increased.
[OLIVEIRA 1981]

Sharing living quarters because of economic necessity, often begun
with good intentions, can lead to friction and stress. When older parents become physically or mentally handicapped, the difference between abuse and good care may depend on being able to hire assistance
or to put the parents in good nursing homes (Crossman, London, and
Barry 1981; Pagelow 1984).

   3. *Characteristics of Abusers and Types of Maltreatment.*   The majority
of abusers live in the same households as their victims (Shell 1982;
Sengstock and Liang 1983), and they are most likely relatives, often the
victims' own children who are in the over-forty "sandwich generation"
(Pagelow 1987). Fulmer, Street, and Carr (1984) have noted that the
caretaker relative most commonly lacks resources to live elsewhere,
thus feels trapped, and may be abusing drugs or alcohol. Other research finds that a majority of the abusers live in the same households
(Shell 1982; Sengstock and Liang 1983). Some reports note that two-
thirds of the abusers were forty years old and over (Sengstock and
Liang 1983; California Department of Social Services 1985), and in one
study, 36 percent were over sixty years old, about half between sixty
and sixty-nine (Shell 1982). Most abusers are relatives, ranging from 70
to 86 percent (Shell 1982; Sengstock and Liang 1983; California Department of Social Services 1985). Abusers most frequently are the
sons and daughters of the victims, and spouses are the second largest
abuser category (Shell 1982; Sengstock and Liang 1983; California Department of Social Services 1985). Few reports mention perpetrators'
substance abuse, but it was suggested by O'Malley et al. (1983).

   It may be premature to speculate, in view of the absence of large-
scale studies using representative samples and the lack of consensus on
definitions, but there are some indications that the type of abuse varies
with the age and sex of the perpetrators (Pagelow 1987). For example,
older caretakers, well-meaning but inept and over-stressed, may be
more likely to neglect or psychologically abuse their charges than youn-

ger, able-bodied caretakers, who may be more likely to commit acts of physical abuse. Caretakers of the "old old" are themselves likely to be in the "young old" category. Soon it will not be unusual for seventy-year-old "children" to be caring for their frail ninety-year-old parents (Douglass 1983). Steinmetz notes: "This is the century not only of old age, but of multigenerational families, often composed of several generations of near elderly, elderly, and frail elderly women. About half of all those over 65 who have living children are members of a four-generation family" (1981*a*, p. 6).

Types of maltreatment may also vary with the sex of the caretaker. Pagelow's (1984) examination of research on child maltreatment found that mothers are more likely to be the physical neglectors and fathers are more likely to be the physical abusers of children. Female caretakers may be more likely to maltreat their elderly charges through psychological abuse or neglect and physical neglect; all are forms of passive resistance. Males may be more likely to abuse the elderly physically, which is forceful and purposive. Males and females may be equally likely to exploit them financially (Sengstock and Liang 1983).

At first it was thought that most abusers were females, as a substantial majority of caretakers are female, often daughters-in-law (Pagelow 1984). Early research seemed to confirm this, but also found that the most common type of abuse was neglect and psychological abuse (Block and Sinnott 1979; Lau and Kosberg 1979; O'Malley et al. 1979). Over half the respondents in the Douglass (1983) study experienced passive neglect but little or no active neglect or physical abuse. In one investigation of the types of abuse committed by different types of abusers, daughters were most frequently perpetrators of psychological neglect (Sengstock and Liang 1983).

Data from over 400 cases showed that the abuser was slightly more likely to be male, and that the two most common types of abuse were physical and financial (Shell 1982; California Department of Social Services 1985). Over half (53 percent) of the physical abusers in the Sengstock and Liang study (1983) were sons, but they also comprised the largest category of psychological abusers. Pillemer's (1985) sample contained only physically abused elders and found that 71 percent of the perpetrators were male, most frequently sons and husbands.

The Pillemer study had a control group of nonabused elders; the mean age of the abused was seventy and the controls' mean age was seventy-five. The small sample ($N = 42$) was selected from physically abused elderly clients in a model project. Pillemer challenged the ideas of earlier researchers and theorists who had almost uniformly agreed that the victims' dependency causes stress for caretakers and the stress increases the likelihood for abuse (Steinmetz 1978, 1981a; Davidson 1979; Pentz 1981; Wilks 1981; Archbold 1983; Ferguson and Beck 1983; King 1983). Pillemer's study (1985) showed a mutual dependency between abusers and victims, but the greatest dependency was financial: 64 percent of the abusers were financially dependent on their victims.

Existing work supports a number of testable hypotheses about the causes of elder abuse. Since almost three-fourths of the abusers of thirty-nine females in his study were male caretakers, Pillemer (1985) suggests that social pressures on men to be financially independent may trigger physical assault because of resentment at their dependency. The perpetrators' ages were not presented in the Pillemer report but financial exploitation should be expected to cross age and sex lines. Younger generation caretakers (victims' offspring) may initially attempt fiduciary abuse but, if thwarted, sons may resort to physical violence. Men of the same generation as the victim, such as husbands or brothers, may be more inclined to direct physical violence, especially husbands who have battered their wives during the length of their marriages.

These sometimes conflicting findings are based largely on rudimentary and exploratory research and indicate the need for more and larger studies. For example, Pillemer carefully selected his sample for physical abuse and found *abuser*-dependency. It is still possible that *victim*-dependency causes abuse in the majority of cases, because the major types of abuse suffered by the elderly appear to be psychological abuse and neglect and physical neglect.

D. Problems in Discovery and Case Processing

Horror stories of physical abuse and neglect, documenting savage and cruel acts, are highly publicized, and the literature is replete with vignettes of these abusive relations (Kelly 1975; Haggerty 1981; Milt 1982; Ferguson and Beck 1983; Rathbone-McCuan and Goodstein 1985; Robinson 1985). These cases invite attention. Sounds of physical abuse are likely to alert neighbors who instigate police intervention. Physical abuse and severe physical neglect can be detected by trained medical personnel who may notify police or social workers. These types of abuse are obvious and provable, and they will probably continue to be overrepresented in the official reports (California Department of Social Services 1985). Horror stories are, however, only the tip of the iceberg of crimes against the elderly.

Although case histories of physically abused elders serve to sensitize people to the problem, most experts believe these are relatively rare (Shell 1982; Sengstock and Liang 1983). Oliveira (1981) reports that physical battery is the *least* common kind of abuse, occurring in only 19 percent of all cases, and that 50 percent of abuse is psychological. Sengstock and Liang (1983) found that the most common abuse was combined psychological abuse and neglect. Abuses that occur in the home can go undetected until their effects are so extreme they are unmistakable to outsiders. Detection may depend on in-home visitors such as other relatives, social workers, visiting nurses, or visiting clerics. Psychological abuse and psychological neglect are probably the most damaging to the victims' mental health and may shorten their lives by reducing their will to live, but they are the least likely to be detected and punished by the criminal justice system.

Some problems associated with detecting and investigating elder abuse are not present in child abuse and neglect cases (Adams 1986).[2] The most important difference is that the law protects adults' rights to privacy; no one can interfere without permission. In many cases, overwhelming evidence is present that adults have been victims of crimes in their homes, but, without their cooperation, it is extremely difficult to build cases sufficiently strong that can be successfully prosecuted. Adults cannot be removed involuntarily from their homes; when the situation appears to be life threatening, there are ways to transfer them to medical facilities, but for only a few hours. It may take months to investigate these cases, and even if victims cooperate at first, they may back out (Adams 1986). Without testimony from the victim, these cases can be carried forward only if there is strong evidence that a crime or crimes occurred, there is a corroborating witness, and it can be shown *why* the victim refuses to testify (e.g., fear of retaliation).

Elder abuse is frustrating to the criminal justice system because the intervenor often knows that crimes have occurred, but victims do not ask for help and may refuse assistance: "Abused elders and their

---

[2] Sgt. Gary Adams of the Santa Ana Police Department (SAPD) has headed, for about seven years, the only specialized unit in California specifically created for investigating crimes against the elderly. Much of the material in this section was obtained during an interview on July 7, 1986, with Sgt. Adams, who now heads the newly created Family Services Unit of the SAPD. This unit investigates other domestic violence crimes as well as dependent adults and elders.

abusers *almost invariably* deny it" (Galbraith and Zdorkowski 1984, p. 23). The elderly seldom report any type of abuse themselves. Elderly victims refuse to assist law enforcement agencies because of their fear of losing independence, fear of retaliation, embarrassment over their state of health, hygiene, or family relations, and fear of forced relocation and institutionalization (O'Malley et al. 1983). In addition, many still love their abusers.

The Sengstock and Liang (1983) cases came from two major sources: senior service agencies, which reported more cases of physical or emotional neglect than any others, including health agencies; and legal aid agencies, which reported the most cases of physical or emotional abuse and financial abuse. Law enforcement agencies reported fewer cases than any of the other agencies.

Discovery of maltreatment of old people depends on indicators that are similar in many ways to indicators of child maltreatment, but they are more difficult to isolate from the normal aging process. For example, physical abuse may be indicated by the types and locations of physical trauma and how well injuries and explanations match. Neglect is indicated by evidence of dehydration, malnutrition, over- or under-medication, household conditions and odors; bedsores are a strong indicator of neglect. Psychological abuse or neglect may be detected by observing how the elders respond to their caretakers or whether their demeanor changes as their caretakers come and go.

Responses by the criminal justice system to victimization of the elderly must be designed on a case-by-case basis, carefully considering many factors, including the victims' ages, their physical and mental health, and their attitudes, as well as the characteristics of suspects, intentionality, and environmental and interpersonal dynamics of the relationship (Adams 1986). Perfect solutions are never found, but some cases are best handled outside the system while others require the strongest legal sanctions possible.

Psychological abuse and neglect are generally beyond the purview of the criminal justice system and, unless they occur in conjunction with criminal acts, are better addressed by training programs, referrals to professional assistance agencies, and provision of social services. Physical neglect is more easily reversible by correcting the deficiencies. When neglect is caused by ignorance or ineptness or stress, nonpunitive, helpful intervention can be most successful. These cases are more appropriately referred to social services than to criminal prosecution.

Financial exploitation often is exposed when victims realize what has happened to their money or property and complain to persons outside the home, usually legal aid agencies or senior service agencies. Law enforcement agencies and prosecutors are more likely to receive elderly victims' cooperation in these cases than in most elder abuse cases, because many victims view this as a theft by a relative rather than as abuse (Adams 1986). If the victims will cooperate, these are appropriate cases for criminal investigation and prosecution.

Deliberate physical neglect[3] and abuse deserve invocation of criminal justice processes. Case development requires the same techniques of identification and medical verification as are used in investigating any other serious crime. The best way to gain victims' trust is by use of a finely-tuned network of caring professionals who assist with their own specialized expertise. If victims' resistance is overcome, the next hurdle is to maintain cooperation. Successful prosecution is most likely when the victim has little or no mental impairment and there is a patient and thorough investigation.

E. Intervention and Prevention

Techniques that are most effective for intervention are also the best for prevention. "Intervention should involve the least restrictive alternative to ongoing abuse or neglect while respecting the rights of privacy and self-determination" (O'Malley et al. 1983, p. 1004). Many professionals have little patience for the desire of victims to protect their abusers or to remain in conditions that, to the professionals, are clearly substandard. They do not understand that victims often have strong ties to their abusers and to their familiar surroundings. Their greatest fear is losing their homes and being institutionalized. Anderson and Thobaben observe that the latter fear is realistic: "All too often, this is the intervention of choice of well-meaning professionals" (1984, p. 9). These writers suggest that intervention should be guided by standardized, preplanned protocols developed by interdisciplinary health care teams, much like those recommended for suspected child abuse.

Although state reporting laws vary considerably (Haggerty 1981; O'Malley et al. 1983), education is an important first step. Health care

---

[3] Physical abuse of an old person is a crime; any assault and battery is criminal and punishable by law. However, neglecting a dependent adult is not always considered a crime. In 1983, the first law prohibiting "endangering health of" dependent adults was added to the California penal code, and in 1984 it was amended to include neglect.

and other social service professionals and the general public must be educated to recognize symptoms and report suspicions. Many people do not report even the most blatant cases because they know the system is not set up to deal with them, and they see no immediate changes as a result of reports (Adams 1986). In addition, the elderly themselves must be informed about their rights and given alternatives to living lives of pain, fear, and degradation.

Another important next step is to compile data from the reports and undertake representative surveys to establish credible information on incidence rates and patterns of abuse. Until policymakers realize the extent and seriousness of the problem, they will not provide mechanisms to deal with it.

Many agencies are concerned and ready to intervene on behalf of victims and to assist abusers to prevent further abuse. For example, the San Bernardino County, California, Agency on Aging distributed a skillfully designed brochure to professionals giving details on how to identify abuse, gather information, and report suspicious events. The brochure notes that intervention should proceed from the least restrictive to the most, and all specific suggestions are ranked in that order. Clients' rights to privacy and to refuse assistance are also stressed. This is important because some professionals may be tempted to "play god" (Pagelow 1984), but, as Adams (1986) notes, there often comes a "time to let go." The agency also provides "When You Need Help . . . A Guide to Senior Services" for professionals to distribute to elderly clients. This slim packet contains a wealth of information on separate inserts about specific needs with descriptions and phone numbers. Examples include "lifeline and postal alert services," legal services, and home repair. Adams (1986) notes, "many instances of abuse or neglect could be prevented if they only knew about services in their own community."

The San Bernardino agency and similar agencies are helping prevent abuse and neglect locally and other public and private agencies are offering services nationally. "Ideally, the services can add up to a 'nursing home without walls,' a combination of health care, day-care supervision, housekeeping services, counseling, meal deliveries, transportation, visits from friendly companions, home repairs and more" (Rosenblatt and Peterson 1986, p. 1).

Agencies dedicated to serving the elderly have been established in many places. In-Home Supportive Services in Orange County, California, hires nonprofessionals to assist the frail elderly with chores such as personal hygiene, preparing meals, and light housekeeping. In some areas, "meals on wheels" brings the mobile elderly to senior centers or brings hot, balanced meals to the house-bound. Nationally, senior centers are providing meals, counseling, recreation, and day care, charging on a sliding scale for these services and providing caretakers respite from twenty-four hour a day responsibility. One Los Angeles center served over 19,000 persons in 1985 (Rosenblatt and Peterson 1986). Some agencies provide emergency housing (Journal of the American Medical Association 1980).

At the same time that programs are expanding and offering more diversified services to meet needs of the elderly and their caretakers, professionals are offering suggestions on intervention that range from individual assistance, family supports, and political activism to push for more government services (Haggerty 1981; Anderson and Thobaben 1984; Giordano and Giordano 1984). Medical professionals are also attempting to educate peers on identification and intervention techniques (Beck and Ferguson 1981; Ferguson and Beck 1983; O'Malley et al. 1983; Rathbone-McCuan and Goodstein 1985). An entire issue of the *Journal of Gerontological Nursing* (1984) was devoted to articles on elder abuse. Although more and larger studies of elder abuse have not appeared in the 1980s, as some had expected, the issue remains of great importance and concern.

II. Abuse of Adolescents by Parents

Abuse of adolescents within families has only recently begun to receive attention. In 1979, the *Journal of Social Issues* devoted an issue to "Violence toward Youth in Families" but, except for articles by Bybee (1979) and Libbey and Bybee (1979), the issue dealt with infant and child abuse, not abuse of youths. Growing interest in adolescent maltreatment is evidenced, however, by the increasing number of recent journal articles on the subject (Garbarino and Jacobson 1978; Herzberger, Potts, and Dillon 1981; Hjorth and Ostrov 1982; Galambos and Dixon 1984; Hoekstra 1984; Wayne and Weeks 1984; Farber and Joseph 1985).

A. Defining Adolescent Abuse

Definitional problems frustrate efforts to isolate adolescent abuse for study. Although there is some disagreement (Libbey and Bybee 1979), most writers accept the definition of *adolescence* used here to include the age span from twelve to eighteen years. The greater problem lies in the definition of *abuse* because of problems in distinguishing among corporal punishment, "normal discipline," and inappropriate violence.

Bybee points out a contradiction in public attitudes toward physical punishment of children: "Simultaneously, there is support for eliminating child abuse and for permitting physical punishment toward youth" (1979, p. 1). During the 1970s, "every state legislated mandatory reporting laws for child abuse, a term that includes physical harm or nonaccidental injury to youth" (Bybee 1979, p. 1), yet in 1977 the Supreme Court held that physical punishment in schools is not unconstitutional in the sense that it constitutes cruel or unusual punishment. The 1974 Child Abuse Prevention and Treatment Act defines child abuse as maltreatment of "a child under the age of eighteen," but does not distinguish adolescent abuse from child abuse (Foreman and Seligman 1983).

There is cultural ambivalence about the extent of children's rights and parents' rights, and about the line between physical punishment and physical abuse. An estimated 80 to 90 percent of all Americans approve of and use physical punishment to discipline children (Stark and McEvoy 1970; Erlanger 1974), yet, as Garbarino (1980, p. 123) notes, "Americans express outrage about child abuse." The National Center on Child Abuse and Neglect (1980a) notes that no state prohibits, and five states expressly permit, parental use of "reasonable corporal punishment" on children. To most Americans, the terms discipline and physical punishment are synonymous; distinguishing between them is a serious problem in studying adolescent abuse.

When definitions of abuse focus on the severity of the injury, this can reduce the incidence rate considerably (Fisher and Berdie 1978; Foreman and Seligman 1983). "Adolescents who are physically maltreated are often not defined as 'abused' because the injuries are not considered sufficiently severe" (Berdie and Medina 1984, p. 15). The same force used against young children and adolescents is more likely to inflict injuries to the younger victims because of their relatively smaller size and strength (Pagelow 1984). A "severity of injury" definition of abuse may also minimize or ignore emotional abuse and neglect suffered by adolescent victims (Hjorth and Ostrov 1982; Galambos and Dixon 1984) because psychological abuse and neglect are less quantifiable and may inflict deep-rooted and long-term injuries that cannot be traced directly to specific persons, places, or events. Berdie and Medina (1984) note that emotional abuse is a particularly common form of maltreatment of adolescents, but it is insufficient as a basis for intervention; few states have established legal definitions with clear standards for emotional abuse and psychological harm.

Compounding the definitional problem is the question of victim provocation—if the youth is perceived by others as deliberately wayward, rule breaking, or being out of control, parental acts that might otherwise be considered abusive may be considered to be appropriate discipline (Libbey and Bybee 1979). Many abusive incidents occur after adolescents have disobeyed or argued with their parents (Libbey and Bybee 1979; Garbarino 1980). Maltreated young children are almost invariably seen as innocent victims, and most people react with sympathy and concern. Adolescents are not generally viewed as being as helpless or as innocent as children under twelve, and many people consider parental abuse as evidence that the children "got what they deserved" (Berdie, Baizerman, and Lourie 1977). Acts that are generally considered criminal when committed against adults outside the home are often viewed as noncrimes when committed against vulnerable young people in the home (Pagelow 1981). Many people consider these acts as "justified" (Foreman and Seligman 1983). "Adolescents are rarely seen as 'victims' in the same way children are" (Berdie and Medina 1984, p. 18).

B. Incidence and Prevalence

A few years ago, the only sources of information on the incidence and prevalence of adolescent abuse were the official reporting centers; as a result, estimates were considerably lower than they are today. The official child abuse and neglect report from 1978 (National Center on Child Abuse and Neglect 1980*b*) showed that youngsters thirteen to seventeen years old constituted 22 percent of the reported victims of substantiated reports. Garbarino (1980) estimates that adolescents are victims in approximately one-third of abuse cases reported to state registries. An American Humane Association report (1983) showed that 29 percent of the minor unspecified physical injuries were suffered by youngsters in the twelve to seventeen age groups.

Researchers tend to find higher proportions of abused adolescents than official reports for several reasons, including the definitions they employ (Berdie and Medina 1984). Lourie's (1977) study found that adolescents constituted 49 percent of the caseload of an affluent northeastern county's social service agency. Libbey and Bybee (1979, p. 101) note: "We now know that almost half of the known cases of abuse involve youth between the ages of 12 and 18"; Fisher and Berdie (1978) reach the same conclusion for the age group ten to eighteen.

Finally, the National Incidence Study (National Center on Child Abuse and Neglect 1981, 1982), provides useful data on the incidence and prevalence of child maltreatment. This is the first national study of child abuse and neglect that used common and consistent definitions at all data collection sites. These sites were located at nearly 600 agencies in twenty-six counties in ten states. Data were collected from child protective services agencies for a year and other community institutions for a four-month period. This carefully designed study found abuse rates that projected up to 652,000 children abused or neglected annually, and an estimate of more than 1 million children maltreated in the United States, on the basis of the rate of nonreporting of known cases to Child Protective Services (National Center on Child Abuse and Neglect 1982). Youths twelve to seventeen constitute 38 percent of the child population, but they are greatly overrepresented as victims. The National Incidence Study (National Center on Child Abuse and Neglect 1981) found that of all forms of maltreatment of children, 47 percent of the victims were aged twelve to seventeen.

In addition, abuse of children increases in severity with age: whereas the fifteen- to seventeen-year-olds make up 19 percent of the child population, they suffered 27 percent of the serious injuries and 23 percent of the fatalities (National Center on Child Abuse and Neglect 1981). The national study shows the lowest incidence rates at the youngest ages and a steady increase with age. Other reports show a curvilinear relation. Straus, Gelles, and Steinmetz (1980), for example, found the highest rates at both ends of the age scale, but they also found that parents use more severe and potentially lethal forms of violence against older children. The American Humane Association report also observed "that major physical injury generally declines with age up until the age of 15, when it increases again" (1981, p. 23).

C. Characteristics of Abused Adolescents and Their Abusers

The overall picture presented in the literature is that abused adolescents are frequently reported by parents or schools to authorities because of disobedience or "acting out" behavior, or that they come to the attention of researchers because of "emotional problems." Their abusers are mostly depicted as middle-aged parents, going through their own mid-life crises, who view their offspring as uncontrollable.

1. *Sex of Victims and Types of Maltreatment.*   Girls are much more likely to be abused in all categories (physical, sexual, and emotional) and physically neglected than boys, whereas boys are more likely to be educationally and emotionally neglected (National Center on Child Abuse and Neglect 1981). Girls are victims of sexual abuse much more often than are boys at all age levels. The National Incidence Study identified "a consistent pattern of sex differences increasing with increasing age, the largest sex differences occurring in the 15–17 group" (National Center on Child Abuse and Neglect 1981, p. 27).

There is a sharp drop in incidence rates of physical abuse of boys in the teenage years, beginning after the age of eleven; the National Incidence Study speculates: "one wonders whether physical abuse of boys occurs less often then, or is just less often recognized" (National Center on Child Abuse and Neglect 1981, p. 27). Lack of recognition by agencies may be one part of the lower report rate, but victims may deliberately avoid recognition. Boys in our culture are taught very early that "big boys don't cry," and teenage boys, even if severely bruised, are likely often to feel shame that would cause them to conceal their injuries. On the other hand, physical abuse of boys may decline with age because of their growth in physical stature and musculature. "It may become less attractive for a parent who is somewhat past his physical peak to continue hitting or punching a boy who now stands eye-to-eye with him. A man who has terrorized his son for years may begin to realize that some day he might get punched back!" (Pagelow 1984, p. 76). Some sons do strike back, but when they do, they tend to enter the system as perpetrators rather than as victims.

All forms of abuse of girls rise sharply at the ages of twelve to fourteen and continue increasing, especially physical and emotional abuse (National Center on Child Abuse and Neglect 1981). The increase may be due in part to their budding sexuality; as girls begin to want independence from parental control, parents simultaneously set rules enforced by physical punishment and restraint. The power differential between parents and sons decreases but the power differential between parents and daughters remains great (Pagelow 1984). Girls in one study were more likely to have experienced the two most severe types of physical violence—being threatened with a knife or gun, or having had a knife or gun used against them (Gelles 1979). Older girls are more likely to respond to severe abuse by the "escapist" crime of running away, which in turn may propel them into prostitution, theft, and substance abuse; thus they too may enter the system as perpetrators, not victims.

2. *Demographic Characteristics.* Although the National Incidence Study data are not presented by age categories, maltreated children showed the following demographic characteristics. The large majority were from white families (86 percent), and black children were underrepresented in all abuse categories and all neglect categories except educational neglect; in that one category, they were substantially overrepresented. Among lower-income groups, incidence rates for all types of maltreatment were consistently higher for whites than for nonwhites; at the lowest income level, overall incidence of abuse was four times higher for whites than for nonwhites. There were virtually no differences between the ethnic groups at the middle- and higher-income levels (National Center on Child Abuse and Neglect 1981).

Low-income families were overrepresented in all maltreatment categories, but there is a stronger association between income and physical and educational neglect (National Center on Child Abuse and Neglect 1981). Children in the middle- and upper-income groups were overrepresented in the emotional neglect and emotional abuse categories. There has been some speculation about the relations between residence patterns and child abuse and neglect, but the National Incidence study did not find as many differences as might have been expected. The distribution of forms of maltreatment in various types of living areas was fairly uniform, with some exceptions. Children in rural areas were overrepresented in the sexual abuse category, educational neglect was much more common in urban areas, and emotional neglect was most often found in suburban areas (National Center on Child Abuse and Neglect 1981).

Nationally, 19 percent of the child population are only children, but they were overrepresented in all maltreatment categories in the National Incidence Study, especially in respect of emotional neglect, for which there were twice as many only children as their proportion of the population. The second largest group of abuse victims was made up of children from families with four or more children; families with two to three children were underrepresented in all categories (National Center on Child Abuse and Neglect 1981). Some researchers have suggested that step-families are at particularly high risk for adolescent maltreatment (Kalter 1977; Daly and Wilson 1981; Burgess and Garbarino 1983), and Garbarino, Sebes, and Schellenbach (1984) found support for that theory in their study of 62 families containing an acting-out adolescent and two parents.

3. *Family Dynamics.*   Depending in large part on how reports reach the system, adolescent maltreatment is often viewed as a problem of deviant individuals—either abusive parents or delinquent children. When cases reach the attention of medical professionals because of severe physical injuries, the victim is likely to be labeled as an abused child and receive sympathetic care (Farber and Joseph 1985). But when adolescents respond to abuse by engaging in typical acting out behaviors and become labeled as drug addicts, status offenders, runaways, or as promiscuous, "the problem becomes one separate from mistreatment and thus subject to a separate remedial approach" (Hoekstra 1984, p. 287). Maltreated children are too often returned to high-risk families for further abuse or are labeled bad or sick by virtue of an expedient placement. "In either case, the problem is no longer viewed as the *family* problem, which a growing body of knowledge indicates adolescent mistreatment is" (Hoekstra 1984, p. 288).

Adolescent maltreatment is increasingly seen as a developmental issue and the family as a system of interacting dependencies and conflicting age-related needs (Lourie 1977; Serrano et al. 1980; Anderson 1984; Garbarino, Sebes, and Schellenbach 1984), in contrast to an earlier characterization of psychopathology of parents and adolescents (Kempe and Kempe 1978). Patterns of adolescent maltreatment are usually divided into three or four etiological types: (1) a continuation of child abuse; (2) maltreatment that began in childhood, ceased, and begins again in adolescence; (3) an escalation of previously used forms of physical punishment (this category is most frequently associated with rigid, controlling parents); (4) maltreatment that begins in adolescence (Berdie, Baizerman, and Lourie 1977; Lourie 1977; Kempe and Kempe 1978; Lourie et al. 1979; Foreman and Seligman 1983; Anderson 1984; Pagelow 1984). The last category is sometimes associated with child-oriented, permissive parents who engage in a struggle over the child's demands for independence.

Lourie (1977) originally proposed a typology of three categories: the first, third, and fourth listed above. Researchers tend to focus on the first category (ongoing child abuse) and the fourth, maltreatment that begins in adolescence (e.g., Pelcovitz et al. 1984). Some studies find that approximately half their samples consist of families in which abuse began when the children reached adolescence (Libbey and Bybee 1979; Garbarino and Gilliam 1980; Pelcovitz et al. 1984). Abuse began at the onset of adolescence in 80 percent of the twenty-five cases studied by Libbey and Bybee (1979). Both rigid and permissive parenting practices in these families were encountered by researchers, who sometimes explain abusive behavior in terms of the dynamics of developmental stresses (Pelcovitz et al. 1984). Some believe that strains introduced into the family system by adolescent development are more important than specific characteristics of the children (Foreman and Seligman 1983).

Anderson (1984) provides a description of interrelated developmental tasks and their implications for intervention and treatment. These tasks, common experiences, and behaviors of all growing youths are identified as separation, identification, peer relations, emerging sexuality, and defiance of authority. Anderson shows how families erupt into maltreatment because they cannot adequately deal with these development tasks, and how other families, where maltreatment is part of their history, are particularly at risk when the maltreated child enters adolescence.

Many parents who abuse adolescents were abusive at earlier stages in their children's lives (Fisher and Berdie 1978). One study of seventy-seven abused adolescents (Farber and Joseph 1985) measured Lourie's (1977) typology of three categories. They found that 21 percent fit the first category (continuing child abuse); 51 percent represented the second (a qualitative change in the severity of punishment); and only 20 percent matched the third (abuse that began at adolescence). They observe: "in over 80% of the cases, there had been a long history of family violence. The use of Lourie's categorization of adolescent abuse does not seem to be related to the forms of the abusive acts, the types of families who abuse, or the reactions of the adolescent victim" (Farber and Joseph 1985, p. 205).

More and larger samples and more rigorous research is needed if our understanding of adolescent abuse is to increase substantially. Most of the existing research consists of surveys based on official reports (with all the report biases and inconsistencies that official reports contain) or on case studies using small or unrepresentative samples. The existing work is heuristically useful and can serve as the basis for developing testable hypotheses, but much more needs to be done.

D. Preliminary Data from a Case Study

In spring 1986, I began a college student survey on the victimization of adolescents by family members and on adolescent violence against relatives. Although my findings cannot be generalized to the population at large because college students are not representative of the total population, they do provide insight into adolescent family relations as reported by unlabeled, presumably well-functioning adults. The study is ongoing and the data base is being enlarged, but some descriptive statistics from the preliminary analysis are available and are outlined here.

1. *The Study.*   Following Finkelhor's lead in his study of sexual victimization of children (1979), the sample was obtained by distributing questionnaires to college students.[4] The survey instrument was distributed to students at three state university campuses in southern California; all of the classes were sociology courses, usually unrelated to the topics under study. Distribution was mostly determined by the willingness of colleagues to devote lecture time to explaining the purposes of the study, the voluntary nature of the students' participation, and assurances of confidentiality. Students were provided a self-addressed stamped envelope and were asked to take the questionnaires home, complete them, and return them by mail. This undoubtedly reduced the response rate, but 473 students nevertheless voluntarily completed the questionnaires, and fourteen of them requested a personal interview.

2. *Demographic Characteristics of the Sample.*   The sample consists of 473 students, 85 percent of whom are female ($N = 399$), with a mean age of twenty-six, ranging from eighteen to seventy-two years.[5] Seventy-one percent have never been married. Eighty percent are Caucasian, 3 percent black, 11 percent Hispanic, and 6 percent Oriental; this distribution is roughly representative of the student populations in the geographic area. Almost all are commuters and employed, the majority on a part-time basis. Most came from small families with a median of two children. Twelve percent were only children, 67 percent grew up in homes with one or two siblings, and 21 percent came from families

[4] The research instrument contains some modified items from the Conflict Tactics Scale developed by Straus (1979) for use in his family violence studies, other modified items from a scale developed by Gwartney-Gibbs (1982) for her study on courtship and dating violence, and others modified from Finkelhor's (1979) study on sexual victimization of children.

[5] Finkelhor attempted to obtain a sample more heterogeneous for age than most college samples and succeeded in obtaining a sample in which 18 percent were over the age of twenty-four. By contrast, 31 percent of this sample was over twenty-four years of age, but that is an artifact of the type of campuses from which samples were drawn. Ninety percent of the respondents were at state-supported, commuter campuses which tend to have a somewhat older student body with diversified ethnic backgrounds somewhat representative of the geographic area.

with more than three children. At the age of twelve, 95 percent lived with their mothers and 81 percent lived with their fathers; a few lived with stepparents, mostly stepfathers. Only 6 percent indicated that another adult relative, usually a grandparent, lived in the same household when they were twelve years old.

3. *Findings on Violence by Parents against Adolescents.* To measure violent acts of parents directed at children, nine items were scaled from least to most violent, and respondents were asked to indicate whether or how frequently these acts were done to them in disputes. Respondents indicated that more of their mothers than their fathers used the less serious forms of violence against them when they were twelve years old or older. For example, 36 percent of the mothers compared with 27 percent of the fathers reportedly slapped or bit them. Ten percent of the mothers were reported to have hit them with a hard object, compared with 6 percent of the fathers.

In the more severe types of violence, fathers were as violent or more violent than the mothers. More of the fathers than mothers "choked" their adolescent child, according to respondents, and more fathers who "beat up" their children did it often. One percent of both mothers and fathers threatened their children with a knife or gun, and two fathers and one mother "used a knife or gun."

There was an open-ended item ("other"), and many questionnaires contained statements about the behavior of the respondents' parents. About half the comments referred to emotional abuse and neglect: "screaming," "yelling," and "swearing at me" were the descriptive terms most often used. One wrote, "You can get over the bruises, but when they play with your head, that's hard to get over." Several said they were shaken or whipped with belts, straps, sticks, boards, and wooden spoons. A mother "pulled [my] hair out" and a father twisted his child's ear. One father hit his child's head on her sister's head and another "forced me to be a mother figure." In a culture where corporal punishment is the rule rather than the exception, most of these behaviors are not shocking, but these forms of punishment were used on children aged twelve years or over, and that the victims recalled them vividly, even years later, shows that they were serious rather than trivial in their younger lives.

4. *Sexual Experiences of Young People in Their Homes.* The survey instrument asked respondents about sexual experiences with members of their families when they were under the age of eighteen. Despite the sensitive nature of these questions, which undoubtedly led to underre-

porting, 26 percent indicated that they had experienced one or more types of sexual encounter. This is comparable to the 26.5 percent of college students in Finkelhor's (1979) study who reported sexual activities between themselves and a family member.[6] (See also West's 1983 review of research on sexual offenses.)

These activities had occurred with more than one person for 29 percent of those who had sexual experiences. The sexual activity was initiated by the other person in 81 percent of the cases, although 44 percent said it involved mutual consent. Much of it was exploratory; one described it as "playing house," usually viewed in retrospect as "neutral" or "mostly positive" experiences, but not always. Some said that teasing and coaxing occurred, but more reported that the activity was engaged in because of threat, fear of force, or force. About half the sexual partners were siblings and the next category of partners of near-age was cousins.

The older partners were at least eight years older than the respondents.[7] In decreasing frequency, they included stepfathers, then fathers, grandfathers and uncles, and brothers-in-law. More respondents indicated that their initial reaction was fear rather than interest. Most respondents (72 percent) told no one about the sexual experience, but about 20 percent told their mothers. The confidant's most common reaction was supportive, but almost as many were unbelieving or unconcerned.

Anderson urges that "the sexual abuse of youth has profound and long-range effects upon adolescents' emerging sexuality" (1984, p. 3). Children are victimized by violence and sexual abuse in the home and it is a serious problem that sorely needs more attention from researchers and policymakers. More descriptive data from this study are presented below to supplement other research findings.

E. Problems of Discovery and Case Processing

It might be expected that maltreated adolescent cases would be far easier for the criminal justice system to discover and process than most

---

[6] In addition, this study did not enjoy the sampling technique used in the Finkelhor study to obtain more highly motivated students (and perhaps more knowledgeable about the research topic) as volunteers.

[7] All females who engaged in these categories of sexual intercourse fit Finkelhor's definition of sexual victimization of children by an older person: children twelve or under who had sex with another child who was "at least five or more years older than the child," or children thirteen to sixteen who had sex with an adult "ten or more years older than the adolescent" (Finkelhor 1979, pp. 56–57).

other types of family violence victims. The victims are neither as non-verbal as little children, nor as dependent on their abusers as the elderly.

Youngsters often complain loudly and to everyone who will listen about how they are abused by their parents. It might be advisable for professionals to view vociferous complainers as "average kids," and to watch more carefully the ones who *never* complain for signs of possible maltreatment. Typically, "gripers" are not victims but rather are young people going through normal stages of growth (Anderson 1984). They may court danger, choose peers their parents dislike, and defy parental restrictions.

There are many reasons why maltreated adolescents are likely to remain unseen by professionals in the system. Abused adolescents are unlikely to turn to outsiders for help except in emergency or severe situations (Pagelow 1984). When adolescents disclose maltreatment to others outside the home, they are often ignored or disbelieved (Lubenow 1983) because they do not fit the image of "victim" like small children (Berdie and Medina 1984). If exploratory attempts at help-seeking are rejected or if they are blamed, this may "prove" to adolescents that no one cares, intensify their low self-esteem, and validate their feelings of unworthiness (Wayne and Weeks 1984). Such children are unlikely to make additional attempts to seek help and instead accelerate their antisocial behavior.

Galambos and Dixon (1984) postulate that adolescents who have been abused since childhood are more likely to believe that events in their lives are outside their control and therefore exhibit frustration, powerlessness, and high levels of hostility and aggression. Adolescents whose abuse began later, according to this theory, are less likely to feel powerless and thus are less fatalistic about their experiences.

The duration of maltreatment may be a key factor in how adolescents respond to abuse. Libbey and Bybee compiled statistical data on the types and degrees of injuries to youth but nothing they found can document the "degree of emotional confusion or disturbance reported by the adolescents" (1979, p. 123). Amsterdam et al. (1979) found that most of the adolescents in their study had experienced some form of physical punishment while growing up, much of it clearly abusive, and only 24 percent told someone about it. This is compatible with my study in which only 28 percent of the children who had sexual experiences under the age of eighteen with family members said they told someone about it.

From studies of sexually abused children, it is clear that many victims are coerced, shamed, or frightened into silence (as are many battered wives and abused elders). We can only guess how many victims never tell anyone (Hunter, Kilstrom, and Loda 1985), but it is known that many keep their "secret" for years (Gruber, Jones, and Freeman 1982; Wayne and Weeks 1984). Some experts believe recovery depends on shattering the silence: "Incest will begin to lose its devastating magic power when women begin to speak out about it publicly and realize how common it is" (Herman and Hirschman 1980, p. 74). The effect of keeping a secret can be devastating to victims, regardless of their ages at the time (see, e.g., Lister 1982, p. 872).

One reason physically abused children often do not report their injuries to outsiders is that many of them justify the use of physical punishment as much as their parents do (Kempe and Kempe 1978; Lourie et al. 1979). The young people studied by Libbey and Bybee (1977) believed that spanking or using a belt was not severe and could be termed discipline, but they felt that hitting the head was abusive.

Amsterdam et al. (1979) found strong supporting evidence that abused adolescents feel that their parents' use of violence is legitimate and their method of punishment is socially acceptable. Their sample of 103 young people came from a diverse population at high schools, colleges, and universities, and twelve were from the California Youth Authority. Respondents in classrooms completed a questionnaire that probed their childhood experiences of punishment and how they coped with them: 96 percent had been physically punished and 11 percent had been severely abused. The majority believed that it was a sign of parental caring and half saw it as a parental effort to make them a "good child." Severity of punishment was correlated with victims' feelings of guilt: the more severely they had been punished, the more they felt they had deserved to be punished. Significantly more females saw parental punishment as justified and tended to withdraw. Victims coped by becoming hypervigilant, inhibited, and withdrawn. Their behavioral responses were delinquency, running away from home, and thoughts of or attempted suicide (Amsterdam et al. 1979).

Herzberger, Potts, and Dillon (1981) tested the attribution of blame theory with a small sample of fourteen abused adolescent boys and ten nonabused matched controls. The abused children described their parents in more negative terms and believed that they had been emotionally rejected by their parents, but not in all cases.

The literature on these issues is sparse, and it is premature to offer firm conclusions. Nonetheless, the general finding that adolescents underreport abuse is consistent with common experience. Many adults describe their own childhood experiences in terms that by today's standards would be clearly abusive, yet they fail to make that connection. Although many respondents in my survey reported extremely violent behavior in their homes, a large majority did not report that their parents *ever* pushed, grabbed, shoved, or slapped them. Since almost all American parents use physical punishment for discipline, many of these students may have underreported violence in their homes. Adults are more willing to accept their parents' punishment practices as just than to define themselves as victims. Finkelhor found that people "react strongly against the idea of seeing themselves as victims under any circumstances" (1979, p. 51). There is no reason to believe that adolescents casually adopt status as a victim either, whether or not they accept parental maltreatment as appropriate.

Wayne and Weeks (1984) suggest that adolescents often gain the spotlight by engaging in antisocial behavior but that authorities may or may not trace this behavior back to its causes. People respond to dangerous and painful situations by enduring it and doing nothing, by fighting, or by flight. The fight response is discussed in the next section of this essay. Flight can be passive or active. Passive flight for adolescents includes substance abuse or multiple personality disorder (Whitman 1982; Fagan and McMahon 1984; Galambos and Dixon 1984; Pagelow 1984; Bowman, Blix, and Coons 1985). Space considerations preclude discussion of passive forms of flight, but the growing literature shows it to be an issue of increasing concern and research attention.

Active flight includes suicide and running away. The ultimate form of escape from parental abuse is suicide; very many attempt it and many succeed (Adelson 1984; Roszell 1985; Shaffer 1986). The rate of suicide by youth has sharply increased in recent years (Koop 1982); it ranks as the second leading cause of death of people between fifteen and nineteen years of age (Anderson 1981).

Running away is another coping response; over a million youngsters run away from home every year in the United States (Ritter 1979). At Senate hearings in 1980 and 1981, experts testified that at least 50 percent are running away from intolerably abusive situations at home (U.S. Congress Committee on the Judiciary 1980, 1982). A large proportion of homeless youngsters are also "throwaways" or "pushouts" (Koestler 1977).

Shelter homes, runaway programs, hotlines, and family intervention on behalf of abused adolescents are badly needed (Fisher and Berdie 1978). Youth services and shelters are few in number and are always financially strapped, and conflicting state laws make it extremely difficult adequately to serve the needs of runaway or throwaway youth (Koestler 1977; Ritter 1979). In the first year of operation, 4,000 children applied for help at the Covenant House crisis center in New York City, but when their needs could not be solved by public assistance, some became victims of the multimillion dollar sex industry that feeds on hungry, homeless children (Ritter 1979). Between 40 and 75 percent of adolescent prostitutes were victimized in their homes, and there are approximately a million juvenile prostitutes of both sexes in the United States (Boyer and James 1982). Thousands of these children were runaways recruited for prostitution and use in pornographic films, books, magazines, and videotapes (Kratcoski, Yonas, and Kratcoski 1979).

Until very recently, when juvenile service workers came in contact with runaways, their primary objective was to return youngsters to their parents' custody, and case workers were unlikely to report suspected cases of abuse (Fisher and Berdie 1978); but that may be changing (Ziefert 1982). Still, minors do not have the option of leaving home to escape mistreatment and, if they do, they are likely to be labeled as "status offenders" or "delinquents." It is bureaucratically easier for child protection workers to seek a Person in Need of Supervision (PINS) petition than to seek a maltreatment petition (Garbarino 1980), which asks the court to remove custody from parents. Compared with younger victims of parental maltreatment for whom the emphasis is on reunification of families, social service professionals are more likely to advocate maintaining the teenager outside the home, but the youngsters are not usually involved in the decision-making process (Garbarino 1980).

A PINS label can lead to prosecution and result in incarceration in detention centers, jail, or even institutions for the mentally retarded (Hoekstra 1984). When homeless youths fall into the juvenile justice system, they often are stigmatized and introduced to even more deviant behavior (Lourie et al. 1979; U.S. Congress Committee on the Judiciary 1982). Smith, Berkman, and Frazer (1980) show that the juvenile justice system, established to process both delinquent youths and abused and neglected youths, often fails to distinguish clearly between victims and accused offenders. "The most important aspect of this link is the labeling and adjudication of abused and neglected children and adolescents as status offenders. Although they are referred to the juvenile court because they are victims, they often leave the system being defined as offenders" (Smith, Berkman, and Frazer 1980, p. 33).

Many writers maintain that abused children are disproportionately at risk of becoming juvenile delinquents (Lewis et al. 1976; Smith, Berkman, and Frazer 1980; Hunner and Walker 1981). Many children begin delinquent "careers" by first committing offenses like running away and truancy (Garbarino 1980; Pagelow 1982a, 1982b). However, Alfaro studied two large data bases of abused children and of delinquent children and concluded that "child maltreatment cannot be used as an indicator or predictor of a particular type of juvenile misbehavior" (1978, p. 16). (See Blumstein et al. 1986 for a recent review of research findings on these issues.)

Smith, Berkman, and Frazer (1980) suggest that maltreated youngsters are most likely to come into the juvenile justice system for status offenses, usually for avoidance or escapist "crimes." Maltreated youngsters are also more likely than children from nonabusive homes to be confined in detention facilities until their hearings, adjudicated as status offenders, and sent to institutions for longer time periods.

Abusive parents may push adolescents out of their homes, or bring charges against them for acts of resistance to parental authority. For staying away from home, a child who spent earlier years alone and neglected, now having reached adolescence, may be stigmatized by a label, incarcerated with other young people who committed criminal acts, and be finally released as a juvenile delinquent with a record— which "proves" what many professionals expected to find all along (Pagelow 1982a, 1982b, 1984).

F. Intervention and Prevention

Many writers have described inadequacies in the established systems for protecting maltreated adolescents (e.g., James 1984; Hoekstra 1984). Hoekstra calls for "stress-reducing intervention quite unlike the standard existing interventions in either the juvenile justice or child welfare systems, which negatively label family members . . . and even subject them at times to situations worse than those for which they needed help originally" (1984, p. 285). Hoekstra observes that families involved in the child welfare system may deal with many agencies at the same time. He also maintains that acting-out behavior by juveniles propels them in one of three directions, each potentially harmful to youths: victimized youths served by the juvenile justice system are likely to be victimized again; youths served by the mental health system are subject to potentially injurious labeling; youths served by alternative youth service programs are often deprived of protection or needed services, and may be pitted against their families (Hoekstra 1984, p. 286). A report by Fisher et al. (1980) is an excellent, comprehensive resource on intervention strategies.

Maltreated adolescents who are in the juvenile justice system because of their behavior may not be recognized as victims and consequently may receive no assistance (Foreman and Seligman 1983). There are a number of promising measures that can be taken: providing individual and family counseling and support services for families; educating parents and children about the developmental stages each is passing through so they can understand each other better; and encouraging parents to join Parents Anonymous.

School administrators have an important role to play. James observes, "school administrators, counselors and teachers are in a strategic position to detect signs of maltreatment due to their high level of contact with youth" (1984, p. 10). The American School Counselor Association in 1981 developed a position statement on counselors' responsibilities to abuse victims (Foreman and Seligman 1983). Because maltreatment often manifests itself in undesirable behavior, such as truancy and poor learning habits, schools often "expend much effort in expelling just the students who are the most likely victims of parental mistreatment—acting out youngsters" (Hoekstra 1984, p. 288). Educators must become familiar with their own state reporting laws.

Police officers often receive reports about suspected maltreatment and they must file reports with the designated state authority. In most states, they have the power to intervene on behalf of the youth and to take temporary custody if it appears that the victim's life or health is in imminent danger (James 1984).

The service delivery system for maltreated youths also includes child protective service agencies, youth-serving organizations, hospitals, and mental health agencies or institutions. James (1984) offers a comprehensive analysis of the entire system and suggestions for overcoming deficiencies. One recommendation calls for increased coordination to facilitate interagency relations for exchange of information and the use of multidisciplinary training teams. Some efforts have been made to establish interagency networks in demonstration projects in

California and Missouri (James 1984), and in a consortium of public and private social and health agencies and private practitioners in St. Paul, Minnesota (Baizerman, Skelton, and Pierce 1983).

These approaches show promise but intervention and prevention work on the individual level must also be strengthened. Wayne and Weeks (1984) made significant progress through group work with abused adolescent girls. However, their system required long-term commitment (in this case, five years) of trained and dedicated caseworkers, continuity of leadership, and willingness to devote large amounts of time to a relatively few youngsters (Wayne and Weeks 1984).

One project for intervention and prevention that warrants replication is sponsored by Boys Town. Called "Youth Helping Youth," its theoretical rationale is that social isolation is a major block to effective intervention (Garbarino and Jacobson 1978; Foreman and Seligman 1983). The Boys Town project involves a youth-staffed hot line, a self-help group for abused adolescents (following the tradition of Parents Anonymous), a pamphlet for young people on recognizing abuse and identifying resources, and a public awareness campaign directed at young people (Garbarino and Jacobson 1978). One pamphlet (Lonnborg 1982) shows how schools and educators can identify maltreated adolescents and intervene on their behalf. Boys Town produced a manual (Lonnborg, Fischbach, and Bickerstaff 1981) that includes a leader's guide for duplication of the six week self-help group meetings. Boys Town also produced a short film for rental or purchase, *Don't Get Stuck There* (Lonnborg 1982), a useful tool for sensitizing adolescents and adults to the issue and to open communication.

These methods for identification point the way to better intervention and prevention strategies. There was a flurry of interest in adolescent maltreatment in the late 1970s and early 1980s, manifested by new laws, demonstration projects, research funded by the National Institute of Mental Health, and congressional hearings (Lourie et al. 1979; Fisher et al. 1980; U.S. Congress Committee on the Judiciary 1980, 1982). Unfortunately, interest has diminished and it is unlikely that major progress will be made in the foreseeable future in funding shelters, programs, and services for homeless and maltreated youth, or support services for beleaguered families.

III. Violence by Children in the Family

Children are both victims and perpetrators of violence, sometimes simultaneously. A child is a minor under the law in most states until reaching his or her eighteenth birthday. Offenders under eighteen years old may be channeled as minors into juvenile court or as adults into criminal court. The ages at which people are prosecuted as adults vary from sixteen to eighteen and above in different states, but with judicial waiver, juveniles may be transferred to criminal court. The laws and procedures governing waiver vary from state to state. This section focuses on what is known about violence by young people against their parents and siblings.

A. Estimates on the Incidence and Prevalence of Violence by Children

Young people are not only victims, but many are victimizers as well; at times their violence is lethal. Thirty percent of persons arrested in 1981 for violent crimes were nineteen or younger, a percentage about equal to their proportion of the population (U.S. Department of Justice 1983). But that statistic masks the overrepresentation of one age group. Whereas children under fifteen are underrepresented in violent crimes, offenders from fifteen to nineteen years old (only 9 percent of the population) made up 25 percent of those arrested for violent crimes in 1981 (U.S. Department of Justice 1983). Victimization studies show that only about half of all crimes that occur come to the attention of authorities (U.S. Department of Justice 1976); underreporting of crimes by youths is probably even greater. Because so much violence by children is perpetrated by adolescents, this section focuses mainly on the age group between twelve and eighteen (see Farrington 1986 for a comprehensive analysis of research on age and crime).

Violent crimes committed by children against family members are difficult to estimate. One nationwide survey of victimization by intimates estimated 1.2 million violent episodes between relatives and, of these, 47,000 involved children's violence against parents (U.S. Department of Justice 1980).

Research concerning the incidence and prevalence of violence by juveniles against family members is presented below according to whether the victims were adults or siblings. There is a high rate of underreporting. Parents may be expected to deny all but the most severe abuse by their children because of shame or a wish to keep these matters private, and sibling violence is underreported even more because victims may not be believed and parents often view their children's violence as normal (Steinmetz 1981*b*; Pagelow 1984).

1. *Sex of Violent Children and Etiology of Violence.* Males are more violent than females: 90 percent of the perpetrators of reported violent

crime are males; this ratio holds for juveniles and adults. Within the family, Straus, Gelles, and Steinmetz (1980) describe many features of sibling violence. They report that families having only sons consistently experience more sibling violence than do families that have only daughters; that the different patterns of sibling violence in these types of families became more pronounced as the children mature; and "for the oldest age group (fifteen through seventeen), the rate for all-boy families is roughly twice as great as that for all-girl families" (1980, p. 89).

Of even more interest to many researchers is whether adolescents are violent because they were abused. Answers to that question are divided. An intergenerational cycle of violence has been taken as a given by Straus, Gelles, and Steinmetz (1980), and they have found support for it in their work together and individually. One of the early articles on child abuse titled "Violence Breeds Violence—Perhaps?" (Curtis 1963), was followed by many others on the same theme (Fontana 1964; Silver, Dublin, and Lourie 1969; Steele 1974). Causality is implied or explicitly claimed by these writers.

Two literature reviews concerning the "cycle of violence" found much supposition but almost no empirical evidence (Pagelow 1984; Stark and Flitcraft 1985). Stark and Flitcraft conclude: "Not only does this view find little empirical support, but the major data set offered to prove 'social heredity' shows the opposite; that the vast majority of persons from violent childhoods do not become abusive and that the vast majority of woman-batterers (and child abusers) do not come from violent families of origin" (1985, p. 168).

One group of researchers suggests that victims of child abuse are *less* likely than their nonabused siblings to commit aggressive acts, and their data support this hypothesis (Bolton, Reich, and Gutierres 1977). Only 7.8 percent of the victims were reported for aggressive acts whereas their siblings had a much higher rate of 17.2 percent; victims of abuse were extremely likely to be reported for escapist behavior (92 percent), and their siblings less likely (83 percent). Control delinquents from nonabusive homes were even less likely to be reported for escapist behavior (Bolton, Reich, and Gutierres 1977). Reich and Gutierres (1979) and Gutierres and Reich (1981) report on two studies assessing juvenile arrest data for a large sample of teenagers who had been abused by their parents. The physically abused children were found to be no more aggressive than controls but their rates of escape infractions were two or three times higher than those of the controls; the sample of sexually abused juveniles, overwhelmingly female, also responded by escape crimes (Gutierres and Reich 1981).

Mouzakitis (1984) argues that abused adolescents respond in one of three ways: by bearing their victimization silently, by fighting back violently, or by running away from home. Mouzakitis finds support for Lourie's view (1977) that there are substantial differences in the effects on children of long-term abuse and of abuse that begins in adolescence. Chronically abused adolescents are seen as more likely to commit aggressive crimes while abuse beginning in adolescence is likelier to result in acting out, escapist behaviors, and minor antisocial acts (Mouzakitis 1984).

Within the family, many children are violent, and unquestionably some are responding to maltreatment by fighting back, particularly at their parents.

2. *Children's Violence against Parents.*   The majority of victims of all types of reported family violence are female (Dobash and Dobash 1978). Kratcoski's (1982) study of violent delinquents found that a sizeable proportion directed their violence toward members of the immediate family or caretakers. Kratcoski (1982, p. 442) observes, "If members of the immediate family were attacked, the mother or stepmother was the most frequent victim, followed by siblings."

In my student survey described earlier in this essay, students were asked if they had committed certain violent acts against an adult member of their families when they were age twelve or older. Thirteen percent had used some type of violence; mostly against parent-figures; 60 percent of the targets were mothers, followed by fathers and stepfathers. In the Straus, Gelles, and Steinmetz (1978) study, 18 percent of their respondents who were parents admitted being targets of their children's violent acts in one year;[8] the sex ratio of the parent-victims is not reported. The rate for more severe acts of violence would suggest that nearly one out of ten children attacks a parent each year (Straus, Gelles, and Steinmetz 1978).

Most of the violence that students reported in my study fell in the less severe range: 57 percent pushed, grabbed, or shoved; 31 percent

[8] Findings of 13 percent from my adolescent study and 18 percent from the survey by Straus, Gelles, and Steinmetz (1978) are not directly comparable. I inquired about violent acts *respondents had committed at any time over the age of twelve* whereas the other questioned respondents about *violence committed by their children of any age during the past year*. The response categories were also different; the instrument used in my study contained more specific acts.

slapped or bit; only 26 percent of the violent adolescents kicked or punched a parent. Two percent said they beat up a parent and 3 percent said they threatened a parent with a knife or gun. These are higher than rates reported by Straus, Gelles, and Steinmetz (1978, p. 10).

The more severe forms of violence in my study were directed at fathers. Some children attempt to kill their parents, most often fathers, as self-defense or as retaliation against abuse. Other times their motives are as obscure as many adult murderers'. Warren (1979) studied fifteen adolescents in a psychiatric hospital who had attacked their parents; eight had attempted to murder a parent. Four parricide cases involved adolescents who were unable to perceive alternatives, for "the family had created an untenable situation in which murder is a reasonable conclusion" (Post 1982, p. 445). Accounts of such killings of violent, abusive fathers occasionally are reported in the newspapers (see, e.g., accounts of the Jahnke case in *Newsweek* [Lubenow 1983] and in the *Los Angeles Times* [1983a, 1983b]; see also the *Los Angeles Times* reports on the Moody case [Murphy 1984]).

The Jahnke and Moody cases closely fit the patterns described by Lubenow (1983, p. 35): "Almost all murders of parents are committed by sons, and in the rare cases that involve daughters, they often recruit a male agent. Usually parent killing involves a drunken, physically abusive father killed by a son who sees himself as the protector of not only himself but also of his mother and siblings." Not all parricides have motives as well documented as the Jahnke and Moody cases. Within fifteen months, there were four murders of parents by children in Orange County, California (Taugher 1984), and one of them was the stabbing death of a mother by her thirteen-year-old daughter and the daughter's boyfriend for no apparent reason. The mother was an advocate of nonviolence and a respected public leader in the domestic violence field.

Some children kill for money, some in retaliation for restrictions on their activities, and others out of rage, but they do not kill only family members. For example, one twelve-year-old boy shot another twelve-year-old boy eighteen times in a dispute over a baseball (King 1985). There is no doubt that some children can be very violent, with or without "provocation."

3. *Sibling Violence.* Violence between children is so commonplace that it is often thought of as normal childhood behavior. Parents take it for granted that "kids will be kids." Violence by children is seen, but

often it is not seen as violence (Pagelow 1984). Steinmetz (1981*b*) found that between 63 and 68 percent of adolescent siblings in the families she studied used physical violence to resolve conflict. Eighty-two percent of the parents of children aged three to seventeen in the Straus, Gelles, and Steinmetz (1980) survey reported sibling violence the highest for all types of intrafamily violence. Rates are highest at the youngest ages, as might be expected, and steadily decrease with age. Rates were 64 percent for the fifteen- to seventeen-year-olds; two out of three teenagers hit a brother or sister each year, averaging nineteen times a year. Of the respondents in my sample, 416 had siblings. Preliminary analysis shows the same or similar rates of violence in some categories as were found by Straus, Gelles, and Steinmetz (1980).

There are few empirical studies of sibling violence. NiCarthy (1983), a specialist educator, estimates that 40 to 50 percent of the teenagers she works with have been assaulted by brothers. One of the few studies of sibling aggression focused only on preschool siblings (Abramovitch, Corter, and Lando 1979). Another researcher surveyed college students about sibling aggression, testing theories of "sibling rivalry" and instrumental conflict over real, tangible issues (Felson 1983). Felson found little support for sibling rivalry as a cause of violence but strong support for the instrumental conflict hypothesis (Felson 1983).

Tooley's studies (1977) of "murderously aggressive" children suggest that younger victims may sometimes be family scapegoats because many parents resist efforts to address the needs of child-victims. Tooley notes that helping professionals, though now alert to signs of child abuse by parents, have difficulty recognizing abuse at the hands of another child. Even when they do, Tooley (1977) says, they are less sure how to proceed.

Some youths both physically abuse and sexually assault younger siblings. Adolescent rapists are often concerned to present themselves in the best possible light and try as hard as they can to play the role of "good boys" (Fehrenbach 1983). Margolin (1983) notes that these young people are often described as lying, sneaky, and manipulative, because their main objective is to control others. "The sexually assaultive adolescent is an individual whose primary concern in social interaction is to make others do his bidding" (Margolin 1983, p. 6). Because they are often likeable and cooperative, Margolin says, "professional staff, community members, and families may find it difficult to accept the idea that a youth is dangerous when he is soft-spoken, friendly, dresses neatly, and is well-liked by little children" (1983, p. 7). Within the family, such children may convince parents by this facade, but it is doubtful that victimized siblings are as charmed (see, e.g., VanBuren 1986, p. 3). Another case of brother-rapist is quoted in Pagelow (1984), and Armstrong (1979) tells of others. My own student survey revealed a sizeable number of sexually abused siblings, although some females and most males indicated sexual activity was initiated by mutual consent. Respondents in Finkelhor's (1979) study who had been involved sexually with siblings were about evenly partitioned into those who viewed their experiences positively, those who viewed the experiences negatively, and those who did not feel strongly either way. Females more often reported their experiences as unpleasant, largely because they were victims in 82 percent of the coercive experiences, and they were more likely to be exploited by older males. The most important feature determining reactions was age differences between siblings: the larger the age gap the more negative the reaction. Next, "If force was used, the experience was more likely to be negative" (Finkelhor 1979, p. 178). Finally, if the sexual activity was primarily genital exhibition, memories were more likely to be positive. Age and coercion may be expected to be strongly correlated; an older sibling usually has greater power to control younger siblings. Finkelhor notes, "It was those with the more exploitative experiences who were most silent. Not a single child who had been involved in sex with a much older sibling confided it to anyone. The fear of being blamed themselves or of not being believed or of suffering retaliation may have made it hard for these children. . . . The pain of secrecy was added to whatever unpleasantness the experience itself involved" (1979, p. 180). These are the silent victims who Lister (1982) hypothesizes may suffer a secondary trauma that makes them more likely to suffer victimization later in life.

B. Problems of Discovery and Case Processing

Children of all ages can be violent and their capacity to engage in violent behavior increases with age, so that more of it is evident and serious when they reach adolescence. When they strike out at adults, they are much more likely to direct aggression at parents than at other adult family members. More than one of every four college students in my sample admitted kicking or punching a parent at least once after the age of twelve. According to Straus, Gelles, and Steinmetz (1978), almost one out of ten parents are subject to severe violent acts by their children each year.

Sibling violence occurs with great frequency in American homes, but it is seen but not seen by parents and outsiders. Children often endure lives of pain and fear, terrorized by siblings who portray the "good boy" image (Fehrenbach 1983).

Helping professionals usually get involved only in extreme cases. It would help to become sensitized to the issues and discard old notions that the "good child" and the "bad child" are readily distinguishable. Criteria for detecting dishonesty of adolescent sex offenders may be useful for professionals trying to identify other abusers (e.g., Margolin 1983, p. 10).

Identifying and processing violent adolescents is as difficult as identifying and processing any other type of violent family members. Professionals are increasingly cognizant of the indications of child abuse and child sexual abuse but are less sensitive to cues. Some parents may be more willing to accept blame for abusing a young child than to expose their other child for his or her crime; many parents try to protect the guilty child (Tooley 1977).

C. Intervention and Prevention

Because there has been so little scientific interest in adolescent violence against other family members, there are few developed and tested intervention and prevention programs. King (1975) writes about a treatment approach for homicidal youth, but on the basis of work with nine young incarcerated killers. Margolin (1983) details a promising treatment model for institutionalized adolescent sex offenders that involves group work and peer confrontation. Psychopathological models for predicting violent adolescent behavior have been tested on hospitalized patients (Sendi and Blomgren 1975), but they are of limited use to other professionals and the public.

Society continues to deal with adolescent violence after the fact; the issue has been ignored far too long. After the problem spills out the front door, agencies and professionals begin to take note, but by that time, it is too late for many. Once a youngster becomes identified as a violent juvenile offender, he or she may be on the way to becoming a career criminal (Blumstein et al. 1986; Farrington 1987).

We must stop looking at children and childhood in stereotypic images of innocence and playtime and realize that adolescent children are not only potential victims of parents and siblings, but they are also capable of violence against parents and siblings. Astute professionals must look beneath the surface and investigate very carefully to determine the difference.

IV. Summary

The three forms of family violence discussed in this essay reveal striking similarities and some differences. The lack of a common definition of abuse is a theme that runs not only throughout this essay but throughout the entire volume. Until there is a degree of consensus on definition, research findings cannot be compared with adequate precision. Important issues like the identification of populations at greater risk of abuse, persons most likely to be abusers, and causal factors cannot be resolved. Estimates on the incidence and prevalence of different types of abuse cannot be derived with confidence. Because of the lack of reliable data on these matters, intervention and prevention methods must be devised on an ad hoc, experimental basis, which requires extensive follow-up and evaluation to test for effectiveness.

Many studies suffer serious methodological problems, including sampling techniques, small samples, lack of controls, and limited generalizability. While most contribute some insight into previously invisible forms of intrafamily violence, many are largely exploratory and are not grounded in sound social scientific theory. Effective intervention and prevention programs cannot be developed until we know more about these issues, and until some of the more rigorous studies have been replicated.

Findings of the studies reviewed here show some patterns and similarities that will probably be supported by further research. It is becoming increasingly clear, for example, that violent families suffer from multiple problems and multiple forms of violence often occur in the same homes (see Loeber 1986 for a review of research on the interaction between family factors and childrens' conduct problems and delinquency).

American families are but a microcosm of American society, which contains many strands of violence and subscribes to values of individualism, competitiveness, and family privacy. Many societal factors contribute to the kinds of family violence addressed in this essay, including the lack of social support systems for individuals in the family. The structure of American families establishes a rank ordering that gives some family members power over others. People who feel powerless in the greater society often demand and exert power and control over those who have less power in the home.

Victims young and old share feelings of powerlessness and shame; they protect the guilty, refuse to seek help, and fear retaliation. People in violent families are reluctant to destroy the image of family harmony by turning to others outside the family for assistance. Denial is pervasive: old people refuse to reveal victimization, adolescents are highly unlikely to disclose abuse from parents or siblings except in the most extreme circumstances, and some parents attempt to protect their abusive children from public stigma. Finally, and of perhaps greatest interest to researchers and investigators, the occurrence of one type of intrafamily abuse is likely to indicate the presence of other types of abuse, previously or concurrently.

Differences between the three subjects discussed here are apparent. Dependent elders are the most invisible to public scrutiny. They are more difficult to identify, being more isolated from the mainstream of society than adolescents. They have no mandatory schooling, employment, or medical evaluations, and they can be kept so well-hidden at home that neighbors may not even know they exist. While the intervention of choice for adolescents may be to remove them from abusive homes or to help them become independent if they run away, moving an elderly person may shorten his or her life. A violent adolescent may be rehabilitated but a violent parent or violent middle-aged caretaker of an elderly person may not be appropriate for, much less amenable to, rehabilitation. Yet elder abuse is the form of family violence most susceptible to deterrence through in-home services and social support systems (Pagelow 1987).

In all these abusive situations, whatever the outcome, intervention itself may serve to prevent abuse. Even when cases cannot be processed through the criminal justice system, intervention may penetrate the wall of privacy. Abusers may be controlled by threat of future prosecution, and case workers may be able to maintain contact with victims. Victims know they are not alone and that options are open to them that they were not aware of before (Pagelow 1981).

REFERENCES

Abramovitch, Rona, Carl M. Corter, and Bella Lando. 1979. "Sibling Interaction in the Home." *Child Development* 50:997–1003.
Adams, Gary. 1986. Interview with author. Santa Ana, Calif., July 7.
Adelson, Andrea. 1984. "Why Do Kids Kill Themselves? Film Probes the Ugly Realities." *Orange Coast Daily Pilot* (May 3), pp. A1–A2.

Alfaro, Jose D. 1978. *Summary Report on the Relationship between Child Abuse and Neglect and Later Socially Deviant Behavior.* Albany: New York State Select Committee on Child Abuse.

Allen, Hugh D., Edward J. Kosciolek, Robert W. ten Bensel, and Richard B. Raile. 1969. "The Battered Child Syndrome." *Pediatrics* 21:155–56.

American Humane Association. 1981. *National Analysis of Official Child Neglect and Abuse Reporting (1980).* Denver, Colo.: American Humane Association.

———. 1983. *National Analysis of Official Child Neglect and Abuse Reporting (1981).* Denver, Colo.: American Humane Association.

Amsterdam, Beulah, Mary Brill, Nova Weiselberg Bell, and Dan Edwards. 1979. "Coping with Abuse: Adolescents' Views." *Victimology* 4:278–84.

Anderson, Linda, and Marshelle Thobaben. 1984. "Clients in Crisis," *Journal of Gerontological Nursing* 10(12):6–10.

Anderson, Luleen S. 1981. "Notes on the Linkage between the Sexually Abused Child and the Suicidal Adolescent." *Journal of Adolescence* 4(2):157–62.

Anderson, Patricia K. 1984. "Issues of Adolescence." In *Adolescent Maltreatment: Issues and Program Models*, edited by the National Center on Child Abuse and Neglect. Washington, D.C.: U.S. Government Printing Office.

Archbold, Patricia G. 1983. "An Analysis of Parentcaring by Women." *Family Relations* 32(1):39–45.

Armstrong, Louise. 1979. *Kiss Daddy Goodnight: A Speak-Out on Incest.* New York: Pocket Books.

Baizerman, Michael, Nan Skelton, and Shirley Pierce. 1983. "Working Together to Treat Adolescent Abuse: Community Agencies Form a Consortium." *Children Today* 12(January/February):18–23.

Beck, Cornelia, and Doris Ferguson. 1981. "Aged Abuse." *Journal of Gerontological Nursing* 7(6):333–36.

Bennie, E., and A. Sclare. 1969. "The Battered Child Syndrome." *American Journal of Psychiatry* 125:147–51.

Berdie, Jane, Michael Baizerman, and Ira S. Lourie. 1977. "Violence towards Youth: Themes from a Workshop." *Children Today* 6(2):7–10.

Berdie, Jane, and Leslie Medina. 1984. "Adolescent Maltreatment: Issues of Definition." In *Adolescent Maltreatment: Issues and Program Models*, edited by the National Center on Child Abuse and Neglect, Department of Health and Human Services. Washington, D.C.: U.S. Government Printing Office.

Block, Marilyn R., and Jan D. Sinnott, eds. 1979. *The Battered Elder Syndrome: An Exploratory Study.* College Park: University of Maryland, Center on Aging.

Blumstein, Alfred, Jacqueline Cohen, Jeffrey Roth, and Christy Visher, eds. 1986. *Criminal Careers and "Career Criminals."* 2 vols. Washington, D.C.: National Academy Press.

Bolton, F. G., Jr., J. W. Reich, and S. E. Gutierres. 1977. *Delinquency Patterns in Maltreated Children and Siblings.* Phoenix: Community Development for Abuse and Neglect.

Bowman, Elizabeth S., Susanne Blix, and Philip M. Coons. 1985. "Case Report: Multiple Personality in Adolescence: Relationship to Incestual Experiences." *Journal of the American Academy of Child Psychiatry* 24(1):109–14.

Boyer, Debra, and Jennifer James. 1982. "Easy Money: Adolescent Involvement in Prostitution." In *Justice for Young Women: Close-up on Critical Issues.* Tucson, Ariz.: New Directions for Young Women.

Burgess, Robert L., and James Garbarino. 1983. "Doing What Comes Naturally? An Evolutionary Perspective on Child Abuse." In *The Dark Side of Families*, edited by David Finkelhor and associates. Beverly Hills, Calif.: Sage.

Bybee, Rodger W. 1979. "Violence toward Youth: A New Perspective. *Journal of Social Issues* 35(2):1–14.

California Department of Social Services. 1985. *Dependent Adult and Elder Abuse: Report to the Legislature, Report Year 1984.* Sacramento: California Department of Social Services.

Cazenave, Noel A. 1981. "Stress Management and Coping Alternatives for Families of the Frail Elderly." Paper presented at the First National Conference for Family Violence Researchers, University of New Hampshire, Durham, July.

Crossman, Linda, Cecilia London, and Clemmie Barry. 1981. "Older Women Caring for Disabled Spouses: A Model for Supportive Services." *The Gerontologist* 21:464–70.

Curtis, George C. 1963. "Violence Breeds Violence—Perhaps?" *American Journal of Psychiatry* 120:386–87.

Daly, M., and M. Wilson. 1981. "Child Maltreatment From a Sociobiological Perspective." *New Directions for Child Development* 11:93–112.

David, Lester, and Irene David. 1980. *Violence in Our Schools.* New York: Public Affairs Committee.

Davidson, Janice L. 1979. "Elder Abuse." In *The Battered Elder Syndrome: An Exploratory Study*, edited by Marilyn R. Block and Jan D. Sinnott. College Park: University of Maryland, Center on Aging.

Dobash, R. Emerson, and Russell P. Dobash. 1978. "Wives: The 'Appropriate' Victims of Marital Violence." *Victimology* 2:426–42.

Douglass, Richard L. 1983. "Domestic Neglect and Abuse of the Elderly: Implications for Research and Service." *Family Relations* 32(3):395–402.

Erlanger, Howard. 1974. "Social Class and Corporal Punishment in Childrearing: A Reassessment." *American Sociological Review* 39:68–85.

Fagan, J., and Polly Paul McMahon. 1984. "Incipient Multiple Personality in Children." *Journal of Nervous and Mental Disease* 172(1):26–36.

Farber, Edward D., and Jack A. Joseph. 1985. "The Maltreated Adolescent: Patterns of Physical Abuse." *Child Abuse and Neglect* 9:201–6.

Farrington, David P. 1986. "Age and Crime." In *Crime and Justice: An Annual Review of Research*, vol. 7, edited by Michael Tonry and Norval Morris. Chicago: University of Chicago Press.

———. 1987. "Predicting Individual Crime Rates." In *Prediction and Classification: Criminal Justice Decision Making*, edited by Don M. Gottfredson and Michael Tonry. Vol. 9 of *Crime and Justice: A Review of Research*, edited by Michael Tonry and Norval Morris. Chicago: University of Chicago Press.

Fehrenbach, P. 1983. "Adolescent Sexual Offenders." *Audio-Digest Psychiatry*, cassette no. 2.

Felson, Richard B. 1983. "Aggression and Violence between Siblings." *Social Psychology Quarterly* 46(4):271–85.

Ferguson, Doris, and Cornelia Beck. 1983. "H.A.L.F.—A Tool to Assess Elder Abuse with the Family." *Geriatric Nursing* 4(September/October):301–304.

Finkelhor, David. 1979. *Sexually Victimized Children*. New York: Free Press.

Fisher, Bruce, and Jane Berdie. 1978. "Adolescent Abuse and Neglect: Issues of Incidents, Intervention, and Service Delivery." *Child Abuse and Neglect* 2(31):173–92.

Fisher, Bruce, Jane Berdie, JoAnn Cook, and Noel Day. 1980. *Adolescent Abuse and Neglect: Intervention Strategies*, edited by the National Center on Child Abuse and Neglect, Department of Health and Human Services. Washington, D.C.: U.S. Government Printing Office.

Fontana, Vincent J. 1964. *The Maltreated Child: The Maltreatment Syndrome in Children*. Springfield, Ill.: Thomas.

Foreman, Susan, and Linda Seligman. 1983. "Adolescent Abuse." *School Counselor* 31(1):17–25.

Fulmer, Terry T., and Virginia M. Cahill. 1984. "Assessing Elder Abuse: A Study." *Journal of Gerontological Nursing* 10(12):16–20.

Fulmer, T., S. Street, and K. Carr. 1984. "Abuse of the Elderly: Screening and Detection." *Journal of Emergency Nursing* 10(3):131–33.

Galambos, Nancy L., and Roger A. Dixon. 1984. "Adolescent Abuse and the Development of Personal Sense of Control." *Child Abuse and Neglect* 8:285–93.

Galbraith, Michael W., and R. Todd Zdorkowski. 1984. "Teaching the Investigation of Elder Abuse." *Journal of Gerontological Nursing* 10(12):21–25.

Garbarino, James. 1980. "Meeting the Needs of Mistreated Youths." *National Association of Social Workers, Inc.* 25(2):122–25.

Garbarino, James, and G. Gilliam. 1980. *Understanding Abusive Families*. Lexington, Mass.: Lexington.

Garbarino, James, and Nancy Jacobson. 1978. "Youth Helping Youth in Cases of Maltreatment of Adolescents." *Child Welfare League of America* 57(8):505–12.

Garbarino, James, Janet Sebes, and Cynthia Schellenbach. 1984. "Families At-Risk for Destructive Parent-Child Relations in Adolescence." *Child Development* 55:174–83.

Gelles, Richard J. 1979. *Family Violence*. Beverly Hills, Calif.: Sage.

Gentry, Charles E., and Barbara D. Nelson. 1980. "Developmental Patterns for Abuse Programs: Application to the Aging." In *Abuse of Older Persons*, edited by David F. Holden and Peggie L. Carey. Knoxville: University of Tennessee, School of Social Work.

Giordano, Hervig, and Jeffrey A. Giordano. 1984. "Elder Abuse: A Review of the Literature." *Social Work* 29:232-36.

Gruber, Kenneth, Robert J. Jones, and Mary H. Freeman. 1982. "Youth Reactions to Sexual Assault." *Adolescence* 17(67):541–51.

Gutierres, Sara E., and John W. Reich. 1981. "A Developmental Perspective on Runaway Behavior: Its Relationship to Child Abuse." *Child Welfare League of America* 60(2):89–94.

Haggerty, Maureen. 1981. "Elder Abuse: Who Is the Victim?" *Gray Panther Network* (January/February), pp. 4–5.

Herman, Judith, and Lisa Hirschman. 1980. "Father-Daughter Incest." In *Sexual Abuse of Children: Selected Readings*, edited by Kee MacFarlane, Linda L. Jenstrom, and Barbara McComb Jones. Department of Health, Education, and Welfare. Washington, D.C.: U.S. Government Printing Office.

Herzberger, Sharon D., Deborah A. Potts, and Michael Dillon. 1981. "Abusive and Nonabusive Parental Treatment from the Child's Perspective." *Journal of Consulting and Clinical Psychology* 49(1):81–90.

Hjorth, Craig W., and Eric Ostrov. 1982. "The Self-Image of Physically Abused Adolescents." *Journal of Youth and Adolescence* 11(2):71–76.

Hoekstra, Kathleen O'C. 1984. "Ecologically Defining the Mistreatment of Adolescents." *Children and Youth Services Review* 6:285–98.

Hunner, Robert J., and Yvonne Elder Walker, eds. 1981. *Exploring the Relationship between Child Abuse and Delinquency*. Montclair, N.J.: Alanheld, Osmun.

Hunter, Rosemary S., Nancy Kilstrom, and Frank Loda. 1985. "Sexually Abused Children: Identifying Masked Presentations in a Medical Setting." *Child Abuse and Neglect* 9:17–25.

James, Linda Rich. 1984. "Systems Issues and Interventions." In *Adolescent Maltreatment: Issues and Program Models*, edited by the National Center on Child Abuse and Neglect. Washington, D.C.: U.S. Government Printing Office.

Journal of the American Medical Association. 1980. "The Elderly: Newest Victims of Familial Abuse." *Journal of the American Medical Association* 243:1221–22.

Kalter, N. 1977. "Children of Divorce in an Outpatient Psychiatric Population." *American Journal of Orthopsychiatry* 47:40–51.

Kelly, John. 1975. "The Battered Parent." *Practical Psychology for Physicians* 2(9):65–67.

Kempe, C. Henry, F. N. Silverman, B. F. Steele, W. Droegemuller, and H. K. Silver. 1962. "The Battered-Child Syndrome." *Journal of the American Medical Association* 181:105–12.

Kempe, R., and C. Henry Kempe. 1978. *Child Abuse*. Cambridge, Mass.: Harvard University Press.

King, Charles H. 1975. "The Ego and the Integration of Violence in Homicidal Youth. *American Journal of Orthopsychiatry* 45:134–45.

King, Nancy. 1983. "Exploitation and Abuse of Older Family Members: An Overview of the Problem." *Response* 6(2):1–2, 13–15.

King, Peter H. 1985. "Boy Dies after Being Shot 18 Times; Playmate Held." *Los Angeles Times* (February 12), sec. 2, p. 18.

Koestler, Frances A. 1977. *Runaway Teenagers*. Public Affairs Pamphlet no. 552. New York: Public Affairs Committee.

Koop, C. Everett. 1982. "Violence and Public Health." National Organization of Victim Assistance, *NOVA Newsletter* 6(10):1–8.

Kratcoski, Peter C. 1982. "Child Abuse and Violence against the Family." *Child Welfare League of America* 61(7):435–44.

Kratcoski, Peter C., David Yonas, and Lucille Dunn Kratcoski. 1979. "Runaways in America: A Look at the Complexities of Youth Flight." *USA Today* (March), pp. 30–32.

Lau, Elizabeth, and Jordan I. Kosberg. 1979. "Abuse of the Elderly by Informal Care Providers." *Aging* 299(September/October):10–15.

Lewis, Dorothy O., David Balla, Shelley Shanok, and Laura Snell. 1976. "Delinquency, Parental Psychopathology, and Parental Criminality." *Journal of the American Academy of Child Psychiatry* 12:660–74.

Libbey, Patricia, and Rodger Bybee. 1979. "The Physical Abuse of Adolescents." *Journal of Social Issues* 35(2):101–26.

Lister, Eric D. 1982. "Forced Silence: A Neglected Dimension of Trauma." *American Journal of Psychiatry* 139(7):872–76.

Loeber, Rolf. 1986. "Family Factors as Correlates and Predictors of Juvenile Conduct Problems and Delinquency." In *Crime and Justice: An Annual Review of Research*, vol. 7, edited by Michael Tonry and Norval Morris. Chicago: University of Chicago Press.

Lonnborg, Barbara. 1982. *Abused Adolescents: How Schools and Educators Can Help*. Boys Town, Nebr.: Boys Town Center.

Lonnborg, Barbara, Marilyn Fischbach, and Melinda J. Bickerstaff. 1981. *Youth Helping Youth*. Boys Town, Nebr.: Boys Town Center.

Los Angeles Times. 1983*a*. "Boy Guilty in Slaying of His Abusive Father." *Los Angeles Times* (February 20), sec. 1, p. 5.

———. 1983*b*. "Wyoming Girl Convicted of Aiding Brother in Slaying Father." *Los Angeles Times* (March 12), sec. 1, p. 23.

Lourie, Ira S. 1977. "The Phenomenon of the Abused Adolescent: A Clinical Study." *Victimology* 2(2):268–76.

Lourie, Ira S., Patricia Campiglia, Linda Rich James, and Jeanne Dewitt. 1979. "Adolescent Abuse and Neglect: The Role of Runaway Youth Programs." *Children Today* 8(6):27–29.

Lubenow, Gerald C. 1983. "When Kids Kill Their Parents." *Newsweek* (June 27), pp. 35–36.

Margolin, Leslie. 1983. "A Treatment Model for the Adolescent Sex Offender." *Journal of Offender Counseling, Services and Rehabilitation* 8(1/2):1–12.

Milt, Harry. 1982. *Family Neglect and Abuse of the Aged: A Growing Concern*. Public Affairs Pamphlet no. 603. New York: Public Affairs Committee.

Mouzakitis, Chris M. 1984. "Characteristics of Abused Adolescents and Guidelines for Intervention." *Child Welfare League of America* 63(2):149–57.

Murphy, Dean. 1984. "Man Convicted of Killing Father Judge Calls 'Scum'." *Los Angeles Times* (January 28), sec. 2, p. 8.

National Center on Child Abuse and Neglect. 1980*a*. *Child Abuse and Neglect: State Reporting Laws*. Department of Health and Human Services. Washington, D.C.: U.S. Government Printing Office.

———. 1980*b*. *National Analysis of Official Child Neglect and Abuse Reporting*

(1978). Department of Health and Human Services. Washington, D.C.: U.S. Government Printing Office.

———. 1981. *Study Findings: National Study of the Incidence and Severity of Child Abuse and Neglect*. Department of Health and Human Services. Washington, D.C.: U.S. Government Printing Office.

———. 1982. *Executive Summary: National Study of the Incidence and Severity of Child Abuse and Neglect*. Department of Health and Human Services. Washington, D.C.: U.S. Government Printing Office.

NiCarthy, Ginny. 1983. Personal communication, October 29.

Oliveira, Odacir H. 1981. "Psychological and Physical Factors of Abuse of Older People." Speech given at the Multidisciplinary Conference on Family Violence, Long Beach, Calif., June.

O'Malley, Helen, Howard Segars, Rubin Perez, Victoria Mitchell, and George M. Knuepfel. 1979. *Elder Abuse in Massachusetts*. Boston: Legal Research for the Elderly.

O'Malley, Terrence A., Daniel E. Everitt, Helen C. O'Malley, and Edward W. Campion. 1983. "Identifying and Preventing Family-Mediated Abuse and Neglect of Elderly Persons." *Annals of Internal Medicine* 98(6):998–1005.

Pagelow, Mildred Daley. 1981. *Woman-Battering: Victims and Their Experiences*. Beverly Hills, Calif.: Sage.

———. 1982a. "Children in Violent Families: Direct and Indirect Victims." In *Young Children and Their Families*, edited by Shirley Hill and B. J. Barnes. Lexington, Mass.: Heath.

———. 1982b. "Child Abuse and Delinquency: Are There Connections between Childhood Violence and Later Deviant Behavior?" Paper presented at the Tenth World Congress of the International Sociological Association, Mexico City, August.

———. 1984. *Family Violence*. New York: Praeger.

———. 1987. "Abuse of the Elderly in the Home." In *Abuse and Religion: When Praying Isn't Enough*, edited by Anne L. Horton and Judith Ann Williamson. Lexington, Mass.: Lexington.

Pedrick-Cornell, Claire, and Richard J. Gelles. 1982. "Elder Abuse: The Status of Current Knowledge." *Family Relations* 31(3):457–65.

Pelcovitz, David, Sandra Kaplan, Carol Samit, Renee Krieger, and Don Cornelius. 1984. "Adolescent Abuse: Family Structure and Implications for Treatment." *Journal of the American Academy of Child Psychiatry* 23(1):85–90.

Pentz, Clyde. 1981. "Stress in the Extended Nuclear Family as a Precursor for Abuse." In *Abuse of Older Persons*, edited by David F. Holden and Peggie L. Carey. Knoxville: University of Tennessee.

Pillemer, Karl. 1985. "The Dangers of Dependency: New Findings on Domestic Violence against the Elderly." *Social Problems* 33(2):146–58.

Post, Shelley. 1982. "Adolescent Parricide in Abusive Families." *Child Welfare League of America* 61(15):296–304.

Rathbone-McCuan, Eloise. 1980. "Elderly Victims of Family Violence and Neglect." *Social Casework* 6(15):296–304.

Rathbone-McCuan, Eloise, and Richard K. Goodstein. 1985. "Elder Abuse: Clinical Considerations." *Psychiatric Annals* 15(5):331–39.

Rawlings, Stephen W. 1978. *Perspectives on American Husbands and Wives.* Bureau of the Census. Washington, D.C.: U.S. Government Printing Office.

Reich, J. W., and S. E. Gutierres. 1979. "Escape/Aggression Incidence in Sexually Abused Juvenile Delinquents." *Criminal Justice and Behavior* 6: 239–43.

Ritter, Bruce. 1979. "The Adolescent Runaway: A National Problem." *USA Today* (March), pp. 24–28.

Robinson, Donald. 1985. "How Can We Protect Our Elderly?" *Parade Magazine* (February 17), pp. 1–3.

Rosenblatt, Robert A., and Jonathan Peterson. 1986. "New Mix of Services: A Little Help Lets Elderly Live at Home." *Los Angeles Times* (June 25), sec. 1, pp. 1–14.

Roszell, Kathleen Chandler. 1985. "Suicide. Why Are Our Young People Killing Themselves?" *California State University Long Beach Review* 13(3):1–4.

Schaie, K. Warner. 1982. "America's Elderly in the Coming Decade." In *Adult Development and Aging,* edited by K. Warner Schaie and James Geiwitz. Boston: Little, Brown.

Sendi, Ismail B., and Paul G. Blomgren. 1975. "A Comparative Study of Predictive Criteria in the Predisposition of Homicidal Adolescents." *American Journal of Psychiatry* 132(4):423–27.

Sengstock, Mary C., Sara Barrett, and Robert Graham. 1984. "Abused Elders: Victims of Villains or of Circumstances?" *Journal of Gerontological Social Work* 8(1/2):101–11.

Sengstock, Mary C., and J. Liang. 1983. "Domestic Abuse of the Aged: Assessing Some Dimensions of the Problems." *Interdisciplinary Topics in Gerontology* 17:58–68.

Serrano, Alberto C., Margot B. Zuelzer, Don D. Howe, and Richard E. Reposa. 1980. "Ecology of Abusive and Nonabusive Families: Implications for Intervention." *Advances in Family Psychiatry* 2:183–95.

Shaffer, David. 1986. "Questions about Teen Suicide." *Sharing* 9(March):1, 2, 7.

Shell, Donna J. 1982. *Protection of the Elderly: A Study of Elder Abuse.* Winnipeg: Manitoba Council on Aging.

Silver, Larry B., Christina C. Dublin, and Reginald S. Lourie. 1969. "Does Violence Breed Violence? Contributions from a Study of the Child Abuse Syndrome." *American Journal of Psychiatry* 126(3):152–55.

Smith, Charles P., David J. Berkman, and Warren M. Fraser. 1980. *A Preliminary National Assessment of Child Abuse and Neglect and the Juvenile Justice System: The Shadows of Distress.* Reports of the National Juvenile Justice Assessment Centers, Department of Justice. Law Enforcement Assistance Administration. Washington, D.C.: U.S. Government Printing Office.

Sommers, Tish. 1982. *Concerns of Older Women: Growing Numbers, Special Needs.* Sacramento: California Commission on the Status of Women.

Stark, Evan, and Anne Flitcraft. 1985. "Woman-Battering, Child Abuse and Social Heredity: What Is the Relationship?" In *Marital Violence,* edited by Norman Johnson. Beverly Hills, Calif.: Sage.

Stark, Rodney, and James McEvoy III. 1970. "Middle-Class Violence." *Psychology Today* (November), pp. 52–54, 110–12.

Steele, Brandt F. 1974. "Child Abuse: Its Impact on Society." Paper presented at the Fiftieth Anniversary Celebration of the James Whitcomb Riley Hospital for Children, Indianapolis, Ind.

Steinmetz, Suzanne K. 1978. "Battered Parents." *Society* 15(5):54-55.

———. 1981*a* "Elder Abuse." *Aging* (January/February), pp. 6–10.

———. 1981*b*. "A Cross-Cultural Comparison of Sibling Violence." *International Journal of Family Psychiatry* 2(3/4):337–51.

Straus, Murray A. 1979. "Measuring Intrafamily Conflict and Violence: The Conflict Tactics (CT) Scales." *Marriage and the Family* 41:75–88.

Straus, Murray, Richard Gelles, and Suzanne Steinmetz. 1978. "Physical Violence in a Nationally Representative Sample of American Families." Paper presented at the Ninth World Congress of Sociology, Uppsala, Sweden, August.

———. 1980. *Behind Closed Doors: Violence in the American Family*. New York: Doubleday.

Taugher, Mary. 1984. "Why Does a Child Kill His Parent?" *Register* (March 5), p. A1.

Tooley, Kay M. 1977. "The Young Child as Victim of Sibling Attack." *Social Casework* 58(1):25–28.

U.S. Bureau of the Census. 1979. *Social and Economic Characteristics of the Older Population: 1978*. Current Population Reports, Series P-23, no. 85. Department of Commerce. Washington, D.C.: U.S. Government Printing Office.

———. 1983. *Characteristics of the Population Below the Poverty Level: 1981*. Current Population Reports, Series P-60, no. 138. Department of Commerce. Washington, D.C.: U.S. Government Printing Office.

———. 1985. *Household and Family Characteristics*. Current Population Reports, Series P-20, no. 398. Department of Commerce. Washington, D.C.: U.S. Government Printing Office.

U.S. Congress. House Select Committee on Aging. Subcommittee on Human Services. 1980. *Domestic Abuse of the Elderly*. Washington, D.C.: U.S. Government Printing Office.

U.S. Congress. Senate Committee on the Judiciary. 1980. *Homeless Youth: The Saga of "Pushouts" and "Throwaways" in America*. 96th Congress. Washington, D.C.: U.S. Government Printing Office.

———. 1982. *Exploitation of Children*. 97th Congress. Washington, D.C.: U.S. Government Printing Office.

U.S. Department of Justice. 1976. *Criminal Victimization in the U.S.* Washington, D.C.: U.S. Government Printing Office.

———. 1980. *Intimate Victims: A Study of Violence among Friends and Relatives*. Bureau of Justice Statistics. Washington, D.C.: U.S. Government Printing Office.

———. 1983. *Report to the Nation on Crime and Justice. The Data*. Bureau of Justice Statistics. Washington, D.C.: U.S. Government Printing Office.

Van Buren, Abigail. 1986. "Dear Abby." *Orange County Register* (April 29), p. D3.

Warren, Carol A. B. 1979. "Parent Batterers: Adolescent Violence and the Family." Paper presented at the annual meeting of the Pacific Sociological Association, Anaheim, Calif., April.

Wayne, Julianne, and Karen K. Weeks. 1984. "Groupwork with Abused Adolescent Girls: A Special Challenge." *Social Work with Groups* 7(4):83–104.

West, Donald J. 1983. "Sex Offenses and Offending." In *Crime and Justice: An Annual Review of Research*, vol. 5, edited by Michael Tonry and Norval Morris. Chicago: University of Chicago Press.

Whitman, Grace. 1982. "Research Links Multipersonality Disorders to Child Sexual Abuse." *Response* 5(5):3–4.

Wilks, Carl. 1981. "Past Conflicts and Current Stress: Factors in the Abuse of the Elderly." In *Abuse of Older Persons*, edited by David F. Holden and Peggie L. Carey. Knoxville: University of Tennessee.

Ziefert, Marjorie. 1982. *Adolescent Abuse and Neglect: Prevention and Intervention*. East Lansing: Michigan State University, Department of Social Work.

*Gerald T. Hotaling and Murray A. Straus with
Alan J. Lincoln*

Intrafamily Violence, and Crime and Violence outside the Family

ABSTRACT

Research on violent behavior over the past fifteen years has generally assumed that violence between family members is fundamentally different from violence "in the streets." Criminologists and family violence researchers have been reluctant to conceptualize family violence as a form of criminal violence, and there has been little theoretical or empirical work on commonalities in violence across family and nonfamily settings. An analysis of three data sets from general populations (two national household surveys and a student survey) shows a link between physical assaults in the family and assaults and other crime outside of the family. Evidence was found for both victimization effects and offender effects. Both adult and child *victims* of violence are more likely to perpetrate assaults and other aggression outside the family than are nonvictims. Violent *offenders* in the family are also more likely to assault nonfamily members. These victim and offender effects do not disappear when controlling for socioeconomic status, gender, or severity of family violence. The findings support the social learning thesis that training in violence is generalizable across settings and across targets.

Gerald T. Hotaling is assistant professor of criminal justice, University of Lowell, and research associate, Family Research Laboratory, University of New Hampshire. Murray A. Straus is professor of sociology and director of the Family Research Laboratory, University of New Hampshire. Alan J. Lincoln is professor of criminal justice, University of Lowell. Funding to obtain the data described in this essay was provided by the National Institute of Mental Health and the Graduate School of the University of New Hampshire. We would like to thank the editors of and referees for this volume and the members of the Family Violence Research Program Seminar for 1986-87 for valuable comments and suggestions.

315

This essay has three major purposes. We consider in Section I why family violence research and criminological research have not taken full account of one another in their work on violent behavior. In Sections II–VIII we review research on the link between family and nonfamily violence and present, for the first time, epidemiological data on the relations between violence in the family and crime and violence "in the streets." We evaluate our current state of knowledge in this area and suggest key issues for future research in Section IX.

I. Criminology and Family Violence Research

Over the past ten years there have been sporadic reports of family violence researchers attending the meetings of criminological research societies. Likewise, there have been rumors of criminologists sighted at conferences on family violence research. Some people say they have actually witnessed family violence researchers and criminologists talking with one another, but there is no hard evidence that these events actually have taken place. The data are not based on a systematic sample and most probably inflate the amount of interaction between these two groups.

Violence between family members has been studied quite separately from the general study of criminal violence. A recent review article on the link between family and stranger violence reported the results of a computer search of professional journals in five data bases and found not a single entry on the relation between family and stranger violence (Fagan and Wexler 1987).

How can this be? Criminologists and family violence researchers have similar academic training, and both are concerned with uncovering risk factors of violent behavior and with the development and testing of theories to explain violent behavior. They use similar measures, and both collect data through surveys, experiments, and case studies in order to understand violent behavior. Even if they never directly interact, these researchers have such common concerns that the intersection of family and nonfamily criminal violence should be an extremely well-researched area. It may be, however, that violence in families is so fundamentally different from violence between strangers that distinctive approaches to separate subjects are necessary and quite appropriate.

A. Reasons for Separate Approaches to Study of Violence in Families

There has been some merging of criminological and family violence research. There has, for example, been research on the response of the criminal justice system to family violence (Bard 1971; Parnas 1972; Lerman and Livingston 1983; Buzawa 1984; Sherman and Berk 1984; Carmody and Williams 1987; Elliott, in this volume). Some family violence researchers have worked from a criminological perspective, and criminologists have incorporated family violence topics into their studies of criminal violence, especially research on family homicide (e.g., Wolfgang 1958; Palmer 1972; Walker 1979, 1984; Straus 1986, 1987; Browne 1987). The nonintegration of these two literatures is most prominent in etiological research and theory development on non-lethal violent behavior.

Gelles (1982) attributes the nonintegration of criminological and family violence to the lack of interest of criminologists in family violence. This may result from a general cultural reluctance to recognize family violence as a problem of significant magnitude or consequence. Only in the mid-1960s did child welfare groups begin to focus on physical abuse, and only in the mid-1970s did the women's movement begin to focus on wife beating. Before that time, neither social institutions, including the academic community, nor the general public paid much attention to assaults on women and children in the home. In short, criminological researchers did not investigate family violence because the prevalent cultural norms and practices did not define it as a problem.

Even in the middle and late 1970s, as evidence accumulated about the high prevalence of family violence (Gil 1970; Straus 1973; Gelles 1974; Steinmetz and Straus 1974; Martin 1976; Gaquin 1977; Dobash and Dobash 1979; Straus, Gelles, and Steinmetz 1980), family violence was still commonly viewed as something different from "real" violence and "real" crime.

The criminal justice system during this time was especially resistant to responding to family violence as criminal violence. Police, prosecutors, and courts regarded violence in the home as a private matter, subject to sanction as a crime only when it resulted in death or serious injury (Fagan and Wexler 1987). The training manual published by the International Association of Chiefs of Police recommended a policy of noninterference, and some cities had an informal "stitch rule" that required a wound needing more than a certain number of stitches to justify an arrest (Straus 1976). Both Straus (1976) and Gelles (1982) view the general cultural tolerance of family violence as authority for the criminal justice system to regard it as something different from criminal violence. The lack of response of the legal system, in turn, reinforced the view that family violence is not a crime. Since family violence was not criminal behavior, no official records needed to be kept about its occurrence, and no criminological research was needed to understand it (Gelles 1982, pp. 202–3).

This explanation is probably largely correct but does not fully account for why little attention is now paid to the criminological aspects of violence in the family. Throughout the 1970s, there was a more general absence of theoretical activity to incorporate knowledge about family violence into existing paradigms. Practitioners and researchers from a number of fields declined to claim family violence as an area of their concern. Thus, child abuse and wife abuse were equally ignored by medicine (Rounsaville 1978; Stark, Flitcraft, and Frazier 1979; Gelles 1982), public health (Bowen et al. 1984), mental health and social services (Martin 1976), religion (Dobash and Dobash 1979), and sociology (Steinmetz and Straus 1974). None of the corresponding research arms of these disciplines rushed to integrate knowledge of family violence into their existing theoretical and methodological work (with the exception of psychiatry; see Gelles [1973] for a review of the psychiatric model of family violence). Not until 1979 was any attempt made to explore the relevance of a number of sociological and psychological theories of violence and aggression to the understanding of family violence (Gelles and Straus 1979).

B. Development of Family Violence Research as a Separate Research Area

Because no one field or academic discipline claimed family violence as a primary focus of research interest, the interdisciplinary area of "family violence research" began to take shape in the late 1970s. Today, this is an area composed of a broad array of researchers and practitioners from sociology, women's studies, psychology, psychiatry, social work, anthropology, medicine, law, human and child development, public health, biology, and other disciplines. Current definitions, concepts, and theories used in family violence research reflect the diverse research traditions of this group. This diversity is one of the primary obstacles to incorporating research on family violence into the study of criminal violence. Paradoxically, family violence research has constructed a knowledge base that depicts violence in families in such a way that criminological methods and theories do not easily apply. In a sense, we have come full circle. At first, criminologists treated family violence as something different than criminal violence; now family violence researchers approach family violence as something different than criminal violence. In the meantime, however, very little empirical evidence has been generated to determine just how different violence in families is from violence "in the streets." We now turn to a discussion of how definitions, knowledge of risk factors, typologies, and theories used to understand family violence can no longer be easily reconciled with the general study of criminal violence.

C. Expansion of the Definition of Family Violence

The greatest convergence between family violence research and criminology occurs in the study of murder (Wolfgang 1958; Palmer 1960; Straus 1986, 1987; Browne 1987; Flewelling and Browne 1987). A major reason is that both fields use the same definition of homicide.

Criminologists adopt a fairly consistent research definition of assault, one that is codified in law and generally agreed on. The same cannot be said for those who study intrafamily assault. The conceptual and definitional development of family violence research has produced a wide array of operational definitions of violent behavior in families. Family violence, such as physical abuse of children and wife beating, has been operationally defined through violent *acts* (Schulman 1979; Straus 1979; Straus, Gelles, and Steinmetz 1980), *injuries* (Kempe et al. 1962; Washburn and Frieze 1981; Berk et al. 1983), both violent *acts and injuries* (McLeod 1983; Pagelow 1984), and through a *"battering syndrome"* involving repetitive acts of physical violence and psychological harm (Walker 1979, 1984).

This diversity accurately reflects a complex reality but is one of the reasons for difficulty in comparing incidence rates and correlates of family violence with knowledge on general criminal violence. More generally, there seem to be three main factors that make it difficult for criminologists to work with the conceptual and operational definitions used in family violence research: normative ambiguity concerning what acts of intrafamily violence are criminal, a tendency for family violence researchers to use injuries rather than acts to conceptualize and measure family violence, and expansion of the terms "abuse" and "violence" to cover many behaviors in addition to assault.

1. *Normative Ambiguity.* Violence in families that has a high probability of producing an injury is typically seen as comparable to criminal violence, but there is a lack of consensus as to whether "minor" violence in families should be similarly conceptualized. Pushing, shoving, or slapping one's spouse or one's child is clearly violent behavior, but is it

criminal to the same degree as pushing or slapping the spouse or child
of a neighbor would be? The reluctance to view "minor" violence in
families as assaults has inhibited research on the links between family
and nonfamily violence. Gelles (1982) argues that the lack of a criminological perspective on family violence is partly due to normative confusion over behavior in families that is clearly violent but not viewed as
criminal because of the implicit cultural support that exists for this kind
of behavior. In addition, there are important ethical and practical problems connected with "criminalizing" all behavior in the family that
would be a crime if the same act took place between strangers (Straus
and Lincoln 1985).

   2. *Acts versus Injuries.*   The legal definition of assault focuses on acts
rather than on injuries. As Marcus (1983, p. 89) puts it: "Physical
contact is not an element of the crime." As the Uniform Crime Reports
puts it: "Attempts are included [in the tabulation of aggravated assault]
because it is not necessary that an injury result" (Federal Bureau of
Investigation 1985, p. 21). However, many (or most) family violence
researchers believe that the criterion should be injury, and this is part
of the reason why the inclusion of "minor" violence is seen as expanding the notion of violence beyond criminal assault. Since minor violence is unlikely to cause an injury that needs medical attention, those
who incorrectly define assault and violence by an outcome such as
physical injury have difficulty including so-called minor violence
within the family as a criminal assault.

   3. *Expansion to Cover Many Types of Maltreatment.*   There is no doubt
that the family and other interpersonal relations are the locus of much
noxious and harmful behavior. In recent years, family violence research
has come to include work on psychological abuse of children and
spouses; child sexual abuse; marital rape; physical, emotional, and educational neglect of children; and other forms of interpersonal maltreatment. All of these behaviors are harmful and are in need of careful
research, but subsuming them under the general heading of "family
violence" has created additional conceptual confusion and probably
inhibited the application of criminological theory to family violence
research (see Gelles [1982] for a discussion of the expansion of the
concept of family violence and Straus and Lincoln [1985] for a theoretical analysis of the implications of such a trend).

D. Belief in Need for Special Theories of Family Violence
   Just as definitions of family violence have expanded to incorporate

notions of harmful behaviors against family members, so have calls for
the development of concepts and theories that are different from those
used to interpret criminal violence. Are unique or special theories necessary to understand family violence? Gelles and Straus (1979) have
argued that physical violence against children and spouses are "special"
cases of violence that require family-based theories to explain them.
Hotaling and Straus (1980) list a number of aspects of family structure
and dynamics to justify the need for special theories of family violence,
and Dobash and Dobash (1979) have argued that violence against wives
is a special and unique type of violence and should not be approached as
a subset of general violent behavior.

Criminologists have generally agreed with this point of view.
Megargee (1982) sees intimacy as a key variable in necessitating a separate theoretical approach to the study of violent families: "Given the
long-standing and intimate nature of the relations between offenders
and victims, it is natural to suppose that to some degree the familial
violence stems from these relationships and constitutes an episode in a
continuing pattern of interactions. This sets familial violence apart
from most other violent offenses and makes it worthy of study in its
own right" (p. 101).

All of these authors make persuasive arguments, but they represent a
decision made within the research community that has discouraged the
application of criminological theory to the study of family violence.
Since "special" theories are needed, it may seem as though there is no
reason to explore theories of general criminal violence. Unfortunately,
assertions about the need for unique theories have never been tested by
empirical evidence. The etiology of violent behavior may be very similar whether it is used against a family member or a nonfamily member.
Notions of intimacy and the primary group nature of the family are
very important for understanding the dynamics of violence in families,
but not necessarily for understanding the motivations of offenders.
Similarly, patriarchal norms may be very important for understanding
the motivation of violent husbands but may also be very important for
understanding violence outside of family relationships (Toby 1966).

The belief in the need for special theories may stem from the fact that
data on violence in families come largely from victims, while data on
nonfamily violence come largely from offenders. Criminology has recognized the need for a victim's perspective as the growing field of
victimology and increased use of victimization surveys attests, but in
family violence research, the victim's perspective is often used to gauge

the offender's motivation. Consequently, criminological theories may appear inappropriate. The need for presumed special theories may mask the need for more direct study of violent offenders in families.

E. Risk Factors in Use of Violence in Families

The violent spouse and violent parent are often seen as different from the violent street criminal in terms of basic demographic and social correlates. How different are adults who are violent in the family from those who are violent outside of it?

The study of criminal violence has produced a number of risk factors that differentiate the criminally violent from the nonviolent. These include being male (Mednick et al. 1982; Elliott and Huizinga 1983, 1984); low socioeconomic status (Elliott and Ageton 1980; Braithwaite 1981); being nonwhite (Hindelang 1981; Weiner and Wolfgang 1985); school adjustment problems (Fagan, Piper, and Moore 1986); disruption in family of orientation (Strasburg 1978); aggressive parental figures (McCord 1984); and a history of juvenile crime involvement (Farrington 1982).

The family violence literature produces a very different image of the abusive spouse and abusive parent. Abusive spouses are also believed to more likely be male but, beyond that, are indistinguishable on the basis of other social and demographic characteristics. Violent males in families are depicted as coming from all socioeconomic backgrounds, races, religions, occupations, and walks of life (Star et al. 1979; Walker 1979, 1984; Giles-Sims 1983; Pagelow 1984; Sonkin, Martin, and Walker 1985). The exposure to violent role models in childhood is also seen as failing to discriminate the violent from the nonviolent (Pagelow 1984).

The image of the "batterer as everyone" is typically based on clinical samples and the reports of victims. Since comparison groups of nonviolent men are not used, there is no way to calculate the risk-to-violence of any social or demographic variable. A recent review of comparison group studies of men violent toward wives (Hotaling and Sugarman 1986) revealed a set of risk factors that are very similar to risk factors of men who are criminally violent. These men report, or are reported to have, lower occupational status, lower income, and lower educational attainment than nonviolent male comparison groups. Violent husbands are also more likely to have had aggressive role models for parents and to be more generally violent (to children and nonfamily members) than comparison group males.

Physical child abusers are also depicted in the family violence literature as coming from all social classes, educational backgrounds, and as
no more likely than anyone else to have a history of abuse (Pagelow
1984). But again, comparison group evidence tends to depict physical
child abusers as somewhat similar to the criminally violent, at least on
the basis of some risk factors. For example, parents who severely assault children do seem more likely than nonchild abusers to have a
history of physical abuse (Melnick and Hurley 1969; Conger, Burgess,
and Barrett 1979; Hunter and Kilstrom 1979; Straus, Gelles, and Steinmetz 1980), lower educational attainment (Hunter et al. 1978; Gelles
1980), and lower socioeconomic status (Giovannoni and Billingsley
1970; Smith, Hanson, and Noble 1973; Gelles 1980).

Violent criminals are portrayed as inhabiting a different sociodemographic space than violent family members. While a profile of the street
criminal begins to emerge through the discovery of risk factors, the
violent family member remains invisible. He is depicted as being anyone. He could possess some of the characteristics of the street criminal,
but that is not seen in the research literature as setting him apart. His
distinctiveness resides in his ability to avoid sociological labels. If those
who assault other family members are depicted as otherwise law-
abiding citizens, there is no compelling reason to apply notions of
criminality to explain their behavior.

F. A Separate Typology of Offenders

If the violent family members cannot be identified sociologically,
then perhaps they can be distinguished psychologically. Specifically,
what is the motivational basis for violence against family members?
The depiction of violent family members in the research literature tells
us that special theories that take into account primary group dynamics
are necessary to understand this violence and that we cannot rely on
risk factors that apply to general criminal violence.

The motivators for violence against family members are depicted as
very different from those influencing violent criminals. One way to
examine these depictions or images is to compare typologies or profiles
of violent family members to those of general violent criminals. Some
common depictions of the reasons for criminal violence are "normal"
(Bromberg 1961), "culturally appropriate" (Glaser, Kenefick, and
O'Leary 1968), "environmental" (Revitch and Schlesinger 1978),
"avenging" (Guttmacher 1960), "instrumental" (Williams 1972; Ochberg 1980), "reputation defending," "norm enforcing," "defending,"

and "pressure removing" (Toch 1969) (see Megargee [1982] for a complete listing). Nonfamily violent offenders are portrayed in these depictions as rational, instrumental, and goal seeking. Based on known risk factors of criminal violence, the use of physical force is seen as a largely rational response to powerlessness and deprivation. Violence is interpreted as being used to deal with threats posed by the immediate social environment or by an unjust and racist society.

Violent criminal offenders also are studied in terms of personal history. They have been conditioned to violence by growing up in a violent family and neighborhood and have a history of violent behavior starting in adolescence. Again, this violent history underscores the rationality of their adult violence.

There are some depictions of violent family members as instrumental (Straus 1973, 1977; Browne 1987), but the general image of the violent spouse and parent in the family violence literature is quite different from the depiction of the violent criminal offender. Profiles and typologies depict violent family members as "overcontrolled loners," "cowards" (Caesar 1985), "approval seeking" (Elbow 1977), "extremely jealous" (Faulk 1974; Pagelow 1984; Walker 1984), "dependent and passive" (Faulk 1974; Sonkin, Martin, and Walker 1985), "fearing abandonment" (Dutton and Browning 1984), "lacking in assertiveness" (Rosenbaum and O'Leary 1981; Pagelow 1984), "having low self-esteem" (Rouse 1984; Telch and Lindquist 1984), "having no impulse control" (Sonkin, Martin, and Walker 1985), "neurotic" (Symonds 1979), "frustration displacing" (Walters 1975; Pagelow 1984), "moody" (Pagelow 1984), "immature and hysterical" (Brandon 1976), "angry" (Walker 1984), and "having feelings of incompetence, inadequacy, and worthlessness" (Kent et al. 1978).

Wife beaters are depicted as psychologically distressed, and their violence as irrational. Wife beating is seen as a response to the husband's dependency, jealousy, and anger. Rather than being depicted as rational and unemotional, violent husbands are characterized as extremely emotional and highly sensitive to situational stress, and their violence is primarily expressive rather than instrumental. The personal inadequacies and frustrations of these people motivate them to victimize the weak and powerless (Finkelhor 1983; Pagelow 1984).

Child abusers are also seen as incompetent and immature. They are unable to cope with the responsibilities of parenting and hold unrealistic expectations of children. They are seen as overwhelmed by the demands of situational stress (see review by Wolfe [1985]).

Current conceptions of the violent offender and of the violent family member are at considerable odds. Street violence is seen as a "deliberate, rational activity to further instrumental goals" (Megargee 1982, p. 106), while family violence is an angry response triggered by psychological flaws and situational stressors.

Megargee (1982, p. 106) has suggested that this conceptual difference may reflect "a real difference between 'street crimes' and 'family crimes,' but it seems equally likely that it is due to the facts that 1) family violence occurs in the home, where the influence of these environmental variables is more readily apparent, and 2) those who have written about family violence have often been more interested in marital dynamics than in criminal behaviors per se." It may be that family violence researchers and criminologists are both correct. The motivations and risk factors associated with why someone is violent toward a relative rather than an acquaintance or stranger may, in fact, be very dissimilar. Unfortunately, the answer will not be known until more direct comparisons can be made between violence in family and nonfamily contexts.

G. Lack of Attention to the Link between Forms of Family Violence

The lack of an examination of the relations between violence across social contexts is also true of types of violence within the family. Family violence research has not explicitly examined the links between violence against children, violence against spouses, sibling violence, or child-parent violence. There is even a lack of epidemiological data on what proportion of families are multiviolent, that is, in what proportion of American families do assaults against children and wife beating coexist?

Within the family violence research area, separate traditions have evolved for the study of physical violence against children and violence against adult partners (Finkelhor 1983). Family violence research is composed of several individual research tracks that have not been linked in any systematic manner. Each area has invested in particular theories and research strategies that do not necessarily lend themselves to a search for common features of violent behavior. This compartmentalization of family violence research may also be another factor that impedes the application of a criminological perspective on family violence.

In summary, current definitions, appraisals of risk factors, and theoretical conceptions of the use of violence in families construe it as something different from criminal violence "in the streets." However, the empirical evidence for this view is weak, relying on clinical accounts and single group studies. In fact, some evidence suggests that violence against family members may be very similar in important respects to violence against nonfamily persons. The important issue, however, is that the possible linkages between family and nonfamily violence have rarely been systematically studied. Before examining the evidence for these linkages in more detail, we turn to a discussion of a major source of conceptual confusion: the terms "violence," "abuse," and "assault."

H. Violence, Abuse, and Assault

The terms "violence" and "abuse" are a source of considerable difficulty and confusion because they cover many types of events, not just acts of physical assault, and, in the case of "abuse," because there is no consensus on the severity required for an act to be considered "abuse." Since there is no standard definition of abuse, and no consensus on severity, the best that can be done is to make clear the way the terms "violence" and "abuse" are used in this essay and their relation to the legal concept of "assault."

"Violence" is defined as an act carried out with the intention, or perceived intention, of causing physical pain or injury to another person. See Gelles and Straus (1979) for an explication of this definition and an analysis of alternative definitions.[1]

Violence as defined here is synonymous with the term "physical aggression" as used in social psychology (Berkowitz 1962; Bandura 1973). However, it is not the same as the legal concept of assault because not all violence is a common-law or statutory crime. Some violent acts, in fact, are required by law—capital punishment, for example.

---

[1] As pointed out in a previous theoretical article (Gelles and Straus 1979), that a physical assault has taken place is not sufficient for understanding violence. Other dimensions also need to be considered. Each of these other dimensions should be measured separately so that their causes and consequences and joint effects can be investigated. Among the other dimensions are the seriousness of the assault (which can range from a slap to stabbing and shooting); whether a physical injury was produced (which can range from none to death); the motivation (which might range from a concern for a person's safety, as when a child is spanked for going into the street, to hostility so intense that the death of the person is desired); and whether the act of violence is normatively legitimate (as in the case of slapping a child) or illegitimate (as in the case of slapping a spouse), and what norms are applicable (legal, ethnic or class norms, couple norms, etc.).

The term "abuse" is restricted to "physical abuse" because we chose in our surveys to concentrate the limited interview time with each family on this phenomenon. This decision was entirely a matter of research strategy. It does not imply that we think physical abuse is more important or more damaging than other types of abuse, such as psychological abuse and sexual abuse.

The difference between violence and abuse is a matter of social norms, either informal or legal or both. Further, the difference depends on both the severity of the act and the relationship between victim and offender. Thus, slapping a child for "talking back" is not an assault, but slapping a store clerk for "talking back" is. Severity of the act (defined as the potential for causing physical injury) is also important in labeling an act as abuse: parents have the right to hit children, but it becomes an assault in the legal sense if they bite, kick, burn, or choke the child.

"Assault" is the term we prefer to use in this essay, rather than "violence," because the focus here is on illegal violence. Moreover, even though there are now statutes that define "child abuse" as a crime, physical assaults on children make up only about one-quarter of the cases identified under these statutes. The remainder are cases of neglect, psychological abuse, or sexual abuse. In view of these considerations, from this point on we try to avoid the term "abuse" in favor of more specific terms such as "child assault" and "spouse assault."

II. Social Learning Theory and the Linkage Issue

Social learning theory would seem to be an excellent starting point for examining the links between assaults in and outside of families. Early studies on social learning suggest that aggressive behavior is learned and is acquired through direct experience (trial and error), by observing the behavior of others (modeling), or in both ways (Singer 1971; Bandura 1973). The learning theory approach to family violence contends that the family serves as a training ground for violence. In terms of modeling, the family provides examples for imitation that can be adopted in later life as the individual draws from childhood experiences to structure appropriate parent or conjugal roles. The family can also encourage and reinforce assaultive behavior in children by rewarding aggressive behavior (e.g., sibling violence). This process is often unintentional but quite effective (Patterson, Cobb, and Roy 1973).

A key issue in the social learning view of assaultive behavior is generalizability. Is learning specific to particular targets, certain contexts, and limited temporally, or do learned responses become a more general mode of behavior? There is some experimental evidence that aggressive models transmit general lessons as well as specific ones and that observers learn general aggressive strategies that go well beyond the specific modeled examples (Bandura 1971, 1973). Straus (1983) presents evidence that also supports the "generalization" hypotheses in that abusive husbands are more likely to have both witnessed and experienced parental assaults as children (see Hotaling and Sugarman [1986] for a complete review of these studies). How generalizable, then, is assaultive behavior in families, particularly across targets within families, across generations, and across contexts?

A. Generalizability of Violence across Targets within Families

Two questions are examined in this essay in relation to the generalizability of assaults across targets. The first, a descriptive issue, is, What proportion of American families during any given year experience both child assault and spouse assault? Families that report *both* child and spouse assault can be called assaultive families. Existing data on this question are based on clinical samples, and there has been no attempt, using epidemiological methods, to estimate the incidence of multiassaultive families. Data from three general population surveys are analyzed later in this essay to examine the extent of multiassaultive families in American society.

The second question about the use of violence across targets within families concerns children. In multiassaultive families, children both experience and observe parental assaults. What short-term effects result from this intensive modeling? Given the power of the models in these roles and the intensity of the modeling, these children may be more likely to learn assaultive responses. But whether they engage in violence in the family is the issue of interest here. The key question is, Are children in multiassaultive families more likely to use violence against siblings and parents than children from families with different assault constellations?

Other factors also affect modeling outcomes. For example, boys seem to be more influenced than girls by the modeling of parental violence (Bandura 1973; Pagelow 1984). The severity of the observed assault may also affect the strength of modeling as may the social class of the family. Consequently, children's violence in families is examined below in terms of its link to intensity of modeling, sex of child, severity of violence observed, and social class.

B. Generalizability of Violence across Contexts

The generalizability of assaultive behavior in families to other contexts remains largely unexplored. This issue must be considered for both children and spouses.

1. *Children.* If children who are exposed to assaultive models are more likely to initiate violence against family members, will they also be more likely to engage in violence against persons outside of the family? The observation and direct experience of assault in the home could spill over into relationships with nonfamily persons. This would be predicted by social learning theory. What about other nonviolent forms of behavior, such as property offenses? Are children from multiassaultive families also more likely to engage in these behaviors? Assaultive behavior is a form of deviant behavior, and the lessons it teaches may also be generalizable. The modeling of violent behavior in the family may weaken one's allegiance to social norms in general and facilitate a more general antisocial response. A third issue to be examined is, Are children exposed to multiassaultive parental models more likely than other children to be violent outside of the family? Are they also more likely to engage in nonviolent delinquent behavior outside the family? Again, the issue of how modeling in this regard is affected by sex of child, severity of violence, and social class is also examined.

2. *Spouses.* Using the notion of multiassaultive families, we examine whether adults in these family contexts are more likely to engage in violence and other antisocial behaviors outside of the family. A major issue here is whether husbands are assaultive only toward their female partners or whether they are more generally assaultive in social relations. Even though assaultive behavior is rare among women (Saunders 1986), we also examine whether the link between assaults inside and outside the home holds for both men and women.

III. Sample and Methods

The issues introduced in the preceding sections are examined through an analysis of data from three studies, each of which contains information on both family and nonfamily violence and crime. The aspects of these issues on which empirical data are presented stem from the contention that assault in interpersonal relationships is a learned response and is generalizable across both targets and contexts. Further, the greater an individual's exposure to assaults in the family, the higher the likelihood of assaultive behavior in both family and nonfamily realms.

A. The Three Surveys[2]

Data to investigate the links between assaults in and outside of families was gathered from three independent surveys. Each of the samples is briefly described in terms of data collection methods and size.

1. *Student Survey.*   The first of the three surveys examined here is variously identified as the "student sample," the "student study," or the "1972 student study." The data were obtained through questionnaires distributed in introductory sociology and anthropology classes at a state university in New England during 1971, 1972, and 1973. The questionnaire asked about family characteristics and about conflict in the family that occurred during the senior year in high school (which in many cases was only two months earlier). The questionnaire was anonymous and voluntary (although completed during the class period). Of the 583 questionnaires distributed, 95.2 percent, or 555, were completed. However, the number of cases for the analyses in this essay, which require data on both parents, is 334 because the remaining students were not living with both parents that year. Data are available for this sample on intrafamily violence by both the parents and the respondents (see Straus 1974), but the crime data is restricted to the respondents.

An obvious limitation of the student sample is that it describes only families with a child in college. Such families and their children are far from representative. For example, since all are attending college, they may be more adequately functioning individuals and families than would be a representative cross section of the general population. Consequently, descriptive statistics on intrafamily violence and on crime by these students are likely to be underestimates. Nevertheless, a great deal of family violence and nonfamily crime was reported. Moreover, the central issue of this essay is not the amount of family violence or the amount of crime, but whether these are correlated. Consequently, since a correlation is not affected by the absolute level of the two variables, valid results are possible, even if the two variables are each severely underestimated (Straus 1970, pp. 572–73), provided there is

[2] The first two of these samples were the source of the data used in a previous analysis of the link between intrafamily assault and crime (Straus 1985). The work reported in this essay refines and extends that work by using a more adequate measure of the independent variable—the "family assault types" given in figure 1—and by a better specified statistical analysis that includes a control for the socioeconomic status of the father.

no "interaction" between the reasons for the underestimate and either the independent or dependent variable.

2. *National Survey.* The second study examined is the National Family Violence Survey conducted by Straus, Gelles, and Steinmetz (1980). (At various places this is abbreviated to "National Survey.") Data for this study come from personal interviews with a national probability sample of 2,143 families in early 1975. The referent period for the data on violence is the twelve months preceding the interview. This sample is not entirely representative of American families because single-parent households were excluded.[3] The cases used for the analyses in this essay are 1,092 families with a minor child living at home. Comparison with census data on husband-wife families show a close correspondence on such variables as income, percentage of women in the paid labor force, and race.

The respondent was the husband for a random half of the national sample, and the wife for the other half. Contrary to our original expectations, the rates of family violence based on interviews with husbands corresponded almost exactly with rates computed from data from interviews with wives. Additional information on the characteristics of the sample, and a table showing correspondence between husband and wife data for a number of variables are in Straus, Gelles, and Steinmetz (1980).

3. *National Resurvey.* The third source of data for this analysis is the National Family Violence Resurvey conducted in the summer of 1985 (which for brevity is referred to as the "National Resurvey" or the "resurvey"). The resurvey replicates part of the National Survey described above, but it is *not* a panel study.

The interviews were conducted by telephone using random-digit dialing to select a nationally representative sample of 4,032 families, plus three oversamples. The analyses reported in this essay use only the national sample, and only cases in which both parents and at least one child were household members ($N = 2,688$). The sample is described in somewhat more detail in Straus and Gelles (1986) and in full detail in a mimeographed report obtainable from us.

---

[3] However, unmarried cohabiting couples were included in this study and in the National Family Violence Resurvey described below. For convenience and economy of wording, terms such as "marital," "spouse," "wife," and "husband" are used to refer to couples, irrespective of whether they are married or nonmarried cohabiting persons. For an analysis of differences and similarities between married and cohabiting couples in the 1975–76 study see Yllo (1978); and Yllo and Straus (1981).

B. Measures

The Conflict Tactics Scales (Straus 1979) violence items were used to measure the incidence of intrafamily assault in all three studies. The methods used to obtain data on nonfamily assault and other crime varied in the three studies. If these different methods were to be described at this point, the details of each procedure would be difficult to recall when the results are presented. Consequently, only the Conflict Tactics Scales is described here. The measures on nonfamily assault and other crime are described in the sections where the data on these variables are presented.

1. *Intrafamily Assault.* Assaults within the family were measured by the Conflict Tactics Scales (Straus 1979, 1988). This instrument has been used and refined in numerous studies (e.g., Straus 1974; Jorgensen 1977; Steinmetz 1977; Allen and Straus 1980; Hornung, McCullough, and Sugimoto 1981; Cate et al. 1982; Giles-Sims 1983; Henton et al. 1983; Arias and Beach 1987; Barling et al. 1987).[4] Four different studies have established that the Conflict Tactics Scales (CTS) measure three factorially separate variables (Jorgensen 1977; Straus 1979; Schumm et al. 1982; Barling et al. 1987): reasoning, verbal aggression, and physical violence. The use of the items in the physical violence factor to measure child and spouse assault is described below.

2. *Format of the CTS.* The introduction to the Conflict Tactics Scales asks respondents to think of situations in the past year when they had a disagreement or were angry with a specified family member and to indicate how often they engaged in each of the acts included in the CTS. The student study version of the CTS contained the following physical violence items: threw something at the other family member; pushed, grabbed, or shoved; slapped or spanked, kicked, bit, or hit with a fist; and hit or tried to hit with something.

For the National Study, the CTS was revised by adding three additional items for purposes of measuring serious assaults: beat up the other family member; threatened with a knife or gun; and used a knife or gun. Finally, still another addition was made in the revised version of the CTS used in the 1985 National Resurvey: an item asking about

---

[4] The reliability and validity of the Conflict Tactics Scales have been assessed in several studies over the fifteen-year period of their development. See Straus (1979) for evidence of internal consistency, reliability, concurrent validity, and construct validity. Other investigators have confirmed some of these findings. See, e.g., Jouriles and O'Leary (1985), Jorgensen (1977), and Schumm et al. (1982).

choking was included in the spouse index, and an item asking about burning or scalding was added to the parental violence index.

3. *Measure of Child Assault.*   Two criteria were used to identify families in which child assault occurred. The first criterion is whether the parent engaged in any assaultive act in the CTS list that is more severe than pushing, grabbing, slapping, shoving, spanking, or throwing things at the child. Thus, the assaultive acts are kicked, bit, hit with fist, hit with an object, beat up, threatened with a knife or gun, and used a knife or gun. If the parent engaged in one or more of the assaultive acts, it was counted as a case of child assault.

The second criterion was high frequency of violence, irrespective of whether it was severe enough to fall into our assault category. If a parent engaged in any of the violent acts more often than 90 percent of the parents in the sample, we classified the family as a case involving child assault. The number of assaults during the year which put a family in the top 10 percent varied from sample to sample: twenty-eight or more for the Student Sample, twenty-five or more for the National Survey, and twenty-three or more for the National Resurvey.

4. *Measure of Spouse Assault.*   The procedure for determining whether spouse assault had occurred was simpler since the legal right to hit a child is not paralleled by the legal right to hit a spouse.[5] Consequently, we classified a family as one in which spouse assault was present if any one or more of the CTS violence acts were reported for the year of the study, regardless of whether they were acts of minor violence (such as slapping or throwing things at the spouse) or acts with a higher risk of injury that we classified as "severe violence," such as kicking, biting, punching, and choking.

5. *Family Assault Type.*   A basic issue addressed in this essay is the extent to which intrafamily violence pervades all family roles or is specific to one role such as that of parent or husband. To answer this question, and to provide a basis for investigating the links between intrafamily violence and violence and other crime outside the family, we created a typology by cross-classifying the child-assault and spouse-assault measures, as shown in figure 1. Four types of family assault are created. They include Type I, nonassaultive; Type II, child assault

---

[5] Under common law, husbands had the right to "physically chastise an errant wife" (see Calvert 1974). Although the courts ceased to recognize this right by the late nineteenth century (see Pleck, in this volume), de facto norms that tolerate such behavior continue to exist (Straus 1976, 1980).

Child Assault

Absent   Present

	Absent	Present
Absent	Type I nonassaultive	Type II child assault only
Present	Type III spouse assault only	Type IV both child and spouse assault

Spouse
Assault

FIG. 1.—Family assault types

only; Type III, spouse assault only; and Type IV, both child and
spouse assult. It should be noted that, although Type I families are
non*assaultive* (as we operationally defined assault), this does not mean
that every family in that category is non*violent* because almost all American parents use physical punishment. For the National Survey sample,
this ranged from 97 percent of the parents of three-year-olds to 28
percent of parents of seventeen-year-olds (Straus 1983). Nevertheless,
for stylistic variation we sometimes refer to violent and nonviolent
families.

IV. Rates of Assault in American Families

The first question to be answered on the basis of these three surveys is
the extent to which a general pattern of family assault cuts across child
assault, spouse assault, and assaults by children within the family.

A. Assault in Multiple Relationships in the Family

Research is accumulating that shows a link between wife assault and
child assault. The extent and nature of this link is difficult to determine
since the data on this issue come largely from clinical samples. Studies
of wife assault among shelter residents consistently find between 25–45
percent of battered women reporting violence against one or more of
the children in the family (Hilberman and Munson 1978; Roy 1982;
Fagan, Stewart, and Hansen 1983; Stacey and Shupe 1983). Studies of
abusive parents also indicate a higher likelihood of spouse assault in
families where a child or children are at risk of physical injury. Case

comparison studies have found abusive parents to be more abusive toward spouses and generally to exhibit more aversive and less prosocial behavior than nonassaultive parents (reviewed in Wolfe [1985]).

It cannot be determined from these studies what proportion of families in the general population are multiassaultive because data are based on clinical samples, and measures of violence and assault are not always standardized. The exact nature of the link between wife assault and child assault is also a matter of some controversy. Is it the assaulter who is generally violent toward wife and children or is it the victim who strikes out against other family members? The existing literature seems to support the idea that violent husbands are also more likely to be violent fathers. Washburn and Frieze (1981) found that 25 percent of the battered women they interviewed reported that their husbands were violent toward their children "several times" or "often" during the last year compared with 4 percent of the nonbattered women they interviewed. Telch and Lindquist (1984) also report that violent husbands are significantly more likely to be violent fathers when compared with nonviolent husbands. Straus (1983), in a national survey of 2,143 households, found that men who frequently and severely assault their wives are significantly more likely than nonviolent husbands to assault their children. This study also found that the more violent a husband is toward his wife, the more violent she is toward her children. Even women who were subjected to "minor" violence such as pushes and slaps had more than double the rate of frequent, severe assaults on their children than wives who were not subjected to assaults by their partners.

The literature does indicate a link between assaults on wives and on children in the family. However, the extent and nature of this link is not well understood. The application of the typology in figure 1 to the three samples in this research provides more definitive information on the extent to which intrafamily violence pervades all family roles or is role specific.

B. Prevalence of Four Patterns of Family Assault

The first column of table 1 shows that almost three-quarters of the families in these three samples were nonassaultive. However, that same column of data shows that some form of assault took place in over one out of four American families during the years of these surveys. The uniformity of results across the three studies is remarkable. As with

TABLE 1

Distribution of Family Assault Types in Three Samples (%)

Study	Family Assault Type				Percentage of Assaultive Families That Are Type IV V
	Non-abusive I	Child Assault Only II	Spouse Assault Only III	Both Child Assault and Spouse Assault IV	
1972 Student Survey (N = 334)	73.1	11.1	10.1	5.7	21.1
1975 National Survey (N = 1,092)	68.1	15.8	9.2	6.9	21.6
1985 National Resurvey (N = 2,688)	69.6	12.4	12.4	5.6	18.4

most findings, one can choose to interpret the results as either "fully 25 percent" or "only 25 percent" (Hirschi and Selvin 1967).

Of particular interest is the uniformity in rates of multiassaultive families, as shown in column 4—between 5.6 and 6.9 percent of all intact families with children report both forms of assault. According to the U.S. Bureau of the Census (1986), in 1984 there were 24,700,000 two-parent families with at least one child in the household. Based on this number, the percentages in table 1 indicate that from 1.4 to 1.7 million children live with parents who assault one another *and* their children. The actual number of children who experience parental assault and who witness assaults between their parents is surely much higher than the 1.4 to 1.7 million estimate because underreporting of assaults is almost inevitable and because many of these families contain more than one child.

Column 5 in table 1 gives the number of multiassaultive families (Type IV) as a percentage of all assaultive families (sum of Types II, III, and IV). Again, there is a good deal of consistency across data sets. These rates indicate that "fully" a fifth of all abusive families are generally assaultive, or that both types of assault occur in "only" a fifth of violent families.

C. *Gender Differences in the Relation between Spouse and Child Assault*

The first column of table 2 shows that, even in the absence of spouse assault, the rate of assaults on children in families is high: about one out of six American children was severely assaulted by a parent in the year

TABLE 2

Child Assault Rate for Each Spouse Assault Type by Gender of
Parent (1985 National Resurvey)

	No Spouse Assault (N)	Wife Only Is Assaultive (N)	Husband Only Is Assaultive (N)	Both Husband and Wife Are Assaultive (N)
A. By mothers	15.5	28.6	28.9	36.1
	(1,213)	(63)	(76)	(138)
B. By fathers	14.7	19.2	15.7	41.1
	(992)	(62)	(41)	(103)

NOTE.—For rate of assault on children by mothers and by fathers: $\chi^2 = 45.81$; df = 3; $p < .001$; $N = 1,198$. Rates are per 100 and are therefore equal to percentages.

of this survey. Moreover, as previously suggested, not all parents who kicked or bit a child will describe such events in an interview, so the actual rate is probably much higher.

The second and third columns of table 2 show that, when either spouse assaults the other, the rate of assaults on children increases, especially assaults by mothers. The last column of the table shows that when both parents physically assault each other, children are at the highest risk of also being assaulted, especially by fathers.

V. Assaultive Families and Violence by Children in the Family

Violence by children in the family can occur against siblings or against parents. Each form is described below.

A. Sibling Violence

Are children who experience physical assault from parents, witness assaults between their mothers and fathers, or both more likely than other children to engage in violence toward family and nonfamily members? Table 3 shows sibling violence rates for children six years of age and older[6] in the four family assault types. The results are very consistent across all three data sets. The rate of sibling violence is higher

---

[6] The measure of sibling violence in this table includes all of the violent acts in the CTS, not just those with a high potential for injury. For the 1975 survey it was also possible to do the analysis using a measure of "severe violence," the results of which are presented below.

TABLE 3

Rate of Sibling Violence by Parent-to-Child Assault and Spouse Assault (Three Samples)

	Child Assault			ANOVA	
Spouse Assault	Absent (N)	Present (N)	Total (N)	Effect	F
A. 1972 student survey (CTS scores):					
Absent	54.5 (189)	78.6 (29)	66.6 (218)	child assault	7.65**
Present	75.9 (28)	93.8 (16)	84.9 (44)	spouse assault	6.04*
Total	65.2 (217)	86.2 (45)	75.7 (262)	child assault × spouse assault df = 3, N = 262	.12
B. 1975 National Survey (CTS scores):					
Absent	67.5 (452)	93.4 (76)	80.5 (528)	child assault	17.11***
Present	85.7 (56)	91.7 (36)	88.7 (92)	spouse assault	4.98*
Total	76.6 (508)	92.6 (112)	84.6 (620)	child assault × spouse assault df = 3, N = 620	3.24
C. 1985 National Resurvey ("fights with children in the family"):					
Absent	3.6 (1,289)	8.5 (141)	6.0 (1,430)	child assault	10.77***
Present	6.0 (168)	11.5 (84)	8.8 (252)	spouse assault	2.99
Total	4.8 (1,457)	10.0 (225)	7.4 (1,682)	child assault × spouse assault df = 3, N = 1,680	.37

NOTE.—Rates are per 100 and are therefore equal to percentages.

* $p < .05$.
** $p < .01$.
*** $p < .001$.

among children in families in which child assault and spouse assault are present and, in two of the three samples, highest of all when both child assault and spouse assault are present. However, the analysis of variance shows that sibling violence is more strongly associated with child assault than with spouse assault.

Several points must be noted about data in table 3. First, the rates that appear in cells for the 1985 survey data are much lower than those in both the 1972 and 1975 surveys. This is because, unlike the two earlier surveys, the 1985 survey did not measure sibling violence through the CTS. Instead of asking whether a variety of forms of physical violence occurred between children, as is done in the CTS, the 1985 survey asked only whether the respondent considered "fights with children in the family" to be a problem. The discrepancy between the CTS rates and the percent of parents who regard violence between siblings as a problem is a reflection of the acceptance of this type of violence in American families. This issue is discussed further in Straus (1983). The important issue for this essay, however, is the pattern of sibling assault in relation to other forms of family violence. All three data sets are in accord on this issue.

Second, these data *cannot* be used to posit a causal relation between sibling assault and other forms of family violence. All three surveys are cross-sectional and can demonstrate only that sibling violence and other forms of intrafamily assault co-occur.

Third, while boys are more likely than girls to engage in sibling violence, separate analysis of the data in table 3 for boys and girls revealed no major differences in main or interaction effects of child and spouse assault on rates of sibling assault. Thus, the pattern of relationships between sibling violence and violence in other family relationships for both boys and girls is very similar, although boys display more assaultive behavior toward siblings.

Fourth, the effect of child assault and spouse assault is more strongly related to rates of sibling violence when severity of sibling assault is taken into account. The version of the CTS used in the 1975 National Survey enables a "severe violence" or "sibling assault" index to be computed on the basis of the occurrence of items such as punching, kicking, biting, and attacking with weapons. Use of that measure reveals a similar but stronger relation of child and spouse assault to sibling violence than is shown in table 3. For example, 37 percent of the 498 children from otherwise nonassaultive families severely assaulted a sibling during the survey year. For children from families in which both child and spouse assault are present, 100 percent of the twelve children in this type of family severely assaulted a brother or sister during the survey year. These results suggest that perhaps not only minor violence, but violence that is severe enough to be classified as a criminal assault, is a learned family behavior.[7]

Part A of table 4 examines the rate of sibling violence controlling for family socioeconomic status.[8] There are no significant differences in rates of sibling violence for children from blue- or white-collar families. Child assault victimization is significantly related to sibling violence for both socioeconomic status groups, and the highest rates of sibling violence occur among children from multiassaultive families regardless of social class.

B. Child-to-Parent Violence[9]

Table 5 indicates that siblings are not the only targets of assault by children from multiassaultive families. Parents are more likely to experience violence from their children when children have been assaulted by their parents or observe assaults between the parents. The results from both the surveys that included the necessary data show that the rate of child-to-parent violence among children six years of age and older is higher for children living in households where both child assault and spouse assault occurred. In the 1975 National Survey there is a very strong main effect for child assault. While the effect for child assault is also strong in the 1985 survey, the interaction between child assault and spouse assault is even stronger. It seems that child-to-parent violence cannot be explained simply in terms of retaliation for child assault. The rate of child violence against parents is eighteen times higher in multiassaultive families than in families in which only one form of assault occurs.

[7] Whether it is sound social policy to invoke the criminal justice process in such cases is another matter, and one that is fraught with dilemmas, some of which are discussed in Straus and Lincoln (1985).

[8] For this analysis, each spouse's occupation was classified as "manual" or "nonmanual" (alternative terms are blue collar and white collar, and working class and middle class) using the Bureau of Labor Statistics revised Occupational Classification system. Each Bureau of Labor Statistics occupation code was classified as either manual or nonmanual using the list of occupations falling into these categories by Rice (see Robinson et al. 1969). All analyses were run separately using wife's occupational ranking and husband's occupational ranking. Results were not significantly different. The analyses presented in this essay were done controlling for husband's occupational ranking.

[9] The measure of child-to-parent violence, like the measure of sibling violence in the previous section, uses all the violent acts in the CTS; i.e., it is not restricted to the acts of "severe" violence.

TABLE 4

Violence Rates of Children by Family Assault Type, Controlling for Socioeconomic Status (1985 National Resurvey)

A. Family Assault Type

	Blue Collar				White Collar			
Dependent Variable[a]	Non-assaultive (N = 631)	Child Assault Only (N = 84)	Spouse Assault Only (N = 93)	Child Assault and Spouse Assault (N = 54)	Non-assaultive (N = 611)	Child Assault Only (N = 54)	Spouse Assault Only (N = 73)	Child Assault and Spouse Assault (N = 28)
A. Sibling violence	3.6	10.1	6.2	13.1	3.1	6.5	5.8	9.1
B. Child-to-parent violence	.2	.4	.6	6.6	.0	.0	.7	.0
C. Nonfamily violence	2.9	10.7	3.4	17.0	1.2	4.9	2.5	3.5

B. ANOVA F-Values

	Sibling Assault	Child-Parent Assault	Nonfamily Violence
Child assault	11.89***	8.17**	28.83***
Spouse assault	3.47	7.81**	1.67
Socioeconomic status	.70	2.60	8.13**
Child × spouse	.01	13.66***	.86
Child × socioeconomic status	1.02	4.91*	6.22*
Spouse × socioeconomic status	.00	4.77*	.27
Child × spouse × socioeconomic status	.01	8.07**	2.14

NOTE.—Rates are per 100 and are therefore equal to percentages.

[a] The dependent variables in this table were measured by a question that asked the respondent if any of a list of social psychological problems caused "any special difficulties" for the child within the past year. Thus, the data reflect a combination of whether the acts occurred and, if they did, whether the parent considered them to be a problem for the child. For this reason, the rates are lower than the rates of violent acts by children obtained using the CTS, which requires only that the act occurred. The three items from the list used to obtain the data in this table are: "physical fights with kids who live in your house," "physical fights with adults who live in your house," and "physical fights with adults who don't live in your house."

* $p < .05$.
** $p < .01$.
*** $p < .001$.

TABLE 5

Rate of Child-to-Parent Violence by Parent-to-Child and Spouse Assault (1975 and 1985 National Surveys)

	Child Assault			ANOVA	
Spouse Assault	Absent (N)	Present (N)	Total (N)	Effect	F
A. 1975 National Survey (CTS scores):					
Absent	7.9	27.6	17.8	child assault	26.40***
	(570)	(87)	(657)	spouse assault	2.45
Present	12.9	37.8	25.4	child assault × spouse assault	.27
	(62)	(37)	(99)	df = 3, N = 756	
Total	10.4	32.7	21.6		
	(632)	(124)	(756)		
B. 1985 National Resurvey ("fights with nonfamily children"):					
Absent	.1	.3	.2	child assault	12.46***
	(1,289)	(141)	(1,430)	spouse assault	11.30***
Present	.3	5.5	2.9	child assault × spouse assault	23.79***
	(168)	(84)	(252)	df = 3, N = 1,682	
Total	.2	2.9	1.6		
	(1,457)	(225)	(1,682)		

NOTE.—Rates are per 100 and are therefore equal to percentages.
*** p < .001.

There are no significant differences between boys and girls on this measure, but there are differences due to family socioeconomic status. Part B of table 4 indicates that the rate of child-to-parent violence is higher among blue-collar families. Furthermore, children from blue-collar, multiassaultive families have rates of violence toward parents that are nine times higher than any other type of family constellation.

VI. Assaultive Families and Violence and Crime[10] by Children outside the Family

A consistent theme in the criminology and family violence literatures is the relation between experiencing violence as part of one's family socialization and later antisocial behavior. Both the experience of parental violence and witnessing spousal violence while growing up have been found in the childhood backgrounds of wife assaulters (see Hotaling and Sugarman [1986] for a review), child assaulters (Alfaro 1978; Potts, Herzberger, and Holland 1979; Gelles 1980), violent criminals (McCord 1979; Sedgely and Lund 1979), and persons who approve of the use of violence (Owens and Straus 1975).

While the *long-term* effects of exposure to family violence are clear-cut, the results of studies of the *short-term* effects are mixed and conceptually confusing. Some research has found a strong link between child assault and adolescent aggression or delinquency (Glueck and Glueck 1950; Strasberg 1978; Conger 1984; Straus 1985), while other research finds little relationship (Morse, Sahler, and Friedman 1970; Elmer, Evans, and Reinhart 1977). Other research suggests that some assaulted children become withdrawn rather than aggressive (Martin and Beezley 1974; George and Main 1979), and still other research suggests that the role of family violence in promoting delinquency is exaggerated relative to the influence of peers, schools, and a host of other socializing influences (Bolton, Reich, and Gutierres 1977; Hawkins and Weis 1980; Fagan and Wexler 1987).

To complicate the issue further, several dimensions of harmful family behaviors are often lumped together as "child abuse" and examined for their effect on children's antisocial behavior, thereby making it difficult to determine whether assault in the family is a true risk factor of adolescent difficulties (Loeber and Dishion 1983; Loeber and Stouthamer-Loeber 1986). Studies have used a variety of measures of

---

[10] Although the term "crime" is used here and in the title of the essay, some items to be analyzed are not criminal but could best be called conduct problems. Nevertheless, the majority of issues addressed in this section concern illegal behavior by children and adolescents.

TABLE 6

Nonfamily Assault Rates of Children by Parent-to-Child and Spouse Assault (Two Samples)

Spouse Assault	Child Assault			ANOVA	
	Absent (N)	Present (N)	Total (N)	Effect	F
A. 1972 student survey ("child used violence against nonfamily person"):					
Absent	34.3	37.1	35.7	child assault	1.41
	(239)	(35)	(274)	spouse assault	2.29
Present	39.4	63.2	51.3	child assault × spouse assault	1.64
	(33)	(19)	(52)	df = 3, N = 326	
Total	36.9	50.2	36.8		
	(272)	(54)	(326)		
B. 1985 National Resurvey ("fights with nonfamily children"):					
Absent	2.1	8.2	5.2	child assault	15.59***
	(1,281)	(141)	(1,422)	spouse assault	.58
Present	3.0	12.1	7.6	child assault × spouse assault	2.75
	(168)	(84)	(252)	df = 3, N = 1,674	
Total	2.6	10.2	6.4		
	(1,449)	(225)	(1,674)		

NOTE.—Rates are per 100 and are therefore equal to percentages.

*** p < .001.

"parental lack of affection," "lack of supervision," "excessive discipline," "rejection," "neglect," and "abuse" but have rarely directly
measured the effects on children of parental assaultive behavior (Lane
and Davis 1987).

Many of the problems involved in establishing a link between childhood exposure to assaultive behavior in the family and juvenile delinquency arise from the use in most studies of samples of children who
have come to the attention of agencies for their delinquency, rather
than general population surveys. Without appropriate control groups,
the proportion of children exposed to violence in their family who do
not become delinquent cannot be determined. It is almost certainly a
large proportion; over one out of four children grow up in violent
families (see table 1).

The data used for the analyses in this essay avoid that problem
because they do not derive from clinical samples. This alleviates one of
the major obstacles to answering the question of whether children who
have been the victim of parental assault, have witnessed spouse assault,
or both are more likely to be violent toward persons outside the family
and to engage in acts of delinquency. Furthermore, the sample for the
1985 National Resurvey contains enough cases to permit use of controls
for the separate effects of sex of child, severity of spousal violence
witnessed by the child, and family socioeconomic status.

A. Nonfamily Violence by Children

Part A of table 6 shows that, in the 1972 student survey, there were
no significant main or interaction effects associated with being the victim of child assault or witnessing spouse assault on assaultive behavior
outside of the family. Nevertheless, the differences are large. The nineteen students who were exposed to *both* forms of assault in the family
have double the high rate of nonfamily assault compared to students
from nonassaultive families (63.2 percent vs. 34.3 percent).

The 1985 National Resurvey (part B of table 6) found a strong relation between parental assault and assaults by children outside the
home. Children who are *both* the victims of parental assaults and who
witness spouse assault have a rate of assault against nonfamily children
six times higher than children from nonassaultive families (12.1 percent
vs. 2.1 percent).[11]

---

[11] The first point in the discussion of table 3 also explains why the rates in part B of
table 6 are so much lower than the rates in part A. In addition, part A is based on self-
reports, and part B is based on those incidents that were known to the parent who was
interviewed.

Separate analyses of the 1985 data for boys and girls indicate that the rate of assault outside the family by boys is much higher than the rate for girls. Despite this, the pattern of findings is very similar for each sex. For boys, a significant main effect was found for child assault victimization, while for girls there was both a significant main effect on child assault and a significant interaction effect between child assault and witnessing spouse assault on out-of-home assault rates.

The findings did not vary when controlling for the severity of spouse assault witnessed by the child. Again, whether children viewed minor or severe acts of violence between their parents, their assault rate outside the family was equally high.

B. Control for Socioeconomic Status

Line C of table 4, part A, shows the relation between family assault type, assaults by children outside the home, and family socioeconomic status using the 1985 Resurvey data. The results show a significant main effect for both child assault and socioeconomic status and a significant interaction effect between child assault and socioeconomic status on outside-family assault by children. The rate of outside assault is significantly higher for children from blue-collar families, compared with the rate for children from white-collar families, but for blue-collar and white-collar children, the rate of extrafamily assault is three times higher for victims of child assault compared with rates for children from nonassaultive families. Children from multiassaultive blue-collar families have an inordinately high rate of assault against nonfamily members.

These results suggest that one of the short-term effects of child exposure to family violence is an increase in assaults by children outside the family. The effect of experiencing assaults by parents is stronger than the modeling effect of observing assaults between parents for children from both blue- and white-collar families. An important conclusion of these analyses is that, while children from white-collar families are less violent than lower socioeconomic status children, there are important within-group differences. Specifically, assaults within the family are related to assaults by children outside the family to the same extent, regardless of social class.

C. Nonviolent Crime by Children

Although social learning theory provides a perspective for understanding the ways in which violence can be learned through direct experience and modeling processes, explanations of nonviolent antisocial acts that focus on these same processes are not plausible. However, it can be argued that being assaulted by a parent weakens the bonds between child and parent and that witnessing physical assaults between parents weakens one's allegiance to societal norms. While the data do not allow for an investigation of the mediating processes, the analyses presented in table 7 do indicate a link between family assaults and nonviolent antisocial acts on the part of children.

Table 7 presents nineteen tests of the hypothesis that nonviolent delinquent acts are related to intrafamily violence. Overall, the highest rates of delinquent behaviors occur in "child-assault only" families (thirteen of nineteen comparisons). This pattern is most prominent for stealing. Three items measuring this behavior—"taking things worth less than $2.00," "taking things worth more than $50.00," and "child steals"—are consistently related to the presence of child assault. Two items measuring property destruction show an inconsistent relation to child assault. A measure of "vandalism" in the 1985 resurvey is strongly related to child assault, while in the 1972 student study, "destroyed property" occurred about equally often among children in nonassaultive and assaultive families. The same inconsistent pattern is evident on items concerning the use of alcohol and drugs.

Perhaps the most sensitive indicator of child problems in the community concerns involvement with police. Two data sets contain items concerning contact with the police. The 1972 student survey asked whether respondents were "questioned by police." Children from families in which multiple assaults occur are significantly more likely to report police involvement. The 1985 National Resurvey asked parents whether the referent child "got arrested" in the last year and found that child assault victims are significantly more likely to have been arrested than are children from other family types.

As is true for other rates of child antisocial behavior, the rate of nonviolent delinquency for boys is significantly higher than the rate for girls. Once again, however, the pattern of findings linking family violence type to delinquency is similar for both sexes, at least for minor acts of delinquency. For more serious problems such as stealing and contact with police, the female offense rate is very low and follows no pattern in terms of exposure to assault in the family.

D. Control for Socioeconomic Status

Data from the 1985 National Resurvey in table 8 examine the link between exposure to family violence and conduct problems, controlling for social class. The most important finding is that socioeconomic status

TABLE 7
Juvenile Delinquency Rates by Parent-to-Child and Spouse Assault (Three Samples)

Data Sets and Indicators	Family Assault Type				ANOVA	
	Nonassaultive (N)	Child Assault Only (N)	Spouse Assault Only (N)	Both Child Assault and Spouse Assault (N)	Effect	F
A. 1972 student survey:						
Nye-Short Delinquency Scale (one or more items)	85.3 (224)	100.0 (36)	93.1 (29)	100.0 (14)	child assault	13.82***
					spouse assault	1.20
					child assault × spouse assault	1.26
Drove with no license	20.3 (237)	40.5 (37)	35.3 (34)	26.3 (19)	child assault	7.88**
					spouse assault	.28
					child assault × spouse assault	4.59*
Took things worth less than $2.00	35.1 (239)	59.5 (37)	29.4 (34)	47.4 (19)	child assault	8.16**
					spouse assault	1.52
					child assault × spouse assault	1.27
Destroyed property	23.8 (239)	29.7 (37)	32.4 (34)	31.6 (19)	child assault	2.00
					spouse assault	.19
					child assault × spouse assault	1.84
Took things worth more than $50.00	2.1 (237)	13.5 (37)	3.0 (33)	.0 (18)	child assault	10.59***
					spouse assault	1.83
					child assault × spouse assault	6.15*
Defied parents	57.6 (238)	80.6 (36)	76.5 (34)	94.4 (18)	child assault	11.46***
					spouse assault	11.69***
					child assault × spouse assault	.88
Used drugs	36.5 (230)	32.4 (37)	31.3 (32)	33.3 (15)	child assault	.53
					spouse assault	1.37
					child assault × spouse assault	.93
Questioned by police	21.3 (239)	29.7 (37)	17.6 (34)	36.8 (19)	child assault	1.94
					spouse assault	.57
					child assault × spouse assault	7.47**

						F
Disciplining problem in school	11.7 (239)	29.7 (37)	20.6 (34)	21.1 (19)	child assault	6.54**
					spouse assault	1.26
					child assault × spouse assault	.12
Kicked out of school	2.9 (239)	2.7 (37)	.0 (34)	15.8 (19)	child assault	1.94
					spouse assault	.57
					child assault × spouse assault	7.47**
B. 1975 National Survey:						
Child caught doing something illegal	4.3 (599)	5.0 (100)	11.3 (71)	4.3 (47)	child assault	.14
					spouse assault	3.16
					child assault × spouse assault	1.87
Kicked out of school/suspended	2.2 (602)	4.0 (100)	5.6 (71)	4.3 (47)	child assault	1.06
					spouse assault	2.63
					child assault × spouse assault	1.84
C. 1985 National Resurvey:						
Vandalism	.9 (1,289)	7.1 (141)	.8 (168)	3.6 (84)	child assault	31.09***
					spouse assault	.96
					child assault × spouse assault	3.59
Stealing	.7 (1,289)	6.7 (141)	.7 (168)	4.6 (84)	child assault	34.05***
					spouse assault	.50
					child assault × spouse assault	4.37*
Drinking	.9 (1,289)	2.9 (141)	1.4 (168)	1.7 (84)	child assault	7.85***
					spouse assault	.44
					child assault × spouse assault	6.14*
Used drugs	.2 (1,289)	1.1 (141)	.5 (168)	1.7 (84)	child assault	8.59**
					spouse assault	5.23*
					child assault × spouse assault	22.99***
Got arrested	.6 (1,289)	3.5 (141)	.0 (168)	.0 (84)	child assault	11.22***
					spouse assault	1.05
					child assault × spouse assault	.95
Disciplining problem in school	4.1 (1,289)	14.7 (141)	4.5 (168)	16.2 (84)	child assault	32.61***
					spouse assault	.83
					child assault × spouse assault	.26
Failing in school	9.1 (1,289)	19.3 (141)	12.3 (168)	17.6 (84)	child assault	15.68***
					spouse assault	2.02
					child assault × spouse assault	.97

NOTE.—Rates are per 100 and are therefore equal to percentages.

* $p < .05$.
** $p < .01$.
*** $p < .001$.

TABLE 8

Delinquency Rate by Family Assault Type and Socioeconomic Status (1985 National Resurvey)

A. Family Assault Type

Dependent Variable	Blue Collar				White Collar			
	Non-assaultive (N = 631)	Child Assault Only (N = 84)	Spouse Assault Only (N = 93)	Child Assault and Spouse Assault (N = 54)	Non-assaultive (N = 611)	Child Assault Only (N = 54)	Spouse Assault Only (N = 73)	Child Assault and Spouse Assault (N = 28)
Vandalism	1.1	7.0	.8	2.8	.5	7.7	.9	.0
Stealing	.5	6.0	1.2	2.8	.9	8.1	.0	8.4
Child drinking	1.0	4.8	2.0	2.7	.7	.0	.7	.0
Child drug use	.2	1.8	.3	2.7	.3	.0	.7	.0
Child arrested	.5	4.1	.0	.0	.8	2.7	.0	.0
Failing in school	10.1	18.1	12.9	19.1	8.2	21.7	11.9	15.9
School discipline problem	4.6	16.3	5.2	19.1	3.8	12.6	3.6	8.2

B. ANOVA F-Values

	Vandalism	Stealing	Child Drinking	Child Drug Use	Child Arrested	Failing in School	School Discipline Problem
Child assault	35.14***	40.51***	3.18	3.97*	9.39**	14.35***	38.04***
Spouse assault	1.19	.41	.01	.55	4.88*	.83	.04
Socioeconomic status	.15	1.17	2.56	.26	.04	.84	1.91
Child × spouse	3.08	1.12	1.18	.12	4.25	.46	.01
Child × socioeconomic status	.74	3.27	4.80*	5.15*	.78	.88	1.88
Spouse × socioeconomic status	.29	.04	.02	.03	.01	.05	.53
Child × spouse × socio-economic status	.10	1.75	.74	.38	.33	.56	.67

NOTE.—Rates are per 100 and are therefore equal to percentages.

$*p < .05$.
$**p < .01$.
$***p < .001$.

exerts no significant main effects on conduct problems of any kind. Even for property offenses such as vandalism and stealing and for arrest rates, there are no significant differences between children from blue- or white-collar families in rates of conduct disorders. In six of seven separate analyses, there is a significant effect due to child assault victimization on conduct problems outside the family but little evidence for an association between growing up in a multiassaultive family and conduct problems.

E. Summary

It appears that children assaulted by parents are more violent toward brothers, sisters, parents, and persons outside the family. They are also more likely to be involved in property crime, to have adjustment difficulties in school, and to be involved with the police. It is not possible to determine the causal direction of this relation with the data used in these analyses, but family assault victimization is clearly linked to antisocial behavior.

Assault by children and other conduct problems are more strongly related to being assaulted by parents than to witnessing assaults between parents. However, children from multiassaultive families have higher rates of child-to-parent violence and violence toward persons outside the family. These two variables are also related to family socio-economic status, with blue-collar children having higher rates of assaulting parents and nonfamily members. No social class differences occur in rates of sibling violence or rates of conduct problems among children.

These results support and specify the theory that family assault trains children in the use of violent behavior. Children who are exposed to multiple forms of assault in the family are more likely to be violent themselves, especially toward parents and peers. These types of assault are also more likely to be committed by boys and children from blue-collar families.

VII. Victimization Effects

The process linking victimization to aggression is not well understood. After all, why would victims of assault be more likely to be violent themselves and more likely to experience a variety of conduct problems? Straus (1985) suggested that victims of violence tend to lose faith in the efficacy and fairness of the world, a belief that is conducive to conforming behavior. Another interpretation may be that victims of violence often see firsthand that violence is effective and that offenders are rarely sanctioned for their behavior. The victim may generalize this to other forms of deviant behavior and feel freer to engage in antisocial behavior.

We have no data to address these speculations. The cross-sectional data presented in this essay cannot demonstrate whether persons are victimized *before* or *after* they become victimizers. But it is clear from previous analyses that there is a strong link between being the victim of assault within the family and assault and other conduct problems on the part of children outside of the family. This section examines whether victimization effects exist among adults who are the targets of assaults within families.

A. Assaults by Assaulted Husbands

Part A of table 9 indicates that husbands who have been assaulted by their wives, and are in a family in which child assault occurs, are more likely to engage in verbal aggression and physical assault outside the family than are men who are not assaulted, and they are also more likely to have been arrested in the previous twelve months. A significant main effect for assault by wives was found for each indicator of the husband's nonfamily aggression and violent behavior. Although the highest rates of nonfamily aggression and assault by husbands occurs when there are both assaults by the wife and assaults on children, the results show a stronger main effect of assault by wives.

This pattern of results is very similar for both blue-collar and white-collar males. Among both groups of men, the rate of nonfamily verbal aggression and assault and the arrest rate is highest for men in multi-assaultive families. However, blue-collar males who are victims of family assaults commit higher rates of outside family assaults.

B. Assaults by Assaulted Wives

The analyses of variance reported in part B of table 9 show that being assaulted by husbands is significantly related to the probability of verbal aggression, assault, and arrest of female victims. Thus, the analysis in part B reveals the same pattern of nonfamily assault and arrest of wives who are the victims of assaults by their husbands as was shown in part A for husbands who have been assaulted by their wives.

Rates of assault outside the family by victims of wife assault show an

TABLE 9

Rates of Nonfamily Verbal and Physical Assault by Family Assault Type and Gender of Adult Victims (1985 National Resurvey)

Dependent Variable	Nonviolent (N)	Family Assault Type			ANOVA	
		Wife-to-Husband Assault, No Child Assault (N)	No Wife-to-Husband Assault, Child Assault (N)	Both Child and Wife-to-Husband Assault (N)	Effect	F
A. For husbands who are victims of assault by wives:						
Husband got angry at nonfamily person and yelled at him/her	49.8 (1,922)	57.9 (359)	68.6 (243)	81.1 (122)	child assault / assault by wife / child assault × wife assault	12.28*** / 51.19*** / .36
Husband got angry at nonfamily person and smashed something	5.9 (1,953)	11.2 (360)	20.6 (241)	26.8 (120)	child assault / assault by wife / child assault × wife assault	11.77*** / 88.28*** / .95
Husband got into fight with nonfamily member and hit him/her	2.3 (1,954)	4.3 (362)	9.1 (242)	9.5 (122)	child assault / assault by wife / child assault × wife assault	3.69 / 34.36*** / .27
Husband got into fight with nonfamily member and injured him/her	.7 (1,959)	.6 (362)	1.7 (242)	5.6 (121)	child assault / assault by wife / child assault × wife assault	2.49 / 16.53*** / 11.33***

Husband got arrested in last twelve months	1.4 (881)	.0 (152)	2.9 (110)	6.5 (54)	child assault	.13
					assault by wife	7.39**
					child assault × wife assault	4.43*
B. For wives who are victims of assault by husbands:						
Wife got angry at nonfamily person and yelled at him/her	42.1 (1,945)	47.9 (360)	54.2 (234)	69.2 (118)	child assault	11.14***
					assault by husband	28.22***
					child assault × husband assault	2.59
Wife got angry at nonfamily person and smashed something	4.0 (1,955)	5.7 (358)	9.7 (233)	18.3 (119)	child assault	7.16**
					assault by husband	35.82***
					child assault × husband assault	5.22*
Wife got in fight with nonfamily person and hit him/her	.7 (1,960)	1.0 (364)	1.8 (237)	3.7 (121)	child assault	1.55
					assault by husband	17.42***
					child assault × husband assault	1.45
Wife got in fight with nonfamily person and injured him/her	.2 (1,965)	.0 (364)	.7 (237)	.0 (121)	child assault	1.34
					assault by husband	4.27*
					child assault × husband assault	1.80
Wife got arrested in last twelve months	.3 (1,067)	.8 (206)	2.8 (142)	1.9 (72)	child assault	.17
					assault by husband	11.84**
					child assault × husband assault	1.23

NOTE.—Rates are per 100 and are therefore equal to percentages.

* $p < .05$.
** $p < .01$.
*** $p < .001$.

identical relation to social class as was the case for males. Both blue-collar and white-collar women in families where multiple assault occurs have the highest rate of outside family aggression.

The uniformity in findings for victims of adult family assault is striking. Whether male or female, blue- or white-collar, the presence of spouse assault appears to be strongly related to aggression against non-family persons.

VIII. Offender Effects

The preceding sections reported a strong victimization effect: victims of intrafamily assault are more likely to engage in assault and verbal aggression outside the family. What of offender effects? Are assaultive husbands and assaultive fathers also violent men outside the family? There are suggestions in the literature that family and nonfamily assault is related among adult men, but this literature is difficult to interpret because only one existing study (an analysis by Straus [1985] of the 1975 National Survey sample) has examined this issue using data from general populations. All the other reports are based on studies of men identified as batterers to determine the proportion who have histories of assault toward nonfamily members, other criminal offenses, and arrest records. These proportions are listed in table 10.

Although the figures strongly suggest that men who assault their wives also engage in nonfamily criminal activities, one cannot be certain because of the absence of comparison groups. However, there have been some case comparison studies of violent and nonviolent husbands. These studies found violent husbands to be significantly more likely than nonviolent husbands to be violent toward nonfamily members (Graff 1979) and significantly more likely to have arrest records for criminal offenses (Hofeller 1980; Dvoskin 1981; Straus 1985).

Two studies examined whether violent family members can be differentiated on the basis of their psychiatric, social, and demographic profile from violent "street criminals." Daniel and Holcomb (1985) compared 213 men who were charged with domestic or nondomestic homicide and given pretrial psychiatric evaluations. Using institutional records, they found that family murder defendants were significantly different from the nondomestic defendants in that they were older, had a more stable adjustment in the community, a prior violent criminal record, to have killed females, had a history of juvenile conduct problems including delinquency and school problems, and were more likely

TABLE 10

Proportion of Male Batterers Who Have Histories of Other Antisocial Behaviors

Study	Antisocial Behavior	Proportion (Percent)
Faulk 1974	previous criminal assault	12
Flynn 1977	nonfamily criminal assault	33
Gayford 1975	previously incarcerated (one-third of above for violent offenses)	50
Stacey and Shupe 1983	arrest record (one-third of above for violent offenses)	80
Walker 1979	previous arrest	71
	violent to nonfamily members	20
Rounsaville 1978	arrest record	35
	previous incarceration	35
	nonfamily violence	51
Fagan, Stewart, and Hansen 1983	previous arrests for other violence	46
Browne 1984 (batterers who were killed by their wives)	previous arrest	92

to receive psychotic diagnoses as a result of pretrial psychiatric evaluations.

In another study of this type, Shields and Hanneke (1981) examined the characteristics of three types of violent men: those violent only toward wives, those violent only toward persons outside the family, and "generally violent" men whose violence was indiscriminate. Their results indicate that generally violent men and men violent only toward nonfamily members are virtually indistinguishable, but wife assaulters were better educated, more law-abiding, and more loyal and concerned about their marital relationships. The authors note that many of the variables suggested by the literature did not differentiate the "family-only" violence group from the "generally violent." However, it is difficult to interpret the applicability of these findings (and those of Daniel and Holcomb [1985]) to more general populations.

A. Child Assault

The child assaulter has typically been depicted as nonaggressive in social relationships and posing no threat to the society at large. Steele and Pollack (1974) describe the abusing parent as not generally violent: "The abusing parents we have seen do not show evidence of an unusually strong basic aggressive drive. They are not fundamentally 'mean' people . . . although their release of aggression is overt and intense, they usually show significant inhibition of aggression in many areas of their lives" (p. 107).

Some evidence, however, shows that fathers of assaulted children have criminal records (Skinner and Castle 1969; Gil 1970; Smith, Hanson, and Noble 1973). Smith, Hanson, and Noble (1973), in a comparison study, found that 29 percent of fathers had a criminal record and Gil (1970) reported that 15.6 percent of abusive fathers had criminal records. By contrast, Steele and Pollack (1974) and Straus (1985) found little relation between child assault and involvement in crime for either mothers or fathers. Gil (1970), however, found that one-tenth of the abusive mothers in his national sample had criminal records. None of this research specifically examines nonfamily assault as an indicator of criminal behavior.

B. Assaultive Families and outside Family Conflict and Violence

To determine whether adults in assaultive families are also more likely to assault persons outside the family, rates of verbal aggression and assault against nonfamily persons and arrest rates were examined for the four family assault types. Table 11 shows that the relation between assaults in the family and crime outside of the family is as strong for adults as it is for children.

1. *Husbands.* Part A of table 11 examines male rates of aggression outside the home in the four family assault types. In every comparison, the analysis of variance shows that there is a significant main effect of assault by husband on the rate of nonfamily verbal aggression, assault, and arrest. For example, the third row of table 11 shows that the rate of hitting a nonfamily member during the study year was four times higher for husbands who had been violent toward their wives than in nonviolent families (2.3 vs. 9.0) and five times higher when there was both wife assault and child assault (2.3 vs. 11.4). In short, men who assault their wives are significantly more likely to have engaged in verbal and physical assault outside the family, and to have been arrested, than men who have not assaulted their wives.

Data in table 12 examine the same issue separately for blue- and white-collar men. In every comparison, the multiassaultive group has the highest rates of verbal aggression and physical assault outside the family, regardless of social class. However, as the outside aggression becomes more serious ("hitting," and "hitting and injuring"), social class differences become more pronounced, with blue-collar men having significantly higher rates of assault against nonfamily persons. Even though social class differences exist in rates of "street violence," we cannot overlook the fact that among white-collar men, the rate of "hitting a nonfamily person" is over five times higher for men in families where there is child assault and wife assault than in families where neither type of assault occurs, while the rate of "injuring a nonfamily person" is almost nine times higher.

2. *Wives.*   Part B of table 11 indicates that the same relation between in-family assault and out-of-family aggression holds for women. In all comparisons, there is a significant connection between intrafamily assault by women and nonfamily assault, verbal aggression, and arrest of women. Although the rate of nonfamily crime committed by women is much lower than for men, women who are assaultive within their family are much more likely to engage in assaultive and other aggressive behavior with nonfamily members.

The analysis shown in table 12 was replicated for women. The findings parallel the pattern for men. For example, as in the analysis of men, "yelling at a nonfamily member" and "getting angry at a nonfamily person and smashing something" was not significantly different for blue- and white-collar women, whereas the rate for assaults against persons outside the family is significantly higher for blue-collar women.

In summary, the results shown in tables 11 and 12 provide substantial support for an association between assaults in the home and assaults and other antisocial behavior outside the family. Those who assault a spouse are more likely to engage in verbally and physically assaultive behavior outside the family and are more likely to have been arrested for some nonfamily crime than are others, and this finding applies to both men and women, and to blue- and white-collar persons.

IX. Summary and Conclusions

There are at least two important and related reasons for a dual focus on violence in the family and violence and other crime "in the streets." The first reason is often overlooked: so much crime takes place in families (Lincoln and Straus 1985). Many of the studies of physical violence within the family discussed in this essay show that the average citizen is much more likely to be assaulted in his or her own home than

TABLE 11

Rates of Nonfamily Verbal and Physical Assault by Family Assault Type and Gender of Adult Offender
(1985 National Resurvey)

Indicator of Nonfamily Aggression	Family Assault Type				ANOVA	
	Non-violent (N)	Child Assault, No Assault by Husband (N)	Assault by Husband, No Child Assault (N)	Both Child Assault and Husband Assault (N)	Effect	F
A. For husbands who assault wives:						
Husband got angry at nonfamily person and yelled at him/her	49.8 (1,931)	59.3 (158)	69.2 (234)	77.3 (120)	child assault	12.84***
					assault by husband	44.46***
					child assault × husband assault	.79
Husband got angry at nonfamily person and smashed something	6.1 (1,960)	11.8 (363)	19.4 (235)	25.7 (118)	child assault	13.03***
					assault by husband	72.03***
					child assault × husband assault	.27
Husband got into fight with non-family member and hit him/her	2.3 (1,960)	3.7 (364)	9.0 (236)	11.4 (120)	child assault	3.30
					assault by husband	41.76***
					child assault × husband assault	.49
Husband got into fight with non-family member and injured him/her	.8 (1,964)	.2 (364)	.9 (236)	6.6 (120)	child assault	2.60
					assault by husband	14.02***
					child assault × husband assault	26.31***
Husband got arrested in last twelve months	1.4 (896)	.6 (158)	3.2 (95)	5.1 (49)	child assault	.82
					assault by husband	5.18*
					child assault × husband assault	1.23

360

B. For wives who assault husbands:

					F
Wife got angry at nonfamily person and yelled at him/her	41.9 (1,937)	46.4 (358)	55.5 (242)	73.7 (120)	child assault 10.40***
					assault by wife 39.73***
					child assault × wife assault 5.18***
Wife got angry at nonfamily person and smashed something	3.8 (1,948)	5.1 (356)	10.7 (240)	20.0 (121)	child assault 6.20*
					assault by wife 53.60***
					child assault × wife assault 8.49**
Wife got in fight with nonfamily person and hit him/her	.6 (1,954)	.9 (362)	2.4 (242)	4.1 (122)	child assault 1.55
					assault by wife 17.42***
					child assault × wife assault 1.45
Wife got in fight with nonfamily person and injured him/her	.2 (1,960)	.0 (362)	.7 (242)	.0 (127)	child assault 1.34
					assault by wife 4.27*
					child assault × wife assault 1.80
Wife got arrested in last twelve months	.3 (1,077)	1.3 (210)	3.0 (132)	.5 (68)	child assault .29
					assault by wife 7.29**
					child assault × wife assault 6.62**

NOTE.—Rates are per 100 and are therefore equal to percentages.
*$p < .05$.
**$p < .01$.
***$p < .001$.

TABLE 12

Rates of Nonfamily Verbal and Physical Assault for Men by Family Assault Type and Socioeconomic Status (1985 National Resurvey)

A. Family Assault Type

	Blue Collar				White Collar			
Dependent Variable	Non-assaultive (N)	Child Assault Only (N)	Spouse Assault Only (N)	Child Assault and Spouse Assault (N)	Non-assaultive (N)	Child Assault Only (N)	Spouse Assault Only (N)	Child Assault and Spouse Assault (N)
Yelled at nonfamily member	51.7 (916)	58.6 (204)	70.4 (137)	73.6 (73)	48.6 (930)	60.2 (147)	65.4 (101)	85.8 (43)
Angry at nonfamily member and smashed something	6.3 (940)	11.3 (207)	24.6 (128)	31.6 (70)	5.8 (942)	10.2 (147)	18.4 (102)	15.2 (46)
Hit nonfamily member	3.4 (941)	6.2 (208)	12.8 (130)	13.1 (72)	1.4 (942)	.4 (147)	2.0 (102)	7.6 (44)
Injured nonfamily member	1.3 (943)	.4 (208)	1.7 (129)	9.4 (73)	.3 (942)	.0 (147)	.0 (103)	2.6 (44)
Arrested in last year[a]	2.1 (402)	.0 (83)	6.1 (50)	7.0 (27)	1.0 (459)	1.4 (72)	.0 (43)	2.7 (21)

B. ANOVA F-Values

	Yelled	Smashed	Hit	Injured	Arrested
Child assault	12.08***	8.70**	2.51	1.58	.17
Wife assault	42.27***	71.47***	30.71***	11.78***	4.73*
Socioeconomic status	.69	4.12*	23.56***	10.22***	2.94
Child × wife	.02	.87	.31	24.65***	1.14
Child × socioeconomic status	1.88	.00***	1.13	.23	1.37
Wife × socioeconomic status	.17	14.92***	7.59**	3.80*	4.90*
Child × wife × socioeconomic status	1.60	.28	3.54	4.79*	.02

NOTE.—Rates are per 100 and are therefore equal to percentages. Number in parentheses are sample sizes.

[a] The N for this row is low because the question was asked only about the respondent. For other questions in this table, respondents were asked parallel questions about themselves and their spouse.

* $p < .05$.
** $p < .01$.
*** $p < .001$.

on the streets of the most dangerous city in the United States (Straus, Gelles, and Steinmetz 1980, p. 49). Likewise, family members commit a high rate of nonviolent crime against each other, including larceny, robbery, and forgery (Straus and Lincoln 1985). If the violent crime and property crime that occurs within the family were aggregated, it would suggest that crime in the family is pervasive, more common than crime in any other setting.

Second, violence in the family and assaults and other crime outside the family are linked in important ways. Evidence was presented in this essay for the existence of both victimization and offender effects. Both offenders and victims of assault in the family have elevated rates of violent and nonviolent crime outside the family.

A. Victimization Effects

Data from three general population surveys found that an assault against a spouse or child takes place in over one out of four American families each year and that in one out of five of these families both spouses *and* children are assaulted. The actual figures are probably much higher because of underreporting. This high incidence of assaults by spouses and by parents constitutes a serious problem in itself, but members of these same families also have higher rates of sibling violence, child-parent violence, and assaults and other crime outside the family.

Children who are assaulted in the family are more likely to assault and commit property crimes outside the family. The relation applies to both genders and cuts across socioeconomic groups but is stronger for males and children from blue-collar families.

Neither previous research nor the current study provide information on why family victimization is linked to outside the family offending behavior. It is not simply the direct experience of being assaulted by a parent that is associated with assaults and other behavioral problems of children outside the family, but the experience of being in a multiassaultive family. Children with the highest rates of outside family violence are from families in which they were not only assaulted by a parent but also witnessed assaults between parents as well.

This pattern also occurs among adults, both male and female and both blue collar and white collar. The highest rates of assault and other crime outside the family occurs among persons in multiassaultive families.

B. Offender Effects

The findings support the notion that assault is a generalized pattern in interpersonal relations that crosses settings and is used across targets. Men in families in which children and wives are assaulted are five times more likely to have also assaulted a nonfamily person than are men in nonassaultive families. These same men are also more severely violent toward fellow citizens, being eight times more likely to have assaulted and injured someone outside the family. Men from multiassaultive families also come to the attention of police more often than others, having an arrest rate that is 3.6 times higher than their less violent counterparts.

This same pattern occurs among women offenders in multiassaultive families although not as strongly as it does for men. These women do have higher rates of assault and other crime against outside family persons, even though severe assaults are very infrequent among all women.

The link between family and nonfamily assault also holds across social class although blue-collar persons report higher rates, especially of more severe assaults outside the family.

C. Research Implications

There are literally hundreds of research questions that spring from these findings, and there would be hundreds more if criminologists and family violence researchers jointly sought a full accounting of the links between crime in the family and crime "in the streets." The first part of this essay explored the problems that might explain why there has been little collaborative work between these two fields. There are no serious structural barriers to discourage joint work, but there is a set of beliefs that continues to define "family violence" as unique and requiring a separate body of theory and separate research approaches.

There is no contradiction between the idea that all violence has something in common and the idea that there are important differences between various types of violence. Both approaches are necessary to understand this complex phenomenon fully. Whether the focus is on the common elements in all violence or on the unique aspects of a certain type of violence depends on the purpose. For purposes of emergency intervention services, it makes sense to have special categories of "battered women" or "abused children" so that such cases can be given appropriate assistance. For some research purposes, it may also be appropriate to examine each of these separately. However, for other research purposes, it may be more important to explore the common elements of etiology and consequences of violent behavior.

Research should be undertaken to specify the conditions under which victimization effects develop. To explain fully the high rate of assault by victims, multivariate analyses must be conducted that simultaneously examine not only childhood exposure to violence but also parental neglect (Loeber and Stouthamer-Loeber 1986), gender sex role socialization (Fagan and Wexler 1987), and social class-related variables. Ideally, this work would be conducted on general population surveys.

There is a need to develop concepts and theories about victimization effects. Aspects of social learning theory may be helpful in this regard (modeling of victim behavior), but other theories and concepts should be explored including work on attribution theory, culture of violence theory, control theory, and feminist theories of patriarchal social structure.

Research is needed to specify the effects of particular types of exposure to family assault on outside family violence and crime. For example, the differential influences of experiencing assault from one's mother or father are not well understood. There is some evidence that fathers' behavior in the family exerts a stronger effect than mothers' on children's antisocial behavior outside the family (Loeber and Stouthamer-Loeber 1986). Information is also needed on whether observing assaultive behavior of father against mother or mother against father or both has a differential impact on children's behavior.

The influence of assaults between siblings on assaults against nonfamily members is rarely studied in terms of victimization effects. Are victims of sibling violence more likely to aggress against peers? Does the effect of sibling victimization vary for boys and girls?

Much needs to be known about the out-of-home assault and other crimes of adults who assault others in their family. A typology of offenders, including "family assault only," "outside-assault only," and "generally assaultive" (Shields and Hanneke 1981) needs to be tested on samples from general populations in order to determine the risk factors associated with each type.

Much research is needed on the links between family and nonfamily violence. This essay is a step in that direction. Further steps would be facilitated by the realization on the part of criminologists and family violence researchers that each contributes to the other in understanding crime and in understanding the family.

REFERENCES

Alfaro, J. 1978. *Child Abuse and Subsequent Delinquent Behavior*. New York: Select Committee on Child Abuse.

Allen, C., and M. A. Straus. 1980. "Resources, Power and Husband-Wife Violence." In *The Social Causes of Husband-Wife Violence*, edited by M. A. Straus and G. T. Hotaling. Minneapolis: University of Minnesota Press.

Arias, I., and S. R. H. Beach. 1987. "Validity of Self-Reports of Marital Violence." *Journal of Family Violence* 2:139–49.

Bandura, A. 1971. *Psychological Modeling*. Chicago: Aldine-Atherton.

———. 1973. *Aggression: A Social Learning Analysis*. Englewood Cliffs, N.J.: Prentice-Hall.

Bard, M. 1971. "The Study and Modification of Intra-familial Violence." In *The Control of Aggression and Violence: Cognitive and Physiological Factors*, edited by J. L. Singer. New York: Academic Press.

Barling, J., K. D. O'Leary, E. N. Jouriles, D. Vivian, and K. E. MacEwen. 1987. "Factor Similarity of the Conflict Tactics Scales across Samples, Spouses, and Sites: Issues and Implications." *Journal of Family Violence* 2:37–55.

Berk, R. A., S. Fenstermaker Berk, D. Loeseke, and D. Rauma. 1983. "Mutual Combat and Other Family Violence Myths." In *The Dark Side of Families: Current Family Violence Research*, edited by D. Finkelhor and associates. Beverly Hills, Calif.: Sage.

Berkowitz, L. 1962. *Aggression: A Social-Psychological Analysis*. New York: McGraw-Hill.

Bolton, R. G., J. W. Reich, and S. E. Gutierres. 1977. "Delinquency Patterns in Maltreated Children and Siblings." *Victimology* 2:349–57.

Bowen, G. L., M. A. Straus, A. J. Sedlak, G. T. Hotaling, and D. B. Sugarman. 1984. *Domestic Violence Surveillance System Feasibility Study: Phase I Report. An Identification of Outcomes and Risk Factors*. Rockville, Md.: Westat, Inc.

Braithwaite, J. 1981. "The Myth of Social Class and Criminality Reconsidered." *American Sociological Review* 46:36–57.

Brandon, S. 1976. "Physical Violence in the Family: An Overview." In *Violence in the Family*, edited by M. Borland. Atlantic Highlands, N.J.: Humanities Press.

Bromberg, W. 1961. *The Mold of Murder*. New York: Grune & Stratton.

Browne, A. 1984. "Assault and Homicide at Home: When Battered Women Kill." Paper presented at the Second National Conference for Family Violence Researchers, University of New Hampshire, Durham, July.

———. 1987. *When Battered Women Kill*. New York: Macmillan/Free Press.

Buzawa, E. 1984. "Patrol Officers Response to Domestic Violence Calls in Massachusetts." Paper presented at the Second National Conference for Family Violence Researchers, University of New Hampshire, Durham, July.

Caesar, P. L. 1985. "The Wife Beater: Personality and Psychosocial Characteristics." Paper presented at the American Psychological Association Meetings, Los Angeles, August.

Calvert, R. 1974. "Criminal and Civil Liability in Husband-Wife Assaults." In *Violence in the Family*, edited by S. K. Steinmetz and M. A. Straus. New York: Harper & Row.

Carmody, D., and K. Williams. 1987. "Wife Assault and Perceptions of Sanctions." *Violence and Victims* 2(1):25–38.

Cate, R. M., J. M. Henton, J. Koval, F. S. Christopher, and S. Lloyd. 1982. "Premarital Abuse: A Social Psychological Perspective." *Journal of Family Issues* 3:79–90.

Conger, R. 1984. "Family Profiles of Serious Juvenile Offenders." Paper presented at the Second National Conference for Family Violence Researchers, University of New Hampshire, Durham, July.

Conger, R. D., R. L. Burgess, and C. Barrett. 1979. "Child Abuse Related to Life Change and Perceptions of Illness: Some Preliminary Findings." *Family Coordinator* 28:73–78.

Daniel, A. E., and W. R. Holcomb. 1985. "A Comparison between Men Charged with Domestic and Non-domestic Homicide." *Bulletin of the American Academy of Psychiatry and the Law* 13(3):233–41.

Dobash, R. E., and R. Dobash. 1979. *Violence against Wives*. New York: Free Press.

Dutton, D., and J. J. Browning. 1984. "Power Struggles and Intimacy Anxieties as Causative Factors of Wife Assault." In *Violence in Intimate Adult Relationships*, edited by G. Russell. New York: Spectrum.

Dvoskin, J. A. 1981. "Battered Women—an Epidemiological Study of Spousal Violence." Doctoral dissertation, University of Arizona, Department of Psychology.

Elbow, M. 1977. "Theoretical Considerations of Violent Marriages." *Social Casework* 58:515–26.

Elliott, D. S. In this volume. "Criminal Justice Procedures in Family Violence Crimes."

Elliott, D. S., and S. S. Ageton. 1980. "Reconciling Race and Class Differences in Self-reported and Official Estimates of Delinquency." *American Sociological Review* 45:95–110.

Elliott, D. S., and D. Huizinga. 1983. "Social Class and Delinquent Behavior in a National Youth Panel: 1976–1980." *Criminology* 21:149–77.

———. 1984. "The Relationship between Delinquent Behavior and ADM Problems." *The National Youth Survey* (project report no. 28). Boulder, Colo.: Behavioral Research Institute.

Elmer, E., S. Evans, and J. Reinhart. 1977. *Fragile Families, Troubled Children*. Pittsburgh: Pittsburgh University Press.

Fagan, J. A., E. S. Piper, and M. Moore. 1986. "Violent Delinquents and Urban Youth." *Criminology* 23:439–72.

Fagan, J. A., D. K. Stewart, and K. V. Hansen. 1983. "Violent Men or Violent Husbands? Background Factors and Situational Correlates." In *The Dark Side of Families: Current Family Violence Research*, edited by D. Finkelhor and associates. Beverly Hills, Calif.: Sage.

Fagan, J., and S. Wexler. 1987. "Crime at Home and Crime in the Streets: The Relation between Family and Stranger Violence." *Violence and Victims* 2:5–24.

Farrington, D. P. 1982. "Longitudinal Analyses of Criminal Violence." In *Criminal Violence*, edited by M. E. Wolfgang and N. A. Weiner. Beverly Hills, Calif.: Sage.

Faulk, M. 1974. "Men Who Assault Their Wives." *Medicine, Science and the Law* 14(18):1–183.

Federal Bureau of Investigation. 1985. *Crime in the United States—1984*. Washington, D.C.: U.S. Government Printing Office.

Finkelhor, D. 1983. "Common Features of Family Abuse." In *The Dark Side of Families: Current Family Violence Research*, edited by D. Finkelhor and associates. Beverly Hills, Calif.: Sage.

Flewelling, R., and A. Browne. 1987. "Female Perpetrated Homicide within American Families." Paper presented at the Third National Family Violence Research Conference, University of New Hampshire, Durham, July.

Flynn, J. D. 1977. "Recent Finds Related to Wife Abuse." *Social Casework* 58:17–18.

Gaquin, D. A. 1977. "Spouse Abuse: Data from the National Crime Survey." *Victimology* 2:632–42.

Gayford, J. J. 1975. "Ten Types of Battered Wives." *Welfare Officer* 25:5–9.

Gelles, R. J. 1973. "Child Abuse as Psychopathology: A Sociological Critique and Reformulation." *American Journal of Orthopsychiatry* 43:611–21.

———. 1974. *The Violent Home: A Study of Physical Aggression between Husbands and Wives*. Beverly Hills, Calif.: Sage.

———. 1980. "Violence in the Family: A Review of Research in the Seventies." *Journal of Marriage and the Family* 42:873–85.

———. 1982. "Domestic Criminal Violence." In *Criminal Violence*, edited by M. E. Wolfgang and N. A. Weiner. Beverly Hills, Calif.: Sage.

Gelles, R. J., and M. A. Straus. 1979. "Determinants of Violence in the Family: Toward a Theoretical Integration." In *Contemporary Theories about the Family*, edited by W. R. Burr, F. I. Nye, and I. L. Reiss. New York: Free Press.

George, C., and M. Main. 1979. "Social Interactions of Young Abused Children: Approach, Avoidance, and Aggression." *Child Development* 50:306–18.

Gil, D. G. 1970. *Violence against Children: Physical Child Abuse in the United States*. Cambridge, Mass.: Harvard University Press.

Giles-Sims, J. 1983. *Wife Battering: A Systems Theory Approach*. New York: Guilford.

Giovannoni, J. M., and A. Billingsley. 1970. "Child Neglect among the Poor:

A Study of Parental Adequacy in Families of Three Ethnic Groups." *Child Welfare* 49:196–204.

Glaser, D., D. Kenefick, and V. O'Leary. 1968. *The Violent Offender*. Washington, D.C.: U.S. Department of Health, Education, and Welfare, Office of Juvenile Delinquency and Youth Development.

Glueck, S., and E. Glueck. 1950. *Unraveling Juvenile Delinquency*. Cambridge, Mass.: Harvard University Press.

Graff, T. T. 1979. "Personality Characteristics of Battered Women." Doctoral dissertation, Brigham Young University, Department of Psychology.

Guttmacher, M. S. 1960. *The Mind of the Murderer*. New York: Farrar.

Hawkins, J. D., and J. G. Weis. 1980. *The Social Development Model: An Integrated Approach to Delinquency Prevention*. Seattle: University of Washington, Center for Law and Justice.

Henton, J., R. Cate, J. Koval, S. Lloyd, and F. S. Christopher. 1983. "Romance and Violence in Dating Relationships." *Journal of Family Issues* 4:467–82.

Hilberman, E., and K. Munson. 1978. "Sixty Battered Women." *Victimology: An International Journal* 2:460–71.

Hindelang, M. J. 1981. "Variations in Sex-Race-Age Specific Incidence Rates of Offending." *American Sociological Review* 46:461–74.

Hirschi, T., and H. C. Selvin. 1967. *Delinquency Research: An Appraisal of Analytic Methods*. New York: Free Press.

Hofeller, K. H. 1980. "Social, Psychological, and Situational Factors in Wife Abuse." Doctoral dissertation, Claremont Graduate School, Department of Psychology.

Hornung, C. A., B. C. McCullough, and R. Sugimoto. 1981. "Status Relationships in Marriage: Risk Factors in Spouse Abuse." *Journal of Marriage and the Family* 43:675–92.

Hotaling, G. T., and M. A. Straus. 1980. "Culture, Social Organization, and Irony in the Study of Family Violence." In *The Social Causes of Husband-Wife Violence*, edited by M. A. Straus and G. T. Hotaling. Minneapolis: University of Minnesota Press.

Hotaling, G. T., and D. B. Sugarman. 1986. "An Analysis of Risk Markers in Husband to Wife Violence: The Current State of Knowledge." *Violence and Victims* 1:101–24.

Hunter, R. S., and N. Kilstrom. 1979. "Breaking the Cycle in Abusive Families." *American Journal of Psychiatry* 136:1320–22.

Hunter, R. S., N. Kilstrom, E. Kraybill, and F. Loda. 1978. "Antecedents of Child Abuse and Neglect in Premature Infants: A Prospective Study in a Newborn Intensive Care Unit." *Pediatrics* 61:629–35.

Jorgensen, S. R. 1977. "Societal Class Heterogamy, Status Striving, and Perception of Marital Conflict: A Partial Replication and Revision of Pearlin's Contingency Hypothesis." *Journal of Marriage and the Family* 39:653–89.

Jouriles, E. N., and K. D. O'Leary. 1985. "Interspousal Reliability of Reports of Marital Violence." *Journal of Consulting and Clinical Psychology* 53:419–21.

Kempe, C. H., F. N. Silverman, B. F. Steele, W. Droegmueller, and H. K.

Silver. 1962. "The Battered Child Syndrome." *Journal of the American Medical Association* 181:17–24.

Kent, J., H. Weisbar, B. Lamar, and T. Marx. 1978. "Physical Abuse of Young Children: A Preliminary Typology of Cases." In *House Committee on Science and Technology, Research into Violent Behavior: Domestic Violence.* Washington, D.C.: U.S. Congress.

Lane, T. W., and G. E. Davis. 1987. "Child Maltreatment and Juvenile Delinquency: Does a Relationship Exist?" In *Prevention of Delinquent Behavior,* edited by J. D. Burchard and S. N. Burchard. Beverly Hills, Calif.: Sage.

Lerman, L. G., and F. Livingston. 1983. "State Legislation on Domestic Violence." *Response* 6(5):1–28.

Lincoln, A. J., and M. A. Straus. 1985. *Crime and the Family.* Springfield, Ill.: Thomas.

Loeber, R., and T. J. Dishion. 1983. "Early Predictors of Male Delinquency: A Review." *Psychological Bulletin* 94:68–99.

Loeber, R., and M. Stouthamer-Loeber. 1986. "Family Factors as Correlates and Predictors of Juvenile Conduct Problems and Delinquency." In *Crime and Justice: An Annual Review of Research,* vol. 7, edited by M. Tonry and N. Morris. Chicago: University of Chicago Press.

McCord, J. 1979. "Some Child-rearing Antecedents of Criminal Behavior in Adult Men." *Journal of Personality and Social Psychology* 37:1477–86.

———. 1984. "Parental Aggressiveness and Physical Punishment in Long-Term Perspective." Paper presented at the Second National Conference for Family Violence Researchers, University of New Hampshire, Durham, July.

McLeod, M. 1983. "Victim Non-cooperation in the Prosecution of Domestic Assault." *Criminology* 21(3):395–416.

Marcus, P. 1983. "Assault and Battery." In *Encyclopedia of Crime and Justice, Volume 1,* edited by S. H. Kadish. New York: Free Press.

Martin, D. 1976. *Battered Wives.* San Francisco: Glide.

Martin, H. P., and P. Beezley. 1974. "Prevention and the Consequences of Abuse." *Journal of Operational Psychiatry* 6:68–77.

Mednick, S. A., V. Pollock, J. Volavka, and W. Gabrielli, Jr. 1982. "Biology and Violence." In *Criminal Violence,* edited by M. E. Wolfgang and N. E. Weiner. Beverly Hills, Calif.: Sage.

Megargee, E. I. 1982. "Psychological Determinants and Correlates of Criminal Violence." In *Criminal Violence,* edited by M. E. Wolfgang and N. A. Weiner. Beverly Hills, Calif.: Sage.

Melnick, B., and J. R. Hurley. 1969. "Distinctive Personality Attributes of Child-abusing Mothers." *Journal of Consulting and Clinical Psychology* 33:746–49.

Morse, C. W., O. J. Sahler, and S. B. Friedman. 1970. "A Three-Year Follow-up Study of Abused and Neglected Children." *American Journal of Diseases of Children* 120:439–46.

Ochberg, F. M. 1980. "On Preventing Aggression and Violence." *Police Chief* 67(2):52–56.

Childhood and Approval of Violence as an Adult." *Aggressive Behavior* 1(2):193–211.

Pagelow, M. D. 1984. *Family Violence.* New York: Praeger.

Palmer, S. 1960. *A Study of Murder.* New York: Crowell.

———. 1972. *The Violent Society.* New Haven, Conn.: College & University Press.

Parnas, R. I. 1972. "The Police Response to the Domestic Disturbance." In *The Criminal in the Arms of the Law,* edited by L. Radzinowicz and M. E. Wolfgang. New York: Basic.

Patterson, G. R., J. A. Cobb, and R. S. Roy. 1973. "A Social Engineering Technology for Retraining the Families of Aggressive Boys." In *Issues and Trends in Behavior Therapy,* edited by H. E. Adams and I. P. Unkel. Springfield, Ill.: Thomas.

Pleck, Elizabeth. In this volume. "Criminal Approaches to Family Violence, 1640–1980."

Potts, D. A., S. D. Herzberger, and A. E. Holland. 1979. "Child Abuse: A Cross-generational Pattern of Child Rearing." Paper presented at the Midwestern Psychological Association Convention, Chicago, May.

Revitch, E., and L. B. Schlesinger. 1978. "Murder: Evaluation, Classification and Prediction." In *Violence: Perspectives on Murder and Aggression,* edited by I. L. Kutash, S. B. Kutash, and L. B. Schlesinger and Associates. San Francisco: Jossey-Bass.

Robinson, J. P., R. Athanasiou, and K. B. Head. 1969. *Measures of Occupational Attitudes and Occupational Characteristics.* Ann Arbor: University of Michigan, Survey Research Center of the Institute for Social Research.

Rosenbaum, A., and K. D. O'Leary. 1981. "Marital Violence: Characteristics of Abusive Couples." *Journal of Consulting and Clinical Psychology* 49:63–71.

Rounsaville, B. J. 1978. "Theories in Marital Violence: Evidence from a Study of Battered Women." *Victimology* 3(1–2):11–31.

Rouse, L. P. 1984. "Conflict Tactics Used by Men in Marital Disputes." Paper presented at the Second National Conference for Family Violence Researchers, University of New Hampshire, Durham, July.

Roy, M. 1982. "Four Thousand Partners in Violence: A Trend Analysis." In *The Abusive Partner: An Analysis of Domestic Battering,* edited by M. Roy. New York: Van Nostrand Reinhold.

Saunders, D. 1986. "When Battered Women Use Violence: Husband-Abuse or Self-Defense?" *Violence and Victims* 1:47–60.

Schulman, M. 1979. *A Survey of Spousal Violence against Women in Kentucky.* Frankfort: Kentucky Commission on the Status of Women.

Schumm, W. R., S. R. Bollman, A. P. Jurich, and M. J. Martin. 1982. "Adolescent Perspectives on Family Violence." *Journal of Social Psychology* 117:153–54.

Sedgely, J., and D. Lund. 1979. "Self-reported Beatings and Subsequent Tolerance for Violence." *Review of Public Data Use* 7(1):30–38.

Sherman, L. W., and R. A. Berk. 1984. "The Specific Deterrent Effects of Arrest for Domestic Violence." *American Sociological Review* 49(2):261–72.

Shields, N. M., and C. R. Hanneke. 1981. "Patterns of Family and Non-family Violence: An Approach to the Study of Violent Husbands." Paper presented at the First National Conference for Family Violence Researchers, University of New Hampshire, Durham, July.

Singer, J. L. 1971. "The Influence of Violence Portrayed in Television or Motion Pictures upon Overt Aggressive Behavior." In *The Control of Aggression and Violence: Cognitive and Physiological Factors*, edited by J. L. Singer. New York: Academic Press.

Skinner, A. E., and R. L. Castle. 1969. *Seventy-eight Battered Children: A Retrospective Study*. London: National Society for the Prevention of Cruelty to Children.

Smith, S. M., R. Hanson, and S. Noble. 1973. "Parents of Battered Children: A Controlled Study." *British Medical Journal* 4:388–91.

Sonkin, D. J., D. Martin, and L. E. Walker. 1985. *The Male Batterer: A Treatment Approach*. New York: Springer.

Stacey, W. A., and A. Shupe. 1983. *The Family Secret: Domestic Violence in America*. Boston: Beacon.

Star, B., C. G. Clark, K. M. Goetz, and C. O'Hara. 1979. "Psycho-social Aspects of Wife-Battering." *Social Casework* 41:479–87.

Stark, E., A. Flitcraft, and W. Frazier. 1979. "Medicine and Patriarchal Violence: The Social Construction of a 'Private' Event." *International Journal of Health Services* 9:461–93.

Steele, B. F., and C. B. Pollack. 1974. "A Psychiatric Study of Parents Who Abuse Infants and Small Children." In *The Battered Child*, 2d ed., edited by R. E. Helfer and C. H. Kempe. Chicago: University of Chicago Press.

Steinmetz, S. K. 1977. *The Cycle of Violence: Assertive, Aggressive, and Abusive Family Interaction*. New York: Praeger.

Steinmetz, S. K., and M. A. Straus. 1974. *Violence in the Family*. New York: Harper & Row.

Strasburg, P. A. 1978. *Violent Delinquents: A Report to the Ford Foundation from the Vera Institute of Justice*. New York: Monarch.

Straus, M. A. 1970. "Methodology of a Laboratory Experimental Study of Families in Three Societies." In *Families in East and West*, edited by R. Hill and R. Konig. Paris: Mouton.

———. 1973. "A General Systems Theory Approach to a Theory of Violence Between Family Members." *Social Science Information* 12:105–25.

———. 1974. "Leveling, Civility, and Violence in the Family." *Journal of Marriage and the Family* 36:13–29.

———. 1976. "Sexual Inequality, Cultural Norms and Wife-Beating." *Victimology* 1:54–76.

———. 1977. "Wife-Beating: How Common and Why?" *Victimology* 2:443–58.

———. 1979. "Measuring Intrafamily Conflict and Violence: The Conflict Tactics Scale." *Journal of Marriage and the Family* 41:75–88.

———. 1980. "The Marriage License as a Hitting License: Evidence from Popular Culture, Law, and Social Science." In *Social Causes of Husband-Wife Violence*, edited by M. A. Straus and G. T. Hotaling. Minneapolis: University of Minnesota Press.

————. 1983. "Ordinary Violence, Child Abuse, and Wife-Beating: What Do They Have in Common?" In *The Dark Side of Families: Current Family Violence Research*, edited by D. Finkelor and associates. Beverly Hills, Calif.: Sage.

————. 1985. "Family Training in Crime and Violence." In *Crime and the Family*, edited by A. J. Lincoln and M. A. Straus. Springfield, Ill.: Thomas.

————. 1986. "Domestic Violence and Homicide Antecedents." *Bulletin of the New York Academy of Medicine* 62(5):446–65.

————. 1987. "Primary Group Characteristics and Intra-family Homicide." Paper presented at the Third National Family Violence Research Conference, University of New Hampshire, Durham, July.

————. 1988. "The Conflict Tactics Scales and Its Critics: An Evaluation and New Data on Validity and Reliability." In *Physical Violence in American Families: Risk Factors and Adaptations in 8,145 Families*, by M. A. Straus and R. J. Gelles. New Brunswick, N.J.: Transaction.

Straus, M. A., and R. J. Gelles. 1986. "Societal Change and Change in Family Violence from 1975 to 1985 as Revealed by Two National Surveys." *Journal of Marriage and the Family* 48:465–79.

Straus, M. A., R. J. Gelles, and S. K. Steinmetz. 1980. *Behind Closed Doors: Violence in the American Family*. Garden City, N.Y.: Anchor/Doubleday.

Straus, M. A., and A. J. Lincoln. 1985. "A Conceptual Framework for Understanding Crime and the Family." In *Crime and the Family*, edited by A. J. Lincoln and M. A. Straus. Springfield, Ill.: Thomas.

Symonds, A. 1979. "Violence against Women: The Myth of Masochism." *American Journal of Psychotherapy* 33(2):161–73.

Telch, C. F., and C. U. Lindquist. 1984. "Violent versus Non-violent Couples: A Comparison of Patterns." *Psychotherapy* 21(2):242–48.

Toby, J. 1966. "Violence and the Masculine Ideal: Some Qualitative Data." In *Patterns of Violence: The Annals of the American Academy of Political and Social Science, Vol. 364*, edited by M. E. Wolfgang. Philadelphia: American Academy of Political and Social Science.

Toch, H. 1969. *Violent Men*. Chicago: Aldine.

U.S. Bureau of the Census. 1986. *Statistical Abstract of the United States*, 106th ed. Washington, D.C.: U.S. Government Printing Office.

Walker, L. E. 1979. *The Battered Woman*. New York: Harper & Row.

————. 1984. *The Battered Woman Syndrome*. New York: Springer.

Walters, D. R. 1975. *Physical and Sexual Abuse of Children*. Bloomington: Indiana University Press.

Washburn, C., and I. H. Frieze. 1981. "Methodological Issues in Studying Battered Women." Paper presented at the First National Conference for Family Violence Researchers, University of New Hampshire, Durham, July.

Weiner, N. A., and M. E. Wolfgang. 1985. "The Extent and Character of Violent Crime in America, 1969 to 1982." In *American Violence and Public Policy*, edited by L. Curtis. New Haven, Conn.: Yale University Press.

Williams, J. E. 1972. "Treatment of Violence." *Medicine, Science and the Law* 12(4):269–74.

Wolfe, D. A. 1985. "Child-abusive Parents: An Empirical Review and Analysis." *Psychological Bulletin* 97(3):462–82.

Wolfgang, M. E. 1958. *Patterns of Criminal Homicide.* Philadelphia: University of Pennsylvania Press.

Yllo, K. 1978. "Nonmarital Cohabitation: Beyond the College Campus." *Alternative Lifestyles* 1:37–54.

Yllo, K., and M. A. Straus. 1981. "Interpersonal Violence among Married and Cohabiting Couples." *Family Relations* 30:339–45.

Jeffrey Fagan

Cessation of Family Violence: Deterrence and Dissuasion

ABSTRACT

Family violence research has only recently begun to investigate desistance. Recent developments in the study of behaviors other than family violence, such as the use of addictive substances, suggest that common processes can be identified in the cessation of disparate behaviors involving diverse populations and occurring in different settings. Desistance is the outcome of processes that begin with aversive experiences leading to a decision to stop. Desistance apparently follows legal sanctions in nearly three spouse abuse cases in four, but the duration of cessation is unknown beyond short study periods. Batterers with shorter, less severe histories have a higher probability of desisting than batterers with longer, more severe histories. Victim-initiated strategies, including social and legal sanctions plus actions to create aversive experiences from abuse (e.g., divorce and loss of children) and social disclosure, also lead to desistance. Batterers are more resistant to change when they participate in social networks that support and reinforce violence to maintain family dominance. Desistance may also actually be displacement, where a violent spouse locates a new victim.

Desistance is one of the most persistent—but least analyzed—findings in the criminological literature. Among both juvenile and adult offenders, the duration and frequency of criminal activities vary extensively (Wolfgang, Figlio, and Sellin 1972; Hamparian et al. 1978; Petersilia,

Jeffrey Fagan is associate director, Criminal Justice Center, and associate professor of law, police science, and criminal justice administration, John Jay College, City University of New York. Sandra Wexler and Patrick Biernacki provided helpful comments on earlier drafts of this essay.

Greenwood, and Lavin 1978; Petersilia 1980; Blumstein, Farrington, and Moitra 1985). Most criminal careers are very short, consisting of only one or two police contacts or criminal events, while others have protracted careers including both petty and serious crimes. Blumstein, Farrington, and Moitra (1985) suggest a model of offender heterogeneity in which "innocents" stop after one or two criminal events, "desisters" have relatively low probabilities of lengthy criminal careers, and "persisters" have high probabilities of lengthy careers with frequent criminal activity. Among the persisters, the probabilities of desistance are lowest for offenders whose careers begin during adolescence and who remain active at thirty years of age.

Blumstein and Cohen (1982) characterize lengthy careers in terms of three phases: an initiation or "break-in" period, a "stable" period where crime rates remain near their peak annual levels, and a "wear-out" period where the career begins to decline rapidly at around forty years of age. Irwin (1970), Petersilia, Greenwood, and Lavin (1978), and West (1982), among others, have found similar patterns. Even the most persistent and lengthy criminal careers have a natural course, tapering off and eventually ceasing as offenders age, possibly "burn out" physically, and ease out of "the life."

The process of desistance may also take different forms. Some shift from "street crime" to a more occupational type of crime (Clarke and Cornish 1985) or into brief lapses followed by sporadic episodes occurring at unpredictable intervals (Petersilia 1980). However, Blumstein and Cohen (1982) found that for violent offenses, including homicide, rape, and aggravated assaults, career lengths are longer, and those involved in violence are less likely to desist in the early years of their careers than are property offenders.

The criminal careers literature also demonstrates that desistance from crime can occur "spontaneously," or in the absence of any external intervention, and also as the result of a legal or social sanction (Clarke and Cornish 1985). Evidence of spontaneous desistance is offered by Sutherland (1937) in *The Professional Thief*, Irwin (1970) in *The Felon*, and Shover (1985) in *Aging Criminals*. In these studies, ex-offenders reflected on the cognitive processes that influenced their decision to abandon their criminal careers. Cusson and Pinsonneault (1986) interviewed seventeen men who had committed several armed robberies and whose decision to give up crime was "voluntary and autonomous" (p. 78). But scant attention to desistance *as a process* leaves many unanswered questions on the social and psychological processes of stopping criminal behavior, the circumstances in which either "spontaneous" cessation occurs or sanctions are effective, and the behavioral antecedents of such processes.

Relatively little is known about desistance from involvement in "stranger" crimes, and even less is known about the "natural" course of crimes in the home. Few studies have examined patterns or careers of family violence to determine when, whether, or under what conditions desistance or cessation occurs. It is uncertain whether desistance occurs in response to societal (or external) interventions, internal strategies, or actions taken by family members, or if "spontaneous" cessation of family violence occurs. How these events vary by family and offender types is unknown. And little is known about the human processes that underlie cessations.

Family violence research has rightly been concerned with understanding the factors that explain initial involvement, patterns of victimization within families, and strategies to protect victims. The methodological difficulties of research on sensitive family topics (Gelles 1978) pose formidable barriers to integrating our general understanding of desistance with the study of "natural" careers of crimes in the home. Accordingly, the process by which criminal behaviors toward family members end remains a neglected topic for both family violence research and criminology.

There is increasing evidence that desistance also occurs in a variety of other antisocial and destructive behaviors, including both criminal and noncriminal acts. These include opiate addiction, eating disorders, tobacco use, and alcoholism (Stall and Biernacki 1986). This literature shows remarkably consistent results, despite wide variation in research strategies. Together with empirical evidence on desistance from stranger crime, this research provides a basis for developing a framework for studying desistance from spouse and child abuse.

The study of desistance has obvious theoretical and practical importance for family violence research. First, the effectiveness of interventions can be weighed by the rates of cessation. Second, understanding the processes that move individuals to desist from family violence may also shed light on the causes or initiation of such acts. Third, whether individuals comply with recent societal "mandates" to end violence in the home through its criminalization can inform future efforts at understanding general deterrence. Finally, understanding desistance can inform or improve treatment intervention by revealing processes that lead to the end of violence. If the treatment of spouse or child abusers appears to be complex or unpromising, an alternative is to focus on promoting or accelerating the processes of desistance. Intervention programs for men who batter[1] focus either on undoing the complex and often intractable causal processes of family violence or on learning new repertoires of behavior.

This essay examines the empirical evidence on the cessation of violence in the home and analyzes its relevance to the literature on desistance from other behaviors. The review is selective in that it focuses on violence against wives, an area where there are extensive data and theory development. Section I examines the limited evidence of desistance in family violence—whether resulting from the effects of interventions or from "spontaneous" recovery. Section II provides an overview of the literature on desistance from other problem behaviors and suggests ways that it is germane to criminology in general and to understanding of family violence in particular. Section III assesses the promise and limitations of a desistance model for theory and policy. Section IV discusses policy implications and areas for further study.

I. Desistance from Family Violence

Unlike several other types of crime, there have been few studies of desistance from family violence.[2] There are no studies that document "natural" or spontaneous desistance without intervention by the victim or as a result of some form of sanction or treatment. The few studies that analyze desistance typically have discussed it as one of three patterns: reductions in violence, or cessation, resulting from interventions, shifts in the victimization patterns of abusers, or cessation resulting from strategies employed by the victim to end the abuse. These three varieties may be called "deterrence," "displacement," and "dissuasion."

---

[1] Spouse abuse is more common among men, particularly when the relative harm or injury of family violence is considered. Though violence by women toward men and children is common, as well as violence by children toward adults, the more severe and harmful behaviors occur when men batter wives and children (Straus 1978).

[2] The terms "desistance," "cessation," and "remission" are used in this essay to describe patterns of stopping family violence. Desistance refers to a process of reduction in the frequency and severity of family violence, leading to its eventual end when "true desistance" or "quitting" occurs. Perhaps more important, desistance implies a conscious behavioral intent to reduce the incidence of violence. In contrast, "cessation" refers to abstention from family violence, either permanent or temporary, often because of legal or other interventions external to the individual. "Remission" is a natural process. It describes a temporary state where there is an episodic lull in violent behavior. Though the lull may become permanent, remission implies that the likelihood of backsliding and recidivism equals that of quitting.

Yet to be studied is "true desistance," or "quitting," which occurs seemingly in the absence of other than internal sociopsychological processes of the violent individual.

A. Cessation by Deterrence

In the 1970s, pandemic violence in American families was disclosed (Straus, Gelles, and Steinmetz 1980). Criminal remedies have been a cornerstone of the societal response. Early research on criminal justice interventions primarily assessed police responses to family violence. Some critics cited weak police responses as tacit societal approval for family violence (Morash 1986). More recently, efforts to halt family violence, particularly violence toward women, have focused on specific deterrence through sanction and punishment. Despite many efforts to improve and strengthen criminal justice interventions, few studies offer conclusive evidence of the deterrent effects of police interventions aimed at family violence. In at least one instance, use of temporary restraining orders seemed to aggravate the situation because of weak enforcement (Grau, Fagan, and Wexler 1984). Until recently, there was little evidence that deterrent approaches could lead to a cessation of family violence.

This changed when Sherman and Berk (1984*a*, 1984*b*) reported the results of a controlled experiment to reduce family violence through the deterrent effects of arrest. They found that apparent cessation of spousal violence was greater when Minneapolis police officers arrested offenders, compared to the effect on violence of counseling or separating the parties. Basing their study on official police records for 314 cases over a six-month follow-up period, Sherman and Berk (1984*a*) found that only 13 percent of those arrested committed a repeat violent act, in contrast to 26 percent of the men in the separated couples. When victim reports were used as the outcome measure, arrest still was the most effective intervention, with a 19 percent failure rate, compared with 37 percent for counseling (mediation).

Looked at another way, nearly 72 percent of assailants, and 87 percent of the arrestees, avoided police contact for family violence for a six-month period. According to victims, desistance was slightly less widespread among arrestees at 81 percent, and 71 percent overall. When a failure-rate analysis was used to determine whether new incidents were delayed, the results again showed that desistance was greater for the arrest group than for those separated or counseled. These promising results were widely embraced, leading to a spate of legislation to man-

Jeffrey Fagan

date arrest in domestic violence cases.[3] These results were then replicated by Berk and Newton (1985) using a nonexperimental sample of domestic disturbance calls to police ($N = 285$) and measures based on official records. The National Institute of Justice is sponsoring six replications of the Sherman and Berk study (see Elliott, in this volume).

The promising findings must be tempered by several factors. First, the follow-up period was relatively short (six months), given the episodic and cyclical patterns of family violence observed by Walker (1979, 1984) and Frieze et al. (1980). Second, self-reports from batterers were not obtained, leaving out the possibility of a "hidden" violence period toward strangers, the original victim, or other victims in the home. Third, distinctions in the level and nature of violence were not made, leaving open questions of the relative harm (e.g., injury, intimidation) that may have accrued from battering incidents. Fourth, the interview process may have depressed recidivism rates. Awareness by offenders of victim interviews may have deterred or simply postponed recidivism during the study period. Fifth, the arrest may have prompted the offender to leave the household and, sooner or later, enter into another relationship where battering may occur. Finally, other forms of abuse, such as persistent denigration or economic reprisal, were not investigated. These forms of abuse, noted in several studies on wife battery (e.g., Walker 1979, 1984; Frieze et al. 1980; Russell 1982), are emotionally harmful, if not threatening to physical safety. Moreover, these forms of abuse may lead to the deprivation of the victim's rights under the law. Noncriminal forms of abuse include psychological abuse (e.g., humiliation), punitive economic deprivation, coerced social isolation, and threatened homicide.

Perhaps the most significant omission from the Sherman and Berk (1984a) study occurred because, for ethical reasons, "Cases of life-threatening or severe injury, usually labelled as a felony . . . were excluded from the design" (p. 263). Any theoretical formulation of cessation via deterrence must take into account the offenders' violence histories. Career criminal studies tell us consistently that persistent offenders differ from the "innocents" or desisters. Fagan, Stewart, and Hansen (1983) report that spouses with histories of severe violence at home are more often violent toward strangers, have more often been arrested for violent offenses, and more often injure both domestic and

---

[3] Washington, Ohio, New Jersey, and Connecticut are among the states enacting such statutes.

stranger victims. Sanctions (including arrests with uncertain outcomes) may affect these persistent offenders far less than they do first- or one-time offenders or men who are violent only within the home.

In another study of the deterrent effects of criminal sanctions, Fagan et al. (1984) evaluated federally supported demonstration programs in six communities testing criminal justice interventions in family violence. The cross-sectional study included more serious cases of violence among the 270 self-selected program clients and analyzed both legal and social interventions such as shelter and counseling. Victim reports for a six-month follow-up period provided data on subsequent abuse and violence.[4] Several measures of subsequent abuse were used to compensate for the limitations of individual measures. The Conflicts Tactics Scale (CTS; see Straus [1978]) was used to measure violence, based on victim reports. The scales were modified to include sexual assault. Also, items measuring verbal threats and harassment were included to provide measures of abuse as well as physical violence. Other measures included injuries before and after the program intervention and subsequent calls to police by the victim due to reoccurrence of abuse or violence, as well as victim and offender background characteristics, especially childhood experiences with violence and violence toward other family members and strangers.

As expected, criminal justice interventions resulted in less frequent and severe violence for the less severe cases—those with little prior history of violence or prior injuries (Fagan et al. 1984).[5] Overall, 72 percent reported no subsequent violence, and 94 percent reported no injuries during the follow-up period. When an arrest occurred, 83 percent reported no subsequent violence, compared with 80 percent of those receiving victim assistance (legal information and referral to advocates) but only 55 percent for "informal" police responses (mediation, separation).

However, the reincidence of abuse was nearly twice that of violence, and criminal justice interventions were more effective in reducing its reincidence only for cases with low prior injury. Overall, over half (56 percent) of the former clients reported reincidence of verbal threats and harassment, compared to 28 percent for violence. Yet abuse in the

---

[4] Abuse was defined as verbal harassment, degradation, threats, and other nonphysical assaults. Violence included only physical assaults.

[5] "Low" prior injury was defined as no injury worse than bruises, while "high" injuries included bleeding, broken bones, lacerations, unconsciousness, or miscarriages due to abuse.

follow-up period was reported by about 15 percent of clients with low prior injury histories, compared to 33 percent of those with more serious prior injury histories. The reincidence of threats or harassment was greater for nonlegal interventions.

After we controlled for the severity of violence, the rates of apparent cessation differed from the Minneapolis study's findings. Table 1 shows that cessation rates varied by the severity of prior injury. For low prior injury, cessation rates were over 90 percent for both victim assistance and arrest but significantly lower (67 percent) for informal police response. Interventions other than police response actually resulted in higher cessation rates than informal police responses. For more severe cases (higher prior injury), the same differentials prevailed, but at a consistently lower cessation rate. The severity of recidivist behaviors was measured with two scales based on a modification of the Conflict Tactics Scales (Straus 1978). An "abuse" scale added verbal abuse (threats, insults, harassment) and sexual assault to the CTS violence items. A violence scale was constructed that added only sexual assault to the CTS violence items and excluded verbal abuse.[6]

The severity of subsequent aggression was lowest following arrest and highest following victim assistance. There were no differences when "abuse" or "violence" served as measures of recidivism. Differences correlated with the severity of prior injury were found only for nonlegal interventions. By comparison, the Minneapolis results also suggested that prior violence at home predicts subsequent violence, regardless of the type of police action (Berk 1986).

In cases where prosecution was attempted, and also where convictions were obtained and offenders sentenced, table 1 again shows that cessation rates were higher for less severe cases.[7] But for assailants with more severe histories of violence, the imposition of more serious sanctions was associated with increased incidence of violence. The results

[6] For the abuse scale, Guttman scaling procedures resulted in a continuous variable. The coefficient of scalability was 0.59, and the coefficient of reproducibility was 0.90. Similar procedures for the violence scale also resulted in a continuous variable. The coefficient of reproducibility was 0.89, and the coefficient of scalability was 0.64, both well within the conventional thresholds for acceptance of scale properties (Edwards 1957). Interestingly, both Guttman procedures placed sexual assault atop the hierarchy of abuse and violence items. Browne (1987) found that sexual assault was one factor that discriminated marital violence cases that resulted in homicide from others. The omission of sexual assault items from the CTS scales suggests a serious flaw in the conceptualization of marital violence in earlier works.

[7] Sentencing categories were collapsed due to their rare occurrence. The sentences included probation, fines or restitution, and jail.

TABLE 1

Prevalence of Subsequent Aggression and Mean Aggression Score
by Legal Sanction and Severity of Violence

Legal Sanction and Incidence of Prior Injury	Sample	% Desisting	Mean Aggression Score of Recidivists
Police response:			
None:			
Low	65	79	3.79
High	79	76	3.23
Informal:			
Low	18	67	3.17
High	33	49	3.18
Victim assistance:			
Low	19	90	4.00
High	32	75	4.00
Arrest:			
Low	12	92	2.00
High	12	75	2.00
		$\chi^2 = 36.1$	$F = 2.76$
		$p = .02$	$p = .05$
Prosecution attempted:			
No:			
Low	88	77	3.50
High	108	65	3.37
Yes:			
Low	26	88	4.00
High	48	67	3.38
		$\chi^2 = 17.4$	$F = 0.08$
		$p = .04$	$p = $ ns
Convicted and sentenced:			
No:			
Low	17	82	4.00
High	39	64	3.50
Yes:			
Low	9	100	0
High	9	78	2.50
		$\chi^2 = 0.2$	$F = 2.95$
		$p = $ ns	$p = .03$

SOURCE.—Fagan et al. (1984).
NOTE.—ns = not significant.

suggest that more serious sanctions may aggravate spousal violence, especially for more serious cases. Cases unsuccessfully prosecuted afford little protection for victims from reprisals by assailants. For cases successfully prosecuted, the apparent increase in abuse and violence may reflect the substantive punishment following conviction for family violence. If the punishments imposed are relatively weak, such as probation supervision on large caseloads with minimal contact, there are also few protections for victims. There may also be counterdeterrent effects that signal the limits on the courts' willingness to impose strong punishment. Assailants in more serious cases usually have extensive prior court involvement for stranger violence as well as having prior family violence arrests (Fagan, Stewart, and Hansen 1983). A weak sentence may actually neutralize the deterrent effects of legal sanctions for spousal violence, particularly for offenders with lengthy criminal histories.

These findings again suggest that sanctions are likelier to deter wife beaters with less severe histories than those with more severe histories.[8] But these less violent offenders tend to be individuals who have little experience with the criminal justice system. They are unlikely candidates for arrest and may be concerned about how employers or neighbors will respond to disclosure of their behaviors. Conversely, the more violent assailants are likelier to be arrested and on average have more often been arrested previously for a violent act. For this group, cessation is less likely, regardless of whether legal sanction or some other societal intervention is attempted (Fagan et al. 1984). Little is known about the outcomes of the previous arrests—whether punishment was imposed, for example. Failure of sanctions in earlier arrests may teach an unfortunate lesson to violent spouses about societal support for wife beating. The often-arrested assailant may already have learned that he has little to fear from the law.

The addition of more serious cases and multiple, continuous measures of violence in the Fagan et al. (1984) study challenges the interpretation from the Minneapolis study of how legal sanctions affect family violence. However, these findings should also be viewed cautiously. As in the Minneapolis study, the follow-up period was limited to six months, and victim reports were the sole data source. Also, the cross-sectional study compared victims who selectively had sought legal or social interventions in several locales, where the context and substance of the interventions varied.

Few studies report the marginal effects of criminal justice responses after arrest on recidivism of wife battery. Dutton (1987) examined data

---

[8] Conclusions about desistance from a six-month follow-up period should be made with caution. Analyses controlling for intact relationships contrasted with separations showed no differences in desistance probabilities. However, this does not rule out the possibility that the violence simply was in remission and might reappear later.

sets from the United States and Canada to construct conditional probabilities for detection, arrest, conviction, and sanction (punishment) of wife battery cases. He identified a "winnowing" process that results in significant case attrition from detection of wife assault through conviction. He concluded that, given the occurrence of wife assault, the arrest probability is 21.2 percent (compared to a 20 percent rate for a composite of other crimes), and the assailant has a punishment probability of 0.38 percent. The analysis illustrated the difficulty of establishing conditions under which general deterrence may occur. The low likelihood of detection and punishment of wife assault makes suspect the attribution of specific deterrent effects to arrests for wife assault.

In sum, we frequently observe apparent cessation from family violence in less serious cases where legal sanctions are imposed, but for serious cases, the rates are no greater than when nonlegal interventions are applied. Because of the short follow-up periods characterizing the major research, we do not know whether cessation is temporary or lasting. Also, the effects of legal sanctions may vary with the severity of prior violence. In the three studies cited here, there are no reported acts of violence in 70 percent or more of cases for the six-month follow-up period. About three in four offenders overall, and nine in ten with less severe prior violence histories, commit no reported acts of family violence. But these rates decline markedly for those with more severe violence histories. Possibly the more serious cases are simply the less serious cases at a later stage in the natural course of battering relations. More serious offenders may follow different causal paths than do less severe or frequent offenders. Accordingly, we may expect that the processes that lead to more sustained, injurious violence may neutralize the processes leading to desistance.

The consistent finding that spousal violence is often repeated and escalates in severity bears on the limits of desistance. Several writers have suggested that the severity of family violence is related to assailant background characteristics, especially to childhood exposure to violence (Walker 1979; Pagelow 1984; Fagan and Wexler 1987). If so, it is not likely that one arrest or a stint on probation will initiate processes of "unlearning" to desist from a pattern of battering. But for those whose socialization is less strongly linked to normative violence, the processes of cessation or desistance may well begin with use of a cultural or legal sanction. For others, more complex processes must precede desistance. These latter strategies are not necessarily stronger medicine but rely on different models of behavioral change.

B. Cessation by Dissuasion: Victim-initiated Strategies

Table 1 suggests that some offenders cease battering even when legal sanctions are not invoked. In fact, until recently, calling the police was an ineffective, if not unavailable, option for battered women. The large volume of these cases, plus the low priority police historically gave them, made it difficult for battered women to obtain help or protection for other than the most violent incidents. In those conditions, victims sought other solutions. However, these victim-initiated strategies long remained unstudied, despite the rapid increase in family violence research in the past decade. The study of cessation without *formal* intervention holds important clues not only to policy on how best to counsel and advise victims but also for understanding the contexts, motivation, and processes of cessation by assailants.

Bowker's (1983) study of victim-initiated strategies was the first research that looked specifically at cessation from family violence. The research focused on victims who had remained in their own homes and minimized abuse by use of social networks, self-help strategies, and available help sources. A self-selected sample of 146 women was recruited from the Milwaukee area to describe and typify the strategies used by former victims to promote the cessation of family violence. Respondents were recruited through social agencies, religious and cultural groups, and media advertisements in the greater Milwaukee area.

Three types of sources were used by victims to promote cessation: personal strategies, formal help sources (legal and social agencies), and informal help sources (social networks). Bowker asked the women to indicate which were most helpful and which were least helpful in ending the abuse. Also, the assailants' self-initiated help strategies were assessed. The questions were posed in such a way as to uncover the factors that enabled women to demand an end to the battering and to reveal the factors that enabled assailants to end the violence. The latter findings may contribute to identifying the sociopsychological processes by means of which batterers ceased their violence.

The preliminary analyses showed that no single tactic was consistently effective or ineffective. Table 2 presents these results in collapsed categories from the original report. Comparing what worked "best" and "least," the patterns reveal three effective types of strategies. The first, social disclosure, "worked best" in 30 percent of the cases. This included disclosure of the violence to neighbors, relatives, friends, and others. Resort to these informal resources helped the violence emerge from the private family realm to social knowledge, and the social sanctions attached to wife beating were invoked. The second

TABLE 2

Victim Reports of Strategies That Worked Best and Least
to Stop Violence

	Worked Best		Worked Least	
	N	Percent	N	Percent
Social disclosure	45	30	14	10
Self-defense	33	23	12	8
Escape or hiding	15	11	3	2
Social or legal intervention	44	30	39	28
Talking	5	4	10	7
Promises from batterer to stop	0	...	21	14
Other	2	1.3	0	...
Nothing	1	.7	46	31
Total	145	100	145	100

SOURCE.—Bowker (1983).

strategy included sociolegal interventions and worked "best" in 30 percent of the cases. This included contacting a social agency or a criminal justice agency. These resources threaten a formal sanction, as opposed to simply a social sanction. Also, contacting the clergy or women's groups often initiated formal help and carried with it the threat of social stigmatization. The third strategy was a group of self-defense efforts, including hiding, taking shelter, and physical self-defense. This was the most effective approach in 23 percent of the cases.

What worked "least" was doing "nothing" (31 percent). Sociolegal interventions (described by 30 percent as working "best") worked "least" for 28 percent! The possibly counterproductive effects of help seeking have been widely documented (Morash 1986) and may underlie these contradictory findings. If legal sanctions promote cessation only for those with less severe histories, these results may reflect the group with more severe histories. The results suggest that external "authorities" and social sources of support are particularly important in promoting the processes of cessation, but not for all victims.

Table 3, also from Bowker's (1983) data, further shows the importance of external authorities. Bowker asked the female respondents to report on their perception of what worked "best" and "least" in helping the batterers to desist. Over half (51 percent) of the males apparently responded to fear of divorce or legal sanction. About one in four also

TABLE 3

Enabling Factors for Batterers to Cease

	N	Percent
Fear of divorce	27	30
Fear of legal sanction	19	21
Want to reestablish relationship*	23	25
Accepted changes in partner	9	10
Other	13	14
Total	91	100

SOURCE.—Bowker (1983).
* Also, fear of loss of partner.

feared loss of their partner and "wanted to reestablish the relationship." Finally, only half of the assailants made any attempt to end the violence. Those who sought help turned mostly to friends and did so when the victims also initiated social or legal sanctions.

Bowker's results once again show the importance of sanctions in initiating cessation. Cessation seemed to occur in response to actions primarily designed to raise the cost of battering to the husband. Bowker's results show that many women victimized by spousal violence raised the stakes in trying to stop it by threatening legal, social, or personal sanctions.

Bowker's findings also suggest that use of sanctions was effective primarily in relations where the history of violence was less severe and power imbalances between partners were minimal (1983, p. 128). For example, the strongest correlates between the relationship history and cessation of violence were duration of violence (Pearson $r = -.31$) and abuse during pregnancy (Pearson $r = -.15$). Again, it appears that more severe and protracted violence may be much more difficult to stop despite formal external interventions, legal or otherwise.

The results of this study stop short of identifying specific processes of cessation or desistance but offer important findings on conditions or antecedents within the relationship. First, a restoration of the balance of marital power is evident in the strategies used by the women studied by Bowker. This notion fits well with other studies (e.g., Frieze 1979; Walker 1979; Pagelow 1984) that correlate marital violence to imbalances in marital power such as in decision making or control of social networks. Second, raising the costs of battering implicitly suggests a social learning approach in which the "costs" of maintaining marital power through force are no longer worthwhile. The actions by victims may represent the introduction of negative reinforcement or aversive social consequences for battering. The removal of the gratifying rewards of battering may also result from these strategies, again opening ways to initiate the processes of desistance.

Third, by establishing social networks with norms and values supportive of marital equality, those norms that reinforce battering behaviors may be effectively neutralized. Such messages to batterers were not consistently communicated, however, in Bowker's Milwaukee study. Informal police responses often deemphasized the illegal status of battering. In contrast, women's shelters effectively communicated societal rejection of battering; shelters create alternatives for women to remaining in violent homes and may neutralize male dominance and control that typifies violence toward wives (Loseke and Cahill 1984; Bowker and Maurer 1985).

Consistent with this is the importance of establishing a "folklore of quitting" for both male batterers and victims. For batterers, a positive social status may be attached to cessation, again neutralizing those values that promote violence. For women, it conveys the availability of paths and "technologies" for ending violence in the home. Part of the process of changing social norms that support battering is the dissemination of these stories of success through broad cultural outlets.

Finally, both Bowker's Milwaukee study and his larger national sample suggest that, for most batterers, "natural" or spontaneous desistance may be a misnomer. Bowker (1984, 1986b) augmented the Milwaukee sample with a similarly recruited sample nationwide for a total sample of 1,000 women. While some batterers may spontaneously desist after one or two incidents, desistance for chronic batterers is often a lengthy process, frequently preceded by specific actions by victims. The incidence of unprovoked "conversions" is extremely rare in theoretical (i.e., purposive) samples of battered women (Walker 1979, 1984; Bowker 1983, 1986a) or probability samples of women (Frieze et al. 1980; Russell 1982). Frieze (1986) found only one case of "spontaneous" desistance in her sample, which included both battered women and matched controls, by a batterer whose childhood background was atypically void of childhood violence experiences. Accordingly, while the decision to stop battering may be "spontaneous," these studies from several locales, involving both clinical and random samples, suggest that desistance is a process that involves a reduction in the frequency and severity of violence, perhaps interrupted by increasingly rare violent episodes.

The roles of various events should be acknowledged and integrated into both victims' and assailants' strategies to end violence. It appears that desistance often begins with provocation from an external source, often a victim-initiated event, usually involving the threat of legal or social sanctions that raise the cost of battering. Only then do the socio-psychological processes of desistance begin for the batterer.

C. Desistance by Displacement: Taking It Elsewhere

Few studies have examined the course of battering careers in terms of changes in victimization patterns within and outside of the family or even compared assailants' violence toward strangers, intimates, or both. Anecdotal data from victims and shelter workers suggest that violent spouses often seek out other victims if cut off from a battering relationship. They move on to other relationships and resume violence, albeit with another victim. Desistance for one victim may be initiation for another. This process may be termed *displacement*, where the violence simply moves (with the assailant) to another relationship.

Only one study has specifically examined displacement, or shifts in victimization patterns, by violent spouses over time. Shields and Hanneke (1981) reported on the intersection of family and stranger violence and also on shifts over time in victim relations. The design compared violent spouses (or partners) with a comparison group of men not known to be violent at home. The study is noteworthy for its direct contact with men, a rare occurrence in research on marital violence (Morash 1986). They recruited subjects from social agencies, newspaper advertisements, and chain referral ("snowball") techniques in metropolitan St. Louis. Respondents were classified as (1) domestic violence only, (2) stranger violence only, or violent only toward persons outside the family, and (3) general violence toward persons in both categories. Data were collected in lengthy interviews that included retrospective accounts of violence histories, childhood socialization patterns, and a variety of personality traits and behaviors.

The findings suggest that victimization patterns of domestic assailants are far from static: nearly 45 percent of the "generally" violent men began their adult violence careers victimizing only strangers. In other words, their circle of victims widened over time to include family members. Yet the researchers rarely found men whose victim circles widened outward *from* the family—few "domestic violence only" men became violent over time toward strangers as well. There were no indications that generally violent men narrowed their circle of victims over time to include one group or the other, an important finding on desistance. For this sample, desistance did not occur, and the number of victims grew over time. However, it was uncertain whether the rate of violent incidents toward the spouse remained constant or whether some violent incidents were displaced from one group of victims to the other. What did *not* occur was displacement of violence within the home to stranger victims.

Comparing the characteristics of men who commit "general violence" and men who commit "stranger violence" only, Shields and Hanneke (1981) found that they were virtually indistinguishable in terms of background characteristics such as age or duration of the relation. The "domestic violence only" men differed from the others in several ways. They were from higher social status groups and had higher educational attainment, though this may well be a sampling artifact.[9] They more often had drug and alcohol problems, they more often had extramarital affairs, and they more often had been exposed to violence as children. They less often exhibited evidence of psychopathology, but they manifested other personality traits often associated with battering: jealousy, low self-esteem, and depression. Naturally, they also had had fewer contacts with the law and were less embedded in violent subcultures.

The lessons for desistance in these findings involve not only the mutability of violence careers over time but also the important fact that "domestic-violence-only" men tend to remain within that pattern. One limitation of this study is its retrospective design—a longitudinal study might reveal shifts in violence patterns or recurring movements between groups that this study could not identify. Desistance is not necessarily permanent and may be "remission"—either a lull in offending or a more casual drifting in and out of a behavior pattern (West 1963). We simply do not know whether violent spouses follow similar career trends.

The differences between groups, and the fact that "domestic-violence-only" men tend to remain in that pattern, suggest plausible hypotheses about desistance prospects and strategies for the different types of offenders. For "domestic-violence-only" men, their violence is instrumen-

---

[9] Higher social status and educational attainment may well affect arrest probabilities, particularly at the ecological or neighborhood level. Smith (1986) illustrated the effects of neighborhood context on police arrest decisions, suggesting that arrest probabilities are higher in lower social class areas for otherwise comparable situations. Accordingly, assignment to a "generally" violent category may be more likely for those subject to higher arrest probabilities.

tal in motivation. Legal and social sanctions will be more meaningful to this (usually) higher social status individual who has much to lose from social disclosure or punishment. Also, psychotherapeutic approaches may be more appropriate for the personality traits associated with that group.

For the "generally" violent men, who had longer histories of violence and arrest, desistance would need to occur through changes in cultural patterns as well as by raising the costs of their well-established behavioral patterns. For them, violence may be expressive and less amenable to external control. It is uncertain whether desistance from family violence would accompany withdrawal from all acts of violence or whether it would mean only desistance from hurting intimate victims. Finally, for all three groups, it is possible that "specialization" follows displacement—that is, ceasing attacks on one group of victims may redirect violence to others. For these answers, a prospective study is necessary.

The Shields and Hannecke research failed to uncover "spontaneous" desistance. In fact, they found quite the opposite—expansion of victim circles for the "stranger only" group and no evidence that victimization patterns contracted in scope. However, sample characteristics may limit the evidence on desistance, whether spontaneous or gradual. Though desistance was far removed from the focus of their research, they did not find assailants within any group who halted their violence. Again, it appears that desistance without a catalyst for change is an extremely rare occurrence. This fact alone bears on our understanding of "recovery" models of cessation.

In sum, the evidence on desistance from family violence suggests several processes leading to its cessation. Recent evidence from studies of legal and social sanctions for spouse abuse suggests that desistance in less chronic or serious (i.e., injurious) cases may occur in response to legal sanctions. However, legal sanctions for more serious cases were less effective and possibly led to escalations in violence. Evidence from theoretical samples of former victims who had ended spouse abuse in their relationships suggests that both legal and social sanctions were important factors in ending violence. Strategies varied, depending on the relationship history and on the assailants' backgrounds. Once again, desistance in severe cases with more injurious and protracted violence was more difficult, regardless of the nature or strength of the sanction. This suggests that habitual or systemic violence may be more amenable to different desistance strategies than less serious cases. Other research suggests that violence in the home may subside or end by displacement to victims outside the home. Actions by victims that deter violence by raising the personal or social costs, together with efforts to re-define the social status of battering, seem to be promising strategies. Questions remain on the processes of desistance—how the decision is made to stop and how the process of stopping occurs. In the next section, evidence from studies of desistance from other patterned be-haviors is examined for its possible contributions to understanding the processes that may end family violence.

II. Spontaneous Cessation from Other Problem Behaviors

In a recent review of research on decision making by criminal offend-ers, Clarke and Cornish (1985) cite a variety of factors that influence burglars to desist from persistent careers. An accumulation of aversive experiences, changes in personal circumstances (what Irwin [1970] has termed "aging out"), and contingencies in the neighborhood or targets may lead to the decision to abandon criminal activity or to displace it elsewhere. Greenberg (1977) and Trasler (1979) both concluded that "occupational" criminality may be incompatible with family demands or with holding down a steady job. Each of these may be viewed as predictable life events that are correlated with age and with the increas-ingly difficult task of maintaining a deviant life-style. Unfortunately, we know little more about the processes that initiate criminals' decisions to quit and that aid them in carrying out the decision. Among violent offenders, there is reason to believe that desistance may run a different course, reflective of the differences in motivation and method that sepa-rate them from chronic property offenders.

Most criminal "careers" end at a young age (Farrington 1986), and there is a general decline in arrest rates with age (Blumstein et al. 1986). Those offenders who continue criminal activity at later ages tend to slow their rate of offending, and the number of crime types tends to decrease (Petersilia 1980). Whether desistance from persistent criminal behavior reflects an age-related phenomenon (Hirschi and Gottfredson 1983) or the influence of social or legal factors associated with desis-tance (Blumstein, Farrington, and Moitra 1985), there is a strong age-skewed distribution to criminal activity. The decline in offending may reflect developmental changes (e.g., maturation effects traditionally ob-served in studies of juvenile offenders) or the conscious decisions of offenders to quit crime.

The epidemiology of wife beating is also age skewed, both in frequency and severity (Shulman 1979; Straus, Gelles, and Steinmetz 1980; Fagan, Stewart, and Hansen 1983). Chronic and injurious violence occurs more often among younger males. These age-correlated drop-offs in spousal assault during early adulthood may similarly reflect decisions or processes among assailants to stop the violence. If the criminal career paradigm applies to family violence, there may be correlates of desistance that apply to the majority of violent males and other correlates that describe persistent assailants.[10] The decisions to quit crime, observed in several studies of desistance from stranger crime (Irwin 1970; Shover 1983; Cusson and Pinsonneault 1986), may also occur among family violence offenders.

For family violence, we know little about how often such decisions occur or the circumstances in which they are made. But the studies cited in the previous section identify external events that may lead to internal decisions to desist from wife abuse. To understand how such decisions are made, we must turn to other research disciplines where the social and psychological processes of desistance have garnered greater attention.

"Spontaneous remission," "natural recovery," and similar terms have been used in the literature on substance abuse and addictions to describe what criminologists now call "desistance." For criminologists, desistance implies the decision to cease behavior, whether or not intervention has occurred. Researchers in the addictions distinguish "treated" and "untreated" cessation and usually apply a criterion of one year of continuous cessation for designating the problem behavior to have ceased. For purposes of this discussion, the "treatment" distinction remains important in understanding the enabling factors leading to cessation.[11]

A. Desistance from Opiate Addiction

Charles Winick (1962, 1964) noted that each year the names of identified addicts disappeared from FBI registers. In general, disap-

---

[10] This raises the likelihood that different intervention strategies will be appropriate for chronic or infrequent assailants.

[11] This by no means constitutes acceptance of a medical or disease model of family violence. It refers only to the distinction between those whose desistance occurs absent formal or lay intervention and those who desist pursuant to some form of "treatment" or social control. Desistance may mean an active decision to stop a behavior or a process leading to behavioral change. It does not suggest that the "causes" of family violence have been addressed or that a pathology has been reversed.

pearance occurred as the addict reached 35–40 years of age. Winick's "maturing out" theory proposed that addiction was a self-limiting process that was abandoned when its purposes were served. Putting aside important but unanswered questions about *how* and *why* the process occurred, there was little doubt that untreated desistance from opiate addiction occurred.

The findings were replicated often in the next decades, in a variety of social surveys, program evaluations, and longitudinal surveys (Waldorf and Biernacki 1979). In general, these studies relied on "alternative survey" populations or theoretical sampling approaches. That is, they oversampled from "high risk" populations in order to increase the prevalence of cases with the behavior of interest. Robins (1973) studied young men who had a unique exposure to drugs while serving as enlisted men in Vietnam in 1970–71, sampling from those who had been detected as drug positive at the time of departure from the war zone. Robins and Murphy (1967) focused on inner-city black males in a study of a general population of urban men. O'Donnell et al. (1976) surveyed a national sample of young men of "high-risk" ages (18–30). Burt Associates (1977) and Macro Systems, Inc. (1975) conducted three-year follow-up studies of treatment populations. While the study designs varied considerably, from survey (polling) methods, to open-ended interviews with recruited samples of current or former addicts, to longitudinal studies of treatment populations, they consistently found occurrences of periods of desistance of varying length. The studies differed, too, in their definitions of addiction and thresholds for determining either remission or desistance.

The process of desistance from opiate addiction was explicated in detail by Waldorf (1983) and Biernacki (1986). They studied the social-psychological dynamics of recovery from opiate addiction through interviews with untreated ex-addicts ($N = 100$) and with treated cases ($N = 100$) from drug treatment programs. Respondents were recruited through chain referral sampling procedures. Addiction was defined as at least one year of daily opiate use and the experience of at least five of ten physiological withdrawal symptoms. Verification was made through short interviews with third parties. Recovery was defined by the length of abstinence—at least two years prior to the interview. Treatment programs included residential and outpatient models, as well as drug-free and methadone maintenance models.

Biernacki (1986) suggested that natural recovery was contingent on reversing the addict's immersion in the subcultures and social worlds of addiction and, conversely, isolation from more conventional roles and norms. Reestablishing ties with legitimate activities and social networks was less difficult for those who had not drifted very far. Once contact with the nonaddict cultures was initiated, successfully recovered addicts relied heavily on appropriate social relations for support and maintenance of their new roles. It was important that these new worlds provided ways for addicts to reinterpret drug use and, in particular, the craving for drugs. The new social roles provided opportunities to substitute legitimate activities—physical exercise or prayer, for example.

Waldorf (1983) noted that, for some addicts, emotional states such as despair preceded the decision to cease opiate use. However, other patterns were noted as well—"drift," rational choice, or "conversion." Conversion was in some cases a religious transformation and immersion in that belief system. In other cases, the ideology of the drug treatment program became a religious attachment. The latter was observed primarily in therapeutic communities that followed the Synanon model. Drift was similar to the patterns cited by Matza (1964) but also involved physical movement away from the old scene.[12] In the instances of rational choice, addicts reported simply tiring of the tenuous life of "spoon calls," crime, and the burden of unmet family and social responsibilities. Whether this was a maturation process, as Winick first called it, or simply an age-correlated phenomenon, remains unsettled. Waldorf (1983), citing recent life-cycle research, terms these evolutions simply "developmental changes."

Still other addicts displace their opiate consumption with alcohol, other substances, or, in rare instances, mental illness. But these were rarely observed. More common was an initiation process in which

---

[12] Synanon was the forerunner of therapeutic communities. Founded in the 1950s, Synanon was a "therapeutic community" that offered a new social world to alcoholics and opiate addicts who had failed in residential drug or alcohol treatment. The principles included abstinence, acknowledgment by residents of the dominance of alcoholic (or addict) personality traits, expunction of those traits through (often harsh) group therapy processes, and immersion in the social and economic activities of the community. In effect, the Synanon world was substituted for the former world that supported addiction or drinking. While not a formally stated theory, the concept of drift (Matza 1964) has been used convincingly to describe delinquent behavior as well as untreated desistance from opiate use (Waldorf 1983). In short, persons give up deviant behaviors because they have only limited commitments to the behavior and any social norms that support it. The behavioral change occurs not because of an emotional experience, an abrupt change in perception or belief, or psychological growth (e.g., maturation). Rather, it simply reflects a drift toward conventional behaviors. Such a drift can occur when individuals move to new social statuses, take up new activities or responsibilities, or enter new social roles (e.g., marriage, becoming a parent, meaningful employment).

addicts decided to stop using drugs when the conditions of maintaining their behaviors became untenable. In these cases, the availability of social worlds and sustaining relations supported the processes of behavioral change. Biernacki (1986) calls this an identity transformation, with attendant changes in self-definition and social roles and vocabularies.

Many of the corollary studies (summarized by Stall and Biernacki 1986) cited similar reasons for quitting drug use: aversive experiences with peers and family members, social stigmatization, geographic changes, and profound personal discoveries. In each instance, the change process involved new social worlds and identities, reinforcing social networks and new (negative) functional values for addictive behaviors, and the development of coping strategies to maintain their abstinence.

B. "Spontaneous Remission" from Alcoholism

Researchers on alcoholism and alcohol treatment use the term "spontaneous remission" to describe the process of untreated recovery from chronic alcohol use. The research on cessation from alcohol abuse is more extensive than that on opiate addiction, and theory development is more advanced. Estimates of spontaneous remission range from a low of 4 percent of "problem alcohol drinkers" to a high of 59 percent, depending on how remission or recovery is defined (Stall and Biernacki 1986). Methodological and measurement strategies account for much of the variability, but differences certainly exist among populations (Roizen, Cahalan, and Shanks 1978). There have been relatively few studies of the processes of spontaneous (untreated) recovery from alcoholism. Such attempts have concentrated on the motivations to stop drinking, rather than on the processes and problems of actual extrication from daily use. A general population survey of adults in Scotland found that new marriage, a change in jobs, problems with health, and short drinking histories were associated with spontaneous recovery (Saunders and Kershaw 1979). Stall's (1983) ethnographic study of Kentucky adults found that untreated ex-alcoholics often were motivated to give up alcohol when they experienced some significant event (e.g., life-threatening accidents, a sudden change in life circumstances such as a job opportunity) that they interpreted as critical to their ability to end problem drinking.

Tuchfeld (1981) studied a small group of former problem drinkers who stopped drinking without the aid of treatment. He found that untreated recovery occurred when problem drinkers identified their role models as negative influences, underwent humiliating experiences, suffered serious health problems, suddenly reorganized their previously intense beliefs concerning alcohol use toward other belief systems (e.g., religious conversion), but who also had had prior success with self-control. Both Tuchfeld (1981) and Stall (1983) noted that recovery proceeded in phases, though they differed in the number and nature of the phases.[13]

Factors often associated with the initiation of spontaneous remission include health problems and social pressures (probably indicating negative social sanctions from problem drinking). Once the decision is made to stop drinking, factors associated with "family life" (especially marital relations) are seen as supports for cessation (Stall 1983). Other factors supporting the process of quitting include increased religiosity, high intensity of beliefs about the negative aspects of alcohol, and positive social reinforcement from more stable social and economic conditions after remission. Stall also described a process of reorganization of beliefs about alcohol as a path to quitting and reliance on these beliefs to sustain the individual's decision in the face of cravings for alcohol. Displacement also occurs in this framework, especially for treated quitters who rely on physical outlets (e.g., running) to manage alcohol cravings, Alcoholics Anonymous models for the sustaining of beliefs and social supports, and other forms of substitution (e.g., excessive work and proselytizing).

The conventional picture of problem alcohol (or opiate) use as a relatively immutable problem may require rethinking (Roizen, Cahalan, and Shanks 1978). As with other problem behaviors, there appears to be a natural process of desistance for some people or lulls in and out of the most severe episodes for others. The biochemical, or even pathological, aspects of problem substance use may be only correlates or contributing factors, not independent causes of addiction. A critical discovery of cessation research is the contribution of social circumstances to sustaining the behavior patterns, initiating the decision to

[13] For example, alcohol researchers strongly disagree on the definition and use of abstinence as a criterion for desistance in studies of "problem drinking." Definitions vary primarily in the length of time of remission, ranging from one to several years before the behavior is regarded as abstinent. Obviously, a lengthy criterion time provides a hedge against false positives among an "abstinent" group, avoiding false "desistance" by those whose behavior may be only a temporary "remission." Whether abstinence is an appropriate measure of change in drinking behavior depends on the social definition of alcohol abuse. Some studies use statistically significant reductions in consumption as measures of decreased alcohol abuse or problem drinking, while other studies regard any use of alcohol as evidence of continued problem use.

break them and reinforcing that decision through developmental changes.

C. Other Addictive Behaviors

Studies of cessation from other addictive behaviors also inform our understanding of desistance by citing factors common across several populations. In particular, the limited research on untreated desistance from smoking illustrates the processes involved in such habituated behaviors. Perri, Richards, and Shulthers (1977) interviewed college students who had quit smoking ($N = 24$) and an equal (but unmatched) sample of those who had failed in their efforts. The successful quitters rated themselves as more motivated and committed to personal change, persisted with a broader repertoire of coping techniques for longer periods of time, and more often used self-reinforcement and problem-solving tactics to evade cravings. Hecht's (1978) small sample of self-quitters ($N = 27$) were mostly males who were well educated, older, and formerly heavy smokers. Among the eight basic reasons for quitting smoking were general and specific health concerns, pressure from significant others, redefinitions of smoking (as a filthy habit) and smokers (a negative self-perception). Most used some substitute to quit, such as food, exercise, or chewing gum to manage cravings for nicotine.

Other studies found similar results. DiClemente and Prochaska (1979) compared treated ($N = 29$) and untreated ($N = 34$) former smokers. Both groups had about the same remission rates after five months: about 60 percent. Those who succeeded in quitting reported processes similar to those shown in other studies (e.g., substitutions to manage cravings, and self-reinforcement). They managed cravings by avoiding situations and settings where they had previously smoked (e.g., bars, and gatherings where there also was heavy drinking). Pederson and Lefcoe (1976) also examined how small samples of self-quitters ($N = 48$), compared with treated quitters ($N = 46$), maintained their decision to stop smoking. Again, processes of substitution were critical in avoiding recidivism, as were acute health concerns. They also found that successful quitters more often lived with nonsmokers.

Stall and Biernacki (1986) reviewed the empirical literature on smoking cessation and eating disorders, especially overeating. Again, as in opiate and alcohol cessation, negative social sanctions or aversive experiences influenced the decision to stop. Among smokers, accidental fires or health problems often preceded the decision to stop. And substitutes such as chewing gum also played an important role. Reorientation of social circumstances to avoid smoking situations helped sustain the decision to stop. The support of friends and intimates, as well as constant reinforcement of the negative consequences of smoking, also sustained the decision to quit smoking.

To study desistance from eating disorders, Stall and Biernacki turned to the popular literature and lay publications. In general, Stall and Biernacki found that the professional literature often overlooked the factors that resulted in weight loss without treatment. While they found ample evidence that people do gain control over their eating problems without formal treatment, they turned to the lay literature to identify the processes of weight loss.

For example, Jeffrey et al. (1984) conducted two obesity prevalence surveys over a decade apart among suburban populations, comparing results in order to separate lasting from episodic weight loss. About half (54.8 percent) of the males and nearly four-fifths (79.8 percent) of the females reported significant weight loss through low-calorie regimens and simple dieting. Schacter (1982) compared an academic department with the working population of a resort town, and found that about two in three had successfully lost significant weight without formal treatment. Only Rosenthal, Allen, and Winter (1980) identified social-psychological processes that contributed to weight loss among obese people, citing differences in weight loss among women in a clinical sample. Those women who more often enjoyed the involvement of husbands had significantly greater weight loss than those without spousal support, a factor that they termed a "nontreatment" variable.

To understand nontreatment factors important to successful weight loss, they reviewed popular magazines such as *Slimming and Nutrition* and *A Silhouette Slimmer*. They found factors contributing to weight loss to be similar to those that supported desistance from smoking, problem drinking, and opiate addiction, albeit in different terminology. "Significant (health) accidents" to increase motivation, social shame and tantalizing new self-images, instigation from family and relatives, redefinition of the social meaning and context of eating, and social reinforcement of cessation decisions were cited as components of desistance from obesity.

D. *Common Factors in Cessation: Making and Sustaining the Decision to Quit*

The common themes in the literature on "spontaneous remission," "natural recovery," or "quitting" other problem behaviors offer useful perspectives for thinking about desistance from family violence. These lessons derive from diverse behaviors—opiate use, eating disorders, alcoholism, and smoking—that have distinctive social meanings in our cultural landscape. Accordingly, their commonalities may offer the beginning of a theory of cessation.

The decision to stop appears to be preceded by a variety of factors, most of which are negative social sanctions or consequences. Health problems, difficulties with the law or with maintaining a current lifestyle, threats of other social sanctions from family or close relations, and a general rejection of the social world in which the behaviors thrive are often antecedents of the decision to quit. For some, religious conversions or immersion into cultural settings with powerful norms (e.g., treatment ideology) provide paths for cessation. Several commonalities appear when these characteristics are compared with the desistance characteristics of the property offenders in Clarke and Cornish (1985), the decisions to quit by the seventeen robbers discussed by Cusson and Pinsonneault (1986), and the experiences of the violent spouses in tables 2 and 3. Notable similarities are the threat of social disclosure (a form of sanction) or sociolegal sanction. For violent men, the threat of loss (of the relationship, in particular) appears to influence a decision to quit.

The literatures on addictions and habituated behaviors also describe processes that sustain and reinforce the changed behaviors on the part of those who have decided to quit. Among these are changes in physical location and social networks, transformations of identity and forming ties to conventional life-styles, changes in the functional definitions of the problem behavior, drift from the preceding social world to new social relations and contingencies that reinforce the decision, displacement of the old behavior with new forms of behavior or expression (from religion, to physical outlets, to strong belief systems), and, occasionally, misuse of substances or substitution of other problem behaviors. The latter, however, were rarely found in the addictions literature.

III. Toward a Model of Desistance
from Family Violence

One need not subscribe to theories of addiction to apply these lessons to spousal violence. There is a basic difference between explaining the *causes* of crime and the *occurrence* of crimes (Clarke and Cornish 1985). The explanatory theories that address initial involvement in a crime may address neither continuance of crime nor desistance. Farrington

(1979) has suggested that the different stages of a criminal career may require different explanations. Theories of desistance may span several behaviors which, at the same time, require quite different causal explanations. There are parallels in desistance from systemic violence toward spouses, problem substance use, and other patterned behaviors. This is not to equate the behaviors but, instead, to suggest that we may understand and model cessation of behaviors whose occurrence results from similar processes, despite radically different origins.

Drawing on the literature discussed in the previous sections, this section proposes a tentative model for understanding desistance from family violence. Three stages characterize the cessation process: building resolve or discovering motivation to stop, making and publicly disclosing the decision to stop, and maintenance of the new behaviors and integration into new social networks (Stall and Biernacki 1986). The disclosure period is particularly difficult, for the old behaviors have been disavowed, but new ones have not yet been developed or internalized. In the third stage, a variety of processes are needed to strengthen the decision, including social sources of identity and definition, social reinforcement of beliefs, and, most important, the immersion into a social world where the old behaviors are conspicuously disapproved while new ones are made available and are approved. Reinforcement may take the form of improved health, social, emotional, or economic conditions, or the substitution of strong belief systems to provide external controls on behavior. These ingredients of a modified social and personal identity, reinforced and supported along the way, provide paths to ending problem behaviors.

A. Catalysts for Change: The Beginning of the End

When external conditions change and reduce the "rewards of violence," motivation may build to end the violence. That process, and the resulting decision, seem to be related to one of two conditions: a series of negative, aversive, unpleasant experiences from family violence, or corollary situations in which the positive rewards, status, or gratification from wife beating are removed. The desistance research discussed earlier shows the potential role of legal or social sanctions in initiating a process of cessation. In the Bowker study (1983), fear of sanction or loss enabled a large percentage of the batterers to stop. From the victims' perspectives, public disclosure (leading to social censure as well as to official scrutiny by social control agents) and sociolegal sanctions contributed most often to desistance. Both the victim and societal responses may combine to bring about these changes in the objective conditions that sustain battering.

The converse of increasing the negative consequence to perpetrators of violence against family members is decreasing the positive consequences of violence. Gratification from family violence may come from achieving or maintaining dominance in a relationship, from the expressive release of anger and aggression, from the attainment of positive social status that domination affords, or even from the "hearts and flowers" aftermath of many battering incidents (see Walker 1979 for examples).[14] Bowker argues that gratification is realized by many men from maintaining, by violence, traditional stereotypes of male dominance: the cultural transmission of values that demand male domination and the reinforcement of those values through socialization as children in male-dominated families and later social embedment in violence-supporting social relations.

The importance of reinforcing societal values, modeled in early childhood and refined in adult years, suggests that both environmental or normative supports for domination of women as a group and situational interactions at a social or subcultural level contribute to male violence toward women. Bowker's (1986a or 1986b) analysis of his study of batterers' battered women ($N = 1,000$) shows the relation between social embedment in male subculture and the severity of husbands' violence toward wives. Figure 1, derived from victim reports, suggests that more frequent contacts with exclusive male subcultures are associated with more severe forms of wife assault. Both trends in figure 1 are significant ($p \le .001$).

Bowker suggests that "the myriad peer-relationships that support the patriarchal dominance of the family and the use of violence to enforce it may constitute a subculture of violence. The more fully a husband is immersed in this subculture, the more likely he is to batter his wife" (1983, p. 135). Less clear, though, are the processes that translate such ecological effects into specific socialization processes that contribute to, or attenuate, a propensity to violence.

---

[14] Walker (1979, 1984) describes the cyclical nature of violence toward wives. There are discrete phases, beginning with the buildup of tension, an explosion of violence, a period of remorse (by the batterer) and contrition, followed again by a buildup of tension. Walker reported that during the remorse stage, many batterers gave the victims flowers, candies, and sometimes elaborate gifts to demonstrate their contrition as well as their love. The batterers tended to be extremely attentive and caring during these periods. This phase is characterized further by the batterer's apparent dependency on the victim, fearing her departure or the loss of her love and craving her nurturing and caretaking.

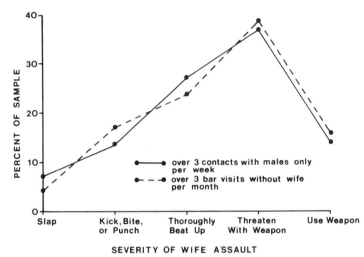

FIG. 1.—Social embedment in male subculture and severity of wife assault. Source: Bowker (1986).

When gratification is neutralized, or when it is overwhelmed by negative experiences, motivation or "resolve" builds to stop. Gelles (1983) calls this "raising the costs of family violence." Batterers will decide to stop when the consequences of violence raise problems that cannot be ignored or have psychic or emotional costs. These include problems with the law or with family members or social sanctions that may in turn lead to economic problems or even punishment. In early years of a battering "career," these problems may not pose difficulties. But in later years, when personal circumstances change, they can become unmanageable, and their "costs" unacceptable.

For the batterer with a lengthy criminal record or for one who knows firsthand that legal sanctions are often weak, legal measures short of incapacitation may be ineffective (Dutton 1987). The career criminal literature shows that sanctions have uncertain effects on criminality. Blumstein et al. (1986) show the difficulty in attributing desistance to arrest and highlight the problem of false desistance in explaining career termination. Further research with batterers may tell us whether weak police interventions (i.e., those with no arrest) reinforce violence by not firmly penalizing it. Other ineffective encounters with the law teach a similar lesson for crimes at home. If this is true, then the costs of an arrest to the offender may not appear to be very high. This would explain the greater frequency of calls to police by victims of batterers with more severe battering histories *and* with arrest records for stranger violence. Other costs or sanctions may be necessary to catalyze these men to change.

It is likely that the forces contributing to a decision to desist will build over time, rather than occur in response to a single event. Unlike substance abuse models, conversion or significant accidents are less likely to occur in the case of batterers. Instead, repeated separations, police calls, or involvement of other help sources are more likely to be necessary. Accordingly, the change in the offender's "cost-benefit analysis" of battering must occur from a series of interventions—from the victim, from a social or legal sanction, or from both. When a victim calls for help or declares limits, how others respond is crucial. Repeated interventions may be needed to build the motivation to stop and change the calculus of violence. The victim-initiated strategies described by Bowker and the *early* responses of police and social networks to a violent family are significant in bringing about conditions leading to desistance. If these succeed in creating a change in the balance of power in the relationship, the batterer may either decide to stop or to move on to another relationship. Whether the battering resumes elsewhere may depend on similar contingencies.

B. Discontinuance

Interviews with victims have shown that violence and injury are frequent, and sometimes daily, occurrences (Walker 1979; Frieze et al. 1980; Russell 1982). Just as the decision to stop violence may take time to build, so, too, may violence take time to discontinue. It is unlikely that the batterer will consider alternatives each time he wants to lash out. Maintaining the resolve to stop will require significant supports for both batterer and victim.

For victims, the resolve to show the batterer, even at personal cost, that battering will have negative consequences is critical to desistance. Economics and emotional ties are often cited as reasons why victims do not abandon violent relationships (Loseke and Cahill 1984). Sidel (1986) provides stark data from interviews with 100 women whose marriages ended precipitately to validate fears of economic loss or loneliness. This study included women with violent episodes in their marriages. The threat of economic and psychological hardship may deter some women from ending a violent marriage (Walker 1984). Browne (1987) reported that threats of harm to children and threats of economic and physical reprisal were tactics commonly used by batterers to deter women from ending the marriage.

For the batterer, the decision to abandon violence may mean loss of social support from peers and uncertainty about how to cope with conflict and anger. Bowker (1983; 1984) interpreted the strong social embedment of the violent husbands as evidence of immersion in a subculture supporting or approving male violence toward family members. Social interactions with only male friends, time spent (without wives) in bars, and participation in male-oriented recreational organizations had the strongest correlations with several dimensions of marital violence, including frequency, duration, and severity of marital violence, and violence toward children. Bowker concluded that the better integrated the battering husband was in male subcultures, the more severe was his violence in the home. Bowker (1984) hypothesizes that violent male subcultures are a major factor in the maintenance and support of marital violence for many men. Dobash and Dobash (1979) describe patriarchal influence as normative, while Straus (1976) describes the marriage license as a "hitting license." The Bowker studies suggest a socialization process that translates normative ecological influences into social processes that operate at the situational and individual levels. While there is no national lobby that supports wife beating, there probably are myriad independent social networks that tacitly condone violence or at least fail to sanction it negatively. Embedment in these cultures poses a high risk of severe violence in the home.

Leaving the subculture is not unlike leaving the world of the addict or the alcoholic. Biernacki (1986) noted the exclusiveness of the social involvements maintained by former addicts during the initial stages of abstinence. With social embedment comes the gratification of social acceptance and social identity. The decision to end a behavior that is socially determined and supported implies withdrawal of the social gratification it brings. For batterers, it also threatens the loss of the gratification from domination in the home. Alternatively, even if the social support for battering is tacit or implied, abandoning violence risks the loss of acceptance in the social environment. The more deeply embedded in that social context, the more dependent the batterer is on that social world for his primary sources of approval and social definition. Similar problems were experienced by the former addicts in Biernacki's study, who reported uncertainty and anxiety that nonaddicts in new daily contacts would not accept them socially.

Addicts develop a number of ruses to deal with withdrawal (Waldorf 1983), while problem drinkers develop similar ruses to manage the urge to drink (Stall 1983). For example, some addicts substituted strenuous athletic activities. Others joined political or religious groups, and still others simply spent all their time at work. Biernacki (1986) reports that one ex-addict moved from southern California to a rural farming area, substituting rigorous farm hours for the relative idleness of urban life. One became a marathon runner, while another organized a union of inmates in state prisons, and a third is now a drug researcher.

It is likely that batterers face similar confusion, but there are few data to describe how they cope with it. Intervention programs for men who batter concentrate on anger management and development of new, nonviolent skills for dealing with situations that in the past led to violent episodes (Gondolf 1985*a*, 1985*b*). Such programs also provide new social worlds in which former batterers can immerse themselves. What is clear is the need for alternatives and substitutes for the now disavowed behavior, but they may be ineffective if not accompanied by revised definitions of marital power and standards of gratification for dominance in the family. (See Saunders and Azar, in this volume, for a review of the effectiveness of treatment programs for batterers.)

Depending on whether such skills are acquired, and also on the responses of victims when discontinuance begins, one of three outcomes of the decision to stop will occur: a return to violence or displacement elsewhere after a short respite, intermittent episodes or a gradual decrease in the frequency and severity of violence, or a complete and abrupt halt.

The processes that *initiate* the decision to stop may not suffice for discontinuance. The decision to abandon violence, and the events preceding the decision, mark the beginning of involvement of both batterer and victim in new social networks and possibly the departure from old ones. This, too, may shift the balance of power in the relationship, creating an immediate change in the calculus of battering. As in other problem behaviors that are not hidden, social relationships (with other family members, peers, and neighbors) especially are contingent on acceptance of the behavior or at least complicity in ignoring it.

But the implications of desistance are clear—social supports for battering, or at least tolerant attitudes toward spouse abuse, may no longer be available. The responses by social control agents, family members, and peer supporters to further episodes of violence are critical in shaping the outcome of discontinuance. New social and emotional worlds to replace the old ones may strengthen the decision to stop. With discontinuance comes the difficult work of identity transformations (Biernacki 1986) and establishing new social definitions of behavior and relationships to reinforce them. Whether desistance can be maintained *without* exchanging social networks and identities remains a question for new research to improve our understanding of these outcomes and the situational factors (especially victim responses) that influence them.

Finally, discontinuance may contradict the cultural norms that contributed to the violence over a lifetime of socialization (Dobash and Dobash 1979). The subcultures and social worlds that reinforce values supportive of violence to women will remain intact, despite the batterer's decision to stop. Yet these values influence some, but not all, men to use violence in families. How men reject those values is an important part of the discontinuance process that is worthy of study. One step involves developing new social definitions of family equalities and new behaviors (e.g., family decision making) that reflect more egalitarian family processes.

If violence is supported through peer cultures to express these broad cultural values, then the development of "immunities" to those influences is critical to discontinuance. Development of new social peers is critical to support a new social identity. And the continued high social and personal costs of violence must be maintained to rationalize the decision to stop.

C. Maintenance

Following the initial stages of discontinuance, strategies to avoid a return to violence build on the strategies to break from a lengthy pattern of violence: further integration into a nonviolent identity and social world, maintaining the costs of battering, acceptance and institutionalization of changes in the balance of power in the relationship, and refinement of the batterer's skills to manage anger and conflict. But immersion into a supposedly nonviolent world does not remove the formerly violent spouse from cultural norms that are ambiguous with respect to wife battery.[15] Men who batter and men who do not batter

---

[15] In analyzing the contributions of patriarchy to family violence, researchers such as Dobash and Dobash (1979), Pagelow (1984), and Browne (1987) specifically focus on economic inequalities and cultural portrayals as manifestations of male orientation and hegemony. The changing role of women in American society and new legislation criminalizing family violence suggest changes in normative values condemning battering. Yet other cultural and economic markers continue to express patriarchal values: the disparity in economic status of women as a group, and the role and portrayal of women in popular culture. Economic inequalities place a lesser value on women's labor and social contributions and reinforce the dominant role played by men in the labor market. Women earn less, and there are fewer women in senior management positions in business or government. There also are fewer women in elective office. Popular culture offers fewer por-

both live out cultural values that are conflicting but nonetheless popular in our culture (Dobash and Dobash 1981). The management of this duality appears to be part of the skill of maintenance.

Two types of strategies appear necessary to maintain nonviolence: substitution and stabilization. Substitution involves the replacement of peer supports and those elements of the social organization of family life that support battering. Stabilization is the process of building social and psychological buttresses to maintain a life free of violence against wives.

1. *Substitution.*   Social supports for battering are the cultural conditions and peer interactions that either afford social status to the assailant or fail to condemn violence toward wives. Empirical studies suggest that social embedment is associated with severe wife battery. Bowker (1984) found strong correlations for 1,000 men between severe wife assault and three measures of social embedment in male culture: exclusive contacts with male friends, time spent in bars without wife, and reading pornography.

Maintenance depends in part on replacing these networks of peers and associates with supports that both disapprove of battering and approve of new nonviolent beliefs and behaviors. This may not be an easy task for those men who are strongly embedded in social worlds at work or in the community. Men's support groups are important sources of alternative social supports to maintain a nonviolent style. In other words, maintenance may depend on immersion into a social world in which wife beating meets immediately with strong formal and informal sanctions.

Bowker (1983) suggests the importance of peer support groups modeled after Alcoholics Anonymous to sustain behavioral and attitudinal changes. But this may not apply to the many batterers who are not embedded in male peer subcultures of violence. For these men, social control is a major restraint on violence, but redefined marital relations can also be such a restraint. Social institutions provide both control and cultural norms of behavior that restrain violence, just as weak societal responses facilitate violence. Their responses convey the supports of or prohibitions against violence.

---

trayals of women than of men in egalitarian social positions or family roles in cinema, television, or print media. These cultural and economic indicators suggest that women occupy a lower status, which in turn reinforces both male attitudes of superiority and the legitimacy of domination.

A more difficult but equally important substitution is the balancing of power. Continued use of informal and formal help sources by the woman maintains high costs for battering as well as social restraints against it. The availability of help sources narrows the inequalities that place women at an economic and social disadvantage. Help sources offer social networks to support decisions to disallow violence and maintain access to legal help and social sanctions. Most important, external resources maintain the victim's option to leave, which is only possible when material and social supports are available to the woman. The high number of separations that preceded desistance in the nationwide study of 1,000 women who overcame battering (Bowker 1986b) supports Walker's (1979) contention that the victim's willingness to leave is the first step to ending the violence.

Other possible causes of battering should also be addressed. For example, problematic alcohol use often is associated with marital violence. Disinhibition theories offer an explanatory bridge to relate substances and behavior. If alcohol is a correlate of abuse, then alcohol treatment should be part of a maintenance strategy.[16]

2. *Stabilization.* Despite these efforts to maintain nonviolence, desistance is likely to be episodic, with occasional bouts interspersed with lengthening of lulls. The linkages of victims with societal supports and responses will determine whether the episodes are part of a declining pattern or the beginning of a resurgence. Age is a critical variable in desistance research, regardless of whether it is associated with maturation or similar developmental concepts. Desistance is part of a social psychological transformation for both victim and batterer. A strategy to stabilize the transition to nonviolence requires the active use of supports by both men and women to maintain the norms that have been substituted for the forces that supported violence in the past.

Careful research is needed to describe and analyze that process. Further empirical data are needed to understand fully what happens to those who discontinue and succeed and those who discontinue and fail. The natural course of family violence remains unknown beyond anecdotal evidence. Cross-sectional data with cohorts of older subjects may develop adequate models for testing in prospective studies with younger subjects.

[16] Alcohol is a correlate of family violence, but its relation to battering varies extensively by study design and samples. Its weaknesses as an explanation of battering lie in two observations: not all the men who drink excessively are wife batterers, and alcohol use by men does not explain why some women are abused and others are not.

IV. Conclusions

Desistance from stranger crime has been well documented by criminologists, as has spontaneous remission from substance abuse. The family violence literature was silent until recently on desistance, but recent evidence suggests that desistance does indeed occur in a variety of circumstances. The evidence on desistance has been generally descriptive and lacks theoretical grounding. The shared characteristics of desistance in three literatures suggest that a preliminary model of desistance may be constructed and put to systematic inquiry.

The evidence on desistance suggests important similarities between family violence and other behaviors whose origins may be quite different. Changes occurred when the pleasurable, gratifying aspects of the old behavior were no longer there. Aversive experiences play an important role in forming the resolve to desist, as does the decline of gratification associated with it. Extraction from the social systems that support and validate wife battery, the substitution of new social networks for batterers with different normative values, balancing marital power (through help sources for victims), and identity transformations that embed batterers within new networks are critical elements of desistance. The maintenance of external restraints, both by significant relationships and others, reinforces the new behavioral norms and restrains the old ones. Also, it seems that desistance is a reciprocal or recursive process, in which the initial effects of aversive experiences initiate a gradual process of decline in the incidence and severity of violence.

Both social and legal sanctions contribute to desistance, though their effects appear to be greater for those with less severe histories of violence. Stronger legal sanctions are required for more severe batterers. Batterers with shorter, less severe histories have a higher probability of desisting than those who are further along in a violence career. In other words, most early desisters stop with little external intervention. But other types of sanctions are effective as well, including victim-initiated strategies and sanctions imposed within the relationship—specifically, the resolve to leave and inflict loss and shame on the batterer. But the situational conditions that make this possible are the help sources that empower women and the access to legal sanctions to maintain restraints. These contextual influences should be integrated into a theory of desistance.

Some aspects of desistance from nonviolent crime and other behaviors are unknown with respect to family violence. "Maturing out" has been cited in several studies of career criminals and addicts, but little is known about age-related desistance from family violence. Also, there is no evidence that the dramatic personality changes or new beliefs ("conversions") that occur for addicts also occur for batterers. But so little research on batterers has been done that this, too, remains an unanswered question.

Is a special theory needed for desistance from family violence? For decades, explanations of crime and violence have differed on whether they are unitary or isomorphic phenomena. Among family violence researchers, similar debates have not yet resolved whether family violence is a special case of violence (Gelles and Straus 1979). One reason has been the concern with understanding the origins of crime (Clarke and Cornish 1985) and predicting its occurrence (Blumstein, Farrington, and Moitra 1985). The policy contributions of these concerns are evident and have led to efforts to prevent or control crimes of social importance. Another reason has been the continuing segregation of family violence from both criminology and violence research. Family violence continues to be viewed as an idiosyncratic crime, much like white-collar crime, and remains outside the mainstream of criminological theory and research (Fagan and Wexler 1987). The result is a focus on unique causes of and solutions to specific crime types, overlooking the common origins of different behaviors and neglecting the importance of situational influences on crime events and later stages of careers.

Whether desistance from family violence parallels desistance from other behaviors may not speak to its origins. But it may yield important clues about the stages of family violence, and the possible convergence of deviant behaviors despite uncommon origins. In other words, the utility of a desistance model may not depend on whether batterers are generalists at violence or specialists within the home. By examining desistance, we force ourselves to rethink the relations among etiological variables—what is important to initiation of violence may be irrelevant to its cessation.

A. *Policy and Applications*

Many of the contributions of feminists to theory, policy, and practice are evident in cessation processes. Shelters are important in balancing the power of victims with batterers and allowing victims to establish internal sanctions absent fears of physical reprisal. Other help sources help victims avoid economic reprisals and provide social supports for demanding an end to violence. They directly allow victims to raise the personal "costs" of continuing violence. Criminal sanctions also restrain battering by raising its social costs. Massive public education can erode the cultural supports for violence by bringing to public debate the consequences of traditional sex roles. In other words, policy must attend to the postcessation environment to provide *cultural* supports for the changing status of women.

How can policy apply knowledge of desistance to decrease battering? Intervention policies can aim to promote desistance processes. Specific policies may be salient for the distinct offender types. Research on batterers suggests the existence of several categories, which in turn supports efforts to taxonomize not only batterers but also policy responses. First, the criminal careers analogy suggests that there is a continuum of battering "types" from a small percentage of chronics, through a middle group whose careers vary in intensity and length, to many who batter only once or twice and never more. Studies of the effects of criminal sanctions imply that early legal intervention in a battering "career" may yield better prospects for desistance than entering later into more serious and protracted battering careers.

Second, Shields and Hanneke (1981) identified distinct violence patterns with both "generally" violent men (who victimize both spouses and strangers) and "domestic-violence-only" men who are violent only toward spouses. Third, Fagan, Stewart, and Hansen (1983) found that the most severe (i.e., injurious) forms of violence occurred most often among the chronic batterers, whose victimization patterns also more often fit the profile of "generally" violent men described by Shields and Hannecke. Fourth, the Bowker studies (1983, 1984) also identify different tactics that battered women used to deal with violence, differential responses used by battered women to deal with violence, and differential responses by batterers to various reactive strategies by women.

Sensible policy-making would recognize the varieties of batterers and develop a range of sanctions and interventions. Sanctions appear to be effective in promoting desistance, particularly for less serious cases or early cases, together with other aversive experiences for batterers. For generally violent men, focusing on stranger crimes may run the risk of displacing stranger violence exclusively into the home. But focusing on family violence may remove the cultural supports for violence by promoting changes in general peer networks supportive of it. Substitution of social supports can maintain the rewards of nonviolence. Treatment interventions may focus on accelerating the processes of desistance by encouraging changes in social networks while teaching new ways to respond to conflict and anger.

Criminal justice policies should promote consistency in establishing the aversive consequences of family violence (protecting victims while sanctioning offenders, for example), but should also take care not to make empty threats through weak sanctions. Monolithic policies, such as presumptive arrest in all cases, may assume that family violence is a homogeneous phenomenon. The variety of patterns of violence suggests a range of policies with diverse approaches to sanctioning assailants and protecting victims. The widespread public promotion of these policies will also signal the new "costs" of violence.

The evidence on victim-initiated strategies suggests that policy should balance sanctions for assailants with supports for victims. Neither is sufficient alone to promote the conditions leading to desistance. Since cultural and situational factors influence each situation, policies should address both areas—for example, presumptive arrest policies still require implementation and coordination in the courts and prosecutors' offices to be effective. Similarly, expanded help sources should be supported by policies that enable victims to avoid the economic hardships of separation.

This economic reality points to the need to coordinate policies that may logically span social arenas. Many communities have formed coordinating bodies for family violence. Recognizing that economic hardship is often a barrier to victim participation in the court process, policies should be coordinated to ease the threat to victims' (and their children's) well-being and should be strategically focused on the weaker areas in the community's response system. This effort, if well publicized, will also add to efforts to reverse cultural supports for battering.

The lessons of desistance also point toward foci for prevention. Beyond policy developments, earlier intervention is needed to sanction the antecedents of marital violence. Recent evidence on "date rape" suggests that aggression toward women is indeed a part of male socialization and is manifested early.[17] Social development curricula in

---

[17] Studies of general adult female populations (Russell 1984), male adolescents (Ageton 1983), and female college students (Malamuth 1981) consistently show that rape or forced intercourse occurs on dates. Ageton's study of a nationwide sample of adolescent males estimated that 5 to 16 percent of the sample reported committing a "sexual assault," and that most are "spontaneous events which occur in the context of a date." In Malamuth's 1977 survey of female college students, over half the women reported that they experienced "offensive male sexual aggression" in the past year. Over half (56

schools should emphasize peer norms that devalue aggression toward intimates and condemn violence in all its sociocultural forms. Peer interventions at that early stage may influence both individual and subcultural processes. Increasing the social status of women will avoid the power differentials that both license violence (Straus 1978) and discourage victims' help seeking (Gelles 1983). These may include such policies as mandatory maternity leave and child care supports to encourage women to remain in the workplace.

B. Research

A desistance approach suggests several complementary directions for research: career studies with cohorts of older respondents to gain longer study periods, replication of deterrence research with more serious (felony) abusers, and desistance studies on other forms of intrafamily violence. As new empirical evidence develops, triangulation of knowledge from separate endeavors will build to refine theory and models.

The examples of desistance research cited above illustrate the methodological dilemmas of family violence research. Retrospective studies and the preponderance of victim reports as data sources highlight limitations on theory and research in the field of offender behavior. Victims may be unaware of displaced aggression on new victims when the assailant leaves home. New efforts are needed to focus on assailants as research subjects, both to validate previous research and to answer new questions on styles of violence. Also, research on men will elucidate the influences, perceptions, and decision processes of offenders in the intervals surrounding battering incidents.

Questions of central importance to desistance research should focus on the role and perception of sanctions, compared with personal circumstances and with the way that formal and informal sanctions are interpreted. Clarke and Cornish (1985) call for research on the heuristic processes that offenders use to assess costs and benefits of crime commission. Similar research should be conducted on violence in the home, examining techniques or processes of neutralization that offset loving, moral, or legal restraints and exploring how situational factors (e.g., drinking and economic stress) affect assailants' actions. These models may also determine how assailants select victims (or joint victimization patterns) within or outside the home.

---

percent) in Russell's 1982 interviews with 930 women in the San Francisco Bay area reported that forced intercourse had been obtained by threat, rather than rape. Of these, 82 percent involved nonstrangers.

The important role of peer supports for maintaining desistance suggests research to describe how norms supportive of violence are communicated and reinforced. Yet it is still unclear how these norms are translated in situational contexts to legitimate the use of violence to maintain dominance in the family. Recent evidence on adolescent aggression toward women suggests that these beliefs develop well before adulthood and marriage. These beliefs express cultural norms and values that reflect a hierarchical, patriarchal social organization. Such norms have been associated with wife assault in empirical studies in the United Kingdom (Dobash and Dobash 1979) and the United States (Bowker 1984; Yllo and Straus 1984). Straus (1976) identified nine specific manifestations of a male-dominant structure that support wife assault.[18]

For questions of this type, ethnographic research in natural settings may be especially valuable for understanding how peer norms are communicated and enforced and how they influence the development of violence careers. Research on the ability of many men to avoid the predictable consequences of patriarchal influences will point out the social, legal, and moral restraints that help them avoid violence in marriage (Morash 1986).

The important deterrence experiments of this decade should be broadened to include other types of family violence and more serious crimes than the misdemeanors in issue in the Minneapolis study. Longer follow-up and more sensitive measures will provide more information on the effects of sanctions and on the deceleration of violence. Experiments on more serious sanctions for felony cases can also further elucidate the relation between sanctions, violence, and individual characteristics. Shorter study periods make certain theoretical assumptions—that desistance is a unitary event, that its effects are not susceptible to erosion, and that offenders are unaware of the surveillant effects of ongoing research. Measurement and design choices often produce artifactual results—the use of dichotomous recidivism variables or emphasis on behavior to the exclusion of consequences,[19] for example—

[18] For example, use of force as defense of male authority, normative attitudes supporting violence toward wives, compulsive masculinity, economic constraints and discrimination, burdens of child care (and failure to provide relief to these burdens), a myth of the intrinsic weakness of the single-parent household, preeminence of the caretaker/wife role for women, women's negative self-image, and male orientation of the justice system.

[19] The debate on husband battering illustrates the ensuing problems that result from overreliance on measures of behavior. Though Steinmetz (1977) found a comparable incidence of violence among women and men, other analysts (e.g., Straus 1978) pointed out the differences in injury from husband-wife violence.

which may mask both good and bad results. Strategies accompanying formal sanctions such as shelter and social disclosure also should be included in desistance research. Designs comparing legal sanctions alone, or combined with social sanctions, can help plan strategies for intervention.

Desistance research requires representative samples of known and self-identified offenders. Research on cessation from substance abuse often has relied on ethnographic samples recruited from populations generally not found through official sources, whose behaviors otherwise remain hidden. Bowker (1983, 1984) and Shields and Hanneke (1981) also relied on recruited samples. The latter study, especially, was noteworthy for its use of violent men as subjects. Each study in turn sheds new light on desistance; these strategies should be part of a coordinated research effort. Clinical studies of violent men from treatment or incarcerated populations are well complemented by research on recruited samples.

Strategies developed by Frieze et al. (1980) for comparison samples can further strengthen these designs. Frieze sampled from the same residential blocks to identify matched cases for comparison with battered women. The natural controls for social structural variables provided a parsimonious alternative to other matching techniques. The results, too, were controversial: over 37 percent of the "controls" also reported wife assaults in the past year.

Desistance research on sexual and physical child abuse has been limited largely to studies of families in treatment or under court sanctions.[20] For all types of violent families, these strategies are powerful tools for sampling from universes of unknown dimensions.

Retrospective study is a basic limitation of such career studies. But recent developments, again primarily in research on narcotics and crime (Speckart and Anglin 1986), offer techniques to minimize recall problems. Using key life events to establish temporal anchors, Anglin has traced the addiction careers of treated and untreated heroin users in

[20] Literature reviewed for this essay revealed very few studies of desistance from other forms of family violence. These were primarily treatment evaluations. Anecdotal information from clinical studies suggests that cessation of child abuse, both physical and sexual, occurs when the child reaches an age where she or he is no longer a salient target. What happens then is unclear. Incest research hints at displacement to grandchildren in some cases, or to other children nearby, where the offender gains access to the child through a trusting role (Finkelhor et al. 1986). For physical child abuse, or abuse where both mother and child are victims, the removal of the child may displace the aggression onto the mother. Most research to date either is epidemiological or clinical, with few efforts to trace the course of abuse in a family.

California. Many of Anglin's subjects were over fifty years of age and were recalling with accuracy events over thirty years old. These methods can be translated to the study of intrafamily violence to construct violence histories that have evolved both over many years and through a variety of influences. Victimization patterns and displacement, other shifts in the frequency or severity of violence (lulls, episodes, relapses after lengthy desistance periods), and contributing situational factors (e.g., peer group roles, legal or social sanctions, and life events such as the birth of a child) can be temporally anchored over a multidecade period to establish "natural" violence careers and the factors that affect their course.

Desistance research is an important part of the study of criminal careers but a neglected one in the literature on violence and aggression in families. Research on desistance from other forms of family violence, particularly incest and child abuse, may also tell us about the relations among them. Desistance research with assailants in both domestic-only and general violence can reveal shifts in victimization patterns and in the factors that influence the choice of victims. The simple integration of questions on violence in and out of the home will add to the explanatory power of theory developed from separate study. The concept of a family violence career, and studies of desistance as well as of displacement within that career, promise to strengthen our understanding of violence. How these patterns vary by social area and the social status of offenders are other important questions.

The systematic study of family violence is a relatively new field. Desistance research should be an important part of it. We must be careful to ask the right questions, not simply whether violence stops within a limited period or in response to a particular policy. Desistance may be a process as complex and lengthy as the processes of initial involvement. Developing empirical knowledge of desistance may require new research strategies that combine both deterministic and voluntary perspectives (Clarke and Cornish 1985). So long as the dimensions of the universe of those violent in families remain unknown, a variety of sampling strategies and research designs will make useful contributions to theory and knowledge. Knowledge of how violence stops does more than lead to new thinking on the prevention of family violence and its control. By framing questions within this perspective, we can begin to understand such important issues as the relations among types of family violence and the bearing of contemporary theories of violence on the special case of the family.

REFERENCES

Ageton, Suzanne S. 1983. *Sexual Assault among Adolescents*. Lexington, Mass.: Lexington.

Berk, Richard A. 1986. Personal communication.

Berk, Richard A., and Phyllis J. Newton. 1985. "Does Arrest Really Deter Wife Battery? An Effort to Replicate the Findings of the Minneapolis Spouse Experiment." *American Sociological Review* 50:253–62.

Biernacki, Patrick A. 1986. *Pathways from Heroin Addiction: Recovery without Treatment*. Philadelphia: Temple University Press.

Blumstein, Alfred, and Jacqueline Cohen. 1982. "The Duration of Adult Criminal Careers." Final report of grant 79-NI-AX-0121, from the School of Urban Affairs, Carnegie-Mellon University, Pittsburgh, to the National Institute of Justice.

Blumstein, Alfred, Jacqueline Cohen, Jeffrey A. Roth, and Christy A. Visher, eds. 1986. *Criminal Careers and Career Criminals*. Washington, D.C.: National Academy Press.

Blumstein, Alfred, David P. Farrington, and Soumyo Moitra. 1985. "Delinquency Careers: Innocents, Desisters, and Persisters." In *Crime and Justice: An Annual Review of Research*, vol. 6, edited by Michael Tonry and Norval Morris. Chicago: University of Chicago Press.

Bowker, Lee H. 1983. *Beating Wife-Beating*. Lexington, Mass.: Lexington.

———. 1984. "Battered Wives and the Police: A National Study of Usage and Effectiveness." *Police Studies* 7(2):84–93.

———. 1986a. "The Meaning of Wife-Beating." *Currents* 2(4):39–43.

———. 1986b. "Empowering Women: The Only Way to End Domestic Violence." Paper presented at the Third National Conference of the National Coalition against Domestic Violence, St. Louis, July.

Bowker, Lee H., and Lorie Maurer. 1985. "The Importance of Sheltering in the Lives of Battered Women." *Response* 9(4):2–8.

Browne, Angela. 1987. *When Battered Women Kill*. New York: Free Press.

Burt Associates. 1977. *Drug Treatment in New York City and Washington, D.C.* Rockville, Md.: National Institute on Drug Abuse.

Clarke, Ronald V., and Derek B. Cornish. 1985. "Modeling Offenders' Decisions: A Framework for Research and Policy." In *Crime and Justice: An Annual Review of Research*, vol. 6, edited by Michael Tonry and Norval Morris. Chicago: University of Chicago Press.

Cusson, Maurice, and Pierre Pinsonneault. 1986. "The Decision to Give Up Crime." In *The Reasoning Criminal*, edited by Derek B. Cornish and Ronald V. Clarke. New York: Springer-Verlag.

DiClemente, C., and J. Prochaska. 1979. "Self-Change and Therapy Change in the Successful Cessation of Smoking Behavior." Paper presented at the annual meeting of the Rocky Mountain Psychological Association, Las Vegas, Nev., April.

Dobash, R. Emerson, and Russell Dobash. 1979. *Violence against Wives: A Case against the Patriarchy*. New York: Free Press.

———. 1981. "Community Response to Violence against Wives: Charivari, Abstract Justice, and Patriarchy." *Social Problems* 28:563–81.

Dutton, Donald G. 1987. "The Criminal Justice Response to Wife Assault." *Law and Human Behavior* 11(3):189–206.

Edwards, Alfred L. 1957. *Techniques of Attitude and Scale Construction.* New York: Appleton-Century-Crofts.

Elliott, Delbert S. In this volume. "Criminal Justice Procedures in Family Violence Crimes."

Fagan, Jeffrey, Elizabeth Friedman, Sandra Wexler, and Virginia S. Lewis. 1984. *National Family Violence Evaluation: Final Report,* vol. 1, *Analytic Findings.* San Francisco: URSA Institute.

Fagan, Jeffrey, Douglas K. Stewart, and Karen V. Hansen. 1983. "Violent Men or Violent Husbands? Background Factors and Situational Correlates." In *The Dark Side of Families,* edited by David Finkelhor and associates. Beverly Hills, Calif.: Sage.

Fagan, Jeffrey, and Sandra Wexler. 1987. "Crime at Home and Crime in the Streets: The Relation between Family and Stranger Violence." *Violence and Victims* 2:5–23.

Farrington, David P. 1979. "Longitudinal Research on Crime and Delinquency." In *Crime and Justice: An Annual Review of Research,* vol. 1, edited by Norval Morris and Michael Tonry. Chicago: University of Chicago Press.

———. 1986. "Age and Crime." In *Crime and Justice: An Annual Review of Research,* vol. 7, edited by Michael Tonry and Norval Morris. Chicago: University of Chicago Press.

Finkelhor, David, Sharon Araji, Larry Baron, Angela Browne, Stephanie D. Peters, and Gail E. Wyatt. 1986. *A Sourcebook on Child Sexual Abuse.* Beverly Hills, Calif.: Sage.

Frieze, Irene H. 1979. "Perceptions of Battered Wives." In *New Approaches to Social Problems,* edited by I. H. Frieze, D. Bar-Tal, and J. S. Carroll. San Francisco: Jossey-Bass.

———. 1986. Personal communication.

Frieze, Irene H., Jaime Noble, Carol Washburn, and Gretchen Zomnir. 1980. "Characteristics of Battered Women and Their Marriages." Final report of grant 1 R01 MH30193, National Institute of Mental Health. Rockville, Md.: U.S. Public Health Service.

Gelles, Richard J. 1978. "Methods for Studying Sensitive Family Topics." *American Journal of Orthopsychiatry* 48:408–24.

———. 1983. "An Exchange/Social Control Theory." In *The Dark Side of Families,* edited by David Finkelhor and associates. Beverly Hills, Calif.: Sage.

Gelles, Richard J., and Murray A. Straus. 1979. "Determinants of Violence in the Family: Toward a Theoretical Integration." In *Contemporary Theories about the Family,* edited by Wesley Burr, Reuben Hill, F. Ivan Nye, and Ira L. Reiss. New York: Free Press.

Gondolf, Edward. 1985a. "Anger and Oppression in Men Who Batter: Empiricist and Feminist Perspectives and Their Implications for Research." *Victimology* 10:311–24.

———. 1985b. "Fighting for Control: A Clinical Assessment of Men Who Batter." *Social Casework: The Journal of Contemporary Social Work* 66:48–54.

Grau, Janice, Jeffrey Fagan, and Sandra Wexler. 1984. "Restraining Orders for Battered Women: Issues of Access and Efficacy." *Women and Politics* 4(3):13–28.

Greenberg, David F. 1977. "Delinquency and the Age Structure of Society." *Contemporary Crises* 1:189–223.

Hamparian, Donna M., Richard Schuster, Simon Dinitz, and John P. Conrad. 1978. *The Violent Few: A Study of Dangerous Juvenile Offenders.* Lexington, Mass.: Lexington.

Hecht, E. 1978. "A Retrospective Study of Successful Quitters." Paper presented at the annual meeting of the American Psychological Association. Toronto, August.

Hirschi, Travis, and Michael Gottfredson. 1983. "Age and the Explanation of Crime." *American Journal of Sociology* 89:552–84.

Irwin, John. 1970. *The Felon.* Englewood Cliffs, N.J.: Prentice-Hall.

Jeffrey, R., A. Folsom, R. Luepker, D. Jacobs, R. Gillum, H. Taylor, and H. Blackburn. 1984. "Prevalence of Overweight and Weight Loss Behavior in a Metropolitan Adult Population: The Minnesota Heart Survey Experience." *American Journal of Public Health* 74(4):349–52.

Loseke, Donileen R., and Spencer E. Cahill. 1984. "The Social Construction of Deviance: Experts on Battered Women." *Social Problems* 31:296–310.

Macro Systems, Inc. 1975. *Three-Year Followup Study of Clients Enrolled in Treatment Programs in New York City—Phase III Final Report.* Rockville, Md.: National Institute on Drug Abuse.

Malamuth, Neil M. 1981. "Rape Proclivity among Males." *Journal of Social Issues* 37:138–52.

Matza, David. 1964. *Delinquency and Drift.* New York: Wiley.

Morash, Merry. 1986. "Wife Battering." *Criminal Justice Abstracts* 18:252–71.

O'Donnell, John A., Harwin Voss, Richard R. Clayton, Gerald T. Slatin, and Robin G. W. Room. 1976. *Young Men and Drugs: A Nationwide Survey.* NIDA Research Monograph no. 5. Rockville, Md.: National Institute on Drug Abuse.

Pagelow, Mildred Daley. 1984. *Family Violence.* New York: Praeger.

Pederson, L., and N. Lefcoe. 1976. "A Psychological and Behavioral Comparison of Ex-Smokers and Smokers." *Journal of Chronic Diseases* 29:431–34.

Perri, Michael G., C. Stevens Richards, and Karen R. Shulthers. 1977. "Behavioral Self-Control and Smoking Reduction: A Study of Self-initiated Attempts to Reduce Smoking." *Behavior Therapy* 8:360–65.

Petersilia, Joan. 1980. "Criminal Career Research: A Review of Recent Evidence." In *Crime and Justice: An Annual Review of Research*, vol. 2, edited by Norval Morris and Michael Tonry. Chicago: University of Chicago Press.

Petersilia, Joan, Peter Greenwood, and Marvin Lavin. 1978. *Criminal Careers of Habitual Felons.* Washington, D.C.: Law Enforcement Assistance Administration, U.S. Department of Justice.

Robins, Lee N. 1973. *The Vietnam Drug User Returns.* Washington, D.C.: U.S. Government Printing Office.

Robins, Lee N., and George Murphy. 1967. "Drug Use in a Normal Population of Negro Young Men." *American Journal of Public Health* 59(9):1580–96.

Roizen, Ron, Don Cahalan, and Patricia Shanks. 1978. " 'Spontaneous Remission' among Untreated Problem Drinkers." In *Longitudinal Research in Drug Use: Empirical Findings and Methodological Issues*, edited by Denise Kandel. Washington, D.C.: Hemisphere.

Rosenthal, B., G. Allen, and C. Winter. 1980. "Husband Involvement in the Behavioral Treatment of Overweight Women: Initial Effects and Long-Term Follow-Up." *International Journal of Obesity* 4(2):165–73.

Russell, Diana E. H. 1982. *Rape in Marriage*. New York: Macmillan.

———. 1984. *Sexual Exploitation*. Beverly Hills, Calif.: Sage.

Saunders, Daniel, and Sandra Azar. In this volume. "Treatment Programs for Family Violence."

Saunders, W., and P. Kershaw. 1979. "Spontaneous Remission from Alcoholism: A Community Study." *British Journal of the Addictions* 74:251–65.

Schacter, Stanley. 1982. "Recidivism and Self-Cure of Smoking and Obesity." *American Psychologist* 37(4):436–44.

Sherman, Lawrence, and Richard A. Berk. 1984a. "The Specific Deterrent Effects of Arrest for Domestic Assault." *American Sociological Review* 49:261–72.

———. 1984b. *The Minneapolis Domestic Violence Experiment*. Washington, D.C.: Police Foundation.

Shields, Nancy, and Christine R. Hanneke. 1981. "Patterns of Family and Non-family Violence: An Approach to the Study of Violent Husbands." Paper presented at the annual meeting of the American Sociological Association, Toronto, August.

Shover, Neal. 1983. "The Later Stages of Ordinary Property Offender Careers." *Social Problems* 31:209–18.

———. 1985. *Aging Criminals*. Beverly Hills, Calif.: Sage.

Shulman, Mark. 1979. *A Survey of Spousal Violence against Women in Kentucky*. New York: Garland.

Sidel, Ruth. 1986. *Women and Children Last: The Plight of Poor Women in Affluent America*. New York: Viking.

Smith, Douglas A. 1986. "The Neighborhood Context of Police Behavior." In *Communities and Crime*, edited by Albert J. Reiss, Jr., and Michael Tonry. Vol. 8 of *Crime and Justice: A Review of Research*, edited by Michael Tonry and Norval Morris. Chicago: University of Chicago Press.

Speckart, George, and M. Douglas Anglin. 1986. "Narcotics and Crime: A Causal Modeling Approach." *Journal of Quantitative Criminology* 2:3–28.

Stall, Ron. 1983. "Spontaneous Remission from Problem Drinking in the Bluegrass Region of Kentucky: An Inductive Study." *Journal of Drug Issues* 13:191–206.

Stall, Ron, and Patrick A. Biernacki. 1986. "Spontaneous Remission from the Problematic Use of Substances: An Inductive Model Derived from a Comparative Analysis of the Alcohol, Opiate, Tobacco, and Food/Obesity Literatures." *International Journal of the Addictions* 2:1–23.

Steinmetz, Suzanne K. 1977. *The Cycle of Violence: Assertive, Aggressive, and Abusive Family Interaction*. New York: Praeger.

Straus, Murray A. 1976. "Sexual Inequality, Cultural Norms, and Wife-Beating." *Victimology* 1:54–76.

———. 1978. "Wife-Beating: How Common and Why?" *Victimology* 2:576–84.

Straus, Murray A., Richard J. Gelles, and Suzanne K. Steinmetz. 1980. *Behind Closed Doors: Violence in the American Family.* Garden City, N.Y.: Doubleday.

Sutherland, Edward H. 1937. *The Professional Thief.* Chicago: University of Chicago Press.

Trasler, Gordon B. 1979. "Delinquency, Recidivism, and Desistance." *British Journal of Criminology* 19:314–22.

Tuchfeld, Barry S. 1981. "Spontaneous Remission in Alcoholics: Empirical Observations and Theoretical Implications." *Journal of Studies on Alcohol* 42:626–41.

Waldorf, Dan. 1983. "Natural Recovery from Opiate Addiction: Some Social-Psychological Processes of Untreated Recovery." *Journal of Drug Issues* 13(2):237–80.

Waldorf, Dan, and Patrick Biernacki. 1979. "National Recovery from Heroin Addiction: A Review of the Literature." *Journal of Drug Issues* 11:61–76.

Walker, Lenore E. 1979. *The Battered Woman.* New York: Harper & Row.

———. 1984. *The Battered Woman Syndrome.* New York: Springer.

West, Donald J. 1963. *The Habitual Prisoner.* London: Macmillan.

———. 1982. *Delinquency: Its Roots, Careers, and Prospects.* London: Heinemann.

Winick, Charles. 1962. "Maturing Out of Narcotic Addiction." *Bulletin on Narcotics* 14:1–7.

———. 1964. "The Life Cycle of the Narcotic Addict and of Addiction." *Bulletin on Narcotics* 16:1–11.

Wolfgang, Marvin E., Robert M. Figlio, and Thorsten Sellin. 1972. *Delinquency in a Birth Cohort.* Chicago: University of Chicago Press.

Yllo, Kirstin A., and Murray A. Straus. 1984. "Patriarchy and Violence against Wives: The Impact of Structural and Normative Factors." *Journal of International and Comparative Social Welfare* 1:16–29.

Delbert S. Elliott

Criminal Justice Procedures in Family Violence Crimes

ABSTRACT

Public attitudes about family violence have shifted during the past decade from indifference to support for use of legal remedies to deter and punish. Few studies adequately describe the methods and differential effectiveness of police and prosecutorial handling of family violence cases. Much of the conventional wisdom concerning justice procedures for dealing with family violence is not substantiated by the available research. Only about one-third of domestic disturbance calls to police involves some form of family violence crime; consequently, studies of police responses to domestic disturbance calls are not generalizable to the subset of calls involving family violence. The claim that the police are less likely to apply criminal sanctions to family violence crimes than to stranger violence crimes is not substantiated by existing research. Few studies support the claim that different factors are involved in decisions to prosecute family violence crimes as compared with stranger violence crimes. Finally, no systematic evaluations identify which sentencing outcomes reduce or eliminate subsequent family violence. The existing research should be improved by resolving definitional problems and ambiguities, by collecting data specific to particular types of abuse, by obtaining more representative samples of offenders and victims, by using better controls and longer follow-up periods on study samples, and by adopting more explicit theoretical and conceptual formulations to guide evaluation research.

Family disturbance calls, the largest single category of calls received by the police, are more common than calls for all other types of violent

Delbert S. Elliott is professor of sociology, Department of Sociology, and associate program director, Institute of Behavioral Science, University of Colorado.

crimes combined (Police Foundation 1977; Breslin 1978; Scott 1981). Family disturbance calls are also reputed to be among the most dangerous types of calls to which police respond (Parnas 1967; Bard 1970; Scott 1981; Bandy, Buchanan, and Pinto 1986; but see Margarita 1980; Garner and Clemmer 1986).

The police and the criminal justice system generally have been criticized for their failure to respond more effectively to family violence. Critics have claimed that the police assign low priority to family violence calls and frequently do not respond at all (Martin 1976, 1978; Fields 1978; Schulman 1979), that they too seldom make arrests or use other criminal sanctions or remedies even when there is probable cause to do so (Roy 1977*b*; Vera Institute of Justice 1977; Dobash and Dobash 1979; Paterson 1979; Goolkasian 1986), and that they mismanage investigations of family violence and thus jeopardize the success of subsequent efforts to prosecute (Field and Field 1973; Martin 1976; Eisenberg and Micklow 1977; Lerman 1986). Critics claim that prosecutors rarely file charges or aggressively prosecute family violence cases, even when a felony assault is involved (Field and Field 1973; Martin 1976; Fields 1978; Brosi 1979; Lerman 1986). In sum, critics claim that perpetrators of family violence are rarely sanctioned by the criminal justice system and, accordingly, that their victims are denied the protections afforded victims of other crimes. If these accusations are true, the criminal justice system may reinforce and perpetuate family violence.

In this essay, I examine the available empirical evidence to determine whether the criticisms summarized in the preceding two paragraphs are borne out by the evidence. By and large they are not. This does not mean that the criticisms do not have merit, merely that the existing data do not sustain them. Nor is the absence of evidence of discriminatory practice evidence of its absence. Perhaps more careful research will document critics' claims. I return to these issues in Section V below.

Underlying these critics' charges are fundamental questions about the criminal justice practices in family violence cases. While some take issue with particular criticisms noted above (e.g., Parnas 1967; Bard and Zacker 1971; Bard 1978; Berk and Loseke 1980–81), virtually everyone agrees that there is room for improvement in handling family violence cases by the criminal justice system. There is, however, disagreement over how to improve the system.

Unfortunately, apart from homicide studies (e.g., Wolfgang 1958; Curtis 1974), criminological researchers have only recently begun to focus attention on criminal justice responses to family violence (Fagan and Wexler 1985; Morash 1986). This neglect reflects the historical focus of criminological work on offenders rather than on victims, and it testifies to the widely shared view that much violent behavior involving family members ought not primarily to be a criminal matter. Much of the criticism of criminal justice system handling of family violence has come from feminists, journalists, and political activists and has by and large been uninformed by the general body of criminological research (Loving 1980, p. 31).

The absence of good descriptive data and the limited number of systematic evaluations of the effectiveness of particular criminal justice strategies to combat family violence make it difficult to evaluate the claims of critics or to make empirically grounded recommendations for criminal justice reforms. The situation has, however, improved in recent years with the publication of results from several major studies providing important new descriptive data and assessments of alternative police responses to family violence crimes (e.g., Fagan et al. 1984; Sherman and Berk 1984b; Erez 1986; Langan and Innes 1986a; Tauchen, Tauchen, and Witte 1986; Smith 1987).

There are a number of conceptual and definitional problems involved in reviewing family violence studies. Many investigators use the terms "domestic violence," "spouse abuse," "wife battering," and "family violence" interchangeably and employ widely divergent definitions for these terms or concepts. Gelles (1987) notes that these definitional problems make it difficult to compare studies or summarize findings. The term "family violence" is used in this essay to refer to forms of physical violence committed, attempted, or threatened by family members on one another. It includes behaviors that police typically classify as menacing behavior, recklessness or endangerment, simple assault, or aggravated assault, in which offenders and victims are related by blood, marriage, or prior intimacy. Many studies include common-law spouses, ex-spouses, and cohabiting adult partners and ex-partners as family members. It is important to note that what may be said of justice system responses to one form of family violence may not be generalizable to other forms of family violence, each of which can involve a unique subset of family violence cases.

Section I surveys what proportion of domestic disturbance calls actually fall within the classification of family violence calls, identifies and describes three distinct police responses to family violence, and discusses the factors involved in the decision to arrest. Section II surveys the evaluation literature on the effectiveness of police responses to family violence and describes the methodological problems that permeate it. Section III reviews research on prosecutorial and judicial handling of family violence cases and the effectiveness of particular court actions or dispositions. Section IV reviews what is known about the collaboration between criminal justice agencies and other public and private agencies that provide services for family violence victims and offenders. Finally, Section V discusses limitations of the current body of research findings, and suggests promising future research directions.

I. Police Responses to Family Violence

One difficulty in attempting to describe police responses to family violence crimes is that there are very few data that are specific to this class of events. Data on alternative responses to particular *types* of family violence crimes (e.g., violence between spouses, siblings, parents and adult children, parents and young children) are even rarer.

Police most typically (but not always) encounter a family violence situation when responding to a "disturbance" call. Police often are dispatched on disturbance calls with little or no information about the nature of the problem or the relationships of the parties involved, and frequently the initial information provided by the dispatcher proves to be incorrect when the officers arrive on the scene (Oppenlander 1982). A substantial proportion of disturbance calls do turn out to involve a problem involving family members.

Unfortunately, much of the available data on police responses to crimes does not distinguish between domestic and nondomestic disturbances. This problem was recently highlighted by Garner and Clemmer (1986), who challenged the widely held view that domestic disturbance calls are among the most dangerous calls to which police officers respond. Prior to 1982, the FBI statistics on types of calls in which police officers are feloniously killed did not distinguish between domestic and nondomestic calls; these data indicated that felonious deaths of officers occurred more frequently on disturbance calls than on burglary or robbery or any other specific offense-type call, and this was widely interpreted as evidence of the danger to police in domestic dispute calls. However, beginning in 1982, the FBI data disaggregated disturbance calls into domestic and other disturbances (e.g., bar fights, man with gun); these data indicate that the felonious police deaths on domestic disturbance calls are not only less than for other disturbance calls but are less than for any other specific offense-type reported.[1]

A. The Proportion of Domestic Disturbance Calls Involving Family Violence Crimes

Police reports on domestic disturbance calls reveal a wide range of domestic problems, including missing persons, trespassing, disturbing the peace, drunk and disorderly conduct, verbal arguments, threats of violence, property damage, minor assaults, and aggravated assaults (Parnas 1967; Berk and Loseke 1980–81). A majority of these incidents do not involve any criminal offense (Black 1971; Emerson 1979), and some of those that do involve offenses do not involve any violence between family members.

Several studies provide estimates of the proportion of domestic disturbance calls that involve family violence. Bard's research (1978, pp. 50–51) indicates that there was no assaultiveness in 56–71 percent of all domestic dispute cases that came to the attention of the police. His estimates were derived from two samples. The first involved 1,388 domestic disturbance calls handled by a special family crisis unit in West Harlem (New York) during a twenty-two-month period in 1967–68. Complainants in 36 percent of these cases made some allegation of an assault; officers determined that there was evidence of an assault in 29 percent of the cases (Bard and Zacker 1974). The second study sample involved 148 domestic disturbance calls in Norwalk, Connecticut; 44 percent of the calls involved an assault (Zacker and Bard 1977).

Faragher (1985) reports that 19 percent of a small sample of domestic disturbance calls in an English community involved an assault, based on his independent judgment at the scene. Breedlove et al. (1977) report that 42 percent of a sample of domestic disturbance calls in Kansas City during five months of 1973 involved some physical force; in those cases

[1] The data presented by Garner and Clemmer (1986) demonstrate a lower risk of felonious death for police officers when responding to domestic disturbances than when responding to other disturbances, burglary, robbery, or traffic events (1983–85). The data on assaults and injuries associated with various types of criminal acts are not as clear. The procedure used for obtaining harm-activity ratios for the latter estimates is questionable (the estimates of harm and activity used to establish a given ratio are derived from different jurisdictions). Some caution is necessary in rejecting the earlier claim that domestic disturbance calls are among the most dangerous calls to which police respond, if dangerousness is defined broadly to include any injury or assault. Further, there is evidence from other sources to substantiate this claim. For example, Breedlove et al. (1977) report that family disturbance calls accounted for 28 percent of all assaults on police in Kansas City in 1975.

432   Delbert S. Elliott

where disputants were married or divorced, 54 percent involved some physical force as compared with 31 percent when disputants were not married or divorced.

· Using the Police Services Study data (Ostrom, Parks, and Wittaker 1977) involving 5,688 observations of citizen-police encounters in twenty-four communities in Rochester (New York), St. Louis (Missouri), and Tampa/St. Petersburg (Florida) during May–July 1977, Oppenlander (1982) reports descriptive data on the subset of cases ($N = 596$) involving arguments and assaults. Trained observers rode with the police and recorded both police actions and citizen complaints and actions. Any case involving physical contact, threat of violence, or physical attack was classified as an assault; those involving only verbal encounters with no threats of violence or physical contact were classified as arguments. Slightly more than 3 percent of the total set of observed encounters involved an assault; slightly over 1 percent involved an assault between family members (i.e., relatives, ex-spouses, and cohabitants). Of those cases involving a family dispute ($N = 259$), 30 percent involved an assault and 70 percent involved an argument. Among disputes involving unrelated participants, 65 percent involved assaults and 35 percent involved arguments.

With the exception of the Oppenlander (1982) and the Bard and Zacker (1974) research, the above studies involved small, nonrepresentative samples. The two studies involving larger, more representative samples produced very similar estimates of the proportion of family disturbance calls involving violent behavior (Oppenlander 1982, 30 percent; and Bard and Zacker 1974, 29 percent). It thus seems reasonable to conclude that a majority of domestic disturbance calls do *not* involve violent crimes.[2]

A recent study by Erez (1986) reports estimates of various types of family violence crimes encountered by police when responding to domestic disturbance calls. All domestic incident reports filed in 1978 by twenty-eight police departments in a midwestern county were examined. All reports indicating violence between family members or cohabiting or dating persons were identified and included in the study

---

[2] The definitions of violence employed in these studies typically involve threatened or actual physical violence between participants and are based on both police definitions and definitions of independent observers riding with patrol officers. Since estimates of family violence vary with the definition of violence employed (Klaus and Rand 1984; Fagan and Wexler 1985; Morash 1986), this conclusion may or may not hold for broader, less restrictive definitions (see Weis [in this volume] for a discussion of these issues).

sample (N = 3,021). A breakdown by type of relationship revealed the following distribution: spouses/ex-spouses, 45 percent; boyfriend/girlfriend, 13 percent; parent/child, 19 percent; in-laws, 5 percent; siblings, 4 percent, roommates, 4 percent, other, 10 percent (Erez 1986, p. 269). This study also indicated how police classified the violence in spousal/ex-spousal and boyfriend/girlfriend violent incidents: threats, menacing behavior, and property damage, 47 percent; minor assaults, 41 percent; aggravated assaults, 6 percent; harassment, 4 percent; suicide, 1 percent; child abuse, 1 percent; sex offense, .5 percent; and homicide, .5 percent. To my knowledge, this is the only general survey reporting the relative occurrence of particular types of family violence incidents coming to the attention of the police through domestic disturbance calls and the distribution of types of criminal charges associated with these violent incidents (limited to spousal/ex-spousal and boyfriend/girlfriend violence).

Several studies report types of family relationships encountered in domestic disturbance calls more generally, without regard to the presence or absence of violence. Emerson (1979) reports on relationships between disputants in a survey conducted by the Los Angeles County Sheriff's Department of all domestic disturbance calls during a two month period in 1978 (N = 1,446). Seventy percent of all disputes were between husbands and wifes; 20 percent between parents and children; and 10 percent involved other immediate family members, including in-laws.

There is some additional evidence that family disputes most frequently involve spouses (Berk and Loseke 1980–81; Dutton 1984) and that physical violence is more likely to be involved in spousal disputes than in other types of family disputes (Breedlove et al. 1977). However, none of these studies provide specific estimates of the frequency at which police encounter various types of family disputes involving violence. For example, in the Emerson (1979) study, 64 percent of these calls were determined to involve no crime, and no breakdown is provided for victim/offender relationships involving violence.

Another source of data on family relationships in family violence crimes is the National Crime Survey (NCS). Klaus and Rand (1984) report that 7 percent of all violent crimes reported in the NCS between 1973 and 1981 involved an offender who was related to the victim. Fifty-seven percent of these family crimes involved spouses or ex-spouses as offenders, 6 percent involved parents, 4 percent children, 9 percent siblings, and 24 percent other relatives.

Langan and Innes (1986*a*) report that 59 percent of domestic violence events (rape, robbery, aggravated assault, or simple assault) reported in the 1984 NCS involved spouses or ex-spouses; other relatives were involved in an additional 6 percent of the reported events. Close friends (including boyfriends and ex-boyfriends) accounted for 35 percent of these events. The most frequent type of family violence reported on the NCS thus appears to involve spouses or ex-spouses (including common-law relationships).

Only half of those who reported family violence crimes to the NCS interviewers reported these crimes to the police (Klaus and Rand 1984; Langan and Innes 1986*a*). There is no reason to believe that those who reported to the police were representative of all of those who were victimized. In fact, there is some evidence to suggest that those persons reporting and not reporting to the police differ in important respects. Bowker (1982), in a 1980–81 study of 146 women reporting 876 family violence incidents, found that calling the police was related to low victim and offender education and frequency of marital violence. It is thus inappropriate to conclude from the NCS distribution of types of family violence crime that the same patterns of family violence events are encountered by the police when responding to family disturbance calls.

The available evidence suggests that about one-third of all domestic disturbance calls to the police involves some form of family violence crime and that the majority of these violent crimes involve violence between spouses, ex-spouses, and heterosexual persons who are or have been living together. Since approximately two-thirds of all domestic disturbance calls appear either to involve no crime or a nonviolent crime, studies of police responses to domestic disturbance calls ought not to be used as the basis for generalizations about the subset of these calls that involve violent crimes. Unfortunately, this is the data base that is most readily available and that is typically cited to support the charge that the police respond differently to violent crimes involving family members than to violent crimes involving strangers.

B. Police Responses to Family Violence

Wilson (1977) has identified three different views about the role of the police when responding to family violence crimes: (1) Family violence is a private matter, and barring very serious injury, disputants should be allowed to resolve their conflict privately. Arrest should be used only as a temporary means to maintain order. (2) The community has a vital interest in family violence, and thus criminal prosecution should be used to remedy this type of violence, even in cases where the victim does not choose to prosecute. And (3), while the criminal justice system should intervene, the police and courts should have a wider range of dispositional alternatives and discretion in their use.

There is little question that the first "hands off" view predominated prior to the early 1970s. Police training materials clearly specified that, when responding to domestic disputes, arrest was to be avoided whenever possible. For example, the International Association of Chiefs of Police (IACP) training materials then stated "in dealing with family disputes, the power of arrest should be exercised as a last resort" (1967, p. 3). The primary focus of training materials prior to 1970 was on the danger to officers in these situations (Parnas 1967).

The second "strict enforcement" view was often put forth in the 1970s (Field and Field 1973; Martin 1976; Eisenberg and Micklow 1977; Roy 1977b). These critics argued that the stricter application of criminal sanctions in family violence crimes would provide better protection to victims and would reduce the risk of subsequent violence. Several class-action suits were brought against police departments for their alleged failure to provide victims of family violence the full protection of the law (Martin 1978; Paterson 1979). The results of the Minneapolis Domestic Violence Experiment (Sherman and Berk 1984b), which suggested that routine use of arrests against alleged assailants reduces the risk of further violence, influenced a substantial number of police departments to adopt a mandatory arrest policy in spousal violence incidents when there was probable cause. Sherman and Cohn (1987) estimate that 48 percent of police departments in cities over 100,000 population now encourage arrest as the preferred response to domestic violence. The IACP has also published new training materials that encourage the use of criminal sanctions in family violence incidents. For example: "A policy of arrest, when the elements of the offense are present, promotes the well-being of the victim. Many battered wives who tolerate the situation undoubtedly do so because they feel they are alone in coping with the problem. The officer who starts legal action may give the wife the courage she needs to realistically face and correct her situation" (International Association of Chiefs of Police 1976, p. 3).

Proponents of the third view warn that mandatory arrest policies will not always help victims or protect citizens' rights (Parnas 1967; Bard 1978; Bard and Connolly 1978). They assert that the mandatory prosecution, particularly when the victim does not want to press charges, can aggravate the situation and increase the level of stress in the family and the risk of further violence. They propose that efforts be directed toward improving, rather than eliminating, police use of discretion by training the police to employ family crisis intervention skills and to make referrals to community service agencies. Arrest, they urge, may be an appropriate response to family violence in some instances, but the police should retain the discretion to use this legal option in response to the particular situation. Bard and Connolly reported in 1978 that 71 percent of police jurisdictions in the United States were delivering some form of training in family crisis intervention. Sherman and Hamilton (1984) more recently estimated that mediation was the preferred approach in over one-third of the large urban police departments.

All three views have proponents in particular police departments. The proportion of family violence cases involving an arrest disposition is thus likely to vary tremendously. In practice, police typically use one of four strategies when responding to family violence crimes: (1) arrest, (2) mediation, (3) separation, or (4) no action. Emphasis on any single strategy depends on the approach endorsed by the department and by the personal view of the officer responding to the call. Parnas (1967) identified some additional options police have employed in domestic disturbance cases (e.g., violation citations and referral memorandums), but these are rarely used.

In most jurisdictions, police are authorized to arrest whenever there is probable cause for a felony charge. The presence of a weapon or serious injury to the victim is, in most instances, sufficient grounds for making an arrest, if the offender is present at the scene, or issuing a warrant for the assailant's arrest if he or she has left the scene. In misdemeanor assault cases, there is considerable variation among the states about legal requirements for arrests (Lerman 1986). In many states, a police officer may make an arrest for a misdemeanor offense only if the offense occurs in the officer's presence (LaFave 1965; Parnas 1967; Emerson 1979; Lerman 1986). In these states, a misdemeanor arrest requires that the victim become legally responsible for the arrest by signing the complaint or warrant. Since most family violence crimes involve misdemeanor assaults, victims' complaints or warrants provide the most common basis for police arrest in these cases. Of course, if an offender assaults the officer responding to a family violence call, is "drunk and disorderly," or commits some other offense in the officer's presence, the officer can make an arrest without a warrant. But this arrest is not for the violent behavior that precipitated the family violence call.

Several studies provide estimates of arrest, mediation, separation, and "no action" rates in family violence cases. Black (1971) reports on a study of 5,713 independent observations of police-citizen encounters in eight police precincts located in Boston, Chicago, and Washington, D.C., during the summer of 1966. This particular analysis involved a 5 percent sample of these observed incidents involving predominantly blue-collar adult suspects and victims and was limited to encounters in which both the alleged offender and victim were of the same race and were present when the police arrived on the scene. Forty-five percent of all felony assaults involving family members ($N = 176$) resulted in an arrest; when the complainant preferred an arrest, 55 percent of the alleged assaulters were arrested. For misdemeanors, 47 percent of all cases resulted in arrest; 80 percent of misdemeanors resulted in arrest when the complainant preferred an arrest. In another analysis of these data, Black (1980) reports that police made arrests in 26 percent of violent disputes involving married couples and attempted to effect separations in 38 percent of these cases.

In a general population survey of 1,793 women in Kentucky in 1979, respondents who had been victims of family violence reported to the police only 10 percent of the violent incidents they experienced (Loving 1980). The police made arrests in 41 percent of the violent incidents reported to them, an arrest warrant was issued in an additional 16 percent of reported violent incidents, a report was filed in 24 percent of the incidents, and no action was taken in 29 percent of the incidents. Oppenlander (1982), using the Police Services Study data described earlier (Ostrom, Parks, and Wittaker 1977), reports on action taken in cases involving an assault by a family member (more than one response is possible for any given case): mediation or referral (20 percent); separation (24 percent); threat of arrest (11 percent); and arrest (22 percent). Essentially, no action was taken in 49 percent of the family assaults in the Police Services Study.

In a slightly different analysis of the Police Services Study data (omitting encounters in which the offender was not present when the police arrived), Smith (1987) reports arrests in 27 percent of assaults involving persons who live together, mediation in 35 percent, and separation in 40 percent of cases. The differences in the Oppenlander and Smith rates appear to reflect the presence or absence of the offender at the scene when the police arrive, with the likelihood of arrest being higher when the offender is present. It follows that the likelihood of mediation and separation would also probably be higher when the offender is present. More important, the comparison of these analyses suggests that when the offender is not present, a "no action" response is much more likely. This observation is confirmed by Berk and Loseke (1980–81), who analyzed incident or arrest reports filed with the district attorney's office in 1978–79 in Santa Barbara. Only those reports that involved adults in a "romantic" or conjugal relationship at the time of the incident or prior to the incident were included in the sample ($N = 262$). The presence of the alleged offender at the scene when police arrived had a significant influence on the type of action taken by police; where the alleged offender was not present, a "no action" response was more likely. Overall, an arrest was made in 39 percent of the incidents. Finally, Erez (1986) reported that arrests were made in 12 percent of spousal/ex-spousal and boyfriend/girlfriend violent incidents.

These few studies suggest that arrest rates (felony and misdemeanor combined) during the periods covered by these studies have been less than 50 percent and may have been as low as 12 percent of reported violent family crimes.[3] There is some evidence that arrest rates may have been higher for incidents involving spouses/ex-spouses and boyfriends/girlfriends as compared to family violence crimes in general. Even when violent family acts are classified as felonies, the arrest rate appears to have been below 50 percent. Separation appears to have been used as often as mediation and, depending on whether the offender was present, no action may have been the most frequent response.

Assuming these are reasonable estimates, are these arrest rates unusually low? Those who have indicted the police for their handling of family violence crimes have portrayed the police response to these crimes as "different" from their response to other forms of violence. Implicit in this position is the assumption that police are less likely to make arrests in violent family crimes than in violent crimes involving

---

[3] I have not included in this review a number of studies involving small, nonrepresentative samples, e.g., samples of battered women or women in shelters (Roy 1977a; Dobash and Dobash 1979; Binney, Harkell, and Nixon 1981; Bowker 1982). Estimates of arrest rates from these studies have been systematically lower than those based on more representative samples.

strangers. Do the police employ different strategies when responding to stranger crimes? Is there any evidence that the rates of arrest are systematically higher in cases involving violent crimes between strangers? Are the factors accounting for arrest decisions different for family violence than for other forms of violence?

Several studies provide comparative estimates. The Black (1971) study is frequently cited as providing evidence about this differential risk of arrest. Black reports that the arrest rate for felony assaults involving strangers is substantially higher than that for felony assaults involving family members (88 percent compared with 45 percent). However, Black offers two caveats. First, the arrest differential between family members and strangers is much smaller for misdemeanor assaults (47 percent vs. 57 percent), and the lowest arrest probability for these offenses is for those involving friends, neighbors, and acquaintances (30 percent). Second, when the complainant prefers that no arrest be made or is uncertain about wanting an arrest, there are *no discernible differences* in probabilities of arrest in various types of violent incidents. The police in this study responded differently to violent incidents involving family members or strangers when the complainant wanted an arrest made. It should also be noted that the estimate of the arrest probability for felony incidents involving strangers was based on eight cases, so that there is some question about the accuracy of this estimate. Further, all of these estimates were derived from a sample that was restricted to adult blue-collar suspects and victims of the same race.

In a study of felony arrests in New York City in 1971, the Vera Institute of Justice (1977) observed that, given a minor injury, police were more likely to make an arrest in cases involving strangers than in cases involving parties having some prior relationship. They also found a lower proportion of serious injuries in stranger arrests than in nonstranger arrests. While the comparisons in the Vera analysis focus more directly on the role of injury in the decision to arrest, these findings indirectly support the claim of a differential risk of arrest in family as compared to stranger crimes of violence.

Several investigators failed to find this differential in arrest rates. In both the Oppenlander (1982) and Smith (1987) analyses of the Police Services Study data, arrest rates for both family and nonfamily assaults were compared (no felony-misdemeanor distinctions were made). In Oppenlander's analysis, the arrest rate for family assaults was *higher* than that for nonfamily assaults (22 percent compared with 13 percent [1982, p. 455]).[4] Further, the police were more likely to ask victims of family violence than nonfamily violence victims if they wanted to sign a complaint. The use of mediation and separation options was also greater in family assaults than in nonfamily assaults. However, the failure to use any of these options (arrest, mediation, or separation) was much more frequent in nonfamily assaults than in family assaults.

Oppenlander notes that the difference in arrest rates is explained by differential rates of injury. This is an important observation because it recognizes the need to control for factors relevant and appropriate to the arrest decision when comparing arrest rates. Seldom have such controls been used in comparisons of arrest rates of violent family and stranger crimes. In this particular case, the effect of a control for victim injury would result in similar rates of arrest for family and nonfamily assaults, but Oppenlander presents no formal analysis involving such controls. Oppenlander claims that arrests in domestic cases are often for another offense such as resisting an officer or public drunkenness. No direct support for this claim is given, and this same possibility exists for stranger assaults.

Smith's (1987) analysis revealed very similar arrest rates for family and nonfamily assaults (28 percent and 30 percent, respectively). The generally higher rates in Smith's analysis are not surprising because this analysis was restricted to cases where the offender and victim were both present when the police arrived. However, Smith notes that when the assault involved males only, the arrest rate was substantially higher than when it involved a male and a female. Unfortunately, this last analysis was not done for family and nonfamily assaults separately. It suggests the need to control for the sex of disputants when comparing arrest rates since arrest rates for spousal assault may well be substantially lower than those for stranger assault when a male offender and female victim are involved. However, I know of no empirical data that addresses this comparison directly. For the general comparison of family with nonfamily assaults, there is no evidence in the Police Services Study data of a differential risk of arrest.

The studies summarized above provide mixed support for the claim that police are less likely to invoke criminal sanctions for family violence than for violent crimes to strangers. The Police Services Study

[4] The arrest rate for incidents involving family arguments was also higher than that for incidents involving nonfamily arguments (9 percent compared to 4 percent).

analyses fail to find a differential response, which could mean that the police departments in this study may have already adopted a policy that encouraged the use of arrest in family violence crimes. This seems unlikely, however, because these data were collected in 1977 when mediation was the preferred approach in most police departments. Further, the overall arrest rates in this study are relatively low. More important, none of these studies involved controls for the major factors known to be involved in the decision to arrest. This is a critical issue since the claim of a differential response to family violence crimes is essentially a claim that different arrest criteria are employed in family violence crimes. It is at least logically possible that similar criteria for arrest are being used but that factors associated with the decision to arrest occur less frequently in family than stranger crimes of violence. If this were to be the case, many of the criticisms of the way the police handle family violence crime would be without merit. The studies providing comparisons of arrest rates for family and stranger assaults have not included the appropriate controls. Without these controls, the available evidence for a differential in arrest rates is simply inconclusive.

C. Factors Involved in the Decision to Arrest

Police officers were asked in several studies to identify the characteristics of a domestic violence situation that are most important in the decision to arrest. Loving (1980) reports on a 1979 survey involving 130 officers from seventeen police departments in cities receiving Law Enforcement Assistance and Administration grants for domestic violence programs. Factors identified as important by 90 percent or more of the officers included the commission of a felony, serious injury to the victim, use of a weapon, use of violence against the police, and the likelihood of future violence. The two factors eliciting the least consensus were the frequency of calls from the household for police assistance and a victim who insists on arrest. When asked to identify factors important in the decision *not* to arrest, the only factor selected by 90 percent or more of these officers was the victim's refusal to press charges.

With the exception of "use of violence against the police," which involves a separate crime, these factors were identified by Parnas (1967) in his seminal article on police behavior as major factors in the decision to arrest in domestic disturbance calls. The same five consensus factors were identified by Dolan, Hendricks, and Meagher (1986) in a study of

125 officers employed in three municipal police departments in a midwestern state.

The Loving (1980) and Dolan, Hendricks, and Meagher (1986) studies involved samples of officers that were neither large nor representative; nonetheless, there does appear to be some consensus from surveys of police officers and informed observers of police behavior that these are the important factors involved in the decision to arrest in family disturbances. However, Dolan, Hendricks, and Meagher (1986) note that these factors are not restricted to family violence incidents and are involved in the decision to arrest in all situations (see Black 1971; Sherman 1980; Sykes, Fox, and Clark 1985).

Another way to identify factors associated with the decision to arrest is to analyze official records or observations of police-citizen encounters to determine what characteristics of the incident or the parties involved are associated with an arrest outcome. Breedlove et al. (1977) report on such an analysis of official contact reports. This study involved reports from a 5-percent sample of 6,480 domestic violence calls received by the Kansas City Police Department during a four-month period in 1973. The three variables that predicted arrest were presence of a firearm, a third party requesting police intervention, and alcohol involvement in the conflict. Unfortunately, it is not clear what other factors were considered in the analysis.

Berk and Loseke (1980–81) report on a much more sophisticated analysis of the arrest decision in spousal violence incidents. This analysis was based on 262 incident and arrest reports of domestic violence, involving heterosexual adults who were, or had been, married or living together, that had been submitted to a special unit in the district attorney's office in 1978–79. Ten incident characteristics (selected as a result of their theoretical relevance and availability in the written reports) were employed as predictors in a multivariate analysis, and they accounted for 45 percent of the variance in arrest decisions.

Four variables had a significant effect on the decision to arrest. The one exerting the strongest effect was the victim's signing or promising to sign a citizen's arrest warrant. The probability of arrest increased by 30 percent with the change from no mention of a warrant to a signed warrant or promise to sign a warrant. Berk and Loseke note that impressionistic data in this study suggest that, if the victim refuses to sign a warrant or complaint, arrest on any grounds is unlikely.

The second and third strongest predictors involved interaction terms in the model: either alcohol use by the male or the allegation of violence by the female, when both parties were at the scene, significantly increased the arrest probability. These findings confirm the earlier observation that the presence of both parties at the scene increases the probability of arrest. Berk and Loseke report that the offender was not present at the scene in 41 percent of the spousal/intimate violence calls in their sample.

The fourth variable influencing the decision to arrest reflected who called the police to the disturbance. If the female called the police, the probability of arrest was *reduced* by 21 percent. Berk and Loseke speculate that the negative effect of the female requesting police intervention resulted from the female's nearly always being the victim; that she could call the police suggested that the conflict was not severe (1980–81, p. 340). They also speculate that the disturbances had not yet come to the attention of neighbors, a circumstance that might demand a more formal response.

The presence or absence of injury to one or both parties was not a significant predictor of arrest, either as a main effect or in interaction with both parties being present at the scene. Police notation of injury was observed in 44 percent of the cases in the sample, a significant proportion. Marital status was also not a significant predictor of arrest, a finding contrary to claims that police are reluctant to arrest husbands (Martin 1976; Roy 1977*b*; Dobash and Dobash 1979). Erez (1986) reports similar arrest rates for married couples, divorced or separated couples, and unmarried couples in an analysis of all domestic incident reports filed in 1978 by twenty-eight police departments in a midwestern county.

Berk and Loseke conclude that the factors most critical to the decision to arrest in domestic disturbance incidents involving present or past cohabitating couples center on the encounter itself: who asked the police to intervene, the presence of both parties at the scene, alcohol involvement, allegations of violence by one of the parties, and the victim's willingness to sign a complaint. The Breedlove et al. (1977) Kansas City study also found that who called the police and alcohol involvement were predictors of arrest in domestic violence cases. Weapons were also identified as a predictor in this study, but this variable was not considered in the Berk and Loseke study; nor is it clear that this study considered the other significant predictors found by Berk and Loseke.

With the possible exception of "who asked the police to intervene," none of the factors mentioned appear unique to family violence. The critical question is whether different factors are involved in the decision to arrest for violent behavior in nonfamily situations.

Smith's (1987) analysis of the Police Services Study data, focusing on arrest decisions in violent disputes in general, partially addresses this question. Both family and nonfamily assaults were included in the sample, and the relationship between the parties in the assault was one of the predictors included in the analysis of the arrest decision. Additional encounter-level variables investigated were the presence of a weapon, the race and sex of the combatants, the private or public setting of the event, alcohol use by one or both of the parties, victim injury, demeanor of the combatants toward the police, prior police contacts with these parties, victim or third party requests for police intervention, and police action requested by the victim. Two general context-level variables were also used as predictors—a measure of neighborhood socioeconomic status and neighborhood victimization.

In a multivariate analysis involving all predictors, the relationship between combatants was not a significant factor in the decision to arrest. This is an important finding because other significant predictors of arrest were controlled for; that is, whether the parties were cohabiting had no independent influence on the arrest outcome, given these other variables. The measure of victim-offender relationship reflected only whether the combatants were cohabiting at the time of the conflict. It does not appear that ex-spouses or those having cohabited at some earlier time were classified as cohabiting persons, and this is an important qualification. Further, cohabiting persons included parents and children and other persons living together. This classification was not limited to spouses or heterosexual partners, so that generalizing to specific types of offender-victim relationships is inappropriate. Still, if present or past family ties had a strong influence on the decision to arrest when responding to violent disputes, some independent predictive influence should have appeared in this analysis.

Those variables that predicted the decision to arrest in violent incidents in general provide an important comparison for the earlier cited studies of arrest decisions in family violence incidents. Significant predictors included the race and sex of the combatants, the presence of a weapon, demeanor toward the police, the victim's willingness to sign a complaint, prior police contacts, and the socioeconomic status of the neighborhood. The victim's willingness to be a complainant, the race of the combatants, and the demeanor of the offender were the strongest predictors of this decision. The location of the violent incident, alcohol involvement, a request for informal action, or whether the disputant or someone else called the police were not predictive of arrest.

Smith's analysis addressed not just the decision to arrest, but the decision to arrest, mediate, or separate. The analysis thus indicates not only that whites are more likely to be arrested for an assault than are blacks but also that the most likely police response to assaults by blacks is separation. With respect to the sex of the disputants, the police are equally likely to mediate an assault between two males and a male and female, but assaults between males are most likely to be resolved by an arrest, whereas assaults involving a male and female are most likely to be handled by a separation. While the location of the violent incident was not related to the use of arrest, it was related to the use of mediation or separation, with a higher probability of mediation in private settings. Likewise, the involvement of alcohol in the dispute increased the probability that the police separated the combatants, but it had no influence on the probability of arrest. This study is easily the most complete analysis of factors involved in alternative responses of the police to violent incidents.

There is some agreement in the findings of the studies reviewed above. The strongest predictor of arrest in both the Berk and Loseke (1980–81) and the Smith (1987) studies was the victim's willingness to sign a complaint. The presence of a weapon was also a significant predictor in the two studies considering this variable (Breedlove et al. 1977; Dolan, Hendricks, and Meagher 1986). Both variables were identified as major factors in the arrest decision for the more general class of violent disputes (Smith 1987).

There was also consensus that the occurrence of injury was *not* a significant predictor of arrest in either violent family disputes or violent disputes in general. Perhaps this is not so surprising, given the way this variable was measured. Unless the level of injury is serious enough to constitute probable cause for a felony assault, the decision to arrest often depends on the willingness of the victim to sign a complaint. Under these circumstances, the critical issue is not whether any injury has occurred, but whether a serious injury has occurred. Neither study including injury as a predictor of arrest measured the severity of injury.

There are mixed findings with respect to other predictors of the police response to family and nonfamily violent crimes. Both alcohol involvement and third-party requests to intervene were identified as predictors of arrest in domestic violence crimes; neither was a significant predictor for violent disputes in general, although alcohol use was related to the use of separation or mediation. Race of disputants was significant in the Smith study but not in the Berk and Loseke study.

What, then, can be said about the evidence for a differential response of the police to violent family disputes as compared to nonfamily violent disputes? First, the available research on this issue is very limited, and the lack of common definitions and samples makes it difficult to compare findings. There is a clear need for more systematic research on police practices with proper controls for legal constraints involved in the decision to arrest. Second, the existing evidence is insufficient to support the claim that police respond differently to violence on the part of family members as compared to persons who are not related. Future research may demonstrate such a difference, but the existing data do not. The most sophisticated study available found no independent effect of the presence or absence of a family relationship on the decision to arrest in violent assault incidents. Third, there is evidence that extralegal factors are involved in the decision to arrest, mediate, or separate. The race and sex of the disputants, alcohol involvement, the private or public setting of the incident, the request for police intervention on the part of third parties, and the socioeconomic status of the neighborhood all appear to have some influence on police response. The police exercise discretion when responding to violent incidents; what is not clear is whether there is any systematic bias in the exercise of discretion in family as compared to nonfamily violent incidents.

There is evidence that police respond differently to violent incidents involving a male and a female compared with those involving two males. Smith (1987) notes that the probability of an arrest is lower when the disputants are a male and female. That the relationship between disputants was not a significant factor in this analysis suggests that this differential response was a general one and not specific to family violence situations.

In large part, those who have been critical of police handling of family violence incidents have reacted to the low frequency of arrest and the frequent use of mediation and separation in these situations. Yet those knowledgeable about routine police work are aware that arrest is in general infrequently invoked (Skolnick 1966; Parnas 1967; Wilson 1968; Bittner 1970, 1974; Black 1971). Whether the police respond to family violence incidents in the same way that they respond to other violent incidents may not be the critical issue. It might reasonably be argued that family violence is a unique situation, one that has a high potential for repeated violence and an escalation in the level of injury, one in which the application of a legal sanction has a unique capacity to deter further violence. On these grounds one might argue for the increased use of legal sanctions in family violence incidents whether or not there is any disparity in police responses to various types of violent incidents. There is clearly some evidence for the assertion that family violence crimes are likely to be repeated (Police Foundation 1977; Bowker 1982; Klaus and Rand 1984; Langan and Innes 1986a). Evidence on the deterrent effect of various responses to family violence is considered in the next section.

II. The Effectiveness of Police Responses

One way to investigate the effect of police responses to family violence is to ask police officers and family violence victims to assess the results of particular police actions. Loving (1980) analyzed the results of a 1979 survey of 130 police officers in seventeen police departments concerning police response to spousal violence. Officers rated separation of the parties as the most effective alternative to arrest, followed by removal of the assailant from the household, removal of the victim from the household, and removal of the victim to a battered women's shelter. These officers rated civil remedies, like restraining orders and protective orders, as low in effectiveness. The officers revealed some frustration over their ability to deal effectively with family violence calls. They attributed their difficulties to poor training, the absence of clear policies and procedures for handling these cases, statutory limitations on their authority to arrest in misdemeanor assault cases, and the refusal of the criminal justice system to prosecute these cases.

Samples of battered women consistently give police services low effectiveness ratings (Roy 1977a; Binney, Harkell, and Nixon 1981; Bowker 1982; Pahl 1985). Bowker (1982) reports on a survey of 146 women who had been victims of marital violence but free from violent incidents for at least a year. Subjects were volunteers recruited from southeastern Wisconsin through newspaper ads, posters, speeches, and appeals on radio and television. Bowker reports that the women gave higher ratings to attorneys, prosecutors, social service agencies, and clergy than to the police, and they gave the highest ratings to shelter services. Unfortunately, these studies involved small, nonrepresentative samples, and none of them differentiated between the types of services delivered by the police in their evaluations of police effectiveness.

A second approach to evaluate police effectiveness is to conduct more formal analyses of objective indicators of effectiveness. Bard (1977), Dutton and Levens (1977), Levens and Dutton (1980), Pearce and Snortum (1983), and Dutton (1984) report on the effectiveness of police use of crisis intervention (mediation) techniques in domestic violence incidents. This series of studies, using quasi-experimental designs, conclude that training the police in mediation techniques reduced the incidence of violence directed toward the police by disputing persons, increased the police use of referrals to community agencies, and increased the dispatch rate to family violence calls. However, there was no evidence that arrest rates were affected or that use of mediation techniques (as compared to arrest) reduced the risk of subsequent violent incidents.

Jaffe et al. (1986) report on the effectiveness of a new policy initiated in 1981 in London, Ontario, that directed officers to make arrests whenever there was probable cause in felony and misdemeanor spousal assault incidents. The study involved independent prepolicy and postpolicy samples of victims of spousal assaults and compared arrest rates, victim-reported violence before and after the police intervention, and officers' perceptions of the impact of the policy. A number of favorable outcomes associated with the implementation of this new arrest policy were reported. First, the arrest rate increased dramatically, from 3 percent of all spousal assault occurrences to 67 percent in the postpolicy year. Second, the proportion of charges withdrawn or dismissed prior to trial decreased significantly. The authors note that this suggests that victims were more likely to follow through when police made arrests than when victims signed complaints. Third, based on victim's self-reports of the frequency of violent incidents before and after the police intervention (obtained in the postpolicy period), there was a significant reduction in all forms of violence during the twelve-month period after the police intervention. Fourth, the level of victim-reported dissatisfaction with the police was substantially lower in the postpolicy sample than in the prepolicy sample. Finally, police perceptions of the effectiveness of the new policy were mixed. Approximately 40 percent of the police believed that the new policy helped battered women, 55 percent indicated that it gave an important message to the community, but only 21 percent believed it was effective in stopping family violence. A majority of officers felt that the courts did not support the arrest policy and that there was no change in the proportion of prepolicy and postpolicy victims reporting satisfaction with the prosecuting attorney's office.

Unfortunately, a number of serious methodological problems in that study limit the significance of these findings. Both the prepolicy and postpolicy victim samples were nonrepresentative samples of spousal assault victims in these two periods. They involved volunteers recruited by a letter from the Chief of Police sent to all spousal assault victims known to the police in 1979 (prepolicy) and 1983 (postpolicy). As a result, self-reported frequencies of violent incidents and victims satisfaction with police service before and after the police intervention cannot be relied on. Further, the claim that there were fewer reported violent incidents in the twelve-month period after the police intervention in the postpolicy period cannot be attributed directly to an arrest disposition by the police; while a higher proportion of all violent incidents in the postpolicy period involved an arrest by the police than in the prepolicy period (67 percent as compared to 3 percent), there was no control for which victims in the sample received or did not receive an arrest disposition from the police. Finally, there were no control groups to reflect the preintervention and postintervention experiences of victims *not* receiving an arrest disposition; without such a comparison, the effectiveness of an arrest compared to any other police response cannot be established. Thus, the only firm finding is that the policy dramatically increased the arrest rate.

Langan and Innes (1986a) provide some evidence that calling the police, as a general strategy for dealing with spousal violence, reduces the risk of further violence. Spousal violence in this analysis involved a rape, robbery, aggravated assault, or simple assault committed against a married, divorced, or separated woman by a relative or other person well known to the victim. Using National Crime Survey data for the period from 1978 to 1982, they found that calling the police after an incident of spousal violence reduced the risk of another violent incident within the next six months by as much as 62 percent. They also reported that subsequent acts of violence against women who called the police were no more serious than those against women who did not call the police.

Since there is a possibility of a systematic selection bias in this analysis, because women who are at lower risk for a repeated assault may be more likely to call the police, some caution is needed in interpreting these results; Langan and Innes (1986a) note this possibility. They also note that the apparent reduction of subsequent violence could have resulted from a particular police action, for example, arrest, rather than a general response. It was also the case that calls to the police in this analysis were not necessarily calls made by the victim (25 percent were not made by the victim). Given the earlier observation that the probability of arrest is related to who makes the call requesting police intervention, it would have been instructive to compare outcomes by this distinction. The analysis of the severity of subsequent assaults by those calling or not calling the police is problematic due to the small number of cases in this analysis (Langan and Innes 1986*b*, tables 4U and 6). The conclusion that subsequent acts of violence against women who called the police declined should thus be viewed with some caution. Langan and Innes are careful to note that it does not necessarily follow from their findings that all victims of family violence should call the police.

The NCS data reveal that victims of violent crimes by relatives were more likely to call the police than were victims of violent crimes by nonrelatives (Klaus and Rand 1984). Although this finding could be an artifact of being willing to report family violence on the NCS, this seems unlikely. Oppenlander's (1982) finding that victims of family assault were more willing to identify their assailants to the police and were more likely to sign complaints than were victims of nonfamily assault supports the NCS finding. These findings clearly challenge the popular view that violent family crimes are more likely to go unreported than are nonfamily violent crimes and that victims of family violence are less likely to sign complaints.

The National Family Violence Evaluation Study (Fagan et al. 1984), a nonexperimental study of 270 victims of spousal violence, attempted to assess the effects of both criminal justice system sanctions and other interventions, such as shelter or counseling services, on subsequent spousal violence. Subjects were women who had sought assistance from one of the federally funded Family Violence Demonstration Programs located in Florida, Vermont, Ohio, and North Carolina. In addition to the data collected at admission concerning the precipitating violent incident, self-reported data were also obtained in face-to-face interviews (in 1980) for a six-month follow-up period.

Four types of police response to the precipitating incident were compared: (1) arrest, (2) victim assistance (legal information and referrals to social agencies), (3) informal action (mediation or separation), and (4) no action. Two measures of recidivism were based on self-reported data obtained during the six-month follow-up period. An abuse measure referred to verbal harassment, degradation, threats, and other nonphysical assaults; a violence measure referred only to physical assaults. Only the findings involving the violence measure are discussed here.

Overall, 72 percent of this sample reported no subsequent violence and 94 percent reported no subsequent injury during the follow-up period. Those cases handled with informal police action had the highest recidivism rates (45 percent), and those involving an arrest had the lowest recidivism rate (17 percent). Of those who received victim assistance, 20 percent reported a repeated violent incident; those receiving a no-action response from the police reported a 23 percent recidivism rate. Interestingly, arrest and taking no action were both associated with a lower rate of subsequent violence than were mediation or separation.

Fagan et al. also attempted to control for the severity of prior violence in their analysis. Recidivism rates were estimated separately for those whose prior injury was minor (i.e., no worse than bruises) or major (bleeding, broken bones, lacerations, unconsciousness, or miscarriage). In this analysis recidivism was clearly related to prior injury level; in every category, those whose prior injury was minor reported fewer repeated violent incidents than those whose prior injuries were major. The rate was lowest for arrest (8 percent) and highest for informal action (33 percent), with intermediate rates for victim assistance (10 percent) and no action (21 percent). For subjects whose prior injury was major, there was a change in the relative ordering of police actions. The recidivism rates for arrest (25 percent), victim assistance (25 percent), and no action (24 percent) are equivalent; the rate for informal actions remains substantially higher (51 percent). These data suggest that arrest is a more effective police response for reducing subsequent violence when prior levels of injury are low; when prior levels of injury are high, arrest appears no more effective than no action or victim assistance. Fagan et al. thus question whether arrest is an effective strategy for serious violent offenders.

Weaknesses in the design of this study require caution in accepting these estimates of the differential effectiveness of various police responses to family violence crimes, and the selection biases in the sample preclude any formal generalization to spouse abuse cases in general. Still, while the evidence is weak, it does suggest that arrest may be the most effective police response to spousal violence, at least for the less serious cases.

To date, a more sophisticated and influential study of the effectiveness of police responses to family violence is the Minneapolis Domestic Violence Experiment (Sherman and Berk 1984a, 1984b) conducted during 1981–82. The design of the study called for the police in two of four precincts in Minneapolis to assign suspects in violent family disputes randomly to one of three police action (experimental) conditions: arrest, separation of the parties, or advise/mediate. The eligible pool was limited to domestic violence cases in which both the offender and the victim were present when the police arrived and in which the incident involved a misdemeanor assault. These were situations in which the police were empowered but not required under Minnesota law to make an arrest. Cases involving aggravated assaults were deliberately excluded because they required an arrest. The design called for a six-month postintervention follow-up period during which interviews were conducted with the victims and official records of subsequent family violence were collected. Interviews involved an initial face-to-face interview followed by telephone or face-to-face interviews every two weeks during the six-month follow-up period and were designed to obtain information on the frequency and seriousness of subsequent assaults by the offender. The follow-up period for the official record data was a minimum of six months and extended to nearly two years for those subjects entering the study early.

Two measures of recidivism were used. The first involved a subsequent police report for domestic violence during the six-month follow-up period. The second was the occurrence of a repeated violent incident (an assault, threatened assault or property damage), as reported in the victim interviews.

The analysis of official records over six months indicated that those receiving the arrest disposition had the lowest rate of recidivism (10 percent) and those receiving the separate disposition had the highest (24 percent). The recidivism rate for those receiving the advise disposition (19 percent) was not statistically significantly different from that for those receiving either an arrest or separate disposition, but the difference between arrest and separate treatments was statistically significant. The analysis of victim-reported violent incidents over the follow-up period again revealed the lowest recidivism rate for those in the arrest condition (19 percent), but the highest rate was observed for those in the advise condition (37 percent). Those in the separate condition had a recidivism rate (33 percent) that again was not significantly different from that in either the arrest or the advise conditions. There was no evidence of a differential effect for different kinds of offenders; arrest worked just as well for those with no prior arrests as for those with prior arrests (Berk and Sherman 1985).

This study provides the most compelling evidence for the effectiveness of arrests as responses to misdemeanor family assaults: it involved a true experimental design and multiple measures of repeated violence. There are, however, some concerns about the internal validity of the study. First, the determination of study eligibility and treatment assignment were not independent. Officers determined the eligibility of a domestic violence incident after arriving on the scene and evaluating the situation. The random assignment to one of the treatment groups for eligible cases was determined by the color of the next investigation report form on the pad. Officers were thus aware of what the assigned treatment would be if the case was determined to be an eligible case, prior to making this determination. Under these conditions, the possibility of a deliberate manipulation of the treatment through the eligibility decision existed. This type of selective exclusion would not have been visible to the project, given the controls established for the assignment process. Nor is it addressed in the analysis of misdelivered treatments presented by Sherman and Berk (1984b). Unfortunately, project controls over eligibility decisions and the random assignment process were rather limited.

Second, there is a potential problem with selective attrition, that is, an attrition linked to the treatment assigned and repeated violence. Only 62 percent of victims in the study could be located and interviewed at the initial scheduled interview. Less than half (49 percent) of victims completed all twelve follow-up interviews. Sherman and Berk tested for selective attrition on initial interviews and report that attrition in general was not significantly related to the nature of the treatment action. The published reports do not indicate that subsequent waves of the follow-up were tested for selective attrition. Nor was the test adequate to cover all potential problems related to selective attrition. For example, it would be important to establish that the proportion of each treatment group moving out of town (one source of attrition) was similar since this particular form of attrition was critical to both the victim-reported and official measures of recidivism. If arrests were associated with a higher probability of moving or break-up of the relationship, this could seriously undermine the deterrence interpretation of these findings. It is not unreasonable to assume that the application of criminal sanctions may increase the risk of break-up, and there is evidence that dissolving the relationship is an effective means of reducing subsequent violence (Ford 1984). Knowledge about the proportion of offender-victim relationships having terminated could be obtained only through the follow-up interviews and accurate estimates of this proportion by treatment are precluded by the high attrition rate.

It is one thing to point to some "potential threats" to internal validity and quite another to demonstrate that these problems exist. Sherman and Berk do an excellent job of addressing those threats to internal validity that they could address with the data available, and they found no basis for a number of other potential problems. No claim is made here that the selective exclusion and attrition problems mentioned are in fact present. However, the possibility suggests some caution in rushing to a policy recommendation on the strength of these findings alone.

There are more serious external validity problems with the Minneapolis Domestic Violence Experiment. There is ample evidence to indicate that the cases included in this study were not a representative sample of all misdemeanor family violence cases encountered by Minneapolis police officers. The two precincts selected as the target area were selected because of the "high density" of family violence occurring in those areas, and in all likelihood they are different from the other two precincts on such variables as socioeconomic status and ethnicity (see Tauchen, Tauchen, and Witte 1986); cases involving assaults on police officers or demands by the victim for an arrest were also excluded by design as were cases in which the suspect was not present when the police arrived. There was a very selective participation by police officers working these areas and reason to suspect that a substantial number of eligible cases were never referred to the project. Since officers typically work particular areas and shifts, this suggests differential representation of particular areas and times within the general targeted areas. In the light of these difficulties, any generalization of these findings to all misdemeanor family violence incidents in Minneapolis, let alone other communities, is problematic.

There is another important concern. This study was not guided by any theoretical perspective that provided an explanation for the apparent effectiveness of arrest and, as a result, provides little insight into the process that links an arrest to a reduction in subsequent violence, although Sherman and Berk (1984*b*) offer some posthoc hypotheses about this relation. Deterrence may operate in different ways, and without measures of intervening variables to help establish causal processes the precise results of these police interventions are unknown (Morash 1986). There are several alternative interpretations to the specific deterrence interpretation offered by Berk and Sherman (1984*b*). Albert J.

Reiss, Jr., for example, offers a displacement interpretation (1986) in which the arrest leads to an increased risk that the offender-victim relationship will be terminated and the offender enters into a new intimate relationship in which he continues his assaultive behavior. Strube and Barbour's (1983) analysis of factors related to termination of an abusive relationship suggests that when women find that their husbands/partners are not deterred by arrest, they are likely to leave the relationship. Without specific data on how being arrested influenced the offenders' attitudes and perceptions relative to their use of violence, the claim that the results demonstrate a specific deterrent effect is not very compelling.

Berk and Newton (1985) report on a nonexperimental replication of the Minneapolis Domestic Violence Experiment involving 783 wife-battery incidents coming to the attention of police over twenty-eight months in a southern California county. Police made arrests in 26 percent of these cases. The initial incident for a couple defined entry into the study; any subsequent incident report involving the same victim and offender was considered a reoccurrence or "failure." The length of the follow-up period thus varied from over two years to less than a month, depending on when a case entered the study. Berk and Newton employed a propensity score analysis, modeling the assignment process and attempting to partial out the effect of nonrandom assignment so as to obtain unbiased estimates of treatment effects. This analysis confirmed the Minneapolis Domestic Violence Experiment findings: arrest resulted in a lower subsequent recidivism rate than did nonarrest. While this analysis involved a very sophisticated approach to estimating the effects of arrest with a quasi-experimental design, the analysis is not as compelling as that based on a true experimental design with random assignment. However, it does increase our confidence in the Minneapolis findings.

Jaffe et al. (1986) note that the Minneapolis Domestic Violence Experiment findings may reflect a temporary, short-term deterrent effect that lasts only while charges are pending some action by the prosecutor and court. Sherman and Berk (1984a) report that only 2 percent of the arrest cases in the Minneapolis study went to trial. What happens when formal charges are dropped or sanctions applied? Is there a possibility of an escalation in the frequency and seriousness of violence in the long run for cases receiving an arrest disposition? Should we not have some knowledge of the long-range consequences of arrest before implementing presumptive or mandatory arrest policies? In contrast, if the arrest operates to reinforce general antiviolence norms, to encourage the victim to take some positive action to terminate the relationship or seek professional aid in dealing with the situation, or to change the balance of power in the relationship, then other types of reinforcements and supports for victims might be employed successfully in conjunction with arrest.

Tauchen, Tauchen, and Witte (1986) report on a reanalysis of a subset of cases in the Minneapolis Domestic Violence Experiment. Only those cases that involved a male and female couple in a romantic relationship were included (approximately 80 percent of the original sample). Also excluded were cases with missing data on the initial or follow-up interviews. The resulting number of cases used in the analysis was eighty-one, approximately 50 percent of the 161 cases completing all interviews.

This analysis differs from Sherman and Berk (1984a, 1984b) in that it focuses on the dynamics of violence and attrition over the follow-up period and makes use of the time-ordered data collected in the twelve follow-up interviews. The attrition in the sample was dramatic. By the sixth follow-up interview only 44 percent (thirty-six cases) were still available and willing to be interviewed. By the last interview (twelfth), only 28 percent (twenty-three) cases were located and interviewed. Repeated violence in this sample was rare; only 7 percent of the couples reported another violent incident in the six-month follow-up period.[5] At the initial interview, 80 percent of respondents ($N = 205$) had reported an assault by the suspect in the prior six months; 60 percent reported a police intervention in the prior six months. Rates of repeated violence in the entire Minneapolis sample were thus quite low compared with these reported rates in the prior six-month period.

Tauchen, Tauchen, and Witte (1986) replicated the earlier finding of Sherman and Berk on this subsample of couples. The lowest recidivism rates were observed for those in the arrest condition; the highest was observed for those in the advise condition. This difference was statistically significant ($p = .10$), but neither arrest nor advise rates were significantly different from the rate for those in the separate condition. This indicates that the general finding from the Minneapolis study held for couples as well as for family violence in general.

[5] This appears to be an unadjusted rate. The rates reported in Sherman and Berk (1984a, 1984b) are adjusted rates that attempt to correct for attrition and other specific data problems (1984a, p. 6). Sherman and Berk do not report the unadjusted victim reported recidivism rates for the general sample. Presumably, they also are quite low, given this rate for 50 percent of the sample.

Their analysis of the dynamics of police treatment effects indicated that the effect of an arrest was greatest in the period immediately following the police action and had essentially worn off by the end of the six-month follow-up period. This result indicates that the effect of arrest was relatively short-term. Unfortunately, the follow-up data were limited to a six-month period; longer term effects cannot be assessed. Tauchen, Tauchen, and Witte also report that the violent episodes, in and of themselves, do not appear to affect the probability of violence in later periods. They then note: "These findings lend no support to the hypothesis that the male is contrite after a violent incident, perhaps because he fears that additional violence may cause her to leave (Walker 1979), or to the hypothesis that violence feeds on itself" (1986, p. 43).

The accumulating evidence from all available studies, experimental and quasiexperimental, supports the claim that arrest is more effective than advisement, separation, or no action in reducing subsequent violence in misdemeanor family violence cases. However, some cautions are in order. Evidence for the generalization of those findings is still quite limited. The Fagan et al. (1984) studies suggest that the differential effect may be minimal for more serious offenders; the Tauchen, Tauchen, and Witte (1986) analysis suggests that the effect may be temporary. None of these studies involved a very long follow-up period, and the longer term effects are still unknown. Whether these results reflect specific deterrence, a displacement effect, or some other explanation is also not yet clear. Nor is it known how a presumptive or mandatory arrest policy will affect the criminal justice system more generally. Once instituted, how will mandatory arrest policies affect victims' decisions to call the police? Many victims do not want their spouses or relatives arrested, and, knowing that a call to the police will result in an arrest, they may not call. Is the reduced probability of subsequent violence following an arrest enhanced by an aggressive prosecution of these cases, or is the arrest itself sufficient?

In an effort to address some of these questions, the National Institute of Justice funded six replications (U.S. Department of Justice 1985), all of which involve true experimental designs. These projects, located in Omaha, Atlanta, Charlotte (North Carolina), Milwaukee, Colorado Springs (Colorado), and Dade County (Florida) will extend the range of police alternatives evaluated (e.g., the use of arrest warrants when the offender is not present at the scene) and the length of follow-up periods and will attempt, at least in some cases, to specify the process by which an arrest leads to a reduced probability of repeated violence (assuming this outcome is replicated). Several of the projects are also conducting baseline studies, that is, they are obtaining descriptive data on all domestic violence incidents in these cities in order to address the representativeness of cases included in the experiment. This initiative also involves the use of shared definitions for treatments and outcomes and the development of a shared core of measures across the project sites to enhance the potential for comparing findings. No results will be available from these replications for several years. In the meantime, the Minneapolis Domestic Violence Study remains the landmark study on the effectiveness of alternative police responses to family violence.

This review of police responses to family violence has focused on family violence generally and on violence between spouses, ex-spouses, and cohabiting adults specifically. There is virtually no empirical data on the effects of alternate police approaches for addressing other forms of family violence, such as child abuse. Erez's study (1986) indicated that police rarely encountered child abuse (1 percent) or interfamily sex offenses (.5 percent) when responding to domestic disturbances. Gelles and Straus (1988) note that the police are "the missing persons of the child maltreatment literature" (p. 13) since there is virtually no research on police responses to child abuse. This is largely because the police are typically bypassed in the identification and reporting of these cases. Reports of child abuse and child sexual abuse from physicians, teachers, and other caretakers are usually made directly to protective service agencies.

III. Prosecuting Family Violence Crimes

Prosecutors have the greatest discretion in the criminal justice system (Reiss 1974). The character, quality, and efficiency of the whole system is heavily influenced by the way prosecutors exercise their discretionary powers. In some jurisdictions, virtually all arrests are taken to the prosecutor, and, in others, the police screen arrests before they are submitted to the prosecutor. In these latter jurisdictions the police can effectively dismiss cases; they can also do additional investigative work before they submit an arrest to the prosecutor. Not all family violence cases reaching the prosecutor involve the police. A victim can sign a complaint that is submitted directly to the prosecutor. Still, the vast majority of all family violence cases coming to the attention of the prosecutor involve arrests. In any event, when a case is submitted, the prosecutor has the discretion to accept, modify, or drop the charge(s).

Critics note that prosecutors rarely file charges or aggressively prosecute family violence cases (Field and Field 1973; Fields 1978; Martin 1978; Dobash and Dobash 1979; Lerman 1986). They argue that the police know this and, on the assumption that prosecutors will dismiss most family violence cases, make little effort to investigate carefully or to obtain the type of evidence necessary for successful prosecutions. From the police perspective, there is little reason to make an arrest if the prosecutor will foreseeably dismiss the case, unless the arrest is necessary as a control mechanism in the immediate situation. If prosecutors pursued family violence cases aggressively, there would be more incentive for police to make arrests.

Prosecutors have traditionally dismissed the majority of family violence cases referred to them by the police or by direct victim-initiated complaints (Parnas 1970; Field and Field 1973; Martin 1976; Fields 1978; Lerman 1986). The critical issue, however, is whether different criteria are used in deciding whether to prosecute family and nonfamily assaults or whether the same criteria are applied and fewer family violence crimes meet the standard criteria.

A. Factors Involved in the Decision to Prosecute

Few empirical studies attempt to identify the factors involved in the decision to prosecute family assault cases, either alone or in comparison with nonfamily assault cases or other types of crimes (Rauma 1984). The vast majority of available empirical studies are general studies of felony case processing. Employing data from the extensive Prosecutor's Management Information Systems (PROMIS), a computer-based management information system, Brosi (1979), Boland et al. (1983), and Boland (1986) document that, for all types of felony crimes, the major factors involved in the prosecutor's decision to reject felony cases at screening or to dismiss them after filing involved problems with witnesses and evidence (also see Forst et al. 1981; Forst and Hernon 1985). Other factors include department policy in a particular jurisdiction, questions of due process, referrals for other prosecution (e.g., for a lesser or different charge), and the possibility of diversion. Neither victim injury nor the defendant's prior record appear to have a significant influence on the decision to prosecute (Forst and Hernon 1985).

Forst et al. (1981) report that, for all types of crime, the availability of at least two witnesses significantly increases the chances of obtaining a conviction. Having only one witness is often deemed insufficient for prosecution and a basis for rejecting a case at screening. Forst et al. also found that cases in which physical evidence was obtained were over two-and-one-half times as likely to result in conviction as cases in which such evidence was lacking.

A higher proportion of felony assault cases than other types of felony cases are rejected at screening (Brosi 1979); a high proportion of felony assault cases, typically 50 percent or more, involve friends and relatives who may drop the charges or refuse to cooperate with the prosecution. Williams (1978) reports similar findings for both felony and misdemeanor assaults. The Vera Institute of Justice's (1977) study of felony arrests in New York City also found that defendants who were charged with assault were less likely to be convicted than defendants on other felony charges. Only 10 percent of the 369 cases were ever decided, and most of these involved a plea to lesser charges rather than trial.

Reporting more specifically on misdemeanor family violence cases, Ford (1984) reports that 70 percent of conjugal cases in Indianapolis during 1978 were dismissed at the victim's request. Field and Field (1973) found that 80 percent of marital violence cases in Washington, D.C., in 1967 had charges dropped, presumably by the victim.

Brosi (1979) and Boland et al. (1983) note that, in general, witness problems are more common for crimes against persons than for crimes against property. However, whatever the type of crime, the proportion of cases prosecuted is lower when the offender knows the victim. When the victim and the offender were friends or acquaintances, cases ended in conviction only half as often as when these cases involved strangers; when family relationships existed, conviction rates ranged from one-fourth to one-half of those involving strangers. Again, this held for *all types* of crimes. The increased risk of conviction associated with the change from family/relative to friend/acquaintance to stranger relationship was even more dramatic for property and robbery crimes than for assault crimes. This is an important observation for it indicates that the effect of the offender-victim relationship on the availability of witnesses and hence the decision to prosecute is a very general one and not peculiar to assault cases.

In a study focusing specifically on domestic violence cases, Rauma (1984) analyzed prosecutorial decision making on the part of a deputy district attorney (DDA) handling domestic violence cases in Santa Barbara (California) as part of a family violence project. The DDA and a criminal investigator were assigned full-time to this project to prosecute domestic violence cases. The analysis involved 199 domestic disturbance cases forwarded to the district attorney's office. Only domestic incidents involving two adults in a present or past heterosexual romantic or conjugal relationship and involving a male offender and a female victim were included. This sample involves a subset of those cases in the Berk and Loseke study (1980–81) described earlier.

Rauma considers three prosecutorial decisions: (1) the decision to follow up a reported incident, (2) the decision to file charges, and (3) the decision to divert to a counseling program (with a threat of future prosecution) rather than go to trial. An arrest at the scene was a major factor in the decision to follow up an incident report. Rauma notes that the incident tends to be better documented when an arrest is made, and this gives the DDA more information with which to make a decision. More severe incidents were also likelier to result in arrest. Arrests thus constitute the better documented and more severe cases. The DDA's decision to follow up an incident was also influenced by negative characteristics of the victim and offender. If the victim was alleged by the offender to have been violent or was noted by the police to have been drinking, the probability of a follow-up was decreased; if the offender was abusive to the police, had a weapon, or was under a restraining order, the probability of a follow-up increased. Rauma notes: "Events that either raise doubts about victims as a 'victim,' or confirm that the offender is guilty of something and deserves attention, affect the DDA's decision about further processing" (1984, p. 339). Injuries to either party also influenced the decision. Injuries to the victim increase the probability of follow-up, whereas injuries to the offender decrease that probability.

Two additional factors were significant in the decision to follow up: being married reduced the probability of follow-up as did the size of the DDA's caseload. The marriage effect appeared to be an indicator of the DDA's assessment of potential problems such as victim noncooperation or possibly a judgment of what a desirable outcome is for married couples. Rauma also noted that increasing the number of cases forwarded and the quality of their documentation had virtually no effect on the number of offenders filed on by the district attorney's office.

Only two factors were observed to influence the decision to file charges: severity of injuries and the offender's prior record. The direction of the injury relationship was unexpected: the more severe the victim's injuries, the lower the probability of filing; injuries to the offender increased the probability of filing. To explain these findings, Rauma notes that 78 percent of the cases forwarded were either arraigned or diverted, and for the vast majority the decision to follow up was, in effect, a decision to prosecute. It may be largely idiosyncratic factors that cause cases to fall apart after the initial decision to pursue them.

Several factors influenced the decision to divert the offender to a counseling program: prior record, negative characteristics of the victim and offender, marital status, and the victim's stated willingness to cooperate with prosecution. As expected, those with prior records were less likely to be diverted. The effect of the victim's drinking and alleged violence increased the probability of diversion while negative aspects of the offender's character decreased the probability of diversion. Married offenders were more likely to be diverted, as were those cases where victims were uncooperative. The severity of the victim's injuries, the quality of evidence, the race of the offender, or the injuries to the offender had little or no effect on this decision. Rauma concludes that good cases have good victims and bad offenders, sufficient evidence, and are serious enough to warrant attention from authorities. Diversion appeared to be an alternative sanction for weak cases or for cases in which counseling would be the outcome in any event. The diversion option allowed the DDA to keep some cases alive that would otherwise have been dropped.

While the empirical evidence is quite limited, there are few data to support the claim that different factors are involved in the decision to prosecute family violence crimes as compared with stranger violence crimes. The differences in prosecution rates appear to be primarily a result of differences in victim/witness cooperation and secondarily a matter of differences in the quality and quantity of the physical evidence available. The victim/witness problem is linked directly to the offender-victim relationship and appears to be the critical factor accounting for the differential rate of prosecution of family violence crimes and other types of violent crimes.

B. Problems in the Use of Victims as Witnesses

Prosecutors view cases primarily with respect to their legal viability. They are thus concerned with the availability of complainants, witnesses, and tangible evidence. In family violence crimes the victim, complainant, and witness are frequently the same person. A number of special problems are associated with requiring family violence victims to be witnesses in the prosecution of their spouses or other relatives. In many jurisdictions, the legal procedures employed in the prosecution of misdemeanor family assault cases require that the victim be the plaintiff in the legal proceeding, not just a witness. Having the responsibility for the prosecution of one's spouse, family member, or lover can clearly create special problems for victims. It may make them more vulnerable to intimidation and retaliation from their assailants. Since the victim has de facto power to terminate the legal proceedings, this will be a problem particularly when victims want to continue their relationship with offenders. The victim is often vulnerable to loss of her or his only source of income; if the offender is the primary wage earner, prosecution may result in financial hardship to the victim. Moreover, victims of family violence are often ineligible for compensation under state statutes providing compensation for crime victims (Carrow 1980; Lerman 1986). It is not surprising that a substantial number drop charges prior to filing or refuse to appear at the trial.

Critics charge that prosecutors deliberately discourage victims of family violence from pressing charges (Martin 1976; Goodman 1977; Roy 1977*b*; Paterson 1979; Lerman 1986). Lerman (1986) maintains that victims are not adequately informed about the process of prosecuting a charge, about what is expected of them, or what they can expect in the way of support and protection. Since defendants can rarely be detained in jail on misdemeanor charges, this last concern is often a vital one.

There are no empirical data available to evaluate the claim that these problems are peculiar to family violence victims. Many of these problems characterize victims and witnesses generally (Cannavale 1976; Forst and Hernon 1985). These general victim/witness studies also confirm that victims who know the defendant are particularly likely to fear retaliation or to want to protect their relationship with the offender. Boland et al. (1983) indicated that problems with witness cooperation when the offender was known to the victim were characteristic of all types of crimes, not just assaults. This suggests that whatever the witness difficulties are, they are fairly common in crimes in which there is some prior relationship between the victim and offender. This finding suggests that the problems of victim cooperation when there is a prior intimate relationship between the victim and offender are neither unique to family violence crimes nor more severe in family violence crimes.

Many states have enacted measures to assist victims and witnesses, provide compensation to victims, and require restitution by offenders (U.S. Department of Justice 1983). A number of programs deal with protection of witnesses from intimidation, counsel or ombudsmen for victims, increased use of deposition in lieu of court appearances, and victim notification of changes and progress in the case. Victims of family violence are often identified as a class of individuals especially vulnerable to crime. Several states have laws that authorize courts to issue protective orders in domestic violence cases to prevent further violence and to establish support services such as shelter facilities, counseling, and hotlines.

A number of cities have established special family violence prosecution units and family victim/witness assistance programs to deal with these victim-related problems. Lerman (1986) describes a number of federally funded programs with mandates to encourage and coordinate the efforts of police, prosecutors, and community agencies and to provide additional services such as shelters, special prosecution units, mental health clinics, protection order clinics, and educational and training programs. Five special prosecution programs in Seattle, Santa Barbara, Los Angeles, Philadelphia, and Westchester County (New York) include a vigorous prosecution of family violence cases (in some sites all arrests are filed), prosecutors signing the complaints and serving as plaintiffs in the prosecution, and the adoption of policies that deny the victim's request for dismissal once the charges are filed. While the program evaluation data reported by Lerman are unsystematic and impressionistic, there is at least some preliminary indication that these programs have achieved higher levels of victim cooperation and lower levels of postfiling dismissals. One program has experimented with continuing the prosecution without victim cooperation, and it reports a 34 percent conviction rate. Unfortunately, it is difficult to determine if the apparent decrease in case attrition is the result of additional support services (most of these sites also had victim/witness assistance programs) or the policy decisions to file on more cases and to resist the withdrawal of the victim from the proceedings. Further, it is not known whether a successful prosecution is any more effective in deterring subsequent violence than is the threat of prosecution alone. The evidence indicates that levels of victim/witness cooperation can be improved with changes in policy and/or special victim/witness support programs; however, a careful, systematic evaluation of these programs is needed.

Forst and Hernon (1985) report that victims were kept better informed in jurisdictions that had victim/witness programs operating out of the prosecutor's office. They recommended the use of a victim impact statement, which is a formal document appended to the presentence investigation report to assist the judge in selecting an appropriate sentence. This statement describes the extent of injuries sustained by the victim, the effect of the crime on the victim's life and, sometimes, the victim's opinion about an appropriate sentence. Victim impact statements are now required in federal courts and are increasingly being used in state courts.

Some argue that mandatory prosecution of offenders in family violence cases is not a wise policy. Gelles and Mederer (1985) and Ford (1984) note that mandatory prosecution may have the opposite effect intended. While designed to empower and aid family violence victims, mandatory prosecution may disempower victims by reducing their control in this situation. Ford (1984) interviewed a small sample ($N =$ 25) of women who requested that charges be filed against their husbands in the Marion County, Indiana, Court in 1981. These interviews focused on motives for filing charges and, in instances in which charges were dropped, the reasons for dropping them. The most frequently stated reason for filing was that the police had advised them to prosecute. Many of the other reasons given implied that the threat of prosecution was being used to bargain with their partners for a desired outcome in the relationship.

In a majority of cases dropped, the victim's reasons were consistent with their stated desired outcome at the time of filing: they believed they had been successful in obtaining agreements from their mates that they considered satisfactory. This typically involved using the leverage of prosecution to control the violence so they could remain in the relationship or to obtain agreements allowing them to leave the relationship on terms more acceptable than had they not threatened prosecution. There were also cases in which women were prosecuting in fulfillment of a threat to prosecute if their mates failed to keep promises made earlier. Ford notes that an awareness of this instrumental use of prosecution may help alleviate problems that often arise between victims and prosecutors when victims initially push for prosecution and then suddenly drop charges. For prosecutors, it generates feelings of being used or wasting time on an unproductive case; for victims, it involves a rational act and a means of altering the balance of power in a conjugal relationship.

The Ford study involved a small and selective sample of victims.

Additional research on this issue is needed to inform prosecution policy. Still, these results do suggest some caution in implementing policies that may inadvertently disempower victims.

C. The Effectiveness of Prosecution and Court-ordered Sanctions

Very few empirical studies address the effectiveness of prosecution, conviction, or sentencing in deterring subsequent family violence. Given the paucity of research, studies of prosecution and court responses are considered together in this section. There are a few scattered references to findings that bear on the effectiveness of prosecution, but only one quasi-experimental study with at least some controls and a comparison group is known to me (Fagan et al. 1984).

The Fagan et al. study was described in detail earlier. It involved a six-month follow-up of 270 women victims of spousal assault who sought help from federally funded family violence programs. Victim reports for the follow-up period provided the data on subsequent violence. The measure of violence included only physical assaults. In the analysis of subsequent violence, controls for the prior history and severity of violence were introduced. Analyses for three types of criminal justice interventions were reported: three levels of police response, prosecution attempted or not attempted, and assailant convicted or not convicted.

The results for the police interventions have been reported earlier. Here the focus is on the effectiveness of prosecution and conviction. Thirty percent of those offenders not prosecuted and 26 percent of those prosecuted had one or more repeated violent assaults in the six-month follow-up period (a nonsignificant difference). However, a more substantial difference in failure rates appeared when the severity of prior violence was controlled. Among those with low levels of prior violence and injury, the recidivism rate was 23 percent for those not prosecuted and 12 percent for those prosecuted. Among those with a high level of prior violence, the failure rates were substantially higher but not differentiated by the treatment condition (prosecuted = 33 percent; not prosecuted = 35 percent). These findings suggest that prosecution was effective in reducing the likelihood of subsequent violence for offenders with a low level of prior violence. There was no evidence of prosecution effectiveness for those with a history of more serious violence.

The analysis of those convicted and not convicted revealed even lower failure rates among those with low levels of prior violence: 18

percent for those not convicted and 0 percent for those convicted. Failure rates for those with high levels of prior violence were 36 percent and 22 percent, respectively. However, the pattern of differences in this analysis was not statistically significant and the N's in the convicted groups were very small.

Fagan (1986) notes that as the legal sanctions became more stringent, assailants with more severe histories of violence were more often violent at least once in the follow-up period. He concludes that these data suggest that sanctions deter only some violent offenders, those with less severe histories of violence. There is little evidence that any legal sanctions were effective in reducing the risk of subsequent violence for those with a history of more serious violent offending.

Unfortunately, the design of this study is weak, and there are potentially serious internal and external validity problems (described earlier). However, apart from the Minneapolis Domestic Violence Experiment, this same criticism could be made for virtually all of the research studies reviewed in this essay. The tentative finding that the effectiveness of legal sanctions (arrest, prosecution, and conviction) is conditioned on the offender's history of prior violence is an important one that needs to be validated. It should also be noted that there is no evidence in the Fagan et al. (1984) study that the deterrent effect of legal action increased with the stage of processing in the legal system or the potential severity of legal sanction. The most effective action as judged by the failure rates for those with low levels of prior violence involved an arrest. Since this study did not involve a nested design or random assignment, this observation may or may not be significant, but it suggests the need to vary the severity of the legal sanction in future research to evaluate this deterrence issue.

There is some research evaluating the efficacy of civil restraining orders to reduce subsequent violence. Only two states had civil restraining-order legislation for battered women prior to 1976. By 1982, thirty-one more states had enacted civil restraining-order legislation (Grau 1982). Before these laws were enacted, the major obstacle to use of restraining orders by spousal assault victims was the requirement that divorce or dissolution proceedings be initiated before a restraining order could be issued. Recent legislation generally does not include this requirement (Grau 1982). While law enforcement procedures in most jurisdictions provide civil sanctions for violating restraining orders, the new restraining-order statutes also provide criminal sanctions for a direct violation of the order (Grau 1982).

Grau, Fagan, and Wexler (1984), employing the Family Violence Evaluation Study data (Fagan et al. 1984), report on the effectiveness of restraining orders in this sample of women victims. All four states involved in the study required a civil court proceeding, although Ohio also permitted access through the criminal court. Thirty-three percent of the subjects in the sample had obtained restraining orders. The orders were in effect for ninety days to one year. Enforcement was primarily through the civil court with punishments including both fines and incarceration for up to six months. All orders forbade violence, and some prohibited threats and verbal abuse as well.

The study involved a quasi-experimental design. The analysis compared repeated violence in the six-month period after entering the family violence program for those having or not having a restraining order. Violence in this study referred to physical violence. Two measures of prior violence on the part of the offender were used as controls in the analysis: the most serious prior injury and whether the offender was violent toward both strangers and his spouse/partner.

Persons obtaining restraining orders tended to be younger, employed, and involved in shorter and less violent marriages. They also had children and a history of prior separations. Grau, Fagan, and Wexler conclude that these are essentially women who have fewer emotional and financial ties to the offender, less severe histories of violence, and have attempted to escape the violence earlier through separation.

A majority (72 percent) of the women with restraining orders thought them effective in reducing further violence. However, postprogram violence was unrelated to the presence or absence of a restraining order; approximately one-fourth of the women in each group were assaulted during the follow-up period. The introduction of controls for the offender's prior history of violence and the severity of the victim's prior injury had no effect on the repeated violence outcome.[6] These findings provide no support for the claim that obtaining a civil restraining order reduces the probability of subsequent violence.

Unfortunately, there are no systematic evaluations of the effec-

----

[6] Grau, Fagan, and Wexler (1984) also report on an "abuse" outcome that included verbal threats and harassment. Overall, rates of subsequent abuse were the same in the restraining order and no order groups. However, prior levels of victim injury did specify the relationship, with less serious cases having a restraining order reporting significantly lower rates of subsequent abuse than those not having a restraining order. Restraining orders thus reduced the likelihood of subsequent abuse for cases involving less severe prior violence.

tiveness of various sentencing outcomes such as incarceration, fines, or probation on subsequent violence. Other important unevaluated research questions include these: Are prosecutors more likely to downgrade charges in family violence cases than in other types of cases? How effective are court ordered diversion programs in reducing subsequent violence? Is the prosecutor or the court more likely to divert family violence cases than other types of cases? And, are prosecutors less likely to obtain pleas or convictions in family violence cases compared to other types of cases? Quality research on the effectiveness of prosecutorial and court sanctions is needed together with descriptions of the processing of family violence offenders and other offenders through the system. The major data collection systems available to describe this flow of cases (e.g., PROMIS) do not break down assaults into those involving relatives, intimates, and others.

IV. Criminal Justice Collaboration with Other Community Service Agencies

To what extent do the police, prosecutors, and courts make use of other private and public services available in the community when responding to family violence crimes? Studies of the police use of referrals in domestic violence cases suggest that referrals to agencies outside of the justice system are rare (Oppenlander 1982; Dutton 1984; Dolon, Hendricks, and Meagher 1986). Loving (1980) reports on a survey of seventeen police departments in which officers were asked about their use of referrals to other community agencies. At least half reported that they made at least monthly referrals to the family court, prosecuting attorney, and marriage counseling services. Over 70 percent indicated that they seldom, if ever, referred victims to any of the following agencies or services: public welfare, battered women's shelters, women's centers, public assistance, victim/witness assistance programs, or churches. Dolon, Hendricks, and Meagher (1986) report similar findings from their survey of 125 police officers in three police departments in a midwestern state. Police referrals are primarily to other justice system agencies and not to service or support agencies in the community.

In practice, referrals to outside agencies are made even less frequently than is suggested by the surveys of police officers. Oppenlander (1982) interviewed a sample of 147 officers who were observed in police-citizen encounters. Over 90 percent indicated that they were aware of referral agencies in the community that were appropriate for persons involved in family violence situations; 50 percent said they frequently made referrals to these agencies, and 30 percent said they sometimes made referrals. However, data from the patrol observations of police-citizen encounters revealed that referrals were made in less than 4 percent of family disturbance or family violence cases. One reason often given for this low use of other community resources is that patrol officers are neither briefed at roll call nor provided with printed listings of these community agencies. Oppenlander concludes, "It appears that both internal procedures and officer predispositions work against the coordination of police services with social agencies" (1982, p. 464).

There is some evidence that crisis intervention or mediation training increases the use of referral to social service agencies. Evaluations of the effectiveness of training programs typically reveal that they increase the referral rate to community social service agencies (Bard 1977; Dutton and Levens 1977; Levens and Dutton 1980; Pearce and Snortum 1983; Dutton 1984). Dutton (1984) reports that after training in one evaluation, the trained officers made referrals in 18 percent of all domestic violence calls. Referrals in the comparison group of untrained officers was 8 percent.

Federally funded family violence programs described by Lerman (1986) frequently included diversion programs and victim/witness assistance programs operating in a number of these cities out of the prosecuting attorney's office. While Lerman does not report on the frequency of use of these services, the number of persons in these programs was often substantial. Involvement in these social service programs typically involved a suspended prosecution arrangement.

The present level of collaboration between criminal justice agencies and social services agencies in general appears to be quite low. At the same time, it appears that police training can increase referral rates to these agencies. Further, new programs designed to prosecute family violence crimes aggressively and to provide victim/witness assistance in response to legislative mandates appear to involve a better level of coordination and collaboration, although the evidence for this coordination is not yet very systematic or comprehensive (Lerman 1986).

V. Overview and Future Research Agenda

Only a handful of good descriptive studies document the response of criminal justice agencies to family violence crimes. There are even fewer sound evaluations of the effectiveness of particular responses. The Minneapolis Domestic Violence Experiment is an obvious exception, and its findings need to be replicated. In addition, research is needed to determine in a more precise way the mechanism that ties arrest to a reduction in subsequent violence and the factors that serve to inhibit or enhance this effect.

A sound empirical base for research requires an adequate description of the range of official responses to family violence, factors involved in the decision to take particular actions, the case flow through the legal system, and victim and offender responses to official actions. In a number of respects the available descriptive research base is simply inadequate for several reasons.

First, major definitional problems are seldom made explicit. Inconsistencies in findings can often be traced to differences in the behavioral content of key measures such as "violence," "abuse," and "assault." Some consensus on the definition and measurement of the central constructs is critical.

Second, there are very few data that are specific to particular forms of family violence, that is, to spouse assault, assaults between unmarried cohabiting adults, assaults involving noncohabiting but intimate relationships, assaults by adults on children in a household, and assaults involving adult siblings. There is a tendency in this literature to interpret data on family violence that aggregates all of the above forms of violence as data on spousal violence. Although the majority of family violence cases involve present or prior intimate, heterosexual relationships, drawing conclusions from analyses of heterogeneous data as if they could be generalized to apply to this specific form of family violence is misleading. Even more questionable is the generalization of findings from domestic disturbance calls to spousal assault. Much more careful research is needed to distinguish between different types of cases.

Third, more representative samples, better controls, and longer follow-up periods are needed to investigate family violence questions. Much of the present work involves very small clinical or institutional samples and other nonrepresentative samples. As a result, findings have only limited generalizability. Further, given the evidence that arrest may involve relatively short-term effects (Tauchen, Tauchen, and Witte 1986), longer follow-up studies are critical for guiding policy decisions that require a longer-term perspective.

The Minneapolis Domestic Violence Experiment has had a very positive impact on the research evaluating the effectiveness of particular police responses to family violence. In the fall of 1985, the National

Institute of Justice released a national solicitation for experiments on alternative police responses to spouse assault (U.S. Department of Justice 1985). Six replications of the Minneapolis experiment are underway. Each involves an experimental design, and several have extended the scope of the experiment, for example, to more serious violent cases or to situations where the offender is not present when the police arrive. The National Institute of Justice has also funded several other major studies evaluating the effectiveness of other legal responses to family violence (e.g., see Ford 1985). The results of these very rigorous and sophisticated studies should advance our knowledge of the effectiveness of legal responses to domestic violence crimes and, in particular, our knowledge of the effectiveness of arrest as a deterrent to subsequent violence. This same level of effort ought to be focused on alternative sanctions available to prosecutors and judges.

One important limitation of the evaluation research is that few studies involve offenders. Offenders are a critical source of data for determining whether arrests or other legal sanctions are a specific deterrent to family violence. The vast majority of evaluation studies are based on information obtained from victims (for an important exception, see Shields and Hanneke [1981]). At least one of the newly funded National Institute of Justice projects is attempting to interview offenders.

Finally, more explicit theoretical and conceptual formulations are needed to guide the evaluation research effort. While deterrence theory is fairly well developed, there is almost no reference to this theoretical framework in the research literature on criminal justice responses to violent family crime. This limitation has important implications for the interpretation of findings and the strength of causal arguments, as well as for identifying the key variables and relationships that need to be examined.

What can be said about the substantive findings in the present body of research on criminal justice responses to family violence crimes? First, the research is so limited that any summary of findings must be tentative. Second, there is little empirical support to date for many of the allegations made about police and prosecutorial practices. For example, the evidence suggests that domestic disputes may not be the most dangerous calls to which police respond (Garner and Clemmer 1986); that being married or living together does not affect the probability of arrest (Berk and Loseke 1980–81; Erez 1986); that victims of family violence are as likely to call the police as are victims of nonfamily violence (Oppenlander 1982; Klaus and Rand 1984); that the police are as likely to inform victims of family violence as victims of nonfamily violence that they can sign a complaint, and that victims of family violence are as likely to sign a complaint as are victims of nonfamily violence (Oppenlander 1982).

At the same time, it should also be acknowledged that there are numerous barriers and disincentives for justice system interventions in family violence cases. Police value their discretion. While the evidence presented earlier demonstrated that the change to a mandatory arrest policy for misdemeanor family assaults clearly affected the rate of arrest (Jaffe et al. 1986), there is also evidence that the police resist the routine use of arrest in misdemeanor domestic violence cases (Ferraro 1985; Ford 1987).

Whether the immediate patterns of increase in arrest that occur after establishment of a mandatory arrest policy will be sustained over time is not known. There are many legitimate, competing demands on an officer's time, and domestic violence cases are likely to be viewed as low-payoff interventions, particularly when prosecutors refuse to file charges on those arrested, as happened in Minneapolis. Prosecutors have their own organizational objectives that may justify this action, but it nevertheless communicates to the police that their use of arrest in domestic violence cases is not supported by the court and is, in effect, only a control mechanism.

Prosecutors certainly view spouse assault charges as a low-payoff effort, given the high probability that the victim will drop the charges or fail to appear as a witness. Yet this option may be very instrumental for victims of spousal violence in assisting them to bargain effectively with their partners for a reduction in violence or a peaceful termination to the relationship (Ford 1984). What may be in the best interest of the victim of family violence may not facilitate personal or organizational goals of those in the justice system. This appraisal led Berk et al. to conclude that "minor tinkering with the system will be unlikely to change matters" (1980, pp. 196–97).

The past decade has witnessed a dramatic shift in public attitudes and orientations toward family violence: a shift from a policy of indifference to one of control, in which legal remedies are more frequently invoked in an attempt to deter this form of violence, provide better protection for victims, and facilitate positive changes in family relationships. There are some who believe this shift has been too sudden, without a careful weighing of the advantages and disadvantages of a control strategy (Gelles and Mederer 1985). In any event, criminal justice responses in many jurisdictions are in a state of transition. Because this essay focuses on the existing research on the justice system's response to family violence, the available data are necessarily dated. Current (that is, 1987) arrest and case attrition rates for family violence cases may be quite different from those examined and discussed in this essay. The same is true for statutory requirements for misdemeanor arrest, legislation affecting prosecution, and the range of alternative responses available to the police or court. Some of these recent changes have been described, but they were not the primary focus in this essay. There are no evaluations or even good descriptions of many of these newly initiated reforms.

The impetus for criminal justice reform has not come from sound, scientific evaluations of past or proposed policies and practices. Although the Minneapolis Domestic Violence Experiment was a landmark study, it served as a reinforcing influence, not a directing one. Political forces were already in motion and changes in police practices had been initiated prior to the publication of these results in 1984 (see International Association of Chiefs of Police 1976), in large part as a result of the women's movement. There is little historical evidence that empirical evaluation results have ever been the primary basis for policy decisions, and there is no compelling logic for claiming that they should be the dominant factor in policymaking (Cook 1983; Cook and Shadish 1986). At the same time we should be concerned that, with the possible exception of the Minneapolis experiment, the present reforms are essentially uninformed by any body of sound empirical investigation. Already there are some preliminary indications that reforms designed explicitly to assist victims may have the opposite effect. The need for a major investment of resources in policy-relevant research on criminal justice responses to family violence is a must if criminologists are to have any significant influence on future justice-system policy in this area.

REFERENCES

Bandy, Carole, Dale R. Buchanan, and Cynthia Pinto. 1986. "Police Performance in Resolving Family Disputes: What Makes the Difference?" *Psychological Reports* 58:743–56.

Bard, Morton. 1970. *Training Police as Specialists in Family Crisis Intervention.* Washington, D.C.: U.S. Government Printing Office.

————. 1977. "Family Crisis Intervention: From Concept to Implementation." In *Battered Women: A Psychosociological Study of Domestic Violence*, edited by Maria Roy. New York: Van Nostrand Reinhold.

————. 1978. "The Police and Family Violence: Practice and Policy (Discussion)." In *Battered Women: Issues of Public Policy.* Washington, D.C.: U.S. Commission on Civil Rights.

Bard, Morton, and Harriet Connolly. 1978. "The Police and Family Violence: Practice and Policy." In *Battered Women: Issues of Public Policy.* Washington, D.C.: Commission on Civil Rights.

Bard, Morton, and Joseph Zacker. 1971. "The Prevention of Family Violence: Dilemmas of Community Interaction." *Journal of Marriage and the Family* 33:677–82.

————. 1974. "Assaultiveness and Alcohol Use in Family Disputes: Police Perceptions." *Criminology* 12:281–92.

Berk, Richard A., and Phyllis Newton. 1985. "Does Arrest Really Reduce Wife Rauma. 1980. "Bringing the Cops Back In: A Study of Efforts to Make the Criminal Justice System More Responsive to Incidents of Family Violence." *Social Science Research* 9:193–215.

Berk, Richard A., and Phyllis Newton. 1985. "Does Arrest Really Reduce Wife Battery? An Effort to Replicate the Findings of the Minneapolis Spouse Experiment." *American Sociological Review* 50:253–62.

Berk, Richard A., and Lawrence W. Sherman. 1985. "Police Responses to Family Violence Incidents: An Analysis of an Experimental Design with Incomplete Randomization." Unpublished manuscript. Department of Sociology, University of California, Santa Barbara.

Berk, Sarah Fenstermaker, and Donileen R. Loseke. 1980–81. " 'Handling' Family Violence: Situational Determinants of Police Arrest in Domestic Disturbances." *Law and Society Review* 15:318–46.

Binney, Val, Gina Harkell, and Judy Nixon. 1981. "Refugees and Housing for Battered Women." In *Private Violence and Public Policy*, edited by Jan Pahl. London: Routledge & Kegan Paul.

Bittner, Egon. 1970. *The Functions of Police in Modern Society.* Chevy Chase, Md.: National Institute of Mental Health.

————. 1974. "Florence Nightingale in Pursuit of Willie Sutton: A Theory of the Police." In *The Potential for Reform of Criminal Justice*, edited by Herbert Jacob. Beverly Hills, Calif.: Sage.

Black, Donald. 1971. "The Social Organization of Arrest." *Stanford Law Review* 23:1087–1111.

————. 1980. *The Manners and Customs of the Police.* New York: Academic Press.

Boland, Barbara. 1986. *The Prosecution of Felony Arrests, 1981.* Washington, D.C.: U.S. Department of Justice, Bureau of Justice Statistics.

Boland, Barbara, Elizabeth Brady, Herbert Tyson, and John Bassler. 1983. *The Prosecution of Felony Arrest.* Washington, D.C.: U.S. Department of Justice, Bureau of Justice Statistics.

Bowker, Lee H. 1982. "Police Services to Battered Women." *Criminal Justice and Behavior* 9:476–94.

Breedlove, Ronald K., Donald M. Sandker, John W. Kennish, and Robert K. Sawtell. 1977. "Domestic Violence and the Police: Kansas City." In *Domestic Violence and the Police: Studies in Detroit and Kansas City.* Washington, D.C.: Police Foundation.

Breslin, Warren. 1978. "Police Intervention in Domestic Confrontations." *Journal of Police Science and Administration* 6:293–301.

Brosi, Kathleen B. 1979. *A Cross-City Comparison of Felony Case Processing.* Washington, D.C.: Institute for Law and Social Research.

Cannavale, Frank. 1976. *Witness Cooperation.* Lexington, Mass.: Lexington Books.

Carrow, Debra M. 1980. *Policy Briefs: Crime Victim Compensation.* Washington, D.C.: U.S. Department of Justice, National Criminal Justice Reference Service.

Cook, Thomas D. 1983. "Evaluation: Whose Questions Should Be Answered?" In *Making and Managing Policy: Formulation, Analysis, Evaluation,* edited by G. R. Gilbert. New York: Dekker.

Cook, Thomas D., and William R. Shadish, Jr. 1986. "Program Evaluation: The Wordly Science." *Annual Review of Psychology* 37:193–232.

Curtis, Lynn A. 1974. *Criminal Violence: National Patterns and Behavior.* Lexington, Mass.: Heath.

Dobash, R. Emerson, and Russell Dobash. 1979. *Violence against Wives.* New York: Free Press.

Dolon, Ronald, James Hendricks, and M. Steven Meagher. 1986. "Police Practices and Attitudes toward Domestic Violence." *Journal of Police Science and Administration* 14:187–92.

Dutton, Donald G. 1984. "Interventions into the Problem of Wife Assault: Therapeutic, Policy and Research Implications." *Canadian Journal of Behavioral Science* 16:281–97.

Dutton, Donald, and Bruce Levens. 1977. "An Attitude Survey of Trained and Untrained Police Officers." *Canadian Police College Journal* 1:75–90.

Eisenberg, Sue, and Patrick Micklow. 1977. "The Assaultive Wife: 'Catch 22' Revisited." *Women's Rights Law Reporter* 3:138–61.

Emerson, Charles D. 1979. "Family Violence: A Study by the Los Angeles County Sheriff's Department." *Police Chief* 46:48–50.

Erez, Edna. 1986. "Intimacy, Violence, and the Police." *Human Relations* 39:265–81.

Fagan, Jeffrey. 1986. "Cessation of Family Violence: Deterrence and Dissuasion." Unpublished manuscript. URSA Institute, San Francisco.

Fagan, Jeffrey, Elizabeth Friedman, Sandra Wexler, and Virginia S. Lewis. 1984. "National Family Violence Evaluation: Final Report. Volume I: Analytic Findings." Unpublished manuscript. URSA Institute, San Francisco.

Fagan, Jeffrey, and Sandra Wexler. 1985. "Complex Behaviors and Simple Measures: Understanding Violence in Families." Unpublished manuscript. URSA Institute, San Francisco.

Faragher, Tony. 1985. "The Police Response to Violence against Women in the Home." In *Private Violence and Public Policy*, edited by Jan Pahl. London: Routledge & Kegan Paul.

Ferraro, Kathleen J. 1985. "Police Response to Domestic Violence." Paper presented at the annual meeting of the American Sociological Association, Washington, D.C., August.

Field, Martha H., and Henry F. Field. 1973. "Marital Violence and the Criminal Process: Neither Justice nor Peace." *Social Service Review* 47:221–40.

Fields, Marjorie D. 1978. "Wife Beating: Government Intervention Policies and Practices." In *Battered Women: Issues of Public Policy*. Washington, D.C.: U.S. Commission on Civil Rights.

Ford, David A. 1984. "Prosecution as a Victim Power Resource for Managing Conjugal Violence." Paper presented at the annual meeting of the Society for the Study of Social Problems, San Antonio, Texas, August.

———. 1985. "The Indianapolis Domestic Violence Project." Grant Number 86-IJ-CX-0012. Washington, D.C.: U.S. Department of Justice, National Institute of Justice.

———. 1987. "The Impact of Police Officers' Attitudes toward Victims on the Discretion to Arrest Wife Beaters." Paper presented at the Third Annual Conference for Family Violence Researchers, University of New Hampshire, Durham, July.

Forst, Brian E., and Jolene C. Hernon. 1985. "The Criminal Justice Response to Victim Harm." *National Institute of Justice: Research in Brief*. Washington, D.C.: U.S. Department of Justice, National Institute of Justice.

Forst, Brian E., Frank Leahy, Jean Shirhall, Herbert Tyson, Eric Wish, and John Bartolomeo. 1981. *Arrest Convictability as a Measure of Police Performance*. Washington, D.C.: Institute for Law and Social Research.

Garner, Joel, and Elizabeth Clemmer. 1986. "Danger to Police in Domestic Disturbances—a New Look." *National Institute of Justice: Research in Brief*. Washington, D.C.: U.S. Department of Justice, National Institute of Justice.

Gelles, Richard J. 1987. "Methodological Issues in the Study of Family Violence." In *Depression and Aggression: Two Facets of Family Interaction*, edited by G. R. Patterson and Elaine Blechman. Hillsdale, N.J.: Erlbaum.

Gelles, Richard J., and Helen Mederer. 1985. "Comparison or Control: Intervention in the Cases of Wife Abuse." Paper presented at the annual meeting of the National Council on Family Relations, Dallas, Texas, November.

Gelles, Richard J., and Murray A. Straus. 1988. *Intimate Violence*. New York: Simon & Schuster.

Goodman, Emily J. 1977. "Legal Solutions: Equal Protection under the Law." In *Battered Women: A Psychosociological Study of Domestic Violence*, edited by Maria Roy. New York: Van Nostrand.

Goolkasian, G. A. 1986. "Confronting Domestic Violence: The Role of Criminal Court Judges." *National Institute of Justice: Research in Brief*. Washington, D.C.: U.S. Department of Justice, National Institute of Justice.

Grau, Janice. 1982. "Restraining Order Legislation for Battered Women: A Reassessment." *University of San Francisco Law Review* 16:702–41.

Grau, Janice, Jeffrey Fagan, and Sandra Wexler. 1984. "Restraining Orders for Battered Women: Issues of Access and Efficacy." *Women and Politics* 4:13–28.

International Association of Chiefs of Police. 1967. *Training Key 16: Handling Disturbance Calls.* Gaithersberg, Md.: International Association of Chiefs of Police.

———. 1976. *Training Key 245: Wife Beating.* Gaithersberg, Md.: International Association of Chiefs of Police.

Jaffe, Peter, David A. Wolfe, Anne Telford, and Gary Austin. 1986. "The Impact of Police Charges in Incidents of Wife Abuse." *Journal of Family Violence* 1:37–49.

Klaus, Patsy A., and Michael R. Rand. 1984. *Family Violence.* Bureau of Justice Statistics: Special Report. Washington, D.C.: U.S. Department of Justice, Bureau of Justice Statistics.

LaFave, Wayne. 1965. *Arrest: The Decision to Take a Suspect into Custody.* New York: Little, Brown.

Langan, Patrick A., and Christopher A. Innes. 1986a. *Preventing Domestic Violence against Women.* Bureau of Justice Statistics: Special Report. Washington, D.C.: U.S. Department of Justice, Bureau of Justice Statistics.

———. 1986b. "Preventing Domestic Violence against Women: Discussion Paper." Washington, D.C.: U.S. Department of Justice, Bureau of Justice Statistics.

Lerman, Lisa G. 1986. "Prosecution of Wife Beaters: Institutional Obstacles and Innovations." In *Violence in the Home: Interdisciplinary Perspectives*, edited by Mary Lystad. New York: Brunner/Mazel.

Levens, Bruce, and Donald G. Dutton. 1980. *The Social Service Role of the Police: Domestic Crisis Intervention.* Ottawa: Solicitor General of Canada.

Loving, Nancy. 1980. *Responding to Spouse Abuse and Wife Beating: A Guide for Police.* Washington, D.C.: Police Executive Research Forum.

Margarita, Mona. 1980. "Killing the Police: Myths and Motives." *Annals of the American Academy of Political and Social Sciences* 452:63–71.

Martin, Del. 1976. *Battered Wives.* San Francisco: Glide.

———. 1978. "Overview—Scope of the Problem." In *Battered Women: Issues of Public Policy.* Washington, D.C.: U.S. Commission on Civil Rights.

Morash, Merry. 1986. "Wife Battering." *Criminal Justice Abstracts* 18:252–71.

Oppenlander, Nan. 1982. "Coping or Copping Out." *Criminology* 20:449–65.

Ostrom, Elinor, Roger B. Parks, and Gordon Wittacker. 1977. The Police Services Study. National Science Foundation Grant GI-43929.

Pahl, Jan. 1985. *Private Violence and Public Policy.* London: Routledge & Kegan Paul.

Parnas, Raymond I. 1967. "The Police Response to the Domestic Disturbance." *Wisconsin Law Review* 31:914–60.

———. 1970. "The Judicial Response to Intra-family Violence." *Minnesota Law Review* 54:585–645.

Paterson, Eva J. 1979. "How the Legal System Responds to Battered Women." In *Battered Women*, edited by Donna M. Moore. Beverly Hills, Calif.: Sage.

Pearce, Jack B., and John R. Snortum. 1983. "Police Effectiveness in Handling Disturbance Calls: An Evaluation of Crisis Intervention Training." *Criminal Justice and Behavior* 10:71–92.

Police Foundation. 1977. *Domestic Violence and the Police: Studies in Detroit and Kansas City.* Washington, D.C.: Police Foundation.

Rauma, David. 1984. " 'Going for the Gold': Prosecutorial Decision Making in Cases of Wife Assault." *Social Science Research* 13:321–51.

Reiss, Albert J., Jr. 1974. "Discretionary Justice in the United States." *International Journal of Criminology and Penology* 2:181–205.

———. 1986. Personal communication.

Roy, Maria. 1977*a*. "A Current Survey of 150 Cases." In *Battered Women: A Psychosociological Study of Domestic Violence,* edited by Maria Roy. New York: Van Nostrand.

———. 1977*b*. "Some Thoughts regarding the Criminal Justice System and Wifebeating." In *Battered Women: A Psychosociological Study of Domestic Violence,* edited by Maria Roy. New York: Van Nostrand.

Schulman, M. 1979. *A Survey of Spousal Violence against Women in Kentucky.* Washington, D.C.: U.S. Government Printing Office.

Scott, Eric. 1981. *Calls for Service: Citizen Demand and Initial Police Response.* Washington, D.C.: U.S. Government Printing Office.

Sherman, Lawrence W. 1980. "Causes of Police Behavior: The Current State of Quantitive Research." *Journal of Crime and Delinquency* 17:69–100.

Sherman, Lawrence W., and Richard A. Berk. 1984*a*. "The Minneapolis Domestic Violence Experiment." *Police Foundation Reports* 1:1–8.

———. 1984*b*. "The Specific Deterrent Effects of Arrest for Domestic Assault." *American Sociological Review* 49:261–72.

Sherman, Lawrence W., and Ellen G. Cohn. 1987. *Police Policy on Domestic Violence, 1986: A National Survey.* Washington, D.C.: Crime Control Institute.

Sherman, Lawrence W., and Earl Hamilton. 1984. *The Impact of the Minneapolis Domestic Violence Experiment: Wave 1 Findings.* Washington, D.C.: Police Foundation.

Shields, Nancy, and Christine R. Hanneke. 1981. "Patterns of Family and Nonfamily Violence: An Approach to the Study of Violent Husbands." Paper presented at the annual meeting of the American Sociological Association, Toronto, Ontario, August.

Skolnick, Jerome H. 1966. *Justice without Trial.* New York: Wiley.

Smith, Douglas A. 1987. "Police Response to Interpersonal Violence: Defining the Parameters of Legal Control." *Social Forces* 65:767–82.

Strube, Michael J., and Linda S. Barbour. 1983. "The Decision to Leave an Abusive Relationship: Economic Dependence and Psychological Commitment." *Journal of Marriage and the Family* 45:785–93.

Sykes, Richard E., James C. Fox, and John P. Clark. 1985. "A Socio-legal Theory of Police Discretion." In *The Ambivalent Force,* edited by Abraham S. Blumberg and Arthur Neiderhoffer. New York: Holt, Rinehart, & Winston.

Tauchen, George, Helen Tauchen, and Ann D. Witte. 1986. *The Dynamics of Domestic Violence: A Reanalysis of the Minneapolis Experiment*. Washington, D.C.: Police Foundation.

U.S. Department of Justice. 1983. *Victim and Witness Assistance*. Washington, D.C.: U.S. Department of Justice, Bureau of Justice Statistics.

———. 1985. *Replicating an Experiment in Specific Deterrence: Alternative Police Responses to Spouse Assault. A Research Solicitation*. Washington, D.C.: U.S. Department of Justice, National Institute of Justice.

Vera Institute of Justice. 1977. *Felony Arrests: Their Prosecution and Disposition in New York City's Courts*. New York: Vera Institute of Justice.

Walker, Lenore E. 1979. *The Battered Woman*. New York: Harper Colophon.

Weis, Joseph G. In this volume. "Family Violence Research Methodology and Design."

Williams, Kristen M. 1978. *The Role of the Victim in the Prosecution of Violent Crime*. Washington, D.C.: Institute for Law and Social Research.

Wilson, James Q. 1968. *Varieties of Police Behavior*. Cambridge, Mass.: Harvard University Press.

———. 1977. "Forward." In *Domestic Violence and the Police: Studies in Detroit and Kansas City, by the Police Foundation*. Washington, D.C.: Police Foundation.

Wolfgang, Marvin E. 1958. *Patterns in Criminal Homicide*. Philadelphia: University of Pennsylvania Press.

Zacker, Joseph, and Martin Bard. 1977. "Further Findings on Assaultiveness and Alcohol Use in Interpersonal Disputes." *American Journal of Community Psychology* 5:373–83.

Daniel G. Saunders and Sandra T. Azar

Treatment Programs for Family Violence

ABSTRACT

Similar issues and similar interventions appear in treatment programs for
child physical abuse, child sexual abuse, and woman abuse. Programs in
all three of these areas make use of crisis lines, temporary shelter for
victims, and professionally guided self-help groups. A wide variety of
treatment orientations are used. However, common to all areas is a
controversy over whether to use a family systems approach or an
individual approach. Critics of family approaches claim that too
much value is placed on family reunion or that they implicitly blame
the victim. There is also a common trend toward closer collaboration
with the criminal justice system. The collaboration is sometimes meant
to convey the message to the family and society that family violence is
a crime but more often it is designed to keep the offender in treatment.
Cognitive and behavioral approaches have been evaluated more often than
other approaches and seem to show promising results. Unfortunately,
serious defects in the designs of nearly all evaluation studies conducted
to date make it impossible to draw definite conclusions about treatment
effectiveness.

As specific types of family violence were brought to public attention,
intervention programs to help the victims were created almost immediately. Programs for offenders followed close behind. Lagging

Daniel G. Saunders is assistant scientist in the Department of Psychiatry at the
University of Wisconsin—Madison and program evaluator for the Program to Prevent
Woman Abuse, Madison, Wisconsin. Sandra T. Azar is assistant professor in the De-
partment of Psychology at Clark University, Worcester, Massachusetts. Support to write
this essay was provided by the Centers for Disease Control and the National Institute of
Mental Health. Other writers in this volume provided useful feedback on earlier versions
of this essay. Special thanks are due to Angela Browne, Jeffrey Fagan, David Finkelhor,
Alfred Kadushin, and Eli Newberger for their help.

much farther behind, however, have been efforts to determine what interventions work to end family violence. For most social and psychological problems, remedies are usually attempted long before their efficacy has been carefully evaluated. This tendency was accentuated for family violence because practitioners quickly realized the drastic effects of child and woman abuse. In recent years, however, some practitioners and social scientists have begun to ask some tough questions about the effectiveness of interventions for both victims and perpetrators.

Treatment is broadly defined here to include psychological, social, and educational interventions that operate outside the formal criminal justice system. The distinction between criminal justice and treatment programs is increasingly difficult to draw. Many communities have formed "coordinated community response" programs that are integrated intervention plans including criminal justice, victim advocate, and abuser treatment agencies. In addition, the theoretical orientations of some therapists lead them to regard arrest or incarceration as part of the therapeutic learning process or as a way to change cultural norms regarding abuse. Despite the blurring of boundaries between criminal justice and treatment approaches, this essay attempts to answer questions about treatment effectiveness outside of traditional criminal justice interventions. Researchers studying the treatment outcomes of the different forms of family violence have generally not benefitted from a sharing of methods and a discussion of the many practical and ethical dilemmas involved in their research. This essay presents the commonalities in treatments and treatment research methods across the forms of family violence. Woman abuse and child physical and sexual abuse have received the most attention and the treatments for these three types are the ones examined in this essay.

Section I examines why much family violence goes undetected and why public officials and professionals are reluctant to report violence even when reporting is required by law. Emergency procedures, including crisis lines, shelters, and removal of victims or offenders from the home are described in Section II. Descriptions and evaluations of programs for victims of woman abuse, child sexual abuse, and child physical abuse appear in Section III. Primary attention is given to evaluations that used standardized measures and samples larger than just a few cases. Section IV provides descriptions and evaluations of programs for offenders. The practical and ethical issues of doing research on family violence treatment programs are discussed in Section V.

I. Detecting and Reporting Abuse

Family members and professionals are often reluctant to face the reality of family violence. For some types of family violence, detection by professionals lead directly to reporting and to intervention. Families' reports to professionals thus can be seen as a step in the therapeutic process.

There is little doubt that most cases of family violence are undetected and that many cases that are detected by professionals go unreported to official reporting agencies. For example, some researchers estimate that only one out of five cases of child sexual abuse comes to the attention of professionals (Finkelhor 1984). Similarly, spouse abuse is underdetected in a number of inpatient and outpatient settings (Hilberman and Munson 1978; Stark, Flitcraft, and Frazier 1979; Mascia 1983). Child physical abuse is underdetected, but estimates vary widely because of use of differing definitions of abuse. There are great disparities between the numbers of abused children and wives reported in official agency records and the number reported in random household surveys (Straus, Gelles, and Steinmetz 1980; Straus and Gelles 1986); some of the disparity results from use of broader definitions of abuse in the random surveys (see Weis, in this volume).

Attempts to detect one form of family violence need to be extended to include attempts to detect all forms. Both offenders and victims of wife abuse, for example, are at risk of abusing their children (Straus, Gelles, and Steinmetz 1980; Walker 1984), and battered women are more likely than other women to have been victims of child sexual abuse (Thyfault 1980; Shields and Hanneke 1984; Truesdell, McNeil, and Deschner 1986).

Family violence goes undetected in part because of the reluctance of victims to report abuse and because of the attitudes and training of professionals. Victims are reluctant to report because of shame, fear of retaliation, or a belief that not much will be done (Gaquin 1978; Finkelhor 1983a). The belief that not much will be done can arise from apathy that victims encounter from friends and relatives. It is reinforced when they seek formal help and feel the indifference of social service providers who are burned out or who are forced by limited resources or policies to place higher priority on other types of cases.

Professionals may sometimes fail to detect abuse because of an overriding concern for the privacy of the family (Pagelow 1984). They may also ignore the violence because they see specific family problems as symptoms of dysfunctional relationships to which all family members contribute equally (Bograd 1984). Few professionals have been trained in abuse detection methods that are direct and yet sensitive. Lack of skills may cause practitioners to avoid problems they feel incapable of treating (Stark, Flitcraft, and Frazier 1979). Legal reporting mandates may discourage detection because professionals fear that reporting will damage their relations with their clients, especially since many cases are ruled later as "unsubstantiated" (often meaning that not enough evidence was found, not that the report was fabricated [Faller 1985]).

In a community survey, Finkelhor (1984) found that the parent is the person most likely to detect child sexual abuse, whether inside the family or outside. Parents are understandably reluctant to report intrafamilial sexual abuse, and quick to report extrafamilial sexual abuse. For those in Finkelhor's survey who indicated a reluctance to report, the major reasons were that they wanted to handle the situation by themselves and that they believed it was "no one else's business." Parents appeared to be more inclined to report abuse if they were aware of community resources such as hotlines and child protection agencies.

Unconscious bias based on class, race, or gender may influence professional detection of abuse. For example, women professionals (psychologists, psychiatrists, pediatricians, and family counselors) in one study were more accurate than male professionals in their estimates of the prevalence of father-daughter incest, and they had a greater willingness to report abuse to official agencies (Attias and Goodwin 1985). The greater willingness of women to report suspected abuse is consistent with the finding that women in a variety of professional groups are more likely than men to view all forms of abuse as more serious (Snyder and Newberger 1986).

Ethnic and race bias may keep some professional groups from seeing injuries as stemming from physical child abuse. Among physicians, for example, there seems to be a tendency to regard more injuries as intentional if the family is of lower social class and from a minority group (Turbett and O'Toole 1980). This same tendency is not apparent among nurses, teachers, social workers, and deputy sheriffs (O'Toole et al. 1987). In general, compared with social workers and nurses, physicians tend to view all forms of child maltreatment as less serious (Snyder and Newberger 1986).

Practitioners who detect abuse are often required by state laws to report the case to child protection or law enforcement agencies. Reporting of child physical and sexual abuse is mandated for most professionals in every state, most states include neglect as reportable child abuse, and about half include some form of emotional or mental abuse. Some states have considered adoption of spouse abuse reporting laws but have rejected the notion because such laws would place victims in a childlike position when what they need is a greater sense of control over their lives.

Despite the existence of mandatory reporting laws for child abuse, many detected cases are not reported to the proper agency. A national study of reporting practices showed that only about one-third of child abuse cases detected by professionals is reported to child protection agencies (National Center on Child Abuse and Neglect 1981); a smaller study of physicians showed the same results (Sandberg, Petretic-Jackson, and Jackson 1986). Professionals report only about half of the detected child sexual abuse cases. A survey by Finkelhor and his associates (Finkelhor, Gomes-Schwartz, and Horowitz 1984), showed that 36 percent of the professionals from a variety of settings admitted that they failed to comply with the mandatory reporting law by not reporting their most recent case of sexual abuse. Criminal justice and mental health agencies had the lowest level of compliance. The authors speculate that mental health workers place the promise of confidentiality over their duty to report. Criminal justice workers may have believed that they had all the tools in their system to protect victims and punish offenders. Another reason for nonreporting is the belief that the intervention, especially court testimony, may create or exacerbate victim trauma. Indeed, there is some evidence that the mental health of incest victims is affected negatively by waiting for the prosecution of the perpetrator; there is also evidence, however, that allowing the child to testify may speed resolution of the child's distress (Runyan et al. 1987). Finkelhor and his associates noted that professionals appeared to refrain from reporting child abuse because they doubted the effectiveness of the official reporting agency, they believed the victim would be further traumatized by the investigation, or they believed the child protection agency would interfere with their plans for treatment.

The evaluation procedure used to assess sexual abuse may drastically affect the number or types of abuse revealed by the offender. In a study by Abel and his associates (Abel et al. 1983), offenders were randomly assigned, after an initial interview, to one of four additional evaluation procedures: (1) a reemphasis of the confidentiality of all their reports; (2) the use of a card sort in which the offender indicated what types of sexual activities were and were not arousing; (3) a reinterview; and (4) confronting the offender with the results of a laboratory assessment of his sexual arousal to different types of sexual stimuli. The most successful procedure was to confront the offender with results of a laboratory assessment of sexual arousal to different sexual stimuli; this increased the number of deviances reported by 62 percent. A reinterview or the use of a card sort to indicate types of arousing stimuli also improved reporting but not as dramatically (about 20 percent more deviances reported). Reemphasizing confidentiality did not improve the reporting. Interview methods with victims of child sexual abuse are also being refined, with a growing consensus regarding the methods to be used (Sgroi 1982; Jones and McGraw 1987; Sink 1988).

In addition to concerns about under-reporting, there is concern that too many false cases are reported. National organizations such as Victims of Child Abuse Laws are receiving the backing of some professionals who point to the large numbers of cases that are "unsubstantiated" (National Center on Child Abuse and Neglect 1981; Besharov 1985). It has become clearer, however, that these reports often are appropriate but lack enough information for substantiation and that "fictitious" accounts number under 10 percent (Jones and McGraw 1987).

In summary, much more needs to be learned about why abuse is not detected and what methods will enhance professionals' abilities to detect abuse. There is some evidence that gender, attitudes, and professional roles play a part in determining whether abuse is detected. These findings have implications for deciding which professionals need the most training and the type of training they need. More also needs to be learned about the reasons why professionals often do not report abuse when they are mandated to do so. This reluctance can have very different motives, from concern about the impact of reporting on the victim to an attempt to minimize the severity of the abuse. Learning more about these motives will help determine what changes are needed: training for the person mandated to report, upgrading of the social service system, or changes in reporting laws.

II. Emergency Procedures

A number of approaches have been developed for dealing with family violence emergencies. These include creation of hotlines and shelters and development of procedures for removing the victim or the offender from the household.

A. Crisis Lines for Victims and Offenders

Crisis telephone services are an essential part of many family violence programs. Some of these services, especially in rural areas, are a part of programs that also serve rape victims or persons with mental health crises. They are often staffed by trained paraprofessionals. Most stress the anonymity and confidentiality of the contact. Crisis lines for victims offer emotional support, immediate assessment of danger, and referral for legal, medical, or other help. If the crisis is not acute, problem-solving counseling might occur as well.

Crisis lines for battered women are usually part of a comprehensive program that includes shelter. Funding for shelter programs from some states is contingent on the provision of crisis line services. While many women call shelter crisis lines to inquire about shelter, a substantial number also want counseling and legal advocacy. Loseke and Berk (1983) found that less than half of the women calling one shelter asked for immediate entry into the shelter. The researchers inspected the shelter's logs of 114 phone contacts with battered women and attempted to see how well the women's requests fit with the workers' recommendations. They found that the majority of requests by women for specific services were matched by the counselors' recommendations for that service. Many times, though, counselors would recommend a service that was not initially requested, possibly because callers were not aware of the service, or because the counselor had knowledge of how effective that service might be.

Crisis lines for both child abuse and wife abuse can be designed preventively. Former or potential abusers can call the line in the midst of a stressful situation to seek support and advice. Crisis theorists note that help provided in the midst of a crisis can produce considerable change, not only for overcoming the crisis but also for overall patterns of functioning (Roberts 1984a). If a call is made after an abusive episode, most abusers seem ready to seek ongoing help; however, this is still an untested assumption. Programs with twenty-four-hour crisis lines are especially well received by law enforcement agencies because officers can refer families to these services immediately.

Evaluations have been conducted of programs that include crisis lines, but no evaluation has been done of crisis lines themselves. It is difficult to evaluate crisis services because many programs offer anonymity to their callers, making follow-ups impossible. One evaluation approach is to compare the types of clients reached through hotlines with those reached by social services. One crisis line reported a self-referral rate of 61 percent for child physical abuse, a figure significantly higher than the rate for most social service agencies (Pike 1973). Since the major function of crisis lines is to make referrals, another form of evaluation would be to determine the proportion of those referred who actually contact the other agency for help.

Crisis lines, therefore, have yet to be evaluated carefully for their impact on rates of violence, on victimization, or on other outcomes. They are, however, an important link to other services. Researchers may do well to focus on programs that only offer crisis lines in order to separate their effects from the effects of other services with which they are often linked. Broadly defined outcomes are needed because crisis lines may decrease levels of abuse not directly but, rather, indirectly through referrals to other programs and services.

B. Shelters for Victims

Provision of a safe environment away from the abuser has been a major source of emergency aid for victims of family violence. For victims of woman abuse, this has included shelter homes, safe home networks of volunteers, or transportation to the home of a relative or friend, where most sheltering actually occurs (Bowker and Maurer 1985). For child abuse victims, a safe environment has usually meant foster care. As a prevention for child abuse, "respite centers," places where children can be cared for on a short-term basis when parents are under stress, are available in some communities.

Shelters for battered women may be operated by traditional agencies like the YWCA, member agencies of Family Service of America, or by independent agencies. About half of the shelters in the United States are the outgrowth of feminist groups or identify themselves as feminist in orientation (Ferraro 1981). In shelters or safe homes, battered women have a chance to overcome some of the emotional effects of battering and to make decisions about their relationships and their careers, and whether to insist that their partners receive help, to get a restraining order, or both.

If a woman brings her children with her to a shelter, the turmoil experienced by the children is increased because they are taken from their home, neighborhood, and school and a father they may fear but also love. One way to avoid this problem is to treat the offender in a residential inpatient setting. Ganley and Harris (1978), for example, used structured group therapy in an inpatient psychiatric unit. There are also disadvantages to involuntary hospitalization or incarceration. The man may retaliate against his partner once he is out of the institution, or the family may suffer economic hardship.

A few attempts have been made to assess shelter services for battered women. Most women who seek help give high ratings to shelters for helpfulness and also to lawyers and women's groups (Saunders and Size 1980; Bowker 1983). In Bowker's (1986) national but nonrandom survey of battered women, 44 percent rated shelters as very effective in decreasing or ending the violence, 12 percent as somewhat effective, 16 percent as slightly effective, and 22 percent as not effective. Shelters were rated as more effective in ending the abuse than other formal sources of help. In another study of women who went to one shelter, matched statistically with women who did not go to a shelter, a decrease in violence two months after leaving the shelter was associated with sheltering, but only if other services were sought (Berk, Newton, and Fenstermaker-Berk 1985). Many other services are often provided by shelters, including supportive counseling and legal advocacy. In British studies, women said that despite the crowding and many rules of shelter life, they preferred shelters over going to an apartment (if that had been provided for them) because of the emotional support found in the shelter (Pahl 1985).

Shelters are often perceived as encouraging family dissolution, but the views of shelter advocates in two states do not support this perception. Saunders et al. (1987) compared the opinions of advocates and undergraduate women on whether women should divorce their partners after being battered. The two groups did not differ in their opinions. Surprisingly, one study found that women who felt most helped by shelters were more likely to plan to return to their partners (Aguirre 1985). Longer shelter stays, however, are associated with leaving the partner (Snyder and Scheer 1981; Grayson 1985). There is some evidence that being able to leave the relationship may be aided by identification with a role model in the shelter, especially if the role model is a former battered woman (Dalto 1983).

To summarize, shelters have received very high ratings for general helpfulness and for effectiveness in decreasing violence. These ratings are based on "consumer survey" studies rather than on measurements of violence before and after shelter residency. Some research suggests that other forms of help seeking are also needed before the violence is reduced. Other studies are needed that include a variety of shelters and that report not only on rates of violence but on a variety of coping abilities as well. The impact on the man's perceptions can also be studied to see if his partner's use of a shelter acts as a deterrent, produces more anger, or has other effects.

C. Removing the Victim or the Offender

One debate in the child abuse field is whether family members should be separated after abuse is discovered, and, if so, who should leave. Some professionals believe that separation is the only way to assure protection for the victim (e.g., Herman 1981). They claim that separation can also be a strong motive for the abuser to change. Other professionals believe that greater trauma will occur to the victim if the family breaks up because of the loss of the parent, guilt for breaking up the family, and social and economic hardships for all family members (e.g., Turbett 1979).

In a survey of professionals conducted by Finkelhor, Gomes-Schwartz, and Horowitz (1984), questionnaires were completed by 790 professionals from the Boston area who were attending community meetings designed to provide information about child sexual abuse. There was consensus that the child should not be removed from the home. Criminal justice workers in the survey were in the minority in favoring prosecution (75 percent) and in placing a low priority on keeping the families together (34 percent). Such divergence of opinion can cause havoc when intervention is needed. When workers involved in a case do not agree on goals for treatment, the family is further victimized through mixed messages, delayed treatment, or, in some cases, no treatment at all (Gelles 1975; Bander, Fein, and Bishop 1982). Despite a general preference for not removing the child, child placement outside of the home is still fairly common (Meddin and Hansen 1985). In a study of sexual abuse cases, 19 percent of the children were placed in foster care or with relatives (Pierce 1985). The placement of the child may occur simply because it is easier from a legal standpoint than removing the offender.

Some advocate out-of-home placement for other reasons: to remove the child from harm, to provide the child with a stable, therapeutic environment, and to provide time for the family to undergo treatment before the child is returned. Anecdotal reports and surveys, however, reveal many unanticipated, negative consequences from social service and court interventions (e.g., Faller 1985).

One question now being raised is whether decisions regarding placement are based on the level of danger to the child. Although some studies have indicated that placements were appropriate because the children had more severe problems (Coombes et al. 1978) and the parents were more abusive or potentially abusive (Miller and Challas 1981), other studies have shown less consistent findings.

For example, in a large-sample study using 250 variables, Runyan et al. (1982) found that none of the variables were strong predictors of foster-home placement. Unfortunately, only the type of abuse, and not its severity, was included in the study. The factors most strongly associated with placement were police referral and the presence of abandonment or neglect. Another study found no relation between children's placement from an emergency service and the type of abuse (physical or sexual abuse vs. neglect) (Segal and Schwartz 1985).

For sexual abuse cases, inappropriate placement of children outside the home may be less of a problem. Finkelhor's (1983b) analysis of data from a national reporting center showed that foster or shelter placement following sexual abuse was more likely in cases in which the parent was the abuser, the family had multiple problems, and the child preferred to leave home. Poor and minority families were not more likely than other families to have children removed.

The therapeutic benefit of foster care has also been questioned. Some authors suggest that the abused child is subject to further maltreatment while in foster care (e.g., Wald 1976), although these claims are difficult to substantiate. One study indicated that the medical care of foster children is often neglected (Schor 1982) and another showed that only about a third of the placed children received clinical services (Meddin and Hansen 1985).

Some theorists argue that separation from the parent is inevitably negative (e.g., Geiser 1973; Arvanian 1975). However, empirical support for this contention is limited or contradictory. For example, although researchers at Tufts University (Tufts New England Medical Center Division of Child Psychology 1984) found that children removed from the home exhibited more behavior problems after being removed, they were also the children who experienced more negative reactions from their mothers. Another study found that abused children placed in foster care exhibited as much delinquent behavior as children remaining at home, but the foster child seemed to be prone to violence initially (Runyan and Gould 1985). Other studies have suggested a number of benefits from placement (for a review see Williams 1983). Comparisons are difficult to make because it is not known how the same child would cope if he or she remained at home. Follow-up studies of foster children as adults show that they differ little from their nonplaced peers (Festinger 1983).

The belief that placements are generally short-term and provide stable environments also lacks empirical support. Multiple placements are fairly common for most children in foster care. Wald (1976) estimated that about 50 percent of all foster-care children experience more than one placement, and at least 20 percent experience three or more. Foster-care placement is also often lengthy. Fanshel and Shinn (1978) found that about half of the abused and neglected children who were placed were still in foster care after five years. Only about one-fourth stayed in foster care for less than a year.

A final questionable belief regarding out-of-home placement is that the parents receive help while the children are in placement. Early reports indicated that only limited treatment was provided to parents (Maas and Engler 1959), and practitioners still tend to be inadequately trained and have large caseloads, making intervention spotty (Williams 1983). In addition, parental contact with a child in foster care may be quite limited. This lack of contact may make reunification of the family difficult. Due to the perceived drawbacks of child placement, laws have been enacted to reduce the time a child can be in placement waiting for permanent arrangements and may require specific plans for treatment of the parents.

1. *Respite Care.*   A very short-term alternative to foster care is the use of respite care or day care. For the young physically abused child, it is often used as such an alternative. It provides the child with a safe setting and monitoring of its condition during the day. Day care also offers the parent relief from the stresses of parenting. A number of reports describe day-care centers designed to deal with the special needs of abused children (Green 1975; H. Martin 1976). When used in conjunction with social learning therapies for parents, such programs have shown reductions in the potential for reabuse (Cohn and Daro 1986) and a positive impact on the children's development (Parish et al. 1985). The usefulness of placing abused children in regular day care, however, has been questioned (Azar and Wolfe 1988).

The effects of protective day care may depend on the age of the child. Crittendon (1983) compared infants who were placed in protective day care with other infants for whom such placement had been sought, but who were not placed. At one year follow-up, the day-care group had higher rates of out-of-home placement and experienced more abuse. The study only suggests poorer results for day care with infants because the day-care group may have had more severe problems initially.

Similar indications come from a summary of findings by Cohn and Daro (1986) of a large number of federal demonstration projects. Out-of-home placement of infants did not appear to have a significant effect on their progress or on the likelihood of future maltreatment (as rated by counselors). However, temporary shelter plus personal skills development and group counseling for adolescents showed positive results. This combination of interventions reduced the reports of abuse or neglect during treatment and contributed to treatment progress as rated by counselors. These results need to be taken cautiously because the study has severe methodological problems, including reliance on counselor ratings, lack of follow-up, and combination of data from different types of programs and types of abuse.

2. *Reducing Out-of-Home Placement.* Recent studies conducted in child protection agencies have shown promising results for decreasing the number of children placed out of the home. Szykula and Fleischman (1985) report on two studies that used a social learning approach. Families were selected because they were considered at risk for protective placement. The treatment package taught child management skills and cognitive self-control. Each family received fifteen to twenty-five hours of treatment, including phone supervision of homework assignments. In the first study, there was an 85 percent drop in out-of-home placements during the program's operation. After the program stopped, the percentage of placements returned to the preprogram levels.

In the second study, families were randomly assigned to either the treatment package described above or to a control condition that received standard social services. The treatment package was more successful in reducing out-of-home placement primarily for the least difficult families (less abusive, more likely employed, and fewer family problems).

To summarize, removal of the child from the home reduces the likelihood of abuse in the short run. Alternatives such as short-term emergency placements and therapeutic day care show promise for children and adolescents. Out-of-home placement for infants appears less promising. Firm conclusions cannot be made at this time, however, because of the methodological problems of the studies reviewed.

More research is needed to assess the short- and long-term impact of each type of placement on the general functioning of the children and on rates of abuse. The child's age, the type and severity of abuse, and family resources are important variables to consider in conducting this research. Studies that evaluate the impact of removing the offender are especially needed. Without such research, it will be impossible to resolve the debate over whether the offender or victim should be removed.

III. Programs for Victims: Description and Evaluation

Programs to help victims of family violence arose from a number of social movements and social concerns. Programs for battered women arose from the grass-roots efforts of the women's movements. Child sexual abuse programs had their origins in the child protection movement and the rape crisis movement. Interventions to aid physically abused children have the oldest history and originated in the medical community in the 1950s. Programs for these three groups of victims are described next.

A. *Woman Abuse*

Shelters for battered women were first established in the early 1970s. Most provide services such as legal advocacy, social service advocacy and employment, and psychological counseling, but few attempts have been made to evaluate these noncrisis services. This section reviews what is known about the effectiveness of services for battered women that go beyond crisis intervention.

Some idea should first be given of the characteristics of women who choose shelter instead of other forms of aid. Kremen (1984) compared women seeking counseling from six community agencies (YWCA, religious agencies, women's coalitions, etc.) with women going to six shelters. The women seeking counseling were more likely to be older, Caucasian, of higher socioeconomic status, and employed, with longer-term relationships. They were less frequently abused and felt in less danger. They were more likely to perceive the psychological causes for the violence. The two groups of women did not differ in how they rated the helpfulness of the agencies they turned to. Similar proportions of the women were living with their partners before and after receiving help (of those choosing counseling, 70 percent lived with their partners before, a figure that dropped to 30 percent after; of those choosing shelter, 87 percent lived with their partners before, while the figure dropped to 33 percent after leaving the shelter). The counselor's opinion about separation was not reported to be a factor in deciding to leave, whereas the best interests of the children and the severity of abuse were factors. Over half of both groups of women (63 percent of those receiving counseling and 57 percent of those choosing shelter) preferred a former abused woman as a counselor.

Washburn and Frieze (1981) compared three groups of battered women: those going to a shelter, those who filed orders of protection, and those who responded to an advertisement seeking subjects for a study of battered women. The shelter women were about twice as likely as the others to be unemployed. These women and those filing protection orders tended to have experienced more severe violence, particularly marital rape. The women who filed protection orders felt the least powerful of the three groups and they realized that they were helping themselves to change their situations.

1. *Legal Aid.*   Most shelters provide legal advocacy for their residents and nonresidents. Many programs publish brochures on legal rights and undertake other public education efforts. Some states require shelters to provide this service as a condition of receiving state funding (Lerman and Livingston 1983). These services are also provided by some victim/witness support programs within prosecutors' offices, by local task forces for battered women, and by other agencies. Typically, these services have the dual function of giving information about laws and criminal justice proceedings and providing support and advocacy to women who choose to use the criminal justice system. Often this information and support are included in the initial phases of counseling or problem-solving groups at shelters and in other victim support programs.

The effectiveness of legal aid needs to be measured not simply by whether victims use the criminal justice system or by rates of successful prosecution but also by whether the women are satisfied with their decisions and their long-term consequences. Criminal justice and therapeutic criteria of success sometimes diverge. For example, criminal justice agencies may be interested in the number of victims who "cooperate" with the system, and therapists may be more interested in whether decisions to initiate criminal justice procedures are carefully thought out by the victim.

There have been no controlled evaluations of the effects of legal aid services. However, some innovative advocacy programs for victims do appear drastically to reduce case attrition. Lerman (1981) reviewed a number of innovative projects that combined victim support with a policy that prosecutors, rather than victims, would take the initiative for prosecution. Attrition rates in these programs ranged from 10 to 30 percent, which is comparable to those in cases involving strangers, and is much lower than the 80 percent attrition rate seen in family violence programs without innovative methods. Seattle has one of the most comprehensive programs of this type. Advocates reach out to abused women whose partners were not arrested by providing information on the criminal court process and assisting with child care and transportation. If a woman wants the charges to be dropped, she is asked to defer her request until the court date. If she still wants charges dropped on that date, the judge is asked to dismiss the charges. Another program, the Domestic Abuse Intervention Project (DAIP) in Duluth, Minnesota, has an intervention plan that coordinates efforts of victim, abuser, and criminal justice agencies (Pence 1984). Novack and Galaway (1982) compared the effects of two approaches. Two groups of patrolmen were part of DAIP and received special training and were instructed to use a pro-arrest policy. Two other groups of patrolmen acted as a comparison. Following an arrest, advocates went to the homes of battered women to explain the court process and to help them make a decision about their needs for legal protection and shelter following their partners' release from jail.

At follow-up, all of the thirty-eight victims contacted by the advocates (out of an initial sample of sixty-five) were "satisfied" or "very satisfied" with the support given, the information provided, and the sharing of personal experiences. The DAIP cases were more likely to result in a guilty plea than in the comparison group where assailants often pleaded guilty but eventually had the cases dismissed. It cannot be concluded that the legal advocacy had an impact on case dispositions, however, because both the assailants and the victims were involved in a variety of crisis and long-term interventions. The two groups also were not comparable before DAIP intervention in terms of race, the assailant's employment and veteran status, prior police involvement, and the presence of injuries.

2. *Counseling.*   Counseling approaches can be roughly divided into supportive, social learning, psychodynamic, and family systems. Supportive counseling is characterized by empathic listening and mutual emotional support, most often in a small group format. By sharing their experiences of abuse and recovery, counselors hope that battered women will feel less isolated, less ashamed, and able to build their self-esteem. Some authors consider supportive peer counseling a "grass-roots, self-help, para-professional" model and distinguish it from a "mental health, professional" model. This dichotomy is probably unfortunate because of the similarity of goals and overlap in methods of the two approaches (cf. Gondolf 1984). For example, the "psychotherapy" group described by Rounsaville, Lifton, and Bieber (1979) alternated between therapy and support depending on clients' needs, and

early sessions included information about legal and practical matters. Many shelter-based "self-help" groups integrate skills and problem solving with mutual support. The benefits of integrating these approaches are shown by Alcorn (1985), who investigated the impact of the shelter experience on the social networks of forty battered women. Advice and information from shelter workers supplemented the natural helping network.

The social learning approach assumes that battered women have a deficit of social skills, particularly assertiveness. Several authors have encouraged assertiveness training for battered women (e.g., D. Martin 1976; Ball and Wyman 1978; Jansen and Meyers-Abell 1981), but the value of this training has been questioned. Battered women may not be generally unassertive (Rosenbaum and O'Leary 1981) or less assertive than other women in troubled marriages (O'Leary and Curley 1984). More important, there are serious risks for women who initiate assertive behaviors with their abusive husbands because the men may view the assertiveness as "provocation" and an excuse to batter (O'Leary et al. 1985). The apparent lack of assertiveness and social skills of battered women may result from the isolation enforced by the abuser (Walker 1984) and from their realistic fears of retaliation (O'Leary and Curley 1984). The nonassertiveness and low self-esteem noted by clinicians may characterize a woman's behavior in the marital relationship, but not outside of it.

A case study by Follingstad (1980) illustrates a cognitive restructuring approach. She theorized that it was necessary to change faulty beliefs and develop skills before behavioral change could be expected in battered women. She helped a twenty-seven-year-old woman who had been in a severely abusive relationship for four years change a number of beliefs, for example: "I have no other alternatives to this relationship," "Maybe I deserve the beatings," and "I can't change anything: I've tried before." Treatment took place in fifteen sessions. The client's Minnesota Multiphasic Personality Inventory (MMPI) scores showed dramatic changes from before treatment to nine months after treatment. The scale profile changed from "a woman exhibiting extreme passivity, dependency, and helplessness, whose interaction style is manipulative and indirect" to "an individual functioning well within normal limits with no current distress and a fairly adaptive interpersonal style." The woman permanently separated from her partner near the end of therapy, but prior to that had been able to modify most of his compulsive questioning and verbal harassment. For some women, this same approach may put them in greater danger, so the strategy needs to be assessed very carefully.

Kelso and Personette (1985) evaluated the outcome of counseling at a shelter and the shelter's off-site "rap" group. The average stay at the shelter was sixteen days. The most common intervention was counseling, for sixteen hours on the average. An attempt was made to follow 140 women monthly for six months. Two-thirds (ninety-four) completed at least one follow-up interview but, of these, only 42 percent to 77 percent could be reached each month. Forty percent were living with their partners after leaving the shelter, and this rose to 57 percent after six months. Physical and sexual violence dropped by at least 62 percent and 54 percent, respectively, but mental abuse decreased by only 24 percent and remained the most frequent form of abuse.

Most of the women kept emergency phone numbers with them during the follow-up period. Only one-fourth of the women used the safety plan worked out with their counselor although many said they needed to use it. There was no significant relation between use of the safety plan—or keeping emergency numbers—and reports of violence, but there was a trend for those who used these methods to report more violence. Over the follow-up period, the women who took an increasingly greater role in household decision making and those who played a relatively larger role reported the least amount of violence. Those who assessed themselves as being capable of managing personal relationships increased from 63 percent initially to 78–91 percent at various points of follow-up. The more capable they felt, the less violence they reported. This increased self-esteem and the sharing of household decisions were goals of counseling but were not related to the completion of counseling, time in treatment, or time in the shelter. It is probably improvement in the abuser's behavior that allowed the women to feel more capable and to share in decisions.

Close friends and parents were the most common sources of help after leaving the shelter. Medical and legal personnel were used less often and the off-site "rap" group was used the least. Victimization was positively related to greater help-seeking from both formal and informal helpers and to the woman's greater average daily alcohol consumption. There was no attempt to untangle the cause-effect relations of these variables.

Weingourt (1985) advocates existential therapy for battered women. She postulates that two major forces rule the lives of most battered women: death anxiety and the need for validation by a powerful other.

According to Weingourt, death anxiety can be either a motivator or a paralyzer. For battered women who have experienced emotional trauma in childhood, death anxiety reaches such awesome proportions that they retreat from life. The need for validation from a powerful rescuer can become so intense that the woman does not believe she can exist outside of an enmeshed relationship. Weingourt provides some case illustrations of therapy but no systematic measurements of change.

Psychoanalytic approaches have probably been the most severely criticized methods for working with battered women, no doubt because of their association with Freud's theory of female masochism. Among those rejecting the notion of battered women's masochism have been psychiatrists (Symonds 1979), psychologists (Walker 1979), and sociologists (Dobash and Dobash 1979). The early psychiatric case examples clearly indicated the authors' belief that the battered women were aggressive and castrating and received direct pleasure from the abuse (e.g., Snell, Rosenwald, and Robey 1964). More recent psychodynamic formulations do not claim that battered women gain pleasure from the abuse but that they receive secondary gains from it; the hypothesis, unsupported by research, is that the battered women may unconsciously be reinforced by the sympathy they receive or from the guilt they produce in their partners (Shainess 1979). The hypothesis is refuted the most thoroughly by Caplan (1985).

Gilman (1980) applies object-relations theory to her work with battered women. She theorizes that most battered women suffer from split self-images, one good and one bad, which alternate in an extreme fashion. She uses this theory to explain how guilt and low self-esteem can exist side by side with "superiority and hostility." For example, a woman may be protective of her child one minute and abusive the next, or be aggressive toward her partner one minute and forgiving and loving the next. Both Shainess and Gilman present case illustrations of therapy but without support for their theories and without systematic measurement of change.

A number of therapists have taken a family systems approach with battered women (e.g., Geller 1982; Deschner 1984; Neidig and Friedman 1984). Geller (1982, p. 201), for example, states that an abusive relationship "is a system that develops long before the abusing couple comes to the attention of a helping person . . . There is a locked pattern of behavior in which the woman is the victim and the man is the assailant. One cannot be without the other." Deschner (1984) used a ten-session cognitive-behavioral couples group in her treatment. The ten women with complete data before and after treatment showed significantly lowered levels of anxiety (self-report and electromyograph), depression, subjectivity, and anger, and improved levels of self-discipline. The women's anger levels were initially higher than the men's and took longer to lower. As victims, they probably had not been allowed to express their anger safely. The number of marital arguments decreased significantly over the course of treatment. The level of violence also decreased but the change was not statistically significant.

Neidig (1986) also used a ten-session cognitive-behavioral approach with couples. Significant changes were noted after treatment for fourteen women on the Nowicki-Strickland Locus of Control Scale and Spanier's Dyadic Adjustment Scale. The women showed higher levels of consensus, cohesion in the relationship, and greater internal locus of control but did not change their levels of relationship satisfaction or expression of affect.

3. *Job Readiness Programs.* Because a battered woman's ability to leave a relationship and remain separated is greatly enhanced if she is employed (for a review see Strube and Barbour 1983), some shelter and nonshelter agencies have begun job readiness programs. Even for women who remain in the relationship, employment is likely to enhance their sense of self-worth and independence. A risk, of course, is that becoming employed may threaten the man's sense of self-worth, especially if he is unemployed or underemployed (Allen and Straus 1980), and thus increase the risk of violence.

A number of studies have evaluated job readiness programs for battered women. Hayman-Rhiannon (1984) conducted an experiment with forty-four women who had been living apart from their partners for at least a month. They were recruited from a crisis service, counseling agencies, and by an announcement for a course for battered women. The women were randomly assigned to either the treatment condition or to a waiting-list control group. The group counseling sessions covered cognitive-behavioral treatment for depression and also training in job readiness (using the Job Club manual [Azrin, Flores, and Kaplan 1975]). The methods used included assertiveness training, relaxation training, discussions of the causes of battery and learned helplessness, and rational-emotive therapy.

The treatment achieved only a slight and nonsignificant impact on reducing depression, with both groups becoming less depressed. Job readiness, defined as making a résumé and having at least one job contact a day, was greater for the treatment than the control group. Actual placement in a job or job training did not differ between the groups. The most dramatic effect was that 33 percent of those on the waiting list returned to their partners compared with only 9 percent of those in the treatment group. Those who were most depressed before the experiment were also most likely to return. Women who were job ready after treatment were the least depressed. It is not known if overcoming depression helped improve job readiness or vice versa.

Caudill, Cline, and Barber (1985) did not use the rigorous design and measures of the above study, but arrived at some useful impressions and conceptualizations. They worked with sixty-five shelter residents, most of whom were white, married, and had one child; vocational tests (which were not specified in the report) showed that they scored low on items measuring ambition and willingness to risk.

The initial goal of placing most of the women in paid jobs had to be modified because psychological and social hurdles appeared to block self-sufficiency; these hurdles included extremely low self-esteem, identity problems, limited work opportunities, and social isolation. The women were assessed as being at one of several stages: (a) crisis (requiring basic physical needs), (b) stabilization (needing emotional stability and access to social service and legal assistance), (c) adjustment and preparation (learning communication skills, developing social network, and building self-esteem), (d) maintenance (educational and vocational testing, job-seeking skills, and keeping job), and (e) independence (school, sheltered workshop, or employed and living independently). Almost all plans were initiated at the first two levels. Those having the greatest exposure to the program were judged to have the most success, while those with the least amount of exposure were judged to have the least amount of success. Those who returned to the abusive situation had the least amount of contact with the program. The authors believe that these women were intimidated by jealous and suspicious partners who tried to keep them isolated from all outside contact.

To summarize the above work with battered women, it is clear that few attempts at evaluation have been made despite the many innovative types of programs that have been developed. Legal advocacy appears to decrease the rate at which victims drop charges. However, this is an area in which better-controlled research is possible and is needed. Counseling with battered women has also not been evaluated to any great extent. There are a number of promising case reports and a few studies of couples therapy that used pre/post designs. The studies of job readiness suggested that many women need to work on psychological problems before they work on job-seeking skills.

B. *Child Sexual Abuse*

The approach taken to the treatment of child sexual abuse depends to a large extent on whether it is viewed as a crime, a mental disorder, or a symptom of family dysfunctioning. Programs that developed out of the child protection movement seem to favor family counseling and family reconciliation (Finkelhor 1984). Legal sanctions are used to keep offenders in treatment rather than to inflict punishment. The rape crisis center movement, by contrast, has led to programs that offer support and advocacy only to victims and that seek the incarceration of offenders for punishment and prevention.

MacFarlane and Bulkley (1982) classify treatment programs in terms of their level of collaboration with the criminal justice system. They note several problems with the traditional use of the criminal justice system for these cases. If prosecution and lengthy incarceration are the goals, they rarely result because, among other reasons, evidence for proof beyond a reasonable doubt is often lacking. They warn about the increased trauma to the victim that often results from multiple interrogations, testimony, and cross-examination and involuntary separation from the family. When prosecution does occur, the perpetrator is often placed on probation with orders to attend therapy. Individual insight therapy for the perpetrator only was most often used in the programs discussed and the therapists typically lacked training to work with these men. In addition, there was often no system of monitoring to see that the men stayed in treatment.

Child protection workers often do not have the time, the training, or the inclination to work with sexual abuse cases (Johnson 1981), and other community agencies often take the lead in developing specialized programs. Most of these programs treat all members of the family either individually, together, or both. However, there is also a growing interest in working with children and adult survivors of child sexual abuse in traditional outpatient and inpatient psychiatric settings (Emslie and Rosenfeld 1983; Carmen, Rieker, and Mills 1984). Treatment in these settings usually focuses on overcoming the initial or long-term traumatic effects of abuse. Some of the treatment procedures are modeled after those used for treating the posttraumatic stress disorder of Vietnam veterans and focus on expression of feelings about the experience, reducing feelings of self-blame, lowering stress, and increasing self-esteem.

MacFarlane and Bulkley (1982) describe the development of five different program models.

The *Victim Advocacy Model* grew out of the victim/witness programs and rape crisis centers. A goal of this model is to soften the aspects of the criminal justice system that are detrimental to children. It focuses on legal advocacy for victims and on short-term counseling.

The *Improvement Model* brings more sensitive intervention and more successful prosecution. Programs in this model advocate prosecution as an action symbolic to the child and to society and as a way to obtain court-ordered abuser treatment. They do not, however, support incarceration of abusers. The criminal justice system is seen as an equal or dominant partner with the treatment program in determining case disposition and ongoing supervision.

The *System Modification Model* also advocates a restructuring of legal procedures to reduce the trauma to the child and family and holds that incarceration is not beneficial to the child, the family, or society. Treatment usually results from postconviction sentencing, pretrial diversion, or coordinated criminal and juvenile court processing. An attempt is made to avoid two separate proceedings. If prosecution is used, the man may be incarcerated in jail with a furlough for work or treatment. Treatment under this model usually focuses on all family members, not to "save" families, but because all family members need treatment, both separately and together.

The *Independent Model* tries to be independent of the legal and political systems. Programs use a psychiatric or family systems orientation. They may use psychiatric counseling, self-help groups, educational techniques, or a combination of these. They are periodically involved with criminal and juvenile justice systems in individual cases.

The *Systems Alternative Model* opposes the use of the courts to punish or to enforce treatment. These programs hold that family members should not be treated as offenders and defendants but as individuals with illnesses or dysfunctional behavior. Cooperation with the criminal justice system is viewed as constituting a conflict of interest, in particular when diagnostic interviews are used to determine legal status.

MacFarlane and Bulkley provide examples of programs across the country that illustrate the above models. Many programs initially restricted their work to child sexual abuse but soon found that most of the families they dealt with had multiple problems, including substance abuse, spouse abuse, extrafamilial sexual abuse, and child physical abuse. In the survey by Daro (1986) of nineteen programs for treating child physical, sexual, and emotional abuse and neglect, 60 percent of the families exhibited more than one type of abuse. Families suffering only from sexual abuse had higher incomes and were more likely to seek help voluntarily. They experienced fewer external pressures than poorer families but more problems with internal functioning such as role reversal between parent and child.

MacFarlane and Bulkley (1982) note that the dominant trend is to offer the defendant treatment as an alternative to prosecution or, following prosecution, as an alternative to incarceration. Conte and Berliner (1981) present evidence from one program to show that once charges are filed, offenders are likely to plead guilty to charges that do not require a prison term, thereby permitting the offender to be treated in the community and the victim to avoid testifying in court.

Few attempts have been made to evaluate programs for sexual abuse victims and the evaluations have not compared different treatment approaches; they have, instead, evaluated comprehensive treatment models for the entire family. Many clinicians prefer comprehensive, interdisciplinary approaches that include the entire family (about 70 percent of the programs) (Forseth and Brown 1981; Cicchinelli, Keller, and Gardner 1987). Such global approaches, however, make the discovery of "active ingredients" of change extremely difficult.

One of the most widely used models, the Child Sexual Abuse Treatment Program (CSATP), was developed by Giarretto (1978, 1982). This is a "Systems Modification" program that works closely with the legal system to coerce abusers into treatment. It combines individual counseling for all family members, mother-daughter counseling, marital counseling, father-daughter counseling, family counseling, and group counseling. The counseling is based on principles of humanistic psychotherapy. Self-help groups are available for each family member through the Parents United Organization. Giarretto (1978) noted that self-abuse (drug use, promiscuity, etc.) among the children was reduced in both intensity and duration in over 500 families. However, he does not report on the source of data or whether standardized instruments were used.

Kroth (1979) evaluated the CSATP by comparing separate groups of family members at intake, midway through treatment, and near termination (after about fourteen months of treatment). The groups were matched on ten criteria, including age and education of family members and type of offender-victim relationship. Nine offenders and eight nonabusing spouses were in each group and provided the data on themselves and the victims. Forty-four separate measures were used. The number of victims who had nervous or psychosomatic symptoms dropped from nearly half in the intake sample to 6 percent in the termination sample. The parents reported that only 4 percent of the children in the intake group had good relationships with friends and peers compared with 46 percent in the termination group. They also reported improved relationships with their parents. Delinquent behaviors (substance abuse, promiscuity, running away, etc.) were apparently at very low levels in the intake group and did not change for the termination group. The results of this study need to be taken cautiously because it is based on the parents' reports, and the matching procedure may not have successfully equated the groups. Also, those who stayed in treatment are least likely to have had severe problems initially.

In Daro's (1986) summary of evaluations of nineteen programs, seven of the programs focused primarily on sexual abuse and the rest on other forms of maltreatment. Classes in personal skill development, temporary shelter, and group counseling were all associated with positive outcomes for adolescents, including lowered risk for future maltreatment. For the children, individual and group counseling were associated with overall treatment progress and therapeutic day care was associated with lower recidivism rates. Of course, the changes could have been due to treatment received by the parents since most of them were involved in treatment. The design of the study is weak because treatments are not carefully described and data are aggregated across programs and types of maltreatment.

Much of the evaluation work in the field of child sexual abuse has been in the area of prevention. Many training aids, curricula, and educational programs have appeared in the last few years to educate children about sexual abuse and how to avoid it. Descriptions of these programs and their evaluation are beyond the scope of this essay. (For descriptions and evaluations of these programs, see Conte [1984] and Finkelhor [1986].)

In summary, there are numerous types of programs for the victim of sexual abuse. Most are multifaceted, include all family members, and can be characterized by the extent to which they collaborate with the criminal justice system. The multifaceted nature of these programs also makes it difficult to evaluate them because, if positive changes are measured, it is impossible to know the "active ingredient." One solution would be to conduct small experiments within treatment programs to test the relative effectiveness of different methods. Combining data from different types of programs should be discouraged in favor of evaluating clearly defined treatment strategies.

C. Child Physical Abuse

Until recently, intervention with abused children focused only on medical needs and physical protection. Today there is growing recognition of the nonphysical effects of child abuse, such as lowered self-esteem, language problems, cognitive delays, aggressive behavior and social withdrawal (Lamphear 1985; Ammerman et al. 1986; Azar 1986). Despite the proliferation of programs to help abused children, the interventions are often not well described and little evaluation work has been done.

Most interventions appear to take a family approach. For example, all eight federal demonstration projects described by Daro (1987) are designed to help the victim use a family approach rather than an individual one. Providers reason that any gains made by children in individual therapy will disappear if the parents do not also change. Most interventions are therefore aimed at the parents and assume that the child's functioning will improve as a result.

Family-oriented interventions have shown positive impact on the physically abused child's functioning. For example, Crozier and Katz (1979), in two case studies, found that child-management training with parents had a positive influence on their behavior and indirectly affected the children's behavior (e.g., increased the target child's positive behavior as well as the behavior of their siblings). It is unclear whether these behavioral changes generalize to other settings where the abused child has demonstrated problems (cf. Hoffman-Plotkin and Twentyman 1984). In addition, the impact of such treatment on more subtle disturbances, both short- and long-term, has yet to be determined. Unlike child sexual abuse and wife abuse, the field of child physical abuse has not focused on the detection and treatment of posttraumatic stress among its victims. The focus on posttraumatic stress and external stress among victims comes about indirectly in programs for abusive parents who were victims as children and who are trying to stop the cycle of abuse.

Foster care is the major form of "individual" intervention used by protective service agencies. The caseloads of child protection workers are generally too large to permit counseling. What little is systematically known about the effects of placement was reviewed at the beginning of this essay. In one study, the other elements of case management thought to be indicators of quality management (e.g., immediacy of response, outside consultation, professional training) were not related to the potential to reabuse (Cohn and DeGraaf 1982). One important ingredient for improving casework seems to be the use of multidisciplinary teams. Hochstadt and Harwicke (1985) present evidence that these teams are more successful than are child protection services in helping families acquire the services recommended to them.

A few reports of individual treatment with physically abused children have appeared. For the most part, these have been case reports of traditional child therapy techniques such as play therapy (e.g., Green 1975; Mann and McDermott 1983). These reports conceptualize the child's problems as being similar to posttraumatic stress syndrome. The reports provide some clues to therapeutic work with children but lack outcome evaluations. Green and his colleagues, for example, use detailed case reports to describe the special issues that arise when doing therapy with abused children, such as the transference of the child's anger onto the therapist and the child's minimization of the abuse (Green 1983).

One study has assessed the outcome of individual treatment. Methods based on social learning theory were used to decrease the socially withdrawn behavior of maltreated children (Fantuzzo et al. 1988). The children were prompted with social overtures (cf., Strain 1981) by peers or adults who were at a higher level of social functioning. The children who were prompted by other children significantly increased their level of social behavior both during and after treatment. The children who received no treatment did not show the same improvements; prompting by adults seemed to have a negative impact. The generalizability of the findings of this study are limited by the small sample size (twelve in each condition) and by the fact that it involved both abuse and neglect cases.

Day care is often recommended to lessen the stresses of child care for the parents; it is viewed less often as a form of intervention for the child. "Therapeutic" day-care programs, designed to address children's special needs, are a special case. Such programs are typically used in conjunction with family treatment, so it is difficult to assess their independent impact. In a study by Parish et al. (1985), fifty-three children between the ages of two and five were involved in daily preschool programs focused on development of motor, language, and social skills.

Parent group programs focused on sharing of feelings and learning of anger management skills. Outside evaluators found that 79 percent of the children showed greater than expected developmental skill gains on standardized measures. Unfortunately, there was no control group against which to measure the children's progress.

Daro (1987), in an evaluation of eight federal demonstration projects, found suggestive evidence that therapeutic day care reduced the likelihood of future maltreatment and contributed to greater progress during treatment. Methodological limitations of this evaluation were noted earlier and further evaluation is needed. A practical drawback of these programs is the costs resulting from the intensity of their services.

The programs evaluated by Daro (1987) also involved a wide range of other services including individual therapy, group counseling, speech and physical therapy, and medical care. Over 70 percent of the young children and adolescents were reported to have made gains during treatment, based on reports of reabuse and counselors' ratings of progress and the likelihood of further abuse. Despite the positive reports from counselors, only 40 percent of the children in these samples were residing with their families at the end of treatment, indicating that there may have been continued risk to the children. It must be emphasized that the majority of clients were being seen for problems of neglect or sexual abuse and not physical abuse, and thus it was impossible to isolate the effects for physically abused children.

In summary, outcome studies of treatments focused on child abuse victims have been limited. Outcome studies now available combine different types of maltreatment or intervene simultaneously with parent and child, making any conclusions difficult to draw. Much more research is needed in this area. As more information is gathered regarding the long-term effects of maltreatment, it is to be hoped that more interventions will be developed and assessed to alleviate these effects.

IV. Programs for Offenders: Description and Evaluation

There are a number of parallels among offender treatment models for the three major forms of family violence. Each has given rise to treatment models based on several different approaches: self-help, social learning, psychodynamic, and family systems. Similar controversies exist within the separate treatment communities over the merits of different approaches. There is a difference, however, in the emphasis placed on any one approach. Treatment for child sexual abuse, for example, is more likely than treatment for wife abuse to emphasize family systems approaches because the family appears more likely to remain together after the abuse (e.g., Giarretto 1982). This section describes the most common treatment models for offenders for each type of abuse and provides what evidence exists to support their effectiveness.

A. Woman Abuse Offender Programs

Treatment models for men who batter their intimate partners can be categorized in a number of ways. Some authors (e.g., Roberts 1984*b*) categorize treatment by the type of setting, for example, volunteer men's collectives, social service agencies, and women's shelters, and Gondolf (1985) argues that the setting influences methods. Eddy and Myers (1984) found that shelter-run programs focused somewhat less on interpersonal dynamics and patriarchal norms than other programs. Feazell, Mayers, and Deschner (1984) found little difference in approach between special abuser programs and traditional service agencies, except that the latter received more voluntary referrals.

There are several major treatment orientations currently in use: self-help, cognitive-behavioral, educational, systems-behavioral, family systems, and a mixture of insight and problem-solving. Some programs use several of these orientations sequentially or integrate them in other ways. Most programs also combine the above methods with sex-role resocialization (e.g., Sonkin, Martin, and Walker 1985). The self-help approach, by its nature, is usually tied to a group format, but the other methods of treatment can be found in programs involving men alone, men in groups, and couples in groups.

The self-help approach was first developed and applied by Goffman (1980, 1984) in Batterers Anonymous Groups. These groups aim to stop woman abuse through peer support and problem solving. They are more like Parents Anonymous than Alcoholics Anonymous, however, because they have a professional consultant or "sponsor" who provides some guidance to the peer group leader during and between group sessions. Jennings (1987) argues that unstructured but closely supervised, supportive self-help groups are the most effective because interpersonal skills, mutual support and confrontation, and examination of sex roles can occur more naturally. He claims that the changes will be longer lasting because they come from within the client. This form of treatment has been used alone and in combination with other modalities such as cognitive-behavioral treatment. There are no reports of outcome evaluations of the effects of these self-help groups.

The cognitive-behavioral approach has been used for individuals, men's groups, and couples' groups (e.g., Ganley 1981; Neidig 1984; Saunders 1984a, 1984b; Edleson et al. 1985) and is currently the most widely used (Feazell, Mayers, and Deschner 1984). Typically, this approach uses a treatment "package" consisting of communication skills training, relaxation training, cognitive restructuring, and building awareness of the personal and social roots of aggression.

Several early case studies indicated that these approaches showed promise. The techniques included thought-stopping (Bass 1973), assertiveness training (Foy, Eisler, and Pinkston 1975), behavioral contracting and communication training (Saunders 1977) and a combination of assertiveness training, relaxation training, and cognitive restructuring (Edleson et al. 1985).

Recently, results from several large-scale studies have been reported. Lund, Larsen, and Schultz (1982) (also reported in Edleson and Grusznski 1988) report on the effects of a comprehensive treatment approach at the Domestic Abuse Project of Minneapolis. The project has programs for men, women, and children. The men's services reported in the study were based on sixteen sessions of cognitive-behavioral treatment followed by a self-help group. Of the sample of eighty-six men, fifty-seven of their partners could be contacted at follow-up. Sixty-seven percent of the partners of men completing the program ($N = 27$) reported at an average of six months follow-up that the violence had not recurred. This figure compared with a reported success rate of 54 percent by the partners of men who dropped out of the treatment program ($N = 30$). However, this form of comparison does not control for factors associated with program completion and higher motivation levels that might be responsible for the positive change. For example, those who completed the program were more likely to be better educated and might have learned to change on their own without treatment. Moreover, when threats were added to the list of abuse items, there was no significant difference between groups. Other limitations of the study were lack of knowledge about the frequency of violence before treatment and use of a nonstandard follow-up period that may not have been long enough.

The men reported that they became less traditional in their views of women's roles and that they improved their levels of affective communication. They did not change, however, in their self-reports of the "need for control."

Two other studies at the Domestic Abuse Project are described by Edelson and Grusznski (1988). In one study, sixteen sessions of a cognitive-behavioral group treatment were followed by sixteen sessions of traditional group psychotherapy. Forty-two women and seventeen men were contacted at a point averaging 9.5 months after treatment. Based solely on the women's reports, 68 percent of the men were nonviolent during the follow-up period. However, only 24 percent were both nonviolent and nonthreatening. The men reported a nonviolence rate of 70 percent. Forty-one percent reported that they were free of both violence and threats.

In a third study from the project, the same two treatments as in the above study were evaluated, but this time completers and noncompleters were compared. There were no significant differences between these two groups on demographic variables, childhood violence, prior help seeking, or source of referral. Of the 159 subjects selected for participation, 112 completers and forty-two randomly selected noncompleters were successfully interviewed. Based on the women's reports approximately six months after treatment, 59 percent of the completers and 52 percent of the noncompleters were nonviolent. This difference was not statistically significant. The difference was greatest for the category of severe violence where the partners of 15 percent of the completers and 22 percent of the noncompleters reported violence. The men in neither of the conditions admitted to severe violence.

The authors speculate that the results of the third study were not as impressive as the other two because the men were more difficult to treat: substantially more were unemployed and had prior mental health and chemical dependency counseling. They also note that, because of a liberal definition of noncompleter, many of the "noncompleters" had undergone all sixteen sessions of the cognitive-behavioral group and some of the therapy group. It is possible that some who dropped out learned the skills quickly and no longer needed treatment. One problem with the study's design, which probably inflated the rate of success, was that the follow-up interviews included couples who were living apart. Violence may not decrease with separation but probably will decrease with separation and no contact (Kelso and Personette 1985).

From a methodological standpoint, these studies underscore the need to rely on reports from the victims of abuse and to include measures of verbal abuse. The authors speculate that "many men who end their violence may resort to the use of threats as a 'legal' but hardly less terrorizing form of control" (Edleson and Grusznski 1988, p. 23).

Dutton (1986) used a quasi-experimental design to compare fifty treated and fifty untreated cases. The untreated cases were deemed unsuitable for treatment by the therapist or were not treated for practical reasons ($N = 42$). Comparison was also made with a sample of men from another study who had been arrested but not treated. The rearrest rate for the untreated group was 40 percent, whereas it was only 4 percent for the treated group. The men and the women completed the Conflict Tactics Scales before treatment and six months to three years after treatment ($N = 37$). On these scales, both husbands' and wives' reports of verbal abuse, all violence, and "severe" violence showed significant pre-post drops. Eighty-four percent of the wives reported no "severe" violence during the follow-up period. Twenty-one percent of the wives, however, reported an increase in verbal aggression. Comparing the wives' reports of severe violence with those of wives whose partners were arrested but not treated (Jaffe et al. 1986), Dutton found significantly greater reductions in violence in the arrested and treated group compared with those who were only arrested.

Hamberger and Hastings (1986) also used a cognitive-behavioral group approach. They compared the self-report or partners' report of thirty-two men who completed treatment and thirty-six men who dropped from treatment. Seventy-two percent of the completers and 53 percent of the dropouts were not violent during one year of follow-up. For those who completed treatment, there were significant decreases in scores on the Conflict Tactics Scale from before treatment to after treatment, with the lower scores still holding at the one-year follow-up. There were significant decreases in self-reported depression and anger over the course of treatment. Scores on a measure of personality (Millon Clinical Multiaxial Inventory) did not change significantly.

Maiuro and his associates (1987) assessed sixty-five men before and after they completed an anger management program and compared them with twenty-five men on a waiting list. Treatment consisted of a structured group using mostly cognitive-behavioral methods. Sex-role resocialization focused on expanding affective repertoires and cognitive distortions regarding women. Group process methods included modeling from a male-female therapy team and mutual support and confrontation among group members. Measures included the Buss-Durkee Hostility Inventory, the Hostility and Direction of Hostility Questionnaire, the Ways of Coping Checklist, and the Beck Depression Inventory. In addition, the men and their partners completed a Brief Anger-Aggression Questionnaire.

The wait-list control group received minimal treatment, which consisted of an intake evaluation, contacts with the program, and probationary monitoring of court-referred cases (60 percent). They were reassessed after a mean of nineteen weeks. The treated men showed significant decreases in anger and aggression by their reports and those of their partners. Decreases in depression and maladaptive coping (wishful thinking and avoidance) and increases in problem-focused coping and seeking of social support were also reported by the treated group. In contrast, the waiting-list group showed positive change on only one of twelve scales. A group of sixteen men was reached one year after treatment and they showed a persistence of treatment effects. This group did not differ from the rest of the treatment sample on demographics, overall level of disturbance, or pretreatment measures.

Shepard (1987) compared the reports of the partners of men in treatment at different phases of treatment, before (N = 30), middle (N = 18), and end (N = 16). There were also follow-up reports received from the women fourteen months after treatment. The men were matched on a number of demographic factors. A questionnaire was used to gather information on physical and psychological abuse. The first three months of treatment consisted of cognitive-behavioral approaches with confrontational techniques for increasing client accountability. The next three months were spent in an educational group that focused on attitudes of control over the victim. Sixty-one percent of the victims reported no violence during their partner's participation in the first group and 69 percent reported no violence either during the men's presence in the second group or at fourteen months follow-up. Psychological abuse did not change over the course of treatment but did over the follow-up period. It should be noted that about 60 percent of the couples were not living together at the time of each phase of the study. This is not a true comparison between the methods because no random assignment was done.

Tolman, Beeman, and Mendoza (1987) also used an approach emphasizing cognitive-behavioral methods and sex-role resocialization. About one-third (N = 48) of the men's partners were contacted an average of twenty-six months after treatment. Fifty-eight percent reported a recurrence of aggression; 35 percent experienced it in the last six months. Length of treatment was not a factor.

Saunders and Hanusa (1986) evaluated ninety-two offenders before and after treatment. Treatment consisted of twelve sessions (thirty hours) of cognitive-behavioral group treatment and eight sessions (sixteen hours) of a guided self-help group. There were significant decreases in the men's self-reported levels of depression, anger toward partner, anger toward work or friend situations, and jealousy, and more liberal scores on the "Attitudes toward Woman Scale," a measure of views of women's roles. These changes were maintained even after controlling for a social desirability response bias. The measure of anger was shown to be related significantly to changes the women reported in aggressiveness from before treatment through a follow-up period.

Douglas and Perrin (1987) noted changes over the course of a six-session cognitive-behavioral program for twenty men diverted from prosecution. The program focused on the causes and effects of abuse, anger regulation, empathic listening, and handling jealousy. Following treatment, the men revealed significantly higher scores on assertiveness and lower scores on the Michigan Alcohol Screening Test. They did not show changes on measures of depression and attitudes about women.

Kelso and Personette (1985) assessed the outcome of a multimethod approach. The goals were to lessen the guilt and isolation of the men, confront their violent attitudes, provide support, and teach interpersonal skills. The skills taught were "time-out" (brief separation when angry), cognitive restructuring, assertiveness, and the use of physical exercise and relaxation for anger reduction. Most of the men received group treatment but about one-third received individual and/or group counseling. The treatment was designed to occur weekly for six months but the average length of treatment was 4.5 months and only 28 percent of the men completed treatment.

Assessment was attempted over the six months when treatment was to occur and was called "follow-up" but was actually an assessment over the course of treatment. Contacts with the men were attempted monthly. Only 48 percent agreed to participate or had complete data. The study measured psychological, physical, and sexual violence. The frequency, severity, and number of different acts of violence were measured separately and in combination.

Comparisons were made with a post hoc baseline six months before treatment. During the assessment period, nonviolence ranged from 68 percent to 96 percent for any monthly period. As in the studies at the Domestic Abuse Project in Minneapolis, mental abuse was most likely to recur (35–61 percent monthly rate) and was almost always present with physical or sexual violence. All of the reports of violence declined over the course of treatment.

Several procedures were likely to inflate the reported success rate:

the sample size fluctuated at each monthly contact (from sixteen to twenty-eight), only the men's reports were used, men are more likely to remain nonviolent during treatment, and the study's major analysis combined those living with and without their partners. When the researchers compared those living with their partners to those living without their partners, each month showed higher rates for those living together and two of the months had significantly different rates.

This study also related client characteristics and their use of therapy skills with outcomes. Court-ordered men reported less violence after treatment but this difference did not exist after controlling for age and the length of the relationship. There was no relationship between social support and violence. Violence did reportedly decrease as alcohol use decreased. Unexpectedly, more frequent use of therapy skills and more frequent contact with public agencies was associated with more reported violence. The authors speculate that the skills may have been used more often but unsuccessfully by those reporting more violence. Likewise, going to a public agency may be a sign of unsuccessful coping.

In a multiple regression analysis, the strongest predictor of violence was the level of pretreatment violence, which was especially high among young, court-ordered men. This study's use of a composite index of violence and its attempts to predict characteristics of successful clients are noteworthy and bear further development.

DeMaris and Jackson (1987) also relied on abusers' self-reports of recidivism. Voluntarily referred men attended an open-ended therapy group that emphasized communication of feelings, coping with stress, and examination of one's expectations of women. Court-ordered men attended a program much more structured and didactic in nature. It covered similar topics and also others, for example, jealousy, substance abuse, and "time out" procedures. Seventeen percent ($N = 53$) of the men returned mailed questionnaires. Those who responded were less likely to have alcohol problems, to have witnessed parental violence, and to have "beaten up" their partners; thus a major bias entered the evaluation.

The total group of respondents reported a recidivism rate of 35 percent, but that figure rose to 40–42 percent for couples living together or currently involved. Significantly higher recidivism rates were reported by those with alcohol problems, with parental violence, and by those who did not call a counselor when violence seemed imminent. Abuse as a child, court-ordered participation, and number of sessions attended did not seem to be related to recidivism, although the dichotomization of the variables may have reduced the chance of finding significant differences. Reduction in the frequency of violence was also reported. The reduction was greatest for men who were voluntary participants, paid attention to physiological signs of anger, used "time-out," and whose partner had also been violent. The authors are aware of the tentative nature of their results because the men are likely to give socially approved answers; the results are more useful if it is assumed that response bias does not differ within their sample.

Three studies report on the use of cognitive-behavioral methods in a couples format. Deschner (1984) reports on a ten-session couples group for treating marital and child abuse that used many cognitive-behavioral methods—relaxation training, cognitive restructuring, time out, and assertiveness training. It also included the assessment and modification of nutritional intake. The ten sessions were each divided about evenly between didactic material and provisions of support. On the Taylor-Johnson Temperament Analysis, a sample of twelve men reported becoming less nervous, less depressed, less inhibited, and less submissive. The scores on "hostility" and five other subscales did not reach significance. Over the course of treatment, the violence of the participants ($N = 47$) decreased by half but the change was not statistically significant. At eight months follow-up, about half of the respondents could be reached. Fifteen percent reported recurrence of violence, but some of the couples were separated; thus the actual success rate is not known.

Myers (1984) also describes a model for couples. Her treatment, however, is much longer, lasting for one year. The first six months emphasizes psychotherapy and skills training and the last six months emphasizes support. Evaluation of twenty-four abusers after six months revealed significant decreases on the Global Distress Scale, the Affective Communication Scale and the Problem-Solving Communication Scale of the Marital Satisfaction Scale, and on the Depression and Psychopathic Deviate Scale of the MMPI. In addition, these men showed significant improvements on the Child Abuse Potential Inventory.

Neidig (1984, 1986) reports on the development and evaluation of a highly structured cognitive-behavioral treatment program for couples. The program includes the basic ingredients of the cognitive-behavioral treatments for individuals that were described above. It is particularly suited for use in the military settings in which it was developed. Data on forty men who completed treatment showed significant improvement on three of the Dyadic Adjustment subscales (consensus, satisfaction, and cohesion) and greater internality on a locus of control scale.

Stacey and Shupe (1984) conducted an assessment of three programs in Texas and combined the data from the three programs. A variety of treatment orientations were used. A project in Austin worked mostly with criminal justice referrals and used three group modules of treatment sequentially: six weeks of a cognitive-behavioral approach, six weeks of an educational approach stressing communication skills and sex-role socialization, followed by six weeks of psychodynamic therapy. The psychodynamic group had no agenda and was tailored to meet the needs of the individuals. A self-help group plus individual, marital, family, and alcohol-drug counseling were used occasionally as adjuncts.

The project at the Tyler Family Preservation Program used a couples counseling format because they assumed the dynamics of abuse to be interactional in nature. During assessment, the background and diagnostic information was shared with each spouse and was considered part of the therapeutic process. The treatment stressed "fair fight" rules, use of humor to defuse anger, sex-role education, and some cognitive restructuring. It was based largely on client-centered (Rogerian) ego psychology and psychodynamic orientations.

The third program, the Arlington Anger Control Program, was described earlier (Deschner 1984). It was designed for couples who intended to stay together and was largely cognitive-behavioral in focus. Individual and couples therapy were also encouraged.

The follow-up assessment of the three programs asked about three broad categories of violence (verbal, physical, and sexual) and the frequency (once, daily, monthly, etc.) and severity of violence. Questions were also asked about awareness of treatment methods. The 235 families who completed treatment among the three programs constituted the sample for follow-up. The majority were from the Austin program.

Of the sample of 235, 148 men and 96 of their partners were contacted and agreed to be interviewed. Cessation of physical violence during counseling was reported by 88 percent of the men and 70 percent of the women. Cessation of violence during the follow-up period, which ranged from months to years, was reported by 72 percent of the men and 55 percent of the women. Rates of nonviolence were lower for those who did not complete treatment: 55 percent according to the men and 33 percent according to the women. Most of the partners of men in treatment reported that physical, verbal, and sexual violence became less severe after treatment; however, 42 percent of them said that verbal abuse was still a problem after treatment. Although the men and women rated the personnel highly and would recommend the programs to others, almost one-third of the women said the programs were "not at all helpful" or "not very helpful." Almost all of the men saw the programs as helpful.

An important aspect of this study was an evaluation of changes in child abuse by the men, based on their partners' reports. Both physical and verbal abuse were reported to decrease substantially, with an overall reduction from 36 percent to 12.5 percent.

Among the weaknesses of this study are the aggregation of data from three programs, the inconsistent follow-up periods, and the lack of baseline data. If the base rate of violence is very low, twice a year for example, then the lack of violence over a six-month follow-up is not much of a change.

There is currently controversy over the respective merits of the use of a couples format and of working with the men and women separately. An advantage of the couples approach is that both partners know exactly what the other is learning and the stigma on the abuser may be lessened, thereby helping him get more readily involved in treatment. Some clinicians who use this approach claim that marital violence is a "relationship" issue to which both partners contribute, therefore indicating the need for couples counseling (Neidig 1984).

Evidence on the causes of woman abuse (Hotaling and Sugerman 1986) and case studies of the couples format have led many treatment programs to insist that abusers undergo assessment and the initial stages of treatment alone. This approach has the advantages of explicitly or implicitly placing more responsibility on the abuser for changing his behavior and avoiding the victim blaming that often occurs; it helps the victim be more open about the history and recurrence of violence and about considering separation (Saunders 1981; Edelson 1985). Eventually, this debate may be decided on empirical grounds. Until then, researchers and clinicians need to be aware of how their values may influence their choice of treatment (Saunders 1981; Bograd 1984) and the risks of violence to the woman if she reports abuse in the man's presence or says that she wants to leave the relationship.

The last study to be reviewed in this section is methodologically the most ambitious but also the most disappointing. The survey by Pirog-

Good and Stets-Kealey (1986) provides a valuable overview of the characteristics of programs for men who batter but falls short in its statistical analysis of treatment outcome. The authors initially identified 314 abuser programs in the United States and found 211 that were still in existence. Seventy-two of these programs responded to a lengthy mail questionnaire. Between 80 and 90 percent of the programs attempted to change attitudes, increase self-esteem, and change sex-role attitudes, in addition to stopping the violence. Most programs used several formats simultaneously or in sequence, with men's groups as the format of choice, followed in frequency by individual counseling, couples counseling, and, finally, family counseling. There were also various combinations of these formats but no particular pattern could be found.

Reports of recidivism were made by program directors and most of the directors said they had to estimate their answers to some questions. Some of the estimates of recidivism were based on rearrest, reentering the program, calls from the wives, and follow-up interviews. The authors state that "this variable should be considered as reflecting program administrators' best estimates of recidivism rates" (Pirog-Good and Stets-Kealey 1986, p. 2). Thus there was no uniformity in criteria for recidivism. Furthermore, relying on rearrest or calls from the partner is likely to underestimate the true incidence rate by a factor of ten (Schulman 1979). The rate of nonviolence estimated by the respondents for a one-year period ranged from 71 percent to 89 percent, which is generally above the rate reported by the men's partners for shorter periods of time in the studies reviewed above.

There were twenty-six programs with enough information for the authors to attempt a multivariate analysis of factors associated with "recidivism." The authors' conclusion that individual and family counseling are the preferred modes is not warranted, in part because of the large number of independent variables and the possibility that correlations among the independent variables could explain the results. For example, it is likely that those in individual and family treatment did better because they were in treatment longer (for a detailed critique see Saunders [1988]).

The research reviewed in this section on programs for men who batter reveals that most of the outcome work has used cognitive-behavioral methods in an individual or couple format. However, because most of the designs so far are before-after comparisons, the studies could not rule out the influence of significant events in the men's lives such as divorce or criminal justice sanctions. The fear of these events may also strongly influence men's behavior. There is some evidence, for example, that both abusers and nonabusers are influenced by the likelihood and severity of legal sanctions and the fear of losing the relationship (Carmody and Williams 1987). In addition, Margolin and Fernandez (1987) report on three couples who stopped the aggression without formal intervention. The couples attributed the change to a variety of factors, including seeing the effects of the violence on the children, stopping drug abuse, a lecture by in-laws to the abuser, and the victim's avoidance of volatile language.

One consistent finding is that rates of physical abuse were lower for treated groups but there was little or no difference in rates of psychological abuse. There are a number of explanations for this: psychological abuse may not be addressed sufficiently in treatment, the men may be able to keep from going over the legal "limit," or this form of abuse may be more difficult to change. A promising result from a couple of studies indicates that sexist attitudes can change over the course of treatment. The next stage of research needs to compare different types of treatment, perhaps including a minimal treatment control group with safeguards for protecting the women and children. In that way, we can move forward in the attempt to discover the most effective forms of treatment.

B. Child Sexual Abuse Offender Programs

A wide variety of treatments have been initiated for sexual abuse offenders. They range from broad, multifaceted therapy and self-help programs, like the Child Sexual Abuse Treatment Program (CSATP), to narrowly focused attempts to recondition the focus of sexual desire (Laws and O'Neil 1979; Kelley 1982). Settings for treatment vary from outpatient psychotherapy to institutions.

A controversy exists in this field, as it does in the field of marital violence, about the importance of family approaches and family reunion. Some programs use family therapy to help the family decide on its options and build more harmonious relationships, or to separate peacefully, whereas the goal of other programs is family reunion.

Although many evaluations of prevention efforts have been conducted, treatment evaluations are less common. Giarretto (1978) summarized the preliminary results of CSATP based on parents' reports: "no recidivism in the more than 500 families receiving a minimum of ten hours of treatment and formally terminated. Two recurrences have been reported, one in an out-of-county family not eligible for individual treatment who attended the group sessions of Parents United, the other in a family in early stages of treatment" (p. 71). Kroth's (1979) evaluation of the CSATP at the beginning, middle, and end of treatment also found no recidivism, but again the reports were only from the parents and only while the family was in treatment. The parents' relationships seemed to improve with significantly fewer in the termination group saying they argued "quite a lot."

Sexual activity and sexual enjoyment between the parents was non-existent for the intake group but was satisfactory for about half the termination group. Of the offenders in the intake group, 78 percent admitted "very much" or "complete" responsibility for the incest, which climbed to 89 percent in the termination group. Twice as many offenders and their spouses felt more "open, honest and in control of themselves" in the termination group. Major flaws in the evaluation design include the total reliance on the parents' reports and the lack of follow-up on those dropping from the program (which probably was not overcome by matching on demographic factors).

Daro's summary of evaluations of nineteen child maltreatment programs (addressing all forms of abuse and neglect), assessed "clinical progress" on three criteria: reincidence of abuse and neglect, clinical judgment of the likelihood of future abuse, and clinician judgment regarding the client's overall progress. Combining programs for all forms of maltreatment, there was a 47 percent recidivism rate. Controlling for a variety of client demographic and functioning characteristics, group and family counseling were consistently associated with client progress.

Clients primarily involved in sexual abuse treatment were reported to show the greatest overall gains; for example, 70 percent were judged as unlikely to abuse again. For these abusers, no particular type of service was associated with treatment progress but two factors stood out as related to progress: accepting responsibility for abuse and being willing to participate in treatment.

The assumption of many community-based therapists is that treatment should focus on the nonsexual aspects of the underlying problems: depression, interpersonal skills, family dynamics, and others. However, as Conte (1985) points out, these are largely untested assumptions. Depression, for example, may be the result of guilt over abuse or being arrested and not the cause of abuse.

Conte also reviews data challenging the assumption that incest offenders do not molest children outside the family; if they do, methods used to treat pedophilia may also be effective with incest offenders. Some of these methods have been based on learning theory and have included age-appropriate heterosexual social skills training, aversive conditioning, and classical conditioning. Aversion therapy usually involves the administration of mild electric shocks concomitant with the client's sexual arousal to pictures of deviant sexual behavior. Most of this work is being conducted in prisons and mental hospitals. One of the most controversial treatments for sex offenders is the use of anti-androgen medication, or "chemical castration." The long-term effects of this medication on recidivism rates are still unknown (Berlin and Meinecke 1981).

A few studies have compared recidivism rates of incest offenders with those of other sex offenders. The rates have generally been lower for incest offenders with follow-up periods of one to twenty-four years (Christenson et al. 1965; Frisbee and Dondis 1965; Tracy et al. 1983). Rates have ranged from 10–12 percent for incest offenders and from 18–24 percent for other offenders. While encouraging, the rates for incest offenders may be deflated because of family members' reluctance to report; or incest may be less prevalent, as a result, not of treatment, but of victims' greater resistance against abuse as they grow older (Finkelhor 1984).

In summary, as with the problem of domestic violence, there is no consensus in the field of child sexual abuse regarding the use of family or individual therapy. Existing evaluations are limited because they do not control for cases that dropped from treatment and because a wide variety of interventions were used both inside and outside of the programs. Because there is recent evidence that incest offenders and child molesters often do not differ significantly, the application of the highly specific treatments now used with child molesters to incest offenders would be a fruitful subject for research.

C. Child Physical Abuse Offender Programs

Treatments for those who physically abuse children are quite diverse. The theories on which they are based include psychodynamic, family systems, cognitive-behavioral, and social support theories (for reviews, see Shorkey [1979] and Azar and Twentyman [1988]). The development of clinical approaches is constrained by an inadequate foundation of theory and knowledge (Newberger and Newberger 1981). A similarity to woman abuse and child sexual abuse treatment is a debate over whether to focus change efforts on an individual or social level. Many researchers point to the evidence that child abuse is associated with social factors such as unemployment and urge that more emphasis be placed on remedying social conditions that place parents at high risk. The assumptions of some researchers, and the evidence they have gathered, leads them to conclude that we need a comprehensive program of prevention (Gelles 1984).

Individual case methods vary a great deal in how extensively treatment outcomes have been evaluated. The psychodynamic model views parents who abuse as suffering from a personality disorder that is due to a lack of nurturing while growing up. Individual therapy of one to two years is recommended. The process involves reviewing the client's developmental history and working through repressed conflicts. However, case reports are often provided with no systematic evaluation. They conclude with vague statements about improvements in client functioning without mentioning whether the abuse has ended (see Shorkey [1979], p. 90, for examples).

Group psychotherapy has also been used. In one group approach, Paulson and Chaleff (1973) attempted to resolve problems related to early developmental phases. Male and female therapists were used to allow abusive parents to identify with positive parent surrogates. After three years of work the authors judged the treatments successful because the parents dealt with intrapsychic problems and they improved their "social and emotional behavior" in therapy and at home. Again, no systematic follow-up with standardized measures was attempted.

The sociological findings on conditions that appear to put families at risk for abuse have led to some interventions. In particular, findings on family isolation and stress have led to creation of self-help groups such as Parents Anonymous. Mutual support and problem solving are stressed but there may also be an educational focus. A professional consultant attends sessions and provides support and guidance to the peer group leaders (Willen 1984). These groups are difficult to evaluate because most of the members also receive individual or family counseling. Multiple forms of intervention occur because many practitioners recognize that the families have multiple problems. For example, self-help and traditional counseling methods may be supplemented with home visits by social workers and nurses (Pagelow 1984).

Cohn (1979), in her evaluation of eleven federal demonstration projects, emphasized the usefulness of lay therapists and Parents Anonymous as components of treatment. The clients who received lay services, often under professional supervision, were seen by the clinicians as having less potential to reabuse than those in group or individual treatment. Volunteers were usually assigned to the parents to serve as a friend and supportive social contact. The apparent effectiveness of such services may be because caseloads were small and volunteers had more energy to devote to individual families.

Families who participated in Parents Anonymous also seemed to fare significantly better than those in other forms of treatment. They were rated as having reduced stress, an improved sense of the child as a person, more appropriate expressions of anger, and a greater sense of independence and self-esteem. Unfortunately, methodological limitations of the study raise doubts about its findings: only clinicians' ratings were used, programs treated a variety of types of maltreatment, with only 34 percent of the cases involving physical abuse, and the lay services and self-help groups were often combined with other forms of treatment. The difference on the perceived likelihood of reabuse between recipients of nonprofessional and professional services was not great (42 percent vs. 53 percent).

A more recent evaluation of nineteen federal demonstration projects (Berkeley Planning Associates 1983) included a higher proportion of programs using a family approach. Outcome measures were similar to the earlier evaluation, and recidivism during treatment was high (47 percent). Across all the projects, group treatment and educational or skills development classes (e.g., household management, health care, and vocational skills) were seen as significantly related to positive outcomes on two of the three outcome measures (Cohn and Daro 1986). Positive ratings of outcome were also associated with lack of substance abuse, higher client motivation, and treatment duration between thirteen and eighteen months. Methodological limitations that apply to the above findings were mentioned earlier.

The best defined and most thoroughly evaluated approaches have been behavioral or cognitive-behavioral in orientation (Gambrill 1983). These approaches differ in the extent to which they focus on the current behavioral patterns between family members, the cognitive distortions of the abuser, and the management of external stress. The most common approach has been to teach child-management skills.

Behavioral parent training has been used in many of the studies. Usually skills in giving positive reinforcement and ignoring a negative behavior are taught didactically and through modeling, role-playing, and feedback (Patterson 1971; Becker 1981). In one of the first studies, home visits by nurses included modeling and reinforcement of "appropriate" methods of child care (Carter, Reed, and Reh 1975). Compared to a no-treatment control group which had a 90 percent rehospitalization rate, the treatment group had no rehospitalizations. Since the treatment package was not well defined, the reasons for the differences remain unclear.

Some case reports give more details about the treatment used. For example, Sandler and his colleagues (Sandler, VanDercar, and Milhoan 1978; Denicola and Sandler 1980; Wolfe and Sandler 1981) and Crozier and Katz (1979) carried out a group of single case studies that used modeling, rehearsal, and feedback. Reading assignments and anger-control training were also provided for the parents. Across the studies, positive parent behaviors increased and negative behaviors declined with training in the home setting. In addition, the changes were maintained over time and the children also improved their social behavior. Similar results were found in a case study with a cognitively impaired parent using a radio transmitter to provide coaching and feedback while she interacted with her child (Wolfe et al. 1982).

A group format has also been used to teach parents new skills. In one study (Wolfe, Sandler, and Kaufman 1981), anger control was included in the package of skills taught and the training included in-home practice. Families in treatment were compared with a matched group of families who received no treatment. The treated group performed better on a contrived parent-child interaction task immediately after treatment than did the control group and at one year follow-up had no reports of child maltreatment.

Stress in the parents has also been the target of change. In a few single-case studies, behavioral methods have been used to reduce parents' extreme negative reactions to aversive child behaviors such as crying (Sanford and Tustin 1974; Sanders 1978; Koverola, Elliot-Faust, and Wolfe 1984). For example, in one of these studies the child's aversive behavior was paired with relaxation to reduce the parent's overreaction (Sanders 1978). While such treatment appeared to be useful, long-term effects are not reported and larger life stresses experienced by the family also needed to be addressed (Wolfe 1985).

Stress-inoculation training has also been used with abusive parents (Novaco 1975). It emphasizes detection of cues related to anger arousal, relaxation training, and replacing anger-producing thoughts with more constructive cognitions. In a set of three case studies, Nomellini and Katz (1983) used these methods in home treatment of lower class families. During and after treatment, these parents showed significant decreases in aversive behavior and "angry urges," as well as substantial decreases on an anger scale. These changes were maintained after treatment. The changes in positive behavior (e.g., positive commands, approval) were small, however, and in two families an increase in aversive behavior of the children occurred. This suggests the need for behavioral training as well.

In another study employing anger-management methods, Barth and his associates (Barth et al. 1983) developed a cognitive-behavioral training package that used videotaped scenarios as a focus for discussion. Parents were trained to identify dysfunctional self-statements that seemed associated with losing control. Relaxation training was used to help parents deal with stress. Communication training was used to enhance parent-child interactions. Along with self-report measures of anger and self-perceptions, a role-play assessment of a stressful parent-child interaction was conducted. Both the performance and self-report measures showed improvement over a comparison group of untreated parents in the areas of effective commands, composure, and blaming statements. Unfortunately, the sources of the subjects for the two groups differed. The treated parents were referred by child protective services, while the controls were recruited from a well baby clinic, suggesting that the groups were not equivalent.

A small group of studies, instead of addressing children's behavior alone, has focused on other stressors that precede abuse. These have included studies focusing on maternal depression, marital problems, headaches, vocational issues, and social skills (Justice and Justice 1978; Conger, Lahey, and Smith 1981; Campbell et al. 1983). While showing some positive effects, these studies, for the most part, employed designs that limit strong conclusions (e.g., single-case designs or no control groups).

A large-scale, behaviorally oriented program has also been evaluated. The program, Project 12-Ways, goes beyond the use of cognitive-behavioral methods of parent training, however, to include various other forms of counseling and concrete services in an "ecobehavioral approach" (Lutzker and Rice 1984). "Ecobehavioral service is provided with the understanding that child abuse and neglect is neither seen nor treated as being as simplistic as parental disciplining deficits or as molecular as parental deficiencies in handling stress. Rather, in-home services are provided in several areas such as parent-child training, stress reduction, self-control, social support, assertiveness training, basic skills, leisure time, health maintenance and nutrition, home safety, job placement, and a variety of pre- and postnatal prevention services for young and unwed mothers" (Lutzker and Rice 1984, p. 520). For evaluation, fifty abuse and neglect families were randomly selected from 150 families previously served by the project. A comparison group was formed of fifty families who were also referred to protective services but were not treated by the project.

Outcomes were assessed by reports to the state's central register of the recurrence of abuse. During treatment, 2 percent of the treated families experienced an abuse or neglect incident compared with 11 percent of the comparison families. For the years after treatment, 8 percent of the treatment group and 11 percent of the comparison group had a report of recidivism. Treated families showed only one incident per family while most of the comparison group families had multiple incidents. The total recurrence frequency of the comparison group was 21 percent, which matched the frequency for the entire state.

A subsequent report from the program includes one- to five-year follow-up data, comparing 352 treated families and 358 comparison families (Lutzker and Rice 1987). For one year of treatment, the two groups did not differ in official reports of recidivism. For the remaining years, the first year of follow-up showed the greatest differences between the groups, with less recidivism for the treated group; the differences narrowed in subsequent years and recidivism increased for both groups. For example, for those treated in 1980, the difference after one year was 12–26 percent, but narrowed to a difference of 35–41 percent after five years. Collapsing data across all treatment years and all follow-up years, there remained a significant difference of 21 percent recidivism for the treatment group and 28 percent for the comparison group.

Two recent studies have evaluated the effects of different treatments with abusive parents. One focused on comparing different types of behavioral approaches (Egan 1983) and the other compared two forms of cognitive-behavioral treatment to an insight-oriented intervention (Azar and Twentyman 1984). Both studies included a waiting-list control condition.

Egan (1983) compared the effect of two behavioral strategies using four study conditions: stress-management training only, child-management training only, a combination of stress management and child management, and a waiting-list control group that received only social service monitoring. Evaluation was conducted using paper and pencil measures of affect associated with life changes and perceptions of family cohesion and conflict, behavioral observations of parent-child interaction patterns, and the parents' reports of child-management strategies in hypothetical situations. Treatment took place over a six-week period. The results indicated some differential treatment effects. Stress-management training led to changes in feelings of the parents, and child-management training produced changes in specific child-management skills. Unfortunately, the results are difficult to interpret because of the way the analyses were conducted.

A second comparison study was done by Azar and Twentyman (1984) with abusive and neglectful parents. Fifty-nine maltreating mothers were assigned to one of four conditions: cognitive-behavioral treatment with generalization (home visitor who did behavioral training), cognitive-behavioral treatment without generalization (home visitor who did supportive listening), insight-oriented treatment (also with home visitor who did supportive listening), and a waiting-list control group. Treatment was carried out over a ten-week period. Outcome measures included parental problem-solving ability and expectations of child behavior as well as home and laboratory measures of parent-child interaction. Measures were administered before treatment, immediately afterwards, and two months afterwards. The results showed no differences among the three treatment conditions. When treated clients were compared with untreated clients, caseworkers rated the treated parents as having fewer problems right after treatment; treated parents interacted more with their children after treatment. They also tended to be more positive toward their children at follow-up. Reports of recidivism at a one-year follow-up showed a trend in support of behavior therapy with the generalization component.

Based on the above studies, there seems to be support for the effectiveness of behavioral approaches and cognitive-behavioral approaches for treating child physical abuse. Results from one of the comparative outcome studies suggest that behavioral training will lead to the development of specific skills. The results of the Azar and Twentyman (1984) study, however, question the superiority of behavioral methods. The results for group plus in-home cognitive-behavioral training were promising because there was no recidivism of the abuse with this treatment. Among the possible reasons that there were no major differences between treatments were the small sample size and the short-term nature of the treatment.

A number of methodological issues must be addressed in future studies. The attrition rate for some studies has been very high. In one, for example, the drop-out rate was 32 percent when families were court-ordered and 87 percent when there was no court order (Wolfe et al. 1980). Positive incentives may need to be added to the treatment. Consideration also needs to be given to the developmental ages of the children being treated. Treatment studies of adolescent victims are completely lacking. Finally, more studies are needed that compare different forms of treatment, including standard case management.

V. Research Needs and Summary

Characteristics shared among the various treatment approaches are described here. In addition, the practical and ethical issues of doing family violence research are examined and recommendations to guide future research are offered.

A. *Common Methods and Treatment Issues*

Treatment approaches for the three major forms of family violence have much in common. Finkelhor (1983*a*) points out common features of the major forms of family violence: the families are isolated; the abuser may hold a powerful position yet feel powerless; and victims are likely to be blamed for the abuse by the abuser, by herself or himself, and by many social institutions. It is not surprising, then, that many similarities have developed in programs for abusers and victims.

First, most programs are willing to coordinate and to collaborate with the criminal justice system. The justice system is viewed as a major force in getting the offender started in treatment and keeping him or her there. The arrest, and sometimes incarceration, of the offender is frequently seen as a symbolic statement to the family and society that the crime is serious and the offender should be held accountable. Use of the criminal justice system may be the only way to rectify the power imbalance between victim and offender. In each treatment area, some believe that coercive intervention is detrimental to the long-term welfare of all family members. Overall, however, it appears that legal sanctions and services for victims and offenders are working toward a common goal and complement one another (Dutton 1986).

Second, many treatment programs for each type of abuse rely, at least in part, on self-help groups. These programs recognize that isolation can be broken in these groups and that mutual support and mutual confrontation are beneficial. Unlike Alcoholics Anonymous, however, these self-help groups rely on professional guidance. This guidance may derive from concern for the ease with which offenders can slip back into norms that support violence.

Third, debates about whether to focus change strategies on the family system or on the individual are ongoing for each area of family violence. A major argument against a family focus is the implicit or explicit blame that may accrue to the victim. Simply having the victim in treatment may imply that the victim is equally responsible for the abuse. For child abuse, particularly where reconciliation of the family is sometimes the goal, there is the realistic fear that abuse will recur. Family systems advocates maintain that a family focus is needed either because they assume that all family members contribute to the abuse or because the change in individuals needs to be integrated into the family's system of interactions. There is increasing evidence, however, that much family violence, particularly wife abuse and child sexual abuse, is the product of offender characteristics rather than of family dynamics (e.g., Hotaling and Sugerman 1986).

Fourth, debates continue on whether to place the highest priority on changing social conditions that produce abuse or on changing individual or family behavior. This debate is less heated than the one over family interventions, and many programs try to keep a dual focus on counseling and social change. In the battered women's movement in particular, program workers speak often about combining social change efforts with work on the individual level.

Finally, many practitioners hesitated to treat victims with traditional mental health methods for fear of stigmatizing victims as ill or deviant and thereby adding to their sense of helplessness. Some of this apprehension is justified, as is illustrated by cases in which battered women are prescribed medication for anxiety or depression or are kept in long-term therapy with no discussion of the abuse. However, with the development of the diagnosis of posttraumatic stress disorder, there is recognition that many distressed victims are reacting normally to an abnormal situation. This diagnosis may not apply very well to sexual abuse victims, however, because of the added weight of betrayal and stigmatization that they suffer (cf. Finkelhor 1987).

The similarities in methods and issues among treatment approaches for the three major forms of family violence has seldom been addressed in the literature but offers much potential for sharing of methods and resources. There has been traditionally little sharing among the fields, perhaps because of their separate historical roots and their association with separate disciplines.

B. Research Issues and Recommendations

Despite the calls for more and better research made throughout the preceding sections, important practical and ethical concerns place constraints on research on treatments for family violence. A number of authors have summarized the methodological problems in treatment studies and have discussed important ethical and practical problems (Blythe 1983; Smith, Rachman, and Yule 1984; Finkelhor 1986; Azar and Twentyman 1988; Saunders 1988).

1. *Control Groups.* Random assignment to a no-treatment control group or even to a waiting-list control group is not ethically justifiable in many cases. Researchers can justifiably attempt to devise minimal treatment or comparison treatments that include close monitoring to protect victims. Even with minimal treatment designs, referral sources are likely to balk at continuing to make referrals to the program, especially if the program has been in place for awhile. A number of patchwork or quasi-experimental designs are more likely to meet ethical standards and be accepted in the community (e.g., Dutton 1986). One example is the comparison over time of offenders in treatment with a group from another community who are not in treatment, matched on such factors as history of violence, prior arrests, and socioeconomic status.

2. *Attrition from Treatment.* Many programs suffer high attrition during treatment and during the follow-up phase. Evaluation efforts need to take attrition into account so that results do not pertain only to "the cream of the crop"—the clients who are most motivated. Reports of research need to describe the attrition rates at various points of assessment and treatment so that readers can make judgments about the generalizability of findings. Comparisons can also be made between persons who complete treatment or who drop out and persons in random community surveys. There is evidence that those who drop out of treatment are similar to those who drop out of psychotherapy in general—the uneducated and unemployed (e.g., Saunders and Hanusa 1986). The factors that predict drop-out can be used to develop strategies to enhance the motivation of those at highest risk to drop out.

3. *Source of Report.* The ideal outcome measure is usually the rate of recidivism as reported by the victim. Several studies show that the offender is more likely to minimize the abuse (e.g., Edleson and Brygger 1988). However, because locating families during follow-up is often difficult and many victims and offenders no longer have contact, this measure is subject to severe limitations. Victims are also subject to

intimidation and other pressures to minimize the extent of recidivism. Thus the development of measures that are difficult to fake and that correlate highly with violence are also needed; the role-play tests and physiological measures used in some programs are examples. There are also times when police records reveal assaults that victims do not report to researchers, making an argument for multiple sources of reporting. Other family members might be an additional source of reports.

4. *Treatment Validity and Process.*   When types of treatment are compared or when treatment is compared to a waiting-list control or dropout group, there is a need to assure the validity of treatment. For example, recordings of treatment can be made and rated to assure that the content of treatment is consistent with the goal of treatment and that the treatments being compared do not overlap too much. Client and therapist manuals for each form of treatment are useful aids for achieving treatment validity. It is more difficult to know what sources of help the clients receive outside of the program being evaluated. Those in the waiting-list or dropout group need to be contacted to see if they are receiving formal or informal sources of help elsewhere. It is also important to document other events in the clients' lives that may dramatically affect them, for example, criminal justice intervention or life stresses.

Researchers can also contribute a great deal by describing the processes of program implementation and the impediments encountered in implementation. Studies that analyze the treatment process are also needed. The treatment setting, therapists' traits, and particular mixtures of client characteristics may have strong effects on outcomes.

5. *What to Measure?*   An encouraging trend, at least for woman abuse, is to go beyond the measurement of physical abuse to measure psychological abuse and the consequences of violence such as physical injuries. A number of efforts are under way to develop measures of emotional abuse and injuries. The victim's ongoing senses of oppression and intimidation in the relationship are important aspects of treatment outcome, especially since several studies have found that treatment stopped short of changing the rates of psychological abuse (see Sec. III). For childhood sexual abuse, there is a convergence of findings on a variety of initial and long-term effects (Browne and Finkelhor 1986) that can point the evaluation researcher to key outcome variables. For physical child abuse, there is a long history of definitional problems, made less opaque by recently developed measures that have been used in nationally representative surveys (Gelles and Straus 1987). The more

we learn about behaviors incompatible with abuse, the more evaluators can focus on positive behaviors such as caretaking skills of parents and couples' communication abilities.

There is also a trend toward measurement of the motives and dynamics of the abusive relationship. When the identified victim has also been violent at some point, researchers need to ask whether violence is self-defense or "mutual" (Saunders 1986). They also need to investigate the relative power of each party. The implications for treatment differ greatly, depending on the answers to these questions.

C. Summary

"Half full and half empty" is the title of Daro's (1986) report on child maltreatment programs. The title implies that, while progress has been made in specifying the types of families that seem to respond to treatment, the recidivism rates during treatment are much higher than hoped for. The same can be said for evaluation results for other forms of family violence treatment. A "half-empty" view emphasizes the many cases of reabuse and a "half-full" view emphasizes that abuse ceased in at least some families and that progress is being made to identify what treatments are most effective with what types of clients. Unfortunately, in almost all studies we examined in preparing this essay, the decreases in the frequency, severity, or prevalence of violence cannot be attributed with any certainty to the treatment. Few interventions have been systematically evaluated, and those that have been evaluated usually measured change before and after treatment without the use of control or comparison groups. Unlike treatments for most human problems, two forces occur simultaneously with treatment for family violence that could explain the observed changes in many of the cases: legal sanctions are applied, the family is separated, or both. To the extent that violence is under the control of the abuser and that norms and beliefs are major factors, legal sanctions and separation may be the most active ingredients of change. This lack of control for extra-treatment conditions is just one of the methodological problems affecting treatment evaluations. Fortunately, better-controlled studies are beginning to appear (e.g., Azar and Twentyman 1984; Dutton 1986), and they provide hope that advances will be made toward discovering effective interventions.

Among the ethical and practical challenges confronting researchers are the problems of contacting clients and their family members for follow-up, the need for designs which approximate no-treatment control groups, and high attrition from treatment. None of these problems is easily resolved. It will take the close collaboration of researchers and service providers to find innovative solutions to the challenges posed by the need for sound evaluation. It is only through the increased sophistication of our evaluation efforts, however, that the suffering caused by family violence can be alleviated.

REFERENCES

Abel, Gene, J. Cunningham-Rathner, Judith V. Becker, and J. McHugh. 1983. "Motivating Sex Offenders for Treatment with Feedback of Their Psychophysiological Assessment." Paper presented at the World Congress of Behavior Therapy, Washington, D.C., December.

Aguirre, B. E. 1985. "Why Do They Return? Abused Wives in Shelters." *Social Work* 30:350–54.

Alcorn, Sandra S. 1985. "The Support Networks of Battered Women before and after Shelter Residents." Ph.D. dissertation, University of Illinois.

Allen, Craig, and Murray Straus. 1980. "Resources, Power, and Husband-Wife Violence." In *The Social Causes of Husband and Wife Violence*, edited by Gerald T. Hotaling. Minneapolis: University of Minnesota Press.

Ammerman, Robert T., Jeffrey E. Cassisi, Michael Hersen, and Vincent B. Van Hasselt. 1986. "Consequences of Physical Abuse and Neglect in Children." *Clinical Psychology Review* 6:291–310.

Arvanian, Ann L. 1975. "Dynamics of Separation and Placement." In *Child Abuse: Intervention and Treatment*, edited by Nancy B. Ebneling and Deborah A. Hill. Acton, Mass.: Publishing Science Group.

Attias, Reina, and Jean Goodwin. 1985. "Knowledge and Management Strategies in Incest Cases: A Survey of Physicians, Psychologists and Family Counselors." *Child Abuse and Neglect* 9:527–33.

Azar, Sandra T. 1986. "A Framework for Understanding Child Maltreatment: An Integration of Cognitive Behavioral and Developmental Perspectives." *Canadian Journal of Behavioral Science* 18(4):340–55.

Azar, Sandra T., and Craig T. Twentyman. 1984. "An Evaluation of the Effectiveness of Cognitive Behavioral versus Insight Oriented Mothers' Groups with Child Maltreatment Cases." Paper presented at the annual convention of the Association for the Advancement of Behavior Therapy, Philadelphia, November.

———. 1988. "Cognitive and Behavioral Approaches to the Treatment of Child Abuse." In *Behavioral Medicine*, edited by Craig T. Twentyman and L. Siegel. New York: Springer.

Azar, Sandra T., and David A. Wolfe. 1988. "Behavioral Treatment of Child Abuse." In *Behavioral Treatment of Childhood Disorder*, edited by Eric J. Mash and Russell A. Barkley. New York: Guilford.

Azrin, Nathan H., T. Flores, and S. J. Kaplan. 1975. "Job-finding Club: A Group Assisted Program for Obtaining Employment." *Behavior Research and Therapy* 13:17–27.

Ball, Patricia G., and Elizabeth Wyman. 1978. "Battered Wives and Powerlessness: What Can Counselors Do?" *Victimology* 2:545–54.

Bander, Karen, Edith Fein, and Gerrie Bishop. 1982. "Child Sexual Abuse Treatment: Some Barriers to Program Operation." *Child Abuse and Neglect* 6:185–91.

Barth, Richard P., Betty J. Blythe, Steven P. Schinke, and Robert Schilling. 1983. "Self-control Training with Maltreating Parents." *Child Welfare* 62:313–24.

Bass, Barry. 1973. "An Unusual Behavioral Technique for Treating Obsessive Ruminations." *Psychotherapy: Theory, Research, and Practice* 10:191–92.

Becker, William C. 1981. *Parents Are Teachers*. Champaign, Ill.: Research Press.

Berk, Richard, Phyllis J. Newton, and Sarah Fenstermaker-Berk. 1985. "What a Difference a Day Makes: An Empirical Study of the Impact of Shelters for Battered Women." Santa Barbara: University of California, Social Process Research Institute and Department of Sociology.

Berkeley Planning Associates. 1983. "Evaluation of the Clinical Demonstrations of the Treatment of Child Abuse and Neglect." Berkeley, Calif.: Berkeley Planning Associates.

Berlin, Fred, and Carl F. Meinecke. 1981. "Treatment of Sex Offenders with Antiandrogenic Medication: Conceptualization, Review of Treatment Modalities and Preliminary Findings." *American Journal of Psychiatry* 138:601–7.

Besharov, D. J. 1985. "An Overdose of Concern." *Regulation Magazine* (November–December), pp. 25–28.

Blythe, Betty J. 1983. "A Critique of Outcome Evaluation in Child Abuse Treatment." *Child Welfare* 62:325–35.

Bograd, Michele. 1984. "Family Systems Approaches to Wife Battering: A Feminist Critique." *American Journal of Orthopsychiatry* 54:558–68.

Bowker, Lee H. 1983. *Beating Wife-Beating*. Lexington, Mass.: Heath.

———. 1986. *Ending the Violence*. Holmes Beach, Fla.: Learning Publications.

Bowker, Lee H., and Lorie Maurer. 1985. "The Importance of Sheltering in the Lives of Battered Women." *Response* 8:2–8.

Browne, Angela, and David Finkelhor. 1986. "Impact of Child Sexual Abuse: A Review of the Research." *Psychological Bulletin* 99:66–77.

Campbell, Randy V., Shirley O'Brien, Alan D. Bickett, and John R. Lutzker. 1983. "In-Home Parent Training of Migraine Headaches and Marital Counseling as an Ecobehavioral Approach to Prevent Child Abuse." *Journal of Behavior Therapy and Experimental Psychiatry* 14:145–47.

Caplan, Paula J. 1985. *The Myth of Women's Masochism*. New York: New American Library.

Carmen, Elaine H., Patricia P. Rieker, and Trudy Mills. 1984. "Victims of Violence and Psychiatric Illness." *American Journal of Psychiatry* 141:378–83.

Carmody, Dianne C., and Kirk R. Williams. 1987. "Wife Assault and Perceptions of Sanctions." *Violence and Victims* 2:25–39.

Carter, Bryan D., Ruth Reed, and Ceil G. Reh. 1975. "Mental Health Nursing

Intervention with Child-Abusing and Neglecting Mothers." *Journal of Public Nursing and Mental Health Sciences* 13:11–15.

Caudill, Mary H., Beverly V. Cline, and R. M. Barber. 1985. "Job Readiness for Battered Women: One Shelter's Experience." *Response* 8:14–16.

Christiansen, Karl, Mimi Ellers-Nielsen, Louis LeMaine, and George Sturup. 1965. "Recidivism among Sex Offenders." *Scandinavian Studies in Criminology* 1:55–85.

Cicchinelli, Louis R., Robert A. Keller, and Debra M. Gardner. 1987. "Characteristics of Child Sexual Abuse Treatment Programs." Paper presented at the Third National Conference for Family Violence Researchers, University of New Hampshire, Durham, July.

Cohn, Ann. 1979. "Essential Elements of Successful Child Abuse and Neglect Treatment." *Child Abuse and Neglect* 3:491–96.

Cohn, Ann, and Deborah Daro. 1986. "Is Treatment Too Late? What Ten Years of Evaluative Research Tell Us." Chicago: National Committee for Prevention of Child Abuse.

Cohn, Ann H., and Beverly DeGraaf. 1982. "Assessing Case Management in the Child Abuse Field." *Journal of Social Service Research* 5:29–43.

Conger, Rand D., Benjamin B. Lahey, and Stevens Smith. 1981. "An Intervention Program for Child Abuse: Modifying Maternal Depression and Behavior." Paper presented at the First National Conference for Family Violence Researchers, University of New Hampshire, Durham, July.

Conte, Jon R. 1984. "Research on the Prevention of Sexual Abuse of Children." Paper presented at the Second National Conference for Family Violence Researchers, University of New Hampshire, Durham, July.

———. 1985. "Clinical Dimensions of Adult Sexual Abuse of Children." *Behavioral Sciences and the Law* 3(4):341–54.

Conte, Jon R., and Lucy Berliner. 1981. "Prosecution of the Offender in Cases of Sexual Assault against Children." *Victimology* 6:102–9.

Coombes, Phyllis, Maureen McCormack, Mary Chipley, and Beverly Archer. 1978. "The INCADEX Approach to Identifying Problems and Evaluating Impact in Child Protective Services." *Child Welfare* 57:35–44.

Crittendon, Patricia M. 1983. "The Effect of Mandatory Protective Day Care on Mutual Attachment in Maltreating Mother-Infant Dyads." *Child Abuse and Neglect* 7:297–300.

Crozier, Jill, and Roger C. Katz. 1979. "Social Learning Theory Treatment of Child Abuse." *Journal of Behavior Therapy and Research* 10:213–20.

Dalto, Carol Ann. 1983. "Battered Women: Factors Influencing Whether or Not Former Shelter Residents Return to the Abusive Situation." Ph.D. dissertation, University of Massachusetts, Department of Psychology.

Daro, Deborah. 1986. "Half Full and Half Empty: The Evaluation Results of Nineteen Clinical Research and Demonstration Projects." Summary of the nineteen clinical demonstration projects funded by the National Center on Child Abuse and Neglect, 1978–81. Berkeley: University of California, School of Social Welfare.

———. 1987. *Confronting Child Abuse: Research for Effective Program Design.* New York: Free Press.

DeMaris, Alfred, and Joan K. Jackson. 1987. "Batterers' Reports of Recidivism after Counseling." *Social Casework* 68:458–65.

Denicola, Joseph, and Jack Sandler. 1980. "Training Abusive Parents in Cognitive Behavioral Techniques." *Behavior Therapy* 2:263–70.

Deschner, Jeanne P. 1984. "The Results of Anger Control for Violent Couples." Paper presented at the Second National Conference for Family Violence Researchers, University of New Hampshire, Durham, July.

Dobash, R. Emerson, and Russell P. Dobash. 1979. *Violence against Wives: A Case against the Patriarchy.* New York: Free Press.

Douglas, Mary Ann, and Sean Perrin. 1987. "Recidivism and Accuracy of Self-reported Violence and Arrest." Paper presented at the Third National Conference for Family Violence Researchers, University of New Hampshire, Durham, July.

Dutton, Donald. 1986. "The Outcome of Court-mandated Treatment for Wife Assault: A Quasi-experimental Evaluation." *Violence and Victims* 1:163–76.

Eddy, Melissa J., and Toby Myers. 1984. "Helping Men Who Batter: A Profile of Programs in the U.S." Austin: Texas Department of Human Resources.

Edleson, Jeffrey L. 1985. "Violence Is the Issue: A Critique of Neidig's Assumptions." *Victimology* 9:483–89.

Edleson, Jeffrey L., David M. Miller, Gene W. Stone, and Dennis G. Chapman. 1985. "Group Treatment for Men Who Batter." *Social Work Research and Abstracts* 21:18–21.

Edleson, Jeffrey L., and Mary P. Brygger. 1988. "Gender Differences in Reporting of Battering Incidences." *Family Relations* (forthcoming).

Edleson, Jeffrey L., and Roger J. Grusznski. 1988. "Treating Men Who Batter: Four Years of Outcome Data from the Domestic Abuse Project." *Journal of Social Service Research* (forthcoming).

Egan, Kelly J. 1983. "Stress Management and Child Management with Abusive Parents." *Journal of Clinical Child Psychology* 12(3):292–99.

Emslie, Graham T., and Alvin A. Rosenfeld. 1983. "Incest Reported by Children and Adolescents Hospitalized for Severe Psychiatric Problems." *American Journal of Psychiatry* 140:708–11.

Faller, Kathleen C. 1985. "Unanticipated Problems in the United States Child Protection System." *Child Abuse and Neglect* 9:66–70.

Fanshel, David, and E. B. Shinn. 1978. *Dollars and Sense in the Foster Care of Children.* New York: Child Welfare League of America, Inc.

Fantuzzo, John, Lisa Jurecic, Alex Stovall, Dirk Hightower, Cynthia Goins, and Daniel Schachtel. 1988. "The Effects of Adult and Peer Social Initiations on the Social Behavior of Withdrawn Maltreated Preschool Children." *Journal of Consulting and Clinical Psychology* 56:34–39.

Feazell, Carann S., Raymond S. Mayers, and Jeanne Deschner. 1984. "Service for Men Who Batter: Implications for Programs and Policies." *Family Relations* 33:217–23.

Ferraro, Kathleen J. 1981. "Processing Battered Women." *Journal of Family Issues* 2(4):415–38.

Festinger, Trudy B. 1983. *No One Ever Asked Us: A Postscript to Foster Care.* New York: Columbia University Press.

Finkelhor, David. 1983a. "Common Features of Family Abuse." In *The Dark Side of Families*, edited by David Finkelhor and associates. Beverly Hills, Calif.: Sage.

——. 1983b. "Removing the Child—Prosecuting the Offender in Cases of Child Sexual Abuse." *Child Abuse and Neglect* 7:195–205.

——. 1984. *Child Sexual Abuse*. New York: Free Press.

——. 1986. *A Sourcebook on Child Sexual Abuse*. Beverly Hills, Calif.: Sage.

——. 1987. "The Trauma of Child Sexual Abuse: Two Models." *Journal of Interpersonal Violence* 2:348–66.

Finkelhor, David, Beverly Gomes-Schwartz, and Jonathan Horowitz. 1984. "Professionals' Responses." In *Child Sexual Abuse: New Theory and Research*, edited by David Finkelhor. New York: Free Press.

Follingstad, Diane R. 1980. "A Reconceptualization of Issues in the Treatment of Abused Women: A Case Study." *Psychotherapy: Theory, Research and Practice* 17:294–303.

Forseth, Laura B., and Art Brown. 1981. "A Survey of Intrafamilial Sexual Abuse Treatment Centers: Implications for Interventions." *Child Abuse and Neglect* 5:177–86.

Foy, David W., Richard M. Eisler, and Susan Pinkston. 1975. "Modeled Assertion in a Case of Explosive Rage." *Journal of Behavior Therapy and Experimental Psychiatry* 6:135–37.

Frisbie, Louise V., and Ernest H. Dondis. 1965. *Recidivism among Treated Sex Offenders*. Research Monograph no. 5. Sacramento: California Department of Mental Hygiene.

Gambrill, Eileen D. 1983. "Behavioral Interventions with Child Abuse and Neglect." In *Progress in Behavior Modification*, edited by Michel Hersen, Richard M. Eisler, and Peter M. Miller. New York: Academic.

Ganley, Anne. 1981. *Court-Mandated Counseling for Men Who Batter: A Three-Day Workshop*. Washington, D.C.: Center for Women's Policy Studies.

Ganley, Anne, and Lance Harris. 1978. "Domestic Violence: Issues in Designing and Implementing Programs for Male Batterers." Paper presented to the 86th annual convention of the American Psychological Association, Toronto, August.

Gaquin, Diedre A. 1978. "Spouse Abuse: Data from the National Crime Survey." *Victimology* 2:632–43.

Geiser, Robert L. 1973. *The Illusion of Caring: Children in Foster Care*. Boston: Beacon.

Geller, Janet A. 1982. "Conjoint Therapy: Staff Training and Treatment of the Abuser and the Abused." In *The Abusive Partner: An Analysis of Domestic Battering*, edited by M. Roy. New York: Van Nostrand.

Gelles, Richard J. 1975. "The Social Construction of Child Abuse." *American Journal of Orthopsychiatry* 45:363–71.

——. 1984. "Applying Our Knowledge of Family Violence to Prevention and Treatment: What Difference Might It Make?" Paper presented to the Second National Conference for Family Violence Researchers, University of New Hampshire, Durham, July.

Gelles, Richard J., and Murray A. Straus. 1987. "Is Violence toward Children

Increasing? A Comparison of 1975 and 1985 National Survey Rates." *Journal of Interpersonal Violence* 2:212–22.

Giarretto, Henry. 1978. "Humanistic Treatment of Father-Daughter Incest." *Journal of Humanistic Psychology* 18:59–76.

———. 1982. "A Comprehensive Child Sexual Abuse Treatment Program." *Child Abuse and Neglect* 6:263–78.

Gilman, Irene S. 1980. "An Object-Relations Approach to the Phenomenon and Treatment of Battered Women." *Psychiatry* 43:346–58.

Goffman, Jerome M. 1980. *Batterers Anonymous: Mutual Support Counseling for Woman-Batterers.* Redlands, Calif.: Coalition for the Prevention of Abuse of Women and Children.

———. 1984. *Batterers Anonymous: Self-Help Counseling for Men Who Batter Women.* San Bernardino, Calif.: Batterers Anonymous.

Gondolf, Edward W. 1984. *Men Who Batter: An Integrated Approach to Stopping Wife Abuse.* Holmes Beach, Fla.: Learning Publications.

———. 1985. "Anger and Oppression in Men Who Batter." *Victimology* 10:311–24.

Grayson, Joan. 1985. "After Shelter What? Service Evaluation and Follow-up of Abused Women." Harrisonburg, Va.: James Madison University, Department of Psychology.

Green, Arthur. 1975. "Psychiatric Treatment of Abused Children." *Journal of the American Academy of Child Psychiatry* 17:356–71.

———. 1983. "Child Abuse: Dimension of Psychological Trauma in Abused Children." *Journal of the American Academy of Child Psychiatry* 22:231–37.

Hamberger, L. Kevin, and James H. Hastings. 1986. "Skills Training for Treatment of Spouse Abusers: An Outcome Study." Paper presented at the annual meeting of the American Psychological Association, Washington, D.C., August.

Hayman-Rhiannon, Nancy. 1984. "A Psychoeducational Approach to Job Readiness and Depression in Battered Women." Ph.D. dissertation, University of Oregon, Division of Counseling and Educational Psychology.

Herman, Judith. 1981. *Father-Daughter Incest.* Cambridge: Harvard University Press.

Hilberman, Elaine, and Kit Munson. 1978. "Sixty Battered Women." *Victimology* 2:460–70.

Hochstadt, Neil J., and Neil J. Harwicke. 1985. "How Effective Is the Multidisciplinary Approach? A Follow-up Study." *Child Abuse and Neglect* 9:365–72.

Hoffman-Plotkin, Deborah, and Craig T. Twentyman. 1984. "A Multimodal Assessment of Behavioral and Cognitive Deficits in Abused and Neglected Preschoolers." *Child Development* 55:794–802.

Hotaling, Gerald T., and David B. Sugarman. 1986. "An Analysis of Risk Markers in Husband to Wife Violence: The Current State of Knowledge." *Violence and Victims* 1:101–24.

Jaffe, Peter, David A. Wolfe, Anne Telford, and Gary Austin. 1986. "The Impact of Police Charges in Incidents of Wife Abuse." *Journal of Family Violence* 1:37–50.

Jansen, Mary A., and Judith Meyers-Abell. 1981. "Assertive Training for Battered Women: A Pilot Program." *Social Work* 26:164–65.

Jennings, Jerry L. 1987. "History and Issues in the Treatment of Battering Men: A Case for Unstructured Group Therapy." *Journal of Family Violence* 2:193–213.

Johnson, John M. 1981. "New Research in Family Violence." *Journal of Family Issues* 2(4):387–90.

Jones, David P. H., and J. Melborne McGraw. 1987. "Reliable and Fictitious Accounts of Sexual Abuse of Children." *Journal of Interpersonal Violence* 2:27–45.

Justice, Blair, and Rita Justice. 1978. "Evaluating Outcome of Group Therapy for Abusing Parents." *Corrective and Social Psychiatry and Journal of Behavioral Technology* 24:45–49.

Kelley, Robert J. 1982. "Behavioral Re-orientation of Pedophiliacs: Can It Be Done?" *Clinical Psychology Review* 2:387–408.

Kelso, Dennis, and Lyle Personette. 1985. *Domestic Violence and Treatment Services for Victims and Abusers.* Anchorage, Alaska: Altam Association.

Koverola, Cathy, Darlene Elliot-Faust, and David A. Wolfe. 1984. "Clinical Issues in the Behavioral Treatment of a Child-Abusive Mother Experiencing Multiple Life Stresses." *Journal of Clinical Child Psychology* 13:187–91.

Kremen, Eleanor. 1984. "Battered Women in Counseling and Shelter Programs: A Descriptive and Follow-up Study." Ph.D dissertation, Columbia University, School of Social Work.

Kroth, Jerome A. 1979. "Family Therapy Impact on Intrafamilial Child Sexual Abuse." *Child Abuse and Neglect* 3:297–302.

Lamphear, Vivian Shaw. 1985. "The Impact of Maltreatment on Children's Psychosocial Adjustment: A Review of the Research." *Child Abuse and Neglect* 9:251–64.

Laws, D. R., and J. A. O'Neil. 1979. "Variations on Masturbatory Conditioning." Paper presented at the Second National Conference on Evaluation and Treatment of Sexual Aggressives, New York.

Lerman, Lisa G. 1981. "Criminal Prosecution of Wife Beaters." *Response* 4:1–19.

Lerman, Lisa G, and Francis Livingston. 1983. "State Legislation on Domestic Violence." *Response* 6:1–28.

Loseke, Donileen R., and Sarah F. Berk. 1983. "The Work of Shelters: Battered Women and Initial Calls for Help." *Victimology* 7:35–48.

Lund, Sander H., Nancy E. Larsen, and Susan K. Schultz. 1982. "Exploratory Evaluation of the Domestic Abuse Project." Unpublished. Minneapolis, Program Evaluation Resource Center.

Lutzker, John R., and James M. Rice. 1984. "Project 12-Ways: Measuring Outcome of a Large In-Home Service for Treatment and Prevention of Child Abuse and Neglect." *Child Abuse and Neglect* 8:519–24.

———. 1987. "Using Recidivism Data to Evaluate Project 12-Ways: An Ecobehavioral Approach to the Treatment and Prevention of Child Abuse and Neglect." *Journal of Family Violence* 2(4):283–90.

Maas, Henry S., and Richard Engler. 1959. *Children in Need of Parents.* New York: Columbia University Press.

MacFarlane, Kee, and Josephine Bulkley. 1982. "Treating Child Sexual Abuse: An Overview of Current Program Models." In *Social Work and Child Sexual Abuse*, edited by Jon R. Conte and D. Shore. New York: Haworth.

Maiuro, Roland D., Timothy S. Cahn, Peter P. Vitaliano, and Joan B. Zegree. 1987. "Treatment for Domestically Violent Men: Outcome and Follow-up Data." Paper presented at the 95th annual convention of the American Psychological Association, New York, August.

Mann, Eberhard, and John F. McDermott, Jr. 1983. "Play Therapy for Victims of Child Abuse and Neglect." In *Handbook of Play Therapy*, edited by Charles E. Schaerfer and Kevin J. O'Connor. New York: Wiley.

Margolin, Gayla, and Vivian Fernandez. 1987. "The 'Spontaneous' Cessation of Marital Violence: Three Case Examples." *Journal of Marital and Family Therapy* 13:241–50.

Martin, Del. 1976. *Battered Wives*. San Francisco: Glide.

Martin, Harold P. 1976. *The Abused Child: A Multidisciplinary Approach to Developmental Issues and Treatment*. Cambridge, Mass.: Ballinger.

Mascia, Cynthia. 1983. "A Study of the Treatment of Battered Women in Emergency Room Settings." Ph.D. dissertation, Kent State University, Department of General Psychology.

Meddin, Barbara J., and Ingrid Hansen. 1985. "The Services Provided during a Child Abuse and/or Neglect Case Investigation and the Barriers that Exist to Service Provision." *Child Abuse and Neglect* 9:175–82.

Miller, Dorothy, and George Challas. 1981. "Abused Children as Adult Parents: A Twenty-five Year Longitudinal Study." Paper presented at the First National Conference for Family Violence Researchers, University of New Hampshire, Durham, July.

Myers, Cheryl. 1984. "The Family Violence Project: Some Preliminary Data on a Treatment Program for Spouse Abuse." Paper presented at the Second National Conference for Family Violence Researchers, University of New Hampshire, Durham, July.

National Center on Child Abuse and Neglect. 1981. *Study Findings: National Study of Incidence and Severity of Child Abuse and Neglect*. Washington, D.C.: Department of Health, Education, and Welfare.

Neidig, Peter H. 1984. "Women's Shelters, Men's Collectives, and Other Factors in the Field of Spouse Abuse." *Victimology* 9:464–76.

———. 1986. "The Development and Evaluation of a Spouse Abuse Treatment Program in a Military Setting." *Evaluation and Program Planning* 9:275–80.

Neidig, Peter H., and D. H. Friedman. 1984. *Spouse Abuse: A Treatment Program for Couples*. Champaign, Ill.: Research Press.

Newberger, Eli H., and Carolyn M. Newberger. 1981. "A Clinical View of Research Needs on Child Abuse." Paper presented at the First National Conference for Family Violence Researchers, University of New Hampshire, Durham, July.

Nomellini, Sharlyne, and Roger C. Katz. 1983. "Effects of Anger Control Training on Abusive Parents." *Cognitive Therapy and Research* 7:57–68.

Novack, Steve, and Burt Galaway. 1982. "Domestic Abuse Intervention Project: Six Month Research Report." Duluth, Minn.: Domestic Abuse Intervention Project.

Novaco, Raymond W. 1975. *Anger Control: The Development and Evaluation of an Experimental Treatment*. Lexington, Mass.: Lexington.

O'Leary, K. Daniel, and Alison Curley. 1984. "Correlates of Spouse Abuse." State University of New York at Stony Brook, Department of Psychology.

O'Leary, K. Daniel, Alison Curley, Alan Rosenbaum, and Chris Clarke. 1985. "Assertion Training for Abused Wives: A Potentially Hazardous Treatment." *Journal of Marriage and Family Therapy* 11:319–22.

O'Toole, Richard, J. Patrick Turbett, John Sargent, and Anita W. O'Toole. 1987. "Recognizing and Reacting to Child Abuse: Physicians, Nurses, Teachers, Social Workers, Law Enforcement Officers, and Community Respondents." Paper presented at the Third National Conference for Family Violence Researchers, University of New Hampshire, Durham, July.

Pagelow, Mildred Daley. 1984. *Family Violence*. New York: Praeger.

Pahl, Jan. 1985. "Refuges for Battered Women: Ideology and Action." *Feminist Review* 19:25–43.

Parish, Ruth A., Patricia A. Myers, Ann Brandner, and Kathie H. Templin. 1985. "Developmental Milestones in Abused Children, and Their Improvement with a Family-oriented Approach to the Treatment of Child Abuse." *Child Abuse and Neglect* 9:245–50.

Patterson, Gerald R. 1971. *Families: Application of Social Learning Theory to Family Life*. Champaign, Ill.: Research Press.

Paulson, Morris J., and Anne Chaleff. 1973. "Parent Surrogate Roles: A Dynamic Concept in Understanding and Treating Abusive Parents." *Journal of Clinical Child Psychology* 2:38–40.

Pence, Ellen. 1984. "Domestic Abuse Intervention Project: Toward a Coordinated Community Response to Domestic Abuse." *Hamlin Law Review* 6:247–75.

Pierce, Robert L. 1985. "Analysis of Sexual Abuse Hotline Reports." *Child Abuse and Neglect* 9:37–45.

Pike, E. L. 1973. "C.A.L.M.: A Timely Experiment in the Prevention of Child Abuse." *Journal of Clinical Child Psychology* 2:43–45.

Pirog-Good, Maureen A., and Jan Stets-Kealey. 1986. "Recidivism in Programs for Abusers." *Victimology* 11 (forthcoming).

Roberts, Albert R., ed. 1984*a*. *Battered Women and Their Families*. New York: Springer.

———. 1984*b*. "Crisis Intervention with Battered Women." In *Battered Women and Their Families*, edited by A. R. Roberts. New York: Springer.

Rosenbaum, Alan, and K. Daniel O'Leary. 1981. "Children: The Unintended Victims of Marital Violence." *American Journal of Orthopsychiatry* 51:692–99.

Rounsaville, Bruce, Norman Lifton, and Margo Bieber. 1979. "The Natural History of a Psychotherapy Group for Battered Women." *Psychiatry* 42:63–77.

Runyan, Desmond K., Mark D. Everson, Gail A. Edelsohn, Wanda M. Hunter, and Martha L. Coulter. 1987. "Impact of Intervention on Sexually Abused Children." Paper presented at the Third National Conference for

Family Violence Researchers, University of New Hampshire, Durham, July.

Runyan, Desmond K., and Carolyn L. Gould. 1985. "Foster Care for Child Maltreatment: Impact on Delinquent Behavior." *Pediatrics* 75(3):562–68.

Runyan, Desmond K., Carolyn L. Gould, D. C. Trost, and Frank A. Loda. 1982. "Determinants of Foster Care Placement for the Maltreated Child." *Child Abuse and Neglect* 6:343–50.

Sandberg, Genell, Patricia Petretic-Jackson, and Thomas Jackson. 1986. "Physicians' Practices in Child Physical Abuse." *Response* 9:6–8.

Sanders, R. Wyman. 1978. "Systematic Desensitization in the Treatment of Child Abuse." *American Journal of Psychiatry* 135:483–84.

Sandler, Jack, Candy VanDercar, and Mariann Milhoan. 1978. "Training Child Abusers in the Use of Positive Reinforcement Practices." *Behavior Research and Therapy* 16:169–75.

Sanford, D. A., and R. D. Tustin. 1974. "Behavioral Treatment of Parental Assault on a Child." *New Zealand Psychologist* 2:76–82.

Saunders, Daniel G. 1977. "Marital Violence: Dimensions of the Problem and Modes of Intervention." *Journal of Marriage and Family Counseling* 3:43–52.

———. 1981. "Treatment and Value Issues in Helping Battered Women." In *Questions and Answers in the Practice of Family Therapy*, edited by Alan Gurman. New York: Brunner/Mazel.

———. 1984*a*. "Helping Husbands Who Batter: Teaching Alternatives to Aggression in a Group." *Social Casework* 65:347–56.

———. 1984*b*. "Issues in Conducting Treatment Research with Men Who Batter." Paper presented at the Second National Conference for Family Violence Researchers, University of New Hampshire, Durham, July.

———. 1986. "When Battered Women Use Violence: Husband Abuse or Self-Defense?" *Violence and Victims* 1:47–60.

———. 1988. "What Do We Know about Abuser Recidivism? A Critique of 'Recidivism in Abuser Programs.' " *Victimology* (forthcoming).

Saunders, Daniel G., and Darald Hanusa. 1986. "Cognitive-Behavioral Treatment for Men Who Batter: The Short-Term Effects of Group Therapy." *Journal of Family Violence* 1(4):357–72.

Saunders, Daniel G., Ann E. Lynch, Marcia Grayson, and Daniel Linz. 1987. "The Inventory of Beliefs about Wife-Beating: The Construction and Initial Validation of a Measure of Beliefs and Attitudes." *Violence and Victims* 2:39–57.

Saunders, Daniel G., and Patricia B. Size. 1980. "Marital Violence and the Police." Madison: Wisconsin Council on Criminal Justice.

Schor, Edward L. 1982. "The Foster Care System and Health Status of Foster Children." *Pediatrics* 69(5):521–28.

Schulman, M. 1979. *A Survey of Spousal Violence against Women in Kentucky*. New York: Louis Harris.

Segal, Uma A., and Sanford Schwartz. 1985. "Factors Affecting Placement Decisions of Children Following Short-Term Emergency Care." *Child Abuse and Neglect* 9:543–48.

Sgroi, Suzanne M. 1982. *Handbook of Clinical Intervention in Child Sexual Abuse.* Lexington, Mass.: Heath.

Shainess, Natalie. 1979. "Vulnerability to Violence: Masochism as Process." *American Journal of Psychotherapy* 33:174–89.

Shepard, Melanie. 1987. "Intervention with Men Who Batter: An Evaluation of a Domestic Abuse Program." Paper presented at the Third National Conference for Family Violence Researchers, University of New Hampshire, Durham, July.

Shields, Nancy M., and Christine R. Hanneke. 1984. "Multiple Sexual Victimization: The Case of Incest and Marital Rape." Paper presented at the Second National Conference for Family Violence Researchers, University of New Hampshire, Durham, July.

Shorkey, Clayton T. 1979. "A Review of Methods Used in the Treatment of Abusing Parents." In *Patterns of Family Violence*, edited by Margaret Elbow. New York: Family Service Association.

Sink, Frances. 1988. "A Hierarchical Model for Evaluation of Child Sexual Abuse." *American Journal of Evaluation of Orthopsychiatry* 58:129–35.

Smith, Jane E., S. J. Rachman, and Bridget Yule. 1984. "Non-accidental Injury to Children—III: Methodological Problems of Evaluative Treatment Research." *Behavior Research and Therapy* 22:367–83.

Snell, John E., Richard J. Rosenwald, and Ames Robey. 1964. "The Wifebeater's Wife." *Archives of General Psychiatry* 11:107–12.

Snyder, Douglas K., and Nancy S. Scheer. 1981. "Predicting Disposition Following Brief Residence at a Shelter for Battered Women." *Journal of Community Psychology* 9:559–66.

Snyder, Jane C., and Eli H. Newberger. 1986. "Consensus and Difference among Hospital Professionals in Evaluating Child Maltreatment." *Violence and Victims* 1:125–39.

Sonkin, Daniel, Del Martin, and Lenore Walker, eds. 1985. *The Male Batterer: A Treatment Approach.* New York: Springer.

Stacey, William A., and Anson Shupe. 1984. *The Family Secret: Family Violence in America.* Boston: Beacon.

Stark, Evan, Anne Flitcraft, and William Frazier. 1979. "Medicine and Patriarchal Violence: The Social Construction of a 'Private' Event." *International Journal of Health Services* 9:461–93.

Strain, Phillip S. 1981. *The Utilization of Classroom Peers as Behavior Change Agents.* New York: Plenum.

Straus, Murray A., and Richard J. Gelles. 1986. "Societal Change and Change in Family Violence from 1975 to 1985 as Revealed by Two National Surveys." *Journal of Marriage and the Family* 48:465–79.

Straus, Murray A., Richard J. Gelles, and Susan K. Steinmetz. 1980. *Behind Closed Doors: Violence in the American Family.* New York: Doubleday/Anchor.

Strube, Michael J., and Linda S. Barbour. 1983. "The Decision to Leave an Abusive Relationship: Economic Dependence and Psychological Commitment." *Journal of Marriage and the Family* 43:623–31.

Symonds, Alexandra. 1979. "Violence against Women—the Myth of Masochism." *American Journal of Psychotherapy* 3:161–73.

Szykula, Steven A., and Matthew J. Fleischman. 1985. "Reducing Out-of-Home Placements of Abused Children: Two Controlled Field Studies." *Child Abuse and Neglect* 9:277–83.

Thyfault, Roberta. 1980. "Childhood Sexual Abuse, Marital Rape, and Battered Women: Implications for Mental Health Workers." Paper presented at the Colorado Mental Health Conference, Keystone, October.

Tolman, Richard M., Sandra Beeman, and Christine Mendoza. 1987. "The Effectiveness of a Shelter-sponsored Program for Men Who Batter: Preliminary Results." Paper presented at the Third National Conference for Family Violence Researchers, University of New Hampshire, Durham, July.

Tracy, Frank, Henry Donnelly, Leonard Morgenbesser, and Donald Macdonald. 1983. "Program Evaluation: Recidivism Research Involving Sex Offenders." In *The Sexual Aggressor: Current Perspectives on Treatment*, edited by Joanne Greer and Irving Stuart. New York: Van Nostrand.

Truesdell, Donna L., John S. McNeil, and Jeanne P. Deschner. 1986. "Incidence of Wife Abuse in Incestuous Families." *Social Work* 31:138–40.

Tufts New England Medical Center, Division of Child Psychiatry. 1984. *Sexually Exploited Children: Service and Research Project.* Final report to the Office of Juvenile Justice and Delinquency Prevention, U.S. Department of Justice, Washington, D.C.

Turbett, Patrick J. 1979. "Intervention Strategies and Conceptions of Child Abuse." *Children and Youth Services Review* 1:205–13.

Turbett, Patrick J., and Richard O'Toole. 1980. "Physicians' Recognition of Child Abuse." Paper presented at the annual meeting of the American Sociological Association, New York, August.

Wald, Michael A. 1976. "Legal Policies Affecting Children: A Lawyer's Request for Aid." *Child Development* 47(1):1–5.

Walker, Lenore E. 1979. *The Battered Woman.* New York: Harper & Row.

———. 1984. *The Battered Woman Syndrome.* New York: Springer.

Washburn, Carol, and Irene H. Frieze. 1981. "Methodological Issues in Studying Battered Women." Paper presented at the First National Conference for Family Violence Researchers, University of New Hampshire, Durham, July.

Weingourt, Rita. 1985. "Never to Be Alone: Existential Therapy with Battered Women." *Journal of Psychosocial Nursing* 23(3):24–29.

Weis, Joseph. In this volume. "Family Violence Research Methodology and Design."

Willen, Mildred L. 1984. "Parents Anonymous: The Professional's Role." In *The Self-Help Revolution*, edited by Alan Gardner and Frank Riessman. New York: Human Sciences.

Williams, Gertrude J. 1983. "Child Abuse Reconsidered: The Urgency of Authentic Prevention." *Journal of Clinical Child Psychology* 12(3):312–19.

Wolfe, David A. 1985. "Child-abusive Parents: An Empirical Review and Analysis." *Psychological Bulletin* 97:462–82.

Wolfe, David A., John A. Aragona, Keith Kaufman, and Jack Sandler. 1980. "The Importance of Adjudication in the Treatment of Child Abuse: Some Preliminary Findings." *Child Abuse and Neglect* 4:127–35.

Wolfe, David A., and Jack Sandler. 1981. "Training Abusive Parents in Effective Child Management." *Behavior Modification* 5:135–48.

Wolfe, David A., Jack Sandler, and Keith Kaufman. 1981. "A Competency-based Parent Training Program for Child Abusers." *Journal of Consulting and Clinical Psychology* 49:633–40.

Wolfe, David A., Janet St. Lawrence, Kenneth Graves, Kathleen Brehony, Drew Bradlyn, and Jeffrey A. Kelly. 1982. "Intensive Behavioral Parent Training for a Child-abusive Mother." *Behavior Therapy* 13:438–51.

Franklin E. Zimring

Toward a Jurisprudence of Family Violence

ABSTRACT

Modern law reform developments have focused increased attention on the jurisprudence of family violence. State intervention in ongoing family relations has been generally constrained by concern for family privacy except when the taking of life, parental incest, or the imminent threat to life or health of a minor child was involved. There are three basic enforcement strategies for dealing with family violence— privatization, contingent intervention, and compulsory intervention— and they represent a continuum of responses to suppress violence among intimates. Privatization is essentially a separation from the formal legal system, contingent intervention makes legal responses available only after the victim has taken action, and compulsory intervention involves full enforcement of the criminal law. Participants in the social and political movement calling for criminalization of family violence would use criminal law powers to regulate family violence by preferring criminal law over other alternatives to deal with family violence, using general crime categories to punish violence within the family as severely as the same acts outside of families, using severe sanctions as instruments of moral education, and reviving interest in the significance of relationships between victim and offender in defining and grading violent offenses.

If privacy has any physical locale in modern society, it is in the home, properly renowned as a haven in the heartless world. If privacy has any social focus, it is in the family, within a set of intimate relationships that can flourish only when sufficiently protected from public scrutiny.

Franklin E. Zimring is professor of law and director of the Earl Warren Legal Institute, University of California at Berkeley.

But privacy can metastasize into a Hobbesian arena where the strong prey on the weak, and the weak prey on those who are weaker still. Life's greatest moments occur behind closed doors. So, too, do some of modern life's most outrageous exploitations.

A jurisprudence of family violence needs to confront the question of the proper public aspects of private life. A coherent policy toward family violence depends on balancing the public value of privacy in family life against the social costs of exploitation and violence in unregulated family relations. In the political and social climate of the 1980s, this task is difficult and complicated.

Family violence is a chronic aspect of American life, but public concern about societal responses to this problem has been unprecedented and acute in the past decade. Violence between spouses and intimates existed before history was written, and little evidence suggests that the incidence or severity of intimate violence is more pronounced in the second half of the twentieth century than it was in earlier eras (Zimring, Mukherjee, and Van Winkle 1983). Yet violence between intimates is a more salient public policy issue in the 1980s than ever before. There is a similar trend toward increased social awareness in regard to the related topics of child abuse and sexual exploitation of children. For example, although incest has a biblical pedigree, it has become the focus of public policy debate only recently. What is called "parental kidnapping" is behavior as old as family dissolution, yet it has become an important legislative concern only in the 1970s and 1980s.

The historical forces elevating public concern about family violence are beyond the scope of this essay. The vindication of minority political and civil rights in the 1960s, increased intellectual and political concentration on questions of gender in the 1970s and 1980s, and the current rethinking of role dependencies and their social implications have all contributed to a political condition in which family exploitation issues are important and policy innovations are quite frequent.

One consequence of increased public concern is legal change. No short list can give credit to the manifold legal changes relating to family violence. Among the more important changes of the last fifteen years are the rapid development of child abuse reporting laws in the states, the creation of shelters for battered spouses, the abrogation of marital status as a defense to forcible rape charges, legal recognition of the battered child syndrome, and debates about expansion of the law of justification in self-defense to include the "battered spouse syndrome."

I do not attempt to catalog in these pages the specific changes in the law of family violence over the past fifteen years. Instead, I focus on one consequence of this new salience: in an era when almost all aspects of legal policy toward family violence are being reevaluated, the basic legal conception of violent activities within the confines of family life—the jurisprudence of family violence, if you will—is particularly important.

This essay attempts to lay a groundwork of basic classifications in order to build toward a coherent legal perspective on family violence as a set of legal problems. Section I sets out what I call the doctrine of family privacy with respect to legal interventions concerning violent acts. Section II presents a range of alternative government responses to family violence and the legal theories that these responses imply. Section III offers reflections on the role of the criminal sanction in response to family violence. Conclusions are offered in Section IV.

I. On Family Privacy

Formulating a family violence policy requires considering family privacy both as a set of legal principles and as a rationale that lies behind much current official behavior. The disputes that involve courts in discussions of family privacy often seem far removed from the control of interpersonal violence but are relevant nonetheless. *McGuire v. McGuire*, 157 Neb. 226, 59 N.W. 2d 336 (1953), a leading case of family privacy doctrine, illustrates the seeming contradictions within the law that result when courts confront the family context, including family violence.

Mrs. McGuire, then sixty-six, sued her seventy-nine-year-old husband in Nebraska to enforce a marital duty to support her that had existed for more than thirty years of their marriage. Her complaint alleged: "For the past four years or more the defendant had not given the plaintiff money to purchase furniture, or other household necessities . . . the house is not equipped with a bathroom, bathing facilities, or inside toilet. . . . [The plaintiff] does not have a kitchen sink" (pp. 228–29).

Mr. McGuire's lapses in generosity were not occasioned by poverty; he was the 1950s equivalent of a 1980s millionaire, with substantial landholdings and cash. Nor was there any doubt that Nebraska law imposed on Mr. McGuire the duty to support his wife.

Yet, the Nebraska court rejected Mrs. McGuire's pleas for indoor plumbing and a kitchen sink. The fatal flaw in her case was that the parties continued to live as husband and wife. The reason this disqualified her claim for support was the doctrine of family privacy: "The living standards of the family are a matter of concern to the household, and not for the courts to determine, even though the husband's attitude toward the wife, according to his wealth and circumstances, leaves little to be said on his behalf" (p. 238). The court emphasized that if Mrs. McGuire were to leave the home, she would be entitled to support from her husband in a style "corresponding to the circumstances and condition" of his financial means. However, while the parties were living together, the wife had either a right without a remedy or no right at all.

The justification for applying the family privacy doctrine in this fashion is the reluctance of government to intrude in the affairs of an ongoing family and to substitute regulatory edicts for family interaction, even if the power relationship within the family leads to regrettable outcomes. As in so many other situations involving the family privacy doctrine, the use of this principle to prevent relief in the *McGuire* case is contingent. If Mrs. McGuire dissolved the marriage relationship, she could sue for support, and no legal concept of marital privacy would stand between her and a flush toilet or any other suitable comfort of life. But the ongoing family presents a higher value than state-imposed concepts of financial equity in family relationships.

Does this doctrine extend to situations of violence within the family? The following excerpt from a 1973 article on parenthood training suggests an affirmative answer.

> A mother and daughter enter a supermarket. An accident occurs when the daughter pulls the wrong orange from the pile and thirty-seven oranges are given their freedom. The mother grabs the daughter, shakes her vigorously, and slaps her. What is your reaction? Do you ignore the incident? Do you consider it a family squabble and none of your business? Or do you go over and advise the mother not to hit her child? If the mother rejects your advice, do you physically restrain her? If she persists, do you call the police? Think about your answers for a moment. Now let me change one detail. *The girl was not that mother's daughter.* [McIntire 1973, pp. 34–36]

Whatever the private citizen's view, as a legal matter it makes all the difference in the world whether we classify this occurrence as a family matter. If the adult were a stranger, it would be considered assault and battery.

As with Mrs. McGuire's illusory right to indoor plumbing in her ongoing marriage, it is difficult to decide whether the parent-child relationship insulates an otherwise minor battery from legal scrutiny because the parent has a "right" to discipline her child (and the child therefore has no "right" to be secure against such discipline), or whether an existing right to be secure against physical battery has merely been subordinated to the values of nonintrusion in the ongoing family. But considerations similar to the doctrine of family privacy in *McGuire* insulate family members from legal responsibility for many unconsented roughings by siblings, parents, and spouses,[1] ranging from physical discipline to minor fights to forcible restraint. Further, the spirit of the family privacy doctrine has led to traditional policies of nonintrusion by law enforcement personnel, juvenile and family courts, and other public agencies when confronting physical interactions within family settings that are far worse then "unconsented touchings" (Clark 1968, p. 257; Areen 1985, pp. 1181–1215).

While notions of husband supremacy and the view of children as chattels are declining, family privacy plays a significant role in many modern reform efforts. The transition from matrimonial offenses as grounds for divorce to neutral standards, such as incompatibility, and finally to no-fault divorce was largely justified by the extensive intrusion on family privacy caused by airing a couple's dirty laundry in open court as the price of matrimonial dissolution (Areen 1985, pp. 267–81). One target of this reform was the notorious "two slap" rule that required public testimony that one spouse had hit the other twice; this was the minimum condition for an Illinois divorce for many years.[2] The movement toward abolition of interspousal tort immunity is best viewed not as a rejection of the family privacy doctrine but as a recognition that such immunity did not serve families well in an era of widespread third-party liability insurance. The decline of immunity does not encourage conflict within family units but instead often makes resources from insurance companies available to families; if one spouse is held liable, homeowners' or car insurance pays for the other spouse's injuries (Clark 1968, p. 253; Prosser 1971, § 122, p. 868; McKinney's

[1] See Thompson v. Thompson, 218 U.S. 611, 618 (1910); Bruno v. Codd, 47 N.Y.2d 582, 393 N.E.2d 976, 419 N.Y.S.2d 901 (1979); Clark (1968, pp. 252–153 [spouses]), 256–25 [parents]; Prosser (1971).

[2] Fritts v. Fritts, 138 Ill. 436, 28 N.E. 1058, 14 L.R.A. 685 (1891); Tuyls v. Tuyls, 21 Ill. 2d 192, 171 N.E. 779 (1961).

Domestic Relations Law [New York], 57; McKinney's Insurance Law [New York], 167[3]).

In the area of child protection policy, family privacy considerations are important in modern reform efforts, but the balance between privacy and public scrutiny varies with the context. The law of child neglect has evolved over the past two decades, requiring greater justification to support state intervention in the ongoing family (Areen 1975; Wald 1976). When the focus shifts from child neglect to child abuse, however, the value accorded family privacy seems to diminish. Child abuse reporting laws, which require individuals to report possible physical mistreatment of minors to state authorities, are the most notable example of recent reforms that give little value to adult autonomy or family privacy. The inconsistent emphasis on values of family privacy, if child neglect is compared to child abuse, is one rather stunning illustration of the current confusion surrounding the aims of and means in child welfare legislation.[3]

In other family violence areas, most notably spousal violence and parental kidnapping, modern reform efforts that increase law enforcement and court presence subordinate family privacy considerations to the public interest in suppressing and responding to the target behavior.[4]

It is important to note, not just as a technical matter, that doctrines of family privacy always apply when the law addresses the relations among members of an ongoing family. The consequences of family privacy doctrine vary, but not its application. Across the range of behaviors to be balanced against privacy, the legal responses that arise when different behaviors are balanced against privacy can be grouped under three headings: categorical exclusion from protection under the privacy doctrine, qualified exclusion, and privilege.

Certain types of behavior are categorically excluded from the application of family privacy theory. The taking of life, parental incest, and the imminent threat to the life or health of a minor child all trigger the

[3] Roe v. Conn, 417 F. Supp 769 (M.D. Ala. [1976]); Areen (1975). The family privacy doctrine has taken on constitutional significance but usually in the context of family members versus state regulation. See Griswold v. Connecticut, 381 U.S. 479, 85 S.Ct. 1678, 14 L.Ed.2d 510 (1965); Roe v. Wade, 410 U.S. 113, 93 S.Ct. 705, 35 L.Ed.2d 147 (1973); but see Eisenstadt v. Baird, 405 U.S. 438, 92 S.Ct. 1029, 31 L.Ed.2d 349 (1972).

[4] Parental Kidnapping Prevention Act of 1980. Pub. L. No. 96–611, § 7, 94 Stat. 3568; Areen (1985), pp. 573–75; Flood v. Braaton, 727 F.2d 303 (3d Cir., 1984) (and in Areen [1985], p. 575); U.S. Attorney General's Task Force on Family Violence (1984); Clark (1968), p. 325.

law's willingness to penetrate the privacy of family life because family privacy considerations are outweighed by other important public goals.[5] An issue in the current debate about spouse battering and the proper threshold for the consideration of child abuse concerns whether other behaviors should be added to the short list that has been a staple element of the jurisprudence of family privacy all along.

What I call "qualified exclusion" from the family privacy doctrine is also a traditional legal approach to problems of family dysfunction. Just as Mrs. McGuire can sue for central heating and a kitchen sink only if she leaves the family home, so there are a number of instances in which the law will not intervene if the family continues to function intact but in which legal institutions will vindicate rights of a spouse or child once the victim and offender are no longer together. The two slaps required for an Illinois divorce on grounds of cruelty would not be the basis for either tort recovery or (by law enforcement tradition) a successful battery prosecution if the parties continue living together.[6] A spouse's right to physical security will be vindicated, however, by finding such an assault to be actionable cause for the dissolution of the marriage. The physical discipline of children is typically insulated from legal review if it does not represent a gross threat to the child, but a court can consider such behavior in a custody contest at divorce when determining the child's future placement (Kay and Philips 1966; Clark 1968, pp. 584–91; Areen 1985, pp. 339–589). Traditionally, law enforcement policy toward spousal abuse was to press formal charges only if there was a high likelihood that the complaining spouse would separate from the offender.[7] In such cases, the right to be secure against physical force may exist in all cases, but the legal remedy has often been available only when the family dissolves.

But not all of the exclusions from normal legal treatment conferred by family status disappear when families break up. For example, traditional exclusion of relationships between spouses from the definition of rape is not contingent in the same sense as Mrs. McGuire's right to

[5] Areen (1975); Wald (1976); People v. Green, 27 Cal. 3d 1, 164 Cal. Rptr. 1, 609 P.2d 468 (1980) (husband charged with robbery, kidnapping, and first-degree murder of wife); State v. Kelly, 97 N.J. 178, 478 A.2d 364 (1984); Areen (1985), pp. 1181–1328.

[6] Compare Kemski v. Kemski, 33 Ill. App. 331 (abstract), 77 N.E.2d 344 (1948); to Prosser (1971), § 122, p. 868.

[7] Bruno v. Codd, 47 N.Y.2d 582, 393 N.E.2d 976, 419 N.Y.S.2d 901 (1979); Marcus (1981), pp. 1657–1733; U.S. Commission on Civil Rights (1982), see esp. pp. 23–34; Lerman (1981).

appropriate support.[8] If the parties were living as husband and wife when forcible sexual relations took place, a later separation or divorce will not retroactively reclassify the earlier event as rape. If tort law immunizes parental spanking, the fact that the spanking parent ceases sometime thereafter to be the child's custodian will not alter the privilege that applied to the earlier behavior. In these fully privileged cases, the complaining family member has no legally enforceable right against the privileged behavior.

On occasion, the same behavior may be the subject of an absolute privilege for some legal purpose but only a qualified privilege for others. The spanking parent may, for example, be immune from tort liability, yet the same inappropriate physical discipline may deprive him or her the custody of a child after divorce. This complexity necessitates review of the wide range of different legal approaches that are alternative responses to family violence in modern American law.

II. Varieties of Legal Response

An exhaustive list of possible legal responses to family violence would include almost all of the law's subtopics. My ambitions here are more limited: I outline three basic strategies of legal control and discuss some legal subsystems currently used in pursuit of each strategic purpose. The three basic strategies I mention, *privatization*, *contingent intervention*, and *compulsory intervention*, parallel the levels of family privacy doctrine discussed in the previous section.

Behavior within the family is privatized when the legal system refuses to attach consequences to the behavior only because of its family context. Not all behavior occurring in family settings that evokes no legal consequences should be considered privatized for family reasons. Verbal exchanges between family members may have no potential legal ramifications because of a societal judgment that such exchanges do not deserve legal consequences in almost all social settings. The mild insult or obscenity does not warrant a legal response because the speech itself is privileged, or because conduct falling below certain thresholds of harm is excluded by a *de minimus* principle. By contrast, the spanking of a child by a parent would constitute battery outside the family context, but it is immunized from legal system response because of the family relationship; this is an example of privatization. Privatization corre-

---

[8] Russell (1982); Schulman (1982), pp. 375–81; People v. Liberta, 64 N.Y.2d 152, 474 N.E.2d 567 (1984).

sponds to the categories of behavior described as privileged in the previous discussion of family privacy doctrine.

Privatization policies span civil law, the administrative and equity jurisdictions of family law, and criminal law. Many examples could be cited. The law has traditionally immunized parents from liability for most batteries involving the physical discipline of children. Detentions that would otherwise constitute false imprisonment are not so considered between parent and child. Contracts between married parties are usually not enforceable by courts during marriage. The law traditionally would not treat forced sex during marriage as rape (Clark 1968; Prosser 1971), and it is notoriously difficult to get police and court agencies, when exercising law enforcement discretion, to view most spousal assaults as other than a private matter.

An alternative description of this process might be "diversion." Describing the pursuit of a privatization strategy as a diversion from the legal system provides an important insight into its modern rationale. An apologist for the privatization of the physical discipline of children need not support spanking any more than the Nebraska court considered Mr. McGuire a model of generosity. Legal solutions are unavailable for conflicts engendered by privileged family behavior because policymakers believe that conflict is better resolved either within the family itself or in alternative dispute-resolving structures rather than by legal institutions (U.S. Commission on Civil Rights 1978, pp. 62–66; Lazlo and McKeen 1978, pp. 327–57).

Despite the increased political salience of family violence, privatization is still a basic and popular response to many problems of parent-child relationships as well as relationships between spouses. The movement to narrow criteria for finding child neglect, and the abolition of grounds for divorce, both discussed earlier, provide evidence of the continued popularity of privatization approaches.

Viewing the consequences of privatization as one form of diversion program suggests another observation: many who advocate legal privatization strategies may do so not because they regard family interaction as unimportant, the traditional rationale for *de minimus* nonintervention policies, but, on the contrary, because they regard such family interactions as very important indeed. If important values are disserved by formal processes, values such as the safety of victims, the result may be advocacy of nonintervention.

If privatization is the strategic equivalent of the unconditional privilege of family privacy, contingent intervention strategies are roughly parallel to the qualified privileges of family privacy discussed in the previous section. Here, legal responses are available only if action is taken—a complaint is made by the victim, charges are brought, suit is filed, or the victim leaves the household (Kohlberg 1982; Fagan et al. 1984).

A contingent intervention strategy for family violence is not limited to circumstances in which qualified privileges of family privacy exist. It may be adopted because a qualified privilege exists, as when we excuse Mr. McGuire from an enforceable obligation to pay for support, unless Mrs. McGuire leaves the household. But contingent intervention programs also can be based on prudential considerations that may apply even when behavior within families is not privileged. Publicly supported aid to battered spouses may be restricted to those willing to leave the house or make complaints, not because passive spouses do not deserve help, but because it is believed that there is no effective way to help them if they remain at home. Contingent intervention strategies are used in civil, administrative, and criminal law systems, but intervention is formally contingent only in civil law and voluntary aid programs: tort and contract remedies only exist if they are pursued by private complainants. Shelters and legal aid programs are voluntary, and thus contingent, for spouses (U.S. Commission on Civil Rights 1978; Jorgensen 1982; Fagan et al. 1984). Traditionally, many forms of child neglect and abuse intervention have in fact relied on the initiative of an adult complainant to mobilize the system (Areen 1975; Wald 1976; U.S. Attorney General's Task Force on Family Violence 1984). Similarly, the refusal of many public authorities to press formal charges in spousal violence episodes unless the abused spouse will separate is explicable as a contingent intervention policy that is based on prudential criteria.

The motives for prudence in family violence intervention vary. One important contrast is between the reluctance to aggravate the situation and the desire to conserve scarce public resources. One reason to limit public intervention in the child-neglect sphere when the child and the target of enforcement will continue living together is to avoid exacerbating the child's situation. The continued proximity of victim and offender might make it impossible to prevent violence. If mobilizing the legal system increases the likelihood or severity of later violence, intervention might be made conditional on family separation to protect the child's best interest.

By contrast, support and intervention may be withheld in the absence of a complainant, or even a separation, simply to conserve re-sources (Davis 1969; Fagan et al. 1984). If interventions are less effec-tive among battered spouses who remain at home, nonseparation might be one rational basis for withholding public funds to conserve program resources and maximize total social benefit. It is not, however, with-held on these grounds when the interests of the individual victim are considered paramount. When program administrators defend the pro-gram's failure to assist victims in order to conserve funds, refusal of service is much more controversial than when the refusal is based on concern for the victim's safety and welfare.

Two tensions caused by contingent intervention strategies seem es-pecially relevant to current debate. The first is the formal inconsistency between the criminal law as a theory and contingent intervention as a strategy. Without delving deeply into the "myth of full enforcement" (the theory that every violation of the criminal law should be discovered by the police and prosecuted in the courts), there is basic conflict between defining behavior as criminal (therefore deserving suppression) and characterizing an optimal law enforcement strategy as conditional (pursuing suppression only under some circumstances).[9]

The second important aspect of this classification scheme concerns the conditions under which policy should change from contingent in-tervention to compulsory intervention and the relation of that decision to the reasons that underlie contingent enforcement strategies. It may be useful to ask whether contingent approaches are defended merely to save money or on the grounds of victim welfare. If scarce resources are the only reason for contingent rather than compulsory intervention, the increased public salience of an issue should favor compulsory interven-tion as a strategy. But if the protection of victims is also an important justification for the contingency of intervention, a heightened sense of priority of the problem has no obvious implications in the choice be-tween contingent versus compulsory intervention.

Thus, if public money is the only factor in the choice between con-tingent and compulsory intervention in child abuse, increased regard for the security of children from physical attacks would encourage compulsory intervention. If compulsory intervention resulted in im-

---

[9] This inconsistency seems a particular irritant to the modern opponents of traditional law enforcement approaches to domestic violence. They have a strong point. But it is a somewhat broader point, involving many behaviors outside the family context, than current discussion recognizes (see Marcus 1981; Russell 1982).

portant child welfare costs, such as excessive removal of children from potentially sustaining family settings, the association between the social importance of the goal and the appropriate strategy of legal response is anything but automatic.[10] When continuity of care is important, the removal of a child will produce suffering even though the child's continued placement risks physical harm. This is a risk that some judges would run for the child's own welfare.

My category of compulsory intervention covers many of those behaviors within the family setting specifically excluded from family privilege doctrine, behaviors such as homicide, grievous assault, and incest. Here, the legal strategy is to pursue full enforcement to its practical limits. The principal tool of compulsory intervention in the United States is the criminal law, often supported with such civil law supplements as juvenile courts, equity courts, and some administrative agencies. But the fact that conduct is unprivileged because of its family status does not necessarily mean that the family context is unimportant in the definition of crime, in law enforcement strategy, or in the choice and level of criminal sanction.

Table 1 presents a visual summary of the relationship between categories of privacy doctrine coverage, discussed in Section I, and the enforcement strategies discussed in this section. The relation between doctrinal categories and enforcement responses is neatly symmetrical, with one important exception. Even when the law categorically excludes behavior from any privilege, we may wish less than full enforcement of the law when victims of violence might be placed at greater risk by universal enforcement of the law.

There exist two fundamentally different methods of using the criminal law as an instrument to control family violence. On the one hand,

[10] One powerful illustration of the point concerns child abuse not only in the family context but also in child-care facilities. The chilling effect of oversensitizing such facilities to the criminal law may also have a significant child-welfare cost. When administrative directives go out to early childhood education teachers and custodial workers on the order of, "Please don't hug the children," child-welfare costs seem obvious. This is one widely reported impact of recent child sexual abuse prosecution. But also see U.S. Attorney General's Task Force on Family Violence (1984). "Contrary to common perception, persons who sexually abuse children tend to be persons of respectable appearance and behavior who are known and trusted by the victim. These abusers tend to use nonviolent techniques, seducing the child through attention, affection, and gifts. One of the common strategies of pedophiles and child molesters is to try to gain employment with organizations whose work involves the care, treatment, transportation, supervision or entertainment of children" (p. 106). The task force urges all states to use fingerprinting and other criminal data-base techniques in screening job applicants for such occupations.

TABLE 1

Privacy Doctrine and Law Enforcement Response

Doctrine of Privacy	Strategic Response by Legal System		
	Privatization	Contingent Intervention	Compulsory Intervention
Unconditional privilege	X		
Qualified privilege		X	
Categorical exemption		X	X

standard proscriptions against crimes of violence can be extended to family violence behavior without major modifications in doctrine, enforcement strategy, or the nature and severity of sanctions. On the other hand, the family context of some violent behaviors can provide the basis for a separate and specific subjurisprudence within the criminal law. The tension between these approaches surfaces in much current discussion (cf. Morris and Hawkins [1970] with Marcus [1981] and U.S. Attorney General's Task Force on Family Violence [1984]). It is revealed in the terminology used to refer to family offenses, in debates on enforcement strategy, and in reaction to verdicts and punishments in particular family violence cases.

Some of the linguistic aspects of modern concern with family violence merit attention. The buzzwords of the 1970s, phrases like "spousal rape" and "parental kidnapping," raise interesting issues. To what extent does the term "parental kidnapping" represent a situation where the adjective defeats the noun, in the sense that what we generally think of as kidnapping cannot by definition be committed by parents, even if the parental behavior is properly regarded as a criminal offense?

Putting aside the issue of whether the forcible imposition of sexual relations within marriage should be criminal, should the crime be considered a species of the genus rape, with the same enforcement policies and sanctions and the same degree of moral condemnation from the community? Indeed, is the same core moral wrong present in sexual predations within marriage as in forcible rape by strangers?

Much, though not all, of the linguistic dissonance of family crime involves matters of public relations. "Parental kidnapping" and "parental abduction" are media phrases; they are the consciousness-raising tactic of those who wish to focus the public's attention on the seriousness of the harm inflicted by noncustodial parents. Most modern legislation defines the offense as the interference with custodial parent-child relationships, an appropriately specific isolation of the harm that fits my category of a separate family jurisprudence in criminal law.

The attempt to assimilate family violence into the existing general jurisprudence of violence is not always confined to public relations terminology. The movement to include behavior between spouses in the category of forcible rape makes spousal rape an undifferentiated part of the general group of rape offenses, with its punishment or defenses correspondingly undifferentiated. This appears to be the intention of some of its sponsors. Similarly, general doctrines dealing with duties, omissions, and negligence are often extended to parent-child interactions. When children die, general doctrines regarding manslaughter liability are invoked, with troubling consequences. Parents who never meant harm are convicted of crimes when children die as the result of innocent ignorance (*State v. Williams*, 4 Wash. App. 908, 484 P2d 1167 [1971]).

One price of extending general doctrine to family violence is a divergence between the formal law that governs family violence and law enforcement policy expressed through police and prosecutor discretion. The intentional nontreatment of severely handicapped newborns in hospitals technically may be murder in the statute books, but that law will rarely, if ever, be enforced. The accidental death of children negligently supervised by parents occurs thousands of times each year, with only a trickle of prosecutions in the United States. Almost all of those cases seem problematic for criminal punishment when intention to injure is absent. Spousal rape, even when criminal in theory, has never been strictly enforced. Whatever symbolic gains are associated with the extension and generalization of standard offenses of violence, the tactic generates a huge gap between doctrine and policy.

A preference for a specific family jurisprudence of violence is usually but not inevitably linked with a desire for less severe criminal sanctions and less rigorous law enforcement. Certainly the harsh sanctions associated with rape are one argument against generalization into the marital context, and the punishments available for manslaughter usually appear too severe for parental negligence.

But a specific jurisprudence of family violence is not necessarily lenient. Extreme and repetitive child abuse may call for more severe, as well as less severe, sanctions than assault by strangers. Certainly the "family context," which is the defining aspect of parental incest, justifies more serious sanctions for the same reasons that embezzlement can be a more severely punished property crime: the penal wrong is exacerbated by abuse of trust (Clark 1968, § 2.8; Comment 1979).

At the enforcement level, the tendency of family violence to represent a continuing threat to the victim's safety may justify both more vigorous enforcement efforts and somewhat more serious sanctions than assaults between strangers that are unlikely to constitute a recurrent threat to an individual victim (Marcus 1981). In this sense, an emphasis on specificity in the jurisprudence of family violence can be considered a neutral principle, not inherently associated with special leniency.

The arguments for assimilation of standard crimes into the family violence context seem a mixture of practical momentum and of the requirements of moral education. Assimilation is a relatively easy legislative remedy: the general offenses of violence already exist. The abolition of special privileges, such as spousal rape, automatically includes the marital offense in the general category.

But more than this momentum supports general extension. Many of those who wish the criminal law extended to forcible sexual relations within marriage also desire that the offense be called rape and treated as if it were as culpable as traditional notions of the crime. Widespread social feeling that the offense is not as culpable in marriage is seen by these advocates as the reason why equal treatment under the general rape rubric is necessary (Russell 1982). The puzzles, manifest and latent consequences, and costs of this approach are issues to which I shall return presently.

III. Family Violence and the Criminal Law

Sections I and II have examined a variety of legal contexts that are involved in the regulation of family violence, viewing the criminal law as one alternative system among many available to respond to and to suppress violence among intimates. In this section, the focus shifts from examining the effect of the criminal law and other legal regimes on family violence to looking at matters from the opposite perspective, discussing the impact of family violence problems on the substantive criminal law.

That topic richly deserves a separate treatment, but I shall use exigencies of time and space to defend my sketchy presentation of five themes as a contribution toward understanding the impact of family violence on substantive criminal law. My short list of impressions gleaned from the family violence literature includes (*a*) criminalization as fashion, (*b*) the preferred position of the criminal sanction, (*c*) the appeal of assimilation, (*d*) the tension between retribution as a limit and moral education as a goal, and (*e*) the continuing challenge of determining the penal significance of relationship in the definition and grading of harms.

A. *Criminalization as Fashion*

The movement to expand the reach of the criminal law over family violence is somewhat at odds with efforts to cut back on the application of penal law in other spheres. In the broad sweep of decades, just when society has begun to recognize the limits of the criminal sanction in areas such as narcotics, gambling, and prostitution, there is a growing emphasis on using criminal law for the regulation of family violence (cf. Vera Institute of Justice [1980] with U.S. Attorney General's Task Force on Family Violence [1984, pp. 22–23]). More striking, the increased salience of family violence has simultaneously led to the quest for alternatives to criminal law sanctions, such as mediation of low-level interspousal violence by some observers, while others press for increased reliance on criminal justice institutions for the same behavior (Goldstein 1960; Morris and Hawkins 1970).

This is not the place to belabor the litany of impediments that limit the effectiveness of the criminal law in regulating human behavior or to attack the special problems associated with low-visibility behaviors that frequently lack complaining parties to mobilize enforcement personnel. Further, the enthusiasm for criminal sanctions against family violence is not necessarily inconsistent with curtailing enforcement in other areas.[11] Many of the problems associated with deterrence and incapaci-

[11] The legal response to family violence must be guided primarily by the nature of the abusive act, not by the relationship between the victim and the abuser. The task force recommends that the legal system treat assaults within the family as seriously as it would treat the same assault if it occurred between strangers. "When an officer enters a home and finds a mother or child who is the victim of an assault, the officer is dealing with a crime—a crime with its own distinctive characteristics, but first and foremost a crime. . . . Because family violence is the only crime in which the victim knows the identity of the offender, the deterrent effects of legal sanctions against the offender are potentially greater than for any other crime. If family violence were always reported and if the legal system always acted on the basis of its knowledge, the deterrent effects of swift and certain legal penalties would be great" (U.S. Attorney General's Task Force on Family Violence 1984, pp. 4–5).

tation for victimless crimes or predatory crimes among strangers are not necessary handicaps for some types of family violence.

Unlike so-called victimless crimes, a potential complainant exists in almost all instances of spousal abuse and most child abuse cases involving children of school age and older. And the victims of family violence, unlike those of many other violent offenses, know their predators all too well. The potential for high levels of detection, with enhanced deterrence and incapacitation, may distinguish family violence from other crimes and justify more optimism about punitive approaches in family violence prevention.

Yet some of the enthusiastic support for penal approaches to family violence is not based on utilitarian calculations about chances of apprehension but on the moral force of criminal law classification. Moreover, many limits of the criminal law that are widely recognized in other contexts—problems of resources, arbitrary enforcement, and limited citizen support—frequently are overlooked by proponents of criminal law solutions in the family.[12]

One irony in the area of child abuse is that the behavior is most visible when it is least dangerous and most dangerous when it is least visible. In the school years, when almost every child participates in a public world that makes his or her bruises and dysfunctions visible, the threat to life from parental abuse is relatively low. During infancy and the early preschool years, when child abuse is of lesser visibility, the life-threatening quality of physical abuse is much greater. A substantial majority of all known child abuse fatalities occur before the age of five, and the rate of such fatalities per thousand children is far higher in the early years.[13] The criminal law may be able to respond to all but the most dangerous forms of child abuse.

Maybe the only way we learn of the limits of the criminal law in an area such as family violence is to depend on it for awhile. If so, the contrast between social confidence in criminal law solutions for the family violence area and social confidence in those solutions for other areas of traditional criminal law enforcement may be a matter of a time lag. However, one wonders about the confident assertion that the discouraging record of criminal law enforcement in areas such as spousal abuse is only a matter of low law enforcement priorities or insufficient

---

[12] McCoid (1965), p. 15; State v. Tanner, 675 P.2d 539 (S.Ct. Utah, 1983); Areen (1985, pp. 1207–8).
[13] U.S. Attorney General's Task Force on Family Violence (1984).

use of sanctions in earlier times. The almost euphoric embrace of the apparent policy implications of the Minneapolis spouse abuse experiment, where the use of arrest and custody led to an apparent decrease in further abuse, may stand the test of time and experience (see Elliott, in this volume). But many observers, including me, have their doubts about whether the criminal law, by itself, can ever be an effective instrument of family safety.

B. The Preferred Position of Criminal Law

Part of the renewed emphasis on criminal law approaches to family violence simply reflects a greater awareness of spousal and child violence as social problems. This would explain the heightened emphasis placed on criminal law approaches by family violence programs, just as it should explain increases in fiscal aid programs, domestic violence shelters, administrative child neglect and abuse programs, and domestic violence programs as part of the civil law of family life. However, there seems to be an ever-increasing trend to favor criminal law approaches over their civil law or regulatory alternatives.

An instructive example of the emphasis and preferred position of the criminal law in family violence is the recent U.S. Attorney General's Task Force on Family Violence, mentioned above. In its report (1984), this body gave no fewer than fifty-eight instances of favorable mention to the involvement of the criminal law, the police, and institutions of criminal justice. The institutions of civil justice, including juvenile and family courts, play a much smaller role in the task force agenda, with a total of four references scattered throughout the document.[14] This pattern of emphasis is not confined to the task force; rather, it seems to be a prominent part of the current debate.

The extent of this "preferred position" emphasis, its origins, and its effects are difficult to document. Part of the climate in which decisions have been made in the late 1970s and early 1980s has been the perception that anything other than criminalization demeans the seriousness of the offenses and the dignity of the victim interests at stake in family violence. If this perception is widespread, it may bias the selection of strategies toward criminal justice as opposed to alternative solutions.

---

[14] U.S. Attorney General's Task Force on Family Violence (1984). Mara Grossman, Boalt Hall, University of California, Berkeley, 1987, coded the references in this report. Her complete count, in the order of frequency: criminal law, criminal law enforcement (58); other governmental responses (excluding criminal law, courts, family courts) (34); communal institutions (29); civil law (including juvenile and family courts) (4).

The feeling that any public regulation other the criminal law confers second-class citizenship on victims may also hinder the identification of promising and creative solutions outside the criminal justice system. The language of blame and the machinery of criminal justice are necessary components of a societal response to serious family violence. Law enforcement institutions, notably the police, are historically the only twenty-four-hour community presence available to respond to family violence. But in this field, as in many others, the search for promising partial solutions can benefit from a deliberate spirit of eclecticism. Peripheral vision is one of the great tools of public policy analysis.

C. The Momentum toward Assimilation

Parental beating of children is not just another form of aggravated assault. The transporting of a child across state lines by his or her noncustodial parent in the wake of a divorce is both harmful and evil, but considering this behavior and abduction for ransom as two kinds of kidnapping is like observing that small families and atomic explosions are both nuclear. Yet the momentum toward extending general crime rubrics is considerable. Parental kidnapping is a metaphor, but the metaphoric definition of substantive crimes can have unintended consequences. So-called statutory rape is one example. When we consider sex achieved by force and sexual relations with a consenting minor to be two forms of rape, does that mean that the same kinds of mistakes and the same threshold for excusable error should apply?[15] Would it not be an amazing coincidence if the proper substantive definition, punishment, and enforcement strategies for parental abduction and kidnap for ransom were parallel?

Specificity in the defining and grading of criminal offenses is always a virtue. In an era of declining confidence in sentencing discretion, narrowing of sentencing ranges associated with specific crimes, and renewed emphasis on retributive equity, specificity is an ever more necessary virtue (Tonry and Zimring 1983). For similar reasons, the shift from total reactivity to management and planning rationality in law enforcement argues for separate harms being defined, punished, and targeted for enforcement resources under separate rubrics. From this perspective, if there were ever a time for marital rape to be blended

---

[15] Compare People v. Mayberry, 15 Cal. 3d 143, 125 Cal. Rptr. 745, 542 P.2d 1337 (1975) (forcible rape), with People v. Hernandez, 61 Cal. 2d 529, 39 Cal. Rptr. 361, 393 P.2d 673 (1964) (statutory rape).

seamlessly into a larger category including predatory stranger rape, that time is not the present.

D. Retribution versus Moral Education

More than novelty made the Rideout trial in Oregon, the first sustained courtroom trial of marital rape, into one of the premier media events of its time. The public reaction was heightened by the prospect of forcible sex in marriage being treated as forcible rape because the majority of the population did not accept the moral equivalence of the two behaviors. The human interest of the trial was the dissonance between the public perception of the behavior and public notions of the seriousness of rape (Russell 1982).

This dissonance was not lost on those who welcomed the trial and hoped the conviction would be accompanied by serious and therefore unpopular punishment. Rape classification was desired by some not in spite of a tolerant public attitude that would view the punishment for the behavior as extreme but because of that tolerant public attitude (Russell 1982). Toleration of forcible sex within marriage, the argument goes, is seen as evidence of the need for public education. Creating a moral equivalence between stranger rape and forcible marital sex was for many a deliberate strategy in pursuing moral education by overshooting the retributive ceiling then existing in the public mind for the marital offense. Almost all thoughtful observers would agree that there was no public consensus on the moral equivalence between the raping stranger and the raping husband. But the trial and the punishment were viewed by some as the mechanism to create that equivalence.

Was this a gamble worth taking? The strategic issue, whether spousal and stranger sexual exploitation should be viewed as equivalent, is beyond the scope of these remarks. The tactical question, whether stretching punishment to and beyond the public perception of what is deserved will underscore the seriousness of spousal exploitation or will produce disrespect and rejection of the legal result, is important in its own right. Whenever the criminal law is used as an instrument of moral education, the legal result must lead rather than follow public perceptions of the seriousness of offenses. But lead by how much? The conventional wisdom is that the criminal law may do this, in exceptional and deserving cases, but that that ground must be chosen carefully. The crusade against drunk driving seems one modern success in this pursuit. Heavy penalties for possession and use of marijuana seems one conspicuous modern failure (Kaplan 1970; Jacobs and Strossen 1985). By my assessment, the Rideout trial overreached the criminal law's capacity for moral leadership, even if one judges the behavior within marriage and among strangers to be equivalent. The drama associated with the criminal prosecution of absconding noncustodial parents is a closer question.

We are on notice that this competition between retributive ceilings and efforts to use severe sanctions as instruments of moral education will be a recurrent element in the new jurisprudence of family violence.

E. The Penal Significance of Relationships

The reexamination of the criminal law of family violence has stimulated, much to our benefit, renewed interest in the significance of a relationship between victim and offender in judging the moral culpability of a variety of offenses. Are sexually exploitative husbands like raping strangers, or is there something in the nature of the relationship that affects our judgment of the harm done or of the offender's culpability and future dangerousness? If husbands are different from strangers, what about those located at midpoints in the continuum between nonrelationship and intimacy? What about date rape (see Kaye 1985; Sweet 1985)?

One of the major contributions made by the renewed interest in the jurisprudence of family violence is its raising of a broader question: the appropriate significance of prior relationship in gauging the seriousness of assaults, sexual impositions, child abuse, and misfeasance in the supervision of the young. The significance of relationship in the definition and grading of offenses of violence has long been neglected. The new emphasis on family violence makes these issues a compulsory part of an agenda for criminal law reform.

IV. Conclusion

Advanced societies take family violence seriously. Thus, the increased attention devoted to intrafamilial violence in the United States is evidence of societal maturity.

Yet the pervasiveness of intimate violence in Western culture suggests that there is a parochial limit to current discussion of the control of such violence in the United States. Child abuse and violence between sexual intimates are recurrent behaviors throughout the Western world. Historical and comparative studies of social control in this area would thus appear to be of substantial potential value.

568   Franklin E. Zimring

What are the practices in those democracies in Europe and Scandinavia with which we usually compare ourselves? How many of the policy options raised in current discussions have been tried elsewhere and with what results? Are there approaches being used by our Western neighbors that we have not yet considered?

Family violence, like the poor, may be always with us, but in different proportions and with different outcomes. Thus, the comparative study of this chronic problem seems particularly important to a balanced agenda of policy research.

REFERENCES

Areen, Judith. 1975. "Intervention between Parent and Child: A Reappraisal of the State's Role in Child Neglect and Abuse Cases." *Georgetown Law Journal* 63:887–937.
———. 1985. *Cases and Materials on Family Law*, 2d ed. Mineola, N.Y.: Foundation Press.
Clark, Homer H., Jr. 1968. *Law of Domestic Relations*. St. Paul, Minn.: West.
Comment. 1979. "Incest and the Legal System." *U.C. Davis Law Review* 12:673.
Davis, Kenneth Culp. 1969. *Discretionary Justice: A Preliminary Inquiry*. Baton Rouge: Louisiana State University Press.
Elliott, Delbert. In this volume. "Criminal Justice Procedures in Family Violence Crimes."
Fagan, Jeffrey, Elizabeth Friedman, and Sandra Wexler, with Virginia Leurs. 1984. *The LEAA Family Violence Program: Final Evaluation Report*. Vol. 1, *Analytic Findings*. San Francisco: URSA Institute.
Goldstein, Joseph. 1960. "Police Discretion Not to Invoke the Criminal Process: Low Visibility Decisions in the Administration of Justice." *Yale Law Journal* 69:543–94.
Jacobs, James B., and Nadine Strossen. 1985. "Mass Investigations without Individualized Suspicion: A Constitutional and Policy Critique of Drunk Driving Roadblocks." *U.C. Davis Law Review* 18:595–680.
Jorgensen, Carol. 1982. "The Role of Shelter Staff in Mediation." In *Alternative Means of Family Disputes Resolution*, edited by H. Davidson, L. Ray, and R. Horowitz. Washington, D.C.: American Bar Association.
Kaplan, John. 1970. *Marijuana, the New Prohibition*. New York: World Publishing Co.
Kay, Herma Hill, and Irving Philips. 1966. "Poverty and the Law of Child Custody." *California Law Review* 54:717.
Kaye, E. 1985. "Was I Raped?" *Glamour* 83:258–59.

Kohlberg, Amy. 1982. "Social and Legal Policy Implications of Domestic Violence." In *Alternative Means of Family Disputes Resolution*, edited by H. Davidson, L. Ray, and R. Horowitz. Washington, D.C.: American Bar Association.

Lazlo, Anna T., and Thomas McKeen. 1978. "Court Diversion: An Alternative for Spousal Abuse Cases." In *Battered Women: Issues of Public Policy*, edited by U.S. Commission on Civil Rights. Washington, D.C.: Commission on Civil Rights.

Lerman, Lisa G. 1981. *Prosecution of Spousal Abuse: Innovations in Criminal Justice Response*. Washington, D.C.: Center for Women's Policy Studies.

McCoid, Allen H. 1965. "The Battered Child and Other Assaults upon the Family: Part One." *Minnesota Law Review* 50:1–58.

McIntire, Roger W. 1973. "Parenthood Training or Mandatory Birth Control: Take Your Choice." *Psychology Today* 7(5):34–36.

Marcus, Maria L. 1981. "Conjugal Violence: The Law of Force and the Force of Law." *California Law Review* 69:1657–1733.

Morris, Norval, and Gordon Hawkins. 1970. *The Honest Politician's Guide to Crime Control*. Chicago: University of Chicago Press.

Prosser, William L. 1971. *Handbook of the Law of Torts*, 4th ed. St. Paul, Minn.: West.

Russell, Diana E., ed. 1982. *Rape in Marriage*. New York: Macmillan.

Schulman, Joanne. 1982. "State-by-State Information on Marital Rape Exemption Laws." In *Rape in Marriage*, edited by Diana E. H. Russell. New York: Macmillan.

Sweet, E. 1985. "Date Rape: The Story of an Epidemic and Those Who Deny It." *Ms.* 14:56–59.

Tonry, Michael, and Franklin E. Zimring, eds. 1983. *Reform and Punishment: Essays on Criminal Sentencing*. Studies in Crime and Justice. Chicago: University of Chicago Press.

U.S. Attorney General's Task Force on Family Violence. 1984. *Final Report*. Washington, D.C.: U.S. Attorney General.

U.S. Commission on Civil Rights, eds. 1978. *Battered Women: Issues of Public Policy*. Washington, D.C.: U.S. Government Printing Office.

Vera Institute of Justice. 1980. *Mediation and Arbitration as Alternatives to Prosecution in Felony Arrest Cases: An Evaluation of the Brooklyn Dispute Resolution Center*. New York: Vera Institute of Justice.

Wald, Michael S. 1976. "State Intervention on Behalf of 'Neglected' Children: Standards for Removal of Children from Their Homes, Monitoring the Status of Children in Foster Care, and Termination of Parental Rights." *Stanford Law Review* 28:625–706.

Zimring, Franklin, Satyanshu K. Mukherjee, and Barrick Van Winkle. 1983. "Intimate Violence: A Study of Intersexual Homicide in Chicago." *University of Chicago Law Review* 50:910–30.

Author Index

Subject Index

Abuse, definitions of, 62, 266–67, 303

Adolescent maltreatment: abuser characteristics, 281–82; and delinquency, 292–93; definitions of, 278–80; demographic and socioeconomic characteristics of, 283–84; developmental issues of, 284–85; incidence and prevalence of, 280–81; intervention and prevention of, 293–95; Pagelow case study of, 285–88, 298–99; reporting of, 282, 289–91; types of, 282, 283; victim characteristics, 282–83

Alcohol and abuse, 63–64, 106, 164, 192–96, 271, 393, 399–401, 445–46

Alderman's courts, 31–32

American Humane Association, 223, 224–29, 235, 241, 246, 280, 281

Arrest decision factors and: alcohol involvement, 164, 445–46; data quality, 446; data sources, 441–44; racial differences, 444–45; sex differences, 444–45, 446

Attitudes toward marital violence, 165–67

Battered child syndrome, 1, 20, 47–48, 60, 264

Biosocial theory: and explanations of child maltreatment, 91–101, 103–4; and explanations of marital violence, 79–91, 102–3; general characteristics of, 71, 74, 75–76, 78–79, 104–6

Body of Laws and Liberties, 22–23, 26, 38, 50

Cessation of spouse abuse (*see also* Victim responses to marital violence): by displacement, 392–95; effectiveness of criminal justice interventions, 381–87, 389, 390, 394; effectiveness of victim-initiated strategies, 388–92; spontaneous (*see* Spontaneous cessation from substance addiction)

Child maltreatment (*see also* Adolescent maltreatment): and coercive interpersonal contingencies, 98–101; and cultural norms (*see* Cultural norms and child maltreatment); and ecological instability, 96–98; criminalization of, 240–42; definitions of, 219–23, 229–30, 247; historical context of, 22, 26–27, 29, 33–34, 47–49, 51–52 (*see also* Societies for the prevention of cruelty to children); incidence of (see Incidence of child maltreatment); policy issues, 254–57; prevalence of, 238–40; research issues, 253–54; severity of, 235, 236–37, 238; socioeconomic and demographic differences in, 61,